George F.L. Marshall

The Butterflies of India, Burmah and Ceylon

A descriptive handbook of all the known species of rhopalocerous Lepidoptera

inhabiting that region, with notices of allied species occurring in the neighbouring

countries along the border. Vol. 2

George F.L. Marshall

The Butterflies of India, Burmah and Ceylon
A descriptive handbook of all the known species of rhopalocerous Lepidoptera inhabiting that region, with notices of allied species occurring in the neighbouring countries along the border. Vol. 2

ISBN/EAN: 9783337244699

Printed in Europe, USA, Canada, Australia, Japan

Cover: Foto ©Andreas Hilbeck / pixelio.de

More available books at **www.hansebooks.com**

THE

BUTTERFLIES

OF

INDIA,

BURMAH AND CEYLON.

A DESCRIPTIVE HANDBOOK OF ALL THE KNOWN SPECIES OF RHOPALOCEROUS
LEPIDOPTERA INHABITING THAT REGION, WITH NOTICES OF ALLIED
SPECIES OCCURRING IN THE NEIGHBOURING COUNTRIES ALONG
THE BORDER; WITH NUMEROUS ILLUSTRATIONS.

BY

LIONEL DE NICÉVILLE,

Fellow of the Entomological Society, London; and Member of the Asiatic Society, Bengal.

VOLUME II.

The Illustrations

DRAWN BY BABU GRISH CHUNDER CHUCKERBUTTY AND BABU BEHARI LALL DASS.
THE AUTOTYPE PLATES BY THE AUTOTYPE COMPANY OF LONDON.

Calcutta:

PRINTED AND PUBLISHED BY THE CALCUTTA CENTRAL PRESS, CO., LD.,
5, COUNCIL HOUSE STREET.

TO BE OBTAINED ALSO OF BERNARD QUARITCH, 15, PICCADILLY, LONDON, W.

1886.

VOL. II.

NYMPHALIDÆ. NYMPHALINÆ.

LEMONIIDÆ,

LIBYTHÆINÆ, NEMEOBIINÆ.

LIST OF ILLUSTRATIONS.

NYMPHALINÆ.

LEMONIIDÆ, LIBYTHÆINÆ.

NEMEOBIINÆ.

VOL. II.

TABLE OF CONTENTS.

PREFACE TO VOL. II.

SOME explanation appears to me to be due to the subscribers to "The Butterflies of India, Burmah and Ceylon" as to the delay which has taken place in the publication of this volume. The second part of the first volume was issued in August, 1883, soon after which date Major Marshall obtained twenty months' sick leave to Europe. He took away with him the rough MS. of this volume, hoping to be able to continue the work at home, but ill-health prevented him from doing so. He returned to India in March, 1885, but the uncertainty of his health even then made it doubtful whether he would ever be able, in addition to his official duties, to conduct to a successful issue a work of this magnitude, and as the publication had already been delayed nearly two years, he most reluctantly decided, in the interests of the work, to abandon his share in it, and, on my expressing my willingness to continue it alone, he forwarded to me all the papers and drawings connected with the publication. Since that date (March, 1885) I have worked steadily and unremittingly at this volume.

It has been a source of great disappointment to me that Major Marshall should have been obliged to retire from the work, and that my name alone should appear on the title-page, especially as his retiring has been so far more nominal than real; every word of the MS. and two proofs have been carefully revised by him, and in every way he has rendered me the greatest assistance and encouragement, and has promised most kindly to continue his valuable help in the future as far as he is able to do so. I can only express a hope in concluding this matter that my readers will not find any falling off in interest or less accuracy in the matter contained in the second than obtained in the first volume, and my deep indebtedness to Major Marshall for his invaluable assistance and advice.

It is my pleasing task to convey my best thanks to the following gentlemen for assistance given, either with specimens or information, during the preparation of this volume, in addition to those mentioned in the preface to the first volume:—To Colonel C. Swinhoe I am indebted for the loan of specimens from his collection, and also for carefully going over all the proofs of this volume and adding many useful notes; to Colonel A. M. Lang, R.E., for the use of his large collection; to Mr. Otto Möller for the loan of any specimens I required from his magnificent Sikkim collection, now numbering some 500 species; and for the gift of specimens from Mr. W. H. Irvine from the Malda district; Major E. Y. Verbury from the Punjab; Mr. A. V. Knyvett from Bhutan, where he has recently obtained *Stichophthalma nourmahal*, (previously only doubtfully recorded from India), the new *Lethe brisanda*, and *Kallima knyvetti*, and the rare *Stiboges nymphidia* and *Armandia lidderdalii*; to Mr. E. H. Man for many rare species from the Nicobars; Mr. R. Wimberley for Andamanese specimens; Mr. J. A. Betham from Central India; Mr. J. L. Sherwill from Assam; Lieutenant E. Y. Watson from Beluchistan and Burma; Mr. W. C. Taylor and Mrs. Wylly from Orissa; Mr. W. F. Hampson from the Nilgiris; Father D. Honoré from extreme South India; and to the Bombay Natural History Society for the gift and loan of specimens. Lastly, I have to express my most grateful thanks to the Superintendent of the Indian Museum, Calcutta, for the facilities he has afforded me, without which it would have been impossible to have carried on the work.

In conclusion, I would express a hope that the succeeding volumes of this work will be issued at shorter intervals than the two first have been, and that the public, professionals and amateurs alike, will extend to this volume the same indulgence as they have shewn to the first, remembering that it is the product of scanty leisure, and carried through in the face of many difficulties and in a trying climate.

LIONEL DE NICÉVILLE.

INDIAN MUSEUM, CALCUTTA. *October*, 1886.

Nymphalinæ, Bates, Journ. Ent., vol. ii, p. 176 (1864); id., Moore, Lep. Cey., vol. i, p. 25 (1880). *Nymphalina*, Distant, Rhop. Malay., p. 83 (1882); *Nymphalidæ* (part) and *Eurytelidæ* (part). Westwood, Gen. Diurn. Lep., pp. 143, 403 (1850, 1851).

"BODY, robust; ANTENNÆ, long, with a broad elongate distinct club; PALPI, *large, protruding, wide apart, scaly, the front edge broadly dilated*; WINGS, large, triangular, but varying much in outline; CELL, sometimes closed in both wings, often open in hindwing, and sometimes open in forewing also; FOREWING, nervures not dilated at base, (except in a few genera, *Ergolis, Eurytela, &c.*, in which the costal nervure only is dilated), the second sub-costal nervule emitted before end of cell*; HINDWING, *channelled* to receive abdomen, no prædiscoidal cell." (*Marshall* and *de Nicéville*, Butt. of India, vol. i, p. 17).

"BODY, more or less robust. HEAD, of moderate size. *Eyes*, large, generally naked. *Palpi*, large, generally obliquely porrected, extending considerably in front of the head, wide apart, generally clothed with scales, with the front edge broadly dilated; the basal joint generally curved, and furnished beneath with a tuft of hairs; the terminal joint small and slender. *Antennæ*, generally rather long, and terminated by a broad or elongated club. THORAX, large. ABDOMEN, moderate-sized or large. WINGS, large, often greatly variegated in the colours, and marked beneath with ocellated spots [in a few of the genera only, the wings are also sometimes marked with ocelli on both sides]. FOREWING, generally more or less triangular, with the discoidal cell closed [usually, though frequently it is entirely open] by slender disco-cellular nervules: *veins*, not dilated at the base [except in the first three genera]; the sub-costal nervure emitting four branches, exclusive of the terminal portion of the vein, which has sometimes been regarded as a fifth branch; the first and second branches generally arising before the anterior extremity of the discoidal cell [in a few genera the first subcostal nervule *only* arises before the end of the cell], and the third and fourth at equal distances apart between the extremity of the cell and the tip of the wing. HINDWING, generally broadly ovate, rarely furnished in the males with tufts of hair; the outer margin often more or less deeply scalloped or dentated, the abdominal margin forming a deep groove for the reception of the abdomen; not furnished at the base with a præliscoidal cell; the præcostal nervure short and arched; the discoidal cell of moderate length, generally closed by slender disco-cellular nervules. FORELEGS, short, and not fitted for walking; the tibia and tarsus of the *male* often clothed at the sides with a fringe of fine hairs, forming a flattened brush; the tarsus consisting of a single elongated joint, obtuse at the top, and destitute of claws; those of the *female* generally rather longer, with the tarsus rather dilated at the extremity, where it is more or less distinctly obliquely articulated; the articulations, as well as the tip of the tarsus, armed beneath with short spines. HINDLEGS, long, with the tibiæ armed with two spurs at the tip, and the underside of the tibia and tarsus armed with rows of short spines. *Claws*, simple, acute, curved; *paronychia*, large, bifid, setose, leathery; the outer division largest; *pulvillus*, dilated."

"LARVA, long, generally cylindric, and more or less spined; not or rarely attenuated behind, and with the hinder extremity of the body generally obtuse. PUPA, elongate, generally more or less armed with angulated prominences; suspended by the tail only, hanging by the extremity of the body, and not girt across the middle." (*Westwood*, l. c., p. 143.)

* The position of the second subcostal nervule of the forewing is very variable, being sometimes given off *after* the end of the cell.

Mr. Westwood in the 'Genera of Diurnal Lepidoptera' included the genera *Euispe*, *Amathusia*, *Zeuxidia*, and *Discophora* in his Family VII, *Nymphalidæ*, they are here placed in the Subfamily *Morphinæ*. In his Family XI, *Eurytelidæ*, he has arranged the genera *Eurytela*, *Ergolis* and *Hypanis* (= *Byblia*), but their more natural position seems to be at the head of the *Nymphalinæ*. They are closely allied to the *Satyrinæ*, but still more closely to the subfamily in which they find a place in this work.

The *Nymphalinæ*, excluding the genera which were placed in a separate subfamily by Westwood under the name of *Eurytelidæ*, comprise two groups in which the form of the LARVA widely differs, the first in which the larva is smooth, limaciform, and having on the head non-retractile horn-like appendages, and of which the typical genus is *Apatura* ; and the second in which the larva is cylindrical, and armed with long spines or with elongated tubercles armed with bristles, and of which the type is *Limenitis*. In the first group also the PUPA is typically without angular projections or metallic spots, and in the second group it usually presents both these features. The European genera have already been divided into these two groups by Dr. Lang ("Butterflies of Europe"), *Apatura* and *Charaxes* coming in the first group under the name of *Apaturidæ*, and *Limenitis*, *Neptis*, *Vanessa*, *Pyrameis*, *Melitæa*, and *Argynnis* in the second as *Nymphalidæ*. The ultimate natural division of the group will no doubt be on these lines, but unfortunately as yet the life-history of many of the Indian genera is so little known that we cannot for want of data work on them, and I have therefore adopted an artificial classification for the present based on the characters of the perfect insect only, and although it is unsatisfactory as separating widely such genera as *Apatura* and *Charaxes*, *Euripus* and *Hestina*, *Argynnis* and *Melitæa*, it is the best that I can offer and will serve its purpose until a more profound knowledge enables us to rectify its errors and shortcomings.

The *Nymphalinæ* contain the typical genera of the entire family of *Nymphalidæ* with the forelegs very feebly developed and unfitted for walking ; they are distinguished from the *Danainæ* by the body being far less leathery in texture, and more densely clothed with hair or furry scales, by the absence of the anal tufts of hair in the males, and by the juices not being acrid ; from the *Elymniinæ* by the absence of the prædiscoidal cell in the hindwing, the greater dilation of the palpi, and the absence (except in *Ergolis*, *Eurytela*, and *Byblia*) of the dilation of the costal nervure ; and from the *Acræinæ* by their having the hindwing channelled to receive the abdomen. But they are linked to the *Satyrinæ* and *Elymniinæ* through the *Eurytelidæ*, and to the *Morphinæ* by the frequent absence of the lower discocellular nervule in the hindwing, and through *Tanæcia* by the arrangement of the subcostal nervules in the forewing. In the typical genera, the long protruding wide-apart palpi dilated on the front edge and the strongly clubbed antennæ are the prominent characteristics ; but the subfamily presents great divergencies in many respects.

There is great diversity in size, *Penthema* and *Kallima* being very large, while *Melitæa* and some species of *Neptis* are very small insects. There is also great variation in form, in many genera the hindwing is tailed and sometimes lobed in addition, in others it is deeply scalloped, while in others again it is slightly waved or entire. The apex of the forewing in some genera is truncate, in others rounded or acute, and lastly in *Kallima* it is produced into a lengthened point. In neuration also there is great variety, in some genera the cells of the forewing and hindwing are closed, in others they are open ; and the subcostal nervules of the forewing are given off from the costal nervure at very different points. It is on this latter character that the key to the genera is primarily based, but it cannot be strictly adhered to, as in four genera (*Hestina*, *Neptis*, *Argynnis* and *Cyrestis*) the species can be divided into two groups, one in which the first subcostal nervule only of the forewing is given off before the end of the cell, in the other the second branch is given off in addition before the termination of the cell.

The genus *Terinos* is remarkable in having the eyes hairy, and in some species the neuration of the male different from that of the female. As a rule, however, in the subfamily there are but few prominent secondary sexual characters. In *Ergolis* and *Terinos* there are large patches of glandular hairs or scales in the male, and in one species of *Cirrhochroa* and some of

Argynnis there is placed on either side of certain of the nervules on the upperside of the forewing a streak of differently-formed hairs or scales. The hairy clothing of the forelegs of different genera of *Nymphalinæ* is exceedingly variable, in *Vanessa* it is carried to the greatest extreme amongst butterflies, both sexes having nearly equally hairy forelegs (hence the name "brush-footed butterflies" often applied to this group), while in other species the forelegs have close-set scales rather than long hairs. The hairy clothing of the palpi exhibits much diversity also. Speaking generally though not always the thorax is very stout, and the abdomen is short with the abdominal margin of the hindwing deeply channelled to receive it.

In their habits in the perfect state they are pre-eminently bold, sunshine-loving insects, never skulking in the shade amongst trees and bushes as do the butterflies of the subfamilies *Morphinæ* and *Satyrinæ*. They also usually rest with the wings widely-spread open; in the preceding subfamilies this is the exception. In the genus *Charaxes* the power of rapid flight is very great, as would be expected from the great strength of the veins and the structure of the stout thorax to which the wings are attached. In the genus *Neptis* and the "White Admiral" group of *Limenitis* the flight is easy, graceful and sailing, while in *Vanessa*, *Argynnis*, *Apatura*, &c., though the flight is rapid and irregular, they are often easily caught owing to their habit of returning again and again to the same resting place on a particular leaf. The flight of *Cyrestis* is weak, and they often when pursued suddenly alight on the underside of a leaf; so also does *Stibochiona nicea*. Many of the species are very foul feeders, the depraved tastes of the "Purple Emperor" are well known, species of *Charaxes* have also been taken on carrion, *C. fabius* is very fond of the juice of the toddy palm, *Euthalia* of rotten fruit, &c. One of the most successful modes of catching many species of rare butterflies is to place rotten fruit or some other attractive, strong-smelling bait on the ground near their haunts, when numbers of specimens may often be found busily regaling themselves where previously not an individual was to be seen.

The *Nymphalinæ* are found throughout the known world, one species, *P. cardui*, being cosmopolitan and found from India to the Polar regions, but the greatest development of the subfamily is in tropical and subtropical regions; out of considerably more than one hundred genera described only eight are found in Europe, while no less than forty-five occur in India including all the European ones, but these latter are for the most part confined in our limits to the Himalayas. The characters of the tropical forms present the greatest difficulty and much less is known about them. Many of the genera are represented by large numbers of species, several by one or two species only, and many of the species are very common over wide areas. The perfect insect appears to have more settled characters and to be less subject to variation than among the *Satyrinæ*, but a notable exception is found in the colouring of the "oak leaf" butterfly (*Kallima inachis*) in which the underside is hardly ever alike in two specimens.

The external structure of the larvæ is very variable. The most usual form is more or less of a cylindrical shape, thickly furnished with rows of branched spines (Plate II, *Athyma leucothoë*), a pair on the head being often more prominent and larger than the rest. In typical *Apatura* however the body is smooth and shagreened, and there are two horns on the posterior portion of the head pointing backwards, and the tail is bifurcated, reminding one at once of the larvæ of the *Elymniinæ* and *Satyrinæ*. The larvæ of the genera *Euthalia* and *Symphædra* are amongst the most remarkable in butterflies. Projecting from the body all round are long widely-branched spines somewhat resembling fern fronds. These spines spring in a single row from the sides, and when the insect is at rest on the surface of a leaf lie flat upon the leaf. The larvæ are usually green, and though so conspicuous-looking when separated from their natural surroundings are exceedingly well-hid and difficult to see when at rest in their usual position in the middle of a leaf, the light-coloured line down the centre of the back answering to the mid-rib of the leaf. An example of this form is given on Plate II, *Adolias* (= *Euthalia*) *garuda*.

The pupæ are always freely suspended by the tail, never girt across the body by a thread (see Plate II). Many of them are beautifully gilt, and from this cause have been termed "Aurelia," hence "Aurelian," an old name for entomologists. They vary very greatly in form.

some are short and thick and quite smooth, others have the head terminating in two points, while others again are much spined and angled.

Key to the Indian Genera of NYMPHALINÆ.

A. Costal nervure of forewing strongly swollen at base.
       a. Male with a large glandular patch of black scales on underside of forewing above submedian nervure.

                    XLIV.—ERGOLIS.

       b No secondary sexual characters in male.
          a^1. Apex of forewing strongly truncate.

                    XLV.—EURYTELA.

          b^1 Apex of forewing rounded.

                    XLVI.—BYBLIA.

B. Costal nervure of forewing not swollen at base.
       a. First* subcostal nervule of forewing only emitted before end of cell.
          a^1. Second subcostal nervule of forewing emitted far beyond end of cell.
             a^2. Cell of both wings open.

                  XLVII.—EURIPUS.

             b^2. Cell of forewing closed, of hindwing open.
                a^3. Costa of forewing much curved, forewing broad.

                  XLVIII.—CUPHA.

                b^3. Costa of forewing nearly straight, forewing narrow.

                  XLIX.—MELITÆA.

             c^2. Cell of both wings closed.
                a^3. Outer margin of hindwing slightly dentate opposite median nervules only.

                  L.—ATELLA.

                b^3. Outer margin of hindwing deeply dentate throughout.

                  LI.—CETHOSIA.

          b^1. Second subcostal nervule of forewing emitted close to end of cell.
             a^2. Male with large patches of black plush-like scales on upperside of both wings.

                LII.—TERINOS.

              b^2. Male unfurnished with prominent secondary sexual characters.
                a^3. Third and fourth subcostal nervules of forewing emitted very close together, the fourth very long.

                  LIII.—CYNTHIA.

                b^3. Third and fourth subcostal nervules of forewing emitted far apart, the fourth short.
                  a^4. Antennæ with club abruptly formed and pyriform.

                  LIV.—HELCYRA.

                  b^4. Antennæ with club gradually formed, long and slender.
                    a^5. Fourth subcostal nervule of forewing long, emitted from subcostal nervure at a distance from the apex of the cell equal to less than two-thirds its length.

                    LV.—SEPHISA.

                    b^5. Fourth subcostal nervule of forewing short, emitted from subcostal nervure at a distance from the apex of the cell equal to three-fourths its length.

                    LVI.—DILIPA.

       b. Second* subcostal nervule of forewing emitted just before end of cell in addition to the first.
          a^1. Cell of both wings open.
              a^2. Antennæ long, more than half the length of the forewing.
                a^3. Fourth subcostal nervule of forewing short, emitted from subcostal nervure at a distance from the apex of the cell equal to more than twice its length.

                  LVII.—APATURA.
                  EULACURA.

                b^3. Fourth subcostal nervule of forewing long, emitted from subcostal nervure at a distance from the apex of the cell equal to less than twice its length.

---

* This character does not always hold good ; in some species of the genera *Hestina, Neptis, Cyrestis* and *Argynnis* the second subcostal nervule of the forewing is emitted after the apex of the cell.

  a^4. Discoidal nervule of hindwing given off from subcostal
   close to origin of first subcostal branch in typical
   species.

       LVIII.—HESTINA.*

  b^4. Discoidal nervule of hindwing given off from subcostal
   some distance beyond origin of first subcostal branch.

       LIX.—HERONA.

 b^3. Antennæ short, less than half the length of the forewing.

  a^3. Costal nervure of hindwing reaching the apex of wing.

       LX.—PRECIS.
       LXI.—JUNONIA.

  b^3. Costal nervure of hindwing short, reaching the margin before the
   apex of the wing.

       LXII.—NEPTIS.*

b^1. Cell of forewing closed, of hindwing open.

       LXIII.—CIRRHOCHROA.

c^1. Cell of both wings closed.

 a^2. Antennæ short, less than half the length of the forewing.

  a^3. Antennæ with club gradually formed and somewhat slender.

   a^4. Third subcostal nervule of forewing given off before
    apex of first.

    a^5. Apex of forewing truncate.

       LXIV.—PSEUDERGOLIS.

    b^5. Apex of forewing rounded.

       LXV.—STIBOCHIONA.

   b^4. Third subcostal nervule of forewing given off opposite
    apex of first.

       LXVI.—HYPOLIMNAS.

  b^3. Antennæ with club abruptly formed and pyriform.

       LXVII.—ARGYNNIS.*

 b^2. Antennæ long, more than half the length of the forewing.

       LXVIII. DICHORRAGIA.

c. Second* subcostal nervule of forewing emitted some distance before end of cell.

 a^1. Outer margin of hindwing more or less entire, not produced into tails or lobes.

  a^2. Apex of second subcostal nervule of forewing beyond origin of fourth.

   a^3. Apex of cell of forewing far beyond origin of second median nervule;

    a^4. Antennæ very short, less than one-third the length of the
    forewing.

       LXIX.—CALINAGA.

    b^4. Antennæ much longer, nearly half the length of the
    forewing.

       LXX.—PENTHEMA.

   b^3. Apex of cell of forewing close to origin of second median nervule.

    a^4. Third median nervule of forewing strongly angled.

       LXXI.—PARTHENOS.

    b^4. Third median nervule of forewing evenly curved but not
    angled.

     a^5. Lower disco-cellular nervule of forewing very
     upright, placed at right-angles to the median
     nervure.

       LXXII.—NEUROSIGMA.

     b^5. Lower disco-cellular nervule of forewing directed
     very obliquely outwards.

       LXXIII.—LEBADEA.
         PANDITA.

  b^2. Apex of second subcostal nervule of forewing before origin of fourth.

   a^3. First subcostal nervule not anastomosing with costal nervure.†

       LXXIV.—LIMENITIS.
       LXXV.—ATHYMA.
       LXXVI.—ABROTA.
       LXXVII—SYMPHÆDRA.
       LXXVIII.—EUTHALIA.

---

 * This character does not always hold good; in some species of the genera *Hestina*, *Neptis*, *Argynnis*, and *Cyrestis* the second subcostal nervule of the forewing is emitted after the apex of the cell.

 † I am unable to find any constant structural character by which to separate these five genera, except that in typical *Symphædra* the cell of the forewing is very short, the upper disco-cellular nervule being emitted from the subcostal nervure at about one-third the length of the wing from the base; in the other four genera it is emitted at much more than one-third distance.

b_1. First subcostal nervule anastomosing with costal nervure.

LXXIX.—Tanaecia.

c^1. Apex of second subcostal nervule of forewing opposite origin of fourth.

LXXX.— Pyrameis.

b^1. Outer margin of hindwing produced into one or more tails and lobes.

a^1. Hindwing with a distinct tooth or tail at third median nervule, no anal lobe.

a^2. Cell of both wings closed.

b_1. Cell of hindwing open.

LXXXI.—Vanessa.

LXXXII.—Symbrenthia.

a^2. Hindwing with a distinct tooth at discoidal nervule.

LXXXIII.—Rhinopalpa.

b^2. Hindwing with narrow curved tail at third median nervule, and a rounded anal lobe.

LXXXIV.—Cyrestis.*

c^1. Hindwing with a narrow tail at submedian nervure.

a^2. Cell of both wings closed.

LXXXV.—Kallima.

b^2. Cell of both wings open.

LXXXVI.—Doleschallia.

d^2. Hindwing with either two long narrow tails at the third and first median nervules, or a distinct tooth at the third and a small one at the first median nervule.

LXXXVII.—Charaxes.

e^2. Hindwing with a broad tail between the second and third median nervules.

LXXXVIII.—Prothoe.

Mr. Westwood, in the Gen. Diurn. Lep., vol. ii, p. 403, placed the first three genera of the *Nymphalinæ* (as here arranged) together with *Elymnias* (= his *Melanitis*), and three American genera which have since been included amongst the *Nymphalinæ*, in his Family XI, *Eurytelidæ*, with the following characters :—

"Insects of moderate size. BODY, moderately robust. *Head*, moderate-sized. *Eyes*, generally naked. *Palpi*, generally elongate, not compressed, clothed with short hairy scales. *Antennæ*, short, slender, not terminated by a decided club. *Wings*, generally large, dentated or angulated, and not ocellated beneath. FOREWING, with the *costal* nervure always greatly swollen at the base ; *subcostal* nervure with the first and second branches arising before the extremity of the discoidal cell, the *discoidal cell* closed with a slender lower disco-cellular nervule. HINDWING, with the abdominal margin moderately developed, so as only to form a slight canal for the reception of the abdomen ; *discoidal cell* closed by a slender lower disco-cellular nervule. FORELEGS, small, those of the *male* more or less hairy, without tarsal articulations ; of the *female* also small, but rather longer, and with the tarsal portion articulated ; without claws. Claws of the MIDDLE and HINDLEGS simple."

"This is another group which I would prefer to regard as a subfamily rather than as a separate family, its characters only appearing sufficiently strong to warrant the latter rank being accorded to it. Of these the elongated palpi scarcely differ from those of many of the *Nymphalinæ*, either in length or the nature of their clothing ; in this latter respect they are well distinguished from the *Satyrinæ*, with which, however, the strongly swollen condition of the costal nervure of the forewing seems to offer a point of connexion, although not a strong one, since it is a character of only generic value amongst the last-named insects. The structure of the forelegs in both sexes is also almost identical with that of many of the *Nymphalinæ*. The species are of moderate size, and for the most part varied in their colouring, although destitute of the beautiful ocelli of many of the preceding groups." (*Westwood, l. c.*)

---

* This character does not always hold good ; in some species of the genera *Hestina*, *Neptis*, *Argynnis*, and *Cyrestis* the second subcostal nervule of the forewing is emitted after the apex of the cell.

Ergolis, Eurytela and *Byblia* certainly seen to form a connecting link between the *Satyrinæ, Elymniinæ* and the *Nymphalinæ*, the structure of the larva and the swollen costal nervure being important points of connection. Mr. Distant in his "Rhopalocera Malayana" places them at the head of his synopsis of the genera of *Nymphalinæ*, but afterwards describes them near the middle of that subfamily, and adds that he is "not at all satisfied with the position in which" he has "placed these genera." Nor am I satisfied with the position they here occupy; they form a small and anomalous group, and it would perhaps have been better to have erected them into a subfamily under Westwood's name.

Genus 44.—ERGOLIS, Boisduval. (PLATE XVIII).

Ergolis, Boisduval, Sp. Gén., vol. i, pl. iv, fig. 4 (1836); Westwood, Gen. Diurn. Lep., vol. ii, p. 409 (1851); id., Moore, Lep. Cey., vol. i, p. 43 (1881); id., Distant, Rhop. Malay., p. 137 (1882); *Ariadne,* Horsfield, Cat. Lep. Mus. E. I. C., pl. vi, fig. 2 (1829).

"BODY, moderate-sized; *wings,* large, broad, thickly ornamented above with numerous slender, dark, undulating lines. *Head,* small, clothed with short scaly hairs. *Eyes,* moderate-sized, naked. *Antennæ,* slender, about two-fifths of the length of the forewing, terminated by a very slight and gradually-formed club, obtuse at the tip, and not more than double the thickness of the basal part of the antennæ. *Palpi,* porrected, but slightly curved, extending considerably beyond the length of the head, and not elevated above the middle of the eyes; the terminal joint a little deflexed at the tip, parallel, finely hairy beneath, the upper edge with a ridge of short hairs from the middle to the end; terminal joint elongate-oval, slender. *Thorax,* oval, woolly in front. *Abdomen,* slender. FOREWING, large, well arched along the *costal margin; outer* margin irregularly waved, about two-thirds of the length of the costal; *inner* margin nearly straight, about one-fourth longer than the outer, so that the wing appears nearly truncate at the tip. *Veins* arranged nearly as in *Eurytela. Costal nervure* dilated at the base; *upper disco-cellular nervule* very short, oblique; the extremity of the [*upper*] *discoidal* nervule extending into the most prominent of the angulations of the forewing; *middle* disco-cellular considerably longer, curved at its base, its extremity directed outwards longitudinally, forming the base of the lower discoidal nervule; *lower* disco-cellular very slender, nearly transverse, uniting with the third median nervule just beyond its origin, closing the *discoidal cell* at about one-third of the length of the wing. HINDWING, very broad, *outer margin* scalloped. *Præcostal nervure* rather oblique, branching at its extremity; *costal* extending to the outer angle of the wing; *subcostal* arising half way between the body and the præcostal, branching at a moderate distance from the base; *upper disco-cellular nervule* arising quite close to the origin of the subcostal branch, forming the very slightly curved base of the discoidal nervule; *lower* disco-cellular nearly straight, slightly oblique, uniting with the median nervure close to the origin of the third median nervule, closing the *discoidal cell* at about one-third of the length of the wing. FORELEGS of the *male* very minute and slender, but slightly and finely hairy; tarsal portion scarcely half the length of the tibia, simple, exarticulate, and destitute of terminal claws or spines; of the *female* somewhat longer than those of the male; *femur* rather shorter than the tibia and tarsus united; *tibia* and *tarsus* of nearly equal length, slender, cylindrical, scaly; the *tarsus* scarcely dilated at the extremity, where it is articulated; the joints with very short spines at their extremity beneath. MIDDLE and HINDLEGS rather short, slender, scaly; *tibia* almost destitute of short spines beneath; *tarsus* more thickly armed with rows of spines at the sides and beneath; *claws,* very slender, curved and entire."

"LARVA, rather short, cylindrical, rather attenuated in front; head armed with two long setose spines; segments of the body armed with fascicles of short setæ, or with small setigerous tubercles, variegated with spots and oblique stripes of different colours. PUPA, rather elongated; head-case obtusely pointed; thorax-case with an obtuse tubercle on the back; base of the dorsum of the abdomen with a larger obtuse tubercle."

"The very broad form of the wings (the forewing appearing almost transversely truncate), and the slender undulating black streaks with which they are adorned on both sides, at once distinguish the species of this genus. On the underside the spaces enclosed between each pair of dark streaks is of a richer hue than the ground-colour of the wings. In their structural generic characters they are, however, very closely allied to the genera *Eurytela* and *Byblia*." (*Westwood*, l. c.)

It is singular that no author, as far as I am aware, has described the very prominent secondary sexual characters that exist in the males of the species of this genus. In all the species on the underside of the forewing there is a very large triangular patch of shining black scales from the submedian nervure extending a short distance into the cell and above the third median nervule, but not reaching the outer margin. In addition to this in *E. ariadne* the subcostal nervure and first subcostal nervule on the upperside of the hind-wing are white and shining for a greater portion of their length ; and in *E. taprobana* in the middle of the disc of the hindwing on the underside there is a large diffused patch of deep maroon scales. All these characters are absent from the female.

Ergolis, as also *Byblia*, is found in Africa, in all parts of India, and extends through the Malay peninsula, Sumatra, Java, &c., to the Philippines. The described species are few in number, several of them are but doubtfully distinct, and some of them range from India to Java. In habits they resemble the *Nymphalinæ* rather than the *Satyrinæ* ; their flight is short and jerky, they frequent bushes and cultivated spots, and always settle with wings widely expanded. They are generally numerous in individuals wherever they occur. It is also a curious fact that two distinct species always seem to occur together in India ; where one species is met with there will be found another species also.

Key to the Indian species of Ergolis.

A. Male with the subcostal nervure and the first subcostal nervule of the hindwing on the upperside concolourous with the rest of the veins.
  a. Male with a subapical white spot on the upperside of the forewing.
   299. E. MERIONE, India, Burma, Malay peninsula.
  b. Male with no subapical white spot on the upperside of the forewing.
   300. E. TAPROBANA, South India and Ceylon.
B. Male with the subcostal nervure and the first subcostal nervule of the hindwing on the upperside
 white.
   301. E. ARIADNE, India, Ceylon, Malayana, Formosa.

299. Ergolis moriono, Cramer. (PLATE XVIII, FIG. 70♂).

Papilio meriona, Cramer, Pap. Ex., vol. II. pl. cxliv, figs G, H (1777) : *P. cortinna*, Herbst, Pap., pl. clxxxi, figs. 1, 2 (1794) : *Ergolis meriona*, Butler, Cat. Fab. Lep. B. M., p. 70, n. 3 (1869) ; id., Wallace, Trans. Ent. Soc Lond., 1869, p. 332, n. 2 ; id., Distant, Rhop. Malay., p. 138, n. 2, pl. xv, fig. 6 (1882), *female* ; *E. tapestrina*, Moore, Journ A. S. B., vol. liii, pl. 2, p. 19 (1884).

HABITAT : Continental India, Burma, Malay peninsula.

EXPANSE : 2·1 to 2·7 inches.

DESCRIPTION : "MALE and FEMALE. UPPERSIDE warm ochraceous ; *forewing* with a subapical white spot placed above the bifurcation of the fourth and fifth subcostal nervules, and with the following blackish markings :—two lines crossing the cell near the base, the outer one continued to the submedian nervure ; two waved and zigzag lines crossing the middle of the cell, and continued to the submedian nervure ; three waved lines at the end of the cell not passing the median nervure ; a pair of curved and very zigzag lines crossing the disc at about the middle of the wing, followed by another very waved line, commencing near the subapical white spot ; a submarginal series of three waved lines, the inner one faint and somewhat macular ; the outer margin black, with the *cilia* alternately greyish. *Hindwing* with the markings similar and generally continuous with those of the forewing, but the inner of the three submarginal lines replaced by a series of castaneous spots placed between the nervules, sometimes at and along the median nervules, divided by the junction of the anterior and posterior waved lines. UNDERSIDE duller and slightly darker than above ; the spaces between the waved lines (excluding the submarginal ones) castaneous, thus showing two very prominent and dark fasciæ on the disc, and a narrower and paler one near the base of both wings ; *body* and *legs* more or less concolourous with the wings." *(Distant, l. c.)*

This species may easily be distinguished from *E. ariadne* by the outer margins of both wings being more even, and the lines across the upperside more numerous and zigzag. The female is altogether paler than the male, the subapical white spot on the upperside of the forewing more prominent. It is a common species ; I have taken it plentifully in Calcutta and in Sikkim at low elevations, but only on one occasion at Simla ; it occurs also rarely at Masuri. Mr. S. E. Peal has sent specimens from Sibsagar in Upper Assam. Mr. Wood-Mason took it in Cachar, and it is common in Orissa, from whence Mr. W. C. Taylor has sent numerous examples. Colonel Swinhoe has taken it at Deesa in Rajputana, and has received it from the Nilgiris ; Dr. Anderson took it in the Mergui Archipelago, and Captain C. T. Bingham in the Thoungyeen Valley, and the Donat range in Upper Tenasserim in the early months of the year. It probably occurs throughout Northern and Continental India, extending eastwards through Assam and Burma to the Malay peninsula. The larva is green, with two branched spines projecting forwards in front of the head, and feeds on the castor-oil plant. Mr. Wallace states that the larva of *Ergolis* " agrees with the *Junonia* type," but the bifurcating branched spines on the head are absent from the larvæ of *Junonia*, their presence would apparently indicate the near relationship of *Ergolis* to the *Satyrinæ* rather than to the *Nymphalinæ*. In *Charaxes*, however, a genus of the latter subfamily, the larvæ of which have a superficial likeness to the *Satyrinæ*, the spines are directed backwards instead of forwards.

The figure shows both sides of a male Masuri specimen in the Indian Museum, Calcutta.

What appears to be an occasional aberration, or " sport," of this species has lately been described by Mr. Moore under the name of *E. tapestrina*. There is a single specimen from the Naga Hills in the Indian Museum, Calcutta, and one from Upper Tenasserim in Major Marshall's collection which agree somewhat with his description ; the latter is given below.*

300. Ergolis taprobana, Westwood.

E. taprobana, Westwood, Gen. Diurn. Lep , vol. ii, p 410, n. 3, pl. lxviii, fig. 4 (1851) : id , Moore, Lep. Cey., vol. i, p. 44, pl. xxiii, figs. 1, 1*b, male* ; 1*a, female* (1880).

HABITAT : South India, Ceylon.

EXPANSE : 1·75 to 2·2 inches.

DESCRIPTION : " MALE and FEMALE. UPPERSIDE, *both wings* dark ferruginous, crossed by four or five basal black sinuous lines, a disco-cellular double line, two medial, two discal, and a marginal line, the discal ones interspaced with indistinct black-speckled spots ; the lines obsolete on the costal border of the *hindwing* ; a small white costal spot near the apex of the *forewing* in the FEMALE. UNDERSIDE dark purple-brown, palest on the outer borders ; transverse sinuous lines indistinct in the male, but very distinct and with four intervening spaces suffused with chalybeate-grey in the female." *(Moore, l. c.)*

In Ceylon " Widely distributed in low country and hills up to 6,000 feet, both in forest and cultivated lands. Found all the year in the hills, variable and not so common in the plains. Flight slow, skimming, but shy, and not easy to capture" *(Hutchinson).* " Common all the year round in low country and up to 4,000 feet" *(Mackwood).*

This species may be distinguished from *E. merione* by its darker colour on the upperside, the outer margin of the forewing less falcate ; it has also no subapical spot on the upperside of the forewing in the male. On the underside of the hindwing in the male there is a large discal round suffused patch of dark maroon scales not mentioned by Mr. Moore. There are specimens in the Indian Museum, Calcutta, from Calicut and Ootacamund (*W. F. Hampson*) in South

* *Ergolis tapestrina,* Moore, Journ. A. S. B., vol. iii, pt. 2, p. 19 (1884). HABITAT : Debra Doon, Manpuri *(Moore),* Naga Hills and Upper Tenasserim EXPANSE : 1·75 to 2·1 inches. DESCRIPTION ; " MALE and FEMALE. Comparatively smaller than *E. merione* ; outline of the *forewing* more irregular. UPPERSIDE paler ; with similar transverse sinuous lines on *both wings*, the two medial lines being somewhat nearer together, the discal cordate marks having their outline of a uniform width, and being somewhat narrower transversely, thus leaving a slightly but perceptibly wider space between the contiguous lines ; the interspaces between the basal lines, the subbasal and medial lines, the discal cordiform marks, and the marginal line and outer margin, are of a more dusky colour, and thus give the wings the appearance of being marked with alternately pale and dusky transverse bands. UNDERSIDE also paler than in *E. merione*, with more regularly alternate pale and dark transverse bands." *(Moore, l. c.)*

India, and from Ceylon, in which places it replaces the common North Indian species, *E. merione*. It has been taken also as far north as Khandalla in the Western Ghâts by Major Yerbury.

301. **Ergolis ariadne**, Linnæus.

Papilio ariadne, Linnæus, Syst. Nat., vol. i, pt. 2, p. 778, n. 170 (1767); *Biblis ariadne*, Godart, Enc. Méth., vol. ix, p. 327, n. 6 (1819); *Ergolis ariadne*, Boisduval, Sp. Gén., vol. i, pl. iv, fig. 4, *larva* and *pupa* (1836); id., (part), Horsfield and Moore, Cat. Lep. Mus. E, I. C., vol. i, p 144, n. 293 (1857); id., Butler, Cat. Fab. Lep. B. M., p 70, n. 2 (1869); id., Wallace, Trans. Ent. Soc. Lond., 1869, p. 332, n. 1; id., Distant, Rhop. Malay., p. 137, n. 1, pl. xi, fig. 6, *female* (1882); *Papilio coryta*, Cramer, Pap. Ex., vol. i, pl. lxxxvi, figs. E, F (1776); id., Herbst, Pap., pl. clxxxi, figs. 3, 4 (1794); *Ariadne coryta?* Horsfield, Cat. Lep. E. I. C., pl. vi, f. 2, *male*; pl. vii, fig 6, *structure of image, larva* and *pupa* (1829); *Ergolis coryta*, Horsfield and Moore, Cat. Lep. Mus. E. I C., vol. i, p. 144, n. 294, pl. vi, fig. 6, *larva*; 6a, *pupa* (1857); *E. minorata*, Moore, Lep. Cey., vol. i, p. 44, pl. xxiii, figs. 2, 2a, *male* (1881); *E. indica*, Moore, Journ. A. S. B., vol. liii, pt 2, p. 20 (1884).

HABITAT: Throughout India, Ceylon, Assam, Burma, Malay peninsula, Sumatra, Java, Borneo and Formosa.

EXPANSE: 1·8 to 2·3 inches.

DESCRIPTION: "MALE and FEMALE rufous or ochraceous. *Forewing* with a small white subapical spot placed just above the bifurcation of the fourth and fifth subcostal nervules, and with the cell crossed by the following dark markings:—a short and nearly straight basal line continued to the submedian nervure, a double-looped and much-waved line in the middle, and two longer, waved, and more widely separated lines at the apex; two waved discal fuscous lines crossing *both wings*, commencing about the subcostal nervure of the forewing, and terminating near the submedian nervure of the hindwing; on both wings these are followed by a waved and more indistinct line, and again by a very dark and situated submarginal line; a similarly dark marginal line, the *cilia* somewhat alternately greyish. UNDERSIDE very dark ochraceous or pale castaneous, crossed by three very irregular dark fasciæ, the first near the base, the second crossing the wings about the apices of the cells, the third between the last and the outer margin; these fasciæ have their margins darker, and the third encloses a series of dark spots placed between the nervules (these are most distinct on the hindwing); marginal and submarginal lines as above, and the subapical white spot on the forewing very distinct. In the MALE the area of the median nervules, on the underside of the forewing, is shining greenish fuscous. *Body* and *legs* more or less concolourous with the wings." (*Distant*, l.c.)

This is as common a species as *E. merione*. I have taken it at all seasons in Calcutta, and rarely in Sikkim. There are specimens in the Indian Museum, Calcutta, from Orissa (*W. C. Taylor*), Sibsagar (*S. E. Peal*), Sylhet, Cachar (*Wood-Mason*), Mergui archipelago (*Dr. J. Anderson*); Bombay, the Wynaad, Calicut, South India, Ceylon, Upper Tenasserim, and Java (*Horsfield*). Mr. Moore has recorded *E. ariadne* from the North-West Himalayas (Proc. Zool. Soc. Lond., 1882, p. 240), but as the specimens referred to were probably those collected in Calcutta and given by me to Mr. Hocking, this is most likely incorrect. Colonel Swinhoe has taken it as far west as Deesa in Rajputana.

Mr. Moore has apparently confined *E. ariadne* to Java, as recently he has described *E. indica* from India. Comparing specimens so named by him with Javan ones collected by Dr. Horsfield, I can find no constant character by which to separate them. The description of *E. indica* is given as a foot-note.* Similarly I am unable to separate the Ceylon specimens which he has named *E. minorata* from Continental Indian ones, except that they are rather smaller. The description is given below.† It would appear from it that there is a wide

---

* *Ergolis indica*, Moore, Journ. A. S. B., vol. liii, pt. 2, p. 20 (1884). HABITAT: Calcutta, Madras, Bombay, Nilgiris. EXPANSE: 1·62 to 1·75 inches. DESCRIPTION: "Differs from typical Javan specimens of *E. ariadne* in its smaller size. UPPERSIDE of a duller colour, the markings more obscure and considerably less sinuous. UNDERSIDE with paler interspaces between the bands, the apical border of the *forewing* and the marginal border of the *hindwing* greyer, and comparatively broader." (*Moore*, l.c.)

† *Ergolis minorata*, Moore, Lep. Cey., vol. i, p. 44, pl. xxiii, figs. 2, 2a, *male* (1880). HABITAT: Ceylon. EXPANSE: *male*, 1·62; *female*, 1·88 inches. DESCRIPTION: "MALE and FEMALE. UPPERSIDE dark ferruginous; both wings with two short black waved lines across the base of the cell, a subbasal line, a disco-cellular line, a medial line, two discal lines, and a marginal line; a small white costal spot before the apex in both sexes. UNDERSIDE dark purple-brown, with the black lines less distinct and with four purple-grey intervening spaces; apical spot distinct." (*Moore*, l.c.)

"Found in low country, and hills up to 4,000 feet. Less common than *E. taprobana*. May to June in greatest number" (*Mackwood*). "Kandy" (*Wade*).

distinction in the colouring of the underside, but in reality this feature is very variable, and a series of Ceylon specimens match in this respect with a series of continental specimens of *E. ariadne.*

Mrs. Wylly of Khorda, Orissa, has furnished me with the following description of the transformations of *E. ariadne.* "LARVA, ·75 of an inch in length. Above black, with a narrow dorsal stripe starting near the head and ending before reaching the tail, composed of transverse stripes and dots of yellow; beneath and legs purplish-red. The body covered with six even rows of 3-branched spines; two long many-branched spines on the small black head; moves its head from side to side when walking. Food-plant, the *Tragia involucrata* (*Bichitee*, Bengali, *Bicha*, Ooriya), a twining plant with hairy and stinging leaves. PUPA, greyish-brown with a few dark shadings, a pointed projection on the thorax. Attaches itself by the tail to its food-plant and stands out from it nearly horizontally, the body of the pupa slightly curved downwards. Emerges in about ten days." The colour of the pupa seems variable; those I have bred in Calcutta when attached to the green stem and amongst the green leaves of the food-plant were coloured green also; the brown pupæ may be attached to dead leaves or stalks.

An allied species to *E. ariadne* from Singapore and Sumatra has been described by Mr. Wallace. Mr. Distant in his "Rhopalocera Malayana" is unable, however, to identify it. The description is given below.*

Genus 45.—EURYTELA, Boisduval. (PLATE XVIII).

Eurytela, Boisduval, Ann. Mus. Hist. Nat., p. 202 (1833); id., Faun. Ent. Madagasc., p. 54 (1833); id., Westwood, Gen. Diurn. Lep., vol. ii, p. 428 (1851); id., Trimen, Rhop. Afr. Austr., p. 211 (1866); id., Distant, Rhop. Malay., p. 135 (1882).

"BODY, and *wings* moderate-sized; the latter scalloped; forewing angulated below the apex. HEAD, moderate-sized, with a tuft of hairs at the base of each antenna. *Eyes,* prominent, naked; hairy in some African species. *Antennæ,* not quite half the length of the forewing, slender; terminated by a slight, gradually formed, but very short club, obtuse at the tip. *Palpi,* elongated, rather slender, finely hairy, porrected further than the length of the head, and elevated to about the middle of the eyes; terminal joint about half the length of the preceding, slender. *Thorax,* of moderate size, woolly in front and behind. *Abdomen,* slender. FORE-WING, moderate-sized; the *costal margin* but slightly arched; *apex* subtruncate; *outer* margin scalloped, angulated below the apex at the extremity of the upper discoidal nervule. *Upper disco-cellular nervule* very short, rather oblique; *middle* scarcely longer, slightly curved; *lower* much longer, straight, transverse, but very slender, uniting with the median nervure exactly at the origin of the third median nervule. HINDWING, moderate-sized, subtriangular-ovate. *Outer margin* strongly scalloped. *Upper disco-cellular nervule* arising very close to the base of the branch of the subcostal nervure; the *lower* very slender, transverse, and uniting with the median nervure at a little distance before the origin of the third median nervule. FORELEGS, of the *male* very slender and short; the *femur* very delicately hairy; the *tibia* and *tarsus* of equal thickness, and of nearly equal length, being together about one-fourth longer than the femur. Of the *female* considerably longer than those of the male, but equally slender; the tarsal portion dilated into an elongate-oval mass, with the three intermediate joints armed at the tip within with a pair of long sharp spines; terminal joint very small and oblique. MIDDLE and HINDLEGS, rather short, thickly scaly; *tibia* armed beneath with rows of short spines; *tarsus* more thickly clothed beneath and at the sides with rows of short spines. *Claws,* small, curved, acute, simple. *Paronychia,* very slender, bifid; the outer division almost setaceous." (*Westwood,* l.c.)

---

* *Ergolis isæus,* Wallace, Trans. Ent. Soc. Lond., 1869, p. 333. n. 4; id., Distant, Rhop. Malay., p. 139 (1882). HABITAT: Singapore, Sumatra. DESCRIPTION: "Size of *E. coryta*" [= *E. ariadne*]. Outline of wings nearly even, with an angular lobe on the *forewing,* waved same somewhat as in *E. coryta* [= *E. ariadne*], but disposed in pairs, no white spot near the apex; on the *hindwing* a series of distinct sublunulate ring markings, each enclosing an obscure reddish spot. UNDERSIDE, *forewing* dusky, the disc reddish-brown, the borders pale, a dusky streak parallel to the outer margin. *hindwing* pale brown, the markings as above, but the lunulate ring spots smaller, the outer border ashy brown. FEMALE, like the male, but paler, especially beneath. This species has probably been confounded with *E. coryta* [= *E. ariadne*] from which the even outline of the wings, and the absence of the white spot, at once distinguish it." (*Wallace,* l.c.) In speaking of *E. taprobana* (l.c.) he also says "A dark rusty-coloured species, with the forewing less angular than in *E. isæus.*"

The larva and pupa of a Natal species (*E. hiarbas*) described by Mr. Gooch are "both conspicuous by their forms. The larva has two long divergent clubbed and rough horns on its head, and the pupa is remarkable by its angulated, excavated, and alated development. Some of the larvæ were green with black marks, and others were green all over."*

Like the genera *Ergolis* and *Byblia*, *Eurytela* is represented in Africa as well as in the Oriental region ; in fact it is in the former continent and in Madagascar that the majority of the species included in it are to be found. Only two species occur in the East, one in the Andaman Isles, Tenasserim and Java, the other in the Malay Peninsula, Sumatra and Borneo. The former is remarkable from the very different aspect of the opposite sexes, the male being dark blue, the female pale ochraceous.

302. Eurytela horsfieldii, Boisduval. (PLATE XVIII, FIG. 69 ♂).

E. horsfieldii, Boisduval, Faun. Ent. Madagasc., p. 54, n. 1, *male*; *E. stephensii*, idem, id., p. 55, n. 2 *female* (1833); *E. horsfieldii*, Wallace, Trans. Ent. Soc. Lond., 1869, p. 332, n. 2.

HABITAT : Andaman Isles, Tenasserim, Java.

EXPANSE : 2·1 to 2·3 inches.

DESCRIPTION : MALE. "Wings dentated, on the UPPERSIDE black-blue, with a common discoidal evanescent pale fascia. UNDERSIDE blackish-grey, with four undulating black lines : the *hindwing* rounded, *forewing* with the apex produced." FEMALE. "Wings dentated, blackish-ferruginous, with four undulating black lines, and a common discoidal fascia, interrupted in the forewing, luteous. UNDERSIDE paler, the *hindwing* rounded, the *forewing* with the apex produced." (*Boisduval*, l. c.)

MALE. UPPERSIDE deep blue-black. *Forewing* with a subapical bluish-white diffused oblique streak, and another wider one across the middle of the disc, commencing just above the second median nervule, and ending on the inner margin, both these streaks inwardly sharply defined, outwardly diffused, and followed by a slaty-blue band extending almost to the margin which is black, and bearing a submarginal waved line dilated at the costa. Within the lower bluish-white streak and below the median nervure to the inner margin the ground-colour of the wing is slaty-blue. *Hindwing* divided into the following bands :—A slaty-blue basal one, a broad bluish-white one, then a narrower blue one, a broad deep blue-black band and the margin blue. The disco-cellular nervules marked with a black line. Cilia white. UNDERSIDE, *both wings* French-grey, mottled with blackish throughout, especially so across the disc, the margin palest ; crossed by a basal nearly straight black line, two hardly-traceable discal ones, which are nearly lost in the dark ground-colour of that portion of the wing, and a very zigzag submarginal one. The disco-cellulars marked with a black line. FEMALE ferruginous-ochreous, instead of deep blue-black as in the male, markings pale ochreous instead of bluish-white ; *cilia* dusky. *Forewing* with a reniform mark near the middle of the cell, followed immediately by a dark line which is continued across the base of the hindwing ; the disco-cellular nervules defined by a dark line. The bluish-white subapical and discal bands of the male replaced by pale clear ochraceous ones, followed by a lunular blackish line, and then a submarginal one as in the male. *Hindwing* with the base ferruginous-ochreous, beyond which the disc is broadly pale ochraceous, the disco-cellulars marked with a dark line, beyond which is an irregular fine dark line from the costa to the submedian nervure, followed by a darker and more regular line, within which towards the anal angle the ground-colour is mottled ferruginous, and beyond it to the margin it is dark ferruginous, with a submarginal black line, which is straight from the anal angle to the third median nervule, from thence to the outer angle it is waved. UNDERSIDE, *both wings* pale ochreous, mottled with blackish ferruginous. The disco-cellulars marked with a dark line, and the wings crossed at nearly equal distances by four dark lines, the third from the base being on the *hindwing* the widest and darkest. The margin defined with a dark line.

---

* Quoted by Mr. Distant in his Rhop. Malay , p 136.

The late Mr. A. de Roëpstorff sent several specimens of both sexes of this species to the Indian Museum, Calcutta.   Captain C. T. Bingham has taken a single male in the Meplay Valley in October, which differs from South Andaman specimens on the upperside in having the marginal blue band obsolete, and in its much lighter colouration on the underside. *E. horsfieldii* also occurs in Java.

The figure shows both sides of a South Andaman male in the Indian Museum, Calcutta.

A very beautiful species of the genus has been described from Malayana; the original description is given below.*   It is quite distinct from *E. horsfieldii*, the ground-colour of the upperside being entirely rich ultramarine-blue to judge from the published figures of it.

Genus 46.—BYBLIA, Hubner. (PLATE XVIII).

Byblia, Hübner, Verz. bek. Schmett., p. 28 (1816) : id., Moore, Lep Cey., vol. i, p. 45 (1881) ; *Hypanis*, Boisduval, Ann. Mus. Hist. Nat., p. 203 (1833) ; idem, id., Faun. Madagasc., Ent., p. 55 (1833) ; idem, id., Spéc. Gén., pl. ix (1836) ; id., Westwood, Gen. Diurn. Lep., vol. ii, p. 410 (1851) ; id., Trimen, Rhop. Afr. Austr., p. 214 (1866).

" BODY, slender, moderately woolly ; *wings*, of moderate size, of a rich orange colour above with black markings, but not ocellated, alike in both sexes.   *Head*, rather small, finely hairy in front.   *Eyes*, prominent, naked.   *Palpi*, elongate, rather slender, not compressed, finely hairy, porrected considerably further than the length of the front of the head ; the terminal joint horizontally porrected, not elevated above the level of the middle of the eyes ; middle joint with a small conical tuft of hairs in the middle, next the face.   *Antennæ*, short, scarcely half the length of the forewing, slender ; joints indistinct, not annulated, with pale scales ; terminated by a rather long gradually-formed club, formed of very short joints, obtuse at the tip, which is curved outwards.   *Thorax*, rather small, woolly in front.   *Abdomen*, very slender. FOREWING, of moderate size, subtriangular ; the *costa* moderately arched ; *apex* rather rounded ; *outer margin* about two-thirds of the length of the costa, convex, very slightly scalloped ; *inner* margin nearly straight, rather longer than the outer.   *Costal nervure* dilated at the base ; *subcostal* with the first and second branches arising before the anterior extremity of the discoidal cell ; third and fourth beyond it, at considerable distances apart.   *Upper disco-cellular nervule* very short, oblique ; *middle* disco-cellular considerably longer, less oblique, slightly curved ; *lower* disco-cellular much longer, transverse, the lower extremity curved a little outwards ; uniting with the median nervure at the origin of the third median nervule, and closing the *discoidal cell* at two-fifths of the length of the wing.   HINDWING, subtriangularly ovate ; *outer* margin scalloped ; *inner* margin forming only a slight gutter for the reception of the abdomen ; *precostal nervure* curved, lightly furcate at the tip ; *costal* nervure extending to the outer angle of the wing ; *subcostal* nervure branching at a moderate distance from the base, followed quite closely by the *upper disco-cellular nervule*, which forms the slightly curved base of the *discoidal* nervule ; *lower* disco-cellular very slender, strongly arched, uniting with the median nervure at a little distance in advance of the origin of its third branch, and closing the *discoidal cell* at about one-third of the length of the wing.   FORELEGS, of the *male* very small, slender, and delicate, very slightly and finely hirsute ; the *femur* rather longer than the tibia ; *tarsus* rather more than half the length of the tibia, quite simple, and destitute of articulations and claws, or terminal spines.   Forelegs of the *female* half as long again as those of the male, slender, scaly, and destitute of hairs ; the proportions of the different parts as in the male, the tarsal portion as thick as the tibia, slightly dilated towards the tip, and armed with three pairs of short spines, indicating the second, third, and fourth articulations.

---

* *Eurytela castelnaui*, Felder. HABITAT : Malay peninsula, Singapore, Sumatra, Borneo. EXPANSE : 2¾ inches. DESCRIPTION : " MALE. Wings insulated with white between the cilia ; UPPERSIDE blue, an undulating black submarginal strga ; UNDERSIDE dusky brown, the base and beyond variegated with white, three common discal black fasciæ." (Felder, Wien. Ent. Monatsch., vol. iv, p. 401, n. 26 (1860) ; id., Reise Novara, Lep., vol. iii, pl. lxi, figs. 5, 6, male (1866) ; id., Wallace, Trans. Ent. Soc. Lond., 1869, p. 331, n. 1 ; id., Distant, Rhop. Malay., p. 136, n. 1, pl. xv, fig. 10, male (1882).

The following short description is taken from the figure in the Reise Novara :—Upperside of a deep ultramarine-blue without gloss, the exterior margin narrowly edged with black, and a submarginal line of narrow black lunules following the contour of the wing which is dentate, and somewhat falcate by the prolongation of the lower discoidal nervule. UNDERSIDE brown, suffused with whitish towards the margin, and covered with minute dark striæ ; *forewing* with two indistinct dark discal bands ; *hindwing* with one indistinct band in continuation of the outer one on the forewing, and two dark sinuous lines between it and the base.

MIDDLE and HINDLEGS, moderately long and slender; the spines on the underside of the *tibia* and *tarsus* rather stronger and more numerous than in *Ergolis* and *Eurytela*; *claws*, strong, simple, entire; *paronychia*, very small." (*Westwood*, l. c.)

This is a genus of very small extent, occurring in Africa, peninsular India and Ceylon only. In Africa the species of *Byblia* present several different forms, some of which have been figured and described by different authors, and are by some authorities still kept distinct, while others unite them under one species. Mr. Trimen remarks (Rhop. Afr. Austr., p. 216) that "There can be no doubt whatever that all the hitherto-recorded species of *Hypanis* [= *Byblia*] are varieties of a single species, *ilithyia* of Drury." They are small insects, bright ferruginous on the upperside with narrow black border and black lines and spots.

Key to the Indian species of Byblia.

A. Underside of hindwing with a black band across the disc beyond the middle of the wing bearing pairs of white dots.
>303. B. ILITHYIA, Africa, Continental and Southern India, Ceylon.

B. This band entirely white, instead of being black, and undulating, and not bearing white dots in pairs.
>304. B. SIMPLEX, Central India.

303. Byblia ilithyia, Drury. (PLATE XVIII, FIG. 68 ♂).

Papilio ilithyia, Drury, Ill. Ex. Ins., vol. ii, p. 29, pl. xvii, figs. 1, 2 (1773), *male; Hypanis ilithyia*, Doubleday and Hewitson, Gen. Diurn. Lep., vol. ii, p. 411, n. 1, pl. lxviii, fig. 1 (1852), *male*; id., Butler, Proc. Zool. Soc. Lond., 1884, p. 483, n. 7; id., Oberthür, Ann Mus. Genova, vol. xviii, p. 725, n. 49 (1883); *Byblia ilithyia*, Hübner, Verz. bek. Schmett., p. 28 (1816); id., Moore, Lep. Cey., vol. i, p. 45, pl. xxiii, figs. 3, 3a (1881), *male; Papilio polinice*, Cramer, Pap. Ex., vol. iv, pl. ccclxxv, figs. G, H (1782), *female; Hypanis polinice*, Boisduval, Sp. Gén., vol. i, pl. ix, fig. 6 (1836), *male*; id., Butler, Proc. Zool. Soc. Lond., 1883, p. 146, n. 6.

HABITAT: Africa, continental and peninsular India, and Ceylon.

EXPANSE: ♂, 1·85 to 2·0; ♀, 2·0 to 2·2 inches.

DESCRIPTION: "MALE. UPPERSIDE, *both wings* bright ferruginous, with black costal and exterior marginal borders. *Forewing* with three short streaks crossing the cell, a disco-cellular lobular streak joined beneath to an irregular band extending across the base of the *hindwing*, and followed on that wing by a lower row of small spots; a submarginal band, broken below the costa of the *forewing*, extending to the anal angle of the *hindwing*, and from which runs a longitudinal line along each vein to the outer border. FEMALE with the black basal markings narrower and more confluent, with suffused dusky basal interspaces, the submarginal band broader, and to which is joined an inner row of lunules, the outer spaces being macular. *Cilia* alternated with white. UNDERSIDE paler, *forewing* marked as above; borders of the costal streaks and a row of spots before the apex pale yellow. *Hindwing* with a basal and medial transverse yellow band, lined externally by a black line, and internally by a row of black spots, an intervening black spot, a submarginal black band spotted with white and bordered outwardly by large yellow spots, a white marginal lunular line." (*Moore*, l.c.)

The Indian Museum, Calcutta, possesses specimens from Kutch, the Deccan, and Bombay, from the late East India Company's Museum; from the Anseba Valley, Abyssinia, collected by Mr. W. T. Blandford, and from Madras. Mr. J. Davidson, C.S., has taken it at Dhulia in the Khandesh district, Bombay, in July, and in Major Marshall's collection are specimens from Poona (October and November), Mhow (October). Depalpore (November) all taken by Colonel C. Swinhoe, from Madras and the Nilgiris. In Ceylon Mr. Moore states that it is "a very rare butterfly." Mr. Butler records B. *polinice* as a distinct species from Madras, probably considering that B. *ilithyia* occurs in Africa and not in India. The Abyssinian specimens above referred to agree, however, with the Indian ones. Colonel C. Swinhoe (Proc. Zool. Soc. Lond., 1885, p. 129, n 32) also records B. *polinice* from "Poona, September to December; Ahmednugger, June to November." From a close scrutiny of the numerous specimens of B. *ilithyia* from various localities which I have examined, I am unable to find any characters by which to separate them into two species. Drury's original figure of B. *ilithyia* is of a male, while Cramer's of B. *polinice* is of a female. It seems more than probable that Cramer did not know both sexes of the species he named, or that his specimen was a female while Drury's was a male of one species, hence the confusion that has arisen.

Mr. E. H. Aitken has furnished me with the following short note on the transformations of this species: "The larvæ of both *Ergolis ariadne* and *Byblia ilithyia* were found on *Tragia cannabina*, and were so similar that the only distinctive mark was the dorsal light-green or greenish-yellow broad band, which in the latter was continued to the anal extremity, while in the former it reached to the middle only. The colour on the sides was sometimes green, but generally almost black. Length about an inch, *E. ariadne* being a little smaller; shape cylindrical, slender for its length, with two longitudinal rows of branched spines. There were twelve pairs of these spines, besides the peculiar pair on the head nearly a quarter of an inch long and not branched, but terminating in a crown-like expansion. The pupa is rather slender, colour sometimes green, sometimes brown. In this stage the two species seem indistinguishable."

The figure is taken from a male Madras specimen in the Indian Museum, Calcutta, and shows both sides.

304. Byblia simplex, Butler.

Hypanis simplex, Butler, Proc. Zool. Soc. Lond., 1885, p. 146, n. 7, pl. xxiv. fig. 8; id., Swinhoe, Proc. Zool. Soc. Lond., 1885, p. 129, n. 1).

HABITAT : Depalpore, a lake-district 30 miles north of Mhow ; Assirghar ; Poona.

EXPANSE : 1·6 inches.

DESCRIPTION : "Allied to the African *H.* [=*B.*] *cora*. UPPERSIDE tawny with black markings as in little-marked females of *H.* [=*B.*] *ilithyia* of Africa. UNDERSIDE very like *H.* [=*B.*] *cora*, but the black discoidal markings of the *forewing* distinctly white-edged, the subapical white spots larger and clearer, the submarginal black band near external angle reduced to a mere undulated stripe ; the first and second white bands of the *hindwing* pure, not crossed by coloured veins, edged on both sides with black dots ; submarginal white spots less widely separated ; an undulated white marginal stripe in place of the pairs of white dots." (*Butler*, l.c.) Mr. Butler does not indicate the sex of the specimen he describes and figures : it appears to be a female however.

B. simplex has as yet only been taken by Colonel C. Swinhoe as far as I know, he has found it at Depalpore in Central India in January ; at Mhow in June, July, and October, common ; at Assirghar in September ; and at Poona in November, December and January, common. I have not seen a specimen of this species. From the figure it appears to be distinct, the hindwing on the underside much paler, with a submarginal chain of large white or yellowish spots inwardly defined with a fine black and then a white line, while in *B. ilithyia* the latter is broken up into white spots in pairs.

The next group of the *Nymphalinæ* contains ten genera, which are distinguished by having only the first of the subcostal nervules of the forewing emitted before the end of the cell ; the second subcostal nervule being emitted beyond the origin of the upper disco-cellular nervule, which marks the end of the cell. This group is further divided into two sub-groups, the first five genera having the second subcostal nervule emitted far beyond the end of the cell, while in the other five it is emitted close to the end of the cell.

With the exception of *Melitæa* which is a Palæarctic genus, only extending into our limits in the high ranges of mountains on the North and North-West, the whole of the genera of this group are either confined to the southern slopes of the Himalayas extending to the hills east of the Brahmaputra, or else are spread through the Indo-Malayan region, one genus extending to Africa and another to Australia. Most of the genera of this group comprise but few species.

Genus 47.—EURIPUS, Westwood. (PLATE XX).

Euripus, Westwood, Gen. Diurn. Lep., vol. ii, p. 293 (1850) ; id., Distant, Rhop. Malay., p. 133 (1882).

"BODY, robust ; hindwing deeply scalloped, with a very short truncated tail in the middle of the outer margin. HEAD, moderate-sized, hairy, scarcely tufted in front. *Eyes*, large, prominent, naked. *Palpi*, scaly, obliquely porrected, not elevated much higher than the middle of the eyes, porrected to about half the length of the head ; the tips converging, scaly, except at the base beneath, and on the back of the terminal half of the second joint, which are hairy. Terminal joint small, ovate-conic. *Antennæ*, strong, rather more than half the length of the forewing ; terminated by an elongated, rather slender club, the tip of which is slightly curved outwardly. *Thorax*, elongate-ovate, robust, woolly, spotted with white in front. *Abdomen*, rather slender. FOREWING, elongate-triangular. *Costal margin* not strongly arched ; *apex* rather obtuse ; *outer margin* about two-thirds of the length of the costa, very slightly scalloped, its anterior portion rather convex, but emarginate below the middle ; *anal angle* strongly rounded ; *inner margin* equal in length to the outer margin. *Subcostal nervure* having the first branch arising at about one-fourth of the length of the wing ; second branch arising rather beyond half the length of the wing ; third branch arising at about two-thirds of its length, and extending to the tip ; fourth branch arising half way between the third and the tip, extending to the outer margin below the apex ; terminal portion of the nervure more oblique. *Upper disco-cellular nervule* extremely short, transverse, arising at about one-third of the length of the subcostal nervure ; *middle* disco-cellular very short, curved, forming the base of the lower discoidal nervule ; *lower* disco-cellular obsolete, so that the *discoidal cell* is open. *Median nervure* strong ; its third branch not strongly arched at the base. HINDWING, subtriangular ; *costal margin* much arched at the base ; *outer margin* deeply scalloped ; the margin between the discoidal and the third median nervule being somewhat elongated into a very short truncated tail. *Precostal nervure* slightly oblique in a direction from the body, and forked at the tip. *Subcostal* nervure branching near the base. *Upper disco-cellular nervule* forming the straight base of the discoidal nervule and the *lower* disco-cellular nervule, the *discoidal cell* being open. FORELEGS, of the *male* small, feathered, the *tibia* shorter than the femur, and the *tarsus* nearly equal to the tibia in length, exarticulate, and destitute of apical claws ; annulated alternately with black and white hairs. Of the *female* about the same length as those of the male, more slender, and clothed with fine scales, the *tarsus* furnished with apical claws. MIDDLE and HINDLEGS, strong ; *tibiæ* and *tarsi* armed beneath with rows of minute spines ; the middle pair longer than the hind ones ; *claws* rather large, sickle-shaped, and very acute." (*Westwood*, l.c.)

This genus comprises about ten species inhabiting the Himalayas extending westwards as far as Masuri, and eastwards through Assam, Sylhet and Burma to the Malay Peninsula. It occurs in the Eastern Ghâts and South India, but has not yet been discovered in Ceylon, the Andamans or the Nicobars. Species are found also in Borneo, Celebes, the Philippines and Japan.

The females of several species are highly mimetic, resembling various species of *Euplœa* so closely as to be easily mistaken for them on the wing, the resemblance being not only in shape and markings but also in manner of flight and in the habit of resting in exposed positions. The males have quite a different appearance, their flight is rapid instead of soaring, and they rest with closed instead of open wings. The females are also very variable, and in some cases distinctly polymorphic. *E. halitherses* has at least three forms of the female which mimic three different species of *Euplœa*. The males are fairly constant in form and style of marking as well as in colour. They are deep indigo blue with whitish elongated patches and spots on the interspaces, most prominent on the hindwing. In the two Indian species the haustellum is black, in the genus *Hestina* which is really closely allied to *Euripus*, but is artificially distantly separated from it in this work, owing to the second subcostal nervule of the forewing in the typical species being given off from the costal nervure before the end of the cell, it is chrome yellow.

Key to the Indian species of Euripus.

A. Both sexes with the base of the hindwing on the underside marked with carmine.

　　305. E. CONSIMILIS, India, Burma.

B. Both sexes with the base of the hindwing on the underside unmarked with carmine.

　　306. E. HALITHERSES, Eastern Himalayas, Assam, Burma.

305. Euripus consimilis, Westwood.

Diadema ensimilis, Westwood, Gen. Diurn. Lep., vol. ii, p. 281, n. 20, note, *female* (1850); *Euripus consimilis*, Wood-Mason, Journ. A. S. B., vol. l, pt. 2, p. 85, n. i, pl iv, fig. 3, *female* (1881); id., Butler, Ann. and Mag. of Nat. Hist., fifth series, vol. ix, p. 405 (1882); *Euripus hallirothius*, Westwood, l. c., p. 293, n. 2, note, *male*; *E. consimilis*, var. *meridionalis*, Wood-Mason, l. c., p. 86, n. 2, pl. iv, fig. 2, *female*.

HABITAT: Himalayas, Eastern Ghâts, South India, Assam, Upper Tenasserim.

EXPANSE: ♂, 2·3 to 2·8; ♀, 2·8 to 3·35 inches.

DESCRIPTION: MALE: UPPERSIDE, "*forewing* black with streaks of whitish elongate spots. *Hindwing* whitish with the veins narrowly black, the border black with white spots, and with four red spots placed transversely at the anal angle. UNDERSIDE, *hindwing* also spotted with red at the base." FEMALE: UPPERSIDE, "wings white, the costa of the *forewing*, the veins, three oblique spots and the outer margin black. *Hindwing* white, the veins narrowly, the outer margin (spotted with white), and a transverse short band beyond the middle black. UNDERSIDE, *hindwing* marked at the base with a small carmine spot." (*Westwood*, l. c.)

MALE: UPPERSIDE, *forewing* deep indigo-blue, with the following pale yellow markings:— a short narrow streak in the cell from the base touching the subcostal nervure, a smaller streak placed outwardly below it, a large somewhat quadrate spot placed obliquely across the end of the cell, beyond it three narrow duplex streaks placed between the nervules, and a spot at the base of each of the median interspaces, the lower much the larger. A discal series of narrow streaks from the costa to the submedian nervure placed in pairs; a marginal series of rounded spots not reaching the apex; a lengthened streak in the submedian interspace with a short one placed below it at its outer end, and an obsolete streak in the internal interspace. *Hindwing* pale yellow, the veins black; the outer margin widely black from the anal angle to the discoidal nervule, thence to the apex narrowly black. A marginal series of small round dots placed two in each interspace; four carmine submarginal spots from the anal angle, the three outer ones rounded, the one at the anal angle somewhat linear. UNDERSIDE as above, the base of the *hindwing* marked with carmine. Thorax black, streaked and spotted with pale yellow, the abdomen black streaked with yellow. *Antennæ, haustellum,* and *cilia* black. FEMALE, ground-colour usually pure dazzling-white, but variable; in an Eastern Ghât specimen it is pale yellow, darker on the hindwing, where it may be described as being of a pale gamboge-yellow colour; in the Travancore specimen, separately described under the name of var. *meridionalis*, it is straw-coloured. Markings deep indigo-blue, almost black, also variable, being much more extensive in some specimens than in others. *Forewing* with the costa black, an oblique black spot across the middle of the cell and a larger one closing it; an angled discal black band from the costa to the first median nervule, the portion below the angle at the third median nervule much wider than the portion above it; the apex widely and the outer margin less widely black and bearing a series of white rounded spots, small at the anal angle, becoming obsolete and lengthened out into streaks at the apex. All the veins marked with black. *Hindwing* with all the veins black, an irregular black patch across the disc from the discoidal nervule to the submedian nervure, sometimes reduced to spots placed on the nervules, in other specimens quite obsolete; the margin black, bearing rounded white spots placed in pairs between the nervules, variable in size. UNDERSIDE much as above, the base of the *hindwing* marked with carmine.

A female from the extreme south of the peninsula has been separately described under the name var. *meridionalis* as follows: "Differs from *E. consimilis* in having the markings of the UPPERSIDE of *both wings* straw-coloured instead of pure and dazzling white; the basal two-thirds of the long streak in the interno-median space, as also the streak below the submedian nervure of the *forewing* obsolete, and the submarginal short streaks at the apex of that wing as prominent as those which succeed them; and all the veins of the *hindwing* much more broadly dark-bordered, with the black patch referred to in the original description of *E. consimilis* consequently much less defined. *Both wings* are bright carmine at their insertion on the UNDERSIDE just as in typical *E. consimilis*." (*Wood-Mason*, l. c.)

With reference to the above Mr. Butler has written the following note:—"It would be supposed from the above description [by Mr. Westwood of *E. consimilis*] that the ground-colour

3

of the wings in this species was pure white; the fact that a pure white form does exist in the North-East Himalayas would convince any Lepidopterist living in India that such was the case. I believe, however, that had Westwood been describing the Darjiling type he would have said 'alis niveis' rather than the more vague 'albis.'"

"The type of *E. consimilis*, which is now in the collection of the British Museum, is of a yellowish cream-colour, not deep enough for 'straw-coloured;' it differs from the white form represented by Wood-Mason by nothing but its yellower colour, in which character it perfectly agrees with its male (*E. hallirothius*). I suspect it to be a dimorphic species; and if so, it would be a mistake to regard the snow-white variety as a local race, and give it a distinctive name. In the case of *E. meridionalis*, however, the pattern as well as the colouring ('straw coloured,' W.-M.) differs not a little; and therefore his name will stand for this race."

"The yellow colour of Westwood's type is not due to age, but is the tint most prevalent in specimens of *Euripus*; were it caused by time it would be rather stramineous than of the pale creamy-sulphur tint which it is. Moreover, of all the examples which I have seen of this species, in both sexes (and I have seen a good many besides the four yellowish ones in our collection), only one female, obtained from Dr. Lidderdale's series, is, as Mr. Wood-Mason says, ' pure and dazzling white.'" (*Butler*, l. c.)

As far as I am able to judge from the specimens to which I have had access, the female is not dimorphic, but is variable and occurs in different forms in different places. I am unable to suggest what butterflies it mimics, unless it be species of the genus *Thyca*, a genus of protected butterflies of the subfamily *Pierinæ*.

Colonel Swinhoe has a female of *E. consimilis* taken in the Deyra Doon; and the Indian Museum, Calcutta, possesses a pair of specimens taken by Colonel Buckley at Masuri; two males from Buxa, Bhutan (*Moti Ram*); one male from Sikkim (there is a female from Sikkim in Mr. Otto Möller's collection); one female from the Thoungyeen forests, Upper Tenasserim (*Captain Bingham*); and a female from Trevandrum, Travancore. In Mr. W. Doherty's collection there are a pair taken in December on a peak 5,000 feet near Potingi, Jaipur State, Eastern Ghâts; a female without locality in Colonel Lang's collection, and another from Cannanore, South India, in Colonel J. H. McLeod's collection. Mr. Westwood records it from Assam, Mr. A. V. Knyvett has taken a single male at Jalpaiguri, and Mr. E. F. T. Atkinson records it as rare from the outer Himalayas of the North-Western Provinces.

306. **Euripus halitherses**, Doubleday and Hewitson. (PLATE XX, FIG. 90 ♂ ♀).

E. halitherses, Doubleday and Hewitson, Gen. Diurn. Lep., vol. ii, p. 293, n. 1, pl. xli, fig. 2, *male* (1850); id., de Nicéville, Journ. A. S. B., vol. l, pt. 2, p. 51, n. 26 (1881); *Hestina isa*, Moore, Horsfield and Moore, Cat. Lep. E. I. C., vol. i, p. 161, n. 333, *female* (1857); *Euripus haliartus*, Felder, Wien. Ent. Monatsch., vol. iv, p. 234, n. 81, *female* (1860); *Diadema nyctelius*, Doubleday, Ann. and Mag. of Nat. Hist., vol. xvi, p. 187, *female* (1845); id., Doubleday and Hewitson, Gen. Diurn. Lep., vol ii, p. 281, n. 22, pl. xxxvii, fig. 1, *female* (1850); *Euripus cinnamomeus*, Wood-Mason, Journ. A. S. B., vol. l, pt. 2, p. 272, pl. iv, fig. 4, *female* (1881).

HABITAT: North-East Himalayas, Assam, Sylhet, Cachar, Manipur, Burma.

EXPANSE: ♂, 2·4 to 2·7; ♀, 3·2 to 3·6 inches.

DESCRIPTION: MALE: UPPERSIDE, *forewing* much as in *E. consimilis*, but the spot at the base of the first median interspace larger, the discal series of spots in pairs shorter, those in the median interspaces V-shaped, three spots in the submedian interspace; the streak from the base in the submedian interspace very much shorter and more prominent, with an elongated spot from its outer end in the interspace below. *Hindwing* with the outer margin more broadly deep indigo-blue, the nervules also more widely defined with that colour, and instead of the carmine spots near the anal angle there is a series of small pale yellow submarginal spots placed in pairs. UNDERSIDE with the markings as above, but the ground-colour pale brown, all except the outer margin of the *forewing* from the anal angle decreasingly to the third median nervule, and the *hindwing* from the anal angle to the discoidal nervule, which is deep indigo-blue like the upperside.

The FEMALE I. Form, which is a mimic of *E. rhadamanthus*, has been described under the name *Hestina isa* by Mr. Moore as follows :—

E. isa. "FEMALE : UPPERSIDE, *forewing* dusky-brown, darker and somewhat bluish on apical half ; a broad oblique short white patch from middle of costal margin, intersected by three of the veinlets ; a whitish mark in middle of discoidal cell, and some narrow longitudinal white marks at the apex ; also an indistinct marginal row of small whitish spots. *Hindwing* dusky-brown, with the middle of the wing to abdominal margin white, intersected by the veins ; also a marginal and submarginal row of small bluish-white spots from anal angle. UNDERSIDE paler brown, and marked as above. Wings shaped as in *H.* [= *Euripus*] *consimilis*." (*Moore, l. c.*) This form is variable ; a specimen from Shillong in the Indian Museum, Calcutta, differs from Sikkim ones in being pale brown on the upperside of the forewing ; the hindwing being almost entirely white, the outer margin only, and a discal series of elongate streaks being very pale brown. Another specimen also from Shillong in Major Marshall's collection differs only from Sikkim examples in having the submarginal series of round spots on the upperside of the forewing larger, while another example has these spots obsolete, the whole of the dark margin which bears them hair-brown instead of purplish.

The FEMALE II. Form, which mimics the male of *E. midamus*, has been described as *Diadema nyctilius* by Mr. Doubleday, and as *Euripus cinnamomeus* by Mr. Wood-Mason, as follows :—

E. nyctilius. FEMALE. "*Forewing* brownish black, the apex broadly shaded with pale blue, the colour varying with the direction of the light ; between the nervules is a series of whitish striæ, becoming less elongate towards the anal angle. *Hindwing* dusky white, fuscous at the base, the outer margin narrowly fuscous, the colour extending inwards between the nervules, which also are fuscous. UNDERSIDE : *Forewing* fuscous, with a marginal series of whitish spots, and two submarginal ones near the anal angle. *Hindwing* fuscous ; the inner margin and a double series of ill-defined spots towards the outer margin, of which those of the inner series are rounded, of the outer elongate, geminate, whitish. *Head* and *thorax* black with white dots. *Antennæ* with an elongate club, fuscous. *Abdomen*, fuscous."

"This species closely resembles some of the Indian *Euplœæ*." (*Doubleday, l. c.*)

E. cinnamomeus. "FEMALE : UPPERSIDE, *forewing* purplish black-brown, darkest at the base and along the edges, and glossed with steel-blue on the disc, with a conspicuous suboval or subtriangular patch of changeable lilac-blue divided by the dark veins, commencing broadly just in front of the ultimate subcostal fork, and rapidly narrowing to the inner angle, and with an indistinct submarginal series of small roundish white spots placed upon the inner edge of the narrow black-brown outer border, and extending from the inner angle up to the third median nervule. *Hindwing* black-brown of a richer tint, broadly and interdigitatingly bordered externally with clear cinnamon-brown, which is traversed by the dark brown veins, and bears, midway between the black base and the wavy purplish-black narrow outer border, a series of four impressed white specks all encircled internally with black-brown, one in each interspace from the first median to the second subcostal nervule, and, at its junction with the wavy black outer border, a similar but more complete series of white specks, two to each interspace (except the second, in which there are four, the middle one of the three being divided) from the internal nervure to the first subcostal nervule, are all roundish, except the first two, which present the form of linear marks parallel to the outer margin. UNDERSIDE, *both wings* cinnamon-brown narrowly bordered externally with purplish black-brown, with the veins rich dark brown, and the submarginal spots more numerous and distinct than above. *Forewing* slightly darker for the basal two-thirds, with a short streak of pale lilac between the first and second median nervules near the base of the cell and an ill-defined roundish clump of scales of the same colour beyond it, an externally forked streak of dark violet-blue occupying the basal two-thirds of the interno-median area and followed by an indistinct clump of violet-grey scales, a grey streak in the apical half of the inner margin, and a submarginal series of violet-white spots situated upon the inner edge of the black outer border, and extending from the inner margin to the apex, with all the spots round except the first six (which have the form of linear streaks), and the last (which is elongate), and arranged two in each interspace except the eighth from the apex (in which there are three), and the last, in which there is only one. *Hindwing* uniformly coloured, with a discal series of seven violet-white spots and dots, arranged in two series, an interior curved one of three, and a posterior straight one of four, the three foremost of which latter, with the last of the anterior series, coincide with the four impressed spots of the upperside; and with a submarginal series of spots of the same colour, situation, and extent as in the forewing, but differing somewhat in shape, the last three being linear streaks parallel to the outer margin, and the rest more or less elongate, and those of each pair divergent externally as if they were the remaining outer ends of lost lunules." (*Wood-Mason*, l.c.)

This form is also variable ; on the upperside of the forewing in *E. nyctelius* described from Sylhet there is a distinct submarginal series of pale streaks placed in pairs between the nervules, and two pale suffused discal spots in the lower median and submedian interspaces, which are not present in *E. cinnamomeus*, the hindwing in *E. nyctelent* is also much paler outwardly.

FEMALE III. Form. UPPERSIDE, *forewing* hair-brown, the outer margin towards the anal angle very slightly paler, and showing just the faintest trace of the discal band from the costa which is present in *E. isa*, the marginal dots and streaks present, but hardly visible. *Hindwing* hair-brown, a discal series of whitish spots between the veins, the four upper ones round and equal-sized, the fifth in the second median interspace larger and diffused inwardly, the one in the space below elongated into a streak, the one in the submedian interspace still longer and bifurcated outwardly, some obscure streaks on the abdominal margin above the anal angle. The usual whitish spots in pairs on the margin. UNDERSIDE, *both wings* paler, the inner margin of the forewing pale purple, the marginal streaks and spots more distinct than above. *Hindwing* with a discal series of even round whitish spots, somewhat blurred at the anal angle, marginal spots as above.

The single specimen described above, which is in Major Marshall's collection, was taken in the Thoungyeen Forests in Upper Tenasserim in April by Captain C. T. Bingham, and apparently mimics *Euplœa alcathoë*, which occurs with it. As the other female forms have been named I propose for the sake of convenience to call this one *E. alcathoöides*.

This species with both female forms *isa* and *cinnamomeus* occurs in Sikkim, there are males in the Indian Museum, Calcutta, from Sylhet, Cachar (*Wood-Mason*); Naga Hills; Sibsagar (*S. E. Peal*); Mr. Sherwill has taken *E. isa* at Jorehat, Assam, in June; Shillong (also type of *E. cinnamomeus*), and Upper Burma (taken by the Yunan Expedition). Mr. E. F. T. Atkinson records it from the outer ranges of the Himalayas of the North-Western Provinces.

The figure shows the upperside of a male and a female I. Form, both from Shillong, in the Indian Museum, Calcutta.

A very slight variety of *E. halitherses* has been described from the Malay peninsula under the name of *E. euplœoides*. The male appears to differ from the Indian form only in having three or four marginal dots only at the anal angle of the forewing on both sides, in the Indian species these dots usually extend as far as the third median nervule. The ground-colour of the female is even paler than the first female from Shillong described above under the name *E. isa*, though the white portion of the hindwing is less extended in the Malayan form. The description is appended.*

* *Euripus euplœoides*, Felder, Reise Novara, Lep., vol. iii, p. 415, n. 618 (1866) ; id., Butler, Trans. Linn. Soc., Zoology, second series, vol. i, p. 541, n. 1 (1877) ; *E. euplœoides*, Distant, Rhop. Malay., p. 134, n. 4, pl xiii, fig 6, *male*, fig. 7, *female* (1882). HABITAT : Province Wellesley, Malacca. EXPANSE : *Male*, 2 8 : *female*, 3·05 inches DESCRIPTION : "MALE : UPPERSIDE very dark indigo-blue. *Forewing* with the following white markings—and spots ; two linear streaks at base of cell, and a large irregularly shaped spot at its termination, which is deeply cleft at its centre ; beneath these are a large subquadrate spot between the second and first median nervules, a series of four linear spots divided by the nervules beyond cell, the lower one very small, and a curved submarginal series, which are centrally cleft and situated between the nervules (between the first median nervule and submedian nervure there are three spots, which are outwardly followed at margin by a few very small pale bluish spots) A long pale bluish streak commencing near base and running above the submedian nervure, and a shorter streak

A second supposed species, of which the female only is known, has been described as below * from Singapore under the name of *E. pfeifferæ*. So far as I can see the male of *E. euplœoides* is inseparable from that of *E. halitherses*, and judging from analogy, it may be predicted that the male of *E. pfeifferæ* when discovered will also be found to be inseparable, and that the whole of these forms belong to one species, *halitherses*, constant (or nearly so) in the male, but exhibiting six, possibly more, forms in the female, *isa, nyctelius, cinnamomeus, alcathoïoïdes, euplœoides* and *pfeifferæ*.

Genus 48.—CUPHA, Billberg. (PLATE XXIII).

Cupha, Billberg, Enum. Ins., p. 79 (1820); id., Moore, Lep. Cey., vol. i, p. 64 (1881); id., Distant, Rhop. Malay, p. 176 (1882); *Messaras,* Doubleday, Gen. Diurn. Lep., vol. i, p. 163 (1848).

"HEAD, rather broad, hairy. *Eyes*, oval, rather prominent, *Palpi*, divergent, ascending, projecting considerably beyond the forehead; first joint subcylindric, slightly curved, scaly, the scales very long; second joint five times the length of the first, large, much swollen beyond the middle, tapering towards the apex, which is truncate, scaly, and in front hairy, the external hairs much the longest, dorsal tuft short; third joint slender, acicular,† equal in length to the first. *Antennæ*, scarcely three-fourths the length of the body, gradually and almost imperceptibly thickening towards the apex into a slender club, the last joint of which is pointed. *Thorax*, oval, moderately stout, hairy. *Abdomen*, rather slender, more than two-thirds as long as the abdominal margin of the hindwing. FOREWING, subtriangular; the *costal margin* considerably rounded; the *outer* margin about two-thirds the length of the costal margin, rounded, slightly sinuate; *inner* margin straight, a little longer than the outer. *Costal nervure* stout, terminating before the middle of the costal margin. *Subcostal* nervure slender, lying close to the costal until the latter turns upwards to the costa; its first nervule thrown off just before the end of the cell; its second at some distance beyond it; its third about as far from the second as this is from the first; its fourth less than half way between the third and the apex, just before which it terminates. *Cell* short, about one-third the length of the wing. *Upper disco-cellular nervule* all but wanting; *middle* much curved inwards; *lower* very slender, almost atrophied, slightly curved, about double the length of the middle

of the same colour near apex of inner margin. *Hindwing* with a very large white spot occupying the larger portion of cell, and narrowly attenuated and extending between the discoidal and third median nervules; on inner side of this are two long and linear white spots divided by the lower subcostal nervule; the upper of these is followed by a whitish spot, and the lower by two very small bluish spots, a pale streak on each side of first median nervule, a long irregular and posteriorly bifid streak on inner side of submedian nervure, and a marginal and submarginal row of small pale bluish spots placed in pairs between the nervules: abdominal margin white, containing two curved fuscous lines. UNDERSIDE pale olivaceous-brown. *Forewing* with the markings as above, but larger, especially the spots beyond the cell, which almost coalesce with the submarginal series. *Hindwing* marked as above, but with an additional linear spot above the upper subcostal nervule, followed by a subquadrate spot near apex; the posterior angle of the *forewing* and the margin of the *hindwing* between the discoidal nervule and the anal angle is indigo-blue as above. *Body* above indigo-blue; the *eyes* castaneous; *head* and *thorax* spotted and streaked with pale bluish; *abdomen* with two prominent basal spots, and the posterior segmental margins of the same colour, beneath marked much as above; *thorax* beneath spotted with whitish, *femora* streaked beneath with the same colour; *forelegs* white, annulated with indigo-blue. FEMALE: UPPERSIDE pale brownish. *Forewing* with the following whitish spots and markings:—a narrow subcostal streak, a basal streak in cell, and a transverse spot at its termination; an oblique macular fascia composed of four large spots beyond cell, above which is a small costal spot, and beneath which are a submarginal series of three spots, one above and two beneath the first median nervule; a marginal series of small spots which become linear at apex. *Hindwing* with the inner basal half whitish, and with the following markings of the same colour; a linear streak on each side of the lower subcostal nervule above cell, an irregular submarginal series placed between the nervules [two between the first median nervule and submedian nervure], and a marginal series of smaller spots. UNDERSIDE as above. *Body and legs* coloured and marked as in male, but paler."

"The female of this species evidently 'mimics' the same sex of *Euplœa diocletiana*, Fabricius, and doubtless thereby obtains similar immunity from the attacks of birds and other enemies as is possessed by that inedible species. *E. euplœoides* is clearly a local race of *E. halitherses*, Doubleday and Hewitson." (*Distant,* l. c.)

* *Euripus pfeifferæ*, Felder, Wien. Ent. Monatsch., vol. iv p 235, n 80, pl. iii, fig. 1, *female* (1860); id., Distant, Rhop. Malay., p. 135. n. 2, woodcut (1882) HABITAT: Singapore. EXPANSE: 3¼5 inches. DESCRIPTION: "FEMALE: *Forewing* with the outer margin convex. UPPERSIDE fuscous, paler at base, darker outwardly, and shot with purple; a spot at the extremity of the cell generally obsolete, and a short transverse subcostal band divided into four subelongate spots by the veins, (the lowest smallest), white. *Hindwing* slightly scalloped. UPPERSIDE purplish-black, the costa and the inner margin paler, an elongate cellular spot powdered with white (and generally with two interior streaks of the same colour). UNDERSIDE deep brown, with a marginal series of elliptical spots white powdered with blue. *Forewing* tinted internally with lilac, the spots and fascia of the upperside, and two powdery bluish spots towards the inner angle. *Hindwing* with the spots and streaks of the upperside more or less distinct, and seven exterior white spots powdered with blue and ringed with black, arranged in a line forming an angle (the first spot the largest). *Abdomen* black above, with the spots at the sides and a double series of abdominal ones white." (*Felder*, l. c.)
Mr. Distant remarks (l. c.) that he only knows this species by Felder's figure and description.
† ACICULAR, with nodulate scratches as if made with a needle, from *acus*, a needle.

one, anastomosing with the third median nervule close to its origin. HINDWING, obovate; the outer margin slightly sinuate-dentate, the longest tooth being at the termination of the third median nervule. *Precostal nervure* simple, bent abruptly outwards. *Discoidal nervule* appearing to be a third subcostal nervule. *Cell* open. Abdominal fold ample. FORELEGS, of the *male* scaly, and slightly fringed with hairs; *femur* longer than the tibia, curved; *tibia* also curved, nearly cylindric; *tarsus* two-fifths of the length of the tibia, subcylindric, slightly tapering towards the apex. Of the *female* with the *femur* longer than the tibia, fringed with hair; *tibia* cylindric, scaly and hairy, spiny within towards the apex; *tarsus* five-jointed; the first joint one-half longer than the rest combined, spiny within, and furnished, as are the three following joints, with a spine on each side at the apex, covered by a tuft of hair at the base of the following joint; fourth and fifth joints transverse, the fifth very small. MIDDLE and HINDLEGS, with the *tibiæ* quite as long as the femora, spiny externally and laterally, the lateral spines longest, spurs rather long; *tarsi* longer than the tibiæ, spiny, the spines of the upper surface slender, the lateral ones the longest, those of the under surface arranged in two regular series; first joint equal in length to the rest combined; the three following joints progressively shorter; fifth elongate, ovate, equal in length to the third." (*Doubleday*, l. c.)

LARVA and PUPA unknown.

Cupha is a genus of moderate extent, about ten species having been described as belonging to it, which occur throughout India except in the dry plains of the North West, in Ceylon, the Andaman and Nicobar isles, Burma, the Malay Peninsula and Archipelago, and reaching into China. They are moderate-sized butterflies, not very strong on the wing, with the prevailing colour ochreous, and the apex of the forewing broadly bordered with black.

Key to the Indian species of Cupha.

A. The black apical area on the upperside of forewing bearing usually two distinct ochreous spots; the black spot in the submedian interspace usually prominent, large and quadrate.

307. C. ERYMANTHIS, India, Burma, Andamans and Nicobars, &c.

B. The black apical area on the upperside of forewing bearing a single indistinct and often entirely obsolete ochreous spot: the black spot in the submedian interspace usually small or obsolete.

308. C. PLACIDA, South India, Ceylon.

307. Cupha erymanthis, Drury. (PLATE XXIII, FIG. 105 ♂).

Papilio erymanthis, Drury, Ill. Ex. Ent., vol. i, pl. xv, figs. 3, 4 (1770); id., Cramer, Pap. Ex., vol. iii, pl. ccxxxviii, figs. F, G (1777); *Argynnis erymanthis*, Godart, Enc. Méth., vol. ix, p. 257, n. 4 (1819); id., Donovan, Ins. China (new edition), p. 64, pl. xxxv, fig. 1 (1842); *Cupha erymanthis*, Distant, Rhop. Malay., p. 176, n. 1, pl. viii, fig. 4, *male* (1882); *Papilio lotis*, Sulzer (*nec* Cramer), Geseh. Ins., pl. xvi, fig. 6 (1776); *Messaras erymanthis* var. *nibasarica*, Felder, Verh. zool.-bot. Gesells. Wien, vol. xii, p. 486, n. 124 (1862).

HABITAT: Kumaon, Nepal, Sikkim, Dacca, Naga Hills, Sylhet, British Burma, Upper Tenasserim, Andaman and Nicobar isles, Malay Peninsula and Archipelago, China.

EXPANSE: 1·9 to 2·5 inches.

DESCRIPTION: "MALE and FEMALE: UPPERSIDE brownish ochraceous, with two irregular dark spots in cell, and two narrow waved dark lines at end of same; a broad and much waved and sinuated stramineous fascia a little beyond cell, which is inwardly margined with blackish, and beyond which the colour is wholly blackish containing a stramineous spot between the discoidal nervules, and a lineate spot between the second and first median nervules; in the pale fascia are two dark brownish spots separated by the second median nervule, and a larger quadrate spot beneath the first median nervule. *Hindwing* with a narrow, black, strongly, and irregularly waved line crossing wing near apex of cell; this is followed by a straighter and broken linear fascia, outwardly margined with ochraceous, again succeeded by an outer discal row of spots placed between the nervules, two submarginal waved and broken fasciæ and a marginal fascia, all blackish. Abdominal margin greyish brown. UNDERSIDE as above, but pale ochraceous. *Forewing* with the pale fascia much broader and beneath the third median nervule, widening to outer margin, where it contains a waved linear fascia before the dark spots; the apical area brownish, containing three pale spots beyond the pale fascia, and separated by the discoidal nervules, and two submarginal narrow waved dark linear fasciæ, which are broken, maculate, and elongate near apex. *Hindwing*, with a distinct lunulate pale violaceous fascia before the black spots, which are more or less surrounded with reddish, the black fasciæ above, pale brownish beneath. *Body* and *legs* more or less concolourous with wings." (*Distant*, l. c.)

Captain Mortimer J. Slater notes[*] that this species was "tolerably plentiful at Dacca, 1844. Flies quietly, and is easily captured. I used to find one or two almost invariably near a deep pool of stagnant water overhung with bamboo jungle." It has been taken at Shelapunji in the Khasi Hills in October, Mr. T. G. H. Moncrieffe took it at Rangoon, Dr. Anderson in the Mergui archipelago, and Limborg from Moolai to Moolat and at Hatsiega in Upper Tenasserim. There is a single specimen from Sikkim collected by Dr. Jerdon in Col. Lang's collection, Mr. A. V. Knyvett and I took it on a flowering tree at Kalimpong, 4,000 feet, also in Sikkim in October, and it occurs in Continental India along the foot of the Himalayas as far west as Kumaon as stated by Mr. E. F. T. Atkinson in his "Notes on the Zoology of the N. W. P., India." In South India it is replaced by the next closely-allied species. Mr. de Roepstorff has sent numerous specimens captured at Port Blair, which are remarkable for the depth of the ground-colour of the upperside, it being deep umber-brown rather than ochreous-yellow ; in this respect they are nearest to some specimens from Upper Tenasserim and Penang.

Var. *nicobarica*, Felder. "Differs from the Indian and Javan types in its much lighter colouration, in the outer spots on the forewing being much larger, and in the opalescent outer series of lunules on the hindwing."

The Nicobarese variety can at once be distinguished from specimens from the Andamans by their much lighter colouration, but they are hardly distinguishable from some examples from Continental India. The Indian Museum, Calcutta, has specimens from Kamorta, Katschall and Great Nicobar.

The figure shows the upper and undersides of a male specimen from the South Andamans in the Indian Museum, Calcutta.

308. Cupha placida, Moore.

C. placida, Moore, Lep. Cey., vol. 1, p. 65, pl. xxxii, fig. 1 (1881).

HABITAT : South India, Ceylon.

EXPANSE : 1·9 to 2·5 inches.

DESCRIPTION : " MALE and FEMALE. UPPERSIDE dark yellowish-ochreous, darkest and tinged with olive on basal areas. *Forewing* with a black apical band, having a waved curved inner border extending from middle of the costa to posterior angle ; a transverse narrow black zigzag line dividing the basal and discal areas ; two lunate marks within the cell and three spots on lower discal area. *Hindwing* with a transverse subbasal black zigzag line, a discal whitish-bordered macular band and outer row of small oval spots, two submarginal lunular darker lines and an outer marginal line. UNDERSIDE pale ochreous, with very pale markings, as above, the discal band composed of white lunules and traversing both wings." (*Moore*, l. c)

The Indian Museum, Calcutta, possesses examples from the Kadur district, Mysore, Oota-camund (*W. F. Hampson*), Wynaad, Canara, Travancore and Ceylon. In the latter island it is recorded as being "a low country insect, found sometimes in the hilly districts. Numerous only about April and May" (*Mackwood*). "Galle and Kandy" (*Wade*). On the upperside of the forewing the pale discal band is darker, and consequently less conspicuous than in *C. erymanthis*, and the apical black area is more deeply coloured and usually immaculate ; in Ceylon specimens, however, it often bears a single obsolete ochreous spot ; the outer edge of the pale discal band also is in typical specimens evenly curved and very slightly sinuate. In its range it is geogra-phically separated from *C. erymanthis*, and differs sufficiently in colouration and markings to entitle it to specific rank ; but the specimens from South India show a gradually increasing resemblance to *C. erymanthis* to the northwards of their range, very marked in some cases.

Genus 49.—MELITÆA, Fabricius. (PLATE XVIII).

Melitæa, Fabricius, Ill. Mag., vol. vi, p. 284, u. 29 (1807) ; id., Doubleday, Gen. Diurn. Lep., vol. 1, p. 177 (1848).

" HEAD, rather small, clothed with hair ; forehead narrow. *Eyes*, oval, not prominent. *Palpi*, divergent, porrect, slightly ascending, projecting considerably beyond the forehead ; all the joints hairy. First joint stout, curved ; second joint subcylindric, rather compressed,

---

* Horsfield and Moore, Cat Lep Mus. E I. C , vol. 1, p. 151.

somewhat stoutest in the middle, twice the length of the first; third joint slender, almost acicular, about the same length as the first. *Antennæ*, short, scarcely half the length of the costal margin of the wing, rather slender, terminating in a short, pyriform, large club. *Thorax*, moderately stout, elongate oval, clothed with long hairs. *Abdomen*, moderately stout, arched, not much shorter than the inner margin of the hindwing. FOREWING, nearly triangular; the *costal margin* scarcely, or not at all, rounded; *outer* margin two-thirds the length of the costal, rounded, often but slightly; *inner* margin nearly straight, longer than the outer. *Costal nervure* rather stout, scarcely extending beyond the middle of the costal margin. *Subcostal* nervure slender; its first nervule thrown off before the end of the cell; its second beyond the cell, opposite, or nearly so, to the termination of the costal nervure; the third nearer to the second than to the fourth; fourth nearer to the third than to the apex. *Upper disco-cellular nervule* very short; *middle* disco-cellular curved inwards, about half the length of the lower, which is but little curved, and anastomoses with the third median nervule not far from its origin. Internal nervure wanting. HINDWING, obovate; the shoulder very prominent; the *costal margin* nearly straight, equal in length to the inner; *outer* margin much rounded, but little more than half the length of the other margins. *Præcostal nervure* simple. *Discoidal nervule* appearing to be a third subcostal nervule, arising from the second subcostal nervule soon after its origin. *Cell* open. *Third median nervule* but little curved. *Inner margin* entirely embracing the abdomen. FORELEGS, of the *male* hairy and scaly; the *femur* and *tibia* of about equal length, unarmed. *Tarsus* smooth, subcylindric, slightly tapering at the base and apex; one-jointed, but sometimes showing slight indications of articulations; shorter than the tibia. Of the *female* with the *tibia* shorter than the femora, unarmed, rather stouter towards the apex. *Tarsus* five-jointed; the first joint cylindric, elongate, equal or more than equal to the rest combined, mostly armed at the apex, as are the three following joints always, with a spine on each side; second joint much shorter; rest transverse; fifth sometimes very small. MIDDLE and HINDLEGS, with the *femora* about equal in length to the tibiæ, rather robust. *Tibiæ* and *tarsi* densely clothed with scales, the former rather longer than the latter, smooth externally, spiny laterally and internally; the lateral spines long, the internal ones very short. *Tarsi* with all the joints nearly cylindric, slightly tapering to the claw, spiny laterally and below, not above; the spines on the lower surface of all the joints arranged in a double series; lateral spines long. First joint not equal to the rest combined; second joint nearly half the length of the first; third and fourth progressively shorter; fifth equal to the third. *Claws* curved, grooved below. *Paronychia* biflaciniate; the outer lacinia slender, nearly strap-shaped, longer than the claw; inner lacinia about half the length of the outer, subtriangular, pointed. *Pulvillus* two-jointed, nearly as long as the claw."

"LARVA subcylindric, rather tapering to the extremities, tuberculate; the tubercules covered with short setæ; or spiny, the spines set round with hairs. PUPA short, obovate, not angular, tuberculate, with the head rounded; or angular, with the head bifid."

"This genus is difficult to characterise in the perfect state, so as readily to distinguish it from *Argynnis*; but there is one important distinctive character, namely, that the tarsi of the middle and hindlegs are not spiny on the under surface, whilst they are so invariably in *Argynnis*." (*Doubleday*, l. c.) But for the single character given above there seems to be nothing to distinguish the species of the two genera, some species of *Argynnis*, like all the species of *Melitæa*, have the second subcostal nervule of the forewing emitted after the apex of the cell, and in both genera there are species with or without silvery markings on the underside.

The genus *Melitæa* is of very large extent, and inhabits the temperate zones of both the Old and New Worlds. In Asia it is found in Siberia, Amurland, the Caucasus, Altai Mountains, Persia, the Mountains of Afghanistan and Bilachistan, and the Himalayas at considerable elevations. They are all small insects, some very small, having the upperside ferruginous with several series of black spots; they are usually abundant in individuals where they occur, and frequent sunny spots in the openings of woods and forests, the banks of streams, and the beds of flowers just below the snow line, except in the case of *M. robertsi*, which is found on bare stony hill sides in Afghanistan and almost in the plains of the Punjab.

Key to the Indian species of Melitæa.

A. Underside with silvery markings.
        309. M. SINDURA, Himalayas.
        310. M. AMŒNULA, Ladak.
B. No silvery markings on the underside.
    a, Upperside of forewing with a prominent black marginal band, enclosing a series of ferruginous lunules.
        311. M. BALBITA, Western Himalayas.
    b, All the markings very small or obsolete, especially on the hindwing; no distinct black marginal band on the upperside of the forewing.
        312. M. ROBERTSI, Afghanistan, Poojab.

309. Melitæa sindura, Moore.

M. sindura, Moore, Proc. Zool. Soc. Lond., 1865, p. 496, n. 64, pl. xxx, fig. 2.

HABITAT : Kongma Pass, North-West Himalayas ; Native Sikkim.

EXPANSE : 1·25 to 1·55 inches.

DESCRIPTION : UPPERSIDE. "Wings ferruginous ; costa and base of wings blackish. *Forewing* with narrow marginal band, two marks within discoidal cell, and two transverse series of discal spots black ; a series of black-margined, pale-centred submarginal lunules. *Hindwing* with the marginal black band and submarginal lunules as in forewing ; also a series of three small black spots from anal angle. *Cilia* white [pale ochreous], spotted with black. *Body* ferruginous black. UNDERSIDE, *forewing* clear ferruginous, yellowish about the apex, with the discal markings as above, but less defined, and a marginal series of yellowish lunules. *Hindwing* with ferruginous base, yellow disc, a pale ferruginous submarginal and marginal band (each with bright ferruginous spots), and an intermarginal series of yellowish lunules. *Sexes* alike." *(Moore, l. c.)*

Note.—"This is very local, apparently. I have seen it but in one place, on one acre of ground I may say, on a patch of very stony pasture-land, at 16,000 feet altitude, on the 'Kongma' pass, leading from Kunawur into the Chinese province of Gughe in Tibet : ground not clear of snow for more than four months in the year. Here one day I saw a great number of these insects flying, an icy-cold wind blowing all the time, so that the insects were blown about, and never more than an inch or so above the ground. No other Lepidoptera near them did I see but a stray *Colias eluza*, and several *Parnassii* coursing up and down the snow-banks a little higher up." *(Colonel A. M. Lang, R.E., l. c.)*

In Colonel Lang's collection are several of the specimens above referred to, which were taken in July. The FEMALE is larger and paler than the male, all the markings more prominent. On the underside of the hindwing in both sexes there is a subbasal band, a spot in the cell, an angulated discal band and submarginal lunulated band all silvery, defined outwardly with a fine black line, not mentioned by Mr. Moore. Captain H. J. Elwes and Mr. Otto Möller have both obtained numerous specimens of this species through their native collectors at high elevations in Native Sikkim, or Chumbi in Thibet. Both above and below these specimens are rather darker and heavier marked than those taken by Colonel Lang, but are otherwise indistinguishable.

310. Melitæa amœnula, Felder.

M. amœnula, Felder, Reise Nov., Lep., vol ii, p. 392, n. 573 (1867).

HABITAT : Western Himalayas, Ladak, Rupshu, Pangchog, Marka.

EXPANSE : Not given.

DESCRIPTION : "MALE. UPPERSIDE fulvous, the *cilia* sulphurous [yellow], in the forewing more distinctly divided with black, with the exterior margin rather broadly blackish-fuscous, inwardly with a series of yellowish lunules, outwardly with [a series of] cinctures divided with black ; *forewing* with the base, and the basal two-thirds of the costal margin powdered with ochraceous, with a cellular mark, another disco-cellular, a spot more or less annular below the former, often another minute one beyond it, an angulate macular discal streak, often evanescent between the median nervules and another one exterior more macular, outwardly more or less edged with obsolete ochraceous patches and the veins towards the margin blackish-fuscous ; *hindwing* with the interno-basal third densely powdered with fuscous, and bearing a subcostal spot and two in the cell outwardly of the ground-colour, with an angulate discal band of obsolete ochraceous spots, surrounded very obsoletely with fuscous as far as the third median nervule, terminated with three powdery spots outwardly on the anal margin, and very often also inwardly with two or three blackish fuscous spots. UNDERSIDE, *forewing* paler, with a dot and two annular cellular marks black, the black spots of the upper-side evanescent, with other outer darker spots interspersed on the ground-colour, the sub-marginal lunules somewhat silvery, surrounded with powdery black in a continuous series, with the margin immediately beyond them ochraceous ; *hindwing* pale ochraceous, the costa, the basal fourth and the cell silvery, an irregular basal fascia, three basal spots (the first near the subcostal fold, the lowest at the internal [fold], the middle one cellular, often interrupted) often confluent, and a disco-cellular spot deep ochraceous, surrounded with black, an angulate submacular silvery discal fascia, surrounded with powdery black, the margin immediately beyond it deep ochraceous, close beyond it with black streaks (the upper often evanescent), then with obsolete fulvous spots, and immediately beyond these a series of joined submarginal lunules, silvery, surrounded with powdery black much broader than in the forewing, a powdery black marginal line."

" Smaller than the allied species, *M. sindura*, Moore, distinguished by the silver bands on the underside." (*Felder*, l. c.)

I have but little doubt that *M. amarula* is synonymous with *M. sindura*. The unac-countable omission by Mr. Moore in his description of the latter species of the silvery markings of the underside doubtless led Dr. Felder to consider his specimens distinct.

311. **Melitæa balbita**, Moore. (PLATE XVIII, FIG. 71 ♂ ♀).

M. balbita, Moore. Proc. Zool. Soc. Lond., 1874, p. 268, n 16, pl xliii, fig. 5.

HABITAT : Sonamurg, N.-E. Kashmir ; Chunpur and the Murbul Pass, Kashmir ; Sanch Pass, Chumba.

EXPANSE : ♂, 1·5 ; ♀, 1·75 to 2·00 inches.

DESCRIPTION : " MALE. UPPERSIDE bright fulvous ; markings prominent ; *cilia* pale yellow, alternating with black ; costal edge and veins black ; base of wings and hind margins fuliginous black ; *both wings* with a broad exterior marginal black band, traversed by promi-nent fulvous dentiform lunules. *Forewing* with a black constricted mark within the cell, a streak at the end, a short longitudinal streak below it from base of wing, and two transverse discal series of spots (the inner row being the largest). *Hindwing* with black subbasal irre-gular transverse series of lunular marks. UNDERSIDE paler. *Forewing* with the veins fulvous ; costa and exterior margin yellow ; markings not prominent ; *cilia* as above. *Hind-wing* with black veins ; a basal band, a prominent disco-cellular spot, a broad curved discal band, and a marginal series of broad lunules yellow, all bordered by a black line ; the discal band traversed by a blackish irregular line ; the interbasal space bright fulvous, and the interdiscal space yellow, with bright fulvous spots ; extreme outer margin and *cilia* yellow. FEMALE. UPPERSIDE dull, clouded fulvous ; *cilia* paler ; markings broader, confluent, the base of the wings more broadly dusky black, the interdiscal space somewhat yellow, and the marginal dentiform lunules more or less yellow. UNDERSIDE as in male, excepting that the exterior marginal lunules of *forewing*, and the basal, discal, and marginal band of lunules, as well as the disco-cellular spot of the *hindwing* is glossy yellow or dull silvery white."

" The nearest European ally of this species is *M. athalia*." (*Moore*, l. c.)

The type specimen was taken by the late Captain R. B. Reed at Sonamurg. I took this species on the Sanch Pass, Chumba, at the end of May ; and at Chunpur, and on the Murbul Pass, Kashmir, in the middle of June.

The figure shows the upperside of both sexes from Kashmir examples in the Indian Museum, Calcutta.

312. **Melitæa robertsi,** Butler.

M. robertsi, Butler, Proc. Zool. Soc. Lond., 1880, p. 406, n. 8, pl. xxxix, fig. 2 ; *M. robertsii,* Swinhoe, Trans. Ent. Soc. Lond., 1885, p. 339, n. 11.

HABITAT : Candahar, Chaman, Afghanistan ; Campbellpur, Attock, Punjab.

EXPANSE : 1·2 to 1·5 inches.

DESCRIPTION : MALE : UPPERSIDE bright fulvous, markings much smaller and generally less prominent than in *M. balbita* ; *cilia* white, alternating with black ; *veins* concolorous with the ground, not black as in *M. balbita* ; base of wings with a few blackish scales ; *both wings* with a narrow black marginal band entirely separate from the submarginal series of black lunules which are small, separate, and on the hindwing often evanescent (in *M. balbita* these latter are confluent with each other and with the marginal band). *Forewing* with two small black streaks across the cell and continued to the submedian nervure, two enclosing the disco-cellular nervules, a twice angulated discal band of spots, the upper four more or less confluent, three or four subapical spots beyond more or less confluent, and a submarginal series of lunules. *Hindwing* with some irregular basal lines, an angulate series of discal spots (in *M. balbita* these are sometimes traceable, but usually entirely absent), and a submarginal series of lunules, often obsolete, black. UNDERSIDE paler : *forewing* marked as on upperside, the exterior markings fainter and evanescent on the anal portion, the apex pale ochreous ; *hindwing* with pale ochreous veins (almost white), and the bands pale ochreous much whiter than in *M. balbita ;* the base of the wing and along the inner margin pale ochreous, the disco-cellular spot extended downwards and coalescing with the ochreous margin, a broad curved discal band and the outer margin broadly pale ochreous, the marginal band is bounded inwardly by the submarginal lunules and bears a marginal series of separate spots besides the interrupted marginal line by which it is bounded ; the discal band is bounded on both sides by fine black lunules and bears an interrupted line of black lunules ; and on each side of the discoidal nervule it is extended outwardly, the extension being again bounded by two black lunules.

The black lines bounding the pale ochreous bands are in all cases composed of separate narrow lunules, while in *M. balbita* the lines are continuous and the bands are yellow, not whitish ochreous.

The above description is taken from the specimens in my collection from Afghanistan and the Punjab, the black markings vary considerably, but in all cases they are more decidedly macular and less confluent than in *M. balbita,* the veins not being black in *M. robertsi* at once distinguishes it from *M. balbita ;* it is also a smaller insect.

Butler's original description is given below.* *M. didyma* is a larger and very variable insect of the same group found in Europe and Western Asia ; the markings are similar in pattern, but much larger, more numerous and more intense, the ground-colour is also much darker fulvous.

" Rather common on the bare uncultivated wastes at the foot of the hills at the end of May

---

* *Melitæa robertsi.* " Allied to *M. didyma* ; colouration and general aspect on the UPPERSIDE more like *M. persea* ; bright fulvous ; wings with the *cilia* white spotted with black, these spots united at their bases by a black line ; a marginal series of black spots alternating with the spots on the cilia. *Forewing* with the ordinary black markings on the basal half and the usual zigzag series of prominent black spots ; four minute black subapical dots. *Hindwing* with a few scattered black scales in the cell and an angular series of seven black dots beyond the middle ; no trace of the ordinary series of submarginal lunules. UNDERSIDE paler than in *M. didyma,* the black markings much smaller, the submarginal series of spots in the *forewing* reduced as on the upperside to four subapical dots (the last two geminate). *Hindwing* with both black and red spots reduced in size, the series of spots placed ordinarily half way between the two red bands closely approximated to the series which bounds the inner edge of the outer band and continued across the wing, so as to make a series of slightly interrupted annular markings ; the series usually bounding the outer edge of the same red band only represented by a few black scales." (*Butler,* Proc. Zool. Soc. Lond., 1880, p. 406, n. 8, pl. xxxix, fig. 2).

† *Melitæa persea,* Kollar, Denksch. Akad. Wien, Math.-Nat. Cl., vol. i, p. 52, n. 6 (1850). HABITAT : Persia. EXPANSE : 1·5 inches DESCRIPTION : " UPPERSIDE fulvous. *Forewing* with three black macular fasciæ ; *hindwing* with two ; the former on the UNDERSIDE with the apex, the latter entirely pale yellow ; with the macular fasciæ in the forewing as on upperside, in the hindwing with two pale yellow fasciæ, and black lunules and dots."

" Allied to *M. casta,* Kollar [also from Persia], but the pattern of the hindwing on the underside, which is very similar to that of *M. didyma,* manifestly differs [from *M. casta*], and comes nearest to *M. didyma,* from which nevertheless it ought to be separated on account of the absence of the black spots chiefly at the base of the wings." (*Kollar,* l. c.)

and beginning of June. I found one chrysalis, but not the larva ; the chrysalis was loose in the middle of a low plant." (*Note by Major Howland Roberts*, l. c.).

There is a single very old specimen of this species labelled " Afghanistan," in the Indian Museum, Calcutta. Major J. W. Yerbury, writing from Campbellpur in the Punjab, states that " *Melitaea robertsi* is an uncommon butterfly here, but on one spur running down to the river Hluron, I took in two days five specimens ; the spur was covered with loose round stones and with scarcely any vegetation. It has a weak flight, but owing to its hugging the ground is at times difficult to catch" He has also taken it at Attock.

It is a very pale, sparsely-marked, species, and easily distinguished from the other Indian species of the genus.

Genus 50.—ATELLA, Doubleday. (PLATE XX).

Atella, Doubleday, Gen. Diurn. Lep., vol. 1, p. 165 (1848) ; id., Moore, Lep. Cey., vol. i, p. 61 (1881) ; id., Distant, Rhop. Malay., p. 173 (1882) ; *Phalanta*, Horsfield, Cat. Lep. E. I. C., pl. vii, fig. 5 (1829).

" HEAD, broad, hairy, the hairs on the crown long. *Eyes*, prominent, nearly round. *Palpi*, divergent, ascending, rising considerably above the forehead. Basal joint very short, curved ; second long, broad anteriorly, very much swollen, scaly and hairy, the outer side of the anterior surface with a fringe of very long hairs, the back with a short tuft towards the apex ; third joint not one-seventh the length of the second, acicular,* scaly. *Antennae*, fully three-fourths the length of the body, terminating in a short but rather gradually thickening club rounded at the apex, with its articulations more distinct than the rest. *Thorax*, short, rather stout, ovate, hairy. *Abdomen*, short, rather stout. FOREWING, subtriangular, the *apex* slightly rounded ; *costal margin* considerably arched, one-half longer than the *outer* margin, which is equal, or nearly so, in length to the *inner*, and, like this last, slightly emarginate. *Costal nervure* stout, extending but little beyond the end of the cell. *Subcostal* nervure slender, lying close to the costal, until this latter curves upwards to the costa : *first subcostal nervule* arising shortly before the end of the cell ; the *second* at rather a long distance beyond it ; the *third* at about one-third the distance between the second and fourth ; the *fourth* about midway between the second and the apex, terminating on the costa just above the apex. *Discoidal cell* short, but little more than one-third the length of the wing. *Upper disco-cellular nervule* extremely short ; *middle* disco-cellular curved, rather more than half the length of the *lower* disco-cellular, which is slightly curved, and anastomoses with the third median nervule at its origin, or shortly beyond it. *Third median* nervule moderately curved. HINDWING, obovate ; the margins all nearly equal in length ; the *outer margin* sinuate, sometimes prolonged into a short tail at the termination of the third median nervule. *Precostal nervure* simple, short, curved outwards. *Costal* nervure considerably curved at its origin. *Upper disco-cellular nervule* slender, directed almost immediately outwards ; *lower* disco-cellular short, slightly curved, very slender, almost atrophied, uniting with the median nervure opposite to the origin of the second median nervule, or with the base of the third median nervule, which is but little curved. FORELEGS, of the *male* clothed with long delicate hairs. *Tibia* shorter than the femur, cylindric. *Tarsus* shorter than the tibia, nearly cylindric, tapering to a point at the apex. Of the *female* scaly and hairy. *Tibia* shorter than the femur, spiny within towards the apex. *Tarsus* shorter than the tibia ; the first joint longer than the rest combined, curved, spiny within and armed, as are the three following joints, at the apex with a stout spine covered by a tuft of hair at the base of the following joint ; fourth and fifth joints transverse, MIDDLE and HINDLEGS, with the *tibiae* shorter than the femora, spiny externally and laterally, the lateral spines longest ; spurs long and stout. *Tarsi* about one-fourth longer than the femora, rather densely spiny all round ; the spines of the upper surface slenderest, the lateral ones the longest, those of the lower surface arranged in two regular series : first joint exactly equal to the rest combined ; second, third and fourth progressively shorter ; fifth of equal length with the third. *Claws* rather short, curved, compressed. *Paronychia* bilaciniate : the outer lacinia as long as, and broader than, the claw, which it quite covers ; inner nearly strap-shaped, slightly tapering, very little shorter than the outer one. *Pulvillus* two-jointed as long as the claw ; the second joint broad."

---

* For explanation of *acicular*, see page 21.

"LARVA cylindrical, spiny ; the spines on all the segments about equal in length.   PUPA elongate ovate, constricted, spiny."   (*Doubleday*, l.c.)

Atella is a genus of rather small extent, occurring in Africa, throughout India and thence through the Malay archipelago.   Two of the Indian species occur in the hills up to 7,000 feet, and are to be met with also in the lower valleys and the plains.   *A. phalanta* (the only species I have seen on the wing) loves the sun, is very active in flight, but settles frequently on flowers.

Key to the Indian species of Atella.

A.   Hindwing with a distinct tail at the end of the third median nervule.

> 313.   A.   SINHA, Himalayas, Orissa, Cachar, Sylhet, Assam, Burma, Upper Tenas-
> serim, Malay Peninsula, Sumatra.

B.   Hindwing with its outer margin rounded ; no tail.

> a.   The cell of the forewing crossed by two irregular black bars besides the two which
> enclose the disco-cellular nervules.

> > 314.   A.   PHALANTA, India, Malayana, China.

> b.   The cell of the forewing crossed by four black lines in addition to the two which enclose
> the disco-cellular nervules.

> > 315.   A.   ALCIPPE, Sikkim, Sylhet, Mergui, Malay peninsula, Andaman and
> > Nicobar Isles.

The first species, *A. sinha*, appears to be at least subgenerically separable from the typical species *A. phalanta*, not only on account of the very different shape of the hindwing, but also in the shape of the discoidal cells in both wings, these being in *A. sinha* much more obtuse at the apex, and in the hindwing ending distinctly short of the origin of the second median nervule, while in *A. phalanta* the apex is slightly beyond it.   The style of marking too is very different, *A. phalanta* closely resembling an *Argynnis* or a *Melitœa* on the upper-side, while *A. sinha* more nearly resembles a *Cynthia*.

313.   Atella sinha, Kollar. (PLATE XX, FIG. 87 ♀).

Terinos sinha, Kollar, Hügel's Kashmir, vol. iv, pt. 2, p. 438, n. 1 (1848) ; *Atella sinha*, Butler, Trans. Linn. Soc., Zoology, second series, vol. 1, p. 544, n. 2 (1877) ; id., Moore, Proc. Zool. Soc. Lond., 1878, p. 828 ; id., Distant, Rhop. Malay., p. 175, n 3, pl. X, fig. 8, *male* (1882).

HABITAT : Himalayas, Orissa, Cachar, Sylhet, Assam, Burma, Malay Peninsula, Banca, and Sumatra.

EXPANSE : 2·45 to 2·80 inches.

DESCRIPTION : " MALE. UPPERSIDE, *forewing* ochraceous ; a dark waved fascia commenc-ing at costa beyond end of cell, concavely extending to third median nervule, and then obliquely deflexed beneath cell to near inner margin ; within the fascia the colour is brownish, the cell being crossed by four narrow black fasciæ ; the apex more or less suffused with blackish, either totally and enclosing some ochraceous spots, or exhibiting two modera-tely well-defined oblique fasciæ ; outer margin broadly blackish, preceded by a narrow submarginal line of the same colour, and with four small blackish spots, of which three—always visible—are placed two above and one beneath the second median nervule, and the fourth—sometimes fused in the apical colouration—situated between the discoidal nervules. *Hindwing* of the same hue as the forewing, but with the outer third brownish, inwardly marked by a series of small dark spots placed between the nervules, and with broad marginal and submarginal dark fasciæ, between which the colour is narrowly pale ochraceous. UNDERSIDE, *forewing* with the basal dark colouration more violaceous, the cell pale, but dark between the narrow black fasciæ, all the dark markings much paler, being brownish or violaceous, and with a series of distinct pale lunulate spots crossing the wing before the dark spots. *Hindwing* more or less violaceous, crossed by two medial and much-waved narrow and darker fasciæ, between the upper portions of which the colour is pale ochraceous, and both of which are more or less outwardly margined with pearly greyish ; a greyish subquadrate spot in cell margined on three of its sides with dark violaceous, the outer discal spots margined with rufous, but with the one above the third median nervule obsolete ; outer margins pale, as on the forewing. *Body* above concolourous with wings, beneath greyish or very pale ochraceous." (*Distant*, l. c.). FEMALE rather darker than the male, the violaceous colouring of the UNDERSIDE less prominent.

Von Hügel described this species from specimens taken in Masuri. It occurs in Nepal, Sikkim (*Otto Möller*), Orissa (*W. C. Taylor*), Subsagar (*S. E. Peal*), Khasi Hills in the autumn (*Johnson*), Naga Hills, Cachar (*Wood-Mason*), Sylhet, Mergui Archipelago (*Dr. Anderson*), Upper Tenasserim, and Moulmein* a " melanoid variety" (*Limborg*). Captain Bingham found it common in the Thoungyeen forests in February, March and April; it occurs throughout Malayana.

A. egista, Cramer, from the Moluccas and New Guinea is a closely-allied species.

The figure, showing both sides of a female example from Shillong, is taken from a specimen in the Indian Museum, Calcutta.

314. **Atella phalanta**, Drury. (PLATE XX, FIG. 88 ♂).

Papilio phalanta, Drury, Ill Ex. Ent., vol. 1, pl xxi, figs. 1, 2 (1773); *Argynnis phalanta*, Godart, Enc. Méth., vol ix, p. 253, n. 10 (1819); *Atella phalanta*, Horsfield and Moore, Cat. Lep. Mus. E. I. C., vol. i, p. 151, n. 313, pl. v. fig. 7, *larva, 7a, pupa* (1857); id., Moore, Lep. Cey., vol. i, p. 62, pl. xxxi, figs. 1, *imago, 1a, larva* and *pupa* (1881); id., Distant, Rhop. Malay., p. 173. n. 1, pl ix, fig. 4, *male* (1882); *Papilio columbina*, Cramer, Pap. Ex., vol. iii, pl. ccxxxviii, figs. A, B (1779); vol iv, pl. cccxxxvii, figs. D, E (1781); *Phalanta Argynnis phalanta*, Horsfield, Cat. Lep Mus. E. I. C., pl. vii, figs. 5, *larva; 5a, pupa; 5b-g, details of Imago* (1829).

HABITAT : Throughout India, Ceylon, the Malay Peninsula, Siam, Sumatra, Java and China.

EXPANSE : 1·9 to 2·6 inches.

DESCRIPTION : " MALE and FEMALE. UPPERSIDE bright ochraceous, with the following blackish markings:—*forewing* with the apical half of the costal margin, four narrow waved fasciæ (arranged in pairs) crossing cell, a waved and broken spot beyond cell extending from costa to the lower discoidal nervule, an oblique series of four spots divided by the median nervules ; a straight discal series of six spots placed between the nervules, followed by a similar series of four spots, the upper of which is placed between the discoidal nervules and the fourth between the second and first median nervules ; a submarginal and much-waved fascia terminating at the first median nervule, where it is followed by an irregular spot, and which is more or less connected along the nervules with a marginal series of spots preceded by a narrow line. *Hindwing* with some transversely waved linear fasciæ on basal area ; a discal series of four rounded spots, the two upper divided by the lower subcostal nervule, and the third and fourth by the second median nervule ; two waved submarginal fasciæ, the innermost particularly waved and sinuated, and a marginal series of elongate spots. UNDERSIDE as above, but with most of the dark markings paler. *Forewing* with the black spots near outer angle very large and prominent ; the straight series of spots beyond cell are outwardly margined with greyish, and beyond this the wing has a violaceous suffusion. [The spaces inclosed by the dark lines across the cell are also violaceous.] *Hindwing* with the outer medial linear dark fascia reddish and outwardly margined with greyish, beyond which the ground-colour has a violaceous tinge, and the black spots are very minute and surrounded with reddish. *Body* above somewhat concolourous with wings, beneath greyish. *Legs* ochraceous, the femora greyish." (*Distant*, l. c.) The intensity and extent of the markings are somewhat variable, specimens from the region of heavy rainfall being as usual darker than those from more arid districts.

The LARVA as figured by "Horsfield is cylindric, green above, whitish below, with the head brown ; each segment bears on the back two branched spines, and those segments which have neither legs nor prolegs have also a similar spine at the side." (*Doubleday* in Gen. Diurn. Lep., vol. i, p. 166). Mr. Moore (Lep. Cey., vol. i, p. 62) describes the larva as "purple-brown ; head armed with two delicate branched spines, each segment with two dorsal rows of similar spines and two lateral rows of shorter spines. Feeds on *Flacourtia, Salix, &c.*"

---

* Moore, Proc. Zool. Soc. Lond., 1878. p. 824

The PUPA, which I found on one occasion in Calcutta attached to the underside of a leaf of a tree resembling the weeping willow, was a beautiful green, with a subdorsal series of five acutely pointed tubercles, marked with red, between each pair another pair of very small blunt ones, the upper edge of the wing-covers and a spot on each side of the head also marked with red. Doubleday (l. c.) describes the pupa as "elongate ovate, constricted across the back ; green with four red dashes on each side, marked in the middle with bluish ; a double series of spines on the back of the same red colour." In Java, Dr. Horsfield notes that the larva "feeds on a species of *Ixora*."

This species is one of the commonest Indian butterflies, occurring throughout the year in the plains and in suitable seasons in the outer Himalayas up to 8,000 feet. The upperside much resembles that of an *Argynnis*. A closely allied species (*A. euytis*, Doubleday, Hewitson) occurs in Africa.

The figure shows both sides of a male Calcutta specimen in the Indian Museum, Calcutta.

315. **Atolla alcippe**, Cramer.

Papilio alcippe, Cramer, Pap. Exo. vol. iv, pl. ccclxxxix, figs. G, H (1782) ; *Atella alcippe*, Distant, Rhop. Malay., p. 174, n. 2 (with a woodcut of a male) 1882 ; *Argynnis alcippe*, Godart, Enc. Méth., vol. ix, p. 259, n. 6 (1819).

HABITAT : Sikkim, Sylhet, Mergui, Tavoy, Malay Peninsula, Andaman and Nicobar Islands, Amboina *(Cramer).*

EXPANSE : 1·8 to 2·2 inches.

DESCRIPTION : " MALE, smaller than *A. phalanta*, but resembling that species in colour and markings, though differing in the following particulars :—UPPERSIDE, *forewing* with the apical half of the costal margin more broadly black ; the outer margin also is broadly black, preceded by a contiguous waved fascia, which is deflected to costa at the lower discoidal nervule, thus enclosing two ochraceous spots ; between these and end of the cell the wing is crossed by a waved series of small spots placed between the nervules ; the cell is crossed by three pairs of linear fasciæ, and is followed by a broader oblique fascia terminating at third median nervule, and beneath the cell are four linear markings, two near base, the third longest and broken, the fourth smallest between the third and second median nervules. *Hindwing* with a broad outer black margin, preceded by a narrower waved and sinuated submarginal fascia ; outer discal spots as in *A. phalanta*, but the upper one very minute ; on inner side of these and extending from about the extremities of the submarginal fascia is a narrow linear and somewhat broken fascia ; other basal markings as in the preceding species, but more distinct. UNDERSIDE marked generally as above, but with corresponding differences as in *A. phalanta*." (*Distant*, l. c.) FEMALE : UPPERSIDE with the ground-colour darker than in the male, all the markings larger and more prominent. In some lights the disc of both wings is suffused with beautiful violascent. UNDERSIDE also with the ground-colour more dusky than in the male, and the markings larger.

The late Mr. A. de Roepstorff has sent numerous specimens of this species to the Indian Museum, Calcutta, taken at Port Blair ; also from Teressa and Katschall in the Nicobars. Dr. Anderson took it in the Mergui archipelago in the cold weather. There are specimens from Sylhet in the Indian Museum, Calcutta, and two specimens from Sikkim in Major Marshall's collection.

Genus 51.—**CETHOSIA**, Fabricius. (PLATE XXII).

Cethosia, Fabricius, Ill. Mag., vol. vi, p. 280, n. 6 (1807), id., Doubleday, Gen. Diurn L ep., vol. i, p. 150 (1848) ; id., Moore, Lep. Cey., vol. i, p. 51 (1881) ; id., Distant, Rhop. Malay., p. 170 (1882) ; *Alacania*, Hubner, Vers. bek. Schmett., p. 46 (1816).

" HEAD, rather narrow, clothed with hair ; *eyes*, oval, prominent ; *palpi*, slightly divergent, ascending, rising considerably above the forehead, clothed with appressed scales ; the first joint stout, short, curved ; second joint more than five times the length of the first, much swollen beyond the middle, smaller towards the apex, which is obliquely truncate, set in front with long erect setæ ; third joint slender, elongate, oval, about equal in length to the first ; *antennæ* about three-fourths the length of the body, gradually clavate ; the club slender, rather pointed, grooved below. *Thorax*, oval, not robust ; the prothorax small, but distinct. *Abdomen*, subcylindric, shorter than the inner margin of the hindwing. FORE-WING, triangular ; the *costal margin* and *apex* slightly rounded ; *outer margin* sinuate-dentate, not two-thirds the length of the costa ; *inner* margin slightly sinuate, , rather longer than the outer. *Costal nervure* stout, not extending much beyond the middle of the wing ; *sub-costal* nervure slender, placed very close to the costal, five-branched, its first branch thrown off just before the end of the cell ; the first and second, and the third and fourth, branches about equally distant from one another ; the third rather nearer to the second than to the fourth. *Discoidal cell* not quite half the length of the wing. *Upper disco-cellular nervule* almost wanting ; *middle* disco-cellular nearly straight, directed slightly inwards ; *lower* disco-cellular twice the length of the middle one, directed first slightly inwards, then curving outwards, uniting to the third median nervule almost immediately beyond its origin. HINDWING, subtriangular, all the margins of about equal length ; the anterior slightly, the outer much, rounded, the latter more or less deeply dentate ; the inner margin forming a distinct channel for the reception of the abdomen, emarginate beyond the termination of the internal nervure. FORELEGS, of the *male* with the *femur* and *tibia* of about equal length, subcylindric, slightly compressed ; *tarsus* one-jointed, shorter than the tibia, subcylindric, slightly compressed, rounded, or rather slenderer, towards the apex. Of the *female* scarcely, if at all, longer than those of the male ; *femur* and *tibia* of about equal length, nearly cylindric, the latter slightly spiny within ; *tarsus* shorter than the tibia, five-jointed ; the first joint nearly double the length of the rest combined, largest towards the apex ; the other joints transverse, successively shorter ; all the joints except the fifth armed on each side at the apex with a stout spine, covered more or less by a tuft of stiff hairs at the base of the following joint. MIDDLE and HINDLEGS, with the *tibiæ* rather shorter than the *femora*, spiny ; the spurs distinct ; *tarsi* about equal in length to the tibiæ, very spiny ; the spines above slender, much stronger at the sides and below, forming three well-defined series along the sole of the foot. First joint equal to the rest combined ; second, third and fourth progressively shorter, and slightly thicker ; fifth longer than the second, rather dilated ; the spines, especially the lateral ones, longer than on the other joints. *Claws* elongate, grooved below, lobed at the base, acute, but little curved except at the base and apex. *Paronychia* and *pulvilli* wanting or rudimentary." (*Doubleday, l. c.*)

The LARVA of two species are known ; they are cylindrical in shape, the third to fifth, the seventh, and the ninth to thirteenth segments marked each with a bright crimson band, the sixth and eighth segments with a bright yellow band, and all the segments bearing several fine and many branched spines, the head with a pair of suberect processes. The PUPA is brown, of different shades, very irregular in shape and foliaceous.

The characteristic features of the *Cethosiæ* are the black outer border, covering the apical half in the forewing and bearing on both wings a series of narrow highly dentate white lunules corresponding with the dentations of the margin ; these lunules are in all cases prominent on the underside, and, except in *C. nikobarica* (in which they are obsolete but traceable), on the upperside also. Also on the forewing a discal series of more elongate white lunules. In the males the ground-colour of the wings is ochreous or fulvous-red, suffused with whitish on the hindwing in a few species only. In the females the prevailing colour is white, often tinged with ochreous. There are two groups,—the first in which the ground-colour is fulvous-red, represented by *C. cyane* in the North-East, *C. mahratta* in the South, and *C. nietneri* in Ceylon ; *C. cyane* having a single prominent black spot below the subcostal nervure in the middle of the hindwing, and the other two bearing numerous black marks on the basal half. This group is also distinguished by a broad, white subapical transverse bar on the forewing, widest and best defined in *C. cyane*, and narrowest and least defined in *C. nietneri*. The second group in which the ground-colour is ochreous-red and the base of the hindwing unmarked below the subcostal nervure except by transparency from the underside, is represented by the typical species *C. biblis*, and an allied species which replaces it in the Andamans and Nicobars.

The species of this genus are all very beautiful, rich red, yellow and black being the chief predominating colours, and in certain lights fresh-caught males have a beautiful purple gloss on the upperside. The deep scalloping of the hindwing is a very remarkable feature. They occur in the eastern Himalayas, Assam, Sylhet, Burma, and thence through the Malay Peninsula and Archipelago to Australia. One species each occurs in Southern India, Ceylon and the Andamans and Nicobars. Where they occur they are usually numerous in individuals, and very conspicuous from their bright colouration. Owing to the strong scent with which their bodies are impregnated, they are probably distasteful to insectivorous animals.

Key to the Indian species of Cethosia.

A. Base of hindwing on upperside marked with black spots below subcostal nervure.

    a. With a single prominent black spot just beyond end of cell, no discal series beyond.

        316. C. CYANE, Oudh, Calcutta, Eastern Himalayas, Assam, Burma.

    b. With two discal series of black spots in addition to those beyond end of cell.

        a¹. Base of forewing on upperside broadly fulvous-red in male, ochreous in female.

            317. C. MAHRATTA, South India.

        b¹. Base of forewing on upperside ochreous, much restricted in male, greyish-blue in female.

            318. C. NIETNERI, Ceylon.

B. Base of hindwing on upperside unmarked with black spots below subcostal nervure except by transparency from underside.

    a. Upperside with a series of fine white lunules on margin following dentation of wings.

        319. C. BIBLIS, Eastern Himalayas, Assam, Burma.

    b. Upperside with margin black, not bearing a series of prominent white lunules.

        320. C. NIKOBARICA, Andaman and Nicobar Islands

316. Cethosia cyane, Drury.

Papilio cyane, Drury, Ill. Ex. Ent., vol. i, pl. iv, fig. 1 (1770), *female.*

HABITAT : Oudh, Eastern Himalayas, Calcutta, Cachar, Sylhet, Assam, Pegu and Upper Tenasserim.

EXPANSE : ♂, 3'4 to 4'0 ; ♀, 3'1 to 4'1 inches.

DESCRIPTION : MALE. UPPERSIDE, *forewing* with the base, the lower half of the cell and the area below the cell obliquely to near the anal angle rich fulvous-red, the rest of the wing black with white markings. A black spot placed just within the red area in the first median interspace, and another smaller one (sometimes a second) placed below it in the submedian interspace. An oblique very irregular subapical white band, bearing two black spots in the lower discoidal and second median interspaces ; a submarginal series of indistinct white spots, the lower one of the series fulvous-red, and a marginal series of fine white very deep lunules, one in each interspace except the anal one where there are two, forming a W-shaped figure ; the discal series of white lunules obsolescent where not merged in the white band. *Hindwing* rich fulvous-red, the outer margin black. Two black spots placed in the interspace above the subcostal nervure, three rounded ones beyond the cell, a discal series of six, and a submarginal diffused series placed on the veins and coalescing with the black margin, the latter bearing a series of lunules as in the forewing. *Cilia* white, black at the ends of the nervules. UNDERSIDE very beautifully marked with black, white, violaceous, fulvous and vermilion. *Forewing* with the cell crossed by several lines of black, vermilion and violaceous, the white subapical band as above, a discal series of white lanceolate markings, the black margin marked as above, except that there is a white streak in the middle of each interspace from the cilia towards the apex of the deep white marginal lunules, the black margin inwardly defined with a fulvous line. *Hindwing* with the base whitish, bearing numerous irregularly-placed black streaks ; then a vermilion irregular band, with a series of rounded black spots placed on the inner side of a whitish band beyond it, then a fulvous band which is continued up to the first median nervule of the forewing, bearing a series of small black marks on its inner edge, one in each interspace ; then a white band bearing inwardly a series of round black spots one in each interspace, and outwardly another series two in each interspace, and lastly the black margin marked as in

5

the forewing and inwardly defined by a fulvous band. Thorax black, with ochreous hairs ; abdomen ochreous. FEMALE : UPPERSIDE, *forewing* black with a greenish tinge, the inner margin and an irregular spot in the middle of the submedian interspace, greenish-white. The subapical white band, submarginal spots and marginal lunules as in the male. *Hindwing* with all but the costal and outer margins greenish-white, markings much as in the male, but there is an additional discal series of black marks one in each interspace. UNDERSIDE with all the black markings as in the male, but lacking the ochreous-red and fulvous bands. In some specimens the base of the forewing on the upperside is ferruginous.

This is a common species in Sikkim, Assam and the Khasi Hills, though less so than *C. biblis*. I have taken a single female in Calcutta in the cold weather. Colonel A. M. Lang, R.E., records "a single specimen only obtained in a wild jungly spot on the Gogra in Oudh."[*] Mr. Wood-Mason took it in Cachar, Mr. S. E. Peal in Sibsagar ; it occurs also in Sylhet, Manipur, Arakan, Pegu, and Upper Tenasserim.

317. **Cethosia mahratta**, Moore. (PLATE XXII, FIG. 98 ♀).

C. *mahratta*, Moore, Proc. Zool. Soc. Lond., 1872, p. 556 ; *Papilio cyane*, Cramer, Pap. Ex., vol. iv, pl. ccxcv, figs. C, D, *male* (1780), *nec* Drury : id., Herbst, Pap , pl. ccxlviii, figs. 3, 4 (1798) ; *Cethosia cyane*, Godart, Enc Méth , vol. ix, p 247, n. 11 (1819) ; *Alaxonia symbiblis* (part), Hübner, Verz. bek. Schmett , p. 46, n. 421 (1816).

HABITAT : South India.

EXPANSE : ♂, 2·75 to 3·5 ; ♀, 3·5 to 4·0 inches.

DESCRIPTION : "MALE. UPPERSIDE bright fulvous-red. *Forewing* with the apical half, transverse discoidal streaks, and spots between the lower veins black ; a broad subapical oblique white band, crossed on its lower part by two black spots which form part of a transverse discal series, the two upper and lower ones of white black and inwardly ringed with white ; beyond these is a submarginal row of small white spots and a marginal series of white angles. *Hindwing* with the anterior and exterior margins black, the latter with a series of white angles ; three transverse discal series of black spots, the inner series small and irregularly disposed, the outer row oval, each ringed with white and bordered outwardly by a black lunule, [the margin as in the forewing]. UNDERSIDE fulvous-red basally, fulvous-yellow exteriorly ; exterior margins with black-bordered, clearly-defined, white angles, each angle including a white streak pointing inwards. *Forewing* with the oblique subapical white band and transverse discal series of oval white-ringed black spots as above, with a parallel outer row of white-bordered black lunules ; transverse discoidal and disco-cellular streaks, small basal spots, three small spots beyond the cell, and spots between the veins below the cell black, the latter series interspaced with pale bluish-green. *Hindwing* with subbasal transverse black streaks, three discal rows of black spots, the outer row of spots conical and broadly white-bordered, each spot having a contiguous outer small black lunule ; interspaces of subbasal streaks and inner discal rows of spots pale bluish-green. FEMALE with markings as in male, but blacker and more prominent. *Hindwing* on the UPPERSIDE having the black borders broader, the discal series of black oval spots larger and partly confluent with the inner series, the outer black lunules being bordered with a mixed white and fulvous lunule. *Head* and *thorax* fulvous-brown. *Abdomen* fulvous. Nearest allied to *C. nietneri*, Felder." (*Moore*, l. c.)

C. mahratta differs from *C. cyane* on the upperside in having the discal series of white lunules more prominent on the forewing, and in having three series of discal black spots on the fulvous ground-colour in both wings ; on the underside the ground-colour of the apical half of the forewing is not black but concolorous with the rest of the wing, and in the hindwing the medial series of discal black spots in much more prominent.

The Indian Museum, Calcutta, possesses specimens from Karwar, Bombay (*J. Davidson*), Calicut, Canara, the Wynaad and Trevandrum. It is a well-marked species, and common along the Malabar Coast at the foot of the Ghâts.

The figure shows the upper and undersides of a female from Calicut in the Indian Museum, Calcutta.

---

[*] Ent. Month. Mag , vol. i, p. 131 (1864-5).

318. Cethosia nietneri, Felder.

C. *nietneri*, Felder, Reise Novara, Lep., vol. iii, p. 380, n. 552, pl. xlviii, figs. 5, 6, *female* (1867) ; id., Moore, Lep. Cey., vol. i, p. 51, pl. xxvii, figs. 3, *male* ; 3*a. female* ; 3*b, larva* and *pupa* (1880).

HABITAT : Ceylon.

EXPANSE : ♂, 3·0 to 4·1 ; ♀, 3·5 to 4·0 inches.

DESCRIPTION : " MALE. UPPERSIDE blue-black. *Forewing* with the lower basal area ochreous merging to ochreous-white ; some pale streaks across the cell ; a bluish-white streak beyond the cell bordered above and below by a blue line, a transverse discal series of narrow conical-lunate marks, a linear row of spots, and a marginal row of narrow sinuous marks ; some black streaks on lower basal area. *Hindwing* with the posterior basal area bluish-white ; some black discoidal streaks interspaced with ochreous ; an upper discal row of black diffused spots and an outer row of larger oval spots followed by a submarginal row of white lunules and a marginal row of slender white sinuous marks. *Cilia* white. FEMALE duller coloured, the white markings dull greyish-blue, no ochreous on the basal area. *Forewing* with broad black streaks between the lower median and submedian veins. *Body* ochreous, *thorax* bluish-grey. UNDERSIDE pale greenish-grey, merging to bluish-grey across the disc, bordered by a submarginal ochreous band, and a black marginal band with white sinuous marks and medial streak. *Forewing* with black discoidal streaks, lower discal spots, transverse discal series of large conical white-bordered spots, followed by a row of white-bordered black lunular spots. *Hindwing* with black basal streaks, large conical discal spots bordered outwardly by a row of white-bordered spots."

" LARVA cylindrical, purple-black, with red medial transverse bands, the sixth and eighth segments with a yellow band ; head armed with two long stout spinous processes, the segments with two dorsal and two lateral rows of long slender finely-branched spines. Feeds on *Modecca.* PUPA ochreous-white, clouded with brown, abdominal segments tubercular, wing-cases dilated and exfoliated beneath, head with two pointed processes." (*Moore,* l. c.)

This species is apparently confined to the island of Ceylon, where it " occurs in the lower lands, but more numerous in the hilly districts ; commoner some years than others" (*Mackwood*). "Taken at Galle and Kandy" (*Wade*). It has the black markings identical in pattern with C. *mahratta* but of greater extent on the upperside, but differs from that species in the far greater predominance of white in the ground-colour, especially on the underside, where in both sexes the fulvous colour is confined to a broad submarginal band.

Two additional and very beautiful species have been recorded from the Malay Peninsula ; the descriptions are given below.* Mr. Butler has recorded C. *methypsea* from Assam and C. *hypsina* from Assam and Nepal, but this is almost certainly an error.

---

* *Cethosia methypsea*, Butler, Trans. Linn. Soc., Zoology, second series, vol. i, p. 543, n. 1 (1877) ; id., Distant, Rhop. Malay., p. 171, n. 2, pl. viii, fig. 9, *male* (1882). HABITAT : Assam ? Perak, Province Wellesley, Malacca. EXPANSE : *male*, 3·2 to 3·35 ; *female*, 2·4 inches. DESCRIPTION : "MALE. UPPERSIDE, *forewing* resembling C. *logani*, but the basal reddish area less black-spotted, and the apical black area crossed a little beyond cell by an oblique series of six pale spots (ochraceous-white or greyish-white) placed between the nervules, the upper three being minute, and the fifth and sixth notched with black : between the lower spot and the costa is a waxed outer series of four small spots. *Hindwing* with the outer black margin narrower than in C. *logani*, and without the numerous black discal spots. UNDERSIDE with the ground-colour and the cellular markings of the *forewing* generally as in C. *logani*. *Forewing* with a broad oblique ochraceous white or greyish-white fascia a little beyond the cell, the upper part of which is margined with small black spots, which are then deflexed and obliquely continued across the wing, where they become the inner margin of an oblique discal subtriangular pale fascia ; both these fasciæ are also outwardly margined with blackish, and the upper one terminates in a narrow pale submarginal fascia, which contains a series of black spots ; outer margin much as in C. *logani*. *Hindwing* with the basal and subbasal fasciæ as in C. *logani*, and with a broad medial irregular and much-waved pale fascia, which is inwardly margined with black spots ; a black spot in cell ; a submarginal narrow pale fascia inwardly margined with small rounded black spots and outwardly by narrow linear black spots ; outer margin much as in C. *logani* FEMALE. More ochraceous than the male ; black area of the *forewing* rather larger, the oblique macular fascia above larger, continuous, and much more pale ochraceous, and the connecting spots with costa also more distinct ; the pale discs of *both wings* are also a little more black-spotted. UNDERSIDE as in male."

" I only possess one female specimen of this species, and should incline to the view that it must be abnormally small in size, as the above-given dimension testifies. The males vary in having the pale markings either ochraceous-white or nearly pure greyish-white." (*Distant,* l. c.)

Cethosia hypsina, Felder, Reise Novara, Lep., vol. iii, p. 385, n. 559 (1866) ; id., Butler, Trans. Linn. Soc. Zoology, second series, vol. i, p. 543, n. 2 (1877) ; id., Distant, Rhop. Malay., p. 172, n. 1, pl. viii, figs. 6, 7,

319. Cethosia biblis, Drury.

Papilio biblis, Drury, Ill. Ex. Ent., vol. i, pl. iv, fig. 2, *male* (1770) ; id., Cramer, Pap. Ex., vol. ii, pl. clxxv, figs. A, B, *male* (1777) ; id , Herbst, Pap., pl. ccxlviii, figs. 1, 2, *male* (1798) ; *P. penthesilea*, Fabricius (*nec* Cramer), Spec. Ins., vol. ii, p. 33, n 370 (1781) ; *Alexonia symbibis* (part), Hübner, Verz. bek. Schmett., p. 46, n 421 (1816) ; *Cethosia biblina*, Godart, Enc. Méth., vol. ix, p. 248, n 12 (1819).

HABITAT : Eastern Himalayas, Cachar, Sylhet, Assam, Upper Tenasserim, Perak, Hainan.

EXPANSE : 2·9 to 3·8 inches.

DESCRIPTION : MALE. UPPERSIDE rich orange red, the apical half of the forewing, and the outer margin of the hindwing black. The *cilia* white, tipped with black at the end of the nervules. *Forewing* with the cell crossed by three pairs of narrow somewhat irregular black lines, a discal series of narrow black linear spots from the third median nervule continued on the hindwing to the subcostal nervure sometimes wanting, three small white subcostal spots beyond the end of the cell, a discal series of five decreasing white elongate lunules, their apices directed inwards, beyond which are seven reniform white spots, the two upper ones very indistinct, a marginal series of deeply indented white lunules. *Hindwing* with a discal series of six oval blackish spots, a submarginal series of faint blackish spots, placed in pairs between the veins, the margin with white lunules as in the forewing, an additional white lunule defined on both sides with black at the anal angle, the abdominal margin yellowish. UNDERSIDE reddish-ochreous. *Forewing* with the cell crossed by three pale greenish bands, each band with two black lines outwardly, the third band at the end of the cell with an additional black line in its middle defining the disco-cellulars. A pale discal band beyond the cell, with black linear spots between the veins on its inner and outer edge ; a discal decreasing series of six white lanceolate spots, each spot outwardly defined with black and with a black centre divided by a white line ; beyond the lanceolate spots is a pale whitish band bearing pairs of small black spots between the veins, the outer margin bearing yellowish lunules outwardly defined with a black line and enclosing a black space, with a short white streak from the margin directed inwards, but not reaching the apex of each lunule. *Hindwing* with the base red ; then a pale greenish irregular band bearing narrow black lines in pairs ; then a red band ; a pale band in continuation of the one beyond the cell of the forewing, and similarly bordered with black linear spots ; a fulvous band ; a white band bearing a series of black conical spots with a black spot on either side of them, the outer edge of the white band with small round spots in pairs ; another fulvous band ; the margin marked as in the forewing. *Antennæ* black ; *thorax* black with long bronzy hairs ; *abdomen* ochreous. FEMALE : UPPERSIDE with the ground-colour, especially of the *forewing*, dusky ferruginous, in some specimens dusky greenish. Otherwise as in the male.

C. biblis is very common in Sikkim at all elevations up to 7,000 feet, also in Assam and the Khasi hills ; Mr. Wood-Mason took it in Cachar ; the Indian Museum, Calcutta, has specimens from Sylhet, Upper Assam (*S. E. Peal*), and Shillong. Captain C. T. Bingham took it in the Thoungyeen forests in March and April and in the Donat range in July, it occurs also in Upper Burma (*taken by the Yunan Expedition*) and Mergui (*Dr. Anderson*), Perak and Hainan, China.

---

male ; 8, *female* (1882). HABITAT : Nepal ? Assam ? Perak, Province Wellesley, Malacca. EXPANSE : *male*, 2·8 to 3·2 ; *female*, 2·9 to 3·1 inches. DESCRIPTION : " MALE. UPPERSIDE as in *C. methypsea*, but the black area larger and occupying the cell, which is crossed by some indistinct reddish fasciæ (obsolete in some specimens) ; an oblique and very much sinuated pale ochraceous or greyish-white macular fascia situated a little beyond cell and terminating a little beneath the second median nervule, but without the outer pale spots as in *C. methypsea*. *Hindwing* as in that species, but with the black margin somewhat broader, its enclosed pale lunate lines clear and distinct, and the discal area more black-spotted. UNDERSIDE as in *C. methypsea*, but the red colouring darker ; the *hindwing* has the medial pale fascia situated further from the base, and the series of linear and rounded black spots are nearer the black margin and not placed at the margins of a narrow pale fascia : on the *forewing* the narrow pale submarginal fascia is replaced by a series of dark spots situated nearer the outer margin. FEMALE UPPERSIDE generally paler and more ochraceous than the male, the black area to the *forewing* much larger and occupying the whole wing, with the exception of the oblique macular fascia beyond the cell, and a large subtriangular space on inner margin, which does not extend above the first median nervule, and is there distinctly paler. UNDERSIDE as in the male."

"The species is a near ally to *C. hypsea*, a Bornean species ; the males are very similar, but the females are sufficiently distinct." (*Distant*, l. c.)

C. methypsea and *C. hypsina* belong to the *cyane* group of *Cethosia*, but differ on the upperside of the forewing in having the subapical band ochreous instead of pure white ; on the underside there is more fulvous in the ground-colour exteriorly, and basally they are ochreous-red rather than vermilion, the whitish band beyond more prominent.

320. Cethosia nikobarica, Felder.

C. nikobarica, Felder, Verh. zool.-bot. Gesells. Wien, vol. xii, p. 484, n. 119 (1862) : idem, id., Reise Novara, Lep., vol. iii, p. 384, n. 557, pl. xlviii, figs. 7, 8, *male* (1867); *C. nicobarica*, Moore, Proc. Zool. Soc. Lond., 1877, p. 583.

HABITAT : Andaman and Nicobar Isles.

EXPANSE : ♂, 2·85 to 3·6 ; ♀, 2·8 to 4·0 inches.

DESCRIPTION : " MALE. UPPERSIDE pale brick red. *Forewing* with the cellular streaks, the costa and the apical half blackish with large white spots and white dots. *Hindwing* with some more obsolete dots beyond the disc and the external border broad blackish, bearing near its inner margin an obsolete series of brick red lunules, the lunulate marginal streaks obliterated above, on the UNDERSIDE alike in both wings, very narrow, less distinct in the forewing." (*Felder*, l. c. in Verh. zool.-bot. Gesells. Wien.) " FEMALE : Blacker than the male. *Forewing* with the lower basal portion and interspaces in cell dark greenish grey ; subapical marks broader, the lower dentate mark formed into a streak. *Hindwing* with the basal portion pale greenish grey. UNDERSIDE, greenish brown (in the male dull vermilion), interspaces of basal streaks greenish (in the male bluish) ; black median transverse zigzag markings and discal dentate marks and spots reddish white-bordered ; a black-and-white marginal sinuous band." (*Moore*, l. c.)

This species is a local race of *C. biblis*, but is sufficiently distinct. It occurs commonly at Port Blair ; and has been recorded from Nankowri, Kondul and Great Nicobar in the Nicobar group of islands. It differs from *C. biblis* in having the black margin of the hindwing broader, the marginal series of white lunules obsolete, and on the underside the black markings much more prominent, except those bordering the medial pale ochreous band which are obsolete on the inner edge, and greatly reduced on the outer. The female is very differently coloured, with a large white patch in the middle of the forewing.

C. logani from Province Wellesley is another local race of *C. biblis*. A description of it will be found below.*

Genus 52.—TERINOS, Boisduval. (PLATE XXIII).

Terinos. Boisduval, Sp. Gén., vol. i, pl. ix, fig. 4 (1836) ; id., Doubleday, Gen. Diurn. Lep., vol. i, p. 159 (1848) ; id., Wallace, Trans. Ent. Soc. Lond., 1869, p. 340 ; id., Distant, Rhop. Malay., p. 181 (1882).

" HEAD, broad, hairy. *Eyes*, oval, prominent, hairy. *Palpi*, porrect, ascending, rising above the forehead, scaly ; the scales on the first joint long ; the second joint hairy at the sides. First joint short, transverse ; second four times the length of the first, subcylindric, slightly swollen in the middle, tapering towards the base, and more so towards the apex ; third joint about one-fifth the length of the second, slender, fusiform, the apex pointed. *Antennæ*,

---

* *Cethosia logani*, Distant, Ent. Month. Mag., vol. xviii, p. 134 (1881) ; idem, id., Rhop. Malay , p. 190, n. 1, pl. viii, fig. 5, *male* (1882). HABITAT : Province Wellesley. EXPANSE : 2·9 inches. DESCRIPTION : " MALE. UPPERSIDE, *forewing* with the basal third bright red, remainder black with white margin ; cell crossed by three pairs of narrow black fasciæ; the last pair somewhat indistinct, owing to the proximity of the black area ; an indistinct arcuated spot beneath cell, and two somewhat waved linear spots separated by the first median nervule ; the dark area contains the following white markings :—four spots a little beyond end of cell, of which the third is very small ; beyond these are three large lanceolate spots, indistinctly margined with white, divided by the discoidal nervules, and outwardly followed by a series of five small spots situated between the nervules ; a very large and irregular subquadrate spot bounded by the third and first median nervules ; a small lunate spot beneath the first median nervule, and a submarginal row of large but somewhat obscure lunately linear spots. *Hindwing* bright red, with the outer margin broadly black, which is inwardly bordered with a series of irregular spots of the same colour, and with nine or ten scattered and irregular black spots on the basal area ; the broad black marginal border contains two small red spots divided by the discoidal nervule, and a submarginal series of large pale, but obscure lunately linear spots. UNDERSIDE, *forewing* much paler, the black apical area being brownish-ochraceous ; cell crossed as above, but the colour between the black fasciæ violescent, all the white markings either larger or more distinct, the lanceolate spots beyond cell being wholly greyish white, containing inwardly an ovate, linear black spot, and outwardly two rounded black spots ; the marginal lunately linear spots paler and with central pale lines. *Hindwing* paler and of the same hue as the forewing, with a black subcostal line at base surrounded with greyish ; an oblique greyish fascia near base margined with black, each margin with a double termination at abdominal margin ; a similar greyish fascia crossing middle of wing, with much broken black margins, the outer of which is very pale ; a broad greyish outer discal fascia containing a series of small black spots near its outer margin, which is black, and with a similar but poorer and more irregular series near its inner margin, which is also more or less black ; outer marginal lunate spots as on forewing, but more broadly margined with black. *Body* more or less reddish ochraceous. FEMALE almost indistinguishable from the male, but with the white markings of the *forewing* a little larger."

" This species is most nearly allied to *C. nicobarica*, Felder, which is found both in the Andaman and Nicobar Islands ; it is somewhat intermediate between that species and *C. methypsea*." (*Distant*, l. c.)

rather short, slender, abruptly clavate ; the club obtuse. *Thorax*, moderately stout, oval, hairy. *Abdomen* about two-thirds the length of the inner margin of the hindwing. FOREWING, subtriangular ; the *costal margin* rounded ; the *apex* somewhat truncate ; *outer* margin sinuate, emarginate, scarcely two-thirds the length of the costal ; *inner* margin nearly straight, about equal to the outer. *Costal nervure* not reaching to the middle of the costa. *First* and *second subcostal nervules* very close together, the latter thrown off exactly at the end of the cell ; *fourth* more remote from the apex than from the end of the cell ; *third* about equally distant from the second and fourth, terminating close to the apex. *Upper disco-cellular* nervule almost wanting ; *middle* disco-cellular curved ; *lower* disco-cellular longer than the middle disco-cellular, directed obliquely inwards to the median nervure, which it joins before the origin of the second nervule. [This is a variable character, as pointed out below.] *Third median* nervule not much curved. HINDWING, almost quadrangular ; the *costal margin* very slightly curved ; the *outer* margin sinuate, produced into an angle at the termination of the third median nervule ; *inner* margin longer than the outer, emarginate towards the anal angle. *Precostal nervure* simple. *Subcostal* nervure dividing very near to the base of the wing. *Discoidal nervule* appearing to be a third subcostal, bent soon after its origin. *Discoidal cell* open, but with a slight indication of a lower disco-cellular in a state of atrophy. Abdominal fold ample. FORELEGS, of the *male* scaly, and fringed with long hairs ; *tibia* shorter than the femur ; *tarsus* shorter than the tibia, one-jointed, subcylindric, pointed. Of the *female* scaly, stouter than those of the male ; first joint three times as long as the rest combined, cylindric, slightly curved, with a few spines below, and two stout spines at the apex, covered with a tuft of hair at the base of the next joint, as is the case also with the three following joints. These are transverse, about of equal length ; the fifth joint is rather longer than the preceding, tapering, terminated by a mucro[*] representing the claw. MIDDLE and HINDLEGS, with the tibiæ rather shorter than the femora, spiny ; the spurs long ; *tarsi* rather longer than the tibiæ, spiny both above and below ; the spines at the sides and below nearly in regular series ; first joint as long as the rest combined ; rest, to the fourth, progressively shorter ; fifth rather longer than the third. *Claws* curved, very slightly grooved below. *Paronychia* bilaciniate ; the outer lacinia elongate, somewhat elliptical, equal to the claw ; inner rather strap-shaped, short. *Pulvillus* jointed, as long as the claw ; the second joint very broad." (*Doubleday*, l. c.)

A single species of this very beautiful genus occurs within Indian limits in Upper Tenasserim ; with this exception, it appears to be strictly confined to Malayana, and comprises some nine or ten species. The males are furnished with prominent secondary sexual characters, a very unusual occurrence in the genera of this subfamily. They consist of a very large patch of blackish velvety scales on the outer margin of the forewing on the upperside extending from the anal angle up to the upper discoidal nervule, and a similar but smaller patch on the hindwing at the apex, posteriorly bounded by the discoidal nervure. Mr. Wallace makes the following remarks on the genus : "The most striking characteristics of these insects are the hairy eyes, and the large plush-like scales which, in the males, form a large patch on both wings, but which are often replaced in the females by blue bands and patches, giving this sex the aspect of a different species. Still more remarkable, however, is the great difference of neuration presented by the sexes in some of the species. Mr. Hewitson pointed out the variation in the position of the lower disco-cellular nervule in relation to the second median nervule, whereby closely allied species may readily be distinguished. This is undoubtedly the case ; but by examination of four species of which I possess both sexes, I find that the difference between the neuration of the sexes is fully as great as between that of the most distant species. I find also by measurement and comparison, that the disco-cellular nervule retains a constant position, so that the length of the cell does not vary, and that it is the branches of the median nervure that alter their position, being, in some cases, very much further from the base of the wing than in others. In *T. clarissa* the sexual difference is perceptible, but slight. In *T. robertsia* and *T. taxiles* it is very easily seen, as in the male the second median nervule springs from the same point as the lower disco-cellular, while in the female it

---

[*] MUCRO, a sharp point or edge.

comes almost exactly midway between the first and second branch. In *T. abisares* the difference is still more marked, since in the male the disco-cellular arises in advance of the second median nervule, while in the female it is nearly midway between them. This is a remarkable illustration of Darwin's law, that when a particular character varies sexually, it also varies specifically. As a rule, differences of neuration are generic, rarely varying much from closely-allied species to species. Here we have them as a sexual distinction ; and we also find them varying in an unusual degree from species to species. It is also very interesting to remark, that in the two species, *T. robertsia* and *T. viola*, the Singapore variety is more highly coloured, and has the branches of the median nervure more distant from the base of the wing than in the more rufous-tinged Sumatran specimens, shewing a remarkable correlation between local modifications of tint, and what are usually important and stable structural characters."

In addition to the single species occurring in British Burma there are two well-marked species of the genus occurring in the Malay peninsula ; a description of them is given below.[*] Mr. Distant remarks of the females that they "appear to be excessively rare, or, as is possible, a difference in their habits may be the cause of their very infrequent capture."

321. Terinos clarissa, Boisduval. (PLATE XXIII, FIG. 101 ♂).

T. clarissa, Boisduval, Sp. Gén., vol. i, pl. ix, fig. 4 (1836).

HABITAT : Upper Tenasserim, Singapore, Java, Borneo.

EXPANSE : ♂ , 2·85 inches (Javan specimen), 3·4 inches (Tenasserim and Bornean specimens).

DESCRIPTION : MALE. UPPERSIDE rich dark violaceous. *Forewing* with the usual deep brown velvety patch occupying about half the wing surface, commencing on the inner margin about one-fourth of its length from the base, extending up the outer margin as far as the lower discoidal nervule, which bounds it anteriorly, then extending obliquely across the wing to the point where it first commences. The apical margin black. *Hindwing* with a similar but smaller apical patch ; the outer margin broadly ochraceous, bearing two obsolete series of blackish lunules, which are most prominent at the anal angle where they approximate. UNDERSIDE dull ferruginous brown marked (in the Tenasserim specimen) with very indistinct darker brown and pale violet irregular lines across the surface. *Forewing* with a subapical

---

[*] *Terinos robertsia*, Butler, Ann. and Mag. of Nat. Hist., third series, vol. xx, p. 399, pl. viii, figs. 2—4 (1867); id , Wallace, Trans. Ent. Soc. Lond., 1869, p. 342 ; id , Butler, Trans. Linn. Soc., Zoology, second series, vol. 1, p. 544, n. 1 (1877) ; id., Distant, Rhop. Malay., p. 182, n. 1, pl. x, fig. 7, *male* (1882). HABITAT : Perak, Penang, Province Wellesley, Malacca, Ayerpanas, Singapore. EXPANSE : 2·5 to 2·9 inches. DESCRIPTION : " MALE. UPPERSIDE dark violaceous. *Forewing* with a large dark brownish silky patch, which occupies about apical half of wing, but not extending above the disco-dal nervules, except at outer margin, where it is continued to apex, it also extends along inner margin to base. *Hindwing* with a similar but smaller silky patch broadly occupying apex and extending from costal margin to the lower subcostal nervule ; two large white submarginal spots separated by the upper median nervule and a third almost obsolete spot between the second and first median nervules ; narrow waved darker marginal and submarginal fasciæ ; cilia greyish UNDERSIDE of a steely-bluish colour, crossed by a number of dull reddish fasciæ, of which five narrow and much waved cross both wings from base to a little beyond cell ; these are followed by a broader and less waved fascia, which on the *forewing* is succeeded by a macular fascia, of which the upper spots are outwardly pointed, and one marginal and two narrow submarginal fasciæ which become fused at apex, and there contain a small white spot placed between the fourth and fifth subcostal nervules ; on the *hindwing* the medial broad fascia is followed by one broader and more irregular, which contains a series of castaneous spots placed between the nervules, one marginal and two submarginal fasciæ, between which the colour is greyish-white, and the inner one of which is waved and at about middle dentate, thus enclosing some apparently large angulated greyish-white spots. *Body* above concolourous with wings ; beneath, with the femora, greyish ; tibia and tarsi ochraceous." (*Distant*, l. c.) " FEMALE. UPPERSIDE fuscous, the basal area, six submarginal discal spots on the forewing placed between the veins and the discal area of the hindwing shining purple. *Forewing* with two equi-distant transverse bands darker fuscous. *Hindwing* with white spots as in the male, and other marginal contiguous lunules whitish." (*Butler*, l. c. in Ann. and Mag. of Nat. Hist.) The hindwing in this species is evenly waved, but not tailed.

Terinos teuthras, Hewitson, Proc. Zool. Soc. Lond., 1862, p. 89 ; id., Butler, Trans. Linn. Soc., Zoology, second series, vol. 1, p. 544, n. 1 (1877) ; id , Distant, Rhop. Malay., p. 183, n. 2, pl. x, fig. 6, *male* (1882) ; *T. viola*, Wallace, Trans. Ent. Soc. Lond., 1869, p. 347. HABITAT : Perak, Penang, Province Wellesley, Malacca, Singapore. EXPANSE : *Male*, 3·2 to 3·6 inches. DESCRIPTION : " MALE. UPPERSIDE dark violaceous. *Forewing* with a large dark brownish silky patch as in preceding species, but which extends a little above the upper discoidal nervule and inwardly to the lower disco-cellular nervule. *Hindwing* with a similar patch near apex, which does not extend to the outer margin, and is continued to between the lower subcostal and the discoidal nervules ; some large marginal conical whitish spots above middle of outer margin, through which extends a waved dark violaceous submarginal fascia ; a dark marginal fascia and the cilia greyish. UNDERSIDE brownish, with steely reflections. *Forewing* with the cell crossed by two narrow waved reddish fasciæ, beyond which is a similar very broad and marginally waved fascia crossing *both wings*; this is also succeeded on both wings by a narrow bluish lunulate line, which on the *hindwing* is placed in front of some reddish spots situated between the nervules ; the *forewing* possesses a pale apical patch enclosing a dark spot and a pale submarginal fascia ; the *hindwing* has an ochraceous much-waved submarginal fascia, on each side of which the colour is pale bluish. *Body* more or less concolourous with wings ; legs ochraceous." (*Distant*, l. c.) The hindwing in this species is prominently tailed.

pale violet oval spot, with a dark brown inner spot attached to it. *Hindwing* with the false end of the cell marked with a prominent white bar, beyond which are a series of five round brown spots placed between the nervules, except in the interspace containing the white bar, a submarginal indistinct lunular ochreous line, and some obscure marginal markings. FEMALE unknown to me.

The single male described above, which was taken by Captain C. T. Bingham at Popee, Thoungyeen, in September, agrees exactly on the upperside with Javan and Bornean male specimens in the Indian Museum, Calcutta, but differs from them and from Boisduval's figure on the underside in the obscurity of all the markings. In them the underside is castaneous, the cell of the forewing crossed by three and the base of the hindwing by two pale violaceous lines, the disc of both wings by three very irregular similar lines, with, on the forewing, some less distinct marginal ones. Hindwing with a discal series of five oval deep castaneous spots between the nervules, the one in the discoidal interspace wanting ; outer margin pale violaceous, bearing two lunulated castaneous lines, the inner one very dentate between the first median and discoidal nervules. The apex of the forewing in the Tenasserim specimen is more falcate than in the Javan and Bornean examples, but not more so than in Boisduval's figure. The length of the tail to the hindwing is variable, but it is longest in the Tenasserim specimen. A large series of specimens alone can determine whether this difference of marking is of sufficient constancy and importance to give the Upper Tenasserim race separate specific rank. Mr. Wallace (Trans. Ent. Soc. Lond., 1869, p. 341) records *T. clarina* from Singapore, as also does Mr. Doubleday (Gen. Diurn. Lep., vol. 1, p. 160), but the species is not included in Mr. Distant's " Rhopalocera Malayana."

The figure is taken from a male specimen from Upper Tenasserim, and now in Major Marshall's collection, and shows both sides.

Genus 53.—CYNTHIA, Fabricius. (PLATE XXI).

Cynthia, Fabricius, Ill. Mag., vol. vi, p. 281, n. 11, (1807) ; id., Doubleday, Gen. Diurn. Lep., vol. i, p. 212 (1849) ; id., Moore, Lep. Cey., vol. i, p. 52 (1881) ; id., Distant, Rhop. Malay., p. 183 (1882) ; *Anartia* (part), Hübner, Verz. bek. Schmett., p. 33 (1816).

" HEAD, of moderate width, hairy. *Eyes*, oval, not prominent. *Palpi*, ascending, convergent, the third joint directed almost immediately forwards ; first joint short, much curved, scaly, with one or two setæ in front ; second joint three times the length of the first, much swollen beyond the middle, rounded at the apex, scaly, and thickly set in front and externally with long setæ ; third joint ovate, about one-fifth the length, and half the breadth, of the first joint, scaly, the scales appressed. *Antennæ*, fully three-fourths the length of the body, terminating in a gradually thickened, short, rather slender club. *Thorax*, elongate, oval, hairy ; prothorax very distinct. [*Abdomen*, stout, somewhat short, about two-thirds the length of the inner margin of the hindwing.] FOREWING, subtriangular ; *costal margin* considerably curved ; *outer* and *inner* margins about equal in length ; the outer emarginate, sinuate ; the inner very slightly emarginate. *Costal nervure* extending to the middle of the costa ; *subcostal* nervure slender, lying close to the costal as far as the end of the cell, five-branched ; its first and second nervules thrown off close together ; the first a little before, the second immediately beyond, the end of the cell ; the third rather nearer to the second than to the apex ; the fourth shortly beyond the third. *Discoidal cell* not half the length of the wing. *Upper disco-cellular nervule* very short, directed obliquely outwards ; *middle* about half the length of the lower, nearly straight, directed obliquely inwards ; *lower* curving inwards, joining the third median nervule soon after its origin ; this latter subsequently considerably curved. HINDWING, with the *costal margin* much rounded, shorter than the *outer*, which is also much rounded, sinuate, often with a short tail in which the third median nervule terminates. *Inner* margin equal to the outer, forming a deep channel for the reception of the abdomen. *Præcostal nervure* bifid. *Costal* nervure not much curved near its origin. *Discoidal cell* open, but with a depression on the underside in the place of the lower disco-cellular nervule. *Discoidal nervule* curved at its separation from the second subcostal nervule. FORELEGS, of the *male* rather slender ; *femur* and *tibia* of about equal length, the latter nearly cylindric, obliquely truncate at its apex, clothed with scales and a few scattered setæ; *tarsus* half as long as the tibia, nearly cylindric, mucronate at the apex. Of the *female* with the *femur* and *tibia* of about equal length, rather slender, scaly; the latter also furnished with some scattered setæ, and with two lateral spines before the apex, which is very obliquely truncate; *tarsus* shorter than the tibia, clavate; first joint nearly cylindric for about two-thirds of its length, then widening to the apex, which is about double the width of the base; second joint transverse, about one-sixth the length of the first; third transverse, shorter than the second; fourth transverse, about half the length of the first; all these joints armed with a spine on each side at the apex; fifth joint very small, shorter than the fourth, armed with two small spines before the apex, and furnished, as are the three preceding joints, with a tuft of hair on each side at the base, covering the spines of the preceding joint. MIDDLE and HINDLEGS, rather robust; *femora* of the middle pair rather longer, of the hind pair rather shorter, than the tibiæ; *tibiæ* spiny all round; the two lateral series distinctly regular; spurs strong; *tarsus* spiny above, laterally, and below; fifth joint less spiny below than the others; the spines below arranged in two tolerably regular series; second joint fully one-third the length of the first; third joint more than two-thirds the length of the second; fourth joint half the length of the fifth, and more than half the length of the second. *Claws* strong, sharp, curved, grooved below. *Paronychia* consisting of one lacinia, broad at the base, then suddenly narrower, nearly linear, rather more than half the length of the claw, very hairy. *Pulvillus* short; the second joint broad, hairy. The sexes differ materially in colour; the males being fulvous with darker markings; the females of a light greyish-brown, both wings being traversed by a broad white interrupted band." (*Doubleday*, l. c.)

LARVA cylindric, head armed with two large erect spiny tubercles, the segments also armed with tubercles from which spring many-branched spines. PUPA irregular-shaped, with numerous projecting processes.

The genus *Cynthia* is found in South India, Ceylon, Andaman Isles, the Eastern Himalayas, Assam, Sylhet, Cachar, Burma, and thence through the Malay Peninsula and Archipelago as far eastwards as New Britain. All the species are very closely allied indeed, so much so that Mr. Doubleday, in the Genera of Diurnal Lepidoptera, confined the species to one only, and Mr. Kirby in his Synonymic Catalogue to one with a variety. In the case of several of them, it is almost impossible to distinguish between them without having both sexes, it being the female which bears the chief specific distinctions.

Three species are found within our limits, while Mr. Distant records two as occurring in the Malay Peninsula. The males of the North Indian and Ceylonese species appear to be almost indistinguishable, so I have based the key below on the principal points of difference in the opposite sex. They are large and handsome insects having the hindwing distinctly tailed in both sexes; the males are bright yellowish-brown, with two macular black lines on the outer margin and one transverse one on the disc across both wings. The females are more or less greenish, with a prominent white band across the disc, with from two to five ocelli on the hindwing.

Key to the Indian species of Cynthia.

A. Female with the white discal band of the upperside reaching the submedian nervure of the hindwing.
      322. C. EROTA, North East India, Burma, Andamans.

B. Female with the white discal band of the upperside reaching the lower subcostal nervule of hindwing only.
    a. Ground-colour of the upperside greenish-olivaceous.
        323. C. SALOMA, South India.
    b. Ground-colour of the upperside dark blue-grey.
        324. C. ASELA, Ceylon.

322. **Cynthia erota,** Fabricius. (PLATE XXI, FIG. 97 ♂ ♀).

Papilio erota, Fabricius, Ent. Syst., vol. iii, pt. 1, p. 76, n. 237 (1793); *Cynthia erota,* Butler, Cat. Fabr. Lep. Brit. Mus., p. 115, n. 2 (1869); id., Moore, Proc. Zool. Soc. Lond., 1877, p. 584.

HABITAT: North East India, Burma, South Andaman Isles.

EXPANSE: ♂, 3·5 to 4·3; ♀, 3·2 to 4·5 inches.

6

DESCRIPTION: MALE. UPPERSIDE bright ferruginous-ochreous, the discal area across both wings slightly paler. *Forewing* with two black lines crossing the middle of the cell, another near its outer end, two very fine lines enclosing the disco-cellulars, a black somewhat lunulated very narrow fascia or line just beyond the cell from the costa to the submedian nervure, a paler much waved discal macular line, followed by a curved series of small black spots one in each interspace, the two on either side of the third median nervule indistinct, a black submarginal waved line enclosing a pale ochreous spot at the apex, and a marginal more waved line. *Hindwing* with a narrow black straight line beyond the cell from the costal nervure to near the anal angle, in continuation of the line on the forewing, beyond which the ground-colour is paler especially towards the costa, the outer margin of this pale band marked by a very irregular deep tawny line, a diffused dusky band bearing two ocelli, the upper one placed in the interspace above the discoidal nervule, the lower one in the first median interspace, these ocelli made up of a fine black outer line enclosing an ochreous space bearing a somewhat diffused blackish excentric spot with a lilac pupil. Marginal and submarginal lines as in the forewing, but enclosing a small patch of violaceous at the anal angle. UNDERSIDE paler, tinged with reddish towards the base, and marked somewhat similarly to the upperside, the basal markings more prominent, the middle bar across the cell of the forewing being produced to the submedian nervure and appearing on the hindwing from the costal to the submedian nervure, an additional line between it and the base across the cell of both wings, and the upper disco-cellular of the hindwing enclosed by two fine lines; the discal line prominent, continued almost straight from the middle of the costa of the forewing almost to the anal angle of the hindwing, near which it curves abruptly upwards and joins the inner margin just below the abdominal fold; a prominent blackish line nearly straight from the outer edge of the apical spot on the forewing to the anal angle of the hindwing, the triangular space between paler and bearing two much waved less distinct lines, the outer of which merges in the outer line on the hindwing, the space beyond much washed with silvery violaceous, the marginal lines paler and indistinct, the apical spot on the forewing large silvery geminate, and followed by two smaller ones corresponding to the black dots of the upperside.

The above description is of the typical form which is found abundantly in North Eastern India from Sikkim, through Assam, the Khasi and Naga Hills, Sylhet, Cachar, Munipore, and Burma to Tenasserim; but there are several more or less well-defined local races in which the characters of the MALE insect differ as follows.

The Andaman race has the UPPERSIDE distinctly paler throughout, but the markings are identical, those on the paler discal area slightly less distinct; the UNDERSIDE is also paler, and more uniformly ochreous in tint, the silvery violaceous washing equally wide-spread but much less brilliant in tone. The ground-colour of the upperside is somewhat variable, in some specimens it is pale ochreous throughout, in others distinctly darker at the base of both wings.

In Tenasserim also there occurs along with the typical form, a local race, nearest to the Andaman form but paler still and more uniformly yellowish in tone; on the UPPERSIDE the markings are all paler and less distinct, those on the pale discal area almost entirely obsolete; the violaceous patch at anal angle indistinct; the UNDERSIDE paler, the markings all less prominent, and the silvery violaceous washings duller and more restricted than even in the Andaman race. This race prominently differs from the South Indian species, *C. saloma*, in the very much paler and more uniform tone of colouring, its smaller size, and the markings throughout being far less prominent.

Lastly, we have a single specimen taken in December by Dr. E. R. Johnson at Harriajan at the base of the Naga hills on the north side towards the Brahmaputra valley; the upper-side of which closely resembles that of the pale Tenasserim local race, but the violaceous patch at anal angle of hindwing is altogether wanting; the UNDERSIDE is darker almost uniform ochreous with a ferruginous tinge, basal half more distinctly ferruginous-red, and barely the faintest trace of the violaceous washing is discernable on the external area.

Males of *C. erota* are very common in Sikkim at all elevations up to 7,000 feet, also in Assam and the Khasi Hills. They are very powerful on the wing, and frequent damp spots where they suck up the moisture. The female is far less frequently seen.

The figure shows the upperside of a male and a female specimen in the Indian Museum, Calcutta, from Shillong.

323. Cynthia saloma, n. sp., Swinhoe, MS.

HABITAT : Nilgiris, Wynaad, Travancore.

EXPANSE : ♂, 4.2 ; ♀, 4.6 inches.

DESCRIPTION : MALE. UPPERSIDE with the basal and external areas of *both wings* much darker than in typical *C. erota*, the black lines broader and more prominent, the violaceous patch at anal angle of *hindwing* wanting, the discal area between much paler, and the markings on it obsolescent. On the UNDERSIDE the discal area is also paler and more conspicuous, the markings on it less prominent, and the silvery violaceous washing of the external area duller and more restricted and in some specimens barely traceable. The FEMALE differs in having the white discal area on the UPPERSIDE of the *forewing* wider and more diffused at the costa and much narrower below, the area beyond being powdered with lilac grey, especially near the hinder angle. On the *hindwing* the white discal band is much restricted, barely extending below the lower subcostal nervule, while in *C. erota* it extends right across the wing to the submedian nervure.

This species, differing as it does in both sexes from the typical *C. erota*, forms a well-marked local race linking *C. erota* with the Ceylon form *C. asela*, on the other hand the pale Tenasserim local race of *C. erota* described above (of which the female is still unknown) appears to link *C. erota* with the Malayan *C. deione*.

Mr. Rhodes-Morgan has taken both sexes of this species in the Wynaad, as also has Mr. Harold S. Ferguson in Travancore. Mr. Frank W. Bourdillon says of this species : "Occurs in Trevandrum at about 2,000 feet elevation, uncommon and difficult to secure owing to its strong flight and habit of settling 20 or 30 feet from the ground." Colonel Swinhoe's original description of *C. saloma* from specimens from the Nilgiris is given below.[*]

324. Cynthia asela, Moore.

C. asela, Moore, Proc. Zool. Soc. Lond., 1872, p. 558 ; idem, id., Lep. Cey., p. 53, pl. xxvi, figs. 1, *male*, 1a, *female* ; 1b, *larva* ; 1c, *pupa*.

HABITAT : Ceylon.

EXPANSE : ♂, 3.4 to 4.0 ; ♀, 4.0 to 4.3 inches.

DESCRIPTION : "MALE, UPPERSIDE bright ochreous-yellow, darkest on basal area and marginal border. *Forewing* with a black medial transverse interrupted line, discoidal streaks, two streaks below the cell, two marginal sinuous lines, and a submarginal row of more or less obsolete lunate spots, the upper spot being pale centred ; an indistinct darker ochreous zigzag fascia across the disc. *Hindwing* with a black medial transverse line, an inner discal zigzag ochreous fascia bordering an outer series of spots, the one between the [lower] subcostal [and

---

" *Cynthia saloma*, n. sp. HABITAT : Nilgheries. EXPANSE : *Male*, 3.7 ; *female*, 4.7 inches. DESCRIPTION : MALE, dull ochreous, basal area and marginal border darker, densely irrorated with reddish grey with a greenish tinge markings as in *C. asela* but the colouration is altogether different and the band between the medial line and outer border is much paler than either in *C. erota* or in *C. asela*, giving it the appearance of a dull pale whitish greyish ochreous band, which gradually darkens on the lower half of the *hindwing*, and becomes suffused into the darker colour of the marginal border. UNDERSIDE as in *C. asela* but paler, colouration duller and less reddish and without the small brown patch at the hinder angle. FEMALE dark greenish grey, outer border dark chocolate grey ; *forewing* with the cell markings as in *C. erota*, female, a central brown line followed by a broad white band divided by the veins and which is narrowest on the hinder margin, where the outer half of the band is greenish, and it expands upwards to the costa to within half an inch of the apex, a suffused black spot on the lower radial interspace, a dentated black line running through the band near its outer margin, a white subapical spot and two very slightly sinuous black submarginal lines very nearly straight and not together as is usual in *C. erota* and *C. asela*. *Hindwing* with a central faint brown line in continuation of the one on the forewing, followed by a broad band also in continuation of the band on the forewing, but this band instead of being white is greenish grey, only slightly paler than the colouration of the basal half, and is quite as opaque as the rest of the wing instead of being semi-hyaline as is the case in the allied species ; there are also the two usual discal ocelli and two submarginal black lines. UNDERSIDE as in *C. erota*, female, but the band on the *hindwing* instead of being white is greyish ochreous and very slightly paler than the colouration of the outer border."

"I compared these insects with many specimens of this genus at the British Museum, and at Mr Moore's, and other collections, and am of opinion that it is a distinct and good species." (*Swinhoe*).

discoidal] nervules and another between the lower median nervules being ocellated, the others indistinct and formed of black speckles; two marginal sinuous lines. UNDERSIDE uniform yellow outwardly from medial dusky line, the base suffused with ochry red; basal streaks bright red. *Forewing* with three contiguous apical white spots, inner marginal straight pale dusky red line, almost obsolete outer marginal zigzag line; a discal transverse zigzag line on *both wings*; marginal lunular lines and extreme margin of *hindwing* from tail to anal angle chestnut-brown; a transverse streak passing the ocelli on the hindwing. FEMALE dark blue-grey, brightest on hindwing, outer borders brown. *Forewing* with a transverse discal band of broad bluish-white traversed exteriorly by a sinuous line; an outer row of blackish spots and two submarginal sinuous lines. *Hindwing* with transverse medial narrow black line outwardly bordered at the costal end by a short broad whitish sinuous-margined band; two large prominent discal ocelli with greenish inner ring; two marginal black sinuous lines. UNDERSIDE similar to *C. erota*."

"LARVA pale yellow, reddish-brown beneath; segments brown streaked, spiracles black; head spinous, armed with two long curved thick spinous tubercles, the segments armed with a dorsal and two lateral rows of long slightly branched spines, the dorsal and upper lateral row arising from a red round tumid spot. PUPA pale reddish-brown, truncated at both ends; head thick, with two short points, thorax conically pointed at top; anterior abdominal segments produced thickly outwards into a point hindwards, and forwards into two lengthened processes, middle segments with a short dorsal tubercle, the two anal segments with longer basally-thickened processes." *(Moore, l. c. in Lep. Cey.)*

In Ceylon "Found everywhere, both in the plains and up to 6,000 feet in forest lands all the year; most plentiful from May to October. Flight slow, very tame; a dozen at a time will alight on the ground close to you." *(Hutchison).*

In the males of *C. asela* and *C. erota* I can detect no single character by which to distinguish them, though strangely enough the South Indian *C. saloma* is very different in aspect from typical *C. erota* and *C. asela*, though placed geographically between them. The female of *C. asela* is a darker insect, especially below, than *C. erota* from Northern India; on the upperside the ground-colour is of a different shade, being blue-grey instead of olivaceous, and the white discal band on the hindwing is less distinct and more restricted. The South Indian species in the female differs much in the tone of the ground-colour on the upperside, which is decidedly bronzy-green; the discal band on the hindwing is also even more restricted.

Two species have been described from the Malay peninsula, one of them, *C. deione,** having a very wide range, the other being as yet known from Province Wellesley only. There are

---

* *Cynthia deione*, Erichson, Nova Acta Ac. Nat. Cur., vol. xvi, Supplement 1, p. 279, n. 3, pl. xl, figs. 2, 2a, *female* (1834); id., Distant, Rhop. Malay., p. 182, n. 1, pl. x, figs. 1, *male*; 2, *female* (1882); *Cynthia erotella*, Butler, Trans. Linn. Soc., Zoology, second series, vol. i, p. 544, n. 1 (1877). HABITAT: Penang, Province Wellesley, Sungei Ujong, Malacca, Singapore, Ilanca, Billiton, Sumatra, Java, Borneo, Labuan, Celebes, Philippines, Luzon. EXPANSE: *Male*, 2 to 3 2; *female*, 3 6 10 3 8 inches. DESCRIPTION: "MALE. UPPERSIDE pale reddish-ochraceous. *Forewing* with the cell crossed by two narrow black fasciæ at middle, a similar waved fascia near end, and two slender and contiguous lines at its termination, enclosing the disco-cellular nervules; an oblique narrow black discal fascia crossing wing beyond apex of cell, after which is a strongly waved fascia, distinct and blackish above the upper median nervule, indistinct and reddish beneath it; a submarginal series of black spots, placed between the nervules, and becoming obsolete towards the apex (which is somewhat infuscated) and outer angle, two narrow waved submarginal black fasciæ and the margin of the same colour. *Hindwing* with a narrow oblique medial fascia, which is either pale fuscous or reddish; two ocellated spots, one between the second and first median nervules, the other above the discoidal nervule; an irregular black spot at apex, and marginal and submarginal lines as on forewing, the inner of which is straight and truncate at median nervules; from the area of the ocellated spots to the posterior margin the colour is distinctly darker. UNDERSIDE paler and marked as above. *Forewing* with three whitish and tale-like apical spots. *Hindwing* with some transverse linear markings near base, and an elongated spot surrounding the upper disco-cellular nervule; beyond the medial transverse fascia on *both wings* the colour is less rufous, and on the *hindwing* an oblique black fascia precedes the ocellated spots. *Body* and *legs* concolourous with wings. FEMALE. UPPERSIDE olivaceous, marked as in the male, but with a whitish medial fascia crossing *both wings*. *Forewing* with distinct white apical spots. *Hindwing* with an additional ocellated and bipupilated spot at anal angle. UNDERSIDE as above, but much paler; *hindwing* with the dark fascia preceding the ocellated spots, as in that wing of the male.' *(Distant, l. c.)*

Mr. Butler (l.c.) in describing *C. erotella* says:—"I have examined a good series of examples, and am therefore confident of the distinctness of this species. In general size and the indistinctness of the lunulated discal line it agrees with *C. deione*; but it is altogether brighter in colour, with longer tails to the hindwing, and a different arrangement of the lines on the underside of the wings."

Cynthia cantori, Distant, Ann. and Mag. of Nat. Hist., fifth series, vol. x, p. 406 (1882); idem, id., Rhop. Malay., p. 183, n. 2, pl. x, fig. 3, *male* (1882). HABITAT: Province Wellesley. EXPANSE: *Male*, 27 inches. DESCRIPTION: "MALE. Closely allied in colour and markings to *C. deione*, from which it differs on the UPPERSIDE by the more angulated markings in the cell of the *forewing*, and by the medial transverse fuscous fascia being placed much nearer to the apex of the cell, whilst on the *hindwing* this fascia is seen to be *abruptly broken and deflected*

specimens of the former from Borneo in the Indian Museum, Calcutta, the male being quite indistinguishable from *C. erota* from North India. The female, however, has the discal white band on the upperside much narrower, and nearly of equal width throughout its length, reach-ing the submedian nervure on the hindwing ; the hindwing on the upperside also has four ocelli.

Genus 54.—HELCYRA, Felder. (PLATE XIX).

Helcyra, Felder, Sitzb. Ak. Wiss. Wien, Math.-Nat. Cl., vol. xl, p. 450 (1860) ; idem, id., Neues Lep., pp. 37, 44 (1861).

"HEAD, small ; eyes, naked ; *antennæ*, medium, the club obtuse ovate. *Palpi*, scaly, ascending, twice as high as the head. *Wings*, with the cells open. FOREWING, with the sub-costal nervure four-branched, the first branch in the middle of the cell, the second beyond the extremity of it, the third arising before the apex of the wing [and the fourth very short], the first disco-cellular rather long, longitudinal, and with the two discoidal nervules arising from the same point. HINDWING, with the præcostal nervure emitted beyond the origin of the subcostal nervure."

"Genus with the neuration of the forewing sufficiently distinct from that of other *Nymphalinæ*, perhaps allied to *Apatura*." (*Felder*, l. c. in Sitz. Ak. Wiss. Wien.)

Two species of the genus only are known, the one inhabiting the hills of North-East India, the other Amboina.

325. Helcyra hemina, Hewitson. (PLATE XIX, FIG. 83 ♂).

H. hemina, Hewitson, Trans. Ent. Soc. Lond., third series, vol. ii, p. 245, n. 1, pl. xv, fig. 1 (1864).

HABITAT : Sikkim, Naga Hills.

EXPANSE : 2·7 to 3·0 inches.

DESCRIPTION : "MALE. UPPERSIDE white. *Forewing* with the apex broadly black, marked with two white spots ; two black spots at the end of the cell, and one near the anal angle of the same colour. *Hindwing* with seven spots beyond the middle, a submarginal line, and the outer margin (which is very narrow) black. UNDERSIDE lilac-white. *Forewing* spotless, with two indistinct lines of brown near the middle, and one scarcely seen near the anal angle. *Hindwing* with the spots of the upperside and the submarginal line indistinctly marked in lilac, preceded by arches of rufous-brown ; the black spot (the outer spot of three near the anal angle) crowned with bright yellow."

"This adds a second species to Dr. Felder's genus *Helcyra*, which he considers nearest to *Apatura*. It differs from the neighbouring genera in the rounded club of the antennæ, which resembles *Argynnis* and *Callithea*. It has the cells of both wings open. In the museum at Leyden this species is put with *Charaxes*, to which it bears a general resemblance." (*Hewitson*, l. c.)

This is a very beautiful species, pure shining white with black markings, quite unlike any other species in the *Nymphalinæ*. It is rare also, Mr. Otto Möller took a single female at Singla near Darjiling, 1,500 feet, in October, which is the only precise record of its capture in my possession. There is a single male from the Naga Hills in the Indian Museum, Cal-cutta. The female does not differ from the male.

The figure shows both sides of a male Sikkim specimen in the Indian Museum, Calcutta.

Genus 55.—SEPHISA, Moore. (PLATE XX).

Sephisa, Moore, Proc. Zool. Soc. Lond., 1882, p. 240 ; *Castalia* (Boisduval, MS.), Horsfield and Moore, Cat. Lep. Mus. E. I. C., vol. i, p. 199 (1857).

HEAD, of moderate size, hairy. *Eyes*, prominent, reddish, naked. *Antennæ*, long, four-sevenths of the length of the forewing, with a distinct gradually-formed club. *Haustellum*, yellow. *Palpi*, porrected obliquely, black above, pale below, clothed with thick short scales.

near the bases of the second and third median nervules ; on the UNDERSIDE this fracture or angulation appears much more distinctly : the basal curved line which crosses the cell in *C. decora* is also broken and looped in *L. cantori*. I have not as yet received a second specimen of this species, nor have I seen its female, which will, however, almost certainly prove to be somewhat like the female of *C. decora*, with the difference of marking detailed above as found in the other sex." (*Distant*, l. c.)

Thorax, robust, wooly ; *abdomen*, rather small. FOREWING, with the *costa* gently arched ; *outer margin* emarginate below the apex and waved, a little shorter than the *inner* margin which is straight. *Costal nervure* reaching the margin about the middle of the costa ; the *first subcostal nervule* given off from the subcostal nervure a short distance before the end of the cell, *second* a little beyond the end of the cell, the *third* given off nearer to the cell than to the base of the fourth, reaching the apex, *fourth* reaching the margin below the apex. *Upper disco-cellular* nervule very small, directed obliquely outwards, *middle* disco-cellular also very short, about three times the length of the upper, directed obliquely inwards, *lower* disco-cellular wanting, thus leaving the *discoidal cell* entirely open. *Third median nervule* moderately and evenly arched. *Submedian nervure* straight. HINDWING, triangular-ovate, *costa* gently curved, *outer margin* sinuate, *inner* margin emarginate at the anal angle, deeply channelled to receive the abdomen. *Precostal nervure* simple, strongly curved outwards. *Discoidal cell* open.

This is a genus of very small extent, two species only being known, which are confined to Northern India extending into Burma. They are handsome insects, the males black and yellow in about equal proportions, one species with some white spots on the forewing. The female of one species *(S. chandra)* is extremely variable.

Key to the species of Sephisa.

A. Male with a discal series of white spots on forewing, female with a single orange spot in cell, no discal spots.

326. C. CHANDRA. N.-E. Himalayas, Assam, Burma.

B. Male with all the markings of the forewing orange, female with discal orange spots in addition to the one in the cell.

327. C. DICHROA, Western Himalayas.

326. Sephisa chandra, Moore.

Castalia chandra, Moore, Horsfield and Moore, Cat. Lep. Mus. E. I. C., vol. i, p. 200, n 400, pl. viz, fig. 4, *male* (1857) ; id., Waterhouse, Aid to the Ident. of Ins., vol. i, pl. 8, *female* (1880) ; *Sephisa chandra*, de Nicéville, Journ. A. S. B., vol. li, pt. ii, p. 60, n. 164 (1882).

HABITAT : Nepal, Sikkim, Upper Assam, Burma.

EXPANSE : ♂, 3·0 to 3·3 ; ♀, 3·40 to 3·65 inches.

DESCRIPTION : MALE. " UPPERSIDE : *Forewing* jet-black, with a greenish gloss at the apex ; a transverse curved row of four orange-coloured spots from costal margin one-fourth of the wing to middle of posterior margin ; a straight row of five *white* spots from middle of costal margin to near posterior angle ; also two small and one minute *white* spot near the apex ; a marginal and submarginal row of spots, those at the apex whitish, the marginal ill-defined, the submarginal rather large and clearly defined, and those to the posterior angle small and bluish. *Hindwing* clear orange-colour, with rather broad black posterior margin, centred with a marginal row of small whitish [bluish] spots ; also a parallel inner zigzag black band from anal angle to anterior angle, and extending along the costal margin, the black extending along the veins upwards and downwards to marginal band ; a small black spot nearly at the base of and within discoidal cell [sometimes absent], and another in the middle of the wing ; on the thickest part of the inner band near anal angle is a small medial bluish-white spot [sometimes absent] ; abdominal margin broad dusky-white. *Body* black ; frontal tuft and neck spotted with white. UNDERSIDE as above, but on the *forewing* the colours are brighter ; the costal margin greenish-white, and there is also a whitish triangular spot at base of discoidal cell : on the *hindwing* along the marginal band is a row of bluish-white lunate l spots ; the spot on the thickest part of the inner band is large, as is also the medial black spot within the discoidal cell ; at the base of the wing are a number of greenish-white spots ; all the veins are broadly lined with black ; *body* and *abdomen* on the sides spotted with white." (*Moore*, l. c.) " FEMALE differs from the male in the outer margin of the *forewing* being less emarginate, the *hindwing* broader and less denticulate. On the UPPERSIDE the rich orange colour of the male has entirely disappeared, except the spot in the cell of the *forewing*, which, however, is much reduced in size. Beyond the cell in that wing in one Sikkim specimen, but hardly observable in another Sikkim example, and in one from Nepal there are four longitudinal white streaks between the nervules, decreasing rapidly from the anterior one placed between the costal nervure and the upper discoidal nervule, and the posterior one between the third and second median nervules. The discal white spots of the male are smaller in the female, the anterior ones whitish, the posterior ones bright steel-blue. There are also other similarly coloured spots and streaks between the nervules just beyond the cell, and below it. In the *hindwing* the ground-colour is black with a marginal and submarginal row of spots, the outer the smaller, and a discal series of streaks between the nervules, all steel-blue. In a specimen from Nepal, these spots and streaks are sullied with tawny. On the UNDERSIDE the orange spot in the cell of the *forewing* is much larger than above, and in the *hindwing* there is a round orange spot on the middle of the costa, and a similar one in the cell, the submarginal spots are yellowish, and all the steel-blue markings of the upperside much paler." (*de Nicéville*, l. c.) The female specimen from Nepal figured by Mr. Waterhouse differs considerably from the females described above, the hindwing is greyish-white throughout except the nervules, a short discal lunular line and two marginal lines which are black.

The Indian Museum, Calcutta, possesses specimens from Nepal, Sibsagar (*S. E. Peal*), and there is one female specimen from Shillong (*Dr. Johnson*) in Major Marshall's collection, and others taken by the Yunan Expedition. Males occur commonly in Sikkim at low elevations, the female, however, is rarely seen. A specimen of the latter sex in Major Marshall's collection probably from Sikkim has four very prominent white streaks from the subcostal nervure to the second median nervule on the upperside of the forewing; in fact, no two specimens of the female as far as I have seen are exactly alike, and many show very great variations in colour and the extent of the markings. They probably mimic the blue species of *Euplœa*.

327. Sephisa dichroa, Kollar.   (PLATE XX, FIG. 93 ♂).

Limenitis dichroa, Kollar, Hügel's Kaschmir, vol. iv, part ii, p. 429, n. 7, pl. viii, figs. 1, 2 (1848); *Castalia dichroa*, Horsfield and Moore, Cat. Lep. Mus. E. I. C., vol. i, p. 199, n. 408 (1857); *Sephisa dichroa*, Moore, Proc. Zool. Soc. Lond., 1882, p. 240.

HABITAT : Western Himalayas.

EXPANSE : 2.6 to 3.0 inches.

DESCRIPTION : "May be distinguished from *Castalia* [= *Sephisa*] *chandra* by the exterior margin of the *forewing* being much less deflexed in the middle, and by having all the markings of the UPPERSIDE of the *forewing* orange colour, and being without the black spots in the discoidal cell of the *hindwing*, and on the UNDERSIDE by the pearly-white on the *hindwing*." (*Moore*, l. c. in Cat. Lep. Mus. E. I. C.) The FEMALE differs but slightly from the male, the ground-colour and markings are paler, especially the apical and two upper of the three spots beyond the cell of the forewing which are almost white.

I have taken this insect commonly at Simla flying round and settling on the oak throughout the summer, also at Kujiah near Dalhousie in June. Colonel A. M. Lang, R.E., records[*] that it is partial to ripe fruit, that he has "seen it in open woods in the interior of the Himalaya, pitching on the sprays of tall shrubs, making rapid flights, and returning to the same spot." The Indian Museum, Calcutta, possesses specimens from the Kulu Valley (*A. Graham Young*), and Masuri (*Templeton*.) Major Marshall possesses specimens taken at Chumba in May and Murree in June. It appears to be confined to the Western Himalayas.

The figure shows both sides of a male Masuri specimen in the Indian Museum, Calcutta.

Genus 56.—DILIPA, Moore.   (PLATE XX).

Dilipa, Moore, Horsfield and Moore, Cat. Lep. Mus. E.I.C., vol. i, p. 201 (1857).

"Differs from typical *Apatura* in having the discoidal cell closed in both wings by a very delicate lower disco-cellular nervule; the palpi and antennæ are, however, like those of *Apatura*." (*Moore*, l. c.) In *Dilipa* the second subcostal nervule of the forewing is given off from the subcostal nervure at about one-twenty-fifth of an inch distance beyond the apex of the cell, in *Apatura* (*namouna*, Kollar) it is given off at about the same distance before the

---

[*] Ent. Month. Mag., vol. i, p. 181 (1864-65).

end of the cell. The outer margins of both wings in *Dilipa* are more even, and the forewing less emarginate, in other respects it does not differ materially from *Apatura*.

A single species of the genus is known, which occurs from Dharmsala to the Naga Hills, but does not appear to be common anywhere. It is a very beautiful insect, upperside swarthy, forewing with two macular yellow bands, hindwing with the disc resplendent shining golden. In the female the yellow markings are replaced by whitish.

328. **Dilipa morgiana,** Westwood. (PLATE XX, FIG. 86 ♂).

Apatura? morgiana, Westwood, Gen. Diurn. Lep., vol. ii, p. 305, n. 22, *note* (1850) ; *Dilipa morgiana,* Horsfield and Moore. Cat. Lep. Mus. E.I.C., vol. i, p. 201, n. 410, pl. viii, fig. 5, *male* and *female* (1857).

HABITAT : Southern India *(Westwood)* ? Himalayas ; the Naga Hills.

EXPANSE : ♂, 2·6 to 2·9 ; ♀, 3·01 inches.

DESCRIPTION : "MALE. [UPPERSIDE?] *Forewing* blackish-swarthy with an irregular oblique median fascia and another beyond the middle golden yellow, and two subapical dots white. *Hindwing* silky golden yellow, with the base and the outer margin broadly fuscous ; the external angle and a wavy streak at the anal angle golden yellow. UNDERSIDE paler, yellowish-white at the base, and pale mouse-coloured at the apex, more or less powdered with grey. FEMALE similarly marked, but with white not golden-yellow, the *hindwing* also irrorated with lilac beyond the middle." *(Westwood,* l. c.)

Mr. Hocking took this species in the Kangra Valley in August at 6,000 feet. Major G. F. L. Marshall found a single female in his house at Summer Hill, Simla, also in August. I have taken several males flying round the temples on the bare top of Tara Devi, opposite Simla, and one in the bed of the Simla river was taken by Mr. C. A. R. Crommelin ; there are males in the Indian Museum, Calcutta, from Masuri *(Colonel Buckley)*, four or five specimens were sent from Nepal by Dr. Scully, and specimens from the Naga Hills also in the Indian Museum, Calcutta. It appears to be a rare species wherever it occurs.

The figure shows both sides of a male Simla specimen in the Indian Museum, Calcutta.

The next group of genera of the *Nymphalinæ* has the second subcostal nervure of the forewing emitted just before the end of the cell in addition to the first, except in certain species of the genus *Neptis* in which it is given off beyond the apex of the cell. These latter species have been generically separated from *Neptis* by Mr. Moore under the name of *Rahinda,* and there is some ground for so doing ; but whether generically separable or not, the species of *Rahinda* are in habits, outline of wings and style of marking, most intimately allied to *Neptis,* and as the arrangement of the subfamily here tentatively adopted would necessitate that the two genera if separated, should be placed far apart, which is manifestly incorrect, I have preferred to class them as comprising a single genus *(Neptis),* with certain aberrant species *(Rahinda).* This aberrant feature also occurs in two other genera of this group, *Hestina* and *Argynnis* ; no generic names have however been suggested for these species, though *Brenthis,* Hubner (type *thore,* Hubner) might be used for the species of *Argynnis* which have the second subcostal nervule of the forewing emitted after the end of the cell.

Genus 57.—APATURA, Fabricius. (PLATE XX).

Apatura, Fabricius, Ill. Mag., vol. vi, p. 280, n. 9 (1807) : id., Westwood, Gen. Diurn. Lep., vol. ii, p. 302 (1850) ; id., Felder, Neues Lep., p. 36 (1861) ; *Potamis,* Hubner, Tentamen, p. 1 (1806) ; *Doxocopa,* Hubner, Verz. bek. Schmett., p. 49 (1816) ; *Rohana,* Moore, Lep. Cey., vol. i, p. 27 (1881).

"BODY, robust ; *thorax,* robust, subovate, very woolly in front and behind. *Abdomen,* small, elongate-conic in the male ; more robust in the female. WINGS, of the male generally with a splendid purple gloss, the forewing emarginate in the middle of the outer margin. *Head,* of moderate size, larger in the male than in the female, hairy, slightly tufted in front. *Eyes,* prominent, naked. *Antennæ,* about equal to three-fifths of the length of the forewing, nearly straight ; terminated by a rather strong elongate-ovate club, compressed and delicately keeled along the inside. *Palpi,* porrected obliquely, the tip rising nearly to the level of the top of the eyes. Inner surfaces parallel, nearly united together, so as to form a conical beak nearly as long as the head, thickly clothed with short scales; the base beneath, the inner surface of the middle joint and the terminal half of the upper surface, furnished with elongated hairs; the basal joint very short; second joint very long, slender, and curved; the third not longer than the basal joint, elongate-conic, pointed at the tip. FOREWING, elongate-trigonate; *costal margin* moderately arched; *apex* subtruncate; *outer margin* more than two-thirds of the length of the costa, slightly scalloped, and more or less emarginate in the middle; *inner* margin nearly straight, a little longer than the outer margin. Veins very strong. *Costal nervure* extending to the length of two-thirds of the costa from the base; *subcostal* nervure with the first branch arising a little before the anterior extremity of the discoidal cell; second branch arising at one-third of the length of the wing, just before or exactly at the extremity of the cell; third branch arising just beyond the middle of the wing, and extending to the apex; fourth branch arising at four-fifths of the length of the wing. *Upper disco-cellular nervule* obsolete, *middle* arising at the anterior extremity of the discoidal cell, at the distance of one-third of the length of the wing from the base, very short, and forming the curved base of the lower discoidal nervule; *lower* obsolete, so that the *discoidal cell* is open. HINDWING, triangular-ovate; the apex more or less elongated; *outer margin* scalloped; *inner* margin deeply grooved to receive the abdomen, with a deep sinus between the body and the anal angle. *Præcostal nervure* strongly curved, its extremity directed outwards from the body; *subcostal* nervure branched at a short distance from its base. *Discoidal cell* not closed, the *lower disco-cellular nervule* being obsolete. FORELEGS, of the *male* very short and slender, clothed with delicate white hairs; *tibia* shorter than the femur; *tarsus* about two-thirds of the length of the tibia, very slender, and, when denuded of its hairs, four-jointed; the joints not indicated by short spines, and the apical joint very minute, simple, and destitute of apical claws. Of the *female* very slender and scaly; *femur* within clothed with short white flossy hairs; *tarsus* two-thirds of the length of the tibia, nearly cylindrical, suboblique at the tip, and articulated, with short spines beneath, indicating the joints. MIDDLE and HINDLEGS, moderately long, scaly; *tibiæ* and *tarsi* finely spined beneath. *Tibia* of the middle legs shorter than the femora; those of the hind legs equal to them in length; tibial spurs short. *Claws, paronychia* and *pulvillus* of moderate size."

"LARVA naked, gradually attenuated behind; the head armed with two spines, and the tail with two obtuse points. PUPA compressed at the sides; the back carinated, and the head bifid." (*Westwood*, l. c.) This diagnosis does not apply to the *Rohana* group.

According to the law of strict priority the name *Potamis*, Hübner, should probably be applied to the genus, as pointed out by Mr. Scudder in his " Historical Sketch of the Generic Names proposed for Butterflies," but I have followed previous writers in retaining the well-known name *Apatura* for it. Mr. Distant remarks on the subject (Rhop. Malay., p. 100) that :—" By the name *Apatura* I allude to the genus as hitherto almost universally understood, and not as recently applied by Messrs. Scudder and Moore to species of *Hypolimnas*. Where an earlier generic name is clearly found to have priority the law should unhesitatingly be applied; but where a certain amount of doubt exists, and the evidence is not convincing, the name generally used should remain unchanged."

Typical species, such as *Apatura iris*, the "Purple Emperor" of Europe, are amongst the most beautiful of butterflies, the males being furnished on the upperside with a resplendant purple or blue gloss, which feature the females more or less lack. Of this group *A. namouna* of Northern India is a worthy representative. *A. sordida* is a plain brown insect in both sexes, with a discal white band and spots beyond on the forewing, presenting, especially in the female, a great resemblance to some species of *Lethe. A. parvata* is also brown with some obscure paler markings; the sexes alike. *A. chevana* is a very remarkable species, alike in both sexes; on the underside it is a typical *Apatura* of the *namouna* group, but on the upperside is a wonderful mimic of a white-spotted and banded *Athyma. A. parysatis* and *A. camiba* are deep purple-black above, the females being coloured somewhat like *A. parvata*, but generally resembling species of the genus *Ergolis*, which they may mimic. Females of all the species are rare, the males are more commonly met with in India, chiefly owing to their habit

7

of frequenting moist spots. In Europe *A. iris* shows a partiality for carrion, I am unaware if its Indian allies possess a similar depraved taste.

The genus *Apatura* is very wide-spread, and occurs in both North and South America, in the West India Islands, throughout Europe and Asia, and in the Malay Archipelago. There are about forty species known.

Key to the Indian species of Apatura.

A. Males with a resplendant blue gloss on the upperside.
> 329. A. NAMOUNA, Himalayas, Assam, Naga Hills.
> 330. A. BHAVANA, N. E. Bengal.

B. Both sexes black on the upperside, with white bands and spots ; the male very faintly blue glossed.
> 331. A. CHEVANA, Sikkim, Assam.

C. Both sexes brown on the upperside.
> a. With a white discal oblique band and apical spots on the forewing.
>> 332. A. SORDIDA, Sikkim.
> b. With obscure ferruginous markings on both wings.
>> 333. A. PARVATA, Sikkim, Bhutan.

D. Males purple-black ; females brown.
> a. Male with one minute apical white dot on forewing.
>> 334. A. (*Rohana*) PARVSATIS, N. E. Bengal, Upper Tenasserim.
> b. Male with three minute apical white dots on forewing.
>> 335. A. (*Rohana*) CAMIRA, South India, Ceylon.

329. Apatura namouna, Doubleday. (PLATE XX, FIG. 91 ♂).

A. namouna, Doubleday, Ann. and Mag. of Nat. Hist., vol. xvi, p. 178 (1845) ; *A. ambica*, Kollar, Hugel's Kaschmir, vol. iv, pt. ii, p. 431, n. 1, pl. xiii, figs. 3, 4 (1848) ; id., Horsfield and Moore, Cat. Lep. Mus. E. I. C., vol i, p. 201, n. 411 (1857) ; id., Moore, Proc. Zool. Soc Lond., 1865, p. 765 ; *A. sansa*, Hewitson, Ex. Butt., vol. iv, pl. i, *Apatura*, figs. 7, 8 (1869).

HABITAT : Himalayas, Assam, Naga Hills.

EXPANSE : ♂, 2·6 to 3·0 ; ♀, 2·9 inches.

DESCRIPTION : " Both wings swarthy black, shot with brilliant shining blue, with a broad transverse band and some spots white. Underside silvery-white, with rufous margins and transverse line."

MALE : " UPPERSIDE *both wings* fuscous black, with a transverse pure white band slightly bordered with bluish, commencing by three rounded dots at the extremity of the discoidal cell of the *forewing*, afterwards widening and attaining the abdominal margin of the *hindwing*[*] ; beyond this band are three white dots towards the apex of the *forewing*, and one or two indistinct ones towards its anal angle ; on the *hindwing* a series of seven [submarginal] whitish dots ; the anal angle rufous. The whole disc and inner margin of the *forewing*, and the whole of the *hindwing*, except [the abdominal margin], the pure white part of the transverse band and the white dots, are in certain lights of the most splendid metallic light blue. UNDERSIDE, silvery white with pearly reflections, a faint indication of the band above ; the costa of the *forewing* except at the base, the outer margins of *both wings*, a transverse band beyond the middle much widened [and suffused with ochreous] towards the anal angle of the *forewing*, rufous. This band is marked at its widest part by a round black spot and bordered there externally with two sublunulate black spots, and an arrow-shaped one. In addition to this are two small black spots in the discoidal cell followed by two short black perpendicular lines, below this is a black spot and two black lunules, and on the *hindwing* a black dot near the anal angle, preceded in the band by a similar one. *Head* swarthy ; the orbits of the eyes, the palpi below, and four spots on the vertex, white ; the antennæ swarthy. *Thorax* and *abdomen* swarthy above, paler below ; legs silvery white." (*Doubleday*, l. c.) "The FEMALE is distinguished from the male in being paler, and having none of that beautiful gloss on

---

[*] This is not correct ; it stops short before the submedian nervure above the inner edge of the abdominal fold.

the UPPERSIDE ; the spots are yellowish-white, and those along the exterior margins are larger." (*Moore*, l. c. in **Cat. Lep. Mus. E. I. C.**)

The males are common in Sikkim at low elevations, and are found more sparingly throughout the outer ranges of the Himalayas westward as far as Murree ; they are not usually difficult to capture, as they come down to the wet sand on the borders of the hill streams to drink. There is a single female from Masuri in the Indian Museum, also males from Buxa, Bhutan (*Moti Ram*), and the Naga Hills ; Major Marshall has taken it below Naini Tal in Kumaon, and Dr. E. R. Johnson at Shillong in the Khasi hills in July.

A curious variety or "sport" of *A. namouna* has been figured and described by Hewitson under the name of *A. zanoa*, in which the discal white band on the upperside has nearly disappeared, the margin of both wings on the underside much more widely rufous, and the discal rufous band of *A. namouna* entirely absent. The description is appended.[*]

The figure shows both sides of a male Sikkim specimen in the Indian Museum, Calcutta.

A variety of *A. namouna* occurs in the interior of the North-Western Himalayas, of which three male specimens are in Major Marshall's collection ; two from Kutabal in Kashmir, taken in June by Mrs. R. Bazett at an elevation of 8,200 feet, and one from Pangi, on the east border of Kashmir, taken by Mr. R. Ellis ; they differ from typical *A. namouna*, and also from the specimen figured by Von Hügel as *A. ambica* in the following particulars :— they are considerably larger than the normal form, their expanse being from 3·15 to 3·50 inches ; on the UPPERSIDE the purple gloss is much duller and less distinctly defined ; and the white discal band is more widely diffused both outwardly and inwardly by white powdering, especially on the hindwing. In the *forewing*, there is an additional white spot above the upper discoidal nervule in prolongation of the discal band, and all the white spots are larger. In the *hindwing* the submarginal series of white dots is expanded into a series of diffuse and almost confluent white lunules. On the UNDERSIDE the discal rufous band is wider, its outer edge less sharply defined with black, and less sinuous ; in the *forewing* the additional white spot also appears, the black spots in the cell are much larger (confluent in one specimen), the black patch at the inner angle is larger and more diffused, and the whitish lunules on the rufous border are reduced to two, and in the *hindwing* the black spot of the rufous band on the lower median interspace, which is found in all typical *Apaturas* in India, is entirely wanting. The absence of this latter spot, and the presence of an additional white spot in the discal band, are probably sufficient to separate this as a distinct species, but in the absence of further specimens and wider knowledge of the insect I prefer to consider it a variety.

330. Apatura bhavana, Moore.

A. bhavana, Moore, Trans. Ent. Soc., Lond., 1881, p. 307 ; id., Waterhouse, Aid, vol. ii, pl cxxvii, fig. 2 (1883).

HABITAT : N. E. Bengal.

EXPANSE : ♂, 3 inches.

DESCRIPTION : "MALE : Allied to *A. ambica*. Differs in its larger expanse, the *forewing* being more deflexed, and of less breadth across : the *hindwing* is also more produced at the anal angle. On the UPPERSIDE the transverse discal white band is similar, but there are only two small apical white spots, and the exterior border of both wings has an unmarked fulvous-brown fascia. UNDERSIDE also similar, the nacreous[†] basal and external areas are

* *Apatura zanoa*, Hewitson, Ex. Butt., vol. iv, pl. i, *Apatura*, figs. 7, 8 (1869). HABITAT : Darjiling. EXPANSE : 2·8 inches. DESCRIPTION : "MALE : UPPERSIDE dark brown, the *cilia* marked by lunules of white. *Forewing* with a large space of brilliant blue on the inner margin, marked by four or five lilac spots, which are again marked with white : three small white spots before the apex. *Hindwing* with a tuft of white hair near the middle, a white spot on the costal margin, an orange spot at the anal angle, and some very slight linear white spots near the outer margin. UNDERSIDE white, tinted with lilac near the inner margin of the *forewing* : both *wings* with the outer margin broadly rufous. *Forewing* with four small black spots in the cell, two larger black spots below these between the median nervules, three lunular spots of white, a spot of the same colour at the anal angle, crossed, together with one of the said lunular spots, by a linear black spot. *Hindwing* with a white spot at the anal angle, also marked by a line of black."

"This is very probably only a remarkable variety of *A. namouna*, such as they designate as " an aberration" on the Continent." (*Hewitson*, l. c.)

† NACREOUS, having a pearly lustre, from *macre*, mother-of-pearl.

bluer and are less black bordered, the apical band broader and showing the white spots more in the middle, and the discal fulvous band on the *hindwing* is narrower." (*Moore*, l. c.)

This species is unknown to me. It is evidently very closely allied to *A. namouna*, if indeed it can be specifically separated from that species. There is a single male from Buxa, Bhutan, in the Indian Museum, Calcutta, which agrees with the description of *A. bhavana* in having only two subapical white spots on the forewing, but it is inseparable from *A. namouna*, in which species the lower of the subapical spots is always small and often obsolescent. The expanse of this specimen in 2·8 inches.

331. **Apatura chevana**, Moore.

Athyma chevana, Moore, Proc. Zool. Soc., Lond., 1865, p. 763, pl. xli, fig. 1.

HABITAT : Sikkim, Assam.

EXPANSE : 2·50 to 3·65 inches.

DESCRIPTION : "MALE. UPPERSIDE dark brown ; markings pale buff yellow. *Forewing* with uninterrupted discoidal streak, terminated by two oblique spots ; a transverse discal series of irregular-shaped spots, a submarginal row of small spots, and indistinct marginal narrow streaks. *Hindwing* with a broad transverse band, a submarginal lunulated band, and indistinct marginal narrow streaks. *Body* with pale buff-yellow waist-band and abdominal rings. UNDERSIDE—*forewing* with the markings as above, the interspaces ferruginous brown, suffused with dark brown posteriorly, except along the base of the costa and triangularly before the apex, which is pale nacreous blue. *Hindwing* with a narrow transverse discal and marginal ferruginous-brown band, the rest of the wing pale nacreous blue, the broad transverse and lunulated submarginal band being paler nacreous white ; a black dot on lower part of disc."

"*Remark.*—The whole underside of this species is very similar to that of *Apatura ambica* ; and Mr. W. S. Atkinson has informed me that in fresh-caught specimens the upperside has also the beautiful reflected purple gloss visible in that insect." (*Moore*, l. c.) The FEMALE differs from the male only in having the upperside entirely unglossed with blue, the markings straw-coloured, and both wings broader, the outer margin of the forewing less emarginate.

This species is a wonderful mimic of the white-spotted and banded group of *Athymas*, and speaking of the latter genus Mr. Distant remarks,[*] it " is supposed to be of a protected nature, owing to the fact of its being apparently 'mimicked' by species of other genera. A most notable instance of this is afforded by the *Apatura chevana*, Moore, a Darjiling species, which, though possessing the beautiful colouration of that genus beneath, is marked above like a species of *Athyma*. This, however, on examination, appears to be a case of 'spurious mimicry,' as the insect when at rest, with its wings folded (and we are not told that it is aberrant in this respect), would exhibit the *Apaturan* distinctiveness, and thus be afforded no protection by the *Athymad* simulation of their upper surface."

Regarding the position *A. chevana* assumes when at rest I can give no direct evidence, having never seen it alive, but as the species of *Athyma* which it apparently mimics have often been seen by me in Sikkim at rest with their wings wide expanded, it is probable that the mimicker assumes the same attitude.

A. chevana is a rare species in Sikkim ; the Indian Museum, Calcutta, possesses specimens from the Naga Hills and Sibsagar in Upper Assam.

332. **Apatura sordida**, Moore.

A. sordida, Moore, Proc. Zool. Soc. Lond., 18/5, p 765, pl. xli, fig. 2, *male* ; *A. phaedra*, Hewitson, Ex. Butt., vol. iv, pl. i, *Apatura*, figs. 1, 2 (1869), *female*.

HABITAT : Sikkim.

EXPANSE : ♂, 2·12 to 2·7 ; ♀, 2·5 to 3·0 inches.

DESCRIPTION : "MALE : UPPERSIDE fuliginous brown. *Forewing* black at the apex, with an oblique discal band of white spots, adjoining which is a single and before the apex two white dots. *Hindwing* with a dark-brown pale-bordered marginal line and submarginal spots. UNDERSIDE brownish grey, brown apically. *Forewing* with the oblique discal band of white spots, the lower spot having a black yellow-bordered ocellus; apical spots and marginal streaks white. *Hindwing* with a transverse discal brown line bordered anteriorly with white spots, a marginal pale-bordered brown line, on the lower part of the disc is an ocellus having a black pupil streaked with blue, yellow iride, and brown outer border. FEMALE. UPPERSIDE paler, with a broad oblique uninterrupted white band; otherwise as in male. UNDERSIDE pale brownish grey; the broad oblique band of forewing as on upperside; the rest as in male." (*Moore*, l. c.)

This is a very rare species. There is a single male in Mr. Otto Möller's collection taken in October at a low elevation, one female in Mr. A. V. Knyvett's collection, and a pair in Colonel A. M. Lang's, taken by Dr. Jerdon, all from Sikkim.

333. **Apatura parvata**, Moore.

A. parvata, Moore, Horsfield and Moore, Cat. Lep. Mus. E. I. C., vol. i, p. 202, n. 412, pl. via, fig. 6 (1857), *male*.

HABITAT : Sikkim, Bhutan.

EXPANSE : 1·9 to 2·3 inches.

DESCRIPTION : " MALE : UPPERSIDE dark ferruginous-brown, darkest at the base, and bright about discoidal cell and along the exterior margin. *Forewing* with blackish marks in the discoidal cell ; marginal and submarginal lines, and indistinct narrow interrupted transverse series of pale ferruginous spots from middle of anterior to posterior margin ; also a series of five small white spots from anterior margin near the apex, below which is an indistinct black spot. *Hindwing* with narrow pale ferruginous band from middle of anterior margin to near middle of abdominal margin ; also, near anal angle, a black spot encircled with ferruginous ; abdominal margin dull ferruginous-brown. UNDERSIDE ferruginous, brightest on the forewing ; markings disposed as above. *Forewing* with the transverse series of spots distinct and white, being bounded inwardly with blackish patches ; near the apex and posterior angle are some patches of black ; the black spot on disc large ; also a black patch on posterior base of the wing ; marginal line ashy. *Hindwing* ferruginous-brown across the disc, with band as above white ; on the lower part of the disc is a small black spot centred with blue and encircled with ferruginous ; a marginal line and submarginal zigzag marks ashy." (*Moore*, l. c.) FEMALE : Duller coloured than the male, the discal series of pale ferruginous spots on the forewing and discal line on the hindwing absent, but replaced by an irregular ferruginous diffused band, which is inwardly sharply defined. *Forewing* with three subapical white dots only, the anal ocellus on the *hindwing* smaller and blind. UNDERSIDE marked much as above, but paler, the discal band outwardly marked with lilac, and a small patch of that colour below the apex of the *forewing*, the white dots larger.

This also is a rare species, the Indian Museum, Calcutta, has specimens from Sikkim, and Buxa, Bhutan (*Moti Ram*).

The next two species have been generically separated by Mr. Moore in his "Lepidoptera of Ceylon," p. 27, from the true *Apaturas* under the name of *Rohana*. I can find no character of sufficient importance in the perfect insect to give these species distinct generic rank, though had the second subcostal nervule of the forewing been given off " beyond the cell," as stated by Mr. Moore, instead of before it as it actually is, they might perhaps have been separated with advantage. The larva (of *A. camiba*), however, is most remarkably different from that of typical *Apatura*, being in fact truly Satyrid in appearance, it is smooth, and furnished with two long spined black processes projecting forwards in front of the head, and other two short pointed smooth greenish processes at the anal extremity. The males are deep purple-black above, paler below ; the females ferruginous ochreous. The description of *Rohana* is given below.*

* Genus *Rohana*, Moore, Lep. Cey., vol. i, p. 27 (1881) : " Wings short : forewing triangular ; first subcostal branch emitted near end of the cell, second at a short distance beyond [immediately before the end of] the cell, third and fourth at equal distances : disco-cellular short, angled close to subcostal, upper radial from the

334. **Apatura parysatis**, Westwood. (PLATE XX, FIG. 9? ♂ ♀).

A. parisatis, Westwood, Gen. Diurn. Lep., vol. ii, p. 305, n. 20, *note* (1850); id., Horsfield and Moore Cat. Lep. Mus. E. I. C., vol. i, p. 202, n. 413 (1857).

HABITAT : Sikkim, Sylhet, Assam, Upper Tenasserim, Java.

EXPANSE : 1·9 to 2·0 inches.

DESCRIPTION : "MALE, with the body above and both wings black, a minute white dot towards the apex of the forewing excepted. UNDERSIDE ferruginous, clouded with fuscous, with two small black dots in the discoidal area [cell ?] and an ear-shaped spot before the middle [of the forewing black], an irregular submedian streak and another subapical greyish-blue, and with small ocellus towards the anal angle [of the hindwing]. FEMALE : UPPERSIDE obscure fulvous, the discoidal area [cell ?] of *both wings* with two dots and a spot black ; an obscure median angulate band, beyond the middle clouded with fuscous, and a submarginal series of small blind ocelli. UNDERSIDE as in the male, but much paler. " (*Westwood*, l.c.)

"*Apatura parisatis* may be distinguished by its small size, and by the uniform jet-black colour of the upperside, the underside being varied with rich red-brown and chestnut, and with a slight whitish macular fascia across the middle of the wings, and a minute eye-spot near the anal angle. The female is dull ferruginous ; both upper and undersides with markings nearly similar to those of the underside of the male, and with a curved row of small white dots near the apex of the forewing." (*Moore*, l. c.)

Males of *A. parysatis* are frequently seen at elevations of 5,000 feet and below in Sikkim, the female being very rare. The Indian Museum, Calcutta, has specimens from Sylhet, Sibsagar (*S. E. Peal*), Naga Hills and Upper Tenasserim.

The figure shows the upperside of both sexes of Sikkim specimens in the Indian Museum, Calcutta.

335. **Apatura camiba,** Moore.

Rohana camiba, Moore, Lep. Cey., vol. 1, p. 27, pl. xiv, figs. i, *male*; 1a, *female*; 1b, *larva*; 1c, *pupa* (1881).

HABITAT : South India, Ceylon.

EXPANSE : ♂, 1·7 to 2·1 ; ♀, 1·6 to 1·9 inches.

DESCRIPTION : "MALE : UPPERSIDE dark purple-black. *Forewing* with a subapical linear series of three minute white spots. *Cilia* white streaked. UNDERSIDE greyish purple-brown, costal area beyond the cell on forewing and exterior border of both wings chestnut-red ; a black-lined chestnut-red mark and two inner small spots within both cells, and a small spot below the cell on forewing ; a slender black zigzag inner-discal line, followed by a suffused black fascia and a submarginal row of purple-grey rings crossing both wings, the latter ending at the apex in a more prominent continuous grey streak, and the inner line bordered externally by purple-white spots which are less distinct on the hindwing ; the three transverse subapical small white spots distinct and followed by two other very minute spots, and then a black spot, all visible on the blackish fascia ; a subanal black spot pupilled with white and circled with chestnut-red on hindwing. FEMALE : UPPERSIDE ferruginous, darkest basally ; markings as in male, but of a ferruginous-brown colour, the transverse discal white spots and subanal ocellus distinct. UNDERSIDE paler, markings less distinct, except the white spots on forewing which are also purple bordered."

"This species is closely allied to R. [A.] *parisatis*, of which a large series of both are under examination, but differs in its slightly more acute angle below the apex of the forewing in both sexes, and a more prolonged anal angle in male, the male also having three white spots on upperside of forewing, one only being present in *A. parisatis*."

angle and lower radial from its end ; cell open ; lower median branch emitted from opposite disco-cellular, the two upper at some distance beyond ; submedian straight ; hindwing triangular ; costal vein curved upward, extending to apex, with a short basal curved spur ; subcostals and radial contiguous at base but divergent ; cell open ; lower median branch emitted at a short distance from base of the two upper, submedian and inner vein recurved. Body short, thorax stout, palpi porrect, pointed, flat beneath, squamose, legs short, squamose, antennae slender. Type, *R. parysatis*." (*Moore*, l. c.)

"LARVA smooth, head small and surmounted by two black spined-processes projecting in front, last segment with two green naked processes ; pale yellowish-green with a dark green dorsal and two lateral bands; face black streaked. Feeds on *Celtis lycodoxylon*. PUPA green, with a pointed angle on middle of thorax and on basal segment of abdomen ; head attenuated, with two points." (*Moore*, l. c.)

In Ceylon it is "common on forest ground in the hills about 5,000 feet near Newera Eliya. Frequently seen basking in the road" (*Hutchison*). In Horsfield and Moore's Cat. Lep. E. I. Museum *A. parysatis* is recorded from Canara, but most probably this species is meant. The Indian Museum, Calcutta, possesses specimens from Ootacamund (*Hampson*) and Pirmad, North Travancore, 2,000 feet (*Doherty*).

The genus *Eulacura* contains but a single species, which hitherto has not been recorded from India, though specimens have been taken near our border in Perak. *Eulacura* is nearly allied to *Apatura*: but the male entirely lacks the brilliant blue gloss which is such a prominent feature in the males of typical species of that genus. The description of the genus and sole species are given below.*

Genus 58.—HESTINA, Westwood. (PLATE XXII).

Diadema, section 6, *Hestina*, Westwood, Gen. Diurn. Lep., vol. ii, p. 281 (1850) ; *Hestina*, Felder, Neues Lep., p. 25, n. 58 (1861).

"*Discoidal cell* of both wings open. *Second subcostal nervule* of the FOREWING arising close to the origin of the upper disco-cellular nervule." (*Westwood*, l. c.)

BODY, moderately robust. *Head*, moderately large, tufted in front, hairy above, usually marked with white spots. *Eyes*, prominent, naked. *Haustellum*, yellow. *Palpi*, porrected, divergent, the tips convergent. *Antenna*, exactly half the length or rather less than half the length of the forewing, terminating in a distinct gradually-formed club. *Neck*, marked with small white spots. *Thorax*, moderately robust, very hairy. *Abdomen*, slender, somewhat long. FOREWING, rather elongated, triangular. *Costal margin* moderately arched ; *outer* margin slightly sinuate, emarginate, rather shorter than the inner margin ; *inner* margin straight. *First subcostal nervule* in the typical species given off from the costal nervure some little

* Genus *Eulacura*, Butler. *Eulaceura*, Butler, Proc. Zool. Soc. Lond., 1871, p. 726; *Eulaccura*, Scudder, Proc. Am. Acad. Arts and Sciences, Boston, vol. x, p. 172 (1875); *Eulacura*, Butler, Trans. Linn. Soc. Zoology, second series, vol. i, p. 541 (1877); id., Distant, Rhop. Malay., p. 99 (1882). DESCRIPTION : " Nearly allied to *Apatura*, but differing in its comparatively longer and more graceful fore and its shorter and more rounded hindwing : antennæ longer, more slender, the club somewhat compressed laterally ; median nervure of hindwing longer, and consequently second and third median branches shorter. Abdomen of male with anal valves composed of an upper hood-like lip, fringed externally with short hair-scales, and sheathing the penis, which is shorter and more spine-shaped than is *Apatura*, and projects obliquely downwards between two bispinose lateral walls of horny texture, and in shape resembling the open beak of a bird ; the lower lip is formed by the union of two closely fitting horny sheaths, deeply excavated within, and terminating abruptly in two strong, perpendicular, somewhat curved, tapering, horny hooks, about a line and a half in length. Typical species *Eulacura osteria*, Westwood." (*Butler*, l. c.)

Eulacura osteria. Apatura osteria, Westwood, Gen. Diurn. Lep., vol. ii, p. 305, n. 19, note (1850) ; *Eulaceura osteria*, Butler, Proc. Zool. Soc. Lond., 1871, p. 726 ; *Eulacura osteria*, Butler, Trans. Linn. Soc. Zoology, second series, vol. i, p. 541, n. 1 (1877) ; id., Distant, Rhop. Malay., p. 100, n. 1, pl xii, fig. 5, *male* ; 6, *female* (1882). HABITAT : Perak, Province Wellesley, Malacca, Singapore, Java, Borneo. EXPANSE : *Male*, 2·6 ; *female*, 2·5 inches. DESCRIPTION : " MALE : UPPERSIDE dark glossy fuscous. *Forewing* with a discal oblique series of five white spots, the uppermost and smallest situated above the third median nervule, remaining four larger, contiguous and only separated by the median nervules and submedian nervure. *Hindwing* with a corresponding but broader oblique series of subquadrate spots, which form a continuous fascia, although apparently divided by the nervules and terminating about middle of abdominal margin, the basal two-thirds of which is pale greyish : a submarginal row of obscure rounded fuscous spots placed between the nervules, and two narrow fuscous marginal lines. UNDERSIDE pale silvery bluish, *both wings* crossed by the pale discal oblique series of spots, forming a more continuous fascia than above, and silvery white inwardly margined with ochraceous ; two narrow ochraceous fasciæ crossing cell of *forewing* : outer margins of *both wings* and apex of *forewing* bordered and suffused with ochraceous, and two ocellated spots (ochraceous with bluish and black centres), the first on *forewing* situated between the second and first median nervules, the second spot situated between the second and first median nervules of the *hindwing*. *Body* and *legs* more or less concolorous with wings. FEMALE : Pale brownish. *Forewing* with two dark fasciæ crossing cell and with a very broad pale submarginal fascia, the outer margin of which is denoted by a series of lunulate white spots, and the inner margin—which is directed outwardly from subcostal nervure to third median nervule and then obliquely reflexed—is marked by a series of irregular white spots ; and an indistinct ocellated spot between the second and first median nervules. *Hindwing* with a narrow pale oblique macular fascia (continuous to the inner margin of the broad fascia of the forewing) obscurely terminating about middle of submedian nervure ; an ocellated spot between second and first median nervules, and a waxed and strongly lunulated ochraceous submarginal fascia, inwardly enclosing obconical fuscous spots, excepting between the second and first median nervules and from thence to anal angle ; two fuscous marginal lines and basal area of abdominal margin pale as in male. UNDERSIDE a little darker and more ochraceous than in male, other markings generally the same." (*Distant*, l. c.)

distance before the apex of the cell; *second* just before the apex; *third* much nearer the origin of the fourth than to the apex of the cell, extending to the apex of the wing. In *H. persimilis* and its allies the first subcostal is given off a short distance before the end of the cell, the second at a considerable distance beyond, the third and fourth at about equal distances apart beyond the second. *Upper disco-cellular* nervule very small, outwardly oblique; *middle* about twice as long as the upper, inwardly oblique, forming the base of the lower discoidal nervule; *lower* entirely absent, thus leaving the *discoidal cell* open. *Third median* nervule moderately curved. *Submedian nervure* straight. HINDWING, with the *costal margin* much arched at base, thence nearly straight, *outer* margin in the typical species forming an angle at the end of the second subcostal nervule, above and below which it is nearly straight but sinuous; *abdominal* margin slightly excavated at the anal angle. *Præcostal nervure* simple, strongly bent outwards at the tip. *Second subcostal* and *discoidal nervules* given off from the costal very close together in the typical species, the latter sinuous. In *H. persimilis* they are given off much further apart, and the discoidal nervule is straight.

Hestina is a genus of very small extent, only six species altogether having been described. The typical species, *H. assimilis*, is found in China, and another, *H. mimetica*, in Java; the remaining four species are all Indian, and, with the exception of one, *H. nama*, which extends through the Eastern Himalayas and the hill ranges east and south of the Brahmaputra into Burma, they are all confined to the Himalayas. The genus is very closely allied to *Euripus*, and like *Neptis, Argynnis* and *Cyrestis*, it comprises two groups, in which the position of the second subcostal nervule of the forewing differs; in *H. nama*, which most nearly resembles the typical species, that nervule is given off before the end of the cell, in the other Indian species it is emitted far beyond the cell. These latter, which in this feature correspond with *Euripus*, and also more closely resemble it in colour and markings, are distinguished from *Euripus* by the more regular and less sinuate outline of the wings, the rounded not linear shape of the pale discal markings and the colour of the haustellum.

All the species are more or less mimetic, and the females of the latter group are variable, but not nearly so variable as in *Euripus*, and so far as is known not dimorphic. The prevailing colouration is very similar to that of the blue *Danais*, subgenus *Tirumala*.

They are not very strong on the wing or rapid in flight, and they frequent glades in forests and orchards at moderate elevations; with the exception of *H. nama* none of them are very common or abundant in any locality.

Key to the Indian species of Hestina.

A. Second subcostal nervule of forewing given off before end of cell.
    336. H. NAMA, N.-E. India, Upper Burma.

B. Second subcostal nervule of forewing given off beyond end of cell.
    a. Discoidal cell of forewing crossed by a black bar.
        337. H. PERSIMILIS, Himalayas.
        338. H. ZELLA, Western Himalayas.
    b. Discoidal cell of forewing with the black bar obsolete.
        339. H. MENA, Kujiah, North India.

The first group is represented by a single species, *H. nama*.

336. Hestina nama, Doubleday. (PLATE XXII, FIG. 99 ♀).

Diadema nama, Doubleday, Ann. and Mag. of Nat. Hist., first series, vol. xvi, p. 232 (1845); id., Doubleday and Hewitson, Gen. Diurn. Lep., vol. ii, p. 281, n. 21, pl. xxxix, fig. 2 (1850); *Hestina nama*, de Nicéville, Journ. A. S. B., vol. li, pt. ii, p. 58 (1882).

HABITAT: N.-E. Himalayas, Sylhet, Assam, Burma.

EXPANSE: 3·2 to 4·3 inches.

DESCRIPTION: UPPERSIDE. "*Forewing* [indigo-blue], with the outer margin sinuate, slightly glossed with purplish, especially towards the apex; with numerous semi-transparent markings of a bluish-white colour, viz., a longitudinal vitta in the cell at the base, followed by two spots, of which the outer one is triangular; above these three indistinct spots, the middle one sometimes wanting; between the lower median nervule and the submedian nervure two vittæ united at the base, the upper one followed by a round spot; above these between the nervules five vittæ, of which the one nearest the costa is pointed, the others bifid externally, each vitta followed by three spots, of which the lower are somewhat lunulate, the upper ones more rounded; four rounded spots near the apex, two near the anal angle. The inner margin is glaucous, the apex tinged with brown. _Hindwing_ castaneous, darker in the female than in the male, with seven whitish subdiaphanous vittæ placed between the nervules, all, except the innermost, followed by a round white dot, beyond which the ground-colour of the wing is slightly darker; towards the outer margin a series of indistinct whitish spots, sometimes nearly obsolete. _Cilia_ of both wings spotted with white. UNDERSIDE. _Forewing_ black with strong blue reflections, the apex broadly chestnut, slightly bronzed towards the disc; the markings as above but clearer, with two additional spots on the costa near the base. _Hindwing_ paler than above, the white portions more or less irrorated with chestnut scales; on the margin a distinct series of whitish lunules. _Head, thorax,_ and _abdomen_ black, clothed with grey hairs; head above, and thorax below, spotted with white; abdomen below grey. _Palpi_ black, spotted with white. _Antennæ_ black. This species, which much resembles _Papilio agestor_ and _Danais tytia_, has the cells of both wings open." (_Doubleday_ l. c.) The FEMALE has " the wings broader than the male, and the ferruginous outer margin on both sides of the hindwing lacks the series of very dark brown lunules between the nervules which are present in the male." (_de Nicéville_, l. c.)

H. nama is common in the Eastern Himalayas extending as far westwards as Kumaon, where however it is rare, and eastwards across the Brahmaputra into the Khasi and Naga Hills and the mountain ranges of Upper Burma. It is the largest of the Indian species, and conspicuously differs from all the others, not only by the castaneous hue of the hindwing, but in the sharply lunulate character of the spots in the discal series, and the corresponding dentation of the streaks preceding them. It most nearly resembles the typical species from China, _H. assimilis,_ but differs from it in not having a submarginal series of red rounded spots towards the anal angle of the hindwing. The female is much less often seen in collections than the male, though at low elevations in Sikkim in the late autumn it is very common, flying or soaring about in open spaces on the borders of forest and exactly mimicking _Danais tytia,_ both in appearance and habits. The Indian Museum, Calcutta, possesses this species from Nepal, Sylhet, Khasi Hills, Sibsagar (_S. E. Poll_), Naga Hills, and specimens obtained by the Yunan Expedition.

The figure shows both upper and undersides of a female from Sikkim in the Indian Museum, Calcutta.

In the second group three species have been described, but owing to the characters on which they are separated not having been recorded, and the great rarity of two of the species, the exact extent of the group is still undetermined. It probably embraces two distinct species only.

The first species, _H. persimilis,_ was described by Westwood in 1850, and his description relates to the male insect only; the female has since been discovered, and is now well known; the male is very constant in the extent of the pale markings, but the female shows considerable variation in this respect.

In 1858 Moore described another species under the name of _H. mena,_ the description also being that of a _male_ insect; but no reference, whatever, was made in it to _H. persimilis,_ nor were the characters stated in which _H. mena_ was considered to differ from _H. persimilis._ The species, however, appears to be a good one, its large size and the character of the forewing referred to above in the key to the species of _Hestina_ being sufficient to warrant its separation.

Again in 1869, Butler described and figured a species under the name of _H. alla_; the specimen described being also a male. It is said to be most nearly allied to _H. mena,_ Moore,

S

and to be "smaller than any species yet described," but in this case too no reference, whatever, is made to *H. persimilis*, to which it is still more nearly allied, and which, judging from the dimensions given, is usually smaller than *H. zella*, and from the description alone it would be impossible to separate them. The question is still further complicated by the fact that the only authentic specimen I know of, which has been identified by Mr. Moore as *H. zella*, lacks the character which distinguishes Butler's figure from *H. persimilis*, and is absolutely identical with *H. persimilis*, male, except that the apex of the forewing is paler and suffused with castaneous. My own opinion is that *H. zella* is simply the paler western form of *H. persimilis*.

337. Hestina persimilis, Westwood.

Diadema persimilis, Westwood, Gen. Diurn. Lep., vol. ii, p. 281, n. 19, *note* (1850).

HABITAT : Himalayas.

EXPANSE : ♂, 2·5 to 2·8 ; ♀, 2·6 to 3·1 inches.

DESCRIPTION : "Black spotted with white. Closely allied to *D.* [= *H.*] *assimilis*, but smaller, with the *forewing* more elongated, the spots on the disc more rounded, and the subapical series obsolete. *Hindwing* with some small white spots in the place of the red spots. UNDERSIDE, *both wings* much paler, the red spots wanting." (*Westwood*, l. c.)

MALE. UPPERSIDE indigo-blue, with the following very pale greenish markings :— *Forewing* with a streak filling the basal half of the cell, and a large oblique spot closing it, three small spots just beyond it, with a large rounded one at the base of the first median interspace, three short streaks divided by the discoidal nervules, a discal series of five increasing round spots, one in each interspace, a submarginal series of eight or nine spots, and a marginal series of obscure dots obsolete and often obliterated. A lengthened bifurcated streak in the submedian interspace, which is broken towards its end, leaving two detached spots. *Hindwing* with all the veins marked broadly with indigo-blue, the margin broadly indigo-blue, leaving a small marginal and a larger submarginal series of whitish spots, with two (sometimes one only) additional ones in the median interspaces, placed internal to the submarginal series. UNDERSIDE much paler, the disc of the forewing only with the ground-colour indigo-blue. Markings as above, but larger. FEMALE differs from the male only in the outer margin of the forewing being less emarginate, both wings broader, the colouration paler throughout. The extent of the pale markings is variable, the spots being generally larger and with a tendency to coalesce. In general appearance the female closely resembles *Danais aglea*, which it probably mimics.

I have taken several specimens of *H. persimilis* in Simla and the neighbourhood chiefly on over-ripe fruit ; it occurs also in Sikkim, but is by no means a common butterfly. Colonel A. M. Lang, R.E, records* it from the "Himalaya, 4,000 to 7,000 feet. I have only seen three specimens. One I caught in a narrow glen, well wooded with undergrowth ; the other two in an orchard of plum and apricot, on the ripe fruit of which these insects were settling, both on the trees and on the fallen fruit below the trees." Males from Sikkim (the only sex I have seen from that locality) have the ground-colour much darker than specimens from the N.-W. Himalayas.

338. Hestina zella, Butler.

H. zella, Butler, Trans. Ent. Soc. Lond., 1869, p. 9, *male* (with a woodcut) ; id., Moore, Proc. Zool. Soc. Lond., 1882, p. 240.

HABITAT : N.-W. Himalayas.

EXPANSE : ♂, 2·7 inches.

DESCRIPTION : "MALE. UPPERSIDE white, with a slightly greenish tinge ; the discoidal cell of the forewing spottedly ashy ; all the veins broadly ashy-blackish. *Forewing* with three

---

* Ent. Month Mag., vol. i, p. 133 (1864-5).

oblique transverse angulate discoidal streaks black, and one connecting the first and second median nervules; the margin and the apex blackish, including three subapical [discal?] and eight submarginal greenish-white spots; seven or eight marginal dots ashy and subobsolete. *Hindwing* with a blackish scaly costal spot, the external margin blackish, and bearing eight submarginal white spots, and eight white marginal dots. *Body* black, *head* spotted with white, *thorax* striated with ashy white, *abdomen* white at the sides, *antennæ* black. UNDER-SIDE whitish-fuscous, the anal area of the *forewing* bluish, the veins in the discal area and the discal fascioles black, other markings as on upperside but pale olivaceous; *body* black, spotted with white; *haustellum* yellow." (*Butler*, l. c.)

According to Butler's figure this species differs from *H. persimilis* in the following points only, the pale streaks in the upper median and submedian interspaces of the forewing, and those in the median interspaces of the hindwing are not divided, and consequently there are no detached pale spots in those interspaces within the submarginal series. The type insect was in a collection made in various localities in the Eastern Islands, and the Continent of India; another specimen in the Hope collection is said to be labelled "East Indies," so the exact locality is unknown, but a specimen seen by me from Mr. Hocking's collection made in Kangra has been identified by Moore as belonging to this species, and, as previously stated, it lacks the special characters noted above which alone separate the species from *H. persimilis*. Kangra is the most westerly known range of this genus, and it is in all probability the locality from which all three specimens were obtained, and bearing in mind the fact that the differences such as they are, are the variations which would naturally be exhibited by *H. persimilis* in its most western range, and that some specimens of *H. persimilis* from the districts immediately east of Kangra do exhibit partial variation in this direction, I cannot avoid the conclusion that *H. zella* is merely a variety of *H. persimilis*, but I keep it distinct for the present until more specimens can be examined. Mr. Hocking records *H. zella* as occurring in the "Kangra district generally."

Mr. Butler in describing it wrote: "This beautiful little species is most nearly allied to *H. mena* of Moore; it is probably intermediate between that species and the *assimilis* of Linnæus, and is smaller than any species yet described."

The female of *H. zella* I have never seen, nor can I get access to any published descrip-tion of it; from information kindly supplied to me by Mr. Butler, I gather that it resembles in essential features the female of *H. persimilis*, the insect described and figured by me as *H. zella*, female,[*] turns out on closer examination to be a male, and is probably referable to the next species.

339. Hestina mena, Moore.

H. mena, Moore, Ann. and Mag. of Nat. Hist., third series, vol. i, p. 48, n. 3 (1858); *Diadema mena*, Butler, id., vol. xvi, p. 398, n. 3 (1865); *Hestina zella*, de Nicéville, (*nec* Butler), Journ. A. S. B., vol. lii, pt. ii, p. 65, pl. i, fig. 2 (1883), *male* (*nec* female).

HABITAT: North India, Kujiah.

EXPANSE: ♂, 3·5 inches.

DESCRIPTION: "MALE. UPPERSIDE pale greenish-white. *Forewing*, with all the veins broadly black; exterior margin black, with a marginal row of small spots, submarginal and third row of large and less distinct spots. *Hindwing*, with all the veins black, also a marginal row of ill-defined, black, lunular spots. UNDERSIDE paler greenish-white: all the veins of *both wings* less black than the upperside, with an indistinct marginal row of spots. *Body* longitudinally striped black and white. Allied to *H.* [*Euripus*] *consimilis*, but may be distinguished by its larger size, and by the absence of the broad, transverse, spotted bands." (*Moore*, l. c.).

Mr. Butler apparently overlooked the description above by Mr. Moore, for in 1865 he redescribed the species as one of "four new Species of Butterflies in the Collection of the

---

[*] Journ. A. S. B., vol. lii, pt. ii, p. 65, pl. i, fig. 2 (1883)

British Museum," giving as synonymy "*Hestina mena*, Moore, MS.," and remarking that "this insect was named by Mr. Frederick Moore, of the Indian Museum." As his description differs considerably from Mr. Moore's, I give it in full.

"UPPERSIDE. *Forewing* pale greenish ; nervures, end of cell, and a submarginal band along the hind margin broadly rich brown ; two indistinct inner submarginal bands of brown scales. *Hindwing* pale ochreous, nervures rich brown ; a submarginal row of brown lunules between the nervures along the hind margin. UNDERSIDE, *forewing* pale greenish ; end of cell, base of nervures, an indistinct band of scales between the nervures just beyond the cell, and an indistinct submarginal row of spots along the hind margin brown ; termination of nervures fulvous. *Hindwing* pale ochreous ; nervures brown ; a submarginal band of indistinct brown spots between the nervures along the hind margin ; front margin darker ochreous. *Body* brown above ; beneath rich brown ; head and thorax streaked with ochreous. Tibiæ and tarsi of *forelegs*, and tarsi of *middle* and *hindlegs* alternately brown and white. Antennæ black." (*Butler*, l. c.)

Mr. Butler kindly informs me th at *H. mena* is a good species, that it is nearest allied to *H. zella*, differing from the female of that species in its "greater size, absence of first discoidal bar in primaries [= forewing], three series of spots (the first subconfluent with ground-colour) on external area. Hindwing white (or cream-coloured) with black veins and submarginal lunules." (*Butler*, in epis.)

On the 22nd May, 1879, I took a single specimen of a *Hestina*, which, misled by the general aspect and outline of the wings I took for a female, and described and figured it (l.c.) as the female of *H. zella* ; on closer examination it turns out to be a male, and it probably belongs to the present species *H. mena*. It corresponds with Mr. Moore's description of *H. mena* in size, and in every other point specified except as regards the melanism of the hindwing ; in typical *H. mena* the black outer border of the hindwing on the upperside has almost entirely disappeared, leaving only a series of ill-defined lunules near the margin. In my specimen the outer half of the hindwing is black, bearing a submarginal series of greenish-white spots, largest on either side of the second subcostal nervule and diminishing towards the anal angle, followed by an incomplete series of much smaller marginal spots of the same colour ; in fact its markings are identical with that of *H. persimilis*, female, but the black outer border is wider, and the submarginal spots are elongate. There is nothing else by which to distinguish it from *H. mena* as described ; but it is abundantly distinct from *H. persimilis*. In the absence of a good series of specimens it must be retained as *H. mena* for the present, but if it is really the same, then *H. mena* is as variable in the male in respect to the relative extent of the pale markings as *H. persimilis* is known to be in the female.

The absence of the discoidal bar in the cell of the forewing and the more elongate character of the pale markings on the border give this species a very different aspect from that of *H. persimilis* ; it mimics with wonderful fidelity in shape, colour and markings, the common *Metaporia agathon*, Moore, (an insect belonging to the sub-family *Pierinæ*), and also in its slow and sailing flight. The similarity is still further heightened by the hindwing being tinted with yellow on the abdominal margin on the upperside, and much more prominently on all the pale markings of the underside, especially on the abdominal fold, which is clear bright yellow, while the dark ground is far more extended, covering the whole of the median and submedian interspaces. *H. persimilis* on the other hand presents the general appearance of *D.* (*Parantica*) *aglea* ; there is no trace of yellow tinting on the hindwing, the underside of which is whitish with a well defined and rather narrow darker border, the veins on the basal half being defined, but scarcely at all bordered with blackish.

Genus 59.—HERONA, Westwood. (PLATE XVIII).

Herona, Westwood, Gen. Diurn. Lep., vol. ii, p. 293 (1850).

"BODY, robust ; *wings*, large ; forewing subangulated below the apex ; hindwing deeply scalloped, and marked with transverse pale bars. *Head*, rather small, especially in the female ;

scarcely tufted in front. *Eyes*, of moderate size, but very prominent. *Palpi*, scaly, porrected obliquely, the tip not reaching much higher than the middle of the eyes, extending in front of the head to about its length ; the insides parallel, but the outsides oblique ; terminating in a point formed by the small terminal joint. *Antennæ*, nearly straight, slender, about half [fully two-thirds] the length of the forewing ; terminated by a slender club, channeled beneath, with the tip slightly curved. *Thorax*, robust, woolly, elongate-ovate. *Abdomen*, elongate, and rather slender. FOREWING, elongate-triangular. *Costal margin* slightly curved ; *apex* rather obtuse ; *outer margin* about three-fifths of the length of the costa, slightly scalloped, obtusely subangulated below the apex, below which the margin is emarginate ; *inner margin* nearly straight, and two-thirds the length of the costal margin. *Veins* not strong. *Subcostal nervure* with its first branch arising before the anterior extremity of the discoidal cell, at about one-fourth of the length of the wing ; the second branch arising close to, but at a very little distance before, the extremity of the cell, at one-third of the length of the wing ; third branch arising near the middle of the length of the wing ; and the fourth at a little more than three-fourths of its length. *Upper disco-cellular nervule* very minute and transverse, emitted from the subcostal nervure at the distance of one-third of the length of the wing from the base ; *middle* curved, short, forming the base of the lower discoidal nervule ; *lower* obsolete, so that the *discoidal cell* is open. HINDWING, subovate-triangular ; *costal margin* straight, except at the arched base ; *outer margin* deeply scalloped. *Precostal nervure* straight, except at the tip, which is turned outwards. *Subcostal* nervure branching at about one-fourth from the base of the wing. *Disco-cellular nervule* arising almost close to the branch, and being almost straight, so as to form portion of the discoidal nervule ; *lower disco-cellular* nervule obsolete, so that the *discoidal cell* is open. FORELEGS, of the *male* small, pectoral, clothed with white downy hairs ; the *tibia* rather shorter than the femur ; and the *tarsus* nearly as long as the tibia, exarticulate. Of the *female* about the same length as those of the male, slender, and clothed with fine white scales ; the *femur* and *tibia* of nearly equal length ; the *tarsus* rather more than half the length of the tibia, obliquely truncate at the tip ; the truncated portion armed with four pairs of minute spines, indicating the articulations, which are very short. MIDDLE and HINDLEGS, rather slender, moderately long, scaly ; the middle pair longer than the hind ones. Tibial spurs short ; *tibiæ* and *tarsi* furnished beneath with several rows of very short spines. *Claws* short, very much curved ; *paronychia* small, bifid." (*Westwood*, l. c.)

Herona, until quite recently when two new species were described, contained but a single species. The three known species are all very closely allied, the males are black above with tawny bands, these bands being paler and whiter in the females ; they are found in the Eastern Himalayas, Assam, Upper Tenasserim and the Andaman Isles.

All the species of *Herona* have an obsolescent ocellular dark spot on the tawny discal band of the hindwing placed in the lower median interspace.

Key to the species of Herona.

A. The maculated bands wide ; the discal oblique band beyond the cell of the forewing straight, entire.

    340. H. MARATHUS, Sikkim, Khasi Hills, Assam.

B. The maculated bands narrow, especially on the hindwing ; the discal oblique maculated band beyond the cell of the forewing broken up into spots, which are outwardly pointed.

    a. Female with the bands on the upperside white.

        341. H. ANDAMANA, Andaman Isles.

    b. Female with the bands on the upperside ochreous.

        342. H. ANGUSTATA, Upper Tenasserim.

340. Herona marathus, Doubleday, Hewitson.

H. marathus, Doubleday, Hewitson, Gen. Diurn. Lep., vol. ii, p. 294, n. 1, pl. xli, fig. 3 (1850).

HABITAT : Sikkim, Khasi Hills, Assam.

EXPANSE : ♂, 2·7 to 3·2 ; ♀, 3·5 inches.

DESCRIPTION : MALE. UPPERSIDE black. *Forewing* with the costa tawny as far as the discal band, the end of the cell marked with a broad oblique tawny band, below which is an elongated tawny spot not reaching the margin, confined between the first and second median nervules. An elongated tawny streak in the submedian interspace from the base of the wing to about its middle. A discal oblique tawny streak from the costa to near the margin, which is joined to a narrow streak on the margin between the first and second median nervules, below which again is a rounded spot, and another elongated spot on the margin near the anal angle. A subapical oblique tawny streak bearing a conical small white spot between the discoidal nervules. *Hindwing* black, the costal margin pale tawny, a broad discal tawny band joined outwardly to a submarginal rather less broad similar band, bearing a small round black spot in the first median interspace, a fine marginal tawny line from the anal angle to the third median nervule, with a similar line beyond but extending to the apex. The abdominal margin pale tawny. UNDERSIDE pale tawny suffused with violascent, the tawny markings alone almost white. *Forewing* with a rounded whitish spot below the bifurcation of the fourth and fifth subcostal nervules. *Hindwing* with a small black ocellated spot in the middle of the first median interspace, and a tawny spot in the cell touching the subcostal nervure. FEMALE similarly marked, but the tawny markings narrower and paler. UNDERSIDE darker than in the male, all the markings more conspicuous.

This is a rather common species in Sikkim, where I have taken it in October between 3,000 and 4,000 feet elevation. There are specimens in the Indian Museum, Calcutta, from Assam.

341. Herona andamana, Moore. (PLATE XVIII, FIG. 76 ♀).

H. andamana, Moore, Proc. Zool. Soc. Lond., 1877, p. 585.

HABITAT : South Andamans (Port Blair).

EXPANSE : ♂, 3·00 : ♀, 3·65 inches.

DESCRIPTION : "Differs from *H. marathus* in the wings being more falcated. On the UPPERSIDE the colour is much darker, the markings are narrower, paler on the forewing in the MALE, and white on both wings in the FEMALE. *Forewing*, in *both sexes* the markings beyond the cell are elongated and pointed at the end. *Hindwing*, the discal band is broken up into spots, and the marginal band from the anal angle is composed of lunules in the MALE, and of large indistinct lunular spots in the FEMALE. UNDERSIDE, the markings are whiter in the MALE, and in the FEMALE white throughout." (*Moore*, l. c.)

The late Mr. A. de Roepstorff has sent numerous specimens of both sexes of *H. andamana* to the Indian Museum, Calcutta. It is a well-marked species.

The figure shows both sides of a female South Andaman example in the Indian Museum, Calcutta.

342. Herona angustata, Moore.

H. angustata, Moore, Proc. Zool. Soc. Lond., 1878, p. 829.

HABITAT : Moolai, 3,000—6,000 feet, Upper Tenasserim.

EXPANSE : 3·0 to 3·2 inches.

DESCRIPTION : "*Female*. Similar to *H. marathus* from the Khasia hills. Differs from same sex of that species in having all the maculated bands narrower, these being but half the width of those in the former species. " (*Moore*, l. c.)

There are five specimens of *H. angustata* in Major Marshall's collection, a female taken in October in Aracan by Captain C. H. E. Adamson, a male from Gawlai in Upper Tenasserim in September, and a male and two females taken in April by Captain C. T. Bingham in the Upper Thoungyeen forests in Upper Tenasserim, in the neighbourhood of which type specimen was taken. The female only differs from the male in having the pale bands much paler and ochreous, not fulvous. The markings are precisely identical with those of *H. andamana*, the pale bands being perhaps a trifle narrower than in the Andaman species.

No reference is made in the description above of *H. augustata* by Mr. Moore to *H. andamana* described by himself in the previous year, and to which it is much more closely allied. It differs from *H. andamana* in the male by having the bands slightly narrower, and in the female by having the bands ochreous, while in *H. andamana* they are nearly pure white.

GENUS 60.—PRECIS, Hübner.   (PLATE XIX).

Precis, Hübner, Verz. bek. Schmett., p. 33 (1816); id., Felder, Neues Lep., p. 33, n. 26 (1861); id., Moore, Lep. Cey., vol. i, p. 59 (1881); id., Distant, Rhop. Malay, p. 89 (1882); *Junonia*, section ii, *Precis*, Doubleday, Gen. Diurn. Lep., vol. i, p. 209 (1849).

"FOREWING, subtriangular, the *costal margin* very strongly arched and convex; *apical angle* obliquely truncate and prominent, and together with remainder of *outer margin* distinctly waved; beneath the apical angle the outer margin is strongly sinuated and concave, after which it is convex to posterior angle; *inner* margin more or less concave. *Costal nervure* short; *first and second subcostal nervules* emitted close together near end of cell; *third* emitted about half-way between end of cell and apex of wing; *fourth* and *fifth* bifurcating at about one-fourth from apex. *Upper disco-cellular* nervules angled at apex of cell and concave to lower discoidal nervule; *lower* disco-cellular nervule slender and indistinct, or somewhat obsolete. *Discoidal* nervules well separated at their base; *third median* nervule rounded at base, where it has an apparently common origin with the second; *second* and *first* median nervules widely separated. HINDWING, subovate, the *costal margin* obliquely convex; *outer margin* very convex, waved, and produced into a short caudate appendage at anal angle. *Abdominal margin* convex and overlapping at base, and then distinctly concave and slightly divergent to anal angle. *Costal nervure* arched and extending to apex; *discoidal nervule* emitted a little beyond the bifurcation of the subcostal nervules; *discoidal cell* with the apex entirely open; *median nervules* arranged much as in the forewing. *Body*, short; *palpi*, long, porrect, and pointed; *antennæ*, slender, gradually thickened towards apex." (*Distant*, l.c.)

LARVA cylindrical, with several series of short branched spines. PUPA with the apex pointed, the dorsal segments with tubercular points.

"This genus is of very considerable extent, and it is in Africa—tropical and subtropical—that its greatest number of species are found; in fact, if we include Madagascar, at least three-fourths of the present known species inhabit the Ethiopian region. *Precis* is also found in Continental India, Ceylon, and onwards, and sparingly—as regards its number of species—through the Malay Peninsula and Archipelago, and is represented in Australia. At this time about forty species have been described." (*Distant*, l. c.) It is very closely allied indeed to *Junonia* in all stages of its existence, so much so that *Junonia atlites* has been recently placed* by Mr. Moore in the former genus, while Mr. Butler† has placed *Precis iphita* in the genus *Junonia*. The two genera can however be distinguished by "the anterior tarsus of the male being about one-third the length of the tibia," while in *Junonia* it is about half the length only. (*Doubleday*, l. c.). In *Precis* the club of the antenna is gradually incrassate, in *Junonia* it is short and rather abrupt. A single species occurs in India proper, and an allied one from the Malay Peninsula and Archipelago. It is a dull brown butterfly with indistinct darker transverse bands, with a series of obscure ocelli on the hindwing, and usually bears on the underside one or two ochreous spots near the costal margin of the hindwing.

343. Precis iphita, Cramer.   (PLATE XIX, FIG. 84 ♂).

Papilio iphita, Cramer, Pap. Ex., vol. iii, pl. ccix, figs. C, D (1779); id, Fabricius, Sp. Ins., vol. ii, p. 86, n. 379 (1781); idem, id., Mant. Ins., p. 46, n. 457 (1787); idem, id., Ent. Syst., vol. iii, p. 109, n. 337 (1793); *Vanessa iphita*, Godart, Enc. Méth., vol. ix, p. 314, n. 40 (1819); *Precis iphita*, Moore, Lep. Cey., vol. i, p. 59, pl. xxi, figs. 1, 1a, *imago*; 1b, *larva* and *pupa* (1881); id, Distant, Rhop. Malay, p. 90, n. 1, pl. xi, fig. 9, *male*; pl. ix., fig. 3, *female variety* (1882); *Junonia iphita*, Butler, Cat. Fabr. Lep. B. M., p. 76, n. 17 (1869); *Precis intermedia*, Felder, Reise Novara, Lep., vol. iii, p. 402, n. 600 (1866).

* Lep. Cey., vol. i, p. 40.   † Cat. Fabr. Lep. B. M., p. 76, n. 17.

HABITAT: India, Ceylon, Burma, Malay Peninsula and Archipelago, New Guinea.

EXPANSE: 2·3 to 3·3 inches.

DESCRIPTION: " MALE and FEMALE. UPPERSIDE fuliginous-brown, variable in intensity of hue. *Forewing* with two transverse fasciæ crossing cell, the margins of which are very irregular and dark fuscous, the first situated about middle and the second near apex ; the apical half of wing is somewhat paler, and inwardly bounded by a dark fascia commencing near costa and outwardly and obliquely directed to third median nervule, from thence reflexed inwardly and terminating near middle of inner margin ; between this and outer margin is a somewhat similar fascia, followed by two very dark submarginal lines, the outer one more prominently waved ; *cilia* and a small subapical spot whitish. *Hindwing* with the apical half paler and with the fasciæ on the forewing continued, the first terminating near abdominal margin about one-third from anal angle, the second broader and more outwardly curved than on forewing, and possessing on its outer edge four or five obscure ocellated spots placed between the nervules ; submarginal lines as on forewing, but the inner one more waved. UNDERSIDE paler ; *both wings* crossed by two somewhat broad, dark, basal fasciæ, the first crossing the middle of cell of the forewing, curved inwardly on cell of hindwing and indistinctly terminating near base of abdominal margin ; the second crossing forewing at apex of cell, and terminating on hindwing a little beyond end of cell ; a similar fascia commencing near costa of forewing, and more or less amalgamating at median nervules, with an oblique fascia crossing both wings, inwardly margined with a dark line commencing near apical angle of forewing, where it is broadest, and terminating near anal angle of hindwing, where it is narrowest ; on the outer margin of this fascia in *both wings* are a series of more or less obscure ocellated spots placed between the nervules ; two submarginal lines as on upperside, but the inner one much waved and sinuated. In some specimens there are two distinct whitish [or ochreous] spots on the underside of the hindwing, separated by the first subcostal nervule, the upper of which is larger. *Body* and *legs* more or less concolourous with wings." (*Distant*, l.c.)

"LARVA cylindrical, dark brown, with dorsal and lateral rows of short delicate branched spines. PUPA short, with tubercular points on dorsal segments, thorax broad." (*Moore*, l. c.)

The intensity of the ground-colour and markings in *P. iphita* is very variable, specimens from the region of the heaviest rainfall being as usual the darkest. On the underside the spaces between the fasciæ are often suffused with violet of varying intensity, and the inner edge of the dark discal transverse line is often defined with yellowish. It is an exceedingly common species as a rule where it occurs ; it has a somewhat bold flight, but not for any great distance, it often (but not always) pitches on the ground, frequently on bushes. It occurs throughout the Himalayas, in Assam, Sylhet, Cachar, Burma, rarely in Calcutta, but commonly in the Wynaad, Nilgiris and Ceylon ; eastwards it extends through the Malay Peninsula and Archipelago as far as New Guinea. In the plains of Upper India it is seldom found, and never in the drier parts.

I also append a translation of Felder's description of *P. intermedia ;** it is in my opinion impossible to separate this form from *P. iphita,* but the species being variable, this description will be useful for reference in further investigation as to the nature of the variations.

The figure shows the upper and undersides of a male Shillong specimen in the Indian Museum, Calcutta.

A species closely allied to, but apparently distinct from, *P. iphita* occurs in the Malay Peninsula and Archipelago. A description of it is appended†.

---

* *Precis intermedia,* Felder, Reise Novara- Lep , vol iii, p 402, n. 600 (1866). HABITAT : Batjan, Macassar, Celebes ; Rambodde, Trincomali, Ceylon ; Cochin ; Calcutta, Darjiling, Bengal ; Kulu, Himalayas. EXPANSE : Not given. DESCRIPTION : " MALE. UPPERSIDE coloured as in *P. iphita,* marked almost as in *P. ida,* but the discal streak of the *forewing* more inflexed and that of the *hindwing* also more flexuous. UNDERSIDE almost as in *P. ida,* but the *hindwing* with the two anterior ochraceous spots most often absent. FEMALE. UPPERSIDE banded with rufescent-brown, *hindwing* on the UNDERSIDE with the two anterior spots most distinct, whitish."

" We have a single female from Celebes, which has the apex of the forewing more produced than those from the above mentioned places, which specimens, however, are all males. The specimens from Trincomali in Ceylon are the smallest, while those from the Moluccas are the largest." (*Felder,* l. c.)

† *Precis (Papilio) ida,* Cramer, Pap. Ex., vol. i, pl. xlii, figs. C, D (1775) ; idem, id., vol. iv, pl. ccclxxiv,

Genus 61.—JUNONIA, Hübner. (PLATE XX).

Junonia, Hübner, Verz. bek. Schmett., p. 34 (1816); id., Felder, Neues Lep., p. 13, n. 23 (1861); id., Moore, Lep. Cey., vol. i, p. 40 (1881); id., Godman and Salvin, Biol. Centr. Am., Rhop., p. 219 (1883); id., Distant, Rhop. Malay., p. 92 (1882); id., sect. i, Doubleday, Gen. Diurn. Lep., vol. i, p. 206 (1849); *Temenis* (part), Hübner, Verz. bek. Schmett., p. 34; *Alcyoneis*, idem, id., p. 35 (1816).

" HEAD, about equal in width to the thorax, thickly clothed with short hair-like scales. *Eyes*, nearly round, rather prominent, smooth. *Palpi*, porrect, ascending, clothed with scales, which are all short and appressed near the base, in part longer and hair-like towards the apex, the second joint with a dorsal tuft. First joint subcylindric, much curved, short; second joint fully three times the length of the first, stout, considerably swollen beyond the middle, then diminishing towards the apex, which is truncate; third joint much longer than the first, slender, elongate, conic, almost acicular. *Antennæ*, about three-fourths the length of the body, slender, terminating in a short, abrupt, obtuse club, grooved below. *Thorax*, rather stout, oval. *Abdomen*, rather small, about two-thirds the length of the inner margin of the wing. FOREWING, nearly triangular; the apex more or less truncate, sometimes falcate. *Costal margin* sometimes but little curved, sometimes considerably arched; *outer* margin about two-thirds the length of the costa, emarginate; *inner* margin equal in length to the outer, straight. *Costal nervure* rather strong, not extending beyond the middle of the costa; *subcostal* nervure emitting its first and second branches close together, a little before the end of the cell; the third at a point rather less than half-way between the origins of the second and fourth branches; this last nearer to the third than to the outer margin of the wing; the third terminating at the apex. *Upper disco-cellular nervule* very short; *middle* disco-cellular about equal in length to one-third the width of the cell. *Discoidal cell* almost always [always in Indian species] open, the lower disco-cellular nervule almost always entirely wanting. *Third median nervule* considerably curved. HINDWING, rounded or angular; the anal angle often produced considerably. *Costal margin* not much curved; *outer* margin sinuate, more or less dentate, often produced into a tooth or short tail at the termination of the third median nervule. *Præcostal nervure* mostly bifid. *Costal* nervure much curved near its origin. *Discoidal nervule* separating from the second subcostal soon after its origin. *Discoidal cell* always open. *Third median nervule* not much curved. FORELEGS, of the *male* slender, clothed with scales and delicate hairs; *femur* considerably longer than the tibia; *tibia* nearly cylindric, slightly slenderer towards the apex; *tarsus* one-jointed, nearly one-half the length of the tibia; slender, subcylindric, sometimes tapering towards the apex, which is not unfrequently truncate. Of the *female* rather small; *femur* longer than the tibia; *tibia* subcylindric, smooth; *tarsus* as long as, or but little shorter than, the tibia; first joint cylindric, twice or three times the length of the rest combined, with a spine on each side at the apex, and sometimes a few scattered spines within; second joint scarcely one-fifth, sometimes scarcely one-seventh, of the length of the first; armed at the apex, as are the two following joints, with two spines; third, fourth, and fifth joints very short, transverse, the fourth the shortest, the fifth sometimes broader than the fourth; all, as is also the second, furnished with a tuft of hairs on each side at the

figs. C, D (1782); id., Herbst, Pap., pl. clxxv, figs. 1-4 (1794); *Precis ida*, Horsfield and Moore, Cat. Lep. Mus. E. I. C., vol. i, p. 142, n. 289 (1857); id., Distant, Rhop. Malay, p. 92, n. 2, pl. xi, fig. 10, *female* (1882); *Apatura iragra*, Hübner, Verz. bek. Schmett., p. 35, n. 295 (1816); *Vanessa idamene*, Godart, Enc. Méth., vol. ix, p. 315, n. 41 (1819). HABITAT: Penang, Province Wellesley, Billiton, Java, Borneo, Celebes. EXPANSE: 2 to 2·8 inches. DESCRIPTION: " MALE and FEMALE. Closely allied to *Precis iphita* but paler and more rufous both above and beneath. UPPERSIDE marked as in *P. iphita*, but the *forewing* having a more or less well developed and distinct series of ocellated spots, placed between the nervules and occupying the middle of the pale apical portion. *Hindwing* with a very distinct and well developed series of ocellated spots placed between the nervules, and continuous with those of the forewing. UNDERSIDE as in *P. iphita*, but paler and more rufous." (*Distant*, l.c.) May at once be known from *P. iphita* by the series of ocelli on the upperside of the forewing, the tone of the ground-colour also is usually distinctly rufous or ferruginous rather than brown. The ocelli of the forewing are, however, distinctly traceable on both sides in many Indian specimens of *P. iphita*, especially on the underside. There are two pairs of this species from Java collected by Dr. Horsfield in the Indian Museum, Calcutta. Herr Snellen is of opinion that *P. ida* and *P. iphita* may be but seasonal forms of one species, which is by no means improbable in the localities where both occur.

base. MIDDLE and HINDLEGS, moderately stout ; *femora* of the former pair longer than, of the latter pair equal to, the tibiæ ; *tibiæ* subcylindric, with two interno-lateral series of spines ; and sometimes a few external spines ; armed at the apex with two stout spurs ; *tarsi* equal to the tibiæ, spiny laterally and below, except the fifth joint, which wants the lateral spines ; the spines below somewhat in two series ; the upper surface sometimes with one or two delicate spines or stiff hairs. First joint more than double the length of the second ; this mostly equal to, but sometimes shorter than, the fifth, always longer than the third ; fourth mostly shorter than the third. *Claws* curved, grooved below. *Paronychia* bilaciniate, outer lacinia broad at the base, then very slender, pointed ; equal, or nearly equal, in length to the claw, sometimes almost strap-shaped ; inner lacinia short, subtriangular. *Pulvillus* shorter than the claw, two jointed ; second joint broad."

"LARVA with the head and all the segments armed with spines. PUPA tuberculated, scarcely angular." *(Doubleday, l. c.)*

The colouration of the Indian species of *Junonia* shows great variety, grey, brown, blue, yellow and ochreous being the predominating colour of the upperside in different species. There is also much variation in the outline of the hindwing, in some species the third median nervule is produced into a short tail, as is also the anal angle, while in others the hindwing is nearly evenly rounded. In India the species occur everywhere up to about 7,000 feet, and are generally numerous in individuals. "The genus is of considerable extent and of wide distribution. It is found in the warmer parts of America, the tropical and subtropical portions of Africa (including Madagascar), Asia, eastwards from Continental India, throughout the Malay archipelago, and onwards amongst the Islands of the Pacific ; it is also represented in Australia. Probably a little over twenty species are known, and though more have been described they are now generally considered as of a varietal character only." *(Distant, l. c.)* They have a rapid flight, but seldom go far before settling, which they do with expanded wings often on the bare ground, frequently on flowers. *J. hierta* and *J. orithyia* delight in the stony beds of dried-up streams in the hills ; in the plains they chiefly frequent fields and gardens. The sexes are very slightly differentiated.

Key to the Indian species of Junonia.

A. Upperside warm ochraceous, with a large ocellus on hindwing, and two smaller ones on forewing.

    a. Underside with prominent ocelli, forewing slightly truncate.

        344. J. ASTERIE, India, Ceylon, Burma, Java, China.

    b. Underside with the ocelli obsolete, forewing highly truncate.

        345. J. ALMANA, India, Burma, Java, China.

B. Upperside grey, with brown lines and a discal series of ocellated spots.

        346. J. ATLITES, India, Ceylon, Nicobars, Malayana, China.

C. Upperside brown, the ocellus on hindwing smaller, and with numerous ochreous spots on the forewing.

        347. J LEMONIAS, India, Malayana, China.

D. Upperside dark brown, with clear golden brown markings.

        348. J HOFFFERI, Sylhet.

E. Upperside black with large patches of blue or bright yellow.

    a. Discal area of both wings yellow, with a large bright blue spot on upperside of hindwing.

        349. J. HIERTA, India, Ceylon, Andamans, Burma, China.

    b. Discal area of hindwing and a patch at anal angle of forewing deep blue.

        350. J. ORITHYIA, India, Ceylon, Burma, China.

The genus is divisible into several sections differing in the outline of the wing and the geographical range of the species.

The first group represented by *J. asterie* and *J. almana* has the outline almost as in *Precis iphita*, the forewing usually highly falcate, and also somewhat produced at the extremity of the third median nervule, and the hindwing prominently tailed at the anal angle, and less prominently at the extremity of the third median nervule. Its range is throughout the plains and hill districts up to 7,000 feet elevation, but it is most abundant in the moist districts, and rare in the desert tracts.

The second group represented by *J. atlites* has the forewing less falcate, and the hindwing evenly rounded and sinuated on the outer margin, tailed at the anal angle. Its range is restricted to the regions of considerable rainfall, in the plains and warm valleys. It seldom ascends the hills to any considerable elevation, being most abundant in the Terais, and altogether absent from the dry plains and desert tracts.

The third group represented by *J. lemonias* has the hindwing more prominently tailed at the third median nervule than at the anal angle, giving the wing a quadrate outline, the forewing as in the second group. Its range is more extended in the hills, reaching 7,000 feet elevation in the Western Himalayas, but more restricted in the plains, it being almost entirely absent from the plains of North India except in Bengal.

The fourth group represented by *J. hierta* and *J. orithyia* has the outline similar to that of the second group, but the margin less sinuated in both wings, and less falcate in the forewing ; the anal angle of hindwing not produced into a tail. Its range is the widest of all, extending in the hills to greater elevations than any of the others, and in the plains it is even more abundant in the desert tracts of the Punjab than it is in the moist plains of Bengal, and wherever found it frequents dry spots and bright sunshine.

344.　Junonia asterie, Linnæus.

Papilio asterie, Linnæus, Syst. Nat., ed. x, p. 472, n. 90 (1758) ; idem, id., ed. xii, p. 769, n. 133 (1767) ; id., Fabricius, Syst. Ent., p. 490, n. 205 (1775) ; idem, id., Spec. Ins., vol. ii, p. 69, n. 312 (1781) ; idem, id., Mant. Ins., vol. ii, p. 34, n. 363 (1787) ; idem, id., Ent. Syst. Nat., vol. iii, pt. 1, p. 83, n. 273 (1793) ; id., Cramer, Pap. Ex., vol. i, pl. lviii, figs. D, E (1775) ; id., Herbst, Naturs. Schmett., vol. vii, p. 131, n. 42, pl. clxxii, figs. 3, 4 (1794) ; *Alcyoneis asterie*, Hübner, Verz. bek. Schmett., p. 35, n. 292 (1816) ; *Vanessa asterie*, Godart, Enc. Méth., vol. ix, p. 321, n. 58 (1823) ; *Junonia asterie*, Horsfield and Moore, Cat. Lep. Mus. E. I. C., vol. 1, p. 142, n. 287, pl. v, figs. 6, *larva* ; 6a, *pupa* (1857) ; id., Moore, Lep. Cey., vol. i, p. 43, pl. xxii, fig. 2 (1881) ; id., Distant, Rhop. Malay., p. 94, n. 2, pl. xi, figs. 1, *female* ; 2, *female* (1882) ; *J. asterie*, var. *nikobaricusis*. Felder, Verh. zool.-bot. Ges. Wien, vol. xii, p. 482, n. 110 ; *J. asterie*, var. *jarama*, idem, id., p. 437, n. 136 (1862) ; *J. asterie*, Moore, Proc. Zool. Soc. Lond., 1865, p. 752 ; *Papilio almana*, Clerck, Icones Ins., vol. iii (ined.), pl. v, fig. 3 (1764) ; id., Linnæus, Mus. Ulr., p. 272, n. 91 (1764).

HABITAT : India, Ceylon, Andaman and Nicobar Isles, Burma, Malay Peninsula, Siam, Malay archipelago, Formosa, Japan, North China.

EXPANSE : 1·90 to 2·55 inches.

DESCRIPTION : " MALE and FEMALE. UPPERSIDE warm ochraceous, with the basal areas of *both wings* slightly infuscated, and with the following markings :—*forewing* with the costal area pale fuscous, and with an irregular fascia denoted by black margins crossing the middle of the cell, and a similar one with its internal area infuscated at end of the cell ; this is followed by a somewhat similar but darker fascia, which terminates at base of the third median nervule, between which and apex is a subtriangular black patch, more or less enclosing two ocellated spots [the upper smaller and sometimes obsolete] divided by the upper discoidal nervule ; a large ocellated spot placed on the middle of the second and first median nervules, with a white centre and black outer margin ; and a marginal and two submarginal black lines, the inner one of which is generally the palest, and the spaces between which are usually more or less infuscated. *Hindwing* with a very large ocellated spot, purplish with two whitish inner spots, an outer black patch and yellow and black margins, the upper surface of which rests on the first subcostal nervule, and its posterior margin is situated between the discoidal and third median nervules ; and a smaller one between the second and first median nervules, in some specimens the latter is practically obsolete ; marginal and submarginal lines as on the forewing, but the inner one darkest. UNDERSIDE pale obscure ochraceous ; the three basal costal fasciæ as on the upperside of the forewing, but their internal areas not infuscated, and the outer margin of the third continued in an oblique line across both wings, terminating near the anal angle of the hindwing, this line being inwardly and broadly margined with white ; a slender, fuscous, irregularly rounded line at the base of the *hindwing* crossing the cell ; ocellated spots as above, but paler, the larger discal spot on the *hindwing* being compressed, irregularly subovate and bipupilate, the lower spot usually larger than above ; marginal and submarginal lines as above, the inner terminating in a small black spot at the anal angle. *Body* and *legs* more or less concolourous with the wings." (*Distant*, l. c.)

LARVA (figured by Horsfield from Java, where it feeds on a species of *Justicia*) is pale brown, the segments more or less marked with black, and bearing numerous many branched spines. Head ochreous, the body with a dorsal line of the same colour. PUPA ochreous, marked and spotted with black, abdominal segments above with tubercular projections.

J. asteric is a common butterfly throughout the tract of heavy rainfall, and is abundant where it occurs ; it frequents gardens and glades in jungles, but shuns the bare open plains. For further remarks, see the next species, *J. almana.*

345. Junonia almana, Linnæus.

Papilio almana, Linnæus, Syst. Nat., ed. x, vol. i, p. 472, n. 89 (1758) ; idem. id., Syst. Nat., ed. xii, vol. i, pt. 2, p 769, n. 132 (1767) ; id., Fabricius, Syst. Ent., p. 490, n. 204 (1775) ; idem, id., Sp. Ins., p. 69, n. 311 (1781) ; idem, id., Mant. Ins., vol. ii, p 34, n. 362 (1787) ; idem, id., Ent. Syst., vol. iii, pt. i, p. 89, n. 278 (1793) ; id., Cramer, Pap. Ex., vol i, pl. lviii, figs. F, G (1775) ; id., Herbst, Pap., pl. clxxii, figs. 1, 2 (1734) ; id , Donovan, Ins China, pl. xxxvi, fig. 2 (1798) ; *Vanessa almana*, Godart, Enc. Méth., vol. ix, p. 313, n. 36 (1819).

HABITAT : India, Burma, Andamans, Java, China.

EXPANSE : 2·1 to 2·6 inches.

DESCRIPTION : MALE and FEMALE. May be known from *J. asteric* by the apex of the *forewing* being usually much more truncate, the outer margin angled at the third median nervule, and the anal angle of the *hindwing* produced into a longer blunt-tipped tail. On the underside all the markings are less prominent, the discal ocelli very obscure, often obsolete.

According to Mr. A. Grote,[*] the "LARVA feeds on *Gloxinia* and *Osbeckia*."

This species occurs throughout continental and peninsular India and in the outer Himalayas up to about 6,000 feet elevation. It is not recorded from Ceylon or the Malay peninsula, but is common through Assam, Sylhet, Cachar to Burma, Mergui and Upper Tenasserim. It occurs in the Andamans, in Java and China, and wherever met with is a common insect.

It will be seen from the localities quoted above that except in Ceylon, the Nicobars and the Malay peninsula, *J. almana* is found wherever *J. asteric* occurs ; and from observations I have made on the time of appearance of the two forms, I have found that *J. almana* is the prevailing form in the dry season, while *J. asteric* abounds in the rains, the times of appearance and periods of existence occasionally overlap somewhat ; a worn *J. almana* may be found early in the rains, or a *J. asteric* now and then in the early winter, but speaking generally the summer brood is *J. asteric*, and the winter brood is *J. almana*, and it is very probable that further investigation will reveal that they are merely seasonal forms of one and the same species. The two forms are variable also both in outline of the wings and in the markings of the underside : in some specimens of *J. asteric* the forewing is almost as truncate, and the hindwing as prominently tailed as in *J. almana*, while the ocelli on the underside are very inconstant ; they vary much in size, and in some specimens they are so pale and obscure as to be barely traceable, and it is difficult, if not impossible, to decide to which form these intermediate specimens belong. The absence of *J. almana* from the localities noted above, if it be a fact, might be accounted for by the seasons in those parts being more equable and more uniformly moist throughout the year ; but the question of the distinctness or otherwise of the two forms can only be satisfactorily settled by a series of experiments in breeding them. Colonel Swinhoe remarks that *J. almana*[†] "is common everywhere [in Bombay and the Deccan] all the year round, *J. asteric* is common in the latter half of the year. I am convinced that although the types of each are so different they are both one and the same insect, one being the normal and the other the dimorphic form, and I have a long series of examples showing every stage of variety between the two."

---

[*] Proc. Zool. Soc. Lond., 1865, p. 761.   [†] Proc. Zool. Soc. Lond., 1885, p. 128.

346. **Junonia atlites,** Linnæus.

Papilio atlites, Linnæus, Cent. Ins., p. 24, n. 72 (Amœn., vol. vi, p. 407), (1763): *Junonia atlites,* Aurivillius, Kongl. sv. vet.-akad. Handl., vol. xix, p. 79 (1882); id., Distant, Rhop. Malay., p. 93, n. 1, pl. xi, figs. 11, *male*; 12, *female* (1882); *Papilio laodamia,* Clerck, Icones Ins., vol. iii (ined.), pl. vii, fig. 5 (1764); *Papilio laomedia,* Linnæus, Syst. Nat., ed. xii, p. 772, n. 145 (1767); id., Drury, Ill. Ex. Ins., vol. i, p. 12, pl. v, fig. 3 (1770); id., Cramer, Pap. Ex., vol. i, pl. viii, figs. F, G (1775); id., Fabricius, Syst. Ent., p. 494, n. 219 (1775); idem, id., Spec. Ins., vol. ii, p. 75, n. 333 (1781); idem, id., Ent. Syst., vol. iii, pt. 1, p. 98, n. 302 (1793); id., Sulzer, Gesch. Ins., p. 144, pl. xvi, fig. 10 (1776); id., Gmelin, Syst. Nat., vol. i, pt. 5, p. 2298, n. 145 (1790); id., Herbst, Nat. Schmett., vol. vii, p. 144, n. 49, pl. clxxiv, figs. 1, 2 (1794); *Temenis laomedia,* Hübner, Verz. bek. Schmett., p. 34, n. 283 (1816); *Vanessa laomedia,* Godart, Enc. Méth., vol. ix, p. 372, n. 59 (1819); id., Lucas, Lep. Exot., p. 112, pl. lviii, fig. 3 (1845); *Junonia laomedia,* Horsfield and Moore, Cat. Lep. Mus. E. I. C., vol. i, p. 140, n 283, pl. v, fig. 4 *larva, 4a, pupa* (1857); id., Butler, Cat. Fab. Lep. B. M., p. 77, n. 19 (1869); *Precis laomedia,* Moore, Lep. Cey., vol. i, p. 40, pl. xxi, fig. 2 (1881) *Papilio jaomedia,* Fabricius, Mant. Ins., vol. ii, p. 37, n. 390 (1787)

HABITAT: Plains of eastern and peninsular India, Ceylon, Nicobars, Assam, Burma, Malayana, China.

EXPANSE: 1·9 to 2·9 inches.

DESCRIPTION: "MALE. UPPERSIDE lilacinous [grey?]. *Forewing* with two waved black lines crossing the middle of the cell, and two similar ones at the end of the cell; a very waved and sinuated fuscous line crossing the wings a little beyond the cell, and between this and the outer margin are two waved fuscous lines (the inner one somewhat faint), between which the colour is distinctly paler, and is marked with a series of six ocellated spots placed between the nervules, of which the first is situated above the upper discoidal nervule, and the first, second, and fifth are largest and most brightly coloured; the first is also preceded by an irregular whitish spot placed at the bifurcation of the fourth and fifth subcostal nervules; fuscous marginal and submarginal lines. *Hindwing* with two waved fuscous lines crossing end of cell, and remaining markings similar and continuous to those on the *forewing,* but with five distinct ocellated spots only (a sixth sometimes obsoletely present between the first median nervule and the submedian nervure), and of which the first, second and fifth are largest and most brightly coloured. UNDERSIDE very pale; the cell crossed by the fuscous lines as above, but fainter, and the two medial ones continued on the *hindwing* and terminating near the median nervure; a distinct fuscous line crossing *both wings,* commencing near the costa a little beyond the end of the cell, where it is angularly waved to the third median nervule and then obliquely and more straightly continued across both wings to near anal angle of the *hindwing;* ocellated spots of the upperside more or less distinctly visible, their outer marginal line present, but the marginal and submarginal lines [almost] absent. *Hindwing* with the two fuscous lines crossing the end of the cell as above, and with a small fuscous spot near the anal angle. *Body* and *legs* more or less concolourous with the wings. FEMALE larger in size and generally darker in colour than the male, the ocellated spots above larger and more distinct, with the area on which they are placed much paler, the fuscous lines deeper in hue. UNDERSIDE also slightly darker than in the male, and the ocellated spots and markings much more distinct, and with the marginal and submarginal lines often distinguishable."

"The principal variation in this widely-spread insect is in depth of intensity of hue. The species has hitherto been almost universally known as *J. laomedia,* Linnæus, but Dr. Aurivillius has recently shown that Linnæus had previously described it under the name of *Papilio atlites,* the law of priority must therefore be followed." *(Distant,* l. c.)

LARVA (as figured by Horsfield from Java) is black, with a white line in the neighbourhood of the spiracles, each segment furnished with several many-branched ochreous spines, the abdomen and legs of the same colour. Feeds in Java on a species of *Achyranthes.* PUPA also fuscous, shaded with black, with two ochreous processes at the head, and numerous ochreous blunt projections all along the upperside.

This is a very common species, seldom if ever occurring in the Himalayas or in the very dry portions of India, but abundant in the plains throughout the area of heavy rainfall. Colonel C. Swinhoe does not record it from Bombay and the Deccan.

347. Junonia lemonias, Linnæus.

Papilio lemonias, Linnæus, Syst. Nat., ed. x, p. 473, n 93 (1758) ; idem, id., ed. xii, p. 370, n. 136 (1767) ; id., Clerck, Icones Ins., vol. iii (ined), pl. vii, fig. 2 (1764) ; id., Fabricius, Syst. Ent., p. 490, n. 207 (1775) ; idem., id., Spec. Ins., vol. ii, p. 70, n. 314 (1781) ; idem., id., Mant. Ins., vol. ii, p. 34, n. 365 (1787) ; idem , id., Ent. Syst., vol. iii, pt. 1, p. 90, n. 282 (1793), *part* id , Sulzer, Gesch. Ins., p. 144, pl. xvi, figs. 7, 11 (1776) ; id., Gmelin, Syst. Nat., vol. i, pt. 5, p. 2292, n. 136 (1790) ; id., Herbst, Natures. Schmett., vol. vii, p. 158, n. 59, pl. clxxvii, figs. 3, 4 (1794) ; *Hamadryas lemonias*, Hübner, Samml. Ex. Schmett., vol. i, pl. 1 (1806-16) ; *Vanessa lemonias*, Godart, Enc. Méth., vol. ix, p. 310, n. 31 (1819) ; *Junonia lemonias*, Horsfield and Moore, Cat. Lep. Mus. E I. C., vol. i, p. 139, n. 281 (1857) ; id., Butler, Cat. Fab. Lep. B. M., p. 74, n. 9 (1869) ; id., Moore, Lep. Cey., vol. i, p. 41, pl. xxi, figs. 3, *male* ; 3a, *female* (1881) ; id., Distant, Rhop. Malay., p. 96, n. 4, pl. xi, fig 5, *male* (1882) ; *Papilio aonis*, Cramer, Pap. Ex., vol. i, p. 55, pl. xxxv, figs. D-F (1775) ; *Junonia aonis*, Hübner, Verz. bek. Schmett., p. 34, n. 284 (1816).

HABITAT : India, Ceylon, Malayana, China.

EXPANSE : 1·8 to 2·55 inches.

DESCRIPTION : "MALE and FEMALE. UPPERSIDE pale brownish ochraceous. *Forewing* with the cell crossed by the following markings :—a slender waved black line near base, two waved black lines enclosing a pale ochraceous fascia a little beyond the middle, and a similarly coloured and enclosed fascia at about end of cell ; beyond this the ground-colour is somewhat darker and marked with the following pale ochraceous spots :—a discal series of six crossing the wing and divided by the nervules, the upper spot beneath the subcostal nervure and with the second and third forming a slightly oblique series ; fourth and fifth directed inwardly, and sixth again deflexed outwardly beneath the first median nervule ; this series is followed by another containing seven spots of the same colour, of which the upper three are divided by the fourth and fifth subcostal nervules ; the fourth and fifth are separated by the third median nervule, and the sixth and seventh—which are small and somewhat indistinct—are placed on each side of the first median nervule ; an indistinct submarginal series of spots placed between the nervules, and two ocellated spots, the first and smallest situated between the discoidal nervules, and the second and largest situated on the second and first median nervules. *Hindwing* with a large elongated and duplex ocellated spot, the smaller portion of which is situated between the subcostal nervules, the larger portion extending over the discoidal nervule, and a very small and indistinct ocellated spot between the second and first median nervules, a broad fuscous submarginal line and two marginal lines of the same colour [enclosing pale ochreous lines]. UNDERSIDE pale and dull ochraceous, *Forewing* with the cell crossed by fasciæ as above ; other markings generally as above ; the upper ocellated spot indistinct. *Hindwing* with several irregular, darker, basal fasciæ, and with a broad submarginal fascia enclosing five dark spots placed between the nervules, of which the second, situated above the discoidal nervule, and the fifth, placed between the second and first median nervules, are largest ; marginal and submarginal lines as above. *Body* and *legs* more or less concolourous with the wings." (*Distant*, l.c.)

LARVA as found in Ceylon, "Cylindrical, smoky black, with a pale dorsal band and paler lateral lower shade ; each segment with eight small branched spines." (*Moore*, l.c. in Lep. Cey.) According to Colonel A. M. Lang it feeds on *Barleria prionitis*.[*]

This is a widely-spread and common Indian species occurring almost everywhere in the plains in the region of heavy rainfall, and extending into the hills up to 7,000 feet elevation. The underside is variable in colour, some specimens having the ground ochreous, others ferruginous and others again beautifully pink or rosy, and there are numerous gradations between them. The markings of the underside also vary much in distinctness, in some examples they are almost obsolete, in others very prominent. These variations are not confined to particular localities, but appear to occur indiscriminately. I possess two "sports," both females, from Bholahât, Malda (*W. H. Irvine*), and Orissa (*W. C. Taylor*), which have all the markings blurred and obliterated on both sides.

---

[*] Ent. Month. Mag., vol. i, p. 137 (1864-5].

348.　Junonia hopfferi, Moschler.

Precis hopfferi, Möschler, Stettin Ent. Zeit., 1872, p. 337; *Junonia hopfferi*, Kirby, Syn. Cat. Diurn. Lep., p. 734 (1877).

HABITAT : Sylhet.

EXPANSE : 1·75 inches.

DESCRIPTION : "*Antennæ* above brown-black, beneath golden-red ; club black with golden-red extremity. *Palpi* golden, the last joint dark brown. *Sternum*, underside of *abdomen* and *legs* golden-white, upperside of *abdomen* and *thorax* with golden-brown pubescence."

"The shape of the *forewing* resembles that of *Precis* [*Junonia*] *erigone* [the Javan form of *J. lemonias*], but the *hindwing* is not angled as in several species of the genus. The ground-colour of *both wings* on the UPPERSIDE is of a clear golden-brown, as in many of the females of *Precis iphita*, Cramer (*ida*, Cramer), but is shaded by a dark brown dusting, so that it [the ground-colour] only appears in a triangular spot at the base of the discoidal cell, in a narrow transverse spot at the end of the cell, in a narrow band behind the transverse series of dark spots which crosses the middle of the wings, and in a broader band in front of the margin. In the discoidal cell in front of the middle are two obliquely-placed round dark brown spots with clear golden-brown centres ; behind these is a large misshapen kidney-like spot surrounded with black. In the middle of the wings the dark dusting is bounded by a series of dark brown transverse spots which enter angularly into the fourth cell. In front of the light margin is placed a series of black-brown, round spots, of which the three upper ones in the fifth, sixth, and eighth cells are only brown on the innerside, being otherwise white, and of these the spot in the fifth cell approaches the margin, thereby dropping out of the line of the others ; the lowest spot in the second cell is the largest and surrounded with a fine golden-brown. Behind these spots runs through all the cells a series of broad lunular spots, and behind this again runs a dark brown undulating streak following the margin which runs in an angle into the fifth cell. The margin is narrowly black-brown in colour, but marked finely with white externally between the veins."

"On the UNDERSIDE the colouring is clearer, brownish ochre-gold, the light parts being almost reddish-gold ; the spots of the cell are encircled with fine black, the series of dark spots through the middle of the wings lighter brown and less distinct on the margin are bordered with white violet-red spots on the *forewing* in cells one *b* and two, also in cells five and six, and in the *hindwing* in all the cells. The dark bands of the upperside between these spots and the clear margin appear narrower in the *forewing*, almost resolved into flecks ; of the round spots immediately behind these the one in the second cell is black bordered, those in the fourth, fifth, sixth, and eighth cells are white bordered, and only the three lowest on the underside are bordered with faint brown, the spot in the third cell is a mere point."

"On the hindwing this band is still more disintegrated, and of the dark spots only the one in the second cell is visible ; it is deep black, on the side towards the margin with a fine white centre. The series of lunulated spots, as also the undulating streak in front of the margin, is a lighter reddish-brown, the border between the two on the forewing in cells five and one *b*, and the *hindwing* in all the cells being tinged with pale violet-red. The margin itself is scarcely darker. Two females from Sylhet." (*Möschler*, l. c.)

I can make nothing out of this species, and can trace no resemblance between it and any species of the genera *Precis* or *Junonia* known to me.

349.　Junonia hierta, Fabricius. (PLATE XX, FIG. 94 ♂ ♀).

Papilio hierta, Fabricius, Ent. Syst., Suppl., p. 424, n. 281-2 (1798); *Vanessa hierta*, Godart, Enc. Méth., vol. ix, p. 318. n. 52 (1819); *Junonia hierta*, Swinhoe, Proc. Zool. Soc. Lond., 1884, p. 505, n. 11 ; *J. hierta*, idem, id., 1885, p. 128, n. 23 ; *Papilio enone*, Cramer, (*nec* Linnæus), Pap. Ex., vol. i. pl. xxxv, figs. A, B, *female* ; C, *male* (1775); id., Fabricius, Ent. Syst., vol. iii, part i, p. 90, n. 280 (1793) ; id., Herbst, Naturs. Schmett., vol. vii, p. 163, n. 61, pl. clxxviii, figs. 1, 2, *female* ; 3, 4, *male* (1794); *Cynthia enone*, Donovan, Ins. China (new edition), p. 66, pl. xxxvi, fig. 1, *male* (1842) ; *Junonia enone*, Hübner, Verz. bek. Schmett., p. 34, n. 291 (1816) ; id., Butler, Cat. Fab. Lep. B. M., p. 77, n. 3 (1869); id., Moore, Lep. Cey., vol. i, p. 40, pl. xxii, figs. 3. *male* ; 3a, *female* (1881) ; id., Forsayeth, Trans. Ent. Soc. Lond., 1884, p. 385.

HABITAT : India, Ceylon, Burma, Andamans, China.

EXPANSE : 1·75 to 2·7 inches.

DESCRIPTION : "MALE. UPPERSIDE black. *Forewing* with a broad medial ochreous [yellow] patch, extending from the base to beyond the disc, and thence narrowed and bent downward ; two short paler ochreous streaks before the apex. *Hindwing* black, with a large broad subbasal ochreous [yellow] patch, and a large distinct blue subbasal spot. UNDERSIDE, *forewing* pale ochreous-brown ; medial patch paler ochreous and suffused outwardly, crossed by black discoidal lines ; two black discal spots. *Hindwing* with basal half greyish-ochreous ; discal area pale ochreous, crossed with brown lunular lines, a medial fascia, and discal row of small brown spots. FEMALE. UPPERSIDE, *forewing* dark ochreous-brown, with the ochreous [yellow] patch paler, shortened basally, and crossed by two black lines on middle of the cell, and a broader disco-cellular band ; a black upper ocellus and a larger lower discal ocellus. *Hindwing* with a very small upper and lower discal ocellus, and two marginal lunular ochreous lines." (*Moore*, l. c.) UNDERSIDE as in the male.

Colonel A. M. Lang records that the LARVA feeds on *Barleria prionites*.[*] Surgeon-Major Forsayeth states that it is "precisely similar to that of *J. orithyia*, but without the orange tip on tail. PUPA also identical in shape and markings."

This species has hitherto been known as *J. œnone*, Linnæus, but reluctant as I am to upset nomenclature that has been for many years in universal use, I fear this identification cannot be maintained. The following is a translation of Linnæus' original detailed description of his *Papilio œnone*.

P. œnone. "UPPERSIDE. *Forewing* blackish, a white fascia, transverse, interrupted, with two white spots towards the apex, a ferruginous ocellus with blue pupil beyond the fascia, two ferruginous lines near the outer margin : *hindwing* blackish, with the margin whitish, divided by a black line, a large blue spot in the middle of the disc, two ferruginous ocelli within the outer margin. UNDERSIDE. *Forewing* with interrupted white fascia undulated with ferruginous and blue towards the base ; fuscous in the middle. *Hindwing* clouded greyish." (*Linnæus*, Mus. Lud. Ulr., p. 274).

To this he appends a description of what he calls a variety of œnone, of which the following is a translation. "*Varietas œnones*. UPPERSIDE. *forewing* with the margin black, two pale unequal spots within the apex, the disc yellow margined with fulvous. *Hindwing* with the margin black, the disc yellow margined with fulvous, the base more broadly black, in the middle of which is a large ovate sericeous blue spot. UNDERSIDE, *forewing* pale yellow, clouded with fuscescent ; a minute black blind ocellus within the apex, a larger black blind ocellus on the disc. *Hindwing* concolourous with the forewing, an obsolete dot in a paler space." (*Linnæus*, Mus. Lud. Ulr., p. 275).

The description of *P. œnone* not only omits all mention of the yellow on the upperside which is so marked a feature of the species we are dealing with, but specifies the existence of a white fascia which is absent, but corresponds with an African insect of the genus which was subsequently figured by Cramer as *P. clelia*,[†] and has hitherto stood under that name ; this name must give place to Linnæus' name. and the African species hitherto known as *J. clelia* stands as *J. œnone*, Linnæus. The description of the "*varietas œnones*," on the other hand, answers almost exactly to a species from Aden, Abyssinia, &c., closely allied to the present species, which has been separated by Trimen under the name *J. cebrene*;[‡] this name will stand since Linnæus, although he correctly described it, confounded it with his *J. œnone*, and gave it no separate name.

In 1798, Fabricius described under the name of *Papilio hierta* a variety of the Indian species in which the blue spot on the hindwing is absent. A translation of his description is given below.

---

[*] Ent. Month. Mag., vol. i, p. 132 (1864-65).
[†] Pap. Ex., vol. i, pl. xxi, figs. E, F (1775).
[‡] Trans. Ent. Soc. Lond., 1870, p. 353.

P. hierta. Female. "Wings denticulate, luteous, with the margin black, both wings with two ocelli, hindwing fuscous at the base. Inhabits the East Indies."

"Shaped like and nearest allied to *P. œnone*," of which I have formerly believed it to be a variety, but it seems distinct. Body fuscous. Both wings yellow with the margin more sinuate, fuscous, the hinder margin fuscous, narrow. Two ocelli on each wing, the hinder one larger in the forewing. Hindwing fuscous at the base. Underside of the forewing concolourous, of the hindwing ashy, densely striated with fuscous, four ocellate dots." *(Fabricius, Ent. Syst., Suppl., p. 424).*

This variety, which lacks the blue spot at the base of the hindwing on the upperside, occurs both in Africa (as pointed out by Mr. Trimen) and in the Indo-Chinese and Malayan regions, is inseparable from the normal form, and the Indian species known hitherto under the name of *J. œnone,* Linnæus, and figured as such by Cramer, Donovan, Moore, &c., must stand as *J. hierta,* Fabricius. This rectification was first pointed out by Mr. Kirby in his Syn. Cat. Diurn. Lep., p. 648; and it has been adopted by Colonel Swinhoe, but by no other author that I am aware of. Dr. Aurivillius, in his critical examination† of the Linnæan descriptions, comes to the conclusion that *J. œnone,* Linnæus, should stand as *J. clelia,* Cramer; and that the variety *œnones,* Linnæus, should stand as *J. œnone,* Linnæus, of which he gives *J. hierta,* Fabricius, as a variety; but I cannot adopt this conclusion.

J. hierta in India presents some considerable variation according to the humidity or dryness of the atmospheric conditions under which it exists, but these variations cannot be maintained as distinct species, as no hard and fast line can be drawn between them. Some male specimens from Kulu and Simla in the Western Himalayas, Sikkim, Calcutta, Orissa, the Wynaad, and Ceylon show no ocellar indentation of the yellow patch on the upperside of the forewing, others from Karachi, Kulu, Simla, Calcutta, Shillong, Upper Tenasserim, and the Andamans have a distinct black tooth, which is most prominent in a specimen from Buxa, Bhutan; in all of these the black inner margin of the forewing on the upperside gives off a projection into the first median interspace, while in examples from Karachi, Simla, Buxa, Calcutta, Shillong, Sibsagar, Rangoon and Upper Burma this projection assumes the form of a more or less separate and distinct spot. The width of the marginal black band on the upperside of the forewing is also variable; and lastly specimens from Bhutan and Upper Assam are very large and heavily marked, owing probably to the greater rainfall of those regions.

This species has a very wide range, occurring at Karachi, thence throughout India, Ceylon and the Andamans to Burma and again in China. It delights in the sun, and to disport itself in the hottest and driest situations.

The figure (incorrectly named *Junonia œnone* on the plate) shows the upperside of a male and a female example from Sibsagar in the Indian Museum, Calcutta.

350. **Junonia orithyia,** Linnæus.

Papilio orithya, Linnæus, Mus. Ulr., p. 278, n. 96 (1764); *P. orithya,* id., Syst. Nat., ed. x, p. 473, n 94 (1758); idem, id., ed. xii, vol. i, pt. 2, p. 770, n. 237 (1767); id., Cramer, Pap. Ex., vol. i, pl. xix, figs. C, D, *female* ; pl. xxxii, figs. E, F, *male* (1775) : idem, id., vol. iv, pl. cexc, figs. A, B, *male* (1780); id., Herbst, Pap., pl. clxxvii, fig 7, *male* ; 5, 6, *female* (1794) ; *Cynthia orithya,* Donovan's Ins. China (new edition), p. 64, pl. xxxv, fig. 2, *female* (1842) ; *Vanessa orithya,* Godart, Enc. Méth., vol. ix, p 317, n. 48 (1819) ; Suppl., p 821 (1823); id., Lucas, Lep. Ex., p. 113, pl. lx, fig. 1 (1845); *Junonia orithya,* Hübner, Verz bek Schmett., p. 34, n. 286 (1816) ; id., Butler, Cat. Fab Lep. B. M., p. 73, n 5 (1869) ; id., Moore, Lep. Cey., vol. i, p. 41, pl. xxii, figs. 1, *male* : 1a, *female* ; 1b, larva and *pupa* (1881) ; *Junonia orithyia,* Doubleday and Hewitson, Gen. Diurn. Lep., vol. i, p. 209, n 8 (1849) ; id , Horsfield and Moore, Cat Lep. Mus. E. I. C., vol. i, p 141, n 285, pl. v, figs. 5, *larva, 5a, pupa* (1857) ; id., Forsayeth, Trans. Ent. Soc. Lond., 1884, p 382 ; id., Butler, Ann and Mag of Nat. Hist., fifth series, vol. xvi, p. 308, n 60 (1885) ; *J. swinhoei,* idem, id., p 309.

HABITAT : India, Ceylon, Burma, China.

EXPANSE : 1·4 to 2·35 inches.

---

† Referring here to the present species figured as *P. œnone* by Cramer ; and not to the true *P. œnone* of Linnæus.

‡ Published in 1852 in Kong. Svens. Vet -Akad. Handlingar, vol. six, part 1, p. 80.

DESCRIPTION: "MALE. UPPERSIDE, *forewing* dark blue-black from base to the disc, outer area fuliginous-black; a purple-tinted ochreous-white short oblique subapical band, and two transverse submarginal narrow lunular fasciæ; on the inner fascia are two small red-ringed ocelli, below which the posterior angle is tinged with blue; costal edge ochreous-white. *Hindwing* blue, suffused with purple; a black basal angular patch curving across the cell towards the anal angle, and merging into brown on the abdominal margin; two ocelli near the outer margin, the lower one red and ringed with black, the upper one almost black and blind; two pale-bordered marginal lines. UNDERSIDE dull ochreous. *Forewing* with three transverse basal ochreous-red bands bordered with black; a discal sinuous black fascia and pale outer lunular fasciæ; ocelli less distinct. *Hindwing* with narrow brown transverse sinuous lines and a brownish discal fascia; ocelli very pale and indistinct. FEMALE differs on the UPPERSIDE in having the basal half of the *hindwing* entirely black, both the ocelli being large and of a bright red."

"LARVA dark purple-brown, each segment with short branched spines, two lateral rows of small yellow spots. Feeds on *Acanthads*. PUPA ochreous, speckled and lined with dark brown." (*Moore*, l. c. in Lep. Cey.) Surgeon-Major Forsayeth describes the transformations of this species somewhat more fully:—"LARVA found on a small labiate herb. Head and body of a very dark shining black, shading into brown when seen by reflected light. Head on a short neck, latter of an orange colour for a short distance; caudal extremity also tipped with orange. Body covered with perpendicular spines armed with strong radial hairs, which, however, have no irritating effect on the human skin. Head bifurcated; reddish spot in centre of face; a small spinous process on each upper angle of eye. Legs 6, 8, 2. PUPA suspended by tail; naked; wing-covers of a muddy yellow; rest of body of a purplish colour, variegated by lines of a dull creamy white. Slight projections of an angular nature along abdomen."

In Ceylon this species is "found at all times in the Western and Central Provinces, both in the plains and up to 3,000 feet in cultivated and open waste ground. Flight rather quick, settles on the ground and seems partial to hot, dusty and sandy spots" (*Hutchison*). "Occurs everywhere, but plentiful only from 2,000 to 4,000 feet, its favourite resort being the *patenas*, and particularly on the pathways or bare places in them" (*Mackwood*). "Taken at Kandy and Galle" (*Wade*). "Observed in the Himalayas. Partial to bare, dry grass-land. To be seen in the hottest hot winds, and in the bleak wintery weather pitched on the grass, flitting quickly away and pitching again after a short circuit. Larva reared on *Antirrhinum orontium*." (*Colonel A. M. Lang*, Proc. Zool. Soc. Lond., 1865, p. 494). Colonel Swinhoe records it from Quetta.

The specimens from Upper Burma, Cachar and Assam are richly marked on the underside, and are almost identical with the typical *J. orithyia* from China, which Mr. Butler has already shown in the Ann. and Mag. of Nat. Hist., fifth series, vol. xvi, p. 60 (1885) to extend to Siam; the western form with the pale, slightly marked underside, has been separated as a distinct local race as *J. swinhoei*,[*] (*Butler*, l. c.). This variety is fairly constant throughout the dry tracts in the west and north-west, and also in the Western Himalayas, but there is no line of demarcation, and the two forms gradually merge into each other; specimens from Ceylon and Travancore are nearly as richly marked as those from Cachar; those from Sikkim and Bhutan, and also from the Western Ghâts are less richly marked; and those from the plains of Bengal and the Coromandel coast still less so; the differences as in all parallel cases following the tropical distribution of the rainfall, the colours being most intense where the rainfall is heaviest.

Another local race, which is probably the *J. œnale* of Hübner, occurs in Java and Sumatra, of which there are two specimens in the Indian Museum; both are females, the one from Sumatra (*Raffles*) has the two ochreous bands in the cell of the forewing on the upperside very prominent, and with slight traces of blue on the hindwing on the disc; the other from

---

[*] *Junonia swinhoei*, Butler, Ann. and Mag. of Nat. Hist., fifth series, vol. xvi, p. 308, n. 60 (1885). HABITAT: Mhow, Poona. DESCRIPTION: "Decidedly paler on the UNDERSIDE than the Chinese insect [*J. orithyia*], the pale markings on the apical area of the *forewing* on the UPPERSIDE quite white. It is uniformly smaller [than *J. orithyia*], and the blue areas upon the wings are less tinged with green."

Java *(Horsfield)*, differs from the Sumatran specimen in having no blue colour on the hindwing, in this respect agreeing with the variety described below under the name of *J. wallacei* by Mr. Distant.

J. orithyia is a common species and appears to occur everywhere in India up to about 6,000 feet elevation. It is exceedingly variable on the underside, specimens from the dry north-west being of pale stone-grey, while examples from Shillong, Assam, have the underside dark brown, richly mottled and shaded with paler brown. On the upperside too there are variations in markings, some males show traces of two ochreous bands across the cell of the forewing, which are usually more or less present in the female, in some specimens of the latter sex, that feature being very prominent. The ocelli vary greatly in size in both sexes, in some specimens they are fully twice as large as in others.

J. wallacei[*] the Malayan form appears to be barely separable from the Sumatran *J. ocyale*, Hübner.

Genus 62.—NEPTIS, Fabricius. (PLATE XXIII).

Neptis, Fabricius, Ill. Mag., vol. vi, p. 282, n. 15 (1807); id; Westwood, Gen. Diurn. Lep., vol ii, p. 270 (1850); id., Moore, Proc. Zool. Soc. Lond., 1858, p. 3; idem, id., Lep. Cey., vol. i, p. 54 (1881); id., Distant. Rhop. Malay., p. 149 (1883); *Pantoporia* (part), and *Acca* (part), Hübner, Verz. bek. Schmett., p. 44 (1816); *Philonoma*. Billberg, Enum. Ins., p. 78 (1820); *Phædyma*, Felder, Neues Lep., p. 31, n. 74 (1861); *Rahinda*, Moore, Lep. Cey., vol. i, p 56 (1881).

"BODY, slender; *forewing* long; *antennæ* short; *palpi* small, hairy, and very acute. *Head*, rather broad, with a frontal tuft. *Eyes*, large, prominent, and naked. *Antennæ*, rather short, not half the length of the forewing; terminated by a short, slender, gradually formed club, the tip of which is curved outwardly, finely keeled beneath. *Palpi*, small, directed obliquely upwards, scarcely reaching above the level of the middle of the eyes. The terminal joint in the same line as the preceding, compressed, clothed with long loose hairs along the whole of the fore edge, and also on the hinder side at the extremity of the second joint; basal joint short; second joint broader and slightly curved at the base; terminal joint, in the typical species, nearly as long as the preceding, slender, and very acute at the tip. *Thorax*, rather slender, scarcely broader than the head, oval, very slightly hirsute, often clothed with metallic scales. *Abdomen*, slender, elongated. FOREWING, elongate, triangular. The *anterior margin* very slightly arched; *apex* rounded; *outer margin* rounded, not, or but slightly, sinuated; *inner* margin three-fourths of the length of the costal margin, more or less emarginate towards the middle. *Costal nervure* moderately strong, not extending to the middle of the costa. *Subcostal nervure* slender; its first branch arising at about one-third of the length of the wing, and uniting with

---

* *Junonia wallacei*, Distant (*Papilio orithya*, Linnæus, var. ?), Rhop. Malay., p. 95, n. 3, pl. xi, figs 3, *male*; 4, *female* (1883). HABITAT: Province Wellesley, Malacca, Java. EXPANSE: *Male*, 1°6 to 2°0; *female*, 2°0 to 2°1 inches. DESCRIPTION: "MALE, *forewing* with the basal portion shining fuscous; costal area—excluding base and apex—very pale ochraceous; cell crossed by two reddish fasciæ, one near middle, the other near termination; a little beyond cell, commencing near subcostal nervure, is an oblique and inwardly much excavated pale ochraceous fascia which reaches outer margin near apices of the median nervules; beyond this is a smaller and shorter fascia terminating at upper discoidal nervule, and a fainter and less continuous submarginal fascia of the same colour; two ocellated spots, the first broadly surrounded with reddish between the discoidal nervules, the second and larger situated between the second and first median nervules; beneath this spot and near outer angle is a small pale bluish patch. *Hindwing* pale bluish, abdominal margin pale fuscous, base and an irregular patch occupying lower half of cell, very dark fuscous or black; two ocellated spots, one black, with an obscure paler centre between the lower subcostal and discoidal nervules, the second and largest red, with a large pale bluish centre and black margins situated between the second and first median nervules; a marginal and irregular waved black lines, between which the colour is more or less distinctly pale ochraceous. UNDERSIDE pale but warm ochraceous. *Forewing* with the base of cell, and two broad irregular fasciæ crossing cell, reddish ochraceous, the one at end of cell continued and terminating a little beneath first median nervule—this is followed by a narrow waved black fascia; remaining markings as above, but the ocellated spots much darker. *Hindwing* darker ochraceous, crossed by several waved and scalloped darker lines, with a wide, distinct, slightly darker submarginal fascia on which are placed the two ocellated spots as above, and a third and much more indistinct spot situated between the subcostal nervules; marginal and submarginal lines as above, but fainter and much paler. *Body* and *legs* more or less concolourous with wings. FEMALE. UNDERSIDE marked and spotted generally as in male, but brownish ochraceous, the blue colour being absent, the ocellated spots larger. UNDERSIDE almost precisely as in male, but the ocellated spot with larger pale margins, and the *hindwing* possessing some irregular reddish ochraceous fasciæ crossing the cell."

"This form is evidently a local race of *J. orithya*, Linnæus, a well-known species in Continental India and elsewhere. It differs from typical forms of that species by the tawny colour of the female, and the absence of the blue and black markings to the wings of the same. The male almost exactly resembles Hübner's figure of *J. ocyale* [Samml. Exot. Schmett., vol. ii, pl. xxxvi, figs. 3, 4]. It is another of the many distinct 'local races' found in the Malay Peninsula and neighbouring islands." (*Distant*, l. c.). There is a female specimen mentioned above from Java in the Indian Museum, Ca cutta, which agrees with the description and figure of this species; but as Mr. Butler says *J. ocyale* occurs in Java, and Mr. Distant that *J. wallacei* is also found in that island, it would appear from this that the latter cannot be maintained as a "local race" even of *J. orithya*.

the costa a little beyond the middle ; second branch, in the typical species, arising close beyond the first, before the anterior extremity of the discoidal cell, [in the *hordonia* group it is given off long after the end of the cell] ; third branch arising at about two-thirds of the length of the wing and extending to the tip ; fourth branch arising at about three-fourths of the length of the wing and reaching to the outer margin below the apex, the apical portion of the vein being deflexed. *Upper disco-cellular nervule* almost obliterated, arising close beyond the origin of the second subcostal branch [in the typical group] ; *middle* disco-cellular short, arched towards the base of the wing in the typical species ; *lower* disco-cellular obsolete, so that the *discoidal cell* is open, its place often indicated by a dark bar having a slightly curved paler line dividing the pale discoidal patch into two parts, and extending to the median nervure just before the origin of its third branch, which is slightly arched. HINDWING, very oval ; the *costal margin* much arched ; the *outer* margin rounded, slightly scalloped. *Præcostal nervure* forming a short straight spur forked at its extremity ; *costal* nervure slightly curved, [usually] reaching only to the middle of the costal margin ; *subcostal* nervure arising from the costal just beyond the origin of the præcostal, and emitting its branch almost at its base. The *upper disco-cellular nervule* forming the curved base of the discoidal nervule ; the *lower* disco-cellular wanting, so that the narrow *discoidal cell* is open. *Median nervure* branching below the branches of the subcostal nervure, with the spaces between the extremities of the branches along the outer margin of the wing wider than usual, in consequence of the costal nervure extending only to the middle of the costa [except in the *columella* group]. FORELEGS, of the *male* very slender and short, more or less clothed with very delicate white hairs ; *femur* slightly curved ; *tibia* scarcely half its length ; *tarsus* very short, not above one-third of the length of the tibia, forming a minute, oval, exarticulate joint, destitute of claws. Of the *female* more robust, and much longer than those of the male, scaly, with but few fine hairs ; *femur* slightly curved ; *tibia* also a little curved, about two-thirds of the length of the femur ; *tarsus* nearly as long as the tibia, well articulated ; the basal joint half the length of the tarsus, the remainder rather dilated, with strong spines on the inside ; the terminal joint minute, spined, but without claws. MIDDLE and HINDLEGS, rather short, scaly ; *tibia* spined beneath, with long tibial spurs ; *tarsus* with four rows of strong spines beneath ; *claws* rather long and very much bent, and acute at the tip ; *paronychia* and *pulvillus* small."

"LARVA slightly elongated ; head armed above with two short conical points ; second and third segments of the body with a pair of diverging, obtuse, setose, fleshy spines, the hinder pair being the largest ; an erect tubercle near the extremity of the body. PUPA with the head bifid, and with the base of the abdomen-case much swollen." (*Westwood*, l. c.)

The genus *Neptis*, like the genera *Hestina*, *Argynnis* and *Cyrestis*, is structurally divisible into two groups, the first of which contains tawny and black species only, and has the second subcostal nervule of the forewing given off from the costal nervure some distance beyond the outer extremity of the discoidal cell ; in the second group some of the insects are tawny and black and some white and black, and have the second subcostal given off just before the end of the cell. The former group has been erected into a genus under the name of *Rahinda** by Mr. Moore.

Neptis differs from all other *Nymphalinæ* in the costal nervure of the hindwing terminating before the end of the costa, instead of reaching the apex of the wing, except in the *columella* group, in which this character is extremely variable and in some localities even sexual. The species are easily captured, they have a floating sailing flight, frequently settling on bushes with spread open wings. "*Neptis* is a very large genus, and is found in the warmer portions of the Old World. Two species inhabit portions of Eastern and South-Eastern Europe, and the genus is represented in Western, Southern and Eastern Africa, Madagascar, and Mauritius. It is very abundant in Continental India, and extends eastward throughout the Malay Archipelago ; it is found as far north as Japan and as far south as Australia." (*Distant*, l. c.)

* *Rahinda*, Moore, Lep. Cey., vol. i, p. 56 (1881). "Differs from *Neptis* (*averis* group) in the wings being comparatively narrower, the forewing more pointed at the apex, having the second subcostal branch emitted at some distance beyond the end of the cell, and the hindwing having the costal and subcostal nervures more curved, the median branches nearer at their base, the short straight basal costal spur slightly furcate. Type, *N. hordonia*, Stoll, Suppl. Cramer, Pap. Ex., vol. v, pl. xxxiii, f. 3, 4, 4D (1791)." (*Moore*, l. c.)

Many of the Indian species are so very closely allied, that it is almost impossible to distinguish between them without comparison with the types. They are also in many cases somewhat variable, which makes correct determination still more difficult. Species of the genus occur in almost every mountainous part of India and at all elevations up to 10,000 feet, and also in the plains of Peninsular and Eastern India where the rainfall is heavy, but they are not found in the dry plains of Northern and Western India.

In the genus *Neptis* the style of markings is extremely constant, more so perhaps than in any genus of large extent. In all the species the ground-colour is black or very dark brown, and the markings which are either white or tawny, are grouped into three almost parallel bands at right angles to the body; the first consisting of a streak from the base of the forewing through the cell and extending into the lower discoidal interspace, sometimes divided abruptly where the cell should end, leaving an elongate triangular spot as the outer portion; this band is termed the discoidal streak of the forewing; following this is the discal band extending from the abdominal margin of the hindwing through the cell to the costa near apex, and continued on the forewing to the costa as an interrupted macular curved band; beyond this again is the submarginal band common to both wings and in both about equidistant from the discal band and from the margin; besides these, there are in many species additional narrower bands on the black space beyond the discal band; but the three bands noted above, the discoidal streak and the discal and submarginal bands are present in all, and usually very prominent. The sexes are but slightly differentiated, the markings being the same in both.

This style of marking is found in many species of *Athyma*, and in one at least of *Apatura* so closely corresponding to *Neptis* as to be almost indistinguishable to an untrained eye, but in all these cases the extension of the costal nervure of the hindwing to the apex distinguishes them at once from all *Neptes* except *N. columella* and allied species.

In the first group the markings are orange, tawny or ferruginous in all the species; it is separable into two subgroups, in one of which the underside is mottled with fine ferruginous striæ; in the other the bands are unmottled. The discoidal streak is entire in some species and indented in others, but in none is it completely divided.

Key to the Indian species of Neptis.
First Group.

A. Second subcostal nervale of forewing given off far beyond outer extremity of discoidal cell. Colouration black, with orange markings.

  a. Underside mottled with ferruginous.

    a.[1] Discal band on hindwing whitish.

        351. N. (*Rahinda*) CYNACALIS, Andaman Isles.

    b.[1] Discal band on hindwing orange.

      a.[2] Orange bands narrow, not extending below median nervure on upperside of forewing, marginal line indistinct.

        352. N. (*Rahinda*) HORDONIA, N.-E. and S. India, Malay Peninsula and Islands.

      b.[2] Orange bands wider, extending below median nervure on upperside of forewing, marginal line prominent.

        353. N. (*Rahinda*) PLAGIOSA, India, Upper Tenasserim.

      c.[2] Orange bands having deeply sinuated borders.

        354. N. (*Rahinda*) SINUATA, Ceylon.

  b. Underside not mottled with ferruginous.

    a.[1] Orange streak in cell of forewing on upperside bounded by median nervure.

      a.[2] Discal orange band on upperside of hindwing broadly coalescing with submarginal band along abdominal margin.

        355. N. (*Rahinda*) ASSAMICA, Assam.

      b.[2] Discal orange band on upperside of hindwing not coalescing with submarginal band, but continued to abdominal margin.

        356. N. (*Rahinda*) DINDINGA, Moulmein, Tenasserim, Malacca.

    b.[1] Orange streak in cell of forewing on upperside extending well below median nervure.

        357. N. (*Rahinda*) VARAKA, Sylhet, Dafla Hills, Chittagong, Mergui, Malay Peninsula, Borneo.

351. Neptis cnacalis, Hewitson.

N. cnacalis, Hewitson, Ann. and Mag. of Nat. Hist., fourth series, vol. xiv, p. 357 (1874).

HABITAT : Andaman Islands.

EXPANSE : 1·45 to 2·1 inches.

DESCRIPTION: " UPPERSIDE dark brown. *Forewing* with the longitudinal spot from the base orange, unusually long, reaching considerably below the middle of the wing, unbroken : crossed beyond the middle by six spots of orange, the two middle spots minute, and outside of this by a narrow band of lilac-white. *Hindwing* crossed before the middle by a broad band of white ; [a submarginal more or less distinct tawny line]. UNDERSIDE. *Forewing* as above, except that the band and spots are much larger and rufous-white, the apex grey-white, and that there are some grey spots near the costal margin. *Hindwing* with the base brown, undulated with grey : below the band lilac-grey, traversed by two bands of brown ; the outer margin brown. On the underside this species resembles *N. hordonia ;* its forewing is unusually prolonged at the apex." (*Hewitson,* l. c.) The female is larger than the male, and has the discal band on the hindwing more distinctly white, but does not otherwise differ.

The paleness of the markings at once distinguishes this species from all others of the *N. hordonia* group. The late Mr. de Roepstorff has sent numerous specimens taken at Port Blair to the Indian Museum, Calcutta. It is apparently confined to the Andaman Isles.

352. Neptis hordonia, Stoll.

Papilio hordonia, Stoll in Suppl. Cramer, Pap. Ex., pl. xxxiii, figs. 4, 4D (1790) : *Nymphalis hordonia*, Godart, Enc. Méth., vol. ix, p. 423, n. 253 (1823) ; *Neptis hordonia*, Horsfield and Moore, Cat. Lep. Mus. E. I. C., vol. i, p. 164, n. 337 (1857) ; id., Distant, Rhop. Malay., p 150, n. 1, pl. xvii. fig. 13, *male* (1883).

HABITAT : N.-E. and S. India, Malay Peninsula, Siam, Sumatra, Banca, Java, Borneo.

EXPANSE : 1·7 to 2·2 inches.

DESCRIPTION : " MALE and FEMALE. UPPERSIDE rich dark brown, with the following orange-coloured markings :—*Forewing* with a long and broad basal cellular streak occupying the lower half of cell and deflexed and extended beyond it at and above the third and second median nervules ; this streak above is distinctly cleft a little beyond its middle, and in some specimens extends a little beneath the median nervure ; a subapical transverse macular fascia, commencing near costa and terminating near third median nervule ; and a short oblique curved and dentate fascia, commencing above the second median nervule and terminating on inner margin. *Hindwing* with a broad medial fascia and a narrow (in some specimens broad) curved submarginal one. *Both wings* with a narrow fuscous submarginal fascia, sometimes that on the *forewing* and sometimes those on *both wings* narrowly outwardly margined with dark ochraceous. UNDERSIDE ochraceous. *Forewing* with a broad costal streak extending to beyond cell, and from thence deflexed and outwardly curved to beyond first median nervule, reddish brown ; two waved reddish brown submarginal fasciæ, and the margin broadly of the same colour, between these the colour is more or less violaceous ; extreme margin fuscous, the *cilia* alternately greyish. *Hindwing* with a broad basal reddish brown fascia or suffusion ; a somewhat curved medial violaceous fascia, narrowly bordered anteriorly and broadly posteriorly with reddish brown, and a submarginal fascia somewhat similarly coloured and bordered. *Body* and *legs* more or less concolourous with the ground-colour of the wings both above and beneath."

" This is a protean species, and varies much both in markings and hue, points of some importance in estimating the specific position of other and closely allied variable species. The specimen figured agrees with the figure of Stoll, and may be considered as typical. Other Malacean specimens have the yellow submarginal fascia on the upperside of the hindwing much wider, but are still inconstant in that respect. The palest specimen I possess, with all the yellow markings broadest, is from Bombay. The mottled markings beneath are always present and always distinctive." (*Distant,* l. c.)

See remarks on the following species.

353. **Neptis plagiosa,** Moore.

N. plagiosa, Moore, Proc. Zool. Soc. Lond., 1878, p. 830.

HABITAT : Upper Tenasserim, Naththoung to Paboga ; Maldá, Sikkim, Calcutta, Sylhet, Assam, Chittagong, Orissa, Nilgiris, Ganjam, and Trevandrum.

EXPANSE : ♂, 1·50 ; ♀, 1·90 inches.

DESCRIPTION. " Allied to *N. hordonia,* Stoll ; differs on the UPPERSIDE in all the ferruginous bands being broader. *Forewing* has the lengthened discoidal band spreading over the median nervure, the marginal line also broader and very distinct. *Hindwing* with the submarginal band nearly as broad as the discal band. UNDERSIDE, the strigæ are more numerous and darker, covering both bands on the *hindwing.*" (*Moore,* l. c.)

This species was originally described from Upper Tenasserim, and I have a specimen named by Mr. Moore from Coonoor. The distinctive characters appear to be the broadness of the orange bands on the upperside, especially the submarginal one on the hindwing, and the ferruginous strigæ or mottling on the underside practically covering the whole of the hindwing ; also the violaceous colour instead of being confined to two bands suffuses the whole outer half of the hindwing. These characters, however, though they enable typical specimens to be distinguished, are very inconstant, and there appears to be every gradation between the narrow-banded form with the underside scantily mottled, to the broad-banded profusely striated form. Neither is the width of the discoidal streak and the marginal line distinctive. I have given above the localities from whence I have seen typical specimens of *N. plagiosa,* but from Sikkim, Sylhet, Assam and elsewhere, I have specimens which are quite intermediate between *N. hordonia* and *N. plagiosa.* In Sikkim typical *N. plagiosa* has been taken in December, and typical *N. hordonia* and intermediate forms from the spring to the autumn ; in Calcutta I have taken typical *N. plagiosa* in February only ; in Orissa Mr. W. C. Taylor has taken typical *N. plagiosa* in February and March, Mr. J. L. Sherwill at Hulunguri, Jorehât district, Assam, in March, the type specimens also were taken in the cold weather ; it appears possible therefore that *N. plagiosa* may be the winter form only of *N. hordonia.*

354. **Neptis sinuata,** Moore.

N. sinuata, Moore, Proc. Zool. Soc. Lond., 1879, p. 136 ; *Rahinda sinuata,* id., Lep. Cey., vol. i, p. 56, pl. xxviii, figs. 3, 3ª (1881).

HABITAT : Ceylon.

EXPANSE : ♂, 1·62 to 1·85 ; ♀, 1·87 to 2·05 inches.

DESCRIPTION : "Allied to *N. hordonia,* Stoll. Differs on the UPPERSIDE in the bands having deeply sinuated borders. UNDERSIDE also paler ; the strigæ less prominent, and disposed in more blotchy patches." (*Moore,* l. c. in Proc. Zool. Soc. Lond.)

In Ceylon *N. sinuata* is "principally a low country insect, difficult to capture perfect as it always frequents the vicinity of thick thorny Acacias. Found at all times, but mostly in March and April" (*Mackwood*). "Western and Central Provinces ; commonest in the plains, but found up to 3,000 feet, in forest land, at all times. Shy, flutters about bushes, alighting on the leaves with wings opened" (*Hutchison*).

This species is a local race of *N. hordonia,* very slightly differing from the North Indian form. It may be distinguished by the discoidal streak on the upperside of the forewing being more distinctly bicleft, and the lower margin of the discal band on the upperside of the hindwing more distinctly sinuous. It is subject to the same variation in the profusion or otherwise of the ferruginous mottling of the underside as is the continental form, the tone of the ferruginous ground-colour below is also very variable.

The next three species differ in lacking the mottling of ferruginous striæ on the underside.

355. **Neptis assamica**, Moore.

Rahinda assamica, Moore, Trans. Ent. Soc., Lond., 1881, p. 311.

HABITAT: Sibsagar and Jorehât, Assam.

EXPANSE: 1·7 to 1·9 inches.

DESCRIPTION: "MALE. Allied to *K*. [= *N*.] *heliodore*, Fabricius [see *N. dorelia*, footnote p. 83]. UPPERSIDE: *Forewing* with the red discoidal streak similar to that in *K*. [= *N*.] *hordonia*, not extending below the cell, the oblique subapical band somewhat narrow, the lower discal band scarcely constricted in its middle. *Hindwing* with a broad subbasal and a discal band, the abdominal margin also broadly of the same red colour as the bands. UNDERSIDE ochreous-yellow, with very narrow ochreous-brown intervening spaces between the bands." (*Moore, l. c.*)

There are two males of this pretty and distinct species in the Indian Museum, Calcutta, from Sibsagar, Upper Assam (*S. E. Peal*); and one in my own collection from Hulunguri in the Jorehât district, Assam, taken by Mr. J. L. Sherwill in March. It can be easily distinguished from *N. paraka* on the underside by the absence of some small black markings on the upper margin of the cell of the forewing and others defining the basal band of the hindwing. The dark markings of the underside of *N. assamica* are also paler in colour and more diffused. The abdominal margin of the hindwing on the upperside being orange is also a very distinct feature. It seems to be rather a variable species, as one Sibsagar and the Jorehât specimen differ from the type in the extent of the orange markings on the upperside, in the type specimen, the oblique subapical and the lower discal bands of the forewing are separated, and the discal black band of the hindwing is wide, while in the other two specimens the former are joined, and the latter is less than half as wide.

356. **Neptis dindinga**, Butler.

N. dindinga, Butler, Trans. Linn. Soc., Zoology, second series, vol. 1, p. 542, n. 10, pl. lxviii, fig. 6 (1877); id., Distant, Rhop. Malay., p. 151, n 3, pl. xvii, fig. 5, *female* (1883).

HABITAT: Moulmein, Tenasserim, Malacca.

EXPANSE: 1·9 to 2·2 inches.

DESCRIPTION: "Larger than *N. heliodora* [*heliodore*], the bands broader, particularly the medial band of the hindwing, which is twice as broad and extends nearly to the base; subapical patch of *forewing* twice as wide, and deeply indented in the middle of its inner border; submarginal tawny streak replaced by pale brown (but intersected by the black line) in the *forewing*, tawny but extremely slender in the *hindwing*. Differences on the UNDERSIDE much as above; discal band of the *hindwing* broad and black, and intersected by a whity-brown streak."

"We have a specimen in the British Museum from Moulmein, which measures 2 inches 2 lines in expanse. It is a well-marked species." (*Butler, l. c.*)

"FEMALE. Allied to *N. paraka*, from which it differs by the different shape of the cellular streak and the absence of the yellow submarginal lines to the *forewing*; the yellow fascia to the *hindwing* are much broader (but this we have already seen is a variable character); the markings on the UNDERSIDE are darker, larger, and more regular, especially on the *forewing*." (*Distant, l. c.*)

I have not seen this species. It may be distinguished from *N. paraka* on the underside by the absence of the small black markings mentioned in the preceding species, and from *N. assamica* by the black discal band on the upperside of the hindwing reaching the abdominal margin.

357. **Neptis paraka**, Butler.

N. paraka (*peraka* on plate), Butler, Trans. Linn. Soc., Zoology, second series, vol. 1, p. 542, n. 9, pl. lxviii, fig. 2 (1877); *N. peraka*, Distant, Rhop. Malay., p. 150, n. 2, pl. xvii, fig. 2, *female* (1883).

HABITAT: Sylhet, Dafla Hills, Chittagong, Mergui, Malay peninsula, Borneo.

EXPANSE: 1·6 to 2·0 inches.

DESCRIPTION : "Almost exactly like *N. hordonia* on the UPPERSIDE, but brighter in colour, and with the tawny bands rather broader ; the submarginal tawny streak of the *forewing* deeply bisinuate so as to form two wide arches, and intersected by a black line. UNDERSIDE ochre-yellow, the black portions of the upperside represented by brownish stains, and partially blotched with grey : the basal area of the *hindwing* crossed by two black oblique lituræ ; the medial band bordered by two interrupted black lines ; the outer border intersected (above the indication of the submarginal tawny line of the upperside) by a slightly waved black line."

"The typical *N. heliodora* [= *heliodore*, Fabricius] very nearly resembles this species on the upperside ; but below it is very different." (*Butler*, l. c.)

"MALE and FEMALE. Closely allied to *N. hordonia*, and on the UPPERSIDE scarcely distinguishable from some of the broadly yellow marked varieties of that species. UNDERSIDE not mottled, and though the pattern of the *forewing* is similar, the markings of the *hindwing* are distinct ; they consist of a basal fascia with dark margins, a regular and similarly coloured and margined fascia near the middle, and a somewhat similar marginal fascia." (*Distant*, l. c.)

Mr. H. M. Parish took this species in the Chittagong district in October and November, and Dr. J. Anderson in the Mergui archipelago in the cold weather ; the black lituræ in the cell of the forewing, and at the base of the hindwing on the underside are very distinctive.

The second group comprises two subgroups, in the first of which the discoidal streak is entire or indented, but never completely divided ; this subgroup contains all the more abnormal forms, and the markings differ greatly in colour and in prominence ; in some they are bright orange as in the first group, in others tinted with fuliginous or brown, in others pure white ; in some again they are very broad and in others very narrow ; and on the underside many of the species have the bands tinted with violet, very brightly in some ; this violet tinting is confined to this subgroup, being absent from all the others.

Key to the Indian species of Neptis.

Second Group.

B. The second subcostal nervule of the forewing given off at the outer extremity of the discoidal cell.
    a. Discoidal streak of forewing not divided by a black bar.
        a^1. Upperside with ground-colour black, with orange or ferruginous markings.
            a^2. Underside with wide orange bands. Of very small size.
                a^3. Upperside with prominent orange marginal band on hindwing.
        358. N. TIGA, Moulmein, Upper Tenasserim, Malay Peninsula, Siam, Java, Borneo.
                b^3. Upperside with orange marginal band obscure or wanting on hindwing.
                    a^4. Underside, margin of hindwing narrowly edged with fuscous.
        359. N. SATTANGA, Burma.
                    b^4. Underside, margin of hindwing broadly fuscous, bearing a narrow orange line.
        360. N. KURASA, Cachar.
        b^2. Underside with whitish bands tinted with shining violet.
            a^3. Upperside with the orange bands narrow.
                a^4. Underside with outer submarginal violet band on hindwing highly lunulate, the points reaching the margin. Of very large size.
        361. N. RADHA, N.-E. Himalayas, Cachar.
                b^4. Underside with the outer submarginal band on hindwing narrow and even.
                    a^5. The orange spot in lower median interspace on forewing almost confluent with the spot in continuation of the discal band of hindwing.
        362. N. MIAH, N.-E. Himalayas, Khasi Hills, Chittagong, Upper Tenasserim.
                    b^5. The above-mentioned spot well-separated from the spot below. Of larger size.
        363. N. ANANTA, Himalayas, Sylhet, Assam, Yunan.
            b^3. Upperside with the orange bands almost as broad as the black interspaces.
        364. N. VIRAJA, N.-E. Himalayas, Orissa, South India, Upper Tenasserim.

II

b^1. Upperside with ground-colour black, with broad ochreous markings.

 a^2. Discoidal streak on upperside of forewing well-separated from spot in first median interspace.

  365. N. ZAIDA, Himalayas.

 b^2. Discoidal streak on upperside of forewing joined to discal spot in first median interspace.

  366. N. MANASA, North India.

c^1. Upperside with ground-colour black, markings almost pure white, broad.

 a^2. End of discoidal streak extending below third median nervule.

  367. N. NATAVANA, N.-W. Himalayas.

 b^2. End of discoidal streak not extending below third median nervule.

  a^3. With a white spot in lower discoidal interspace of forewing.

   368. N. AMBA, N.-W. Himalayas, Nepal, Yunan.

   369. N. AMBOIDES, Kashmir, Kangra district.

  b^3. No white spot in lower discoidal interspace of forewing.

   370. N. BURMANA, Upper Tenasserim.

d^1. Upperside with ground-colour brown, markings more or less fuliginous, narrow.

 a^2. Discal band of hindwing white, all the rest tinted with fuliginous.

  a^3. Underside of hindwing with no white band between basal and discal bands.

   371. N. CARTICA, Nepal, Sikkim.

  b^3. Underside of hindwing with a prominent white band between basal and discal bands.

   372. N. CARTICOIDES, Sikkim, Naga Hills, Yunan.

 b^2. Upperside with all the bands brown.

  373. N. FULIGINOSA, Tenasserim.

 c^2. Upperside with all the markings tinted with pale fuliginous, very narrow.

  a^3. Inner submarginal line on hindwing prominent, straight.

   374. N. VIKASI, Sikkim, N.-E. Bengal, Mergui, Malay peninsula and islands.

  b^3. Two submarginal lines equally obscure, coalescing and enclosing a series of black spots.

   375. N. HARITA, E. Bengal, Assam, Cachar, Upper Tenasserim.

e^1. Upperside with ground-colour black, with markings brown, very narrow. Underside, the bands bright violaceous.

  376. N. ANJANA, Upper Tenasserim.

The first three species very closely resemble the last two of the preceding group in which the underside has the bands unmottled, in colouration, and in their small size, but the orange bands of the upperside are not so broad, while the orange marginal line of the forewing is much more prominent. They have no trace of violet tinting on the underside.

358. Neptis tiga, Moore.

N. tiga, Moore, Proc. Zool. Soc. Lond., 1858, p. 4, n. 3; id., Butler, Trans. Linn. Soc., Zoology, second series, vol. i. p. 547, n. 8 (1877); id., Distant, Rhop. Malay, p. 151, n. 4. pl. xvii, fig. 4, male (1883).

HABITAT : Moulmein, Donat Range, Upper Tenasserim ; Province Wellesley, Malacca, Siam, Java, Borneo.

EXPANSE : 1·7 to 1·9 inches.

DESCRIPTION : "MALE and FEMALE. UPPERSIDE rich dark brown, with the following orange-coloured markings :—*Forewing* with a large cellular streak much resembling that of *N. dindinga*, but sometimes more or less truncate at its apex ; this is followed by a subapical transverse streak and two irregularly shaped spots, situated one on the area of the median nervules and one on the inner margin ; a broad submarginal fascia, strongly sinuated and toothed interiorly, followed by a submarginal line of the same colour. *Hindwing* crossed by two broad fasciæ, one near base and the other near outer margin, and a submarginal line of the same colour. UNDERSIDE ochraceous, the *forewing* with a broad subcostal pale fuscous fascia, which is obliquely deflexed beyond cell, and forms a large looped spot extending from costa to third median nervule ; a pale fuscous fascia beneath cell, which forms an irregularly looped spot beneath and attached to the other looped spot, and which outwardly extends to inner margin ; a pale fuscous submarginal line and the outer margin broadly of the same colour. *Hind-*

wing marked as above, but the colour much paler and the dark portions much narrower. *Body* above rich dark brown, the thorax with some frontal yellow markings, and the disc of the abdomen beyond base much suffused with the same colour ; body beneath and *legs* more or less concolourous with wings. " (*Distant*, l.c.)

"This species agrees with an example in the Banksian cabinet, but not with the Fabrician type ; there are two medial brown curved lines across the underside of the hindwing, partly or wholly filled in with paler brown." (*Butler*, l.c.)

There is a single specimen of this species taken by Captain C. T. Bingham in the Donat Range in Upper Tenasserim in January in Major Marshall's collection. A variety of it differing principally from the typical form in being smaller, and the markings on the underside darker, has been described as a distinct species under the name of *N. dorelia*, Butler.[*]

A species apparently allied to *N. tiga* (but which may however belong to the *Rahinda* group) has been described under the name *N. camboja* from Cambodia, as below.[†]

359. Neptis sattanga, Moore.

Rahinda sattanga, Moore. Trans. Ent. Soc. Lond., 1881, p. 311.

HABITAT : British Burma.

EXPANSE : 1·75 to 2·15 inches.

DESCRIPTION : "FEMALE. Allied to the Malayan *R.* [= *N.*] *dorelia*,[‡] Butler. UPPERSIDE blacker, the markings paler, but more sharply defined. *Forewing* with the discoidal streak entire, the subapical patch of equal width with that beneath it ; submarginal band slender and lunular. *Hindwing* with only two bands, both of which are straight, the submarginal band narrow and only half the width of the inner band ; no marginal line." (*Moore*, l. c.)

In the above description Mr. Moore states that *dorelia* belongs to the group of *Neptis* to which he has applied the name *Rahinda*, but Mr. Distant places it with those species which have the "second subcostal nervule of anterior wings emitted at extremity of cell," and therefore it belongs to the typical group of *Neptis*. *N. sattanga* appears to differ chiefly from *N. tiga* in the absence of the marginal line on the upperside of the hindwing in the male, it is present but less distinct in the female.

There are numerous specimens of a species of *Neptis* taken by Dr. Anderson in the cold weather in the Mergui Archipelago which agree exactly with Mr. Moore's description of *N. sattanga*, and to which species they probably belong. The second subcostal nervule is given off at the end of the cell in these specimens, so they belong to the typical group of *Neptis*. There is also a male of this species taken in April in the Upper Thoungyeen forests and another in Tenasserim in November, in Major Marshall's collection.

---

[*] *Neptis dorelia*, Butler, Trans. Linn. Soc. Zoology, second series, vol. i, p. 542, n. 7, pl. lxvii, fig. 3 (1877); *N. tiga*, var. *dorelia*, Distant, Rhop. Malay., p. 152, pl. xvii, fig. 3 (1883); *Papilio heliodore*, Fabricius (nec Cramer, nec Moore), Mant. Ins., vol. ii, p. 52, n. 516 (1787); idem, id., Ent. Syst., vol. iii, pt. i, p. 130, n. 401 (1793); *Neptis heliodore*, Butler, Cat. Fab. Lep. B. M., p. 62, n. 4 (1869); *N. heliodora*, Druce, Proc. Zool. Soc. Lond., 1873, p. 343, n. 7. HABITAT : Malacca, Singapore. EXPANSE : 1·5 to 1·6 inches. DESCRIPTION : " The type of the Fabrician species differs from the examples of *N. tiga* in the Horsfield Cabinet from Java in having a single instead of a double medial arched line across the UNDERSIDE of the *hindwing* ; this line is, in some examples, slightly thickened." (*Butler*, l. c.)

[†] *Neptis camboja*, Moore, Proc. Zool. Soc. Lond., 1879, p. 136. HABITAT : Cambodia. EXPANSE : 1·5 inches. DESCRIPTION : "MALE. UPPERSIDE—*forewing* with a pale ferruginous broad longitudinal band from the base to beyond the cell, a broad oblique subapical and a constricted lower band ; also two very narrow indistinct ferruginous marginal lines. *Hindwing* with a broad ferruginous transverse discal, and narrow slightly curved submarginal band ; also a single very narrow and indistinct ferruginous marginal line. UNDERSIDE pale yellowish ferruginous ; bands as above, but indistinctly defined."

"Allied to *N. dindinga*, Butler, from Malacca ; also allied to *N. heliodore*,[*] Fabricius, from Siam (the *type* specimen of which is in the Banksian Cabinet in the British Museum), but differs above on the forewing in the discoidal streak not extending over the median nervure, and in the submarginal band on the hindwing being narrower. On the underside these differences also occur, and the dark interspace between the bands on the hindwing is also narrower." (*Moore*, l.c.)

[*] Mr. Distant in his Rhop. Malay., gives *N. heliodore*, Fabricius, as a synonym of *N. dorelia*, Butler, *N. heliodore*, Cramer (Pap. Ex., vol. iii, pl. ccxii, figs. F, F (1779), is a black *Neptis* with white markings from Amboyna. In his Index, Cramer spells this name *heliodora*, but in the text it is given both as *heliodore* and *heliodora*.

[‡] See foot note above.

Another species of this group, *N. nolana*, has been described as below from Siam.[*] It may belong to the *Kalinda* group.

360. **Neptis kuhasa**, de N., n. sp.

HABITAT : Cachar.

EXPANSE : ♂, 1·9; ♀, 2·0 inches.

DESCRIPTION : MALE. UPPERSIDE black with orange markings. *Forewing* with a broad discoidal streak bounded below by the median nervure, obscurely separated from the large triangular spot beyond by two fine black lines ; a broad subapical patch well-separated from a rather less broad discal one which reaches the inner margin, and is strongly constricted at the first median nervule ; a prominent submarginal somewhat lunate band, with a very obscure and fine pale marginal line. *Hindwing* with a broad straight even discal band, and a narrower (about one-third the width) submarginal similar band ; marginal line as in forewing. UNDERSIDE with the ground-colour much paler, and the bands also paler, ochreous rather than orange. *Forewing* marked as above. *Hindwing* with an additional ochreous band at the base of the costal margin, the discal and submarginal bands broader (much reducing thereby the width of the band of the ground-colour between them), the outer margin broadly fuscous bearing a prominent ochreous line. FEMALE slightly paler. *Forewing* with the apex less produced. *Hindwing* with the discal band narrower, the submarginal band wider than in the male. UNDERSIDE with the same differences as above.

N. kuhasa differs from Upper Tenasserim specimens of *N. sattanga* in both sexes in the submarginal band on the upperside of the hindwing being narrower, the band of the ground-colour on the underside of the hindwing between the discal and submarginal ochreous bands is twice as wide, and in addition the outer margin of that wing is broadly fuscous, bearing a prominent ochreous line. In *N. sattanga* the margin is equally broadly ochreous inwardly bounded by a narrow black line, the extreme margin being defined by a very fine black line.

Mr. Wood-Mason took one male on the 29th July, and two females on the 8th August at Irangmara in Cachar.

The next four species have the bands of the underside tinted with violet, comparatively slightly in *N. viraja*, very brightly in the other three ; the bands of the upperside are orange, broad in *N. viraja*, much narrower in the others.

361. **Neptis radha**, Moore.

N. radha, Moore, Horsfield and Moore, Cat. Lep. Mus. E. I. C., vol. i, p. 166, n. 343, pl. iva, fig. 4 (1857) ; id., Moore, Proc. Zool. Soc. Lond., 1858, p. 6, n. 9.

HABITAT : Sikkim, Bhutan, Cachar.

EXPANSE : 2·9 to 3·4 inches.

DESCRIPTION : "UPPERSIDE brownish-black : markings ferruginous. *Forewing* with a long discoidal streak, narrow at base, and extending to a short distance between the third and second median nervules ; two small spots on costal margin, and two larger oblique spots near the apex ; a large spot on disc, and an elongate spot to middle of posterior margin ; marginal line pale. *Hindwing* with rather broad inner and narrower outer band, both extending across the abdominal margin ; a marginal line and line between the two bands pale brown. UNDERSIDE ferruginous-brown ; markings as above, but indistinct, owing to the surface being mottled over with ashy-blue." (*Moore*, l. c. in Cat. Lep. Mus. E. I. C.) FEMALE differs from the male only in the ferruginous markings being broader and paler.

[*] *Neptis nolana*, Druce, Proc. Zool. Soc. Lond., 1874, p. 105. HABITAT : Chentaboon, Siam (September). EXPANSE : 2·25 inches. DESCRIPTION : " UPPERSIDE dark brown, all the bands and spots rufous-orange. *Forewing* with a longitudinal band from the base to beyond the cell, with a broad band from the costal margin to the anal angle curved inwards and narrower in the middle, with a narrow band round the outer margin. *Hindwing* crossed by three rufous-orange bands, the first and third narrow. UNDERSIDE as above, only much paler in colour, with all the bands indistinctly marked." (*Druce*, l. c.)

This species appears to have only one marginal line on the upperside of the forewing ; and is singular in having the discal band of the hindwing as well as the marginal line narrow.

N. radha is the largest of the Indian species of *Neptis*, and one of the most distinct. On the upperside of the forewing it has two small pale streaks on the costa within the subapical band and divided by the second subcostal nervule as in *N. narayana* and *N. manasa*, but in no other Indian species. The underside is beautifully variegated with violaceous, there is a conspicuous violet spot closing the upper outer end of the cell of the forewing; five spots in a transverse band from the costa to the third median nervule beyond the cell divided by the veins, and a large irregular divided subapical violet patch. The hindwing is widely banded with violet, there is a small ferruginous ring near the middle of the cell, beyond which is a curved pair of fine ferruginous lines joined at each end, all the bands on the outer half of the hindwing are highly lunulate.

N. radha is a rare species. Mr. Möller has obtained a single specimen in Sikkim in the spring; I took a worn male at about 4,000 feet elevation below Darjiling in October; and Mr. Wood-Mason obtained a single male on Nemotha, Cachar, in September.

362. Neptis miah, Moore.

N. miah, Moore, Horsfield and Moore, Cat. Lep. Mus. E. I. C., vol. 1, p. 164, n. 330, pl. iva, fig. 1 (1857); idem, id., Proc. Zool. Soc. Lond., 1858, p. 4, n. 5.

HABITAT : Sikkim, Bhutan, Khasi Hills, Assam, Chittagong, Upper Tenasserim.

EXPANSE : 2·25 to 2·40 inches.

DESCRIPTION : " UPPERSIDE brown-black. *Forewing* with a longitudinal streak from base of wing [indented at the end of the cell], an oblique transverse short apical fascia, and which nearly meets a reversely-oblique fascia on posterior margin, rufous. *Hindwing* with a nearly straight broad inner band, and a narrow [curved] submarginal band, rufous. UNDERSIDE dark ferruginous. *Forewing* with the longitudinal and oblique marks pinky-white; two narrow submarginal lines purple. *Hindwing* with inner band pinky-white; two submarginal and a less distinct middle line purple; costal margin at the base whitish." (*Moore*, l. c. in Cat. Lep. Mus. E. I. C.) The markings of the FEMALE are rather paler than in the male.

N. miah is a fairly common species in Sikkim throughout the summer, and I have taken numerous male examples in October sucking up moisture from damp sand in the beds of streams. Mr. H. M. Parish has taken a single female in the Chittagong district in November, and Mr. J. L. Sherwill a male at Hulunguri in the Jorehát district, Assam, in March. In Major Marshall's collection there is a male taken in February at Sekkan, and two females taken in March and April in the Thoungyeen forests, Upper Tenasserim.

363. Neptis ananta, Moore.

N. ananta, Moore, Horsfield and Moore, Cat. Lep. Mus. E. I C., vol. i. p. 166, n. 342, pl. iva, fig. 3 (1857); idem, id., Proc. Zool. Soc. Lond., 1858, p. 5, n. 7; idem, id, in Anderson's Anat. and Zool. Researches, p. 924 (1878).

HABITAT : Himalayas, Sylhet, Assam, Yunan.

EXPANSE : 2·5 to 2·8 inches.

DESCRIPTION : " Upperside brownish-black; markings ferruginous. *Forewing* with discoidal streak straight [indented at the end of the cell]; a curved twice-interrupted band from anterior margin near apex to middle of posterior margin; a pale marginal line. *Hindwing* with rather broad inner and narrow outer band, both extending across the abdominal margin; also a pale marginal line and line between the bands. UNDERSIDE very deep ferruginous. *Forewing* with discoidal streak, spots near apex and from posterior margin, ferruginous-white; posterior margin broadly patched with black; a marginal and submarginal bluish-ashy line. *Hindwing* with inner band white, outer band grey and indistinct; a marginal line and zigzag line between the two bands bluish-ashy." (*Moore*, l. c. in Cat Lep. Mus. E. I. C.) FEMALE has the markings rather broader and paler than in the male.

The Western Himalayan specimens of *N. ananta* differ from those from Sylhet and Assam in having the bands of the upperside much paler; in the former they are ochreous, in the latter ferruginous. On the underside also the same differences occur in the colour of the ground, the more eastern examples being much darker. It is rather a rare species. I met with it at Kujiah near Dalhousie and at Ulwas, Chumba, in wooded streams at the end of May, Mr. A. Graham Young has taken it in Kulu at the same period, and Colonel A. M. Lang, R. E., took it at Kandloo, Kunawur, in July, Mr. C. Templeton took it at Masuri, Mr. J. L. Sherwill at Hulunguri, Jorehât district, Assam, in March, April and June, and Mr. A. V. Knyvett has taken it in Sikkim and Bhutan.

It is closely allied to *N. miah*, but is a much larger insect ; the bands too are rather narrower, and the outer discal violet line on the underside of the hindwing is lunulate and more prominent. In *N. ananta* the spot in the first median interspace on the upperside of the forewing in well separated from the spot below, in *N. miah* they are joined.

364. Neptis viraja, Moore.

N. viraja, Moore, Proc. Zool. Soc. Lond., 1872, p. 563, pl. xxxii, fig. 6.

HABITAT : N.-E. Bengal, Sikkim, Bhutan, Orissa, S. India, Upper Tenasserim.

EXPANSE : ♂, 2·12 to 2·30 ; ♀, 2·4 to 2·8 inches.

DESCRIPTION : "MALE and FEMALE. UPPERSIDE black ; markings ferruginous. *Forewing* with a broad discoidal streak extending to two-thirds the length of the wing [sometimes indented at the end of the cell]; a large broad subapical oblique spot, and a broad band beneath extending to hind margin ; an indistinct pale brown marginal line, *Hindwing* with a broad transverse inner band and narrow submarginal band. UNDERSIDE ferruginous-brown in male, blackish ferruginous in female ; markings as above, pale glossy ferruginous-white, and tinted with blue in some lights ; a marginal line on *both wings* ; a narrow median discal line, basal and a subbasal streak on *hindwing* bluish-white. Allied to *N. radha*." (*Moore*, l. c.)

This is a rare species. I took a single female in the Sikkim Tarai in October, and Mr. Möller has one specimen in his collection, also from Sikkim, taken in May. The Indian Museum, Calcutta, has examples from Buxa, Bhutan, a single female taken by Mr. W. C. Taylor in Orissa in March, another from the Wynaad, taken by Mr. Rhodes-Morgan, and a third from Cannanore. In Major Marshall's collection there is a single female taken in the Thoungyeen forests in Upper Tenasserim in March. The four latter specimens differ from Himalayan females in having the submarginal band on the upperside of the hindwing nearly as broad as the discal one, *i.e.*, much broader than in examples from the Himalayas. On the underside the markings are much the same.

N. viraja has the bands of the underside broader than in the three preceding species, and the violet tinting is less pronounced ; in these respects it more nearly resembles the next two species, but it is distinguished from both *N. zaida* and *N. manasa* by the deep orange colour of the bands of the upperside, and by the complete fusion of the lower discal spots of the forewing into a band in continuation of the discal band of the hindwing.

The next two species have the bands broad, tinted with ochreous, but not deep orange ; the bands of the underside are tinted with violaceous, but not very prominently : the principal distinctive feature in these is in the medial spot of the discal band on the forewing : in *N. zaida* it is well separated from both the discoidal streak and the spot in continuation of the discal band of the hindwing ; in *N. manasa* it coalesces with the discoidal streak but is well separated from the spot on the inner margin, while, as pointed out above, in *N. viraja* it is well separated from the discoidal streak, but it coalesces with the spot below.

365. Neptis zaida, Doubleday, Hewitson.

N. zaida, Doubleday, Hewitson, Gen. Diurn. Lep., vol. ii, p. 272, n. 9, pl xxxv, fig. 3 (1850) ; id., Moore, Proc. Zool. Soc. Lond., 1858, p. 6, n. 10.

HABITAT : Himalayas.

EXPANSE : 2·6 to 3·0 inches.

DESCRIPTION : MALE : UPPERSIDE black, with pale ochreous or almost white markings. *Forewing* with a narrow discoidal streak not extending below the median nervure or indented at the end of the cell, ending in an acute point on the third median nervule ; a subapical streak composed of four spots divided by the nervules, the upper two on the costa very small ; a large rounded spot in the first median interspace, extending into the interspace above ; a streak below it ending on the inner margin, a very pale indistinct submarginal line to *both wings*. *Hindwing* with a broad discal band and a narrow submarginal one, less than half as wide as the discal one. UNDERSIDE ochreous, markings as above, but whiter on the hindwing, the marginal line on both wings tinted with lilac, the submarginal band of the *hindwing* bordered within and without with lilac followed by diffused yellow lines, a diffused black median patch near the inner margin of the *forewing*. FEMALE larger, the markings broader.

There is much difference in the intensity of the colour of the markings on the upperside ; in some specimens from Masuri and Sikkim in Colonel Lang's collection they are almost pure white, in other Sikkim and Masuri examples they are pure ochreous, and there are intermediate specimens taken by Mr. C. Templeton at Masuri in the Indian Museum, Calcutta. Colonel Lang's Masuri specimens were taken in June at 7,000 feet elevation. It is recorded by Mr. Moore from Simla, and he remarks : " *N. zaida* has the wings more rounded than in the other allied species, and on the hindwing the inner band is very broad, the outer band narrow and *much curved*." (*Moore*, l.c.) It is a rare species.

366. Neptis manasa, Moore.

N. manasa, Moore, Horsfield and Moore, Cat. Lep. Mus. E. I. C., vol. 1, p. 165, n. 341, pl. iva, fig. 2 (1857) ; idem, id., Proc. Zool. Soc. Lond., 1858, p. 5, n. 6.

HABITAT : N. India.

EXPANSE : 2·5 inches.

DESCRIPTION : "UPPERSIDE dull dusky-brown : markings white, tinged with very pale ferruginous. *Forewing* with the discoidal streak long, and continued in a curve to near the posterior angle ; an apical oblique streak ; two small spots on costal margin, and one below the margin ; a spot on middle of posterior margin ; a marginal row of small indistinct spots. *Hindwing* with broad inner and narrower outer band, both extending across the abdominal margin ; an indistinct marginal line and line between the two bands. Narrow *cilia* white. UNDERSIDE pale ochreous, with indistinctly-defined white markings ; the discoidal streak is continued uninterruptedly to the middle of posterior margin, the space within being blackish ; on the *hindwing* are some small white markings between the inner band and costal nervure."

" *Neptis manasa* may be distinguished on the upperside by the discoidal streak being nearly confluent with the spot on the middle of posterior margin, it being quite confluent on the underside." (*Moore*, l.c. in Cat. Lep. Mus. E. I. C.)

This is a very remarkable and distinct species, of which I have never seen a specimen.

The next four species have the markings almost pure white ; the underside has the bands tinted with violet, prominently in *N. narayana*, faintly in the other three, as in the preceding species to which they are closely allied.

367. Neptis narayana, Moore.

N. narayana, Moore, Proc. Zool. Soc. Lond., 1858, p. 6, n. 8, pl. xlix, fig. 3.

HABITAT : North India, Kulu Valley, Chini.

EXPANSE : 2·5 to 2·7 inches.

DESCRIPTION : "MALE. UPPERSIDE black ; markings white. *Forewing* with the discoidal streak narrow [indented at the end of the cell] ; along costal margin towards the apex some narrow spots, with two large spots descending obliquely across the apex [two small spots in continuation on the costa divided by the third subcostal nervule] ; a quadrate spot in middle of disc, and another on posterior margin ; two submarginal narrow spots parallel with the quadrate discal spot. *Hindwing* with straight inner and narrower nearly straight outer band. UNDERSIDE glossy ferruginous, darkest about the middle of the wings, very pale at the base of costal margin, and blackish along posterior margin of the forewing. *Forewing* with markings as on upperside ; *hindwing* with submarginal line, zigzag line between the two bands, greyish-white."

"Allied to *Neptis zaida*, but may be known from that and other allied species by the markings on the upperside being *pure white*." (*Moore, l. c.*)

The Indian Museum, Calcutta, possesses specimens of both sexes (which do not differ from one another) from the Kulu Valley taken in May by Mr. A. Graham Young, and there are others from Kunawar in Colonel Lang's collection. Mrs. Deane took a single female at Chini in June. The markings of the upperside are more usually just tinted with ochreous, the forewing has three very minute streaks divided by the veins on the upperside of the forewing below the costa within the subapical spots as in *N. radha* and *N. manasa*; there also a marginal pale line which becomes very distinct below the third median nervule. It appears to be a rare species, and confined to a very limited area.

368. Neptis amba, Moore.

N. amba, Moore, Proc. Zool. Soc. Lond., 1857, p. 7, n. 11, pl. xlix, fig. 4 ; idem, id., in Anderson's Anat. and Zool. Researches, p. 924 (1878).

HABITAT : N.-W. Himalayas ; Nepal, Yunan (*Moore*).

EXPANSE : 2·4 to 3·0 inches.

DESCRIPTION : "MALE. UPPERSIDE smoky-brown ; markings white. *Forewing* with long discoidal streak indented at the extremity of the cell ; two oblique spots near the apex, and four reversely oblique spots to middle of posterior margin ; an indistinct marginal and submarginal black line. *Hindwing* with rather broad inner band and narrow brownish-white outer band ; marginal and submarginal line darker. UNDERSIDE dark ferruginous ; markings as on upperside ; but the marginal and submarginal lines, base of costal margin, and streak near base of *hindwing* also white." (*Moore, l. c.*)

There are numerous specimens of *N. amba* in the Indian Museum, Calcutta, all from the Himalayas west of Nepal, one of which from Masuri has been identified by Mr. Moore. It differs from the description above, and also from Mr. Moore's figure in having four instead of two oblique spots near the apex of the forewing, the upper one often divided by the subcostal nervules.* There is also a submarginal white line between the two black lines described by Mr. Moore. The type specimen is from Nepal. We have no specimens from Nepal, but those we possess from the Western Himalayas show very little variation in the markings ; they all have the additional spots in the discal series, and differ markedly from Mr. Moore's figure also in having the discal band of the hindwing very broad, and all the markings pure white, and but for Mr. Moore's identification of one of them as *N. amba*, I should not have included them with the specimen he has figured. The additional white subbasal band on the underside of the hindwing allies this species with *N. carticoides*, but the width and extent of the white markings render *N. amba*, as now identified, conspicuously distinct from all allied species. Mr. Moore's figure would lead to the conclusion that the Nepal race is nearer to *N. carticoides* of Sikkim than to *N. amba* of the Western Himalayas, the specimen he records from Yunan is almost certainly *N. carticoides*, and it will probably turn out on further research that *N. carticoides* is really synonymous with *N. amba*, and that the Western Himalayan species here called *N. amba* requires a new name. The FEMALE has the forewing broader, the outer margin straighter, and the apex less produced than in the male. It is a common species in Simla, and there are specimens in the Indian Museum, Calcutta, from the Kulu valley and Masuri, and in Colonel Lang's collection from Kunawur. Mrs. Deane took it at Chini in June.

369. Neptis amboides, Moore.

N. amboides, Moore, Proc. Zool. Soc. Lond., 1882, p. 241.

HABITAT : Ruttun Pir, Kashmir ; Kangra district.

EXPANSE : ♂ , 2·1 ; ♀ , 2·25 inches.

---

* The fourth spot in this series in the lower discoidal interspace completing the broad discal series is a conspicuous feature ; it is present in all our specimens, and it is this that gives the very white appearance by which *N. amba* is so easily recognised.

DESCRIPTION : " Allied to but smaller than *N. amba. Forewing* with the discoidal streak broader ; the discal spots also broader and more compactly disposed. *Hindwing* with a broader subbasal band, and a more uniformly curved and narrower submarginal band," (*Moore,* l. c.)

The expanse of the type specimen of *N. amba* from Nepal taken from Mr. Moore's figure is 2·7 inches, considerably larger than the dimensions given above for *N. amboides*. The smallest specimen of *N. amba* (out of thirty-two) in our collections is 2·4 inches· Except in size the other differences as given above by Mr. Moore seem but slight. I have never seen a specimen.

370. Neptis burmana, de N., n. sp.

HABITAT : Upper Tenasserim.

EXPANSE : 2·4 inches.

DESCRIPTION : MALE. UPPERSIDE black with prominent pure white markings. *Forewing* with the discoidal streak narrow, deeply indented at the end of the cell ; the discal series of spots large and well separated, the submarginal macular band distinct, with a pale line on either side. *Hindwing* with the discal band somewhat broad, straight and even, followed by a pale line, the submarginal white macular band prominent, with a pale line beyond. UNDERSIDE dull ferruginous. *Forewing* with the triangular spot less prominently separated from the discoidal streak beyond, and the pale lines on either side of the submarginal macular band more distinct. *Hindwing* with a broad white basal band, two marginal white lines (there is only one pale line on the upperside), other markings as above.

Nearest to *N. cartica*, from which it differs on the upperside in having all the markings prominent and pure white, in *N. cartica* the markings are all obscure and tinged with fuliginous, except the discal band of the hindwing and the four spots on the forewing in continuation which are white ; the submarginal band also on the hindwing is more macular in *N. burmana* ; and on the underside there are two marginal lines on the hindwing, in *N. cartica* there is only one, thereby increasing the width of the band of the ground-colour between the discal and submarginal bands in that species.

There are two male specimens of *N. burmana* in Major Marshall's collection, both taken by Captain C. T. Bingham, one at Donat in January, the other at Sekkan, Thoungyeen, in February.

The next two species have the bands of the upperside white, but all except the discal band are suffused with fuliginous brown ; the bands of the underside are faintly tinted with violet as in the three preceding species.

371. Neptis cartica, Moore.

N. cartica, Moore, Proc. Zool. Soc. Lond., 1872, p. 562.

HABITAT : Nepal, Sikkim.

EXPANSE : 2·25 to 2·75 inches.

DESCRIPTION : " MALE and FEMALE. UNDERSIDE dark fuliginous black. *Forewing* with long fuliginous-white discoidal streak, indented at the end of the cell, beyond which is a maculated band curving from costa before the apex to middle of hind margin, and bordered outwardly by a narrow wavy line and a submarginal row of whitish lunules, the marginal line being black. *Hindwing* with straight inner whitish band and less distinct outer submarginal band, between which is a pale brown line, and a similar line along outer margin [this pale line is also present on the forewing]. UNDERSIDE dark ferruginous, banded as above [but all the bands white], the marginal lines on *forewing* more prominent and tinged with purple, the median discal line and marginal line on *hindwing* also purple-tinged ; base of hindwing with a broad white streak." The FEMALE is larger than the male, wings broader, markings similar, but more tinted with fuliginous on the upperside.

12

" Allied to *N. amba*, specimens of which, from the same locality, are under examination."
(*Moore*, l. c.)

The markings of *N. amba* are very wide, and pure white ; those of *N. cartica* are narrow and tinged with fuliginous, and there is no difficulty in distinguishing between them. *N. cartica*, however, is very close to *N. vikasi*, from which species on the upperside it differs in having the markings less fuliginous, especially the discal band which is pure white, and broader, the apex of the forewing also is somewhat less produced. On the underside the ground-colour is ferruginous rather than fuliginous-brown. On both upper and undersides the ground-colour is suffused darker in each interspace between the white bands, forming rows of diffused dark maculæ bands. In *N. vikasi* these dark bands are even more prominent. *N. cartica* is rather a rare species, but occurs in Sikkim from April to October.

372. Neptis carticoides, Moore.

N. carticoides, Moore, Trans. Ent. Soc. Lond., 1881, p. 309.

HABITAT : Darjiling, Naga Hills, Yunan.

EXPANSE : 2 inches (*Moore*) ; 2·8 to 3·0 inches.

DESCRIPTION : " Allied to *N. cartica*. MALE differs from the same sex of that species in being somewhat smaller and of a fuliginous-brown colour, not black ; markings similar, but of a pale fuliginous tint, and, therefore, less prominent ; the subbasal band on the *hindwing*, and the lower discal spots on the *forewing* only being whitish. UNDERSIDE of a brighter chestnut colour, and the bands less prominent." (*Moore*, l. c.)

A male specimen of a *Neptis* from the Naga hills was sent to Mr. Moore for identification ; he returned it to the Indian Museum, Calcutta, labelled " *N. ? carticoides*, larger than type." It agrees very fairly with the description above, but is much larger in size. From *N. cartica* it may be distinguished on the underside by the forewing lacking the white irregular line between the discal curved series of spots and the inner of the two submarginal lines, and by the hindwing having an additional subbasal streak and two submarginal whitish lines, in *N. cartica* there is only one. On both sides of the forewing also *N. carticoides* has the discal curved series of spots more diffused and elongated and completed by the addition of a spot in the lower discoidal interspace. This extra spot on the forewing and the additional white subbasal band on the underside of the hindwing are also characteristic of *N. amba*, to which species *N. carticoides* is nearest allied, but differs in having the markings narrower and tinged with fuliginous. Mr. Otto Möller has a single male in his collection from Sikkim ; there are two males from the Naga hills, and one obtained by the Yunan expedition in the Indian Museum, Calcutta. The latter is the specimen probably that Mr. Moore named *N. amba* in " Anderson's Anat. and Zool. Researches," p. 924.

In the next species all the bands are fuliginous brown on the upperside, and the underside has no trace of violet tinting.

373. Neptis fuliginosa, Moore.

N. fuliginosa, Moore, Trans. Ent. Soc. Lond., 1881, p. 310.

HABITAT : Moulmein, Mergui.

EXPANSE : 1·9 inches.

DESCRIPTION : " MALE. Allied to *N. ebusa*, Felder [from Mindoro, one of the Philippines]. UPPERSIDE fuliginous olive-brown. *Forewing* with fuliginous olive-white slender discoidal streak, transverse discal interrupted macular band, and two slender submarginal lunular lines. *Hindwing* with a broad subbasal and a discal band, a narrower less distinct slender intervening medial line, and an outer marginal line. UNDERSIDE paler fuliginous-brown, with markings as above, but more prominent and whiter, the *hindwing* having also an additional subbasal band." (*Moore*, l. c.)

This is a very distinct and well-marked species. The apex of the forewing is much more rounded than in *N. vikasi*, and all the markings more distinct, broader and more macular. It is very distinct from all the other species of this group, the wings being shorter and broader, and the outline more evenly convex. It more nearly resembles the *N. varmona* group in general aspect, but the markings of the upperside being fuliginous, and the discoidal streak uninterrupted readily distinguish it. The type specimen from Moulmein is in the Indian Museum, Calcutta, taken by Major C. H. E. Adamson ; and Dr. Anderson took a pair in the Mergui archipelago during the cold weather.

The next three species are the darkest of all, the bands being very narrow and fuliginous or brown not white. On the underside *N. vikasi* and *N. harita* have only a very faint trace of violet, and the markings correspond in general style with those of *N. cartica*. *N. anjana* has all the bands violet, and is as distinct in its markings from its allies as *N. radha* is among the species with orange bands.

374. Neptis vikasi, Horsfield.

N. vikasi, Horsfield, Cat. Lep. E. I. C., pl. v, figs. 2, 2a (1829) ; id., Horsfield and Moore, Cat. Lep. Mus. E. I. C., vol. i, p. 165, n. 340 (1857) ; id., Distant, Rhop. Malay., p. 152, n. 5, pl. xvi, fig. 13, *female* (1883).

HABITAT : Sikkim, Cachar, Assam, Mergui, Malay Peninsula, Java, Borneo, Celebes.

EXPANSE : 2·25 to 2·80 inches.

DESCRIPTION : "MALE and FEMALE. UPPERSIDE dark shining fuliginous-brown, with paler and darker markings. *Forewing* with the following very pale fuliginous markings :— a long basal cellular [discoidal] streak about reaching the lower discoidal nervule [distinctly indented at the end of the cell by a pair of five black lines enclosing a pale space], beyond which the wing is crossed by a strongly curved series of spots, [a highly irregular narrow line following the outer margin of the curved discal series of spots] and two almost straight submarginal fasciæ, which are denoted and separated by two very dark fuscous and abruptly sinuated narrow fasciæ, the outer margin with a distinctly darker patch near apex and about middle. *Hindwing* with an almost straight, transverse, and very pale fuliginous fascia near base, followed shortly beyond by a narrow and obscurely paler linear fascia, and a very dark fuscous macular fascia crossing middle of wing ; a submarginal series of very dark fuscous spots placed between the nervules, preceded and followed by pale fuliginous, the outer margin being broadly fuscous and very obscurely spotted. UNDERSIDE very much paler, marked generally as above, but the pale markings nearly white, and the spots on the outer margins of *both wings* very distinct. *Body* and *legs* more or less concolourous with wings." (*Distant, l. c.*) The FEMALE is larger, has the wings broader, and the apex of the forewing less produced than in the male, the outer margin of the forewing also is not emarginate.

N. vikasi is not uncommon throughout the warmer months in Sikkim. Mr. Wood-Mason took it in Cachar in July and August, and Dr. Anderson at Mergui during the cold weather. It is a very distinct and well-marked species.

Mr. Moore has described a species of *Neptis* from Penang which Mr. Distant places as a variety of *N. vikasi* with the following remark :—" I cannot, however, believe that Penang possesses a different species to the widely ranging one [*N. vikasi*] found in Province Wellesley ; and a drawing of *N. omeroda* kindly made for me by Professor Westwood has, in my mind, confirmed this view." (Rhop. Malay., p. 153). Mr. Moore's original description of *N. omeroda* is appended below. *

---

* *Neptis omeroda*, Moore, Proc. Zool. Soc. Lond., 1874, p. 571. HABITAT : Penang. EXPANSE : 1·37 inches. DESCRIPTION : " Allied to *N. vikasi*, but is a much blacker insect both above and below. UPPERSIDE blackish, glossed with greenish olive-brown ; banded with olive-brown, as in *N. vikasi*. *Forewing*, upper portion of transverse discal series of spots oval, lower portion rounded. UNDERSIDE black, paler externally, with a glaucous gloss ; veins brown ; discoidal streak, lower portion of transverse discal series of spots of *forewing*, and inner band of *hindwing* pale fuliginous ; the subapical spots and outer bands greyish white, the scales on the latter being raised or depressed, and thus having the appearance of short strigæ." (*Moore, l. c.*)

375. Neptis harita, Moore.

N. harita, Moore, Proc. Zool. Soc. Lond., 1874, p. 571, pl. lxvi, fig. 8.

HABITAT : E. Bengal, Assam, Cachar, Upper Tenasserim.

EXPANSE : 2·0 to 2·3 inches.

DESCRIPTION : " MALE and FEMALE. UPPERSIDE olive-brown. *Forewing* with paler and rather indistinct discoidal streak and dentate disco-cellular mark ; two transverse discal series of pale black-bordered zigzag lunules, and a submarginal similar lunular line. *Hindwing* with pale narrow subbasal transverse band, with dark outer border, beyond which is a blackish fascia, and then a submarginal row of pale-bordered dark lunules (these lunules being triangular in the female). UNDERSIDE olive-brown ; markings as above, but whiter."

" Allied to *N. vikasi*, but may be distinguished from it by its smaller size, less-distinct markings, and in the submarginal band of the hindwing being formed of distinct lunules." (*Moore*, l. c.)

In the Indian Museum, Calcutta, is a single specimen of this species from the Dunseri Valley, Upper Assam, a male taken in July in Cachar by Mr. Wood-Mason, and one male taken by Capt. C. H. E. Adamson in February in the Meplay Valley and another from Kannee in October, both in Upper Tenasserim, in Major Marshall's collection. They are smaller than typical *N. vikasi*, but differ in other respects only in the two submarginal pale lines on the upperside of the hindwing being lunular, coalescing and enclosing a submarginal band of dark spots.

376. Neptis anjana, Moore.

N. anjana, Moore, Trans. Ent. Soc. Lond., 1881, p. 309.

HABITAT : Moulmein, Meplay Valley.

EXPANSE : 2·5 to 2·7 inches.

DESCRIPTION : " MALE. UPPERSIDE very dark olivaceous-brown. *Forewing* with a slender, but not very prominent, ochreous-brown narrow discoidal streak, a curved discal macular band, a submarginal and a less distinct marginal line. *Hindwing* with a slender transverse subbasal band, a recurved discal band, and narrower but less distinct marginal line. UNDERSIDE dark chestnut-red. *Forewing* with the discoidal streak, transverse outer bands glossy purplish blue, the lower part of the discal band being pale ochreous. *Hindwing* with two medial, two discal bands, a very slender marginal glossy purplish blue and a broad paler basal band. Allied to *N. ananta*." (*Moore*, l. c.)

N. anjana on the upperside is nearest allied to *N. vikasi*, the markings, however, being even more obscure, but is altogether much blacker, and the brown streaks narrower and straighter. On the underside the ground-colour is very different, being dark chestnut-red, in this respect being nearest to *N. ananta*. The markings are distinctly glossed with purplish. There is a single male in the Indian Museum, Calcutta, obtained by Captain C. T. Bingham in the Meplay Valley, Upper Tenasserim, and one from the Donat range taken in January in Major Marshall's collection, also obtained by Captain Bingham. Mr. Moore has noted on the former specimen that it is " darker than type," so like most of the species of *Neptis*, *N. anjana* is subject to variation ; it is, however, one of the most distinct species of the genus.

The second subgroup has the discoidal streak completely divided below the base of the discoidal nervules, leaving a triangular white spot beyond. It contains the typical species of the genus allied to the European forms. The bands are white, pure white in most, but slightly tinted with fuliginous in some. On the underside, there is no trace of violet tinting except in three species (*N. nata* and its allies) in which the bands on both sides are tinted with blue ; the ground-colour is ochreous or ferruginous on the underside, very uniform in the typical species, and the bands and spots are more sharply defined than in the preceding groups.

Key to the Indian species of Neptis.

Second Group—(Continued)

B. The second subcostal nervule of the forewing given off at the outer extremity of the discoidal cell.
   A. Discoidal streak on upperside of forewing completely divided across by a black bar opposite the
       origin of the discoidal nervules ; markings almost always pure white on a black ground.
       a^1. All the markings of the underside with sharply defined edges, ground-colour of uniform
              tint throughout.
          a^2. Discal white band on underside of hindwing distinctly defined with black, ground-
                 colour ochreous.
             a^3. Submarginal band on upperside of both wings very narrow, and usually
                    sullied-white.
                              377. N. ANDAMANA, Andamans.
             b^3. Submarginal band on upperside of both wings prominent, white.
                a^4. Three marginal lines on underside of hindwing prominent.
                              378. N. NICOBARICA, Nicobars.
                b^4. Two outer marginal lines on underside of hindwing obsolescent.
                   a^5. Marginal line on upperside of hindwing obscure fuscous.
                      a^6. Submarginal band on hindwing evenly curved ;
                             white bands and spots on underside broadly
                             margined with black.
                              379. N. VARMONA, India, Ceylon.
                              380. N. DISRUPTA, Ceylon.
                              381. N. ADARA, Burma.
                              382. N. MEETANA, Upper Tenasserim.
                      b^6. Submarginal band on hindwing deflected to-
                             wards anal angle ; white bands and spots on
                             underside narrowly margined with black.
                              383. N. SWINHOEI, Nilgiris, Rajputana, Assam.
                              384. N. KAMARUPA, Calcutta, Assam.
                   b^5. Marginal line on upperside of hindwing prominently
                          white.
                              385. N. EURYMENE, North-Western and Central Pro-
                                    vinces.
          b^2. Discal white band on underside of hindwing distinctly defined, obsoletely mar-
                 gined with black ; the marginal line on upperside obsolete ; ground-colour
                 chocolate.
                              386. N. ASTOLA, India.
                              387. N. EMODES, North India, Yunan.
       b^1. All the markings of underside with edges more or less blurred.
          a^2. Discal white band on upperside narrow.
             a^3. Bands and spots white, tinted with blue.
                a^4. Submarginal band composed of well-separated rounded spots
                       on upperside of hindwing.
                              388. N. KHASIANA, Bhutan, Khasi Hills.
                b^4. Submarginal band composed of almost confluent and more pro-
                       minent linear spots on upperside of hindwing.
                              389. N. MAGADHA, N. India.
                              390. N. NATA, Mergui, Malacca, Singapore, Borneo.
             b^3. Bands and spots white, sometimes sullied with fuliginous.
                a^4. The discoidal streak very narrow.
                   a^5. The submarginal band on upperside light brown.
                              391. N. MANANDA, Andamans, Assam.
                   b^5. The submarginal band clouded with fuliginous.
                              392. N. SOMA, North-East India, Yunan.
                   c^5. The submarginal band pure white.
                              393. N. ADIPALA, Sikkim, Khasi Hills, Upper Tenas-
                                    serim.
                              394. N. CACHARICA, Cachar.
                              395. N. KALAURA, Nilgiris, Travancore.
                b^4. The discoidal streak broad.
                              396. N. SUSRUTA, North-East India, Upper Tenasserim.
       $ᵇ$. Discal white band on upperside broad.
          a^3. Discal spots in median interspaces of forewing close to and in continua-
                 tion of the two spots below.

a⁴. Discoidal streak of forewing not completely separated from spot beyond on underside.
    a⁵. Submarginal band on upperside of both wings prominent, white.
        397. N. NANDINA, India, Java.
    b⁵. Submarginal band on upperside of both wings narrow, brownish-white.
        398. N. CLINIA, Bengal, Siam.
b⁴. Discoidal streak of forewing well separated from spot beyond on both sides.
    399. N. MAHENDRA, N.-W. Himalayas.
b³. Discal spots in median interspaces of forewing well-separated from the two spots below, the spot in the submedian interspace much reduced or wanting.
    a⁴. With a prominent submarginal macular white band on hindwing.
        a⁵. Discoidal streak of forewing on upperside only divided below base of discoidal nervules.
            400. N. OPHIANA, India, Malay Peninsula.
        b⁵. Discoidal streak of forewing on upperside again divided nearer the base forming a short streak with two white spots beyond.
            401. N. MARTABANA, Rangoon, Upper Tenasserim.
    b⁴. With no submarginal white band on hindwing.
        402. N. JUMBAH, India, Ceylon, Burma, Andamans.

377. **Neptis andamana,** Moore.

N. andamana, Moore, Proc. Zool. Soc. Lond., 1877, p. 586.

HABITAT : South Andamans (Port Blair).

EXPANSE : ♂, 1·9 to 2·1 ; ♀, 2·2 to 2·4 inches.

DESCRIPTION : "MALE and FEMALE. UPPERSIDE, black. *Forewing* with a prominent white broad cell-streak and dentate spot beyond, a curved transverse discal series of widely separated spots, and two marginal rows of pale lunules, the outer row most distinct. *Hindwing* with a white subbasal [discal] band, somewhat irregular, bordered and crossed by the veins ; a submarginal row of whitish lunules and a very indistinct pale median and submarginal line. UNDERSIDE dusky ferruginous, markings as above, including a basal and subbasal streak, all very prominent and with black margins." (*Moore,* l. c.)

There are numerous specimens of both sexes of this species in the Indian Museum, Calcutta. It is a local form of *N. varmona,* on the upperside the small marginal spots are nearly obsolete, and the submarginal band on the hindwing is narrow and usually sullied with black scales, giving the outer half a very black appearance. The width of the discal band on the hindwing is variable. On the underside all the white markings are very prominent, including those which are obsolete above, and broadly margined with black. *N. andamana* appears to be confined to the Andaman Isles.

378. **Neptis nicobarica,** Moore.

N. nicobarica, Moore, Proc. Zool. Soc., 1879, p. 586 ; ? *N. matuta,* Felder (*nec* Hübner), Verh. zool.-bot. Gesells. Wien, vol. xii, p. 483, n. 114 (1862).

HABITAT : Nicobars.

EXPANSE : ♂, 1·9 to 2·2 ; ♀, 2·15 to 2·40 inches.

DESCRIPTION : "MALE and FEMALE. Nearest allied to *N. varmona,* markings similar ; also nearly allied to *N. mamaja,* Butler, from Malacca. *Forewing* with the discal series less curved, thus giving a wider marginal space ; the marginal row of lunular spots very prominent. *Hindwing* with outer or discal series of spots smaller and terminating more towards anal angle ; the marginal lunular line distinct. UNDERSIDE also similar, the marginal markings broader." (*Moore,* l. c.)

N. nicobarica is altogether a whiter insect than *N. varmona,* to which species however it is very closely allied. The series of submarginal small white spots on the upperside of the forewing is complete and the spots are prominent, the marginal line on the upperside of the hindwing is distinctly lunular, it is usually quite straight in other species of *Neptis* ; in the male it is obscure, in the female prominent. The white spots and bands are prominently black bordered on the underside, and the hindwing bears three prominent white macular bands on the margin, the inner one lunular, the other two straight.

The Indian Museum, Calcutta, has received specimens of this species from the following islands in the Nicobars :—Kamorta, Takoin, Nankowri, Katchall, Kar Nicobar and Great Nicobar.

A closely-allied species* from the Malay Peninsula has been described by Mr. Butler under the name of *N. mamaja*. Mr. Distant considers it to be, however, a variety of *N. eurynome*, Westwood, from China.

The next four species are, as far as I can see, nothing but different forms of *N. varmona*. *N. disrupta* is clearly a "sport" or casual variety. I have specimens of *N. adara* and *N. varmona* identified by Mr. Moore, and there is no single character sufficiently fixed and definite which I can discover either from the descriptions or from properly authenticated specimens to distinguish between these two. I have no authenticated specimen of *N. mectana*, but there is a large series of the *N. varmona* type in our collections from Upper Tenasserim from whence the *type* specimen of *N. mectana* was obtained, and in these the markings of the underside are less prominently black bordered than in those taken farther north and in India, thereby agreeing with *N. kamarupa* ; but this character is variable in intensity.

The three species which follow are also varieties of the same type. Typical specimens of *N. swinhoei* and *N. kamarupa* from India can be separated by the shape of the submarginal band, but the points of separation are variable, and neither form is confined to a distinct geographical range. Further, although the deflection of the submarginal band of the hindwing at anal angle is prevalent in these three forms it is not constant, and intermediate forms are frequently met with ; further *N. eurynome* in which typically the marginal line is pure white and prominent passes by insensible gradations into the *swinhoei* form, in which the marginal line is well nigh obsolete, and the conclusion to which an examination of large series of all the forms in which the discal band of the underside is distinctly defined with black leads me is that they represent a single species, *N. varmona*, with *N. nicobarica* as a well marked local form, *N. andamana* a less well marked local form, *N. disrupta* a casual aberration, and *N. swinhoei*, *N. kamarupa* and *N. eurynome* as inconstant varieties, while *N. adara* and *N. mectana* are inseparable from the typical form.

379. **Neptis varmona,** Moore.

N. varmona, Moore, Proc. Zool. Soc. Lond., 1872, p. 561; idem, Id., Lep. Cey., p. 54, pl. xxviii, figs. 1, 1a (1881) ;? *N. matuta*, Moore (*nec* Hübner), Proc. Zool. Soc. Lond , 1865, p. 763.

HABITAT: Mountains of South India (Matheran, Nilgiris), Ceylon (*Moore*); Sikkim, Sylhet, Assam, Cachar, Continental India.

EXPANSE : 1·75 to 2·50 inches.

---

* *Neptis mamaja*, Butler, Trans. Linn. Soc., Zoology, second series, vol. i, p. 541, n. 1, pl. lxix, fig. 3 (1877); *N. eurynome*, var. *mamaja*, Distant, Rhop. Malay., p. 156, n. 12, pl. xvi, fig. 14, *female* (1883); *Limenitis eurynome*, Westwood, Donovan's Ins. China, p. 66, pl. xxxv, fig. 4 (1842). HABITAT : (var. *mamaja* only) Province Wellesley, Penang, Malacca. EXPANSE : 2·00 to 2·25 inches. DESCRIPTION ; "Nearly allied to *N. eurynome*, but always to be distinguished by the narrower externo-discal band of white spots on the *hindwing*, colouring on the UNDERSIDE rather brighter than in *N. eurynome*."

"This appears to be the commonest *Neptis* in Malacca." (*Butler*, l. c)

"MALE and FEMALE. UPPERSIDE closely resembling *N. duryodana*, but the pale markings more or less tinged with lemon-colour (very strongly so in the specimen figured), the spot at the end of the cell in the *forewing* smaller, but variable in size, and the narrow pale submarginal linear fascia of the *hindwing* almost obsolete. UNDERSIDE warm ochraceous ; markings resembling those of *N. duryodana*, but more or less tinged with lemon-colour as above, and with the outer pale discal fascia to the *hindwing* more macular than in that species."

"Typical specimens of *N. eurynome*, localised as from N. India (*sic*) and China, which I have examined, appear to be sufficiently distinct from the European *N. aceris*, Lepechin, to have specific differentiation, though I consider the *N mamaja*, Butler, to be better expressed as a variety only of Professor Westwood's species, especially as I have received another very close variety from North Borneo. Even in my Province Wellesley specimens considerable variation is found, such as the basal cellular streak of the *forewing* being either broken, or entire as in the figure given." (*Distant*, l. c.)

DESCRIPTION : " Has much the appearance of the European *N. accris* in the more elongated form of the wings and in the less defined markings of the UPPERSIDE, which, in the male, are more like those of the European species than in *N. astola*. The colour of the UNDERSIDE is duller and more yellow, and the black borders of the markings are still more prominent than in *N. astola*, the veins of the *forewing* being streaked with black in front of the triangular discoidal spot." (*Moore*, l. c. in Proc. Zool. Soc. Lond.)

" MALE and FEMALE. UPPERSIDE black. *Forewing* with a white longitudinal streak within the cell, a lengthened triangular spot beyond it, a discal transverse curved series of seven oval spots, and a submarginal row of small lunate spots; a very indistinct pale waved line between the discal series and another along the outer margin ; the discoidal streak slightly black-speckled near its thickest end. *Hindwing* with a white broad recurved medial transverse band, and a discal linear series of six quadrate spots ; a pale linear indistinct line intervening across the disc, and another along the outer margin. UNDERSIDE ferruginous ; with white markings more prominent than above and all black bordered ; the *hindwing* having a short white streak on base of costa and another below it."

" LARVA pale green, with an oblique lateral pink fascia from top of anal segment ; head armed with two short conical points, third, fifth and anal segments with a dorsal pair of short fleshy setose spines and two longer divergent spines on fourth segment. Feeds on *Leguminosæ*. PUPA short, pale reddish-brown, wing cases dilated laterally, head bluntly cleft. (*Moore*, l. c. in Lep. Cey.)

In Ceylon *N. varmona* is " Widely distributed, occurring in the hills and plains, both in forest and cultivated land all the year. Flight slow, floating, alights on bushes with wings generally if not always open" (*Hutchison*). " Found everywhere, and below 3,000 feet in great abundance nearly all the year" (*Mackwood*).

The Indian Museum, Calcutta, possesses specimens of *N. varmona* named by Mr. Moore from Bombay, the Khandesh District, and two from Ceylon, also one from Sikkim with a query. Even these five examples show considerable variation, in one Ceylon specimen the seventh upper spot of the discal series of the forewing on the upperside is wanting, in the Khandesh specimen the marginal line to the hindwing on the upperside is very prominent and pure white, less so in one Ceylon specimen, and obscure and sordid white in the others. The marginal spots on the forewing on the upperside are inconstant in number, size and distinctness. On the underside of these specimens the shade of the ground-colour is very variable, in some it is bright light ochreous, in others dull umber brown, and there are intermediate forms between these extremes. In some specimens the three upper spots of the discal series in the forewing on the underside are completely joined, forming a continuous white band, in others well separated by the black-edged veins. The prominence of the black edging to the bands and spots is variable, and so is the black streaking between the veins. In fact *N. varmona* is one of the most variable as well as wide-spread species of the genus. In addition to the specimens mentioned above which have been named by Mr. Moore, the Indian Museum, Calcutta, possesses examples from Malda, Calcutta, Cachar, Silsagar, Madras, Bangalore, Calicut, and Trevandrum.

380. Neptis disrupta, Moore.

N. disrupta, Moore, Ann. and Mag. of Nat. Hist., fourth series, vol. xx, p. 339 (1877); idem, id., Lep. Cey., p. 55, pl. xxviii, figs. 4, 4a (1881).

HABITAT : Ceylon.

EXPANSE : ?, 2·12 inches.

DESCRIPTION : " FEMALE. UPPERSIDE black. *Forewing* with whitish discoidal streak and triangular terminal spot ; three spots from middle of hind margin and a fourth smaller spot beyond the triangular discoidal spot [all that is left of the usual curved discal band]; between this series and a submarginal series of somewhat conical spots is a discal series of indistinct pale dusky oblique spots ; a linear marginal row of narrow indistinct dusky streaks. *Hindwing*, with a discal [our submarginal] white maculated band, a quadrate spot on abdominal margin near the base, and two narrow parallel spots and streak on anterior margin [these spots are all that remain of the discal band] ; a linear row of marginal white streaks. UNDERSIDE, dull ferruginous, with black-bordered white markings as above, and black confluent spots across the disc of *both wings*." (*Moore*, l. c. in Ann. and Mag. of Nat. Hist.)

"A very rare species. A single specimen is in the collection of Mr. F. M. Mackwood at Colombo, which was taken at Ambegamoa, in the Central Province." (*Moore*, l. c. in Lep. Cey.)

This supposed distinct species, the type and only known specimen of which I have examined, is almost certainly a melanoid aberration, occasional variety or "sport" of *N. varmona*.

381. Neptis adara, Moore.

N. adara, Moore, Proc. Zool. Soc. Lond., 1878, p. 830.

HABITAT : Upper Tenasserim, Moulmein to Meetan, Ahsown, Naththoung to Paboga, Moolai, 3,000 to 6,000 feet.

EXPANSE : ♂, 2·0 ; ♀, 2·2 inches.

DESCRIPTION : "Allied to *N. varmona* from South India. UPPERSIDE. Differs in the maculated bands being narrower, the discoidal terminal spot broader and less pointed, the discal series of spots more oval in shape, and the submarginal series not so prominent. On the UNDERSIDE, the ground-colour is much brighter, and the markings are less black-bordered." (*Moore*, l. c.)

There is a single male specimen of this species from Rangoon in the collection of the Indian Museum, Calcutta, which has been named *N. adara* by Mr. Moore. In every respect it agrees with some Ceylonese specimens of *N. varmona*, except that the discoidal terminal spot on the upperside of the forewing is slightly broader and more obtuse. It is more than doubtful whether, if the locality labels were removed, the Burmese specimens could be distinguished from South Indian ones of *N. varmona*. In the Indian Museum, Calcutta, there are other examples from Rangoon and also from Upper Tenasserim taken by Limborg with the type specimens. Like *N. varmona* they show variation in details.

382. Neptis meetana, Moore.

N. meetana, Moore, Proc. Zool. Soc. Lond., 1878, p. 830.

HABITAT : Upper Tenasserim ; Meetan, 3,000 feet (March) ; Taoo, 3,500 feet.

EXPANSE : ♂, 2·00 ; ♀, 2·12 inches.

DESCRIPTION : "Allied to *N. adara*, but with the markings on the UPPERSIDE more like those in *N. andamana*. It is a somewhat narrower-winged insect, the spots of the discal band relatively narrower in both sexes, the UNDERSIDE of a brighter red, and the markings less black-bordered." (*Moore*, l. c.)

This species is quite unknown to me. From the description it would appear to be nearer to *N. andamana* than to *N. adara*, as it is said to be more like the former than the latter species on the upperside. On the underside the differences between these two species are very inconspicuous. *N. andamana* on the upperside is easily distinguished by the submarginal macular bands on both wings being nearly obsolete.

The next three species differ typically from the four species which precede them in having the white bands and spots of the underside slenderly defined with black, and the ground-colour of a lighter, more ochreous tint. It appears to me by no means improbable that they are all the dry-season form of *N. varmona*.

383. Neptis swinhoei, Butler.

N. swinhoei, Butler, Proc. Zool. Soc. Lond., 1883, p. 145, n. 4, pl. xxiv, fig. 9 ; idem, id., Ann. and Mag. of Nat. Hist., 6th series, vol. xvi, p. 305, n. 42 (1885).

HABITAT : Mount Abu, Nilgiris, Assam.

EXPANSE : 1·8 inches.

DESCRIPTION : "Only differs on the UPPERSIDE from *N. aceris* in the narrower black border beyond the white discal series of spots on the *hindwing* ; it differs from *N. eurymene*

13

in this character, and in the reduction of the subapical series of white spots on the *forewing* to three, also in the absence of the submarginal white line on the *hindwing*. UNDERSIDE yellower even than *N. eurymene*, the white cuneiform spot beyond the cell of the *forewing* shorter, the white band of the *hindwing* broader and straighter, and the yellow belt following it also broader, straighter, and less tapering ; from *N. aceris* the yellow colouration on the UNDERSIDE at once distinguishes it" [the latter being red-brown]. (*Butler*, l. c.)

N. swinhoei evidently has a wide range. It is very near indeed to *N. eurymene*, but as described and figured it may at once be known from that species by having only three marginal white spots on the upperside of the forewing and no marginal white line on the hindwing. I have no authenticated specimens, and not one which answers exactly to the original description and figure, but I have numerous specimens that evidently belong to the form described ; both the above given characters are variable.

384. Neptis kamarupa, Moore.

N. kamarupa, Moore, Proc. Zool. Soc. Lond., 1874, p. 570.

HABITAT : Continental India, Assam, Burma.

EXPANSE : ♂, 2·12 ; ♀, 2·25 inches.

DESCRIPTION : " MALE and FEMALE. UPPERSIDE fuliginous black ; markings white, broad, prominent. *Forewing* with the discal series of spots at very oblique angles, the first spot of the lower portion small ; a prominent marginal linear series of white quadrate spots. *Hindwing* with the subbasal band evenly margined ; outer band broad and composed of quadrate spots ; a prominent narrow white marginal line. UNDERSIDE ferruginous yellow ; markings as above ; very slightly black-bordered."

"Nearest allied to *N. varmona*, but may be distinguished from it on the underside by the delicate narrow black bordering of the bands and the absence of the black streaks on the veins of the forewing." (*Moore*, l. c.)

There are numerous specimens of *N. kamarupa* from Calcutta so named by Mr. Moore in the Indian Museum, Calcutta, only one of which has a prominent narrow white marginal line on the hindwing ; also one from Shillong which possesses this character, and another from the Dafla Hills which has the line, but it is not prominent. The narrow black edging to the white bands and spots of the underside will suffice however to distinguish typical specimens from *N. varmona* ; the ground-colour is also usually lighter and brighter. It is the commonest species of *Neptis* in Calcutta, and the Indian Museum, Calcutta, possesses specimens from Sikkim, Bhutan, Malda, Cachar, Shillong, Assam, Chittagong, Orissa, Mysore, and Oota-camund. In Major Marshall's collection are numerous examples from Akyab, Tavoy and Upper Tenasserim. These latter agree with the description of *N. mectana* on the underside, but are not the least like *N. andamana* on the upperside, and in fact agree exactly with the description of *N. kamarupa.*

385. Neptis ourymene, Butler.

N. eurymene, Butler, Proc. Zool. Soc. Lond., 1883, p. 145, n. 3, pl. xxiv, fig. 5.

HABITAT : Mhow, Central India ; Mirzapore district, N.-W. Provinces.

EXPANSE : 2 inches.

DESCRIPTION : "Nearly allied to *N. eurynome*, Westwood, but smaller, with the costal and outer margins of the *forewing* straighter. UPPERSIDE blacker, with purer white markings ; spots on the disc smaller ; *hindwing* with an ill-defined whitish streak in the medial black belt and a slender white submarginal line. UNDERSIDE of a purer ochre-yellow colour ; the white markings, excepting the discoidal streak of the *forewing*, narrower." (*Butler*, l. c.)

" Common here [Mhow] in February ; have one also from Paras Pani, Mirzapore district, N.-W. Provinces, taken in the same month." (*Note by Colonel Swinhoe*, l. c.)

This species is very close indeed to *N. kamarupa*, if in fact the latter species is typically held to have a prominent narrow white marginal line on the upperside of the hindwing, I do not know how to separate them. All the markings of the upperside of *N. eurymene* are very pure white and distinct, the ground-colour of the underside pure light ochre-yellow.

There are two specimens of this species from Akrain in the Satpuras in my collection ; the specimen also from the Khandesh district, named *N. varmona* by Mr. Moore, and referred to under that species, seems to be nearer to *N. eurynome*. Major Marshall's collection contains specimens from Mhow, from the South Concan and from Khandalla.

The two next species are quite distinct from either those that precede or those that follow them. The wings are short and broad, colouration of underside chocolate, discoidal streak of forewing broad and well-separated from the spot beyond ; bands and spots of underside obscurely defined with black.

386. Neptis astola, Moore.

N. astola, Moore, Proc. Zool. Soc. Lond., 1872, p. 560; id., Butler, id., 1883, p. 246, n. 5; idem, id., Ann. and Mag. of Nat. Hist., fifth series, vol. xvi, p. 305, n. 41 (1885); id., Swinhoe, Proc. Zool. Soc. Lond., 1885, p. 129, n. 37.

HABITAT : Kangra, Simla, Masuri (*Moore*) ; Belgaum, Assam (*Butler*) ; Bombay (*Swinhoe*).

EXPANSE : ♂, 1·62 ; ♀, 1·87 inches (*Moore*) ; 2·2 inches (*Butler*).

DESCRIPTION : "Allied to, but differs from, *N. aceris* of Europe in having the wings shorter and broader, the markings on the UPPERSIDE more prominent, and those on the UNDERSIDE more clearly defined by a black border, by which they are all margined." (*Moore*, l. c.)

"Allied to *N. varmona*, but the submarginal series of white spots on the *forewing* five in number towards apex ; the white subbasal band of the *hindwing* straighter and of more even width throughout ; the interrupted submarginal pale line whitish towards anal angle, but sometimes wanting. UNDERSIDE red-brown, redder than in *N. varmona* ; the white subbasal band of the *hindwing* not distinctly black-edged, the reddish belt following it even and tapering towards the apex ; the macular discal band a little narrower and not distinctly black-bordered ; the interrupted white submarginal stripes wider." (*Butler*, l. c.)

In the Indian Museum, Calcutta, there are named specimens by Mr. Moore of *N. astola* from the Kulu Valley and Simla. It is easily distinguished from *N. kamarupa* by the ground-colour being chocolate-red rather than ochreous. Mr. Butler says that the marginal spots are reduced to five in number towards the apex on the upperside of the forewing ; there appear to be always, however, in Western Himalayan specimens two additional spots towards the outer angle. It is the common *Neptis* of Simla and surrounding hills, and in old lists and collections stood as *N. aceris*. In Colonel Lang's collection there is a single specimen from Umballa. He writes of it[*] under the name of *N. aceris* as follows :—"Common in woods and gardens in the Himalayas ; also taken in winter in gardens at Umballa. It has a beautiful flight, floating in and out of the sunlight in the shade of trees ; occasionally basking on the sun-bathed foliage, or resting, in groups of half-a-dozen or more, on the moist fern-covered rocks in the midst of the stream in some Himalayan glen." Colonel Swinhoe (l. c.) records *N. astola* from "Matheran, May ; Sattara, November ; Poona and Bombay from September to December. Found in hilly districts." Its occurrence in Bombay is singular, and I have never seen a specimen from that Presidency.[†]

387. Neptis emodes, Moore.

N. emodes, Moore, Proc. Zool. Soc. Lond., 1872, p. 561, pl. xxxii, fig. 2; idem, id., in Anderson's Anat. and Zool. Researches, p. 924 (1878).

HABITAT : N.-W. and S.-E. Himalayas (Nepal, Sikkim, Khasia Hills), Yunan.

EXPANSE : ♂, 2·00 ; ♀, 2·37 inches.

DESCRIPTION : "MALE and FEMALE. UPPERSIDE blackish fuliginous ; markings disposed as in *N. astola*, but smaller, narrower, and of a brownish-white colour. UNDERSIDE bright dark ferruginous-red ; markings very prominent and black-bordered." (*Moore*, l. c.)

In the Indian Museum, Calcutta, there is one Kulu valley, two Sikkim, and one Shillong example of *N. emodes* named by Mr. Moore. Judging from these specimens and the description

---

[*] Ent. Month. Mag. vol. i. p. 132 (1864-65).

[†] A specimen sent by Colonel Swinhoe as *N. astola* since this was written turns out to be *N. varmona* ; and I have now little doubt that the records of the occurrence of *N. astola* in South India are based on a misapprehension.

above *N. emodes* can only be distinguished from *N. astola* by the markings being smaller (this however does not hold good even in the specimens Mr. Moore has named), and sullied instead of pure white (this character is also variable). Under these circumstances it appears to me that the latter of these names should be sunk as a synonym, as there is apparently no character by which they can be separated.

The next three species are distinguished by having the white bands tinted with bluish on both upper and undersides ; the markings are as in *N. astola*, the bands being rather narrow.

388. Neptis khasiana, Moore.

N. khasiana, Moore, Proc. Zool. Soc. Lond., 1872, p. 560, pl. xxxii, fig. 7.

HABITAT : Bhutan, Khasia Hills.

EXPANSE : 2·25 inches.

DESCRIPTION : " MALE. UPPERSIDE dark fuliginous black. *Forewing* with an elongated bluish-white narrow discoidal streak, and small terminal contiguous spot, two oblique subapical spots, and a row of four spots to middle of hind margin ; an indistinct submarginal row of very small spots, each side of which has a pale wavy line. *Hindwing* with a narrow subbasal bluish-white band, and a submarginal row of five small spots. *Cilia* alternated with white. UNDERSIDE dark brown ; markings as above, but more prominently bluish-white. *Hindwing* with a white band along base of anterior margin, and a pale median and marginal lunular line." (*Moore*, l. c.) The two latter lines are faintly visible on the upperside.

This very distinct species has all the markings extremely small, smaller than in any other species known to me, and distinctly tinged with bluish. The shade of the ground-colour on the underside is unusual, being a dead hair brown. There are two specimens in the Indian Museum, Calcutta, obtained from Buxa, Bhutan.

389. Neptis magadha, Felder.

N. magadha, Felder, Reise Novara, Lep., vol. iii, p. 427, n. 675 (1867).

HABITAT : North India.

EXPANSE : Not given.

DESCRIPTION : " FEMALE. UPPERSIDE as in *N. nata*, but the *forewing* with all the white spots smaller, especially the two near the internal margin, the lowest subapical spot more separated from the two upper ones, the innermost submarginal streak less wavy. *Hindwing* with the bands narrower, the outer one more macular, the streaks more obsolete than in *N. nata*. UNDERSIDE more ferruginous than *N. nata*, with the spots and bands of the upperside but larger, opalescent, the streaks opalescent-white. *Hindwing* from the costal lobe to the costal nervure white, the greyish subcostal fasciole absent."

" Smaller, and the wings shorter, than *N. nata*, Moore." (*Felder*, l. c.)

A comparison of the types of *N. khasiana* and *N. magadha* will probably show that these two species are identical.

390. Neptis nata, Moore.

N. nata, Moore, Horsfield and Moore, Cat. Lep. Mus. E. I. C., vol. i, p. 168, n. 346, pl. iva, fig. 6 (1857); idem, id., Proc. Zool. Soc. Lond., 1858, p. 10, n. 22 ; id., Distant, Rhop. Malay., p. 154, n. 7, pl. xviii, fig. 1 (1883).

HABITAT : Mergui, Malacca, Singapore, Borneo.

EXPANSE : 2·2 to 2·3 inches.

DESCRIPTION : " SEXES alike. UPPERSIDE deep black, markings very white. *Forewing* with discoidal streak long, in two portions ; curved series of spots small. *Hindwing*, with the bands narrow. UNDERSIDE dusky-brown, inner band of *hindwing* not extending to anterior margin ; a marginal line *only* between outer band and exterior margin, the submarginal line being obsolete." (*Moore*, l. c. in Cat. Lep. Mus. E. I. C.)

This species may be known from *N. khasiana* by the bands and spots being larger, especially the submarginal ones on the hindwing, which in *N. nata* are almost confluent and linear, being divided only by the nervules ; they are also but very slightly tinged with bluish. On the underside the discal band of the hindwing in this species and in *N. khasiana* does not reach the costa, ending in the subcostal interspace. There is a single male and two females of this species in the Indian Museum, Calcutta, taken in the Mergui archipelago by Dr. Anderson in the cold weather, one of which has been identified by Mr. Moore.

Four apparently allied species of this group have been described from the Malay peninsula. One of them (*N. gononata*) Mr. Distant says "is an undoubted local race" of *N. soma*, from the figure, however, it appears to be nearer to *N. nata*, but without specimens it is impossible to say for certain. The descriptions are appended.*

The five species which follow have the discoidal streak of the forewing on the upperside very narrow and well-separated from the spot beyond ; the discal series of spots on the forewing are well-separated, and on the underside all the bands and markings are very white and distinct but their edges blurred, owing to the absence of any black bordering. The ground-colour of the underside is ferruginous, not ochreous as in the *tarmona* group.

391. Neptis mananda, Moore.

N. mananda, Moore, Proc. Zool. Soc. Lond., 1877, p. 586, pl. lviii, fig. 4, *female* ; id , Butler, Ann. and Mag. of Nat. Hist., fifth series, vol. xvi, p. 305, n. 40 (1885).

HABITAT : South Andamans (Port Blair), Car Nicobar ; Assam.

EXPANSE : ♂, 1·85 to 2·30 ; ♀, 2·25 to 2·60 inches.

DESCRIPTION : "MALE and FEMALE. UPPERSIDE, black. *Forewing*, with narrow dusky-white cell-streak and elongated pointed streak beyond ; a discal curved transverse series of small white spots and two marginal rows of indistinct pale lunules. *Hindwing*, with broad white subbasal band, an indistinct pale brown submarginal narrow line, and a less distinct

---

* *Neptis leuconota*, Butler, Trans. Linn. Soc., Zoology, second series, vol. i, p. 541, n. 2, pl. lxix, fig. 1 (1877) ; id., Distant, Rhop. Malay., p. 154, n. 8, pl. xvii, fig. 14 (1883). HABITAT : Malacca. EXPANSE : 2 inches. DESCRIPTION : " UPPERSIDE olive-brown, banded and spotted with cream-colour ; arrangement of markings as in *N. nata*, but the bands of the *hindwing* wider and nearer together ; pale brown intermediate streaks better defined. UNDERSIDE slightly redder ; bands and spots as above ; intermediate streaks white." (*Butler*, l. c.)

Neptis gononata, Butler, Trans. Linn. Soc., Zoology, second series vol. i, p. 547, n. 3, pl. lxix, fig. 2 (1877) ; id., Distant, Rhop. Malay., p. 151, n. 9, pl. xviii, fig. 2, *male* (1883). HABITAT : Singapore. EXPANSE : 2·1 inches. DESCRIPTION : " Wings of the same shape and with the same spots and bands as *N. soma* ; but all these markings pure white instead of scmid yellowish white. UNDERSIDE chocolate-brown ; bands below straighter ; submarginal line of *hindwing* below white. Intermediate in character between *N. nata* and *N. soma*." (*Butler*, l. c.)

Neptis duryodana, var., Distant, Rhop. Malay., p. 155, n. 10, pl. xvi, fig. 15, *female* (1883) ; *N. duryodana*, Moore, Proc. Zool. Soc. Lond., 1858, p. 10, n. 21, pl. xlix, fig. 6. HABITAT : Province Wellesley, Malacca, Borneo. EXPANSE : *female*, 2·2 inches. DESCRIPTION " FEMALE. UPPERSIDE dark fuscous. *Forewing* with the following white spots and markings :—a long basal cellular streak gradually widening and terminating about apex of cell ; this is followed by a long subtriangular spot placed between the lower discoidal and the third median nervules ; two large subapical spots placed obliquely, divided by the upper discoidal nervule and preceded by two very small subcostal spots ; two rounded discal spots divided by the second median nervule ; two smaller spots on inner margin divided by the submedian nervure, and a submarginal series of small spots directed obliquely inward at apex, which are outwardly and inwardly margined with black ; cilia alternately white. *Hindwing* with the following white markings :—a nearly straight transverse fascia near base and a series of small subquadrate spots on outer third of wing, which are divided by the nervules, with the innermost obliquely deflexed towards anal angle ; between these transverse white markings is a very narrow pale fascia, and there is also a narrower and greyish submarginal one, cilia alternately white. UNDERSIDE much paler and more or less olivaceous ; white markings as above, but larger ; on the *forewing* the submarginal series of spots are preceded and followed by grey hues, the inner one very strongly waved ; the *hindwing* has the basal costal margin white, an additional subbasal narrow whitish fascia, the narrow discal intermediate fascia much paler and the submarginal one nearly white. *Body* above fuscous, beneath greyish ; *legs* greyish, the intermediate and posterior tibiæ and tarsi brownish."

" I have compared the female specimen here figured and described with the Bornean type in the British Museum, and find the following slight varietal differences :—on the underside of the forewing the cellular streak is not so strongly divided from the adjacent and following spot ; the broad white fascia on the hindwing reaches the costal margin, (in another Malaccan specimen in the British Museum this fascia does not extend to the costal margin, thus agreeing with the typical form of the species), and the colour beneath is also darker, but this is an inconstant character." (*Distant*, l. c.)

Neptis charon, Butler, Ann. and Mag. of Nat. Hist., third series, vol. xx, p. 400, pl. ix, fig. 1 (1867) ; id., Distant, Rhop. Malay., p. 155, n. 11, with a woodcut (1883). HABITAT : Singapore. EXPANSE : 2·50 inches. DESCRIPTION : " UPPERSIDE very black. *Forewing* with a triangular discoidal streak, a contiguous cuneate spot, three unequal subapical spots, three subanal placed obliquely and eight submarginal dots, snowy-white ; eight marginal dots and a very indistinct irregular discal stria somewhat ashy. *Hindwing* with a subbasal band and another discal one of seven spots snowy-white ; a macular submarginal stria somewhat ashy, an indistinct fuscescent median band ; *body* black, greenish ; *antennæ* black, tipped with yellow. UNDERSIDE paler, the discal streaks of the forewing and the median of the hindwing tinged with violet, the submarginal streak hoary-whitish, the marginal streak ashy ; the costal base of the hindwing snowy-white : otherwise as on upperside ; *body* bluish-white ; the *legs* ochreous, the *antennæ* ferruginous."

" Near to *N. duryodana* of Moore, but quite distinct." (*Butler*, l. c.)

medial and marginal line. UNDERSIDE, dark chestnut-brown, markings as above, prominent, and purplish-white, including a narrow basal and sub-basal streak on *hindwing.*" (*Moore*, l. c.)

This species is very closely allied to *N. soma*, and appears to differ chiefly in the discal band of the hindwing being somewhat broader in both sexes. Mr Butler records it from "Near Assam," this is the only record of its occurrence on the Continent, but the appearance of a *N. soma* with the discal band of the hindwing a little wider than usual need cause no surprise.

392. **Neptis soma**, Moore. (PLATE XXIII, FIG. 108 ♂).

N. soma, Moore, Proc. Zool. Soc. Lond., 1858, p. 9, n. 17, pl. xlix, fig. 6 ; idem, id., in Anderson's Anat. and Zool. Researches, p. 924 (1876).

HABITAT : Sikkim, Bhutan, Cachar, Sylhet, Naga Hills, Assam, Yunan.

EXPANSE : 2·10 to 2·65 inches.

DESCRIPTION : "*Sexes* alike. Allied to *N. nandina*, but differs on the UNDERSIDE in having the discoidal streak narrower, and the seven spots of the curved row are much smaller, being only half the size, and are wider apart ; the submarginal row of spots is also smaller ; the bands on the *hindwing* are also narrower. UNDERSIDE, deep maroon, the markings as on upperside, but those on the hindwing less straight." (*Moore*, l. c.)

All the markings in this species are very small and narrow and more or less sullied, not clear pure white, the submarginal series of small white spots on the upperside of the forewing complete. On the underside the markings are pure white and of nearly equal width throughout. It appears to be a constant and well-marked species. In the Indian Museum, Calcutta, there are specimens from Buxa, Bhutan, Sikkim, Cachar, Sylhet and Assam.

The figure is taken from a male Cachar specimen in the Indian Museum, Calcutta, and shows both upper and undersides. The markings in the figure have come out too white, and the discoidal streak is drawn rather too wide, so that it is not a good representation of typical *N. soma.*

393. **Neptis adipala**, Moore.

N. adipala, Moore, Proc. Zool. Soc. Lond., 1872, p. 563, pl. xxxii, fig. 8 ; idem, id., 1876, p. 830.

HABITAT : Sikkim, Khasi Hills, Naga Hills and Upper Tenasserim.

EXPANSE : 2·0 to 2·6 inches.

DESCRIPTION : "MALE. UPPERSIDE fuliginous-black ; markings white. *Forewing* with a narrow discoidal and elongated triangular contiguous streak ; spots of curved discal band small ; a submarginal row of black-bordered lunules. *Hindwing* with moderately broad inner band, and outer band of narrow quadrate spots. UNDERSIDE deep bright ferruginous. *Forewing* markings as above. *Hindwing* with the bands and two basal streaks similar to those of *N. nandina*, except that the narrow outer line is in this nearer the margin." (*Moore*, l. c.)

In the Indian Museum, Calcutta, is a single male specimen from Sikkim of *N. adipala* named by Mr. Moore. On the upperside all the markings are very clear and pure white, on the underside the ground-colour is rich ferruginous. The Museum possess specimens also from the Naga and Khasi Hills. Mr. Moore records it from Moulmein to Meetan and Hatsiega in Upper Tenasserim. Mr. S. E. Peal has sent me a single male from Sibsagor in Upper Assam, and Mr. J. L. Sherwill from Jorehát.

394. **Neptis cacharica**, Butler.

N. cacharica, Butler, Trans. Ent. Soc. Lond., 1879, p. 3.

HABITAT : Cachar.

EXPANSE : 2·25 inches.

DESCRIPTION : "FEMALE. Allied to *N. adipala*, but of a more rufous-brown colour, the three oblique spots beyond the cell more elongated or less widely separated, the oblique series below the cell, near external angle, also more elongated, the first two being only separated by the internal vein ; the oblique white dashes beyond these spots replaced by a regular lunulated pale brown stripe ; the submarginal lunules more regular, with black internal borders ; the inner belt of *hindwing* wider and more incurved towards the costa ; the outer belt farther from the outer margin, consisting of seven instead of six spots ; the pale brown submarginal stripe narrower and farther from the margin. UNDERSIDE golden-brown, with white bands, stripes and spots as above, excepting that the lunular submarginal series of forewing and the discal macular belt of hindwing are wider, with their divisions less distinctly separated ; two whitish stripes close to the outer margin, interrupted upon the forewing by a patch of the ground-colour upon the second median interspace, the outer one diffused and interrupted a second time at apex, the inner stripe of forewing interrupted by the veins ; the undulated pale brown lunulated stripe of the upperside replaced by a whitish stripe ; base of costa orange. *Hindwing* with the base, a subcostal streak near the base, and a nearly straight stripe through the second brown belt (beyond the broad white belt), whitish. *Body* below white. *Tibiæ* and *tarsi* of second and third pairs of legs testaceous."

"A well-marked form of this puzzling group, quite distinct from any named species in Mr. Moore's collection or that of the British Museum." (*Butler*, l. c.)

I have never seen this species, nor did Mr. Wood-Mason obtain it during the summer months he collected in Cachar.

395. **Neptis kallaura**, Moore.

N. kallaura, Moore, Trans. Ent. Soc. Lond., 1881, p. 309.

HABITAT : Nilgiris ; Kallaur Road, Travancore, 1,200 feet, April ; Mynall, 2,000 feet.

EXPANSE : ♂, 2·1 ; ♀, 2·35 inches.

DESCRIPTION : "Allied to *N. adipala*. Markings of UPPERSIDE pale yellow ; *forewing* with the discoidal streak and its terminal pointed spot more rounded at the edges where divided by the disco-cellular vein ; discal series of spots smaller and more oval ; *hindwing* with comparatively narrower inner band and broader outer band." (*Moore*, l. c.)

There is a single female specimen of this species named by Mr. Moore from Trevandrum in the Indian Museum, Calcutta. It is very close indeed to *N. adipala*, even if it can be considered specifically distinct. The markings are slightly tinged with palest yellow, the other characters given seem trifling. Mr. W. F. Hampson has sent me three specimens taken in the Nilgiris, they have the bands very irregular in width.

The next species differs from the preceding group by having the discoidal streak broad. On the underside the bands of the hindwing are very faintly defined outwardly with black. The bands of the upperside are sometimes sullied with fuliginous, sometimes pure white.

396. **Neptis susruta**, Moore.

N. susruta, Moore, Proc. Zool. Soc. Lond., 1872. p. 563, pl. xxxii, fig. 4.

HABITAT : Sikkim, Dhutan, Cachar, Sylhet, Assam, Khasi Hills, Chittagong, Upper Tenasserim.

EXPANSE : 2·0 to 2·4 inches.

DESCRIPTION : "MALE. UPPERSIDE brownish black. *Forewing* with ferruginous [? fuliginous] white narrow discoidal and attenuated contiguous streak ; curved discal band of small and widely separated spots, an ill-defined black-bordered submarginal lunular line. *Hindwing* with white inner band, and ferruginous [? fuliginous] white outer narrow lunular curved band. UNDERSIDE deep ferruginous : markings prominent, and suffused with pale ferruginous [? fuliginous] ; those of the hindwing similar to *N. soma*, but narrower." (*Moore*, l. c.)

There are four specimens named by Mr. Moore of this species from Sikkim, Assam and Upper Tenasserim in the Indian Museum, Calcutta. As a rule they average smaller than *N. soma*, all the markings are wider and more prominent, especially the discoidal streak in the forewing ; in many specimens they are tinged with greenish-yellow as in *N. nandina*.

The next two species have the bands and spots of the upperside very wide and prominent, in this respect allying them to *N. amba*, from which species, however, they differ in many important particulars.

397. Neptis nandina, Moore.

N. nandina, Moore, Horsfield and Moore, Cat. Lep. Mus. E. I. C., vol. i, p. 168, n. 347, pl. iva, fig. 7 (1857) ; idem, id., Proc. Zool. Soc. Lond., 1858, p. 9, n. 18.

HABITAT : Himalayas, Eastern and Southern India, Java.

EXPANSE : 2·25 to 2·70 inches.

DESCRIPTION : " UPPERSIDE black ; markings white. *Forewing* with discoidal streak in two portions ; the curved row of seven spots broadly interrupted ; and submarginal row of small less-defined spots. *Hindwing* with inner band, and narrow outer row of less-defined square spots ; indistinct marginal line, and line between the bands, brown. UNDERSIDE deep chocolate-brown, with markings as above, but more defined and of a brighter colour ; those of the hindwing gently curved. *Sexes* alike."

" This species may be known from *Neptis aceris* by the deep chocolate colour of the underside, by the anterior margin of hindwing being evenly arched to beyond the middle ; all the markings of this wing being nicely curved." (*Moore*, l. c. in Cat. Lep. Mus. E. I. C.)

This is a distinct and well-marked species. The white bands and spots are often tinged with pale greenish-yellow. On the underside the discal band of the hindwing suddenly widens out at the costa, a feature peculiar to this and the next species. From *N. mahendra* it may be known by the discoidal streak and the spot beyond being placed much closer together ; the ground-colour of the underside is also of a richer chocolate-brown in *N. mahendra*. In the Indian Museum, Calcutta, there are specimens of *N. nandina* from the Kulu Valley, Simla, Sikkim, Calcutta, Cherrapunji, Upper Burma, and Ootacamund. Major Marshall has specimens from Chini taken in June, Chumba in March, and from Shillong.

398. Neptis clinia, Moore.

N. clinia, Moore, Proc. Zool. Soc. Lond., 1872, p. 563, pl. xxxii, fig. 5 ; id., Druce, Proc. Zool. Soc. Lond., 1874, p. 105.

HABITAT : Bengal (*Moore*) ; Chentaboon and Nahconchaisee, Siam (September).

EXPANSE : 2 inches.

DESCRIPTION : " MALE. UPPERSIDE black ; markings white. *Forewing* with a rather broad discoidal and short contiguous streak ; curved discal band of broad closely united spots ; marginal black-bordered lunular line indistinct. *Hindwing* with a very broad straight inner band and narrow brownish-white outer lunular line. UNDERSIDE bright ferruginous, markings as in *N. soma*, but very prominent." (*Moore*, l. c)

I have never seen this species, and the locality given by Mr. Moore is very vague ; as, however, Mr. Druce records it from Siam, the species may be confined to that region, and may not occur within our limits at all. From the figure it seems to be allied to *N. mahendra*, but is smaller, the spot beyond the discoidal streak of the forewing much longer and narrower, and the marginal white spots obsolete and replaced by brownish marks. On the hindwing the discal band is as wide as in *N. mahendra*, but the submarginal band of white spots is entirely wanting, there being a pale brownish narrow band in its place.

399. Neptis mahendra, Moore.

N. mahendra, Moore, Proc. Zool. Soc. Lond., 1872, p. 560, pl. xxxii, fig. 3.

HABITAT : N.-W. Himalayas.

EXPANSE : ♂, 2·0 ; ♀, 2·5 inches.

DESCRIPTION : " MALE and FEMALE. UPPERSIDE black ; wings elongated, as in the European *N. aceris* ; markings white, and disposed as in that species, but more prominent and broader than in any other known allied species of this group, being broader even than in *N. nandina*. UNDERSIDE deep brownish ferruginous ; markings white, broad, their borders imperceptibly black-margined, not prominently so as in *N. astola* or *N. varmona* : middle band of *hindwing* narrowing to abdominal margin." (*Moore*, l. c.)

This also is a very distinct species, occurring only in the N.-W. Himalayas. The discal band of the hindwing on the underside is widened out at the costa. All the white markings are very prominent, especially the discal band of quadrate spots on the hindwing. I took this species at Kujiah near Dalhousie, and at Ulwas, Chumba, in May; Mr. A. Graham Young obtained it in the Kulu Valley in April and May; it occurs also in Simla, Kasauli and Masuri. Major Marshall possesses specimens from Kashmir, 8,200 feet, taken in June; Chumba in May and June; Pangi, 8,000 feet. in July; and Chini in June.

The three last species are very distinct, and differ from all the others in having the discal spots of the forewing arranged in pairs, each pair of spots being well-separated from the pair or pairs next it. The discoidal streak is narrow and short, the spot beyond far distant from the outer end of the discoidal streak, very broad and short. The white markings in *N. jumbah* are usually and in *N. ophiana* occasionally tinged with very pale green.

400. **Neptis ophiana**, Moore.

N. ophiana, Moore, Proc. Zool. Soc. Lond., 1872, p. 561; id., Distant, Rhop. Malay., p. 153, n. 6, pl. xvii, fig. 12 (1883); *N. columella* (part), Moore (*nec* Cramer), Proc. Zool. Soc. Lond., 1858, p. 7, n. 13, pl. xlix, fig. 5, *male* and *female*; idem, id., 1865, p. 763; id., Butler, Trans. Linn. Soc. Lond., Zoology, second series, vol. i, p. 542, n. 6 (1877).

HABITAT : Eastern and Southern India, Burma, Malay Peninsula.

EXPANSE : 2·5 to 3·0 inches.

DESCRIPTION : "MALE. UPPERSIDE dark fuliginous black, markings white. *Forewing* with very narrow terminally-indented discoidal streak, and large broad triangular spot beyond; a curved discal transverse series of five [or six] spots, the two upper obliquely before the apex, the next pair on the middle of the disc, the lower one of which points to the angle of the wing, the fifth elongated and extending along posterior margin [sometimes with a smaller one above it]; a submarginal interrupted row of whitish lunules with black borders. *Hindwing* with broad inner band ; and a less prominent submarginal series of six rather quadrate spots. UNDERSIDE brownish-ferruginous, markings as above, white, prominent. *Forewing* with three marginal series of lunules. *Hindwing* with bluish-white basal streak, subbasal fascia, a narrow transverse median discal and a marginal lunular bluish-white line ; median band terminating on third [? second] subcostal vein. Allied to *N. columella*, Cramer." (*Moore*, l. c.)

Mr. Distant remarks that "Malaccan specimens agree thoroughly with the type of the species [*N. ophiana*], save that the discal spots are somewhat larger, and the basal streak is entire, though in other specimens from the same locality it is abbreviated and somewhat cleft. It appears to be sufficiently distinct, however, from *N. columella*, which was described by Cramer as from China, and as figured is a much larger insect [3·4 inches in expanse], with a *concave* spot on the inner margin of the forewing."

"In two specimens now before me, viz., the 'type' from Darjeeling and a Malaccan example, the neuration of the hindwing is aberrant, the costal nervure being placed low down and reaching the apex, whilst the subcostal nervules are thus forced close together." (*Distant*, l. c.) On examination of the long series of specimens of this species in the Indian Museum, Calcutta, I find this latter feature very inconstant, in all the female examples and also the males from South India, the costal nervure of the hindwing does not nearly reach the apex of the wing, the subcostal nervules being therefore well-separated, while in males from Sikkim, Calcutta, Cachar, North Khasi Hills and the Meplay Valley, it reaches the margin at or even below the apex, the subcostals being consequently placed very close together.

There is a single male from the North Khasi Hills in the Indian Museum, Calcutta, named *N. columella* by Mr. Moore. As its expanse is half an inch less than that of Cramer's figure, and as the spot on the upperside of the forewing in the submedian interspace is not curved, I prefer to consider it to be one of the numerous forms of *N. ophiana*. The ground-colour of the underside of this specimen is distinctly bright ochreous (as in Cramer's figure), but this character is extremely variable, in Sikkim and South Indian examples it is dark brownish-ferruginous. In female examples from Orissa, Rutnagherry, Bangalore and Ootacamund the discal white band of the hindwing on the underside reaches to the interspace below the costal nervure, in male examples from Ootacamund only to the interspace below that, while in many North Indian specimens it does not extend beyond the interspace below that again;

14

and in all South Indian examples the markings on the underside, especially of the hindwing, are longer and more prominent. *N. ophiana* is a well-marked species, its only near ally in India being *N. martabana*.

401. Neptis martabana, Moore.

N. martabana, Moore, Trans. Ent. Soc. Lond., 1881, p. 310.

HABITAT : Rangoon, Upper Tenasserim.

EXPANSE : 2·3 inches.

DESCRIPTION : "MALE. Intermediate between *N. columella* and *N. ophiana*. From the former it is one-fourth smaller in size. From the Darjiling type of *N. ophiana* it differs on the *forewing* in having the discoidal streak more distinctly broken near the end, and in there being a wider space between its end and the large conical spot beyond. On the *hindwing* the subbasal transverse band is somewhat broader, and the submarginal spots smaller, more rounded, and less prominent. UNDERSIDE of a much darker chestnut purplish-brown, the markings showing out much more strongly." (*Moore*, l. c.)

There is a single male of this species in the Indian Museum, Calcutta, taken in the Thoungyeen forests in the autumn, and named by Mr. Moore. It is smaller than the average specimens of *N. ophiana*, the discoidal streak of the forewing is more distinctly broken near its extremity, but in other respects it differs but slightly from some examples of *N. ophiana*, and should I think be considered as a variety only of that species, especially as the true *N. ophiana* is known to occur in the regions north and south of that from whence *N. martabana* has been recorded.

402. Neptis jumbah, Moore.

N. jumbah, Moore, Horsfield and Moore, Cat. Lep. Mus. E. I. C., vol. i, p. 167, n. 345. pl. iva, fig. 5 (1857) ; *N. jumba*, id., Proc. Zool. Soc. Lond., 1858, p. 7, n 14 ; idem, id., Lep. Cey., vol. i, p. 55, pl. xxviii, figs. 2, 2a, *imago* ; 2b, *larva* and *pupa* (1881).

HABITAT : Eastern and Southern India, Ceylon, Burma, Andamans.

EXPANSE : 2·2 to 2·7 inches.

DESCRIPTION : " UPPERSIDE smoky-black. *Forewing* with a narrow longitudinal discoidal streak, and a triangular spot in continuation, white ; a transverse curved row of interrupted white spots from apical third of costal margin to near middle of posterior margin, composed of two very narrow longitudinal spots on the costal margin, beneath which are two large spots, then a very small streak, then two large spots, and lastly two narrower spots terminating on posterior margin ; between this band of spots and exterior margin are two rows of more or less defined lunular-shaped white spots, these being bounded exteriorly by a shade of deep black. *Hindwing* with a broad white band from costal to abdominal margin, being intersected by the veins ; near outer margin a row of ill-defined white lunated marks, bounded exteriorly by deep black, then a submarginal row of black lines ; between the white band and row of white lunated marks is a broad band of black. UNDERSIDE ferruginous. *Forewing* with markings as above, but the four rows of markings along exterior margin white, and suffused at the apex and near the middle with ferruginous. *Hindwing* with the broad white band ; abdominal margin, base of costal margin, and broadly across parallel with the band, suffused with white ; a marginal and two submarginal rows of whitish marks, between which and the broad band a series of five dark ferruginous spots from abdominal margin, and terminating in white marks on costal margin. *Body* above, black ; beneath, white. *Sexes* alike." (*Moore*, l. c. in Cat. Lep. Mus. E. I. C.)

" LARVA pale brownish-purple, anal segments below dark purple-brown spotted with green, and bordering an oblique line extending laterally from anal spines obliquely to base of spines on fourth segment ; anterior and anal segments narrowed, the middle segments thickened laterally ; head armed with two short points, two long divergent fleshy spiny tubercles on fourth segment, two short dorsal fleshy tubercles on third, fifth, and sixth segments. Feeds on *Byttneriaceæ*, &c. PUPA pale brownish-ochreous, head with two short points, thorax angulated." (*Moore*, l. c. in Lep. Cey.)

This is an exceedingly well-marked and distinct species, and differs from all others in having a small round brown spot placed near the base on the underside of the hindwing on a white band. It is somewhat variable; in some specimens the marginal markings on the upperside are very prominent, in others they are obsolete; the ground-colour of the underside is sometimes ochreous, sometimes ferruginous, and sometimes dark hair-brown coloured. In Ceylon it is "Found in the Western and Central Provinces; plains and up to 4,000 feet, in forest land, at all times, but chiefly during the S.-W. monsoon. Flight slow, heavy; settles with wings open, easily captured" (*Hutchison*). "Occurs everywhere: joins in the up-country flights, February and March in fair numbers" (*Mackwood*). It is very common in Calcutta, and the Indian Museum, Calcutta, possesses specimens from Cachar, Rangoon, Upper Tenasserim, Mergui, Orissa, Trevandrum, Ceylon and the South Andamans.

Genus 63.—CIRRHOCHROA, Doubleday. (PLATE XXIV).

Cirrochroa, Doubleday, Gen. Diurn. Lep., vol. i, p. 157 (1848); id., Moore, Lep. Cey., vol. i, p. 62 (1881); id., Distant, Rhop. Malay., p. 177 (1883).

"HEAD, of moderate size, clothed with hairs. *Eyes*, ovate, not remarkably prominent. *Palpi*, slightly divergent, ascending, rising above the forehead, scaly; the second joint furnished with a slight dorsal tuft, and externally with numerous erect setæ. First joint curved, very short; second joint five times as long as the first, swollen at the middle, tapering almost to a point at the apex; third joint slender, acicular, barely one-seventh the length of the second. *Antennæ*, of moderate length, gradually thickening into a slender club, the articulations of which are not more distinct than those of the other portion of the antennæ. *Thorax*, moderately stout, oval, hairy. *Abdomen*, small, scarcely half the length of the inner margin of the hindwing. FOREWING, subtriangular; the *costal margin* rounded; the *outer* margin about two-thirds the length of the costal margin, nearly straight, or slightly concave [sometimes convex]; *inner* margin rather shorter than the outer, slightly emarginate. *Costal nervure* not extending to the middle of the costa. *Subcostal* nervure emitting its *first* nervule shortly before its *second*, at the end of the cell; its *third* at about two-thirds the distance between the cell and the apex; the *fourth* nearer to the third than to the apex; the third terminating at the apex. *Upper disco-cellular nervule* nearly wanting; *middle* disco-cellular curved inwards, or slightly angular; *lower* disco-cellular very slender, nearly straight, more than double the length of the middle disco-cellular, joining the median nervure at a short distance before the origin of its second nervule. *Internal nervure* wanting. HINDWING, obovate; the *outer margin* slightly sinuate; the *inner* emarginate near the anal angle. *Præcostal nervure* simple, curved outwards. *Discoidal nervule* appearing to be a third subcostal nervule, but little curved. *Discoidal cell* open. Abdominal fold ample. FORELEGS, of the *male* scaly, the femur and base of the tibia slightly, apex of the tibia and the tarsus thickly covered with long hairs. *Tibia* shorter than the femur, but longer than the *tarsus*, which is subcylindric, slightly pointed, one-jointed. Of the *female* scaly. *Tibia* smooth, slightly shorter than the femur. *Tarsus* about the length of the tibia, five-jointed; its first joint cylindric, slightly curved, smooth, about twice the length of the other joints combined; second and third joints transverse, of equal breadth, the latter rather shorter than the former; fourth joint rather tapering; all these with a spine on each side at the apex, covered by a tuft of hairs at the base of the following joint; fifth joint narrower, tapering towards the apex, which is mucronate. MIDDLE and HINDLEGS, with the femora, tibiæ, and tarsi nearly of equal length. *Tibiæ* spiny, especially towards the apex; their spurs distinct. *Tarsi* nearly cylindric, spiny; the spines at the sides longest, those of the lower surface arranged in two nearly regular series. First joint longer than the rest combined; second, third, and fourth progressively, though but little, shorter, all of similar form, as is the fifth, which is about equal in length to the second. *Claws* curved, grooved below. *Paronychia* bilaciniate; the outer lacinia subtriangular, broader than, and about as long as, the claw; inner shorter, strap-shaped. *Pulvillus* jointed, as long as the claws; the second joint broad." (*Doubleday*, l. c.)

LARVA with two dorsal series of long and two lateral series of shorter delicately-branched spines, also a similar spine projecting on each side in front of the head from the second segment. PUPA bluish-purple marked with black, head ending in two points, two long spines projecting from the back of the thorax in front of the head, a hump on the back of the thorax, which, with the abdominal segments above, bear pairs of spines.

"This genus has a singular character on the hindwing of the male [it occurs in both sexes]. Between the third subcostal [discoidal] and third median nervule, the upper surface of the wing is marked by a transverse depression, extending nearly, or quite, across the space between the nervules, causing a corresponding elevation of the lower surface, which, but for its breadth, might be mistaken for the indication of a disco-cellular nervule." (*Doubleday*, l. c.) In one species only, *C. fasciata*, the male has distinct secondary sexual characters, *viz.*, on the forewing on either side of the discoidal nervules from their origin rather more than half way to the margin and also on the first and second subcostal nervules of the hindwing on the upperside, there is a narrow streak of modified ochreous scales, which gives this portion of those veins the appearance of a feather of which the vein itself is the shaft, and the scales the barbs. Typically they are fulvous or tawny insects with the outer margin black, and with a discal and three marginal sinuous black lines, the hindwing also has a discal series of six black spots ; on the underside there is always a more or less prominent pale discal band from middle of costa of forewing to anal angle of hindwing, and the black marginal lines are replaced by yellow or olivaceous.

"In some species, as in *C. aoris*, the sexes differ widely in appearance, the female being of a more obscure and duller colour above. This, however, is not the rule with the majority of the species of the genus." (*Distant*, l. c.) In *C. olivacea* the difference in the colouration of the opposite sexes is even more marked than in *C. aoris*. Except in *C. fasciata*, which is an altogether aberrant form, the females differ also in having the outer margin of the forewing much more emarginate than in the males ; this feature is most prominent in the South Indian and Ceylon species.

Cirrhochroa is somewhat widely distributed ; it occurs in the Eastern Himalayas, in Eastern and Peninsular India, Ceylon, the Andamans and Nicobars, throughout Assam, Burma, the Malay peninsula and islands to New Guinea and Australia. Many of the species are very plentiful where they occur, are strong and very conspicuous on the wing, but frequently settle, often in swarms, on a damp spot in the hills. Many of them are very closely allied, and their specific determination and range by no means easily determined. The distinctness or otherwise of many of the described species is still uncertain and can only be determined by experimental breeding.

Key to the Indian species of Cirrhochroa.

A. Males without secondary sexual characters.
    a. Male with apex of forewing truncate.
        a¹. Male with outer margin of forewing narrowly black, female with prominent series of ochreous lunules on outer margin of forewing on upperside.
                403. C. AORIS, Eastern Himalayas, Cachar, Sylhet, Assam.
                404. C. ABNORMIS, Sikkim.
        b¹. Male and female with outer margin of forewing broadly black, female without the series of prominent ochreous lunules on outer margin of forewing on upperside.
                405. C. OLIVACEA, Upper Tenasserim.
    b. Male with apex of forewing rounded.
        a¹. Inner edge of discal band of forewing on underside not constricted at lower discoidal and first median nervules.
            a². Colouration of upperside of male fulvous, female brownish-ochreous.
                a³. Apex of forewing on upperside of male broadly black, discal black spots on hindwing very large.
                    406. C. NICOBARICA, Nicobars.
                b³. Apex of forewing on upperside of male narrowly black, discal black spots on hindwing small.
                    a⁴. Discal band on underside of forewing much wider at costa, tapering to inner margin.
                      407. C. SURYA, Upper Tenasserim.

b^4. Discal band on underside of forewing of even width throughout.

　　408. C. MITHILA, Bengal, Yunan.
　　409. C. ROTUNDATA, Sikkim, Assam, Malacca.
　　410. C. ANJIRA, Barrackpore, Andamans.

b^2. Colouration of upperside of male ferruginous, female somewhat paler.

a^1. Discal band on underside obsolescent in male, black border prominent on upperside.

　　411. C. LANKA, Ceylon.

b^1. Discal band on underside very prominent in both sexes, black border much less prominent on upperside.

　　412. C. RELATA, South India.

b^3. Inner edge of discal band of forewing on underside strongly constricted at lower discoidal and first median nervules.

a^2. Colouration of upperside of male ferruginous, female somewhat paler.

a^1. Discal band on underside usually silvery white and prominent in both sexes. The wings larger, the forewing more emarginate in both sexes.

　　413. C. THAIS, South India.

b^1. Discal band on underside obsolescent in male, often prominent in female; black border of upperside, especially in the male, much darker and more uniform.

　　414. C. COGNATA, Ceylon.

b^2. Colouration of upperside of both sexes ochreous.

　　415 C. SWINHOEI, South India, Ceylon.

B. Male with discoidal nervules of forewing and first and second subcostal nervules of hindwing on upperside with a streak of differently-coloured scales on either side for about two-thirds of their length.

　　416. C. FASCIATA, Upper Tenasserim, Sumatra.

C. aoris and *C. oliveus* are distinguished from all the other Indian species by their large size, and by the males as well as the females having the apex of the forewing distinctly truncated. The females too are more widely different in both than in the remaining Indian species of this genus. They are confined to North-Eastern India and Burma.

403. **Cirrhochroa aoris**, Doubleday, Hewitson.

Cirrhochroa aoris, Doubleday, Hewitson, Gen. Diurn. Lep., vol. i, p. 138, n. 1, pl. xxi, fig. 2, *male* (1847); id., Westwood, Trans. Ent. Soc. Lond., 1880, p. 113, pl. ii.

HABITAT: Sikkim, Cachar, Sylhet, Upper Assam, Naga Hills.

EXPANSE: 2·8 to 3·6 inches.

DESCRIPTION: MALE. UPPERSIDE, *both wings* bright fulvous, powdered with dusky at the base. *Forewing* with the apex strongly truncated, the outer margin slightly emarginate and sinuous; the disco-cellular nervules slightly defined with dusky on either side; a very irregular and somewhat indistinct discal fuscous line, beyond which are a series of diffused, very indistinct, often obsolete fuscous rounded spots between the nervules, the margin narrowly black, widely black at the apex, two submarginal lunular black lines, of which the outer one is the more prominent and becomes merged in the black apex. *Hindwing* with a very irregular discal black line, with the usual whitish spot on the middle of the costa; a discal series of six round black spots one in each interspace except the discoidal; two deeply engrailed submarginal lines, the outer one the darker, a marginal narrow nearly straight black line: all the veins defined with black on the disc. UNDERSIDE, *both wings* much paler, all the markings of the upperside more or less obliterated; a common discal whitish fascia, narrowest in the middle of each wing, its outer edge very straight and even, its inner edge irregular, defined by a pair of dark lines enclosing a pale yellow line; submarginal and marginal yellow lunular lines, divided and inwardly bounded by whitish lunules; a pale brown subbasal streak. *Forewing* with a whitish patch at the apex. *Hindwing* with the six round black spots of the upperside but smaller. FEMALE much darker, the ground-colour of the UPPERSIDE ochreous, thickly irrorated throughout with fuscous scales. Markings as in the male, but heavier and darker throughout. UNDERSIDE pale buff, washed throughout with obscure violaceous; the markings of the outer half more obscure, of the inner half more prominent and wider than above, the discal fascia less distinct, almost concolourous with the ground, inwardly defined with a dark band (this band edged on both sides with pale fuscous), outwardly by a straight pale fuscous or purple line. *Forewing* with a narrow band crossing middle of the cell to origin of first median nervule, from thence crossing the interspace below and continued across the base of the hindwing from costal to submedian nervure, with a spot beyond in the cell in the latter wing. The disco-cellulars of the forewing defined with a similar line. The tone of the ground-colour of the upperside in the female varies, in some it is ochreous, in others fuscous.

C. *aoris* may be distinguished from *C. olivacea*, the only other species in which the forewing of the male is truncate, by the narrow black border to the forewing and the more uniform colouration of the upperside, these characters being common to both sexes. It is one of the commonest and most distinct as well as the largest species of the genus. It is met with in Sikkim up to about 6,000 feet elevation, almost throughout the year, and occurs equally commonly in the hills to the eastwards as far as Sibsagar in Upper Assam.

Professor J. O. Westwood (l. c.) has described and figured two gynandromorphous specimens of *C. aoris* contained in the collection of the British Musuem ; in one of these "the gynandromorphism is exactly bilateral, the wings on the right side of the insect having the colouring and markings of the male strongly defined, whilst the wings on the other (left) side are those of the female equally strongly marked." In the other specimen "a singular mixture of the characters of the two sexes" is exhibited in the wings on the right-hand side of the insect.

Mr. Moore has described a species of *Cirrhochroa* from Sikkim under the name of *C. abnormis* ; the description corresponds very closely with some specimens of *C. aoris*, and I can find no reliable character by which to distinguish between them. No indication is given by Mr. Moore as to which species it is most closely allied, or of the outline of the wings, and I place it here provisionally pending further information.

404. Cirrhochroa abnormis, Moore.

C. *abnormis*, Moore, Journ. A. S. B., vol. liii, pt. 2, p. 19 (1884).

HABITAT : Sikkim.

EXPANSE : 2·62 inches.

DESCRIPTION : " MALE. UPPERSIDE ferruginous-yellow. *Forewing* with a medial discal transverse black lunular waved band, which is broadest at the costal end, a narrower submarginal sinuous band, and a nearly straight marginal line, the interspace from the submarginal band and edge of the wing being suffused with black towards the apex ; an indistinct dusky streak at end of the cell. *Hindwing* with a medial discal transverse angulated black lunular band, which is broadest at the costal end ; a submarginal lunular line, and a slender nearly straight marginal line ; a row of minute black discal dots. UNDERSIDE brownish-ochreous ; a transverse medial slightly purpurascent band, with waved suffused dusky lunular inner border and slender almost straight outer border, the band being quite narrow where it crosses from *fore-* to *hindwing*, and broadly dilated at the costal end on the forewing and at anal end on the hindwing : contiguous to the inner border of the band is a similar dusky suffused lunular fascia, the interspace being of a slightly pale yellowish colour ; at end of each cell is a dusky double lunular mark, a similar double lunular waved line also extends from middle of the cell on the forewing to below the cell on the hindwing ; outer border of *both wings* traversed by faint traces of a yellowish submarginal lunular band ; on the *forewing* is a conspicuous whitish apical patch, and on the *hindwing* is a row of very small blackish transverse discal dots." (*Moore*, l. c.)

405. Cirrhochroa olivacea, de N, n. sp. (PLATE XXIV, FIG. 111 ♀).

HABITAT : Upper Tenasserim.

EXPANSE : ♂, 2·4 to 3·0 ; ♀, 3·3 inches.

DESCRIPTION: MALE. UPPERSIDE bright fulvous, in some specimens the basal area bounded by the discal line dark fulvous ; all the veins on the disc distinctly defined with black. *Forewing* with the disco-cellular nervules marked as usual with a dark fine line on either side, a very irregular black discal line which becomes obsolete before reaching the inner margin, and is widest at the costa ; the outer margin, especially at the apex, broadly black, decreasing towards the anal angle, where it includes one, two or three fulvous lunules. Outline truncate at the apex, sinuous below. *Hindwing* with the usual pale quadrate spot on the middle of the costal margin, a somewhat even discal line, obsolete in some specimens, the usual six round discal black spots, two lunular submarginal and marginal straight black lines beyond, the inner one obsolescent towards the costa. UNDERSIDE opalescent buff, but variable in depth of shade. The usual discal fascia across *both wings*, its outer margin defined by a prominent straight fine purple line, its inner edge with an irregular brown yellow-bordered line : the fascia broad on the costa of the forewing, narrowing gradually and regularly to the inner margin, of nearly equal width throughout on the hindwing. Other markings as above, but paler ; the marginal lunular lines yellow, not black ; a prominent pale apical patch on the forewing. FEMALE. UPPERSIDE dark olivaceous, all the markings heavier and darker than in the male. *Forewing* with a prominent broad discal whitish band stained with pale fulvous towards the inner margin, its outer edge very irregular, and the outer edge of the discal fascia below showing through. Towards the anal angle it bears two series of very indistinct submarginal black lunules. *Hindwing* with the costal white spot much larger, narrowly prolonged to the discoidal nervule. UNDERSIDE purplish-white, the discal fascia much more prominent and paler, otherwise as in the male.

In Major Marshall's collection are two males taken at Lampha by Captain C. H. E. Adamson in March, three males and a female taken in the Thoungyeen Forests in that month, and one male (the darkest) in the autumn by Captain C. T. Bingham. The male is nearest to a Perak specimen of *C. bajadeta*, but the apex of the forewing is truncate and less produced, and does not bear the pale spot on the upperside ; the ground-colour is also lighter, especially below. The female is quite different from that sex of *C. bajadeta*, and may be distinguished from *C. aoris* in having the discal band whitish instead of ochreous, and the black margin beyond untraversed by a series of prominent ochreous lunules ; the veins of the forewing also across the disc are more distinctly black in the male than in any other Indian species.

The figure, showing both the upper and undersides, is taken from the type female specimen in Major Marshall's collection.

Two allied species, *C. bajadeta* and *C. malaya*, from the Malay peninsula are described below. *

---

* *Cirrhochroa bajadeta*, Moore, Horsfield and Moore, Cat. Lep. Mus E. I. C., vol. i, p. 150, n. 309; pl. iiia, figs. 3, 3a (1857) ; id., Distant, Rhop. Malay., p. 170, n. 4, pl xix, figs. 2 *male* ; 2, *female* (1883) ; *Cirrhochroa ratnana*, Moore, l. c., n. 310. HABITAT : Perak, Penang, Province Wellesley, Malacca, Borneo, Java, EXPANSE : 2·6 to 3·0 inches. DESCRIPTION : " MALE. UPPERSIDE reddish-ochraceous *Forewing* with the costa, a narrow transverse fascia near end of cell, and the outer margin—very broad at apex—black ; beyond the cell the colour is somewhat paler, giving the appearance of a broad transverse fascia ; and a small ochraceous subapical spot. *Hindwing* with the outer area from end of cell paler, its inner area marked on each side of the submedian nervure with a lunate black linear spot, and by a similar spot above the upper subcostal nervule ; an irregular series of small black spots placed between the nervules (absent between the third median and the discoidal nervules), and three waved submarginal black fasciæ, the outer one more or less fused with the dark outer margin. UNDERSIDE paler in hue. *Forewing* with the cell crossed by two linear darker fasciæ, one at its termination, the other beyond middle and extending beneath the median nervure ; a somewhat violaceous area crossing wing beyond cell, broad at costa and very narrow and attenuated at inner margin ; apex obscurely infuscated, and containing two subapical greyish white spots and a marginal waved fascia, the edges of which are distinctly pale fuscous ; beneath the first median nervule and in front of the pale fascia is an irregularly formed fuscous spot. *Hindwing* crossed by a narrow and a very pale violaceous fascia, which is distinctly narrowed and attenuated between the upper subcostal and the discoidal nervules ; black spots as above, but margined with reddish-ochraceous ; marginal and submarginal fasciæ as on the forewing. *Body* and *legs* more or less concolourous with the wings. FEMALE. UPPERSIDE as in male, with the pale area better defined and inwardly but narrowly margined with blackish. UNDERSIDE with the medial fasciæ paler."

" The female of this species appears to have been described by Mr. Moore under the name of *C. ratnana*, but having received both sexes from Java, Borneo, and the Malay Peninsula, I feel no doubt as to its sexual relation to *C. bajadeta*." (*Distant*, l. c.)

In the Indian Museum, Calcutta, is a single male of this species from Perak.

Cirrhochroa malaya, Felder, Wien. Ent Monatsch., vol. iv, p. 399, n. 18 (1860) : id., Distant, Rhop. Malay., p. 180, n. 5, pl x, figs. 4, *male* ; 3, *female* (1883) ; *Cirrhochroa johannes*, Butler, Proc. Zool Soc., 1868, p. 221, pl. xvii, fig. 10 ; idem, id., Trans. Linn. Soc., Zoology, second series, vol. i, p. 545, n (1877). HABITAT : Perak, Province Wellesley, Malacca. EXPANSE : 2·5 to 2·8 inches. DESCRIPTION : " MALE and FEMALE. Resembling the corresponding sexes of *C. bajadeta*, but with the pale violaceous fascia crossing the underside of the hindwing entire and not attenuated at the subcostal and discoidal nervules as in that species ; the underside of both wings is also generally rather darker and more violaceous than in *C. bajadeta*."

" Both Mr. Butler and Mr. Kirby incline to the opinion that the *C. malaya*, Felder, is more or less synonymous with *C. bajadeta*, and the reasons why I have differed from these authorities and identified it with *C. johannes* are contained in Felder's diagnosis. Thus the description of the underside of the wings as " blacino suffusis," and the pale fascia to the hindwing as " angusta recta," thoroughly applies to the species figured and

406. Cirrhochroa nicobarica, W.-M. and de N.

C. nicobarica, Wood-Mason and de Nicéville, Journ. A. S. B., vol. l, pt. ii, p. 231, n. 15 (1881); idem, id., vol. li, p. 16, n. 17, pl. iii, fig. 5, *male* (1882).

HABITAT : Great Nicobar.

EXPANSE : 2'35 and 2'50 inches.

DESCRIPTION : "MALE. UPPERSIDE bright fulvous powdered with fuscous scales at the base of *both wings*, and along each side of the disco-cellular nervules. *Forewing* with the costal margin narrowly, the apex broadly, and the external margin decreasingly fuscous, and with a small obscure patch of fuscous scales near the inner angle. *Hindwing* with a thin discal striga somewhat discontinuous and nearly straight anteriorly but zigzaged posteriorly ; six rather large rounded spots, and a short streak between the third median and discoidal nervules in the same line as the spots, black ; and beyond the spots three regularly engrailed fuscous strigæ, one of which is marginal and the innermost of which is the darkest and is connected with the discal thin striga by the dark brown margins of the nervules ; with the usual white blotch between the anterior black spot and the discal striga ; and with the dusky fulvous interval between the two outermost marginal fuscous strigæ continued for a short distance on to the fuscous margin of the forewing at the inner angle. UNDERSIDE, *both wings* much paler, faintly suffused with lilac ; with a common opalescent discal band inwardly bounded with dusky, scarcely perceptible in the forewing but prominent in the hindwing, in which it is nearly straight externally but dentate internally. *Hindwing* with five of the black spots of the upperside (two interspaces being devoid of a spot) smaller than above, seated, the foremost one wholly, the second and last (which is twinned) partially, upon a dusky ground, the remaining ones upon fulvous of a brighter shade than the rest of the wing ; beyond the spots with two opalescent lunular bands, the first the broader and internally margined with diffused dusky, and the second the narrower and sharply defined, both of which bands are continued faintly and diffusedly on to the forewing ; and with the usual basal and disco-cellular pale fuscous marks."

"Apparently most nearly allied to *C. malaya*, Felder, from the Malay Peninsula." (*Wood-Mason* and *de Nicéville*, l. c.) It is even more closely allied to *C. surya*, but may be at once distinguished from that species and from all Indian species by the large size of the discal series of black spots on both the upper and undersides, and the prominence of the discal and submarginal opalescent bands on the underside of the hindwing. It is, however, most closely allied to *C. clagia*, but the outer black border on the upperside of both wings is far less prominent, in *C. clagia* it includes the discal spots more or less, and is also more prominent on the underside than in *C. nicobarica*.

Mr. de Roepstorff obtained two males at Great Nicobar.

407. Cirrhochroa surya, Moore.

Cirrhochroa surya, Moore, Proc. Zool. Soc. Lond., 1878, p. 827.

HABITAT : Moulmein to Meetan ; Taoo, March, 3,000—5,000 feet ; Moolai, 3,000—6,000 feet ; Upper Tenasserim.

EXPANSE : ♂, 1'87 to 2'25 ; ♀, 2'5 inches.

DESCRIPTION : "Allied to *C. lanka*, Moore. MALE differs above on the *forewing* in the narrower marginal band, a single sinuous line extending with fulvous interspaces to near the apex. *Hindwing* with the submarginal line more sharply sinuous ; other markings similar.

---

described by Mr. Butler, and the last character especially, in contradiction to the suddenly or attenuated fascia in the other species. Felder naturally compared it to *C. bajadeta*, *C. johannes* not having been then described, and the fact of his having thus compared it would naturally lead to the supposition that he must have been cognisant of Mr Moore's species."

"I am inclined, however, to the view that specimens will be obtained of a completely intermediate character between *C. bajadeta* and *C. malaya*." (*Distant*, l. c.)

There is a single male of this species from Perak in the Indian Museum, Calcutta. It differs from a Perak example of *C. bajadeta* in the colouration being paler above, the outer margin of the forewing less excavated below the apex, and wanting the subapical spot. On the underside the discal fascia of the hindwing is distinctly narrower and quite even in width throughout. Judging from the single specimens I have seen of these two species, I should have no hesitation in considering them distinct.

UNDERSIDE purplish fulvous grey ; the discal transverse band broader, and pale bluish purple on the forewing, bluish purple-white on the hindwing, its outer border being dark blue, and its inner border red and waved ; other markings red. FEMALE darker above, the discal black line sinuous at the costal end ; a double sinuous marginal line ; other markings and underside as in male." (*Moore*, l. c.)

C. surya is a much paler and yellower insect than *C. lanka*, and the margin of the hindwing on the upperside is concolourous with the ground and bears a distinct black marginal line ; in *C. lanka* the margin is black, the black line merging in the black border which extends nearly to the lunular submarginal line, the inner submarginal lunular line also is prominent, but in *C. surya* is almost entirely obsolete ; the character of the markings is, however, similar on both upper and undersides. *C. surya* is still more nearly allied to *C. olivacea*, the males of which may be distinguished from those of *C. surya* by their larger size, the veins on the disc of the forewing being distinctly defined with black on the upperside, and the marginal fulvous lunules being obsolescent, leaving a more uniform black border ; on the underside the pale discal band in *C. olivacea* is much wider at the costa of the forewing, and its outer margin is defined by a much darker more prominent purple line. I have not seen the female of *C. surya*, but the discal band on the upperside not being white, would readily distinguish it from the female of *C. olivacea*.

It appears to be a good species confined to Upper Tenasserim, and is usually of very small size, averaging a little over two inches in expanse only. The black border to the forewing on the upperside is very prominent, as the rest of the wing is hardly marked at all. Dr. Anderson took several specimens in the Mergui archipelago in the cold weather, and there are numerous examples in Major Marshall's collection taken by Captain C. T. Bingham in the Thoungyeen forests and the Donat range from December to April.

Three species, *C. satellita*, *C. clagia*, and *C. orissa*, of which the descriptions are given below, have been recorded from the Malay Peninsula.* In the shape of the discal band on the underside of the forewing they correspond with *C. surya* and *C. olivacea*.

* *Cirrhochroa satellita*, Butler, Cist. Ent., vol. 1, p. 9 (1869) ; id., Lep. Ex., p. 103, pl. xxviii, fig. 7 (1871) ; id., Distant. Rhop. Malay., p. 176, n. 2, pl. xix, fig. 9, *male* (1883). HABITAT : Perak, Borneo, China. EXPANSE : 2.6 to 2.7 inches. DESCRIPTION : "MALE. Upperside brownish-ochraceous, *both wings* closed a little beyond the cells by a broad bright ochraceous fascia, after which the wings are blackish ; the pale fascia of the *hindwing* consists an incomplete series of black spots placed between the nervules—that at anal angle largest—and two narrow, waved, black submarginal fascia, the outer of which, above the median nervules, is blended with the posterior black area. Underside paler, the black areas [of the upperside] brownish, the medial pale fascia containing at their inner margins a narrower greyish fascia, widest on the forewing, where it is also more ochraceous. *Forewing* with a submarginal, lunately macular, violaceous fascia, beyond which is a straighter and more distinct pale fascia. *Hindwing* with a macular violaceous fascia as on the forewing, followed by two dark, narrow, waved fascia, the series of black spots larger and more continuous. Body and legs more or less concolourous with wings."

" This species is slightly variable in the number of black spots visible on the upperside of the hindwing." (*Distant*, l. c.)

Cirrhochroa (*Argynnis*) *clagia*, Godart, Enc. Méth., vol. ix, Supple., p. 816 (1823) ; id., Boisduval, Spec. Gén., vol. i, pl. x, fig. 6 (1836) ; id., Distant. Rhop. Malay., p. 179, n. 3, pl. xvii, fig. 7, *male* (1883). HABITAT : Singapore, Sumatra, Java. EXPANSE : 2.1 to 2.5 inches. DESCRIPTION : "MALE. Upperside reddish-ochraceous, *both wings* with a broad outer marginal blackish fascia, which on the *forewing* is rectuved and broadest at the apical angle, these blackish areas possess two indistinct narrow dark submarginal fascia ; and that on *hindwing* is either preceded or inwardly margined by a series of black spots placed between the nervules ; a very narrow and non-continuous blackish fascia also crosses the hindwing a little beyond the cell, which at the costal margin has an adjacent greyish spot. Underside much paler, crossed by a greyish fascia, as in *C. satellita*, which is margined with reddish ochraceous, and beyond which their area is distinctly darker and somewhat tinged with violaceous, containing the narrow submarginal fasciae as in *C. satellita* ; the *forewing* has a greyish subapical spot, and the cell is medially crossed by a sinuated dull reddish line, which is continued beneath the median nervure, the lower diven-cellular norvule being similarly coloured ; the *hindwing* has the black spots margined with reddish, and the cell crossed by a sinuated dull reddish line, which extends from near the costal margin to near the submedian nervure. Body and legs more or less concolourous with wings ; the femora, sternum, and abdomen beneath greyish. FEMALE differs from the male on the *upperside* by having distinct traces of a medial broad yellowish fascia on the *forewing* ; the *hindwing* having the outer black area narrower, leaving the two narrow waved fasciæ very distinct, the spots thereby appearing further removed "

" The principal variation in the forms of this species appears to consist in the breadth of the outer black margin to the hindwing, and the thereby sometimes consequent assimilation or fusion of the black spots." (*Distant*, l. c.) *C. nicobarica* is a pale local form or race of this species.

The Indian Museum possesses two specimens of this species collected by Dr. Horsfield in Java.

Cirrhochroa orissa, Felder, Wien. Ent. Monatsch., vol. iv, p. 399, n. 19 (1860) ; idem, id., Reise Nov., Lep., vol. iii, p. 388, n. 562, pl. xlix, figs. 7, 8 (1866) ; id., Wallace, Trans. Ent. Soc. Lond. 1869, p. 340 ; id., Distant, Rhop. Malay., p. 178, n. 1, pl. x, fig. 9, *female* (1883). HABITAT : Penang, Province Wellesley, Malacca, Singapore, Borneo. EXPANSE : 2.3 to 2.7 inches. DESCRIPTION : "MALE. Upperside, *forewing* brownish-ochraceous, with a broad transverse yellow fascia crossing the wing at end of cell and the whole apical area black. *Hindwing*

The next three species have a very wide range. In their detailed descriptions I have given only the localities from which they have individually been recorded by competent authorities. It will be at once apparent by examining these localities how erratic is the distribution of each ; moreover the characters given in the descriptions are all inconstant, and this being so I would prefer to consider them as one species only, which would best stand as *C. mithila*. Treated as a single species it occurs in Fyzabad, Oudh ; Bholahát, Malda ; Barrackpore near Calcutta ; Sikkim ; Assam ; the Naga Hills ; Sylhet ; Cachar ; Manipur ; British and Upper Burma ; the Andaman Isles ; Malacca and Java (*Horsfield*).

C. mithila in a comprehensive sense is of a lighter colouration on the upperside than *C. lanka* and *C. cognata*, the forewing of the male is evenly rounded, of the female usually more or less truncated, but never to the extent that it is in *C. aoris* and *C. olivacea*. In the male none of the markings of the upperside are very prominent, the inner lunular line of the forewing is usually obsolescent, and the margin beyond much less prominently black than in *C. lanka*, *C. surya*, &c. The colouration of the underside is extremely variable, some specimens are pale buff almost throughout, others are bright ochreous with the discal band prominently margined outwardly with purple, in others again the ground-colour is darker, but the discal band lacks the outer purple margining ; all these variations are common to the species whereever it occurs. The discal band across the wings on the underside is of nearly equal width throughout in the forewing, slightly narrower on the hindwing and constricted in the middle, its inner edge usually, but not always, irregularly bounded by a fine double line constricted at each vein with the intervening space yellow, this feature linking it with *C. aoris*. The female is darker than the male, the colour of the upperside as well as the underside being variable.

408. Cirrhochroa mithila, Moore.

Cirrochroa mithila, Moore, Proc. Zool. Soc. Lond., 1872, p. 558; idem, id., in Anderson's Anat. and Zool. Researches, vol. i, p. 924 (1878).

HABITAT : Bengal, Upper Tenasserim.

EXPANSE : 1·37 [2·37 ?] inches.

DESCRIPTION : " MALE. UPPERSIDE pale ferruginous. *Forewing* with the blackish marginal band narrow, its inner row of lunules palely defined ; medial transverse line scarcely visible on either wing ; the row of black spots, white spot on anterior margin, and outer marginal lunular lines of *hindwing* also very palely defined. UNDERSIDE dull testaceous, glossed with greyish purple ; medial band obsolete, its place faintly defined by a dusky straight outer streak and narrow inner line ; spots on *hindwing* partly obsolete." (*Moore*, l. c.)

Mr. Moore has very kindly furnished me with a sketch of *C. mithila* taken from the type specimen. In the Indian Museum, Calcutta, there are numerous males taken by Dr. Anderson in the Mergui archipelago in the cold weather, and in Major Marshall's collection there are several others taken in Tenasserim, in the Thoungyeen forests in January, March and April, and in the Donat range in January and April, which agree more or less with Mr. Moore's description and drawing. The prominence of the markings and colour of the ground on the underside is variable, but it is impossible to separate the heavier-marked darker-coloured ones from the others which agree exactly with the type.

409. Cirrhochroa rotundata, Butler.

Cirrochroa rotundata, Butler, Trans. Linn. Soc. Lond., Zoology, second series, vol. i, p. 543, n 4 (1877); id., Distant, Rhop. Malay., p. 181, n. 6, pl. x, fig. 10, *female* (1883); id., Butler, Ann and Mag. of Nat. Hist., fifth series, vol. xvi, p. 303, n. 27 (1885).

brownish-ochraceous, with the following black markings :—a narrow, linear waved fascia crossing wing near end of cell and strongly angulated at first median nervule, followed by a row of spots placed between the nervules (absent between the discoidal and third median nervules) and a marginal and two submarginal much-waved fascia. *Upperside paler*. *Forewing* with the medial fascia whitish, containing a triangular brownish spot at inner margin ; apical area brownish, with two long, ovate, contiguous greyish spots at apex, and an indistinct waved darker submarginal lineate fascia. *Hindwing* with the medial black fascia above replaced by a broader pale violaceous fascia beneath, beyond which the colour is more or less shaded with violaceous, the black spots margined with reddish, and two submarginal pale violaceous fascia. *Body and legs* more or less concolorous with wings. FEMALE resembles the male, but the *forewing* on the upperside with a small subapical greyish streak, and on the under surface, with the pale medial fascia crossed by a narrow pale sinuated brownish fascia attached to the triangular spot at inner margin ; the apical brown area also possesses an indistinct violaceous much-waved fascia." (*Distant*, l. c.)

HABITAT : Sikkim, Assam, Malacca.

EXPANSE : 3 inches.

DESCRIPTION : "FEMALE, nearly allied to *C. mithila*, Moore, the wings more rounded, *forewing* less produced ; markings of the forewing above almost obsolete ; outer undulated line of *hindwing* much more distinct. UNDERSIDE, all the bands and spots tawny instead of ochre yellow."

"I have no doubt that this species is distinct from *C. mithila ;* the colouration of the bands below is strikingly different." (*Butler*, l. c.)

In the Indian Museum, Calcutta, is a single male of this species from Sikkim so named by Mr. Moore. The outline of this specimen agrees with that of Mr. Moore's sketch of *C. mithila*, and also with Mr. Distant's figure of *C. rotundata*, the markings of the forewing on the upperside are nearly obsolete, but the bands of the underside are buff rather than tawny. Out of six Sikkim males that belong certainly to one species no two are marked alike on the underside, some are very pale buff, one is ochreous, one is tawny, and some are ferruginous marked with deep purple, but the bands are in almost every case tawny not ochre. *C. rotundata* cannot, I think, be maintained as a distinct species. Mr. Butler records it from "near Assam."

410.　**Cirrhochroa anjira,** Moore.

Cirrochroa anjira, Moore, Proc. Zool. Soc. Lond., 1877, p. 584 ; id., Rothney, Ent. Month Mag., vol. xix, p. 34 (1882).

HABITAT : Barrackpore ; S. Andamans (Port Blair).

EXPANSE : ♂, 2·62 to 3·00 ; ♀, 2·87 to 3·30 inches.

DESCRIPTION : "Nearest allied to *C. aoris* ; differs in being less falcate in the *forewing*, the MALE above having similar but more prominent black markings. In the forewing the transverse discal sinuous line is more erect, and in the FEMALE is less pointed at the angles ; the marginal double sinuous band is broader. UNDERSIDE, darker in colour, the transverse pale lilac band broader on the *forewing* and narrower on the *hindwing* ; this band is also much less sinuous on its inner border." (*Moore*, l. c.)

C. anjira is of course widely distinct from *C. aoris*, the forewing in the male being rounded at the apex or hardly perceptibly truncate ; in the female it is often distinctly truncate, but never to the extent that obtains in *C. aoris*. The colouration of the upperside in the male is also of a much deeper fulvous than in *C. aoris*. Comparing South Andaman males and a Sikkim male identified by Mr. Moore as *C. rotundata*, I can find no character by which to segregate them into distinct species. The females of *C. anjira* are extremely variable in colouration, some are deep tawny above, others coloured like the females of *C. aoris*. The colouration and distinctness or otherwise of the markings on the underside are even more variable.

The remaining species of this group represent the genus in South India and Ceylon : they are restricted to those regions, and are the only species known to occur there ; with the single exception of *C. swinhoei* they are darker in tone than the North Indian and Indo-Malayan species, and their ground-colour is ferruginous not fulvous. In all the species the difference between the sexes in outline of wing is more marked than in the northern species, the female having the forewing much more emarginate and consequently falcate than the male. They comprise two groups distinguished by the form of the pale discal band on the underside, and comprise three distinct species all found both in South India and in Ceylon, and in each case the Ceylon specimens have the pale discal band of the underside much less prominent than in the South Indian specimens, especially in the males, thus forming more or less defined local races or subspecies, the Ceylon subspecies being best defined in the case of *C. thais* and least defined in that of *C. swinhoei*.

In the case of *C. thais* the Ceylon race has been separated by Mr. Moore under the name of *C. cognata* ; he also records *C. thais* from Ceylon, but all the Ceylon specimens of this type that I have seen belong to *C. cognata*, and are separable from the South Indian *C. thais* not only by the obsolescence of the discal band on the underside in the male, but by the much more prominent and uniform black border of the upperside.

In the case of *C. lanka* the Ceylon race only has been named, but there is in South India a local race which stands in precisely the same relation to *C. lanka* as *C. thais* does to *C. cognata*, for which I here propose the name *C. relata*.

In *C. swinhoei* the differences are less well-marked. I have specimens from Ceylon which are referrable to this species, but they do not appear sufficiently distinct to constitute a separate subspecies.

411. **Cirrhochroa lanka**, Moore.

Cirrochroa lanka, Moore, Proc. Zool. Soc. Lond., 1872, p. 557; idem, id., Lep. Cey., vol. i, p. 63, pl. xxxii, figs. 4, 4a (1880)

HABITAT: Ceylon.

EXPANSE: ♂, 2·2 to 2·5; ♀, 2·5 to 2·8 inches.

DESCRIPTION: "MALE. UPPERSIDE bright ferruginous. *Forewing* with medial transverse black line, which is oblique in front of the cell, nearly obsolete hindward; marginal band black, traversed by an inner row of ferruginous lunules, the outer series being more or less obsolete. *Hindwing* with the white spot on the anterior margin large, the median transverse line from it faintly defined; the parallel row of black spots, outer and second marginal lines prominent. UNDERSIDE dusky ferruginous, somewhat fulvous at the base, glossed with purple-grey; a broad transverse medial prominent purple-white glossy band; indistinct lunules on outer margin of wings with purple-grey borders; black spots on *hindwing* prominent." (*Moore*, l. c. in Proc. Zool. Soc. Lond.) Mr. Moore also records it from South India.

In Ceylon it occurs in the "Western, Central, and Southern Provinces; plains and up to 6,000 feet in forests; flight moderately rapid, settles on the ground and on bushes. Easily captured" (*Hutchison*).

I possess eight specimens, three males and five females, of *C. lanka* from Ceylon. The males differ somewhat in the depth of the colour of the ground on the upperside, and also in the width of the outer black border to both wings, the discal band on the underside is very obscure, but the comparative straightness of its inner edge at once distinguishes it from *C. cognata*. The females are also variable in the ground-colour of the upperside and also in the prominence of the discal band on the underside, though it is always much wider and more distinct than in the male. In two specimens it is slightly paler than the ground-colour and glossed with purple, in the other three it is silvery purplish-white.

412. **Cirrhochroa relata**, de N., n. sp.

HABITAT: South India.

EXPANSE: 2·5 to 3·1 inches.

DESCRIPTION: MALE. UPPERSIDE, *both wings* bright fulvous, the disc crossed by a more or less prominent black line, much deflexed inwards at the third median nervule of the forewing, with the usual white spot placed outwardly against it on the costa of the hindwing very large and quadrate; two submarginal lunular and a marginal straight black line, the two outer lines anteriorly widening out and amalgamating towards the apex. *Forewing* with the discocellulars defined by a fine black line. *Hindwing* with a discal series of six round black dots. UNDERSIDE, *both wings* paler, a very obscure subbasal fine black line, usually with an extremely prominent pure white discal band, its outer edge very straight, its inner edge somewhat less so, and defined by a narrow fuscous line; the marginal lines of the upperside but very indistinct, with a pale patch at the apex and inner angle of the forewing, enclosing two pale bands on the hindwing. *Hindwing* with the discal dots as above, but smaller and placed on an obsolescent diffused darker band, which is obscurely continued on to the forewing. FEMALE. UPPERSIDE, *both wings* paler than the male, all the black markings more prominent, the disc beyond the medial black line on the *forewing* paler than the rest of the ground; the outer margin highly emarginate, thereby giving the wing a very falcate appearance. UNDERSIDE, *both wings* with the ground-colour more ochreous than in the male, markings similar, but the discal pure white band still more prominent, its outer edge defined with a somewhat broad deep purple line. Other markings as in male.

The above description is made from three males and four females from the Nilgiris, two males and two females from North Canara, and one male and two females from Travancore. They exhibit extremely little variation; the male differs from *C. lanka* in being larger, the ground colour of the upperside paler, the outer black border much less prominent, and the discal white band on the underside being usually very wide and conspicuous. The female differs from that sex of *C. lanka* in the ground-colour of the upperside also being paler, and the outer black border less prominent. One male from the Nilgiris and the North Canara example differ from the other typical specimens described above in being smaller, and the discal band of the underside very obscure.

413. Cirrhochroa thais, Fabricius.

Papilio thais, Fabricius, Mant. Ins., vol. ii, p. 64, n. 601 (1787); idem, id., Ent. Syst., vol. iii, part i, p. 149, n. 436 (1793); *Cirrochroa thais*, Butler, Catal. Fabr. Lep. B. M., p. 116, n. 1 (1869); id., Moore, Proc. Zool. Soc. Lond., 1872, p. 557.

HABITAT : South India.

EXPANSE : 2·8 to 3·0 inches.

DESCRIPTION : " MALE and FEMALE. UPPERSIDE, pale ferruginous, glossed with green at the base. *Forewing* with a prominent medial transverse black line, which is oblique and zigzag in front of the cell and lunular hindward ; exterior margin broadly dusky black and traversed by a double row of ferruginous lunules, the marginal row obsolete at the apex ; a dusky streak lining the disco-cellular nervules. *Hindwing* with a large round white spot on anterior margin, from which proceeds the medial transverse black lunular line, between which and the exterior margin is a parallel row of six small black spots, two dusky lunular lines and a third outer line. UNDERSIDE pale ferruginous brown in male, brown in female, with a transverse medial irregularly dentated purple-white glossy band on both wings, the outer margin of the band being straight, and the dentations disappearing towards anal angle of hindwing ; transverse row of black spots on hindwing smaller than on upperside, marginal dusky lunules hardly visible."

" *Note.*—The above is the description of the insect which, according to Mr. Butler's determination, is the *C. thais* of Fabricius." (*Moore*, l. c.)

I possess one male of this species from Calicut, three males from Travancore, three males and one female from North Canara, and one male and four females from the Nilgiris. They show but little variation, and differ from the Ceylon form of *C. thais* (*C. cognata*) in being larger, the outer margin of the forewing more emarginate, and the black markings on the outer border far less prominent especially on the hindwing, in the colouration of the ground of the upperside being usually paler, the discal white band on the underside nearly always prominent and highly dentate in both sexes, in one Nilgiri male specimen only is it obscure ; in *C. cognata* it is never nearly as prominent and usually quite obsolete. The female is also paler above and the black margin less prominent, the forewing more deeply emarginate, the discal band below also more distinct. Messrs. Butler and Moore (Cat. Fab. Lep. and Proc. Zool. Soc. Lond. 1872) give *C. thais* from Ceylon, the description above applies best, however, to the South Indian form.

414. Cirrhochroa cognata, Moore.

Cirrochroa cognata, Moore, Lep. Cey., vol. i, p. 64, pl. xxxii, figs. 3, 3a, *male*; 3b, *larva* and *pupa* ; *C. thais*, Moore (*nec* Fabricius), id., p. 63, pl. xxxii, figs. 2, 2a, *female* (1881).

HABITAT : Ceylon.

EXPANSE : 2·0 to 3·0 inches.

DESCRIPTION : MALE. " UPPERSIDE differs from *C. thais* in the *forewing* being shorter, the apex broader and not falcated ; medial sinuous line indistinct, the marginal black band narrower and traversed by a row of dentate spots. *Hindwing* with a small white costal spot ; the discal transverse markings similar, but the outer marginal line blacker. UNDERSIDE dark ferruginous, the medial transverse band narrower, less defined, and in some specimens nearly obsolete."

" LARVA pale purplish-brown, yellowish beneath ; head yellow, spotted in front with black ; with two dorsal rows of long delicate branched spines and two lateral rows of shorter spines, a similar spine projecting on each side of the head from second segment. Pupa pale bluish-purple, spotted with black, with lengthened dorsal tubercles and two longer tubercular processes projecting from front of thorax; head cleft." (*Moore*, l. c.)

The above description is that of *C. cognata*. Mr. Moore does not state what sex he is describing, but from the outline of the wings he has evidently figured a male. He also records *C. thais* from Ceylon and describes both sexes as below. but figures a female only.

"MALE and FEMALE. UPPERSIDE pale ferruginous, glossed with green at the base. *Forewing* with a prominent medial transverse black line, which is oblique and zigzag in front of the cell and lunular hindward; exterior margin broadly ferruginous-black and traversed by a ferruginous sinuous line; a dusky streak lining the disco-cellular nervules. *Hindwing* with a large quadrate white spot on anterior margin, from which proceeds a medial transverse black lunular line; a discal row of six small black spots, two submarginal lunular lines and a third outer line. UNDERSIDE pale olive-brown in male, ferruginous-brown in female; with a transverse medial irregularly dentated purple-white glossy band on *both wings*, the outer margin of the band being straight and the dentations disappearing towards the anal angle of hindwing; a transverse row of black spots on *hindwing* smaller than on the upperside; marginal lunular lines indistinct and suffused with glaucous-purple. EXPANSE : ♂, 2·75; ♀, 2·25 inches " (*Moore*, l. c.) The above given dimension for the female is probably incorrect, that sex averages larger than the male.

I have but little doubt that the descriptions above of *C. cognata* and *C. thais* apply to one species only, as it appears from the former that Mr. Moore was unaware of the fact that the falcation of the forewing is a sexual and not a specific character in this group of *Cirrhochroas*, and I can find no character by which to separate the Ceylon specimens into two species.

C. cognata, judging from the large number of specimens that have been sent me, is by far the commonest species of the genus occurring in Ceylon. It is recorded (of *C. thais*) that it have been "taken at Galle and Kandy" (*Wade*), and (of *C. cognata*) that it is "a low country insect, found chiefly in the interior" (*Mackwood*). The males have the discal band of the underside usually quite as obscure as in *C. lanka*, but with the inner edge highly irregular and dentate, and the black outer border of both wings on the upperside very broad. The female is paler ferruginous than the male, the discal black line on the upperside much more distinct, the costal white spot of the hindwing much larger and quadrate; on the underside the discal band is always wider and more prominent, but is somewhat variable; in some specimens it is comparatively obscure, in others very prominent and highly dentate, in others again less prominent and its inner edge more regular, but always far less regular than in the same sex of *C. lanka*. The outer edge of the discal band is usually defined by a purple line, which in some examples is outwardly broadened out into a diffused band.

415. Cirrhochroa swinhoei, Butler.

Cirrhochroa swinhoei, Butler, Proc. Zool. Soc. Lond., 1881, p. 604, n. 8.

HABITAT : Nilgiris, Wynaad, Trevandrum, Ceylon.

EXPANSE : 2·2 to 2·9 inches.

DESCRIPTION : "FEMALE. Allied to *C. thais* of Ceylon, but of a clear bright fulvous colour above, almost as bright as in *C. aoris* and *C. mithila*, the *forewing* more falcate than in *C. thais*, the inner or discal zigzag line less strongly defined and more completely separated into <-shaped markings, the very irregular series just beyond the cell considerably more slender. *Hindwing* with all the markings less pronounced. *Body* considerably paler, the thorax pale greenish. UNDERSIDE stone-colour, with greenish and flesh-coloured tints, the basal area to the middle being flesh-coloured, the discal lines and outer borders washed with pale olivaceous; the band across the middle rather paler than the ground-colour, but not white or silvery in the type specimen; a diffused double pearly white spot at apex of forewing. *Pectus* whitish; *legs* flesh-coloured." (*Butler*, l. c.)

I possess three males and four females from the Nilgiris, one male from the Wynaad, two males and one female from Travancore, and three females from Ceylon which I identify as belonging to this species. The colouration of all of them on the upperside is very pale fulvous, in the males the outer border of the forewing on the upperside is somewhat wide at the apex enclosing four fulvous lunules, but rapidly narrowing towards the inner angle, the discal line on both wings is very obsolete, as are the three marginal lines on the hindwing. On the underside the tone of the ground-colour is very even and regular, all the markings are very obscure, except in one Travancore specimen in which the discal band (which has its inner edge always highly irregular and dentate) is white and somewhat prominent. The female is even paler on the upperside than the male, the markings somewhat more prominent, the discal band on the underside wider and usually more prominent, in one Ceylon example it is outwardly bounded by a broad diffused deep purple band which on the forewing occupies the whole of the upper half of the wing between the discal band and the margin. Mr. Moore does not record *C. swinhoei* from Ceylon, but the three female specimens I possess from that island must, I think, be placed under that specific name.

416. Cirrhochroa fasciata, Felder.

Atella fasciata, Felder, Wien. Ent. Monatsch., vol. iv, p. 236, n. 83 (1860); *Cirrochroa fasciata*, idem, id., vol. v, p. 301, n. 14 (1861); idem, id., Reise Novara. Lep., vol. iii, p. 389, n. 567, pl. xlix, figs. 9, 10 (1867).

HABITAT : Mergui, Upper Tenasserim, Sumatra, Mindoro.

EXPANSE : 1·8 to 2·2 inches.

DESCRIPTION : " Wings widely-dentate. UPPERSIDE brownish-fuscous, with a narrow common discal fascia extending from the first median nervule of the forewing to the anal angle of the hindwing, lutescent [yellowish]. *Forewing* with a subcostal spot, a submacular external fascia, and six posterior lunules, lutescent [yellowish]. *Hindwing* subangulate, with a posterior fascia inwardly marked with six black spots and six elongate submarginal lutescent lunules, separated by a streak, with an obsolete marginal concolourous line UNDERSIDE pale yellowish-brown, with the fasciæ of the upperside much paler. *Forewing* with a black spot near the inner angle." (*Felder* l. c. in Wien. Ent. Monatsch., vol. iv.)

This is a very distinct species, possessing alone in the genus the curious secondary male characters given at page 108. The female differs from the male only in not having these male marks. The colouration of the upperside is blackish, thickly irrorated with ochreous scales. There is a common discal band broken between the third median and lower discoidal nervules of the forewing, beyond which is a maculated band inwardly marked with six round black spots on the hindwing, and one black spot at the inner angle of the forewing, a submarginal series of lunules between the veins and an indistinct marginal line all pale clear ochreous. The underside is much paler throughout, but is similarly marked, the forewing has the round black spot near the outer angle, with sometimes a smaller one above it in the first median interspace very prominent.

Dr. Anderson took two males and a female in the Mergui archipelago during the winter months ; there are specimens in Major Marshall's collection taken by Captain C. T. Bingham in April in the Upper Thoungyeen forests, the Donat range and at Munwaddy, Kankaret, all in Upper Tenasserim.

Genus 64.—PSEUDERGOLIS, Felder.   (PLATE XXIII.)

Pseudergolis, Felder, Reise Novara, Lep., vol. iii, p. 404 (1867).

" *Antennæ*, rather long, beneath scarcely annulated, terminating gradually in a rather narrow club. *Palpi*, as in section *kedonia* of *Precis*, but a little shorter and stouter. *Wings*, with the discoidal cells slenderly closed. *Forewing*, with the discal " geniculum" * greater than in *P. kedonia* and its allies, with the second subcostal nervule a little more distant from the end of the cell, the third given off in the middle of the wing. *Hindwing*, with the discoidal nervule more distant from the lower subcostal nervule than in *Precis*. General appearance scarcely different from *Ergolis*." (*Felder*, l. c.) Only two species are known.

The type of the genus is *P. avesta* from Celebes, a species very closely allied to but larger than the Indian *P. wedah*. Structurally *Pseudergolis* is very nearly allied to *Precis*, but may be at once distinguished from it by the discoidal cells of both wings being slenderly but distinctly closed ; on the other hand in colouration and general style of markings it more nearly resembles *Ergolis*, being a ferruginous insect on the upperside with several dark sinuous transverse lines ;

Probably the bend in the lower disco-cellular nervule is meant

it may of course be distinguished from *Ergolis* by the costal nervure of the forewing not being dilated at the base. The Indian species, the only other one known besides the type, is apparently confined to the Himalayas and the tracts east of the Bramaputra.

417. Pseudergolis wedah, Kollar. (PLATE XXIII, FIG. 109 ♂).

Ariadne wedah, Kollar, in Hügel's Kaschmir, vol. iv, pt. 2, p. 437, n. 1 (1848); *Pseudergolis wedah*, Moore, Proc. Zool. Soc. Lond., 1882, p. 240; *Precis veda*, Kirby, Syn. Cat. Diurn. Lep., p. 191, n. 27 (1871); *Precis hara*, Moore, Horsfield and Moore, Cat. Lep. Mus. E. I. C., vol. i, p. 143, n. 291, pl. iiis, fig. 1 (1857); idem, id., Anderson's Anat. and Zool. Researches, p. 923 (1878).

HABITAT : Himalayas, Sylhet, Assam, Chittagong, Burma.

EXPANSE : 2·2 to 2·6 inches.

DESCRIPTION. "UPPERSIDE golden-brown, darker on outer margins. Both wings with three narrow transverse black bands on the anterior half, the outer band on the hindwing being zig-zagged, with a parallel row of small black spots between the outer and middle bands ; within each discoidal cell are two narrow and rather square-shaped spaces, those on the hindwing being the narrowest. UNDERSIDE dull brown, marked as above, with deep brown, but the two inner bands broad, the outer very narrow ; on the hindwing, above the marks, within [above] discoidal cell, is a narrow brown mark ; the outer margins are also deep brown." (Moore, l. c.) On the underside this species is more or less, especially on the outer margins, glossed with pale violet. The FEMALE differs from the male only in being somewhat paler.

In the N.-W. Himalayas and in Sikkim I have always met with this species near water. It occurs at Shillong in May ; Mr. H. M. Parish has taken it in the Chittagong Hill Tracts in November ; Captain C. T. Bingham has taken it in October in the Donat Range, Upper Tenasserim, and the Indian Museum, Calcutta, possesses specimens obtained by the Yunan expedition. It is not a rare species where it occurs, and has a very pretty soaring flight, and usually settles with wide outspread wings on the upper surface of a leaf.

The figure is taken from a male Masuri specimen in the Indian Museum, Calcutta, and shows both upper and underside.

Genus 65.—STIBOCHIONA, Butler. (PLATE XIX).

Stibochiona, Butler, Proc. Zool. Soc. Lond., 1868, p. 614.

"Allied to *Diadema* [= *Hypolimnas*] *alimena*, but differing from it, from *Apatura*, and from *Adolias* [= *Euthalia*] in having the discoidal cells of both wings distinctly closed, the middle and lower disco-cellulars of forewing forming a continuous arch, the upper disco-cellular of hindwing obliquely arched, the lower a little longer than the upper, slightly arched, and meeting the median nervure somewhat obliquely at the origin of the second and third branches. Colours intermediate between *Adolias* [= *Euthalia*] *coryta* and *Diadema* [= *Hypolimnas*] *alimena*. Typical species, *S. coresia*, Hubner." (Butler, l. c.)

This is a genus of very small extent, but two species being known, one occurring throughout the Himalayas from Kulu to Assam, the other in Sumatra and Java. The colouration of the Indian species is very deep blue, with a few lighter blue and white spots and markings. The wings are very evenly rounded, and the sexes very slightly differentiated.

418. Stibochiona nicea, Gray. (PLATE XIX, FIG. 81 ♂).

Adolias nicea, Gray, Lep. Ins. Nepal, p. 13, pl. xii, fig. 1 (1846); id., Moore, Trans. Ent. Soc. Lond., new series, vol. v, p. 83, n. 43 (1859); *Stibochiona nicea*, Butler, Proc. Zool. Soc. Lond., 1868, p. 614, n. 1; *Adolias dolofe*, Felder, Wien. Ent. Monatsch., vol. iii, p. 184, n. 6 (1859).

HABITAT : Himalayas, Sylhet, Assam.

EXPANSE : ♂, 2·25 to 2·75 ; ♀, 2·75 to 3·10 inches.

DESCRIPTION : "MALE. UPPERSIDE velvety-black. Forewing with a marginal, short submarginal, and a shorter third row of small white spots, the marginal row bordered inwardly by a row of small indistinct blue spots ; also indistinct blue marks within discoidal cell. Hindwing with a marginal row of black spots encircled with blue inwardly, and with white outwardly ; [within which is a lunular blue line becoming obsolescent towards the apex]. *Cilia* white. UNDERSIDE brown-black. *Forewing* as above [but all the markings more prominent]. *Hindwing* with marginal row of white lunulated spots, and a submarginal row of minute white dots. [A discal angulated series of bluish-white spots, with some bluish markings in and about the cell] FEMALE. UPPERSIDE marked as in male, but washed with olive-green, the marginal row of encircled spots of *hindwing* larger, and with a submarginal narrow greenish line. UNDERSIDE with the three rows of white spots on *forewing* extending to posterior margin. On the *hindwing* the marginal row of lunulated spots are larger, and there is a submarginal row of white spots, also a third inner row of bluish-white spots." (*Moore*, l.c.)

Mr. Hocking took this species in the Kangra Valley, and states that it " flies like *Papilio pammon*, following the line of a hedge and passing in and out between the bushes." Mr. A. Graham Young has taken it in the Kulu Valley, I met with it in August below Kotgarh, fifty miles north of Simla, and Mr. Templeton has taken it in Masuri. It is common in Sikkim, and the Indian Museum, Calcutta, has specimens from Sylhet, Cherrapunji, Naga Hills, Sibsagar (*S. E. Peal*), and examples brought by the Dafla Expedition. It is a very pretty insect on the wing, has a quick flight, but settles often, always with wings widely distended, and frequently on the underside of a leaf.

Mr. Butler (l. c.) records a variety from Northern India, with the following description :— " Variety. Male smaller, with the spots distinctly green not blue." I have seen no male specimen answering to the above, but the spots on the margin of the upperside in the female are of a green rather than of a blue tint.

The figure shows both sides of a male Sikkim example in the Indian Museum, Calcutta.

Genus 66.—HYPOLIMNAS, Hübner. (PLATE XX).

Hypolimnas (also spelt *Hipolimnas*), Hübner, Verz. bek. Schmett., p. 45 (1816); id., Distant, Rhop. Malay., p. 164 (1883); *Esoptria*, Hübner, Verz. bek. Schmett., p. 45 (1816); *Diadema* (nom. praeoc.), Boisduval, Voy Astr., Lep., p. 135 (1832); id., Felder, Neues Lep., p. 25, n 57 (1861); id., Wallace, Trans. Ent. Soc. Lond., 1869, p. 277, *Monograph*; id., sect. 1, *Diadema*, and sect 5, *Euralia*, Westwood, Gen. Diurn. Lep., vol. ii, pp. 279—281 (1850); *Apatura*, Moore, (*nec* Fabricius), Lep. Cey., vol. i, p. 57 (1881).

" BODY, moderately robust, *wings* large, those of the male generally more brilliantly coloured than those of the female ; head and neck often marked with small white spots, *Head*, moderately large, with a frontal tuft nearly reaching to the tip of the second joint of the palpi. *Eyes*, prominent, naked. *Palpi*, porrected, rather more than twice the length of the head, ascending obliquely, but scarcely elevated above the level of the middle of the eyes, rather flattened beneath, scaly ; the scales lying flat except at the base, beneath which they are slightly elongated, and also near the middle of the upperside of the second joint, where there is an elongated tuft of white scales, and another near the tip within, which causes the apical joint to be as wide apart as the space between the eyes ; the terminal joint is elongate ovate, slightly pointed at the tip, and about one-fourth of the length of the second joint. *Antennae*, short, scarcely above three-fourths of the length of the body, and not half the length of the wings, slender, slightly curved ; terminated by a distinct, rather small club, not occupying more than one-fifth of the length of the antennæ. Club obovate, terminated by a very minute acute point. *Thorax*, moderately robust, hairy, especially on the metathorax ; neck short, marked with small white spots ; wings large. FOREWING, subtrigonate. *Costal margin* much arched ; *apex* not regularly rounded ; *outer margin* about three-fourths of the length of the costa, angulated below the apex, emarginate below the angle ; margin slightly scalloped ; *inner margin* slightly concave, about the same length as the costa. *Costal nervure* extending beyond the middle of the costa ; *subcostal* nervure with its first branch arising about one-fourth [less than one-third] from the base of the wing ; second branch arising at a little distance beyond the first, and before the anterior extremity of the discoidal cell ; third branch arising at about [before] two-thirds of the length of the wing, and extending to the tip ; fourth branch arising [less than] half way between it and the apex, and reaching the outer margin at a little distance below the apex, the terminal portion of the

16

vein slightly deflexed. *Upper disco-cellular nervule* very short, almost obsolete, arising from the subcostal at about [more than] one-third of the length of the wing; *middle* disco-cellular short, curved obliquely outwards; *lower* disco-cellular slightly curved, about three times as long as the middle one, and uniting with the third branch of the median nervure at a little distance beyond its origin, closing the *discoidal cell* at a little more than one-third of the length of the wing; the third [median] branch is considerably curved beyond the discoidal cell. HINDWING, broad, nearly rounded; *costal margin* much arched; *outer margin* somewhat longer than the costal, rounded, and scalloped. *Precostal nervure* curved outwardly. *Costal* nervure much curved, extending to the outer angle. *Subcostal* nervure branching at about one-fifth of the length of the wing. *Upper disco-cellular nervule* arising very close to the base of the subcostal branch; *lower* disco-cellular arising at about the same distance from the base of the upper disco-cellular, curved, and united with the median nervure exactly at the origin of its third branch, closing the *discoidal cell*. FORELEGS, of the *male* short and pectoral, scaly; *femora* clothed beneath with rather long scaly hairs; *tibia* and *tarsus* scaly, the tibia slightly curved, the tarsus not more than one-third of the length of the tibia, elongate-ovate, exarticulate. Of the *female* considerably larger; *femur* and *tibia* similarly clothed; *tarsus* scaly, more than two-thirds of the length of the tibia, distinctly articulated, the basal joint occupying nearly three-fourths of the whole tarsus, with two strong spurs at its tip beneath; second, third, and fourth joints very short, obliquely truncate, spined beneath at the tip; fifth joint minute, but with similar spines. HINDLEGS, rather long, scaly; *tibia* with two rows of short spines, and rather long tibial spurs; *tarsi* with several rows of shorter spines beneath and at the sides; *claws* moderate."

"LARVA cylindrical; head with two erect spines, each of the following segments with several shorter spines. PUPA robust; hunched on the back; abdomen-case spined." (*Westwood, l. c.*)

Mr. Wallace, in monographing the genus in 1869, wrote: "Two of the commonest species, *Diadema* [= *Hypolimnas*] *bolina*, Linnæus, and *D. misippus*, Linnæus, have an immense range, from Australia and the Pacific to India and Africa, but no other species of the restricted genus is found in continental India, and all but two are inhabitants of the Austro-Malayan region, which we may therefore look upon as the probable birth-place of the group. This genus, and those which have been separated from it, furnish us with examples of almost all the anomalies of variation. Some species present an amount of variation perhaps greater than any to be found among butterflies; others scarcely vary at all. The sexes are, in some species, absolutely without a feature of their colouration in common; in others, they are hardly distinguishable. In a large number of species there is the most wonderful mimicry of other groups, so that they have been mistaken for *Danaidæ* and *Acræidæ*, and there is, perhaps, nothing more striking than the accurate manner in which some African species imitate the striped and spotted *Acræa*, which inhabit the very same districts. In the Eastern islands the protective mimicry has sometimes caused the usual sexual characters to be completely reversed, which has led to confusion in the determination of the species." (*Wallace, l. c.*)

The males of the two Indian species are among the most beautiful of butterflies, being black on the upperside, with a large pale-centred patch of resplendent irridescent purple on each wing, this colour, however, being quite invisible when seen from behind, though it is most brilliant when seen in front, *i.e.*, with the head of the insect turned towards the observer, "in which position, as Dr. Schulte remarks, the male would be seen by the female when approaching her," as Mr. Darwin has quoted. The two Indian species occur abundantly throughout the country, and in the hills are met with up to 6,000 feet at any rate.

Key to the Indian species of Hypolimnas.

A. Both sexes with the ground-colour black. Apex of hindwing on underside black.

419. H. BOLINA, India, Malayana

B. Male, ground-colour black with purple and white spots on the upperside; apex of hindwing on underside ochreous. Female with ground-colour tawny, as in *Danais chrysippus*.

420. H. MISIPPUS, America, Africa, India, Malayana.

419 **Hypolimnas bolina**, Linnæus.

Papilio bolina, Linnæus, Syst. Nat., ed. x, p. 479, n. 124 (1758) ; idem, id., Mus. Ulr., p. 295, n. 113 (1764); idem, id., Syst. Nat., ed. xii, vol. i, pt. 2, p. 781, n. 188 (1767) ; id., Clerck, Icones Ins., vol. ii, pl. xxi, fig. 2, *male* (1764) ; id., Fabricius, Syst. Ent., p. 507, n. 269 (1775) ; *Diadema bolina*, Wallace, Trans. Ent. Soc. Lond., 1869, p. 278, n. 1, *part* ; *Hypolimnas bolina*, Kirby, Syn. Cat. Diurn. Lep., p. 274, n. 1 (1871), *part* ; id., Distant, Rhop. Malay., p. 165, n. 1, pl. xii, figs. 10, 12, *male* ; pl. xv, fig. 12, *female* (1883) ; *Apatura bolina*, Moore, Lep. Cey., vol. 1, p. 58, pl. xxx, fig. 1, *male* ; 1b. *larva* and *pupa* (1881); *Papilio auge*, Cramer, Pap. Ex., vol. ii, pl. cxc, figs. A, B, *male* (1777); *Diadema auge*, Horsfield and Moore, Cat. Lep. Mus. E. I. C., vol. 1, p. 158, n. 328, pl. v, figs. 9, *larva* ; 9a, *pupa* (1857); *P. jacintha*, Drury Ex. Ent., vol. ii, pl. xxi, figs. 1, 2 *female* (1773); id., Donovan, Ins. China, pl. xxxvii, fig. 1, *female* (1798); id., Fabricius, Ent. Syst., vol. iii, pt. 1, p. 60, n. 187 (1793) ; *Apatura jacintha*, Moore, Lep. Cey., p. 58, pl. xxx, fig. 1a, *female* (1881); *Papilio avia*, Fabricius, Ent. Syst., vol. iii, pt. 1, p. 111, n. 342 (1793) ; *Hypolimnas charybdis*, Butler, Cist. Ent., vol. ii, p. 432 (1881).

HABITAT : Throughout India, Ceylon, Andaman and Nicobar Islands, the Malay peninsula, Siam, Sumatra, Java, Australia.

EXPANSE : ♂, 2·5 to 4·3 ; ♀, 2·9 to 4·8 inches.

DESCRIPTION : " MALE. UPPERSIDE very dark indigo-blue. *Forewing* with a large elongate and macular white spot at [beyond] end of cell, margined with bright bluish, commencing near the upper discoidal nervule and terminating near the second median nervule ; two or three small sub-apical white spots divided by the fourth and fifth subcostal nervules ; and sometimes followed by a few minute submarginal whitish spots placed between the nervules. *Hindwing* with a large medial white spot, broadly and irregularly surrounded by pale bluish, which commences on lower half of cell, and is bounded by the upper subcostal and the first median nervules ; a series of minute and frequently subobsolete submarginal white spots placed between the nervules. *Cilia* of both wings alternately white. UNDERSIDE dark olivaceous-brown. *Forewing* with the white markings as above, but with the large macular spot at [beyond] end of cell almost extending to costa, not prominently margined with bluish, and followed by a small pale spot be-neath the second median nervule ; submarginal spots distinct, one on each side of first median nervule largest and bluish ; a pale lunulate submarginal fascia and a similar but more linear marginal fascia, which are almost obsolete above the lower discoidal nervule ; basal half of costal area minutely irrorated with greyish ; cell with three upper small and irregular white spots more or less surrounded with dark fuscous. *Hindwing* with a broad medial whitish fascia, com-mencing near upper subcostal nervule, where it is preceded by a subcostal spot, and terminating near anal angle (this fascia is variable both in size and shape) ; a submarginal series of small bluish white spots placed between the nervules, followed by a submarginal series of greyish subconical spots placed in pairs between the nervules ; marginal linear lunular spots as on forewing. *Cilia* as above. *Body* above dark indigo-blue, the head marked with a few pale spots ; body beneath and *legs* more or less concolourous with wings ; the *palpi* beneath white, the legs beneath more or less greyish, and the *abdomen* and *thorax* with a few whitish spots. FEMALE. UPPERSIDE dark olivaceous-brown. *Forewing* with a few small bluish subcostal spots above cell ; a transverse blue macular fascia beyond end of cell (corresponding to the white fascia of male) ; a submarginal series of white spots placed between the nervules, the two uppermost of which are largest and contiguous, followed by a submarginal and marginal series of waved and linear greyish spots, between which the colour is somewhat paler. *Hindwing* with a submarginal series of greyish spots placed between the nervules, followed by a series of subconical spots of the same colour, which are placed conjointly in pairs between the nervules; marginal spots as on forewing, but more lunulate. *Cilia* of both wings alternately greyish. UNDERSIDE brownish ochraceous. *Forewing* with the marginal and submarginal markings as above, the macular fascia at [beyond] end of cell subobsolete and greyish ; the basal half of wing is pale castaneous, with the costal area and cell marked as in male. *Hindwing* with the marginal and submarginal markings as above, and the middle crossed by a faint greyish fascia more or less corresponding to that on the wings of the male." *(Distant, l.c.)*

" LARVA purple-brown, head armed with two long erect branched spines, the segments with a dorsal row of three (two only on the anterior and posterior segments) long branched red spines, and three lateral rows of spines. PUPA thick, purple-brown, blotched with black ; ab-dominal segments with stout pointed dorsal tubercles ; head obtuse, pointed in front, thorax angular at top." (*Moore*, l. c. in Lep. Cey.) Surgeon-Major Forsayeth found the "larva on a small herb with a purple flower. It somewhat resembled that of *Junonia orithyia*, but the head is entire, of a red colour, and armed with two fleshy horns covered with short spines. The body is also armed with similar processes. The pupa also resembles that of *J. orithyia* in form and colouring, but of course much larger in size, and has spinous projections along the middle of abdomen and dorsum of thorax."

Mr. Wallace writes (l. c.) :—" This is an exceedingly wide-spread and variable species. The male is tolerably constant, but presents three decided modifications. That which extends over the whole continent of India, is generally distinguished by a row of white points behind the blue and white spot on the hindwing, and the white bands across the wings on the underside are well marked. Those of the Malayan and Polynesian countries never have the white dots, and seldom have the bands beneath so distinctly marked. In the British Museum are some remarkable specimens from the Philippine Islands, in which the male has the spot on the hindwing reduced to a mere blue gloss without any paler centre, so that in most lights it is invisible ; but without a large series from this locality it would be impossible to determine how far this is linked to the more ordinary forms by intermediate types." Regarding this latter point there are two male specimens in the Indian Museum, Calcutta, and several in my own collection, obtained by Mr. S. E. Peal at Sibsagar in Upper Assam, which agree with the specimens from the Philippine Islands referred to, in the character of the blue spot without white on the upperside of the hindwing, but although they are alike in this respect they differ in size and in the markings of the underside. Mr. W. C. Taylor has also taken a small specimen in Orissa, which shows but very faint traces of the white colouration in the middle of the blue spot ; in fact there are gradations from a perfectly uniform blue spot to others in which the white spot is fully developed.

In India *H. bolina* is represented by several fairly well-marked forms in the male, but they are neither confined to particular localities nor constant in their characters, each form being linked to the others by numerous intermediate gradations. The female is much more constant comparatively, though it too shows variation in the extent of the markings, especially on the upperside.

The typical male which was described by Linnæus under the name *bolina*, and figured by Clerck under the same name and by Cramer under the name *auge*, has on the upperside the patches white, bordered with blue ; the white central portion being untinted with blue in any light ; on the underside there is a prominent white bar or band on each wing, and the submarginal band of whitish spots between the discal dots and marginal lunules is obsolescent. This form, so far as I am aware, usually appears during the rainy season.

Next there is a larger form in which on the upperside the patch on the hindwing is tinted or irrorated with blue throughout, but much paler in the centre ; and on the margin they frequently show more or less prominent traces of whitish markings corresponding with the border markings of the underside. The underside is very variable, typically lighter and more uniform brown, the white band on the forewing much reduced and irrorated with brown, the white discal band of the hindwing very diffused and obsolescent ; and the submarginal band on the other hand much more prominent and almost filling the entire space between the discal dots and the marginal lunules. The larger size, paler and more uniform colouration of the underside, and the absence of pure white markings, those on the upperside being irrorated with bluish, and those on the underside with brown, are the distinguishing characters of this form. As far as I am aware, it usually appears during the dry season.

Again, each of these forms exhibits, but not commonly, a striking variety in which the patch on the upperside of the hindwing is uniform black, shot in certain lights with brilliant deep blue, but showing no trace of pale centering. These varieties are not casual isolated forms, but linked by numerous gradations in which the pale centering gets gradually less.

In the variety allied to the smaller typical form there is a striking difference on the underside also, in extreme cases the white discal band of the hindwing and all the whitish

---

* Trans. Ent. Soc. Lond., 1884, p. 384.

markings on the border of both wings entirely disappear, except a white dot on the cilia in each interspace, and there appears a deep violet suffused patch on the disc just beyond the cell ; the ground-colour is darker throughout, and the discal white markings of the forewing though narrower are prominent.

In the variety allied to the larger form the underside is less strikingly different, the markings are even more obscure and suffused as well as irrorated with brown, and the discal dots on both wings are more prominently tinted with violet.

The female was figured by Donovan and Drury under the name *jacintha*, and later on was described by Fabricius under the name *aria*. The variations of it, which are casual and inconstant, are mainly confined to the greater or less prominence of the blue macular fascia on the upperside of the forewing, and the greater or less prominence of the whitish submarginal band on the hindwing, in one extreme consisting of small conical spots in pairs between the nervules, in the other extreme these spots are greatly elongated, entirely filling the spaces between the veins, and coalescing with the discal spots towards the anal angle. On the underside the females in all cases appear to correspond with the larger form, and not with the typical smaller form in style of markings. Mr. Moore in his "Lepidoptera of Ceylon" gives *H. jacintha* as a distinct species from *H. bolina*, but remarks that the former "may probably be a seasonal variety of" the latter.

H. bolina is in most parts of the country one of the commonest as well as one of the most beautiful of the Indian butterflies ; in the drier portions of Western Continental India it is rare, but even there it may occasionally be found in gardens. In the moister regions, particularly in the warm valleys and submontane tracts, it abounds, and the flash of the brilliant purple as it opens and closes its wings while sunning itself on some flower or spray of foliage meets the eye at every turn.

Mr. Butler has recently described as a distinct species under the name of *H. charybdis* some specimens which I cannot recognise even as a distinct variety of *H. bolina*. He apparently considers the larger form described above to be distinct and to stand as *H. jacintha*, but in this I cannot follow him. The original description of *H. charybdis* is appended for reference.[*]

A closely-allied species or local race which has been described apparently from a single pair by Mr. Butler as *H. incommoda* occurs in Malacca ; it is almost identical with the Javan species which has been identified as *H. lasinassa* of Lucas (*nec* Cramer), the female of which presents the characters noted but is extremely variable (one form of it is figured by Cramer as *P. proserpina*). The description of *H. incommoda* is appended for reference.[†]

In the Malay peninsula and archipelago several species of this genus occur which apparently mimic certain species of *Euplœa*. Two species of this group have been described as occurring within our limits, *H. wallaceana* (India ?), and *H. interstincta* (Assam, *Warwick*), but the authority for the localities appears to be in both cases doubtful, and I am not personally aware of any instance of the occurrence of any species of this group even in Tenasserim.

---

[*] *Hypolimnas charybdis*, Butler, Cist. Ent., vol. ii, p. 432 (1883). HABITAT : Bombay. EXPANSE : *Male*, 3⅝ ; *female*, 4 ½ inches. DESCRIPTION : "Nearly allied to *H. bolina*, rather larger ; the white fascioles on the bright ultramarine patches of the upperside narrower and more elongated ; the white discal spots on the female reduced to dots (excepting two near the costa of the forewing) ; the submarginal notched spots and the crescents close to the margin narrower and suffused with brown. UNDERSIDE intermediate in character between *H. bolina* and *H. jacintha*, the oblique white belt beyond the cell of the forewing being distinct, but broken up into spots ; the belt beyond the middle of the hindwing sordid whitish, with a brownish tint in the male, and a creamy tint in the female, corresponding with the submarginal belt in colour ; the latter, the undulated whitish marginal stripe and the discal series of pearly white spots as in *H. jacintha*. Nearest to D. [= *H.*] *incommoda* in general appearance." (*Butler*, l c.)

This species appears to be one of the almost innumerable varieties of *H. bolina*.

[†] *Hypolimnas incommoda*, Butler, Trans. Linn. Soc., Zoology, second series, vol. i, p. 543, n. 2 (1877) ; id., Distant, Rhop. Malay., p. 162, n. 2, pl. xvi, figs. 8, *male* ; 9, *female* (1883). HABITAT : Malacca. EXPANSE : *Male*, 3¼ ; *female*, 3⅞ inches. DESCRIPTION : "MALE very similar to the male of *H. bolina*, but with the unbanded band of the *forewing* straighter on the UNDERSIDE, and the pale brown submarginal spots narrower and darker. FEMALE differs from the female of *H. bolina* in having a broad oblique subapical white band on the UPPERSIDE of the *forewing*, a large diffused sordid white patch just beyond the cell of the *hindwing*, and the submarginal spots all separated, small, and pale brown."

"This form seems to replace *H. bolina* in Malacca ; in some respects it approaches the Javan species *H. nerina*." (*Butler*, l c.)

Mr. Distant states (l c.) that "The male and female typical specimens, which are contained in the British Museum, and here figured, constitute at present our sole knowledge of the species."

I append descriptions of these species for reference, also of *D. anomala*[*] to which they are both evidently very closely allied.

420. **Hypolimnas misippus,** Linnæus. (Plate XX. Fig. 85 ♂, ♀ I. Form).

Papilio misippus, Linnæus, Mus. Ulr., p. 264, n. 83 (1764) ; idem, id., Syst. Nat., ed. xii, vol. 1, pt. 2, p. 767, n. 118 (1767); *Diadema misippus,* Wallace, Trans. Ent. Soc. Lond., 1869, p. 280, n. 2 ; id., Trimen, Trans. Ent. Soc. Lond., 1870, p. 356 ; *Apatura misippus,* Moore, Lep. Cey., vol. i, p. 59, pl. xxix. figs. 1, *male;* 1b, *female I form ;* 1a, *female II form ;* 1c, *larva* and *pupa* (1881); *Hypolimnas misippus,* Kirby, Syn. Cat. Diurn. Lep., p. 225, n. 2 (1871); id., Distant, Rhop. Malay., p. 167, n. 3, pl. xii, figs. 9, 11, *male ;* pl. xv, fig. 11, *female I form* (1883); id., Butler, Proc. Zool. Soc. Lond., 1884, p. 481, n. 3; *Danais misippus,* Godart, Enc. Meth., vol. ix, p. 188, n. 40 (1819); *Nymphalis misippe,* idem, id., p. 394, n. 153 (1823); *Papilio bolina,* Drury (*nec* Linnæus), Ill. Ex. Ent., vol. i, pl. xiv, figs. 1, 2, *male* (1770); id., Cramer, Pap. Ex., vol. i, pl. lxv, figs. E, F, *male* (1775); *Diadema bolina,* Trimen, Rhop. Afr. Austr., p. 152, n. 91 (1862); *Papilio diocippus,* Cramer, Pap. Ex., vol. i, pl. xxviii, figs. B, C, *female I form* (1775); id., Fabricius, Ent. Syst., vol. iii, pt. 1, p. 51, n. 158 (1793); *Euplœa diocippe,* Hübner, Verz. bek. Schmett., p. 15, n. 83 (1816); *Papilio inaria,* Cramer, Pap. Ex., vol. iii, pl. ccxiv, figs. A, B, *female II form* (1779); *Papilio chrysippus,* Sulzer, Gesch. Ins., p. 144, pl. xvi, fig. 3 (1776).

HABITAT : America (Florida), Cuba, Antigua, Trinidad, Africa, Madagascar, Aden, throughout India up to 6,000 feet in the Himalayas, Ceylon, Andamans (*Doherty*), Nicobars, Burma, Siam, Malay Peninsula, Sumatra, Java, Celebes, Borneo, Lombock, Timor, Formosa.

EXPANSE : ♂, 2·45 to 3·30 ; ♀, 2·85 to 3·90 inches.

DESCRIPTION : "MALE. UPPERSIDE very dark indigo-blue. *Forewing* with an oblong subapical white spot divided by the fourth and fifth subcostal nervules ; a large elongated white spot on disc passing [beyond] apex of cell, commencing beneath subcostal nervure and terminating between the second and first median nervules. *Hindwing* with a large irregularly rounded discal white spot, commencing on lower half of cell and bounded by the first subcostal and the first median nervules ; these spots on *both wings* are surrounded by bright but evanescent

---

* *Hypolimnas anomala,* Wallace, Trans. Ent. Soc. Lond., 1869, p. 285, n. 15; id., Distant, Rhop. Malay, p. 169 (1883). HABITAT : Malacca, Java. EXPANSE : n.t given. DESCRIPTION : "MALE. Form of *P.* [=H.] *antilope,* rather smaller. UPPERSIDE bronzy or olive-brown, with a blue gloss on the costal and outer margins of the *forewing,* and the outer part of the *hindwing,* paler. A row of white round spots parallel to the outer margin as in *D. antilope,* but larger and more distinct ; a band of three white or bluish-white marks, sometimes very indistinct, across the *forewing* beyond the middle ; marginal and submarginal spots as in *D. antilope.* UNDERSIDE olive-brown, spots and markings as above, with one additional white spot on the costal margin. FEMALE UPPERSIDE rich purple-brown, the whole surface of the *forewing,* except the basal third, richly glossed with satiny blue, a transverse band of three bluish elongate spots beyond the cell, and a fourth much smaller ; the two white spots of the intra-marginal band nearest the costa large and confluent, while those nearest the anal angle are small and indistinct. UNDERSIDE as in the male "

" *Diadema* [= *Hypolimnas*] *anomala* offer- the most remarkable case known among butterflies of a reversal of the usual sexual colouring, the males being always dull brown, the females glossed with rich blue. The reason for this exception to the ordinary rule is, I believe, to be found in the fact that the brilliant blue gloss causes the female to resemble or mimic the *Euplœa midamus,* one of the very commonest butterflies of the East, and one that belongs to the pre-eminently protected group of the *Danaidæ.* The two insects frequent the same places, and the resemblance on the wing was such as to deceive myself, and it is perhaps owing to this cause that I captured so few specimens of this interesting butterfly. That protection which female insects usually obtain by being less brilliant and conspicuous than the males, is here given by exactly opposite means ; a remarkable proof, as it appears to me, that female butterflies would be more generally brilliant than they are, were not their variations in this direction checked, and eliminated by the danger they incur through it. It may be observed, that in the allied species *Diadema antilope,* the female resembles *Euplœa climena* (a common species in the countries it inhabits) much more than the male does. It also closely resembles *Elymnias vitellia,* a species which has long figured in our lists as a *Diadema;* and there is reason to believe that the *Eurytelidæ,* to which *Elymnias* belongs, are themselves a protected group, though perhaps not so perfectly so as the *Danaidæ."* (Wallace, l. c.)

Hypolimnas wallaceana, Butler, Cist. Ent., vol. i, p. 157, n. 15 (1873). HABITAT : India? EXPANSE : 3·33 inches. DESCRIPTION : "MALE. Allied to *D. antilope* and *D. albula;* but still more like *D. anomala,* from which it differs in the absence of any blue gloss above, in the presence of three white streaks placed obliquely beyond the discoidal cell of the *forewing,* and in the larger discal spots towards the costa of the same wing. UNDERSIDE (in addition to the above distinctions) the submarginal spots of the *forewing* are more evident, and the whitish streaks beyond the cell of the *hindwing* are wanting."

" Mimics *Euplœa kinbergi* of Wallengren ; and was supposed by Mr Wallace to be the male of *D. anomala;* the latter species, however, is nearly alike in both sexes, as evidenced by examples from Borneo now in the collection ; and, were it not so, no advantage could accrue to the female over the male from the blue spot of the forewing since the supposed male is equally well protected in its brown dress by its resemblance to another species of *Euplœa."* (Butler, l. c.)

Hypolimnas interstincta, Butler, Cist. Ent., vol. i, p. 157, n. 16 (1873). HABITAT : Assam (*Warkwick*). EXPANSE : Male, 3·5 inches. DESCRIPTION : "MALE. Allied to *D. wallaceana* and to *D. anomala,* from which it differs in the absence of the blue shot on the UPPERSIDE of the *forewing,* and the presence of a creamy discal band in the *hindwing,* interrupted by the nervures and internervular folds. UNDERSIDE only differs in the greater length of the whitish streaks towards the abdominal area of the *hind wing.*

" This species was considered by Mr. Wallace to be a variety of the male of *D. anomala;* it is, however, clearly distinct, and is a mimic, probably of the female of *Euplœa alcathoe."* (Butler, l. c.)

blue, *Cilia* alternately greyish. UNDERSIDE, *forewing* with the large discal spot as above, but extending to costa, and more or less margined with fuscous, and before which the colour is pale castaneous, beneath it fuscous and beyond it ochraceous ; basal half of costal area fuscous, irrorated with minute bluish-grey spots ; cell with three upper white spots broadly and irregularly surrounded with black ; subapical spot as above, followed by a small spot on each side of lower subcostal [discoidal] nervule and a minute spot on each side of first median nervule ; two narrow submarginal bluish-grey fasciæ, bordered on each side with fuscous. *Hindwing* reddish ochraceous, crossed by a broad white fascia, commencing at costal nervure where it is broadest, and terminating near the internal nervure where it is narrowest, and which is inwardly straight and anteriorly margined with fuscous ; it is outwardly notched at upper subcostal nervule, and then rounded to submedian nervure, where it is somewhat prolonged towards anal angle, and there contains an angulated black spot, and also an irregular black spot situated between the costal nervure and upper subcostal nervule ; a basal black spot before the præcostal nervure, a submarginal series of small bluish-white spots placed between the nervules, and submarginal fasciæ as on forewing. *Body* above concolourous with wings, and with the *head* spotted with white ; body beneath fuscous, spotted with white ; *legs* fuscous, greyish-white beneath ; *palpi* (excluding apices) white beneath." (*Distant,* l. c.)

FEMALE 1. FORM (*P. diocippus* of Cramer). " UPPERSIDE reddish ochraceous. *Forewing* with rather less than apical half, beginning at base, gradually widening across apex of cell and narrowly terminating at posterior angle, black, containing a waved series of five white spots placed between the nervules, the first smallest and linear, the second and third subquadrate, fourth and fifth more or less rounded ; this series is preceded by about two small subcostal white spots and followed by a waved series of four small subapical white spots, the two uppermost largest ; two submarginal series of small bluish-white spots, not distinctly extending beyond the first median nervule. *Cilia* alternately greyish. *Hindwing* with a large medial black spot beneath the costal nervure, and a marginal black fascia preceded by some small paler and indistinct spots, and containing a series of lunate ochraceous spots placed between the nervules, bluish at anal angle. *Cilia* as on the forewing. UNDERSIDE, *forewing* as above, but with the apex beyond the transverse spots ochraceous and not black. *Hindwing* with the disc whitish ; a basal spot and a medial subcostal spot as in male, and a black spot at end of cell ; a broad white marginal fascia containing three waved black lines, and preceded by a series of small white spots."

This form "affords one of the best and strongest examples of ' mimicry,' it being a true and startling mimic of *Danais chrysippus,* a protected species which is found with it in its different habitats, excluding America, where, however, it is evidently an introduced species. According to Boisduval, this resemblance is even found at first sight, in the larvæ of the two species, which in South Africa feed upon the leaves of the Oleander." (*Distant,* l. c.)

This form of the female is the most widely distributed, probably occurring everywhere with the male. I am aware of its occurrence in South Africa, Aden, Karachi, Simla, Oudh, Malda, Calcutta, North Canara, Bombay, the Nilgiris, Bangalore, Trichinopoly, Travancore, Ceylon, Katchall in the Nicobars, the Malay peninsula and Batavia.

At Aden (*Major Yerbury*), Ootacamund (*G. F. Hampson*), and probably elsewhere in India a variety of this form occurs with the disc of the hindwing on the upperside white ; it mimics the variety of *Danais chrysippus* named *alcippus,* which also has white on the hindwing.

FEMALE II. FORM (*P. inaria* of Cramer). " This differs from the ordinary female in the absence of the black ground-colour (at the apex of the forewing), and the oblique white band, these parts being of the some ferruginous colour as the other parts of the wing." (*Moore,* l. c.)

This form occurs less commonly than the other, examples of it have been taken in South Africa, at Aden, Karachi, Bombay, Rajputana, Oudh, Malda, Calcutta, Bhadrachallum, Madras, Bangalore, Ceylon, Java and Amboyna. Its model is an unnamed form of *Danais dorippus* in which the hindwing is entirely red.

At Aden this form also varies, examples occurring in which the hindwing is suffused with white on the disc, its model being the true *Danais dorippus* of Klug. This variety of *Hypolimnas* has been separately described by Mr. Butler as *H. alcippoides*.[*] It occurs in the Victoria Nyanza, Africa, as well as in Aden.

"LARVA purple-brown, numerously covered with minute white spots, cylindrical, thickest towards the middle; head armed with two erect rugose spines, the segments with three dorsal rows of branched pale spines and three lateral rows of shorter spines. Feeds [in Ceylon] on *Abutilon*, *Abelmoschus*, &c." In Calcutta it feeds on *Portulaca quadrifida*, and Colonel Lang has reared it on *Portulaca oleracea*. "PUPA purple-brown, thick, abdominal segments tubercular, head obtusely pointed, thorax convex." (*Moore*, l. c.) I can see no resemblance between the larva of *H. misippus* and that of *Danais chrysippus*, although Boisduval is said to have seen some.

H. misippus appears to be almost as universally met with in India as is *Danais chrysippus*, which is the model of the I. Form of its female. The apex of the forewing on the underside being ochreous will at once distinguish the males of this species from that sex of *H. bolina*, though in size and general style of markings the small rainy season brood of the latter resembles it somewhat closely, but it always has the apex of the forewing black beneath.

The figure shows the upperside of a male from Kulu, and of a female I. Form from Ceylon in the Indian Museum, Calcutta.

Genus 67.—ARGYNNIS, Fabricius. (PLATE XVIII).

Argynnis, Fabricius, Ill Mag., vol. vi, p. 283, n. 19 (1807); id., Latreille, Enc. Méth., vol. ix, p. 10 (1819); id., Doubleday, Hewitson, Gen. Diurn. Lep., vol. i, p. 171 (1848); *Dryas*, Hübner, Tentamen, p. 1 (1806); *Brenthis, Argynnis, Acidalia* and *Argyronome*, id., Verz. bek. Schmett., pp. 30—32 (1816); *Argynnis* and *Brenthis*, Felder, Neues Lep., pp 9, 10, nos. 13, 14 (1861); *Acidalia*, Moore. Lep. Cey, vol. i, p. 60 (1881).

"HEAD, rather broad, hairy. *Eyes*, nearly round, smooth. *Palpi*, porrect, slightly ascending, divergent, projecting considerably beyond the head: the first and second joints clothed with scales and long setiform divergent hairs; the third joint with scales, and more or less appressed hairs. First joint subcylindric, curved, about one-fourth the length of the second; second joint slightly curved, much swollen beyond the middle, then narrowed towards the apex, which is truncate; third joint very small, acicular, about one-fourth the length of the second. *Antennæ* rather short, terminating in an abrupt pyriform club. THORAX, rather stout, rounded, oval. ABDOMEN, moderate, about two-thirds the length of the inner margin of the wing. FOREWING, trigonate; the *costal margin* rounded; the *outer* about two-thirds the length of the costa, sometimes slightly concave, sometimes nearly straight, often rounded; *inner* about equal in length to the outer margin, nearly straight. *Costal nervure* stout, extending about three-fifths of the length of the wing; *subcostal* slender, sometimes emitting its first and second nervules near together before the end of the cell, the third at less than half the distance between this and the apex, the fourth rather more remote from the apex than from the third; sometimes emitting its first nervule before the end of the cell, its second [after the end of the cell] at about an equal distance from the first and third, its fourth nearer to the third than to the apex. *Upper disco-cellular nervule* very short, sometimes almost wanting; *middle* curved inwards, longer [? shorter] than the *lower*, which is nearly straight, and anastomoses with the third median nervule at some distance from its origin. HINDWING, obovate; the margins about equal, all rounded. *Precostal nervure* simple, slightly curved, directed outwards; *discoidal nervule* appearing to be a third subcostal nervule. *Discoidal cell* closed by a slender disco-cellular, sometimes flexuous, sometimes nearly straight. FORELEGS, of the *male*, fringed with long delicate hairs; *tibia* smooth, rather shorter than the femur; *tarsus* shorter than the tibia, one-jointed, subcylindric, tapering towards the apex. Of the *female* scaly, slightly fringed with hairs; *tibia* fully as long as the femur, smooth, slenderest in the middle; *tarsus* shorter than the tibia, smooth, five-jointed; the first joint twice the length of the rest combined; the second barely one-fourth the length of the first; the third one-half

---

* Ann and Mag. of Nat. Hist., fifth series, vol. xii, p. 102, n. 2 (1883).

the length of the second ; the fourth transverse, three-fourths the length of the third ; these joints all armed at the apex with a short spine on each side, not covered at the base by any bunch of hairs or setæ situated on the next joint ; fifth joint smaller than the fourth, transverse, unarmed. MIDDLE and HINDLEGS, with the *femora* and *tibiæ* of about equal length, the latter spined all round ; the lateral spines much the longest ; the spurs very distinct. *Tarsi* about as long as the tibiæ ; all the joints nearly cylindric, spiny all round ; first joint nearly equal to the others combined, the spines below arranged in two alternating series ; second, third and fourth joints progressively shorter ; the fifth longer than the third ; all these with the spines of the lower surface arranged in two regularly opposed series. *Claws*, curved, grooved below. *Paronychia*, bilaciniate ; the outer lacinia rather slender, tapering, equal to the claw ; inner much shorter. *Pulvillus*, jointed, nearly equal in length to the claw."

"LARVA, cylindric, spiny, the spines verticillate ; the prothoracic segment always with at least two spines. PUPA, angular, tuberculate, the head mostly bifid." (*Doubleday*, l. c.)

Like the genera *Hestina*, *Neptis*, and *Cyrestis*, *Argynnis* is divisible into two groups by the position of the second subcostal nervule of the forewing. The first, which contains all the larger Indian species, has the "second subcostal nervule thrown off before the end of the cell, and the second joint of the palpi mostly much swollen." The second group contains but two species within Indian limits, which are of small size, and in general appearance are very like species of the genus *Melitæa*. This group has the "second subcostal nervule thrown off beyond the end of the cell, and the second joint of the palpi not remarkably swollen." In the males of some of the Indian species of the first group the two lower median nervules and the submedian nervure are clothed for a portion of their length with modified hairs and scales, this "sexual mark" appearing on different veins in different species.

The genus is a very extensive one, occurring in both the Old and New Worlds up to the extreme northern limit of vegetation : the great majority of the species belong to the Palæarctic and Nearctic regions, but a single species is found in the tropics of the Old World, and one is recorded from Jamaica, and several species from Chili and Buenos Ayres in the new. One species, *A. niphe*, occurs throughout India from the outer ranges of the Himalayas to Ceylon, also in Assam, British Burma, Java, Australia and China. All the rest of the Indian species (except *A. rudra* which has as yet been found only in the Khasi Hills, and *A. childreni* which occurs also in the Khasi Hills as well as in the Himalayas) occur only in the Himalayas, some at very great elevations. The species are all "more or less of a bright fulvous orange, marked with black spots, arranged in transverse bands ; and, below, the same or similar spots are repeated on a rather paler ground, mingled on the hindwing, and at the apex of the forewing with silvery or pearly spots, sometimes also with green ; on the hindwing they are often shining green, splashed with silver. The larvæ are always spiny ; the spines set round with numerous stiff hairs ; the prothoracic segment always has two spines, which sometimes are longer than the others. The general colour is brown or fuscous, with longitudinal bands of either a darker or paler hue. Some are bluish white, with longitudinal fuscous lines ; the spines being brown. The food of most of the species consists of some species of violet, but some feed on the bramble, nettle, some *Cruciferæ* and *Papilionaceæ*, and also on *Anchusa officinalis* and *Polygonum bistorta*. Lying hid under the leaves the greater part of the day, they are difficult to find. The pupæ are more or less angulated, constricted across the back, the head often bifid, the abdominal segments furnished with a double row of tubercles on the dorsal surface. They are generally of some shade of brown, often marked with metallic spots. The pupæ of the species composing the second section are rounder at the head, and altogether less angular than those of the first section." (*Doubleday*, l. c.)

The key below is mainly based on certain structural characters of both sexes, the next division having been made on the colour and markings displayed. The males of the first five species in addition differ from all those which follow in having the "sexual marks" mentioned above, this feature being absent from all the rest. It is to be noted however in the case of *A. niphe* that this character is only prominent in specimens from South India (the Nilgiri and Pulni Hills, and Travancore), it being barely traceable in Ceylon specimens or in those from elsewhere.

17

Key to the Indian species of Argynnis.

A. With second subcostal nervule of forewing given off before end of cell.

    a. Male and female differing widely in colour and markings of forewing, male with ground-colour fulvous throughout, female with apical half deep purple crossed by an oblique white band. Upperside of hindwing in both sexes with bluish lunules on the black outer margin.

        421. A. (*Acidalia*) NIPHE, India, Java, China, Australia.

    b. Male and female similarly marked.

        a¹. Silvery markings on underside of hindwing in the form of distinct bands.

            a². No silvery markings on basal half of hindwing.

                422. A. RUDRA, Assam, Yunan, Kashmir ?.

            b². Basal half of hindwing with silvery markings.

                a³. Outer margin of hindwing on upperside broadly bluish-greenish.

                    423. A. CHILDRENI, Himalayas, Assam, Burma.

                b³. Outer margin of hindwing concolourous with rest of wing.

                    a⁴. With a single short subbasal silver band in addition to the discal one.

                        424. A. PANDORA, Eastern Europe, North Africa, Central Asia, Gilgit.

                    b⁴. With three more or less complete subbasal silver bands in addition to the discal one.

                        425. A. KAMALA, North-West Himalayas.

        b¹. Silvery markings on underside of hindwing consisting of isolated well-separated spots.

            a². Outer margin of both wings evenly curved without any angulation.

                a⁴. Submarginal silvery band on underside of hindwing composed of lunular spots. Apex of forewing on upperside concolourous with rest of wing.

                    a⁴. Underside of hindwing with a series of ferruginous spots with silver centres between the discal and submarginal series of silver spots.

                      426. A. JAINADEVA, North-West Himalayas.

                    b⁴. Underside of hindwing lacking the series of ferruginous spots with silver centres between the discal and submarginal series of silver spots.

                      427. A. VITATHA, Kashmir.

                b⁴. Submarginal silvery band on underside of hindwing composed of triangular spots joined at the base. Apex of forewing marked with whitish streaks between the nervules.

                  428. A. CLARA, Kumaon.

             b². Outer margin of forewing emarginate, hindwing angled at discoidal nervule and anal angle, silvery markings on underside extremely large and prominent.

                429. A. LATHONIA, Europe, North Africa, Central Asia, Himalayas.

         c¹. Outer margin of forewing slightly convex, apex very sharply angled, costal margin of hindwing very straight, outer margin slightly angled at third median nervule, anal angle rounded.

            a¹. Upperside bright fulvous, cilia fulvous throughout.

                430. A. GEMMATA, Native Sikkim, Chumbi.

            b¹. Upperside ochreous, cilia spotted with white.

                431. A. ALTISSIMA, Native Sikkim, Chumbi.

B. With second subcostal nervule of forewing given off after end of cell.

    a. Costal and outer margins of hindwing nearly straight, apex angled.

        432. A. SIPORA, Kashmir, Lahoul.

    b. Costal and outer margins of hindwing curved, apex rounded.

        433. A. JERDONI, Kashmir.

Mr. Moore places the first species, *Argynnis niphe*, in a distinct genus named *Acidalia*, of which it is the type. His description is given below.*

---

* *Acidalia*, Hübner, Verz. bek. Schmett., p. 31 (1816) ; id., Moore, Lep. Cey., vol. i, p. 60 (1881) : *Argynnis* (part), Doubleday, Gen. Diurn. Lep., vol. i. p. 171 (1848). "FOREWING triangular ; *costa* much arched, *apex* rounded, *exterior margin* oblique, sinuous, convex (? concave) below the apex ; *costal nervure* extending two-thirds of the margin ; first and second *subcostal nervules* emitted before the end of the cell, third at nearly one-half beyond, fourth and fifth at two-thirds beyond ; *upper (middle) disco-cellular nervule* shortest, deeply concave, *lower* slightly concave ; *upper discoidal* nervule from the end of the cell in a line with the subcostal, *lower* from the middle of the disco-cellulars ; *second median* nervule emitted at nearly one-third before the end of the cell ; *first* from two-thirds before its end ; *submedian nervure* recurved. HINDWING short, broad ; *costal margin* very convexly angular at the base ; *costal nervure* much arched from the base, the basal spur curved outward ; *first subcostal nervule* emitted at nearly one-half distance before the end of the cell ; *disco-cellular nervules* of equal length, *upper* curved very obliquely outward, *lower* slightly curved ; two *upper median nervules* from end of the cell, *lower* from one-third before its end ; *submedian* and *internal nervures* slightly recurved at the base.

421. Argynnis niphe, Linnæus.

Papilio niphe, Linnæus, Syst. Nat., ed. xii, vol. i, pt. ii, p. 785, n. 208 (1767¹; id., Drury, Ill. Ex Ent., vol. i, pl. vi, fig. 1, *female* (1770); id., Cramer, Pap Ex, vol. i, pl. xiv, figs. D, E, *male*; B, C, *female* (1775); id., Herbst, Pap., pl. ccliv, figs. 3, 4, *female* (1798); *Argynnis niphe*, Godart, Enc. Méth., vol. ix, p. 261, n. 17 (1819); id., Kollar, Hügel's Kaschmir, vol. iv, pt ii, p. 440, n. 2, pl. xiii, figs. 1, 2, *male* (1848); *Acidalia niphe*, Hubner, Verz. bek. Schmett., p. 31, n. 256 (1816); id., Moore, Lep. Cey., vol. i, p. 60, pl. xxvi, figs. 2, *male*; 2a, *female*; 2b, *larva* and *pupa* (1881); *Papilio hyperbius*, Johansson, Amœn. Acad., vol. vi, p. 408, n. 75 (1764); *P. argyrius*, Sparrman, Amœn. Acad., vol. vii, p. 502, note f, *male* (1768); *P. argynnis*, Drury, Ill. Ex. Ent., vol. i, pl. vi, fig. 2, *male* (1770); *P. arginnis*, Herbst, Pap., pl. ccliv, figs. 5, 6, *male* (1798); *Argynnis tephnia*, Godart, Enc. Méth., vol. ix, p. 262, n. 18 (1819); *A. aruna*, Moore, Horsfield and Moore, Cat. Lep. Mus., E. I. C., vol. i, p. 156, n 322, pl. iiia, fig. 4. *male* (1857).

HABITAT: Himalayas, Oudh, Assam, Burma, South India, Ceylon, Sumatra, Java, Formosa, China, Australia.

EXPANSE: 2·4 to 3·7 inches.

DESCRIPTION: "MALE. UPPERSIDE bright dark ochreous. *Forewing* with black discoidal marks, a transverse discal zigzag series of six large spots, two submarginal rows of slightly smaller spots and a marginal dentate line. *Hindwing* with slender black discoidal marks and transverse discal spots, a submarginal inner row of small spots and outer row of broad conical spots bordered towards the anal angle by a blue line; a marginal dentate line bordered by a blue line. FEMALE brownish-ochreous on basal area; markings broader; apical area of *forewing* with blue-black interspaces and obliquely crossed by a white band, the spots also bordered by blue. UNDERSIDE, *forewing* red on basal area, pale ochreous and greenish at apex; MALE with two apical series of white spots; FEMALE as above; other markings as on upperside. *Hindwing* greenish ochreous-brown, crossed by three black zigzag lines and a submarginal line broadly bordered by silvery-white; a discal row of spots centred with silvery-white." (*Moore*, l. c.)

Mr. Moore in his "Lepidoptera of Ceylon" has figured the larva and pupa, but has not described them. Mr. A. Graham Young has however furnished me with a description of the transformations of a Kulu specimen.

"LARVA. Head and legs black, body black, this colour, however, almost obscured by the orange-tawny markings. A broad orange-tawny dorsal stripe. Four straight horizontal simple black spines on head; spines on pectoral segments black; on abdominal segments pink, tipped with black; on caudal segments pink, faintly black tipped. PUPA. Head and wingcases pale Indian red; ten pale metallic spots on back; abdomen dark pink; spines faintly black tipped." The head ends in two well-separated blunt points; there are a pair of spines anteriorly, another pair in the middle, and a third smallest pair posteriorly on the thorax, the latter being hunched and keeled, on the abdominal segments there are eight pairs of spines, the third anterior pair the largest.

Of all the species of the genus, *A. niphe* has probably the widest geographical range. In India it is found throughout the outer ranges of the Himalayas, in Assam, and Burma. I have taken it at Agra in the winter, it occurs again in Bombay, the Nilgiris, Travancore, and Ceylon, where it is "found in the hills from 2,000 to 6,000 feet, in the neighbourhood of waste grass-lands and swamps. Larva feeds on wild violet" (*Mackwood*). Colonel Lang writes of it: "Tolerably abundant in certain localities, 6,000 to 8,000 feet in the North-West Himalayas. The males seem much more abundant than the females." It has not been recorded from the Andamans and Nicobars nor from the Malay peninsula, but occurs again in Sumatra, Java, Formosa, China, and North Australia. The male may be distinguished from all other Indian species of the genus by the blue marginal markings on the upperside of the hindwing, and the female by the whole apical half of the forewing being purplish-black, crossed by an oblique white band intersected by the nervules. In South Indian specimens of the male the first median nervule on the upperside of the forewing is furnished for a portion of its length with raised modified scales, this character being obsolete in specimens from other localities.

Body robust; *palpi* ascending, finely pilose, second joint long, extending to top of the head, third joint short, pointed and naked; legs slender; antennæ with a short spatular club. Sexes dissimilar. *Type, A. niphe.* (*Moore, l. c.*)

Mr. Moore has described an accidental variety or "sport" of *A. niphe* under the name of *A. aruna*. There is a somewhat similar but less heavily marked example from the Khasi Hills in the Indian Museum, Calcutta. A description of *A. aruna* is given below. *

422. Argynnis rudra, Moore. (PLATE XVIII, Fig. 75 ♂).

A. rudra, Moore, Horsfield and Moore, Cat. Lep. Mus. E. I. C., vol. i. p. 157, n. 325 (1857); idem, id., Proc. Zool. Soc. Lond., 1874, p. 267, n. 22; idem, id., Anderson's Anat. and Zool. Researches, p. 924 (1878).

HABITAT : Kashmir, N. India *(Moore)*; Assam, Upper Burma.

EXPANSE : 2·7 to 3·1 inches.

DESCRIPTION : "UPPERSIDE bright fulvous, duller and slightly tinged with green at the base. *Forewing* with the markings disposed as in *A. childreni*, but somewhat smaller, but with a marginal row of small spots. *Hindwing* with the spots also disposed as in *A. childreni*, but with a marginal row of spots. UNDERSIDE, *forewing* fulvous-yellow, greenish at the apex ; the spots on the exterior half indistinct. *Hindwing* light green, palest on abdominal margin ; a ferruginous irregular band crossing the basal half ; an irregular more or less white line crossing from anterior margin near the angle to abdominal angle ; also some white disposed from anal angle and enclosing the green colour, and thus forming a subinarginal row ; along the outside of the white line some ferruginous spots, centred with white. Wings shaped as in *A. laodice*, which appears to be a near ally." *(Moore, l. c.)*

A. rudra is a very beautiful species, and is quite distinct from all the other Indian ones, though closely allied to the Eastern European, Northern Asiatic and Japanese *A. laodice*, Pallas, but is more heavily marked, and the outer margin of the hindwing on the underside not so distinctly vinous coloured. The male has the dark raised scales on the upperside of the forewing on either side of the submedian nervure and first median nervule for a portion of their length. I have not seen a female, but it will probably differ from the male only in having the ground-colour on the upperside somewhat duller, and all the black markings heavier, and in lacking the dark raised scales on the nervules. It is fairly common at Shillong in June, and the Indian Museum, Calcutta, possesses specimens from Cherrapunji, Sibsagar *(S. E. Peal)*, and others from Pousee in Upper Burma taken in March by the Yunan Expedition. I have no knowledge of its occurrence in Sikkim or indeed anywhere west of the Brahmaputra. Mr. Moore records it from Kashmir in describing the collection of the late Captain R. B. Reed, but it is quite possible that the specimen was obtained by exchange ; no other collector has, so far as I know, found it there nor in the vast intervening tract of country from Kashmir to Bhutan ; and if a species of this type were found in the western Himalayas it would more probably be the eastern European *A. laodice* than the Indo-Burmese *A. rudra*. The figure shows both sides of a male Shillong specimen in the Indian Museum, Calcutta.

423. Argynnis childreni, Gray.

A. childreni, Gray, Zool. Misc., vol. i, p. 33 (1831); id., Lep. Ins. Nep., p. 11, pl. xi, *male* (1846); *A. sakontala*, Kollar, Hügel's Kaschmir, vol. iv, pt. ii, p. 439, n. 1, pl. xii, *male* and *female* (1848); id., Moore, Anderson's Anat. and Zool. Researches, p. 924 (1878).

HABITAT : Himalayas, Assam, Burma.

EXPANSE : 3·1 to 3·8 inches.

DESCRIPTION : "Wings fulvous, spotted with black ; the anal half of the posterior margin of the *hindwing* tinged with blue. UNDERSIDE of the *forewing* with the basal portion crimson, spotted with black, an oblique medial band which extends along the margin to the posterior angle, and the apex pale green with two short white lines. *Hindwing* greenish-bronze with oblique silvery white bands, narrowly margined with blue on each side." *(Gray, l. c. in Lep. Ins. Nepal.)*

---

* *Argynnis aruna*, Moore, Horsfield and Moore, Cat. Lep. Mus., E. I. C., vol. i, p. 156, n. 322, pl. iiir, fig. 4, *male* (1857). HABITAT : N. India. EXPANSE : 3·12 inches. DESCRIPTION : "UPPERSIDE, wings fulvous. *Forewing* with a broad black patch in discoidal cell and between the nervules, and duller markings on the exterior margin. *Hindwing* having the whole space between the nervules posteriorly occupied with black, and leaving only small lunular markings on the exterior margin, the latter becoming bluish at the anal angle. UNDERSIDE with the *forewing* broadly suffused with black. *Hindwing* with the basal half silvery, and with black markings across the wing from outer to anal angle. Shape of wings as in *A. niphe*" *(Moore, l. c.)*

MALE: UPPERSIDE, *both wings* rich fulvous marked with black. *Forewing* with two narrow sinuous lines across the middle of the cell, a spot beyond touching the subcostal but not reaching the median nervure, and two spots at the end, the lower the larger; a twice-angled discal series of rounded spots, a spot below the origin of the fourth and fifth subcostal nervules, two submarginal series of rounded spots, a submarginal broad and marginal narrow line. On either side of the submedian nervure and the first and second median nervules for a portion of their length are placed raised modified blackish scales. *Hindwing* with a streak at the end of the cell, a discal angular series of six spots beyond the cell, an inner submarginal series of five round spots, another series of eight spots beyond, becoming somewhat lunular towards the anal angle; marginal lines as on the forewing. The outer margin from about the discoidal nervule increasingly to the anal angle and ascending the abdominal margin for a short distance is bluish-greenish, which constitutes the most prominent feature of this species. UNDERSIDE, *forewing* red, almost crimson in freshly emerged specimens, the apex at first ochreous, then greenish, crossed by two silvery lines; other markings as above, but more prominent. *Hindwing* rich shining greenish ochreous, crossed by numerous silvery lines and bands, defined on one or both sides with black. A subbasal band from the costa to the median nervure, below which is an annulated spot, a band from the subcostal to the median nervure crossing the middle of the cell, the disco-cellulars defined with a silvery line, another band from the subcostal nervure to the discoidal nervule where it merges into a broad discal band from the costa to the anal angle, from whence it extends up the abdominal margin; the internal and submedian nervures and the first median nervule all broadly defined with silvery till they meet a cross silvery band which extends from the internal nervure to the third median nervule, where it becomes merged in the discal band; beyond this latter band is a series of obscure dusky spots with ochreous centres, a submarginal line, and two marginal ones divided by a fine black line, a similar black line on the margin. *Cilia* of the forewing fulvous, of the hindwing white tipped with black at the ends of the nervules. *Head* and *body* thickly clothed with fulvous hairs. FEMALE differs from the male only in the ground-colour of the UPPERSIDE being much duller, dusky-ochreous instead of rich fulvous. No raised modified scales on the upperside of the forewing along the veins.

A. childreni is the finest species of the genus occurring in India, probably in the world. It attains its largest size and greatest richness of colouring at Shillong, the species becoming smaller and less brightly coloured the further west it extends. I have taken it in Kashmir, Kulu, Simla and Sikkim; it occurs in Masuri, Kumaon, Nepal, Shillong, the Khasi Hills, and Manipur, and it was obtained by the Yunan expedition. Colonel Lang states that it is "a North-West Himalayan species, frequenting grassy slopes near woods, open copses and gardens, 7,000 to 10,000 feet elevation. Flight bold and very fast. Affects *Compositæ* and *Cruciferæ*. Not a very common species."

424. Argynnis pandora, Wien. Verz.

Papilio pandora, Wien. Verz., p. 176, n. 1 (1776); id., Hübner. Eur. Schmett., vol. i, figs. 71, 72 (1793, 1794); figs. 606, 607 (1800—1803); *P. cynara*, Fabricius, Gen. Ins., p. 266 (1777); id., Herbst, Pap., pl. cclxi, figs. 1, 2, *male*; 3, 4, *female* (1798); *Argynnis cynara*, Godart, Enc. Méth., vol. ix, p. 269, n. 29 (1819); *Papilio maja* (*recto maia*), Cramer, Pap. Ex., vol. i, pl. xxv, figs. B, C, *female* (1775).

HABITAT: South-Eastern Germany, South Europe. Algeria, Western Asia, Gilgit.

EXPANSE: 2·25 to 2·90 inches.

DESCRIPTION: MALE. UPPERSIDE greenish fulvous. *Forewing* with a pair of black bars crossing the cell near its middle, another broader pair at its outer end, with an oblique black line joining them; a discal much angled band, a diffused subcostal spot, a series of seven even rounded spots, two submarginal series of oval spots, the outer series touching each other on the interspaces, the first and second median nervules for a portion of their length in the middle of the wing clothed with upright modified scales, which form a prominent ridge along that portion of the nervules. *Hindwing* more greenish, the disco-cellulars marked with a duplex black line, a discal irregular somewhat lunulated line from the costal nervure to the first median nervule, a series of five round spots beyond, a series of seven submarginal spots, the three anterior ones rounded, the rest lunular, a marginal series of joined lunules. UNDERSIDE, *forewing* rosy red, the costa, apex broadly and outer margin decreasingly to anal angle pale yellow, the black spots at the apex on the upperside greenish on the underside, other markings as above, but more prominent. *Hindwing* deep green; the costal lobe, a spot within from the base of the præcostal along the costal nervure, a curved spot from the costal nervure to the point where the first subcostal nervule is given off, inwardly defined with black, a similar spot towards the end of the cell (all these spots often more or less wanting), a discal irregular somewhat narrow band, inwardly defined with black towards the costa, a series of five minute spots placed on round diffused fulvous patches, and a submarginal narrow line, all silvery. FEMALE. UPPERSIDE darker than in the male, all the markings more prominent. UNDERSIDE also with the markings more prominent, especially the silvery ones on the hind-wing. All the *cilia* fulvous.

I am indebted to Mr. J. F. Duthie for a single male specimen of this species taken by a native botanical collector attached to Colonel Lockhart's mission, probably near Gilgit, on the north-eastern frontier of Kashmir. It has already been recorded from Turkestan,[*] and from Kouldja.[†] The species should be known by its oldest name, *A. maia*, as Cramer described it a year in advance of Schiffermüller in the Wiener Verzeichniss, but as it has almost uniformly been known as *A. pandora*, I have retained that name.

425. **Argynnis kamala**, Moore.

A. kamala, Moore, Horsfield and Moore, Cap. Lep. Mus. E. I. C., vol. I. p. 156, n. 324 (1857) ; id., Moore, Proc. Zool. Soc. Lond., 1874, p. 267, n. 20 ; *A. enidia*, Felder, Reise Nov., Lep., vol. iii, p. 392, n. 574, pl. l, figs. 5, 6, *male* (1867).

HABITAT : Western Himalayas.

EXPANSE : 2·70 to 2·87 inches.

DESCRIPTION : " UPPERSIDE golden-yellow ; forewing somewhat dusky at the base, hind-wing tinged in parts with yellowish-green. *Forewing* with all the veins and veinlets deeply defined with black ; the black markings disposed exactly as in *A. paphia* [the " Silver-washed Fritillary" of England] but larger and duller, and in *A. kamala* the submarginal row of spots are less defined and continuous, rather forming a stripe than a linear series of spots ; the marginal row is connected between the veinlets by a narrow line. *Hindwing* with an irregular zigzag inner black band, then a row of five round black spots, and a submarginal row of seven linear-shaped spots (the anterior and third being smallest), also a marginal black line ; the angles and end of veinlets also black. UNDERSIDE, *forewing* yellow, the markings within discoidal cell and about the disc as above, but the submarginal row paler ; none on margin ; near the apex a green patch, containing three silvery-white spots. *Hindwing* beautiful metallic green, with a broad submarginal and inner band, and a series of marks about the basal half silvery-white, all margined more or less on one side with black ; between the submarginal and inner band some small spaces of yellow, and an indistinct row of reddish spots. Wings shaped as in *A. paphia*." *(Moore,* l. c.) The FEMALE has the base and inner margin of the forewing and all but the anterior margin of the hindwing on the upperside thickly powdered with dull green, the markings are similar to those of the male.

This is a much smaller species than *A. childreni* ; the colouring of the upperside is dusky ochreous like the female of that species, the outer margin of the hindwing concolourous with the rest of the wing, not greenish-bluish as in *A. childreni*. On the upperside of the forewing in the male the first and second median nervules only have the raised modified scales. The hindwing is much less deeply scalloped than in *A. childreni*. It is a fairly common species in Chini, Kulu and the Simla district in the late summer. Mr. Moore records it from Kashmir, where I found it the commonest species of the genus in June. Colonel Lang remarks that *A. kamala* is "abundant throughout a tract of 120 miles, at an altitude of 6,000 to 10,000

---

[*] Erschoff's Lep. Turkestan, p. 17, n. 54 (1874).
[†] Alphéraky, Hor. Soc. Ent. Ross., vol. xvi. p. 412, n. 82 (1881).

feet, in the summer and autumn months, in the Simla district and Lower Kunawur. It affects open glades and the borders of forests, pitching on low shrubs, brambles, and banks of thyme, thistles, scabious heads, &c." Mr. W. Doherty took it in the Pindari Valley in North-West Kumaon at 8,000 feet elevation.

Dr. Felder has described *A. cnidia* as a distinct species; it appears however to be only *A. kamala*. His description is appended.*

426. Argynnis jainadeva, Moore.

A. jainadeva, Moore, Ent. Month. Mag., vol. i, p. 131, *note* (1864); idem, id., Proc. Zool. Soc. Lond., 1865, p. 495, n. 63, pl. xxx, fig. 1; idem, id., Scien. Res. Second Yarkand Mission, Lep., p. 2, n. 5; id., Butler, Ent. Month. Mag., vol. xxi, p. 66 (1884).

HABITAT: Upper Kunawar, Kulu, Kashmir, Ladak.

EXPANSE: ♂, 1·75 to 2·80; ♀, 2·00 to 3·00 inches.

DESCRIPTION: "MALE. UPPERSIDE rich fulvous; markings black. *Forewing* with four discoidal streaks, the fourth double and closing the cell; a transverse discal series of narrow lunulated spots irregularly disposed, but each joined to the other by being continued in a line on the vein; a small suffused spot before the apex; a second discal series of round spots, a submarginal row of lunules, and a double marginal line. *Hindwing* with a double mark closing the cell; an irregular transverse discal series of lunules; a second discal series of three round spots and an upper intermediate dot; a submarginal row of well-defined lunules, and a double marginal line. *Cilia* pale fulvous yellow. UNDERSIDE, *forewing* pale fulvous, greenish yellow apically; markings as above, except that those at the apex and the marginal line are pale green, the inner apical spaces being silvery white. *Hindwing* pale green, yellowish across the disc and along exterior margin, basal and a transverse discal series of spots, and a marginal row of lunules, silvery white, those of the two former more or less with a black border, the latter bordered by a black marginal line; a few rufous-brown spots outside the discal series. FEMALE of a deeper colour; markings the same, but larger."

"This species is allied to *A. clara*, Blanchard." (*Moore*, l. c. in Proc. Zool. Soc. Lond.)

"*Note.*—Very common in Upper Kunawur; not appearing in Lower Kunawur. This is a companion to *A. kamala*, but only for some twenty miles of its furthest northern range, appearing first on the meadows of 'Chini,' 10,000 feet elevation, the fittest village of Kunawur; this and the next ten miles appear its head-quarters. I caught it, however, far to the eastward, on the bare, treeless, shrubless regions of the Zungcham river, in Tibet (an affluent of the Spiti). It flies from May to November." (*Colonel A. M. Lang, R.E.*, l. c.)

"Mr. Elwes has frequently urged upon me the importance of the expanded fusiform patches upon the median branches in the males of many species of *Argynnis*, as probably constant and therefore valuable characters for the determination of otherwise nearly allied forms; in this opinion I have no doubt he is right, and therefore I do not hesitate to regard *Argynnis adippe†* (the male of which has two such patches on the forewing) as perfectly distinct from *A. jainadeva*, in which these patches have not been developed." (*Butler*, l. c.)

---

* *Argynnis cnidia*, Felder. HABITAT: Kulu, Pangi. EXPANSE: 2·7 inches. DESCRIPTION: "MALE, UPPERSIDE, *forewing* fulvescent, the basal area yellowish-brown, hairy, a cellular mark, another at the extremity of the cell, a little band placed between, a macular broken discal band, a small subapical band, a bent series of external spots, others submarginal, with the margin divided by a series of streaks of the ground-colour and the nervules blackish. *Hindwing* yellowish-brown, with a disco-cellular mark, a broken macular discal striga, external spots, others submarginal bent, and the margin divided by little streaks of the ground-colour much wider than in the forewing, all blackish, with obsolete fulvous spots in three series between these (the inner series short). UNDERSIDE, *forewing* much paler, the spots blacker, the apical margin greenish, with two or four silvery spots. *Hindwing* greenish, tinted throughout with fulvescent, the costal margin on the lobe, a basal fascia, another subbasal banded inwardly with black, a third very macular, a fourth wider and a fifth before the margin all outwardly banded with black, silvery, external obsolete silvery dots, widely circled with ferruginous and outwardly widely defined with fulvous. FEMALE: UPPERSIDE darker, the spots larger." (*Felder*, l. c.)

† *Argynnis adippe*, Linnæus. "The MALE closely resembles *A. aglaia*, but the black lines along the nervures of the *forewing* [on the UPPERSIDE] are thicker. UNDERSIDE, *Forewing* brighter fulvous than in *A. aglaia*, with distinct silvery markings near the apex. *Hindwing* light yellow, with a fulvous tinge; spots well defined and silvery; between the hind-marginal and medial rows is a series of reddish spots with silvery centres; the inner margin is greenish, with a silvery gloss. FEMALE brighter fulvous [than in *A. aglaia*], and the dark markings are not so intense, neither is there the black shading towards the base of the wings found in that species. EXPANSE: 1·9 to 2·2 inches. HABITAT: Europe, Asia Minor, Armenia, the Altai, and the Amur." (*Lang* in Butt. of Europe, p. 111).

I took *A. jainadeva* in several places in Kashmir in June and also in Ladak ; the latter owing to the scanty vegetation and dry climate are much smaller and lighter coloured than specimens from elsewhere. Kulu female specimens are exceedingly dark on the upperside, the ground-colour basally being fuscous tinted with deep vinous purple. As pointed out by Mr. Butler the male has no secondary sexual characters on the upperside of the forewing, though some specimens show traces of thickening on the first and second median nervules, *A. adippe* possessing this character to a greater extent. It does not appear to occur on the outer ranges of the Himalayas ; it seems to be confined to the inner ranges of the Western Himalayas at elevations above 8,000 feet. Mr. W. Doherty took it at Dhankri in Western Kumaon at 11,000 feet.

427. **Argynnis vitatha,** Moore.

A. vitatha, Moore, Proc. Zool., Soc. Lond., 1874, p. 568.

HABITAT : Kashmir, North side of Rajdiangan pass and Gurais ; Gilgit.

EXPANSE : 2·25 inches.

DESCRIPTION : " Allied to *A. aglaia* ; markings similar but more prominent. UNDERSIDE of *hindwing* with the whole of the space from base to the transverse discal series of silvery spots, as well as their outer bordered spots and marginal lunules, dark powdery green." (*Moore,* l. c.)

Through the kindness of Mr. J. F. Duthie I have lately received three males and a female of this species obtained probably near Gilgit under the same conditions as the *A. pandora* mentioned above. They may at once be distinguished from *A. jainadeva* by all the markings on the upperside being much smaller ; the apex of the forewing, the whole basal area of the hindwing up to the discal series of silver spots, also a series of spots placed outwardly against these latter, rich powdery green ; the marginal silver lunules also surrounded with that colour (assuming the form of lunules within). On the hindwing also on the underside there is no series of rufous-brown spots with silver centres between the marginal and discal series of silver spots, nor a silver spot on the costa between the discal and subbasal series of silver spots as in *A. jainadeva*.

A description of *A. aglaia* is appended for reference, *A. vitatha* being at best but a very slight variety of it.*

428. **Argynnis clara,** Blanchard.

A. clara, Blanchard, Jacquemont's Voy. dans l' Inde, vol. iv, p. 20, n. 14, Insectes pl. ii. figs. 2, 3 (1811).

HABITAT : Tihri Garhwal, North-West Himalayas.

EXPANSE : 2·3 inches.

DESCRIPTION : " UPPERSIDE golden-yellow, with small black spots arranged in transverse rows. [UNDERSIDE], *hindwing* greenish-golden, with irregular basal spots and spots arranged in two rows, silvery."

" UPPERSIDE orange-yellow, with the base of *both wings* thickly irrorated with black ; the *forewing* has a kidney-shaped spot towards the middle of the discoidal cell, a little beyond a second comma-shaped spot, and at the end a third elongated spot ; the *hindwing* also has a black spot at the end [of the cell]. *Both wings* have three transverse series of spots, the first placed a little beyond the discoidal cell is sinuous, the second is more

---

* *Argynnis aglaia,* Linnæus. "Cilia black and whitish. Nervures of the forewing with black lines [on the upperside] in the male. Both wings bright fulvous in the male, duller in the female. Hind margins black ; bases dusky, darkest in the female ; the markings consist of the usual black spots and black marginal lunules ; the square spots near the middle of the wings are joined so as to form a narrow wavy band. UNDERSIDE, *forewing* light reddish brown, spotted with black, apex with green and silver marginal spots. *Hindwing* bronze-green, with a band of straw-colour tinged with green running parallel to the hind margin ; silver spots large and distinct, arranged in three rows ; first a row of semi-lunar spots along the hind margin, then a medial ro v, internal to this a row of three spots, and then three more at the base. There are never any brown, silver-centred spots between the marginal and medial rows ; or any costal silver spot between the medial and internal rows. EXPANSE : 2·25 to 2·5 inches. HABITAT : Europe, the Canaries, Asia Minor, Syria and Persia." (*Lang* in Butt. of Europe, p. 90.)

regular and composed of six small rounded spots, of which only five are well marked on the hindwing, the third placed in front of a black streak before the outer margin is formed of triangles resembling a festoon. UNDERSIDE, *forewing* coloured as above but slightly paler, as are also the spots, the apex slightly tinged with green, the marginal series of spots silvery, as are also some others near the second series of spots. *Hindwing* yellowish-green, slightly gilded, the black spots of the upperside silvery, rather larger ; in addition, between the marginal band composed of triangular spots and the band which precedes it there is a series of five small yellow spots. *Body* blackish, covered with yellow hairs." (*Blanchard*, l. c.)

A. *clara* is a very beautiful and distinct species. In Blanchard's figure the upperside of the forewing at the apex above the third median nervule has some whitish streaks between the nervules, there are three spots in the cell, the outer and inner ones reniform, two discal series, a submarginal dentate line and two straight marginal lines all black. Hindwing with a spot in the cell, two discal series and the marginal markings as in the forewing, but beyond the dentate line there is a series of whitish or silvery lunules. Underside, forewing paler than above, the spots smaller, the apex broadly whitish. Hindwing golden green, two series of subbasal spots, an elongated discal series and a marginal highly dentate series all silvery ; beyond the discal series are five round yellow spots between the nervules.

The exact locality where Jacquemont took the type specimen is unknown, but Mr. J. C. Pyne who accompanied Mr. J. F. Duthie on a trip into the Garhwal Himalayas took several examples of A. *clara* "about the middle of August, 1883, on the side of a mountain called Phuláldára in the Nila valley, the Nila being a tributary of the Bhagiráthi or Ganges. The elevation must have been about 12,000 feet, and the locality in the territory of Tihri Garhwál." (*Duthie* in epis.) This is the only certain locality known for this species, which was rediscovered on this occasion ; these specimens are now in the British Museum.

429. **Argynnis lathonia,** Linnæus.

Papilio lathonia (recte *Latonia*) Linnæus, Faun. Suec., p. 282, n. 1068 (1761) ; idem, id., Syst. Nat., ed. xii, vol. i, pt. 2, p. 786, n. 213 (1767) ; id., Hübner, Enr. Schmett., vol i, figs. 59, 60 (1793 ?) ; figs. 613 (1823 ?) ; id., Herrich-Schäffer, Schmett. Eur., vol. i, figs. 152—154 (1844) ; id , Flwes, Proc. Zool. Soc. Lond., 1882, p. 404 ; *Argynnis latonia*, Godart, Enc. Méth., vol. ix, p. 267, n. 28 (1819) ; id , Kollar in Hügel's Kaschmir, vol. iv, pt. 2, p. 440, n. 4 (1848) ; *Papilio Athalia valdensis*, Esper, Schmett., vol. i, pt. 2, pl. cxv, fig. 4 (1800 ?) ; A. *issea*, Gray, Lep. Ins. Nepal, p. 11 (1846) ; A. *issea*, Horsfield and Moore, Cat. Lep. Mus. E. I. C., vol. i, p. 156, n. 323 (1857) ; id., Moore, Proc. Zool. Soc. Lond., 1865, p 495. n. 60.

HABITAT : Europe, North Africa, Central Asia, Himalayas.

EXPANSE : 1·7 to 2·4 inches.

DESCRIPTION : MALE. UPPERSIDE fulvous, with black spots ; forewing with the base, costa and inner margin, hindwing with the basal and abdominal area widely, mottled with darker coloured scales. *Forewing* with a reniform spot enclosing a portion of the ground-colour, a transverse spot beyond and one closing the end of the cell. A discal twice-angled series, with an additional spot towards the base in the submedian interspace ; a suffused subcostal spot ; a submarginal series of six spots, of which the three upper ones are small and round, the lower three larger and less regularly shaped ; a marginal row of lunules ; a black marginal band bearing a series of fulvous linear spots ; towards the apex this border in some specimens coalesces with the marginal spots, leaving three fulvous spots between. *Hindwing* with a spot closing the cell, three angled series of black spots in continuation of those on the forewing, the outer margin as on the forewing. UNDERSIDE paler. *Forewing* with the submarginal series of black spots pupilled with silver, a prominent silver spot within the uppermost spot of this series, and five apical marginal silver spots increasing to the third which is the largest. *Hindwing* with a silver spot at the base just beyond the præcostal nervure, a very large silver spot between the costal and subcostal nervures, with a triangular one beyond reaching the interspace below ; two small silver spots towards the base of the cell, a very large one beyond extending beyond the cell, an elongated silver spot at the base of the submedian interspace, with another somewhat quadrate one beyond it ; two elongated

18

silver spots below divided by the internal nervure. A small round silver spot towards the base of the first median interspace, a discal series of three silver spots increasing from the first median to the submedian interspace, a twice curved discal series of small dark spots with silver pupils and outer fulvous ring, a very prominent marginal series of sub-triangular spots, of which the first, fourth and seventh are smallest, the intermediate pairs of spots about twice the size. *Cilia* pale fulvous. The margin bears two fine dark ferruginous lines, and all the silver spots are more or less defined with black. FEMALE similarly marked, but the dark basal ground-colour of the upperside distinctly greenish.

"Moore seems to have followed Gray, who followed Doubleday, in separating the Himalayan form from the European one [under the name of *A. issæa*]. I cannot find that any description of it has been published; and I agree with Kollar in saying that it is identical with *A. lathonia*, though a large series of specimens seem somewhat larger and darker than a series from various parts of Europe." (*Elwes*, l.c.) There are slight differences in the markings of the hindwing on the underside, European specimens being more uniform, but in my opinion these differences are not sufficient to constitute a separate species, especially as it is not known if they are confined to Himalayan specimens.

This is one of the commonest Himalayan species of *Argynnis*, occurring in Simla almost throughout the year. It occurs as far west as Kashmir, thence eastwards to Sikkim, where, however, it occurs plentifully in native territory only, but has occasionally been taken in the station of Darjiling. Colonel Lang writes of it: "Very abundant in the North-West Himalayas, 5,000 to 8,000 feet. At all seasons of the year, even in winter, when snow lies deep on sheltered slopes, this insect may be seen on open sunny sites."

430. Argynnis gemmata, Butler.

A. gemmata, Butler, Ann. and Mag. of Nat. Hist., fifth series, vol. vii, p. 32, n. 1, pl. iv, fig. 1 (1881); id., Elwes, l. c., p. 467: idem, id., Proc. Zool. Soc. Lond., 1882, p. 404, pl. xxv, figs. 6, *male*; 7, *female*.

HABITAT : Eastern Himalayas.

EXPANSE : 1·45 to 1·93 inches.

DESCRIPTION : UPPERSIDE "fulvous, with the body and basal third of the wings shining coppery brown, wings with three transverse series of black spots, the first bi-angulated in zig-zag fashion on the *forewing*, and simply angulated on the *hindwing* ; this series is placed just beyond the middle of the wings ; the second and third series united at their costal extremities near the apex [of *forewing*] ; a nearly marginal interrupted black line. *Forewing* with thick black discoidal markings, much as in *A. cashmirensis* [= *A. jerdoni*] ; a subcostal, ill-defined, blackish, triangular spot between the first and second series. UNDERSIDE, *forewing* paler than above, with smaller black spots, the basal area not brown, but uniform with the rest of the ground-colour, the costa ochreous towards the apex, and the outer margin and *cilia* spotted with the same colour ; an oblique apical chestnut-red stripe, margined internally by a conspicuous spot and a minute dot of silver, and bounded externally by an abbreviated submarginal series of six oval silver spots, which decrease in size at both extremities of the series ; the first two visible spots of the second series of the upperside greyish green. *Hindwing* somewhat like that of *A. myrina* (but altogether brighter and prettier, with the central silver spot more as in *A. lathonia*), bright ferruginous, varied with patches of ochreous, the basal half occupied by about fifteen silver spots and streaks of various sizes and shapes, the two middle ones united and passing through a post-median arched series of sagittate silver spots ; a marginal series of large triangular spots, abdominal margin and the base of the costal margin silver ; all these markings are slenderly edged with black ; a discal series of dull green rounded spots with silver pupils. *Cilia* bright ochreous spotted with ferruginous : *body* below ochraceous." (*Butler*, l. c.) *A. myrina*, Cramer, occurs in North America.

Until lately *A. gemmata* was considered to be a very rare species. Two examples taken by Major Charlton have been in the British Museum since 1852, which were captured somewhere between Nepal and Thibet ; Dr. Lidderdale has also recently obtained a specimen. Its habitat is probably restricted to the higher elevations.

Mr. Elwes writes : " Of this distinct and lovely species I received a considerable number of both sexes, which I take the opportunity of figuring here, as a coloured plate is necessary to give an idea of its beauty. The FEMALE differs from the male in having the base and posterior margin of the *forewing* grey, and the marginal spots pale outside ; the *cilia* also are pale-spotted, which is not the case in the male. This species must be very abundant at some localities, probably at a great elevation ; and it is just possible that *A. altissima* is a still more alpine form of it, analogous to *Melitæa aurinia*, var. *merope*, though more different from *A. gemmata* than *M. merope* is from *M. aurinia*." (*Elwes*, l. c.) Mr. Elwes' and Mr. Otto Möller's native collectors obtained this species in large numbers in Native Sikkim.

431. **Argynnis altissima,** Elwes.

A. altissima, Elwes, Proc. Zool. Soc. Lond., 1882, p. 403, pl. xxv, fig. 8.

HABITAT : Native Sikkim or Chumbi.

EXPANSE : 1·1 inches (one specimen 1·4 inches).

DESCRIPTION : " MALE. UPPERSIDE, markings generally similar in arrangement to those of *A. gemmata* ; but the row of spots on the exterior margin are usually whitish, the ground-colour is paler, and the *cilia* spotted with white. UNDERSIDE, the position and arrangement of the markings are very similar to those of *A. gemmata* ; but all the silvery spots are more elongated and less brilliant, and the deep fulvous markings are almost absent."

" A single specimen is at least a quarter larger in size than the other nine, and has the wings broader and less pointed. In fact it has the appearance of a less alpine variety than the others, which, judging from the collector's marks, were taken with *Œneis pumilus* and *Parnassius* at a very great elevation. This species has a very distinct and peculiar appearance, quite unlike any other *Argynnis*." (*Elwes*, l. c.) I have not seen a specimen of this species.

432. **Argynnis sipora,** Moore. (PLATE XVIII, FIG. 72 ♂ ♀).

A. sipora, Moore, Proc. Zool. Soc. Lond., 1874, p. 568, pl. lxvi, fig. 11 ; *A. baralacha*, idem, id . 1882, p. 242, pl. xi, figs. 1, 1a.

HABITAT : Kashmir, near Gungabul lake, at foot of Haramook peak ; Zoji-la, Kashmir ; Baralacha Pass, Lahoul.

EXPANSE : ♂, 1·37 to 1·80 ; ♀, 1·5 to 1·8 inches.

DESCRIPTION : " Allied to *A. pales*. UPPERSIDE pale fulvous in the male, dusky fulvous in the female. MALE. *Forewing* with black narrow short streak, two small spots [one above the other] and a recurved streak within the cell, a curved streak at its end, a dentate spot beneath, and an irregular transverse discal series of lunules beyond the cell ; a transverse discal row of conical spots, a submarginal row of triangular spots, and a marginal line formed into less-defined spots, one being at the end of each vein. *Hindwing* with two narrow streaks at end of the cell, a transverse discal series beyond, two outer and a marginal row of spots. FEMALE, black markings broader, the submarginal row of spots on both wings large, and with pale whitish outer marginal border. *Cilia* white. UNDERSIDE. MALE. *Forewing* paler, markings indistinct, apex and exterior border yellow, streaked with red. *Hindwing* yellow, abdominal margin greenish ; a broad irregular subbasal and discal transverse red band, the basal band enclosing a pearly-white round spot within the cell and an elongated spot beneath it, the band bordered exteriorly by three pearly-white transverse streaks ; within the discal band the upper and lower portions are slightly streaked with pearly-white, and on the middle portion is a series of five blackish spots ; on the outer margin of the wing is a row of quadrate pearly-white spots. FEMALE. *Forewing* dark fulvous, markings more prominent, apex and margin greenish. *Hindwing* with the base and middle portion dark green, the subbasal and discal bands dark chestnut-red ; markings as in male." (*Moore*, l. c.)

Mr. Moore has described as a distinct species under the name of *A. baralacha* some specimens which appear to me to be inseparable from *A. sipora*. I have taken a large series of *A. sipora* in June and July in Kashmir and Lahoul, and find that the markings vary slightly, for instance in many examples the spots in the cell of the forewing on the upperside are reduced to one, while in others there are three ; the intensity of all the markings is also variable. I also took numerous specimens of a small *Argynnis* in July below the Baralacha pass at about 12,000 feet elevation, one of which now in the Indian Museum, Calcutta, was identified by Mr. Moore as *A. baralacha*; they differ from the single specimen from the Zoji-la, Kashmir, at about 11,000 feet elevation, taken by me a month earlier, and which from the locality should be *A. sipora*, in not having the discal series of spots quite so triangular or conical, but this is the only difference I can detect, and is barely sufficient for a specific separation even if constant. The species is nearly allied to the European *A. pales*, but the ground-colour of the underside, especially on the hindwing, is not so dark. A description of *A. baralacha* is appended.*

The figure (named *A. baralacha* on the plate) shows the upperside of both sexes from Lahoul examples in the Indian Museum, Calcutta.

433. Argynnis jordoni, Lang.

A. jordoni, Lang, Ent. Month. Mag., vol. v, p. 34 (1868) ; *A. cashmirensis*, Moore, Proc. Zool. Soc. Lond., 1874, p. 267, n. 25, pl. xliii, fig. 4.

HABITAT : Goolmurg, Sonamurg, Chunpur ; all in Kashmir.

EXPANSE : Wings, 1·5 inches. Body, ·5 inch.

DESCRIPTION : " UPPERSIDE fulvous, markings black. *Forewing*, base, and interior margin, below submedian nervure, dark fuscous; two spots (first circular, second lunular) within, and a streak closing the cell ; a large spot below the origin of the first median nervule ; a transverse, curved, discal series of seven spots ; a suffused spot on costa at two-thirds from the base ; a nearly straight, exterior, transverse series of seven spots ; a submarginal series of lunules ; and a very slender marginal line, which expands into an angle at the end of each nervule. *Hindwing*, the basal half dark fuscous, with a sinuous exterior margin ; an exterior, transverse series of six spots ; a submarginal series of five lunules ; and a very slender marginal line expanding into an angle at end of each nervule. UNDERSIDE. *Forewing* pale fulvous ; markings as above, with the exception of the fuscous of the base and interior margin, which is wanting, but is replaced by an additional narrow, lunular, basal mark within the cell. *Hindwing* fulvous ; base deep ferruginous, including a basal series of three small silvery spots ; a broad, curved, transverse, discal fascia (with acutely angulated black margins), silvery, white, except where interrupted by two yellowish-white patches ; an exterior transverse curved series of six small ocelli ; the sixth (near anal angle) geminated ; ocelli black, with minute white pupils ; marginal series of large silvery spots, each bordered interiorly with a narrow black lunule. *Thorax, abdomen, palpi, antennæ,* dark fuscous ; the latter with ochreous tips to the large, flat, pyriform clubs." (*Lang*, l. c.)

I have carefully compared the type of *A. jordoni* which is in Colonel Lang's collection with specimens of *A. cashmirensis* so named by Mr. Moore, and can find no single character by which to distinguish them. I took a large series of both sexes of *A. jordoni* at Chunpur, Kashmir, in June, which show slight variation in the intensity of the black markings, the paler ones agreeing almost exactly with the unique type specimen. Mrs. R. Bazett also took it in considerable numbers at Bayadmulla, 6,500 feet, and elsewhere in Kashmir at 8,500 feet, in June. The description of *A. cashmirensis* is given below † for reference.

* *Argynnis baralacha*, Moore, Proc. Zool. Soc. Lond., 1882, p. 242, pl. xi, figs. 1, 1a. HABITAT : Ladak. EXPANSE : 1·62 inches. DESCRIPTION : " MALE. UPPERSIDE fulvous ; lower basal area of both wings minutely black-speckled. *Forewing* with a black recurved streak within the cell, a lunular streak at its end ; a discal transverse zigzag series of broader streaks, two outer rows of small spots, which are indistinct at the apex, and a marginal, indistinct, dentated lunular speckled line. *Hindwing* with two less distinct and more slender cell-streaks, discal row of spots, two outer rows of spots (of which the inner row is indistinct), and a marginal speckled line. UNDERSIDE. *Forewing* paler fulvous, with the cell, discal, and inner row of black spots as above showing very indistinctly ; the costal border, two streaks from the apex, and short X-shaped marginal marks being yellow. *Hindwing* yellow, with a very irregular transverse subbasal, discal, and a marginal fulvous-red band ; the subbasal band bordered outwardly by linear pearly streaks, the discal band by indistinct pearly lunules, and the marginal band traversed by pearly X-shaped marks ; the discal and marginal bands more or less confluent ; a small pearly spot also within the cell." (*Moore*, l.c.)

† *Argynnis cashmirensis*, Moore, Proc. Zool. Soc. Lond., 1874, p. 267, n. 25, pl. xliii, fig. 4. HABITAT : Soonamurg, N.E. of Kashmir Valley. EXPANSE : *Male*, 1·37 ; *female*, 1·62 inches. DESCRIPTION : " MALE and FEMALE. UPPERSIDE bright ferruginous, markings black and very prominent. *Forewing* with the costa, base,

Genus 68.—DICHORRAGIA, Butler. (Plate XIX).

Dichorragia, Butler, Proc. Zool. Soc. Lond., 1868, p. 614 ; *Adolias*, sect. 6, Felder, Neues Lep., p. 35 (1861).

" Most nearly allied to *Apatura* (*A. erminia*), but differing slightly in the neuration, the discoidal cell of the hindwing partially closed by an interrupted and rather delicate lower disco-cellular nervule. In colouring the type more nearly resembles *Symphædra cyanipardus* ♀ than anything else, which probably accounts for its retention in *Adolias* [= *Euthalia*]. Typical species *Dichorragia nesimachus*." (*Butler*, l. c.)

Antennæ very slightly more than half the length of the forewing. Forewing with the *costa* gently arched, *outer margin* slightly emarginate and waved, *inner* margin straight, about equal in length to the outer. *First subcostal nervule* given off near the end of the cell, *second* just before its end, *third* opposite the termination of the costal nervure, reaching the apex of the wing ; *upper disco-cellular* nervule obsolete ; *middle* obliquely inwardly straight for a greater portion of its length, then sharply angled outwards ; *lower* at first straight, upright, then angled outwards, joining the median nervure a little beyond the origin of the second median nervule ; *third median* nervule much arched, *submedian nervure* sinuous. Hindwing with the *costa* moderately curved ; *outer margin* gently waved, *inner margin* deeply channelled to enclose the abdomen ; *præcostal nervure* upright, simple ; *discoidal cell* closed by a fine sinuous lower disco-cellular nervule, joining the median nervure exactly at the origin of the second and third median nervules ; *third median nervule* arched at the base, then straight, *first* median nervule slightly sinuous, *internal nervure* very sinuous.

Dichorragia is a genus of very small extent containing two species only, *D. nesimachus* confined to the hills to the north-east of India and occurring again in Borneo, and *D. ninus*, Felder, in Amboyna and Ceram. The Indian species is of a dark greenish blue with numerous irregularly disposed pale spots, with a highly dentate pure white marginal narrow band.

434. **Dichorragia nesimachus,** Boisduval. (Plate XIX, Fig. 82 ♂).

Adolias nesimachus, Boisduval, Cuv. Règne Anim., Ins., vol. ii, pl. cxxxix *bis*, fig. 1 (1836) ; id., Moore, Trans. Ent. Soc. Lond., new series, vol. v, p. 83, n. 16 (1859) ; *Argynnis? hippomenes*, Herrich-Schaffer, Ex. Schmett., pp. 54, 77, figs. 11, 12 (1850); *Dichorragia nesimachus*, Butler, Proc. Zool. Soc. Lond., 1868, p. 614 ; id., Druce, Proc. Zool. Soc. Lond., 1873, p. 346.

Habitat : Sikkim, Assam, Sylhet ; Borneo (*Druce*).

Expanse : ♂, 3'00 ; ♀, 3'37 inches.

Description : " Upperside black, suffused more or less with green. *Forewing* with a number of whitish spots disposed about the basal half ; at the extremity of discoidal cell three longitudinal streaks, and above these on costal margin some narrow streaks, white ; a double submarginal row of narrow white zigzag lines, and a marginal row of white spots. *Hindwing* with whitish spots about the middle ; a curved row of black spots above a submarginal row of narrow zigzag white marks, the latter more or less geminated about the middle ; and a marginal row of narrow lunulated white lines. Underside black, with markings as above on *forewing*, and tinged with blue, the spots on the *hindwing* bluish, but more or less obsolete, the surface of the wing being tinged with green ; the row of deep black spots as above. *Sexes* alike." (*Moore*, l. c.) The colouration of the female is somewhat paler

and hind margin brown ; three lunular marks within and an outward curved streak closing the cell ; a dentate lunule below the cell ; a transverse discal confluent zigzag series of spots ; a suffused subapical patch ; a submarginal recurved row of broad oval spots ; a marginal row of dentate spots, and narrow exterior line which is angled on the veins. *Hindwing* with the base brown, indistinctly streaked with black, and bordered by a distinct black zigzag lunular band ; the outer portion marked as in forewing. Cilia alternately white and black. Underside : *forewing* fulvous, apex and exterior border streaked with yellow ; markings narrower and less defined ; anterior spots in submarginal and marginal rows with white dots ; a black patch at base of hind margin. *Hindwing* dark ferruginous ; disc clouded with yellow ; two small pearly-white streaks at base of wing, one above, the other below the cell ; a small black narrow streak at base and a white-bordered black spot within the cell ; a curved median transverse band with irregular black angulated borders, composed of three pearly-white portions and yellow intervening spaces, the former disposed thus :—(1), between the costal and subcostal ; (2), at end of the cell and divided by the disco-cellular ; (3), between the first and second median, the first and third being much constricted ; a submarginal series of six white-centred black spots ; a marginal row of pearly-white quadrate spots, each well separated by a dark ferruginous streak, and bordered interiorly with a narrow blackish dentate lunule. *Body* above blackish brown, beneath and *legs* dark yellow."

" This species belongs to the " *selene* " group, and is allied to *A. jerdoni*, Lang, from Goolmurg on S.-W. side of the valley." (*Moore*, l. c.)

than in the male, and on the upperside of the forewing the double submarginal row of narrow white zigzag lines are completely joined, thus forming arrow-headed figures.

D. nesimachus is a common species in Sikkim at low elevations, and occurs as far east as Sibsagar in Upper Assam.

The figure shows both sides of a male Sibsagar example in the Indian Museum, Calcutta.

Genus 69.—CALINAGA, Moore. (FRONTISPIECE).

Calinaga, Moore, Horsfield and Moore, Cat. Lep. Mus. E. I. C., vol. i, p. 162 (1857) ; id., Lucas, Ann. Soc. Ent. France, sixth series, vol. iv, p. lxxxvi (1884).

"HEAD, small, with a somewhat long frontal tuft. [*Eyes* densely hairy]. *Thorax*, large, hairy, neck covered with long velvety hairs. *Abdomen*, long, slender. *Palpi*, porrected, ascending, elevated to the level of the middle of the eyes, slender, covered with fine hairs, those in front very long ; apical joint ovate-cylindric. *Antennæ*, [short, less than one-third of the length of the forewing, stout, with a gradual, but rather prominent club, articulations distinct]. FORELEGS, short, pectoral ; *femur* clothed with fine long hairs ; *tibia* and *tarsus* hairy ; tarsus two-thirds the length of tibia, armed with a single claw. MIDDLE and HINDLEGS, rather stout ; *femur* clothed with hairs ; *tibia* the same length as the femur, and partially covered with short spiny hairs, with two short tibial spurs ; *tarsus* with several rows of shorter spines ; of five joints, the first as long as the other four together ; second, third, and fourth short ; fifth rather long, half the length of the first ; claws sharp. FOREWING, elongate-trigonate ; *costal margin* slightly arched, *apex* rounded ; *exterior margin* about half the length of the costa ; *posterior margin* slightly convex, two-thirds the length of costa. *Costal nervure* strong, and extending to two-thirds of the costal margin ; *subcostal* nervure separated from the costal, its first branch arising at two-fifths from the base ; second branch at a little distance off, and at equal distance from the first as from the extremity of discoidal cell, and both running parallel with the costal ; third and fourth branches arising at equal distances from each other and from the extremity of the discoidal cell and the tip of the wing. *Upper disco-cellular nervule* very short, almost obsolete, arising from the subcostal at about the middle of the wing ; *middle* disco-cellular four times the length of first, extending downwards, and slightly convex ; *lower* disco-cellular long, curving obliquely downwards and outwards, and uniting with the third branch of the median nervure at its origin, closing the *discoidal cell*. HINDWING, elongate-trigonate ; *costal margin* convex at its base, then quite straight ; *outer* margin rounded ; *abdominal* margin nearly straight, slightly rounded ; *præcostal nervure* rather indistinct, curved inwards ; *costal* nervure arched near the base, then straight, extending to costal margin on three-fourths of the wing ; *subcostal* nervure straight to two-fifths of the wing, where it branches slightly upwards, and extends to the apex ; *upper disco-cellular nervule* short, straight, arising at the subcostal branch ; *middle* disco-cellular slightly oblique, concave ; *lower* disco-cellular oblique, convex, uniting with the third branch of the median nervure a little beyond its origin, closing the *discoidal cell*." [Third median nervule strongly arched]. (*Moore*, l. c.)

There appears to have been much uncertainty as to the correct position of this genus. Mr. Kirby in his Catalogue of 1871 placed it second in the subfamily *Papilioninæ*, but in his Supplement of 1877, placed it in the *Nymphalinæ*, in which subfamily it was originally described by Mr. Moore. M. Oberthür as lately as 1881* remarked that the characters furnished by the antennæ would indicate that the position of the genus lies between *Leuconea* (a genus of the subfamily *Pierinæ*, of which the European Black-veined White, *Aporia cratægi*, is the type) and *Parnassius*. Mr. Butler has recently described a species from "near Assam," and has prefixed the following note† regarding the genus, which, however, he retains in the subfamily *Nymphalinæ* between the genera *Hestia* and *Ergolis*. " The genus to which the following species [*C. brahma*] belongs has hitherto been placed in this part of the *Nymphalinæ* ; I have, however, not the least doubt (in spite of its short thickened antennæ) that its proper place is in the *Satyrinæ* between *Zethera* and *Orinoma* ; the neuration of the wings is almost identical

---

* Études d'Ent., vol. vi, p. 11 (1881).

† Ann. and Mag. of Nat. Hist., fifth series, vol. xvi, p. 309 (1885).

with that of the latter genus." As the forelegs of *Calinaga* are completely pectoral and unfitted for walking, the proper position of the genus is among the *Nymphalidæ*, though a knowledge of its transformation is necessary for determining its exact position in that family.

The genus *Calinaga* is of very small extent; three species have been described, but the describer of one of them afterwards considered that it was synonymic with one of the other two, and so far as I can ascertain at present there is but a single species. All the forms described "occur in the central plateau of Asia and upon the southern and eastern slopes of this plateau." They are smoky-black insects with whitish spots and streaks, the thorax in front thickly clothed with long ferruginous hairs, the abdomen leathery and somewhat like that of a *Danais* or *Euplœa*, being also bare of hairs. The antennæ are very short, and the texture of the wings papery, somewhat like those of *Hestia* or *Parnassius* (a genus of *Papilioninæ*). The species are exceedingly rare and are probably mimetic.

435. Calinaga buddha, Moore. (FRONTISPIECE, FIG. 122 ♂).

C. buddha, Moore, Horsfield and Moore, Cat. Lep. Mus. E. I. C. vol. i, p. 163, n. 336, pl. ixa, fig. 7 (1857); *Parnassius davidis*, Oberthür. Etudes d' Ent., vol iv, p. 108, n. 17 (1879); *Calinaga buddha*, idem, id., vol. xi, p. 11, n. 1, pl. viii, fig. 6, *male* (1881); *C. brahma*, Butler, Ann. and Mag. of Nat. Hist., fifth series, vol. xvi, p 309, n. 63 (1885).

HABITAT: Himalayas, Assam, Eastern Thibet.

EXPANSE : 3·5 to 3·9 inches.

DESCRIPTION : "UPPERSIDE smoky-brown. *Forewing* with a submarginal row of rounded creamy-white spots ; also a parallel row of irregular-shaped longitudinal whitish streaks from costal margin, widening to posterior margin ; space within discoidal cell whitish, divided transversely in the middle by a blackish bar. *Hindwing* with a submarginal row of white oval spots ; another row from anterior margin narrowing towards anal angle ; interior of discoidal cell and abdominal margin broadly whitish, the latter tinged at the anal angle with ochreous. *Thorax* ferruginous. *Abdomen* black. UNDERSIDE : *Forewing* as on the upperside, but the markings less defined ; [the apex broadly dull ochreous], *Hindwing* dull ochreous, paler at the base and on abdominal margin ; whitish markings rather indistinct ; sides of thorax ferruginous." (*Moore*, l.c.) The FEMALE appears to be like the male, as Mr. Butler in describing *C. brahma* states that he possesses a female, but gives no separate description of it.

C. buddha is decidedly a rare species. In the collections of the Indian Museum, Calcutta, Major Marshall and M. Oberthür are specimens from Sikkim, and Mr. A. Graham Young writes to me as follows regarding his experiences of it in the Western Himalayas : "Five specimens, Kujiah near Dalhousie, 6,000 feet, May, 1867 ; one specimen, Kulu, 3,600 feet, March, 1871 ; one specimen, Kulu, 3,500 feet, March, 1872 ; and one specimen, Kulu, 3,700 feet, May, 1885. In July, 1872, I saw three in Kulu at 4,500 feet flying together ; and on three different dates in May, 1885, I saw three more specimens." From the above it will be noticed that *C. buddha* occurs in Kulu from March to July. The single male specimen he has sent me agrees very closely in outline and markings with Mr. Moore's original figure and description.

The type specimen, judging from the figure of it, has the apex of the forewing rounded, and the outer margin of the hindwing evenly rounded also, which characters are noticeable in the specimen from Mou-Pin figured by M. Oberthür. The Indian examples, however, that I have seen have the outer margin of the forewing somewhat emarginate, that margin of the hindwing angled at the apex and third median nervule, giving it two nearly straight edges, these characters being less pronounced in the Kulu example. It was these differences and also some others in the details of colouration and markings which led M. Oberthür to describe the Mou-Pin form as a distinct species, but he afterwards received an intermediate specimen from Kouy-Tchéou, which convinced him that there is but a single somewhat variable species of the genus.

The form which Mr. Butler has very recently described from "near Assam" agrees very minutely with our four Sikkim male specimens, which differ from the North Indian type form collected by Colonel Buckley (probably at Masuri) described by Mr. Moore, and from my

Kulu specimen in having the markings smaller and more irrorated with grey, and also in having the forewing proportionally longer, the outline of the Sikkim form being very similar to that of *Danais tytia*; the greater depth of colouring is exactly what might be expected in the Sikkim race, but I have not sufficient materials to enable me to decide whether the difference of outline is constant; it is not referred to by Mr. Butler in his description of *C. brahma* given below.* The type specimen of *C. buddha*, and also my Kulu specimen, have the pale markings pale ochreous throughout and tinted with yellow at the anal angle of the hindwing, the abdominal margin being entirely pale coloured, and on the underside the hindwing and the apex of the forewing are pale ochreous. In the Sikkim specimens the markings are whiter, and the underside is pale fuliginous brown. It may be that the Eastern and Western forms are distinct species, but it cannot be proved till we know what forms occur in the Central region. Mr. Butler's species *may* be distinct from either, but so far as the description goes it is identical with the Sikkim form.

The figure shows both sides of a Sikkim male specimen in the Indian Museum, Calcutta.

Genus 70.—PENTHEMA, Westwood. (FRONTISPIECE).

Diadema, section 2, *Penthema*, Westwood, Gen. Diurn. Lep., vol. ii, p. 281 (1850).

" Wings elongate-triangular. Club of antennæ slender." (*Westwood*, l.c.)

Antennæ long, rather less than half the length of the forewing, the club very slender and gradually-formed. FOREWING, *costa* moderately and evenly arched; *apex* rounded; *outer margin* even, very slightly emarginate; *inner* margin straight, rather longer than the outer; *first subcostal nervule* given off at about two thirds of the length of the cell, *second* some distance before its end, *third* considerably beyond the apex of the costal nervure and before the apex of the first subcostal, not reaching the apex of the wing, *fourth* reaching the apex of the wing; *upper disco-cellular nervule* short, outwardly oblique; *middle* more than twice as long, outwardly curved, throwing out a spur into the discoidal cell, *lower* sinuous, directed outwards, joining the median nervure far beyond the origin of the second branch, at a distance equal to that between the bases of the first and second median nervules; *submedian nervure* sinuous. HINDWING with the *præcostal nervure* simple, straight, at right angles to the costal nervure; *costal* nervure evenly curved; *upper disco-cellular nervule* slightly curved outwards. *lower* almost in the same line as the upper, slightly more directed inwards, faintly sinuous, joining the median nervure just after the emission of the second median nervule; *submedian* and *internal nervures* gently curved.

The genus *Penthema* contains three closely allied species only, which inhabit the north-east of India and Burma. They are amongst the largest insects in the subfamily; the colouration is dark blue with white streaks and spots. They are forest-loving insects.

Key to the species of Penthema.

A. With a white streak at the base of the cell of the forewing and two spots beyond.
　436. P. LISARDA, Sikkim, Assam, Sylhet, Cachar.
B. With all the markings much reduced, the basal streak in the cell divided into two small spots.
　437. P. DARLISA, Upper Tenasserim.
C. With all the markings still further reduced, no spot or streak in the cell of forewing.
　438. P. BINGHAMI, Upper Tenasserim.

436. Penthema lisarda, Doubleday.

Diadema lisarda, Doubleday, Ann. and Mag. of Nat. Hist., first series, vol. xvi, p. 233 (1845); *Penthema lisarda*, Doubleday and Hewitson, Gen. Diurn. Lep., vol. ii, pl. xxxix, fig. 3 (1850); id., Wood-Mason, Journ. A. S. B., vol. i, pt. 2, p. 86, n. 3, pl. iii, fig. 1, *male* (1881); *Nymphalis euphrone*, Westwood, Cab. Or. Ent., p. 55, pl. xxvii, fig. 1 (1848).

HABITAT: Sikkim, Assam, Sylhet, Cachar.

EXPANSE: 4·7 to 6·0 inches.

* *Calinaga brahma*, Butler, Ann. and Mag. of Nat. Hist., fifth series, vol. xvi, p. 309, n. 63 (1885). HABITAT: Near Assam. EXPANSE: *Male*, 3·6; *female*, 4·0 inches. DESCRIPTION: "Nearly allied to *C. buddha*, but both sexes suffused with greyish, especially in the discoidal cell of the *forewing*, so that the bands across and at the end of the cell are blurred and indistinct; the elbowed discal series of spots more or less suffused and reduced in size, as are also the spots beyond the cell of the *hindwing*; the extremity of the cell in that wing is partly filled in with grey; the *thorax* is of a more orange tint than in *C. buddha*. Two males and a female were obtained." (*Butler*, l.c.)

DESCRIPTION : " UPPERSIDE, brownish-black, marked with numerous white spots and stripes. UNDERSIDE, fulvous-brown, the *forewing* darker brown, except at the tips, *both wings* marked as above with white spots. *Abdomen*, white, with a dorsal stripe of blackish-brown."

"There is scarcely any distinction between the appearance of the two sexes. The wings are large and broad, with the outer margins slightly sinuose ; the costal margin of the fore-wing is rounded."

The detail of the markings is as follows : " UPPERSIDE brownish-black, the discoidal cell [in the *forewing*] with three large oval white spots, one near the base and the two others placed obliquely. These are followed by a very much curved series of about ten white stripes, varying in size and length, the innermost one occupying nearly the whole of the inner margin of the wing ; beyond these are two rows of white spots, seven in each row, the innermost one in the anterior row being confluent with the preceding white dash. In the *hindwing* the discoidal cell is white, separated by brown veins from a series of white streaks, the innermost of which occupies nearly the whole of the anal area ; beyond these are two rows of white spots, some of those in the anterior row being more or less confluent with the preceding white dashes. UNDERSIDE, the wings are marked as on the upperside, the ground-colour of the *hindwing* being of a fulvous-brown, whilst that of the *forewing* is brown, gradually becoming paler to the tip. The *head*, *palpi*, and *thorax*, are black, spotted with white ; and the *abdomen* is white, with a dorsal band of blackish-brown, the sides also with a row of small black dots." (*Westwood*, l.c.) " The setose clothing at the base of the hindwing [on the upperside] between the median and submedian nervures is scanty and cretaceous-white like the markings." (*Wood-Mason*, l.c.)

P. lisarda occurs commonly in deep forest in Sikkim in the summer, and appears to be single-brooded. Mr. Wood-Mason obtained numerous specimens in Cachar ; Mr. S. E. Peal has taken it at Sibsagar, and Mr. J. L. Sherwill at Jorchât, both in Assam. It occurs also in Sylhet, Munipore, and the Dafla and Naga Hills.

437. Penthema darlisa, Moore.

P. darlisa, Moore, Proc. Zool. Soc. Lond., 1878, p. 800 ; id., Wood-Mason, Journ. A. S. B., vol. l, pt. 2, p. 87, n. 4, pl. iii, fig. 2, *male* (1882).

HABITAT : Upper Tenasserim, Meetan 3,000 feet (April), Thoungyeen forests.

EXPANSE : 5·0 to 5·4 inches.

DESCRIPTION : MALE and FEMALE. Allied to *P. lisarda* from North India, differs in the following particulars:—" *Forewing*, all the markings, except the streak along posterior margin, are bluish-white and smaller, those within the cell oval, two at the base and two near the end ; the marks of the discal series also are short and conical (not continuing outwards to the inner transverse series), the streak between the lower median nervule and submedian nervure only being elongated. *Hindwing*, the pale luteous interspaces between the veins are deeply excavated at their end, and partly coalesce with the inner transverse series of spots (the spots being larger), the outer row are also larger, conical, and deeply excavated externally ; a black streak traverses the cell." (*Moore*, l. c.) " This species also differs from *P. lisarda* in its broader wings, a character not mentioned by Mr. Moore in his description of the species. The scanty setose clothing of the base of the hindwing [on the upperside] is fuscous." (*Wood-Mason*, l. c.)

Captain C. T. Bingham has obtained numerous specimens of this species in the Thoungyeen forests in Upper Tenasserim. It has been found nowhere out of Upper Tenasserim at present. In fine fresh specimens the whole of the markings on the upperside of the hindwing and the long streak in the internal interspace with the duplex spot in the interspace above on the forewing being straw colour, while all the other markings on the forewing are bluish-white, makes a strong contrast between this species and *P. lisarda* ; in the latter all the markings are whitish or just tinged with palest ochreous.

438. Ponthema binghami, W.-M. (Frontispiece, Fig. 121 ♂).

P. binghami, Wood-Mason, Journ. A. S. B., vol. l, pt. 2, p. 87, n. 3, pl. iv, fig. 1, *male* (1881); i.d., Butler, Ann. and Mag. of Nat. Hist., fifth series, vol. x, p. 372 (1882).

HABITAT : Thoungyeen forests, British Burma.

EXPANSE : 5 inches.

DESCRIPTION : "MALE, differs from *P. darlisa* in having fully the basal half (including the same extent of the abdominal area in the hindwing) of *both wings* devoid of markings, the submarginal and discal series of spots alone remaining ; these two series of spots are blinish-white in the *forewing*, and of a beautiful straw-yellow in the *hindwing* ; they are, in fact, of the same colour, size, and shape as in *P. darlisa* ; but *the inner of the latter two series is closer to the outer*, which is placed at the same distance from the external margin of the wings. Both wings are also somewhat narrower than in *P. darlisa*, thus approaching those of the typical species ; and the *hindwing* is furnished on the basal half, between the median and submedian nervures and in the discoidal cell, with a thick and conspicuous furry clothing of rich dark fuscous setæ exactly matching the dark ground-colour of the wing and the abdomen of the insect in shade, which setose clothing is so scantily developed as to be quite inconspicuous in *P. darlisa* and *P. lisarda*. The whole body, too, but especially the abdomen, is much darker-coloured than in either of them. Shadowy traces of the lost spots are faintly discernible on the *forewing*." (*Wood-Mason*, l. c.)

The type specimen was obtained by Captain C. T. Bingham, after whom it is named, and is now in the Indian Museum, Calcutta ; he has presented other examples to the British Museum. The figure showing both sides is taken from the type.

Genus 71.—PARTHENOS, Hübner. (PLATE XXI).

Parthenos, Hübner, Verz. bek. Schmett., p. 38 (1816) ; id., Moore, Lep. Cey., vol. i, p. 46 (1881) ; id., Distant, Rhop. Malay., p. 143 (1883) ; *Minetra*, Boisduval, Voy. Astrolabe, Lep., p. 126 (1832) ; i.d., Westwood, Gen. Diurn. Lep., vol ii, p. 265 (1850).

"BODY, robust ; *abdomen*, small ; *wings*, elongated. *Head*, broad, hairy, without a frontal tuft. *Eyes*, large and naked. *Palpi*, compressed, parallel, not forming a conical projecting beak, directed upwards. The terminal joint nearly erect, and elevated to the level of the top of the eyes, thickly clothed with short scaly hairs, and with longer loose hairs on the whole of the front surface of the middle joint, and with a tuft of hairs at the extremity of the upperside ; terminal joint small and conical. *Antennæ*, half the length of the forewing, nearly straight, terminated by a very long and slender, gradually formed club, slightly grooved on its interior lower surface. *Thorax*, robust, thickly clothed with short woolly hairs, and marked with transverse bars of different colours. *Abdomen*, small, rather slender. FOREWING, elongate triangular. *Costa* slightly arched ; *outer margin* three-fourths of the length of the costa, scarcely emarginate, and slightly scalloped ; *inner angle* rounded ; [*inner margin*] not much more than half the length of the costa, very slightly emarginate. *Costal nervure* strong, and extending more than two-thirds the length of the wing ; *subcostal* slender ; its first branch arising at the distance of one-fourth of the length of the wing from the base ; the second branch arising at two-fifths of the length of the wing, beyond which for a short distance the subcostal nervure is a little deflexed, it then runs parallel with the costa, until the branching off of the third branch at the distance of two-thirds from the base of the wing ; which is immediately followed by the branching off of the fourth branch. The *upper disco-cellular nervule* is almost obsolete, it branches off from the subcostal nearly at half the length of the wing, just beyond the origin of the second branch of the subcostal ; *middle* disco-cellular short, straight, and rather oblique, being directed from the side of the costa towards the base of the wing ; *lower* disco-cellular much longer, obliquely arched, so that it closes the *discoidal cell* by uniting with the median nervure close beyond the origin of its third branch (being preceded on the upperside of the wing by a slender, arched, black line, dividing the second white subcostal patch into two irregular-shaped portions). *Median nervure* strong ; its third branch strongly angulated at about one-third of its length from its origin. *Submedian* nervure considerably curved. HINDWING, subquadrangular ovate. *Costal margin* nearly straight : *outer* margin rather deeply scalloped, with the portion between the first and third branches of the median nervure somewhat prolonged ; *anal angle* rounded. *Precostal nervure* distinct from the base, throwing off a forked branch towards the costa immediately before its junction with the *costal* nervure, which is considerably arched ; *subcostal* nervure branched at not more than one-eighth of an inch from its base. *Upper disco-cellular nervule* curved at its base, which is at about the same distance from the base of the branch of the subcostal nervure ; *lower* disco-cellular slightly arched, closing the short and narrow *discoidal cell* with an acute point, terminating at the base of the third branch of the median nervure. FORELEGS, of the *male* small, pectoral, very hairy ; *tarsus* about half the length of the tibia, slender, cylindrical, simple, exarticulate. Of the *female* small, not much longer than those of the male, rather slender, scaly ; *femur* beneath with long hairs ; *tibia* as long as the femur, with delicate setæ on the outside ; *tarsus* nearly as long as the tibia, slightly dilated towards the apex, with the articulations distinguished by slightly elongated spines beneath ; the basal joint about three-fourths the length of the limb ; apex destitute of claws. MIDDLE and HINDLEGS, moderately long and strong, scaly, and very much spined ; the middle *tibia* with a patch of short incurved hairs on the underside near the base ; spines on the underside of the tibiæ forming two rows ; tibial spurs long ; *tarsi* more numerously spined, especially at the sides, where the spines form longitudinal rows, beneath with two rows of smaller spines, except on the terminal joint ; *claws*, large, hooked, as long as the setæ at the extremity of the upperside of the last joint of the tarsus ; *paronychia* with two divisions, the outer nearly as long as the claw, slightly curved, finely setose ; inner lacinia shorter, obtuse ; *pulvillus* broad, short." (*Westwood*, l.c.)

LARVA cylindrical, anal segment spined, the third to twelfth segments furnished with pairs of long branched spines. PUPA smooth, boat-shaped, the head ending in two obtuse points.

There are many peculiarities in the neuration of the genus *Parthenos* ; the subcostal nervure of the forewing is bent downwards about the end of the cell and with its second branch encloses a small triangular space ; the third and fourth subcostal nervules both branch from nearly the same point, and the nervure itself is bent at the origin of the fourth branch ; the third median nervule is highly angulated. In the hindwing the precostal nervure is of very unusual form, being distinct from the base, and running some distance parallel with the costal nervure to which it is joined, but before the point of junction throws off a Y-shaped spur ; the third median nervule is angled in the hindwing also ; the discoidal cell is abnormally small. In markings also it is peculiar in having several of the black bars at the base of the wings on the upperside continued across the thorax and base of the abdomen. The colouration of all the species is some shade of green or bronze with darker markings, and the forewing furnished with a broad fascia of white semi-transparent spots and streaks. The genus is of moderate extent, containing several closely-allied species which are found in Eastern and Southern India, and Ceylon, the Andamans and Nicobars, the Malay Peninsula and Islands to New Guinea. In all the species the sexes are alike.

Key to the Indian species of Parthenos.

A. Upperside, ground-colour olivaceous green.
　　439. P. GAMBRISIUS, N.-E. India, Upper Tenasserim, Malay peninsula, Andamans and Nicobars.
B. Upperside, ground-colour light brassy green.
　　440. P. VIRENS, South India.
C. Upperside, ground-colour greyish-blue.
　　441. P. CYANEUS, Ceylon.

439. Parthenos gambrisius, Fabricius.

Papilio gambrisius, Fabricius, Mant. Ins., vol. ii, p. 12, n. 113 (1787) ; idem, id., Ent. Syst., vol. iii, pt. i, p. 85, n. 264 (1793) ; *Minetra gambrisius*, Butler, Cat. Fab. Lep. B. M., p. 101 (1869.)

HABITAT : Eastern Bengal, Assam, Sylhet, Cachar, Upper Tenasserim, South Andamans ; Nicobars, Malay Peninsula (*P. lilacinus* only).

EXPANSE : 3·7 to 4·7 inches.

DESCRIPTION. MALE and FEMALE. UPPERSIDE greenish olivaceous. *Forewing* with two basal black streaks which are continued across the thorax, the upper one in the cell giving off a curved fine line to the subcostal nervure, followed in the cell by a pair of black lines placed obliquely, joined posteriorly, then a semi-hyaline band, a black triangular and another triangular semi-hyaline spot, the latter outwardly defined with a fine black line following the contour of the disco-cellular nervules. The disc crossed by a broad band of semi-hyaline spots all defined with black, arranged as follows :—a triangular spot at the base of the lower discoidal interspace, six or seven elongated ones from the costa to the third median nervule, the subcostal interspace in some specimens containing a single spot which entirely fills it, in others it bears two distinct spots, being divided in the middle by a streak of the ground-colour. In those specimens which have two spots in the subcostal interspace, the lower one of the two and the spot below it in the next interspace have two smaller spots placed interior to them. Two large rounded spots towards the base of the median interspaces, and a small irregular one in the space below, placed on a bluish diffused patch, sometimes geminated. A submarginal and marginal even black band, with a black spot placed within the submarginal band in the submedian interspace. *Hindwing* with two basal black bands much as in the forewing, both terminating outwardly in a white spot ; a discal series of black spots, beyond which are placed five black lines in pairs between the nervules, which are concavely joined outwardly, the nervules on this portion of the wing being broadly bordered with black ; a submarginal series of acutely-pointed black lunules placed between the nervules, and a marginal lunulated broad black band. UNDERSIDE much paler, all the markings less prominent. *Forewing* with two distinct black spots in the submedian interspace near the inner angle divided by a fold in the wing, and a curved black line towards the base from the median nervure to the fold. *Hindwing* with a very fine black line near the base from the costal nervure to the first subcostal nervule, another irregular discal one, beyond which are a series of five duplex black spots, three placed anteriorly (the upper one very large and prominent) and two posteriorly, the ends of the nervules marked with a black spot on the margin. *Cilia* prominently white on the interspaces. The specimens here described are from Sylhet.

This species has been recorded from Dacca.* Mr. Wood-Mason obtained numerous specimens in Cachar in the summer months ; it occurs also in Sylhet, Assam, the Andamans, and Dr. Anderson obtained it in the Mergui Archipelago in the cold weather.

Var. *apicalis.* "Distinguished from *P. gambrisius* by the forewing having the white band quite diaphanous, without any borders to the veins, and extending broadly and uninterruptedly to the costal margin, thence continuing along it to the extreme apex." (*Moore*, Proc. Zool. Soc. Lond., 1878, p. 829.)

Mr. Moore records this form from "above Ahsown ; Taoo, 3,000—5,000 feet," and in Major Marshall's collection are specimens taken in the Donat Range and the Thoungyeen forests in Upper Tenasserim near the locality from which the type was obtained. In his collection there are examples from Shillong and the Andamans which also possess the characters given by Mr. Moore as distinctive of *P. apicalis*; he possesses other examples from Upper Tenasserim which exhibit these characters, but have in addition the distinctive feature of *P. lilacinus, viz.,* the basal bands of blue on the upperside of the hindwing and a patch of the same colour on the forewing below the first median nervule. *P. apicalis* appears therefore to be an inconstant and casual form of *P. gambrisius,* and occurs wherever that species is met with, and in each locality exhibits the other features of the local race with which it occurs.

Var. *lilacinus.* "UPPERSIDE. Differs from *P. gambrisius* in the lilac internal area of the forewing and basal area of the hindwing. UNDERSIDE. In the blue-green basal area of the hindwing, and the much better defined series of black lituræ beyond the hyaline band of the forewing."

"I have seen long series of both the Indian and Malayan forms, and am, therefore,

---

* Horsfield and Moore, Cat. Lep. Mus. E. I. C., vol. i, p. 148, n. 303 (1857).

satisfied that the differences are constant. The Fabrician type agrees with examples from Sylhet." (*Butler*, Trans. Linn. Soc., Zoology, second series, vol. i, p. 544 (1877); *Minetra gambrisius*, Doubleday and Hewitson (*nec* Fabricius), Gen. Diurn. Lep., vol. ii, pl. li, fig. 2 (1850); *P. gambrisius*, var. *lilacinus*, Distant, Rhop. Malay., p. 143, n. 1, pl. xi, fig. 7, *female* (1883) ; *P. sylla*, Donovan, Ins. China, pl. xxxviii (1799).

Mr. Butler records this form from Assam and Nepal (*sic*), Penang and Malacca, and in Major Marshall's collection are numerous specimens from Upper Tenasserim, many of which have the patch of blue on the upperside of the forewing on the inner margin and the two similar subbasal bands on the hindwing quite as distinct as examples from the Malay Penin-sula in the Indian Museum, Calcutta, and others with this colour becoming gradually less till they are almost as green throughout as the typical *P. gambrisius*. Some specimens of *P. lilacinus* from Upper Tenasserim also have the white discal band of the forewing almost or entirely continuous to the costa, being occasionally only slightly broken at the subcostal interspace, where the white spot is divided by a diffused blackish line ; the discal band also continued along the costa to the apex, but sordid-white and opaque, not semi-diaphanous, which characters are distinctive of the form *apicalis*. It appears, therefore, from our speci-mens that both *P. gambrisius* and *P. lilacinus* occasionally assume the white apex to the fore-wing of *P. apicalis*, and that though *P. lilacinus* may be quite constant in the Malay Peninsula, it becomes gradually merged into the typical form *P. gambrisius* in Upper Tenasserim. On this subject Mr. Distant writes :—" Many reasons advocate the view that the *P. lilacinus*, Butler, is but a slight local variety of *P. gambrisius*, Fabricius." (Rhop. Malay., p. 144.) Mr. W. Doherty has shown me specimens of *P. lilacinus* taken by him on Great Nicobar.

440. **Parthenos virens**, Moore.

P. virens, Moore, Ann. and Mag. of Nat. Hist., fourth series, vol. xx, p. 47 (1877).

HABITAT : Calicut, Malabar coast ; South India.

EXPANSE : 3·75 to 4·60 inches.

DESCRIPTION : " Form and pattern of *P. gambrisius*; ground-colour of the wings light brassy green. *Forewing* with the white spots as in *P. cyaneus* ; black markings not so prominent, but somewhat confluent and leaving little interspaces between the marginal series, the sub-marginal row on *hindwing* being very broadly conical." (*Moore*, l. c.)

P. virens appears to be a sufficiently distinct species. The colouration of the upper-side is of a different tone, being yellower than in *P. gambrisius*, and even more distinct from *P. cyaneus*. The two spots of the discal diaphanous band of the forewing in the subcostal interspace are usually joined into one constricted spot, thus giving the band a more conti-nuous appearance. The lower spot in the submedian interspace in this species and in *P. cyaneus* is usually obsolete ; the submarginal black spots on the upperside of the hindwing are larger and inwardly more convex than in *P. gambrisius*, and the whole outer border is blacker than in that species, very markedly so in some specimens.

There are numerous specimens of this species in the Indian Museum, Calcutta, from Calicut and Trevandrum ; it also occurs in the Wynaad and North Canara.

441. **Parthenos cyaneus**, Moore. (PLATE XXI, FIG. 95 ♂).

P. cyaneus, Moore, Ann. and Mag. of Nat. Hist., fourth series, vol. xx, p. 46 (1877) ; idem, id., Lep. Cey., vol. i, p. 46, pl. xxiv, figs. 1, *imago*; 1a, *larva* and *pupa* (1881).

HABITAT : Ceylon.

EXPANSE : ♂, 3·75 to 4·00 ; ♀, 4·25 to 4·50 inches.

DESCRIPTION : " Form and pattern of *P. gambrisius* from Sylhet, but of larger size, the ground-colour throughout the wings greyish blue, the white spots on *forewing* prominent, the two elongated subapical spots entire and not broken [inwardly] at their costal end ; the two median transverse black bands [on hindwing] broken up into spots, the discal series of longitudinal streaks very narrow, and the submarginal lunules also narrow." (*Moore*, l. c. in Ann. and Mag. of Nat. Hist.)

"LARVA cylindrical, pale purplish-brown, darker beneath, with dark brown longitudinal dorsal lines and transverse white spotted lines ; head and anal segment spined, other segments slightly hairy. third to twelfth segments armed with branched spines which are longest on third, fourth, eleventh, and twelfth segments. Feeds on *Modecca*. PUPA pale purplish-brown, somewhat fusiform, head pointed and cleft." (*Moore*, l. c. in Lep. Cey.)

In Ceylon this species "occurs everywhere. Plains and up to 6,000 feet, in forest land, I believe all the year round. A slow flier, rather shy. Sits on large leaves with wings spread" (*Hutchison*). "Very swift of flight, and difficult to capture" (*Mackwood*). "Galle ; Kandy. Common" (*Wade*).

This species is easily distinguished from *P. gambrisius*. The tone of the ground-colour is quite different, the three subapical semi-hyaline spots of the forewing are well-separated and distinct from the next group of three spots, and the submarginal black lunules on the hindwing above are much narrower and with rounded apices. The lower semi-hyaline spot in the submedian interspace is obsolete in this species, but is almost always present in *P. gambrisius* in all its forms.

The figure shows the upper and undersides of a male specimen from Ceylon in the Indian Museum, Calcutta.

Genus 72.—NEUROSIGMA, Butler. (PLATE XIX).

Neurosigma, Butler, Proc. Zool. Soc. Lond., 1868, p. 615 ; *Acontia*, Westwood, Cab. Or. Ent., p. 76 (1848).

"Nearly allied to *Romaleosoma* [an African genus], of which it is probably the eastern representative ; it differs, however, in neuration. BODY, *palpi* and *antennæ* formed and coloured as in *Romaleosoma*; the wings coloured as in some Eastern species of *Argynnis*: the *discoidal cells* closed ; the *upper disco-cellular nervule* of the FOREWING extremely minute ; the *middle* short and transverse ; the *lower* long, transverse, and gently waved, meeting the third median nervule close to the origin of the second ; the *upper disco-cellular nervule* of HINDWING short and arched inwardly ; the *lower* long, arched outwards, slightly angulated in the middle, and meeting the third median nervule just beyond the origin of the second. Typical species, *Neurosigma siva*." (*Butler*, l. c.)

Antennæ, exactly half the length of the forewing, with a long slender but distinct club ; *eyes*, naked ; *palpi*, with closely appressed scales. FOREWING, triangular ; *costa* gently arched, *apex* rounded ; *outer margin* slightly emarginate, even ; *inner* margin sinuate, rather longer than the outer *margin* ; *costal nervure* reaching to more than half the length of the wing ; *subcostal* throwing off its first branch at two-thirds of the length of the cell, its second branch emitted some little distance before the end of the cell, its third branch opposite the apex of the costal nervure, at first running almost parallel with the subcostal nervure, then arched forwards and reaching the apex of the wing. *Middle disco-cellular nervule* at first straight, inwardly oblique, angled just beyond its middle, from the angle outwardly oblique ; *lower* disco-cellular sinuous, meeting the median nervure a little beyond the origin of the second median nervule ; *third median* nervule slightly curved ; *submedian nervure* very sinuate. HINDWING, with the *præcostal nervure* long, stout, evenly curved outwards, emitted from the costal nervure exactly at the point from which springs the subcostal nervure ; the *lower disco-cellular nervule* joined to the median nervure immediately after the point where the second median nervule is given off.

Neurosigma contains but a single species, which occurs in Sikkim, Assam, Cachar, Chittagong, and Upper Burma. It is rich tawny in colouration with black spots and markings, the apex of the forewing and the outer margin of the hindwing broadly black with whitish spots. In the female the tawny colouration is reduced to a small patch at the base of both wings.

442. Neurosigma siva, Westwood. (PLATE XIX, Fig. 80 ♂).

Adolias siva, Westwood, Gen. Diurn. Lep., vol. ii, p. 291, n. 18 (1850); id., Moore, Trans. Ent. Soc. Lond., new series, vol. v, p. 85, n. 49 (1859); *Neurosigma siva*, Butler, Proc. Zool. Soc. Lond., 1868, p. 615; *Acontia doubledaii*, Westwood, Cab. Or. Ent., p. 76, pl. xxxvii, fig. 4 (1848).

HABITAT: Nepal, Sikkim, Assam, Sylhet, Cachar, Upper Burma, Chittagong, N. India.

EXPANSE: 2·74 to 4·5 inches.

DESCRIPTION: UPPERSIDE. "*Forewing* luteous at the base, with spots and margins of black, the outer portion of the wing broadly black, with three rows of white markings, the first irregular, the second formed of elongated lunules, and the third formed of oval spots. *Hindwing*, with the basal half varied with white, black, and luteous, the outer border broadly black, with a double row of white spots, the first larger and oval-shaped, the second smaller and rounded. UNDERSIDE, coloured and marked as above, but rather paler." (*Westwood*, l. c. in Cab. Or. Ent.) The specimen described and figured by Westwood from its large size (4·5 inches in expanse) and markings is probably a female. I have not seen that sex, but Mr. Otto Möller describes it from a Sikkim example in his collection as "identical with the male in the shape of the wing and the markings, but the fulvous colour on the forewing confined to the base, hardly perceptible on the hindwing, being replaced by creamy-white on both wings." This species was first described under the name of *doubledaii*, by which it should probably be known.

The male has been described by Mr. Moore as follows:—"MALE. UPPERSIDE: *forewing* ochreous-yellow, with spots on the basal half, and irregular lines across the disc and along exterior margin, and the apical portion of the wing broadly, black. *Hindwing* from the base to disc ochreous-yellow, barred with black; within, and spot below discoidal cell, white; rest of the wing black, with two rows of whitish spots; abdominal margin whitish; *body* spotted with pale ochreous. UNDERSIDE nearly as in upperside; markings and colours paler." (*Moore*, l. c.) *N. siva* is somewhat variable in the extent and prominence of all the spots and markings. It appears to be a rare species. Mr. Otto Möller has obtained it in Sikkim in the Spring, Mr. Wood-Mason obtained three males in September on Nemotha, Cachar, Mr. J. L. Sherwill has taken it at Jorehát, Assam, in April; it occurs also at Cheerapunji, on the Naga Hills, in Sylhet, Mr. W. Doherty has taken it in the Chittagong hill tracts, and it was obtained by the Yunan expedition.

The figure shows both sides of a male Sikkim example in the Indian Museum, Calcutta.

Genus 73.—LEBADEA, Felder. (PLATE XIX).

Lebadea, Felder, Neues Lep., p. 28, n. 68 (1861); id., Distant, Rhop. Malay., p. 144 (1883).

"Club of *antennæ* slender, much prolongated. *Palpi* scaly. *Eyes* naked. *Discoidal cell* of both wings closed. *First subcostal nervule* of forewing given off after the middle of the cell, the *second* before the end of the cell, curved downwards, the *third* ascending far beyond the middle of the wing, curved downwards, the *fourth* originating soon afterwards at the vertex. *Disco-cellular* nervules of the forewing curved inwardly. *Second* and *third median* nervules somewhat distant from each other. *Precostal nervure* of the hindwing curved outwards, simple, ascending far beyond the origin of the subcostal nervure."

"Differs from *Limenitis*, under which Westwood has placed the species belonging to this genus, by the closed cell of the hindwing and the position of the precostal nervure." (*Felder*, l. c.)

Several of the aberrant species of *Limenitis* have the cell of the hindwing distinctly closed by a slender disco-cellular nervule, but in all of them the precostal nervure of that wing is emitted opposite the origin of the subcostal nervure; in *Lebadea* it is emitted a considerable distance beyond that point; the most obvious character of *Lebadea* is, however, the shape of the forewing, it is much elongated, the apex being broadly produced and the outer margin being emarginate between the upper discoidal and the first median nervules. The inner margin is also very short, much shorter than the outer margin, whereas in *Limenitis* it is always the same length as, or in a few cases longer than, the outer margin. The shape of the cell of the forewing too is very different; in *Lebadea* the lower disco-cellular nervule is directed outwards from the median nervure, closing the cell with an acute apex at its junction with the subcostal nervure: in *Limenitis* it is directed at right angles to both the median and subcostal nervures.

The genus *Lebadea* contains but few species—*L. ismene* occurs in North-Eastern India, *L. attenuata* in Upper Tenasserim, *L. martha* in the Malay Peninsula and Islands including Borneo, and *L. paduka* also in Borneo. *L. ismene* much resembles *Limenitis procris* in colouration, but the discal white band is narrow and directed to the apex, which latter is generally suffused with whitish, and the discal band is followed outwardly by a series of white lunules; the ground-colour is rich fulvous. It has a weak flight, always settles with outspread wings, usually on a leaf.

Key to the Indian species of Lebadea.

A. Upperside with the medial band comparatively broad.
    413. L. ISMENE, North-Eastern India.
B. Upperside with the median band very narrow.
    444. L. ATTENUATA, Upper Tenasserim.

413. Lebadea ismene, Doubleday, Hewitson. (PLATE XIX, Fig. 79 ♂).

Limenitis ismene, Doubleday, Hewitson, Gen. Diurn. Lep., vol. ii, p. 276, n. 10, pl. xxxiv, fig. 2 (1850).

HABITAT: Sikkim, Assam, Cachar, Sylhet, Chittagong.

EXPANSE: ♂, 2·35 to 2·70; ♀, 2·7 to 2·8 inches.

DESCRIPTION: MALE. UPPERSIDE, *both wings* rich fulvous, with a white discal band, its inner edge somewhat straight and even, in the forewing somewhat macular, and above the third median nervule directed somewhat inwardly to the subcostal nervure; followed by a series of deep white lunules outwardly defined with black, on the forewing also with white powdering beyond, a submarginal irregular dentate fine black line narrowly defined with whitish on both sides. *Forewing* with a short irregular black line at the base of the cell continued to the submedian nervure, a pair of zigzag lines in the middle of the cell and another pair in the interspace below, both pairs enclosing a space brighter coloured than the ground, often with a whitish bar in the cell beyond; another pair of black lines enclosing the disco-cellular nervules; the apex more or less broadly white. *Hindwing* with the usual fine black basal and cellular lines. UNDERSIDE pale ochreous, the base of both wings and the abdominal margin of the hindwing greyish, all the markings as above, but less distinct. FEMALE with the ground-colour on the UPPERSIDE much richer and darker; the discal white band more macular on the *forewing*, the white lunules beyond with the black lunules placed outwardly against them more prominent, the apical white patch smaller. *Hindwing* with the series of black lunular spots beyond the discal band larger and more prominent than in the male, with a discal series of diffused black spots placed between the nervules, sometimes faintly present in the male. UNDERSIDE darker than the male, all the markings more distinct.

L. ismene occurs somewhat commonly at low elevations in forest in Sikkim, Mr. Wood-Mason took it in Cachar, it occurs also in Sylhet, Assam, and the Naga Hills, and Mr. H. M. Parish took it at Rangamutti, Chittagong, in October. In Major Marshall's collection is one male taken in March at Toungboak, Akyab, by Captain C. H. E. Adamson. The figure shows both sides of a male Sikkim specimen in the Indian Museum, Calcutta.

444. Lebadea attenuata, Moore.

L. attenuata, Moore, Proc. Zool. Soc. Lond., 1878, p. 829.

HABITAT: Hatsiega; Naththoung to Paboga, Upper Tenasserim.

EXPANSE: ♂, 2·0; ♀, 2·5 inches.

Description : "Male and female. Differs from *L. ismene*, Doubleday, in being smaller and of a brighter colour, the white medial transverse band narrower, the apical portion on the *forewing* more angular in position and extending to the costa, the outer series of narrow lunules being present on the *hindwing* in both sexes." (*Moore*, l. c.)

The Indian Museum, Calcutta, possesses several specimens of this species which were taken by Limborg with the types. It appears to be a very doubtfully distinct species, none of the characters given above being confined to examples from Upper Tenasserim ; specimens from Cachar have the ground-colour of the same tint, one specimen from the Naga Hills, and another from Sylhet have the medial white band as attenuated, its upper portion extending to the costa and placed at almost right angles to it, and so on. Female specimens taken by Dr. Anderson in the Mergui Archipelago in the cold weather are very dark ferruginous, but not more so than one female example from Sylhet in the Indian Museum, Calcutta. In Major Marshall's collection are numerous examples taken by Captain C. T. Bingham in the Donat range and Upper Thoungyeen forests in Upper Tenasserim, and one taken by Captain C. H. E. Adamson at Moulmein.

An allied species, *L. martha*, occurs in Malayana. The description is appended.*

The small genus *Pandita*, Moore, which includes about three species, is confined to the Indo-Malayan region. A description of it and the single species which occurs in the Malay Peninsula is given below.† *P. sinope* is a butterfly of moderate size, the wings broad and rounded, the basal half on the upperside fuscous, crossed by black waved lines, the outer half ochreous crossed by fuscous bands.

---

* *Lebadea (Papilio) martha*, Fabricius, Mant. Ins., vol. ii, p. 56, n. 555 (1787) ; idem, id., Ent. Syst., vol. iii, pt. i, p. 139, n. 429 (1793) ; *Limenitis martha*, Butler, Cat. Fab. Lep. B. M., p. 59, n. 1, pl. i, fig. 4 (1869) ; *Lebadea martha*, Distant, Rhop. Malay., p. 145, n. 1, pl. xvii, figs. 10, *male*, 11, *female* (1883) ; *Acanthea alankara*, Horsfield, Cat. Lep. E. I. C., pl. v, fig. 6, *male* (1829) ; *Limenitis alankara*, Horsfield and Moore, Cat. Lep. Mus. E. I. C., vol. i, p. 179, n. 364 (1857). Habitat : Malacca, Sumatra, Banca, Java, Borneo. Expanse : *Male*, 2½ ; *female*, 2⅔ to 2¾ inches. Description : "Male. Upperside brownish ochraceous. *Forewing* with the cell crossed by three pairs of blackish lines, of which two are basal, two medial enclosing a large whitish spot, and two at apex ; beneath cell and between the first median nervule and submedian nervure are some black linear markings ; beyond cell the wing is crossed by an irregular series of eight white spots divided by the nervules, of which the sixth and seventh are largest, and separated by the first median nervule ; these are followed by a straight series of six lunulate white spots margined with fuscous, that beneath the first median nervule being duplex ; apex somewhat broadly white ; a waved fuscous submarginal line, margined with white, and commencing beneath the fifth subcostal nervule. *Hindwing* with the cell crossed by two medial, waved, black lines, which are continued to near submedian nervure, and two short contiguous black lines near apex ; a discal oblique white fascia (continuous to the series of spots on the forewing), narrowing towards anal angle and margined on each side with fuscous ; this is followed by a series of fuscous lunulate spots, inwardly margined with whitish ; a submarginal line as on the forewing, but preceded by some obscure fuscous lunulate spots ; margins of *both* wings narrowly fuscous, with the *cilia* greyish ; abdominal margin greyish. Underside pale ochraceous. *Forewing* marked as above, but much paler. *Hindwing* marked generally as above, but much paler, the medial series of fuscous lunulate spots almost obsolete, and with two fuscous lines between the bases of the costal and subcostal nervures. *Body* and *legs* more or less concolourous with the wings. Female. Upperside as in male, but broader, and with the discal series of white spots much attenuated, the submarginal line extending to apex, which is not white, and with the white spot absent from cell. *Hindwing* as in male, but with the medial white fascia very narrow, and its following fuscous spots not margined with white. Underside much paler than above, and with the markings bearing the same relation to those of the upperside as obtains in the male."

"All the specimens of *L. alankara*, Horsfield, which I could examine, having proved of the male sex, whilst those of *L. martha*, Fabricius, have been invariably females, I have felt no hesitation in considering them as but the sexes of one species, and treating them here as such." (*Distant*, l. c.) Mr. Distant in describing the generic characters of *Lebadea* states that the lower disco-cellular nervule of the hindwing is "obsolete." This may be so in *L. martha*, but in both the Indian species it is distinctly present.

† Genus Pandita, Moore, Horsfield and Moore, Cat. Lep. Mus. E. I. C., vol. i, p. 181 (1857) ; id., Distant, Rhop. Malay., p. 146 (1883). "Head, rather small ; *eyes*, prominent, naked ; *palps*, rather short, directed upwards to about the middle of the eyes, extended a little in front of the head, hairy, the hairs at the base long, apical joint conic ; *antennæ*, rather longer than half the length of the forewing, straight, with an elongated slender club. Thorax, moderately robust, covered with scales, the sides hairy. Abdomen, rather small, slender, hairy. Forewing, elongate-trigonate, *anterior margin* arched ; *apex* rounded ; *exterior margin* two-thirds the length of the anterior, more or less scalloped ; *posterior margin* about the same length as the exterior, somewhat rounded near the base and the angle. *Costal nervure* moderately strong, extending to the middle of the anterior margin ; *subcostal nervure* with its first branch arising at one-fourth of the wing from the base, and extending to the costal margin at one-third from the apex ; second branch arising a little beyond the first, some distance before the extremity of the discoidal cell, and terminating one-fourth from the apex ; third branch commencing at one-third from, and extending to, the apex ; fourth branch at one-fifth of the wing, and terminating a little below the apex ; *upper disco-cellular nervule* very short, almost obsolete, commencing obliquely a little beyond the base of the third subcostal branch ; *middle* disco-cellular five times the length of the first, descending in an oblique inward curve ; *lower* disco-cellular rather slender, but distinct, long, descending straight, but uniting in a curve with the third median nervule immediately above its origin, thus closing the *discoidal cell*. Hindwing, quadrate-trigonate ; the extreme base of the *anterior margin*

20

The next five genera *Limenitis*, *Athyma*, *Abrota*, *Symphædra* and *Euthalia* are very closely allied ; the neuration of the wings is practically identical, and the small divergencies that are exhibited are in some cases wider among species of the same genus than between the different genera taken as a whole. The outline of the wings, too, the robustness of the body and the length of the antennæ, though typically distinct in each, vary within as well as between the different genera. With the perfect insect alone the outline of the wings taken in conjunction with the style of markings is sufficient with a little practice to identify the genus of any insect of this group, but until the life-history of each is known the divisions of this group into genera must be considered as tentative ; so far as is known, the caterpillar of *Athyma* is distinct from but closely allied to that of *Limenitis*, the caterpillar of *Abrota* is unknown, and the caterpillar of *Symphædra* is widely distinct from that of *Limenitis* and closely allied to that of *Euthalia*.

In *Limenitis* all the Indian species have a broad discal band, generally white and almost always prominent, extending from the costa of the forewing to the submedian nervure of the hindwing near the anal angle. In *L. danava*, the only Indian species in which this band is obsolescent (in the male only, it is prominent in the female) the elongated forewing and comparatively straight costa distinguish it as a *Limenitis*. In *L. austenia* the band is very similar in character in both sexes to that in the male of *L. danava*, but is a little more prominent.

In *Athyma* the markings are typically white and sometimes tawny, being in form and colour as in *Neptis*, but in some species the discal band only is prominent ; the body is almost always barred with white ; the discal band reaches the submedian nervure of the hindwing near its base, its *outer* edge never being beyond the origin of the second median nervule, while in *Limenitis* the *inner* edge of this band is close to the origin of the second median nervule, the outer being far beyond it. In outline *Athyma* has the forewing less elongated and the costa more arched than in most of the species of *Limenitis*.

In *Abrota* the markings are much as in *Athyma*, but the outline is more like that of *Euthalia* ; the markings are tawny on a black ground, but in the male the tawny markings are much wider and more diffused than in any of the tawny species of *Athyma*.

In *Symphædra* the markings present several distinct types ; this genus consists of a few species differing widely from each other, and there appears to be no more reason for grouping them together than there is for uniting them one and all to *Euthalia*. So far as the perfect insect is concerned there is no character, structural or otherwise, by which the genus as a whole can be separated. Seven species are represented within our limits, two of which are closely allied (*teuta* and *teutoides*) if not inseparable, and are marked as in *Limenitis* but shaped like *Euthalia* ; a third is allied to these, but has the discal band on the forewing more even, and a fourth has this band reduced to five spots only on the forewing, and entirely absent on the hindwing ; the remaining three present two distinct types of markings unlike each other and unlike anything else in the group.

In *Euthalia* the markings are of several distinct types ; a few species are marked some-what as in *Limenitis*, and are very similar in general aspect to both *L. dudu* and *S. teuta* ; the others present two dominant types, in one of which the body is very stout, the apex of

---

arched, the rest of it nearly straight ; *exterior* margin somewhat rounded, scalloped ; *abdominal* margin grooved, about the same length as the anterior. *Præcostal nervure* curved outwardly ; *costal* nervure arched to about the middle, and then straight to the apex ; *subcostal* nervure breaking off nearly straight, opposite the junction of the præcostal ; *upper disco-cellular nervule* straight, oblique, arising a little beyond the subcostal ; *lower disco-cellular* obsolete : *discoidal cell* open. FORELEGS, very small, with fine silky hairs ; *femur* rather longer than the tibia, *tarsus* half the length of the tibia, simple."

"This genus is somewhat allied to *Limenitis* and *Heterochroa*" [an American genus]. (*Moore*, l. c.)

Pandita sinope, Moore, Horsfield and Moore, Cat. Lep. Mus. E. I. C., vol. i, p. 192, n. 372, pl. viii, fig. 3 (1857) ; id., Distant, Rhop. Malay., p. 146, n. 1, pl. xii, fig. 13, *female* (1883). HABITAT : Penang, Province Wellesley, Malacca, Singapore, Banca, Java. EXPANSE ; 2·0 to 2·2 inches. DESCRIPTION : " UPPERSIDE bright fulvous. *Forewing* with the costal margin and basal half of wing golden-brown ; exterior margin, submarginal line, a pale inner parallel line, also a rather broad zigzag band, curving outwards across the disc from the apical third of the costal margin to inner margin near angle, and transverse markings within and below discoidal cell, black. *Hindwing* with the base golden-brown ; abdominal margin plain dull brown ; a broad exterior marginal band, a submarginal line, an inner broad band, also a rather zigzag ill-defined band across the disc, and markings about the discoidal cell, black, the black colour being darkest on the submarginal lines and discoidal markings. UNDERSIDE paler fulvous, the markings the same as on the upperside, but very indistinct ; *body* and abdominal margin grey. *Sexes* alike." (*Moore*, l. c.)

forewing and anal angle of hindwing in the male are sharply angulate ; in the other the body is comparatively slender, the apex of the forewing in the male is more or less falcate, and the anal angle of the hindwing is rounded. In all the inner margin of the forewing is long, and in many the anal angle of the hindwing is somewhat produced.

Genus 74.—LIMENITIS, Fabricius. (PLATE XXIV).

Limenitis, Fabricius, Ill. Mag., vol. vi, p. 281, n. 10 (1807) ; id., Hübner, Verz. bek. Schmett., p. 44 (1816) : id., Westwood, Gen. Diurn. Lep., vol. ii, p. 274 (1850) ; id., Felder, Neues Lep., p. 29, n. 71 (1861) ; id., Distant, Rhop. Malay., p. 147 (1883) ; *Callianira*, Hübner, Verz. bek. Schmett., p. 38 (1816) ; *Basilarchia*, Scudder, Syst. Rev., p. 8 (1872) ; *Nymphalis*, Boisduval, (*nec* Latreille), Ind. Méth., p. 14 (1829) ; idem, id., Gen. Ind. Méth., p. 16 (1840) ; id., Boisduval and Leconte, Lep. Amer. Sept., p. 197 (1833) ; *Moduza*, Moore, Lep. Cey., vol. 1, p. 47 (1881) ; *Najas*, Hübner, Tentamen, p. 1 (1806).

" BODY, moderate ; *abdomen*, rather short and small ; *wings*, long, trigonate. *Head*, rather small, with a small tuft of hair at the base of each antenna, and a small, conical, frontal tuft. *Eyes*, but slightly prominent, naked. *Palpi*, rather short, thick, directed obliquely upwards, reaching rather above the middle of the eyes ; the tips convergent, thickly clothed with short hairs, especially upon the underside of the basal joint, and the upperside of the terminal half of the second joint ; the third joint short, oval, obtuse at the tip. *Antennæ*, scarcely half the length of the costal margin of the forewing, straight ; terminated by a very slender, gradually-formed club, which is nearly one-third of the length of the whole antenna, rather obliquely truncate at the tip, with a very shallow double groove on the underside. *Haustellum*, long and strong. *Thorax*, oval, hairy ; tippets and sides of the metathorax more hirsute. FOREWING, elongate-trigonate ; *costal margin* very little arched ; *apex* rounded ; *outer margin* rather more than two-thirds of the length of the costa, emarginate, and very slightly scalloped ; *inner margin* a very little longer than the outer margin, nearly straight. *Costal nervure* strong, extending to three-fifths of the length of the costa ; *subcostal* nervure with the first and second branches arising close together before the extremity of the discoidal cell ; third branch arising just beyond the place of junction of the costal nervure with the costa, and extending to the tip of the wing ; fourth branch arising at about four-fifths of the length of the wing, reaching the outer margin a little below the apex, the terminal portion of the subcostal nervure very slightly deflexed. *Upper disco-cellular nervule* arising at four-ninths of the length of the wing, extremely short ; *middle* disco-cellular short, curved outwards ; *lower* disco-cellular slender, nearly straight,* uniting with the third branch of the median nervure just beyond its origin, closing the *discoidal cell*, which is rather narrow, and reaches nearly to half the length of the wing. *Median nervure* strong, its branches wide apart, the third gradually arched. HINDWING, subtriangular ; *costal margin* not much curved ; *outer margin* of the same length as the costal, somewhat truncate from the extremity of the subcostal nervure to that of the first branch of the median, scalloped. *Præcostal nervure* well-defined and curved outwardly ; *costal* nervure arched, extending to the outer angle of the wing ; *subcostal* nervure arising just before the præcostal, its branches arising at the same distance from its base as exists between the base of the wing and that of the præcostal nervure. *Upper disco-cellular nervule* forming the base of the discoidal nervule, and arising at a similar distance from the base of the subcostal nervule ; *lower disco-cellular* [usually] wanting, so that the *discoidal cell* is open. *Median nervure* and its branches moderately robust. FORELEGS, of the *male* small, pectoral, clothed with rather short loose hairs ; *femur* slightly thickened at the base ; *tibia* nearly straight, as long as the femur, slightly thickened at the tip ; *tarsus* two-thirds of the length of the tibia, gradually attenuated, and, when denuded of scales and hairs, consisting of three distinct joints, the basal joint more than half the length of the tarsus, the second and third of nearly equal length. Of the *female* longer than in the male, more scaly, and much less hairy ; the *femur* and *tibia* of nearly equal length, the *tarsus* two-thirds of the length of the tibia, and of equal thickness with it to the tip, composed of five joints, the basal joint occupying half the length of the

---

* See detailed description of the subgenus *Moduza* on page 163, in which the lower disco-cellular is outwardly convex, meeting the median nervure far beyond the origin of the second median nervule ; in typical *Limenitis* it is nearly straight, and is joined to the median nervure at the origin of the second median nervule.

tarsus, the second, third, and fourth gradually shortening, each with a pair of short spines at the tip, on the lower side, the terminal joint very small, with two very short straight spines. MIDDLE and HINDLEGS, moderately long and robust, scaly; *femur* hairy beneath; *tibia* of equal length with the femur, with strong spines beneath (except at the basal one-third) and at the tip, tibial spurs strong; *tarsus* equal to the tibia in length and thickness, with four rows of spines beneath; *claws* rather large, but not so long as the terminal setæ of the tarsus, strongly curved, and very acute; *paronychia* bifid, setose, nearly as long as the claws; *pulvillus* short."

" LARVA, subcylindrical, narrowed behind, with setose tubercles on the sides of the body, and with several pairs of elongated, obtuse, hairy spines on the back, those towards the head being the longest. PUPA, suspended by the tail, head-case beaked or bifid, gibbose on the back of the thorax." (*Westwood*, l, c.)

The genus *Limenitis* contains about thirty species, and occurs in North America, Europe, and almost throughout Asia; no species, however, has been described from the Southern Hemisphere. The Indian species are very varied in colouration, but all of them have a broad band of a lighter colour than the ground across the upperside of both wings, white in most species. They are very beautiful insects on the wing, almost always found in forests or amongst trees; they have a particularly graceful sailing flight, and settle on leaves with fully expanded wings. The well-known European "White Admiral" (*L. sibylla*) has three or four closely-allied forms occurring in the Western Himalayas; several very beautiful species occur in Sikkim and eastwards, while *L. procris* is met with throughout Eastern and Southern India, the Malay Peninsula and in Java, having allied forms in Ceylon and the Andamans. *L. procris* and its allies have been separated by Mr. Moore under the generic name of " *Moduza*." All the species of true *Limenitis* occurring within Indian limits are confined to the hilly regions of Northern and North-Eastern India; one species, *L. daraxa*, extending as far south as Upper Tenasserim.

Key to the Indian species of Limenitis.

A. Discoidal cell of both wings closed.

　　a. Lower disco-cellular nervule of hindwing joining the median nervure immediately before the point where the second median nervule is given off. Colouration brown, forewing with a prominent discal series of dark brown sagittate markings narrowly defined with white.

　　　　445. L. AUSTENIA, Cachar, Khasi Hills.

　　b Lower disco-cellular nervule of hindwing extremely slender, joining the median nervure exactly midway between the points where the first and second median nervules are given off.

　　　　a[1]. Colouration brown, the outer half crossed by paler (brown in the male, white in the female) bands, no sagittate markings on forewing.

　　　　　　446. L. DANAVA, Himalayas, Assam.

　　　　b[1]. Colouration fuscous, both wings crossed by a pale green discal band, macular and directed towards the apex in the forewing.

　　　　　　447. L. DARAXA, N.-E. India, Upper Tenasserim.

B. Discoidal cell of hindwing open.

　　a. Lower disco-cellular nervule of forewing nearly straight, joining the median nervure at the point where the second median nervule is given off.

　　　　a[1]. With the discal band straight or nearly so on the forewing.

　　　　　　a[2]. The discal band rich ochreous on the forewing, white on the hindwing.

　　　　　　　448. L. ZAYLA, Sikkim, Assam, Sylhet.

　　　　　　b[2]. The discal band white on both wings.

　　　　　　　a[3]. With a prominent ferruginous submarginal line on both wings.

　　　　　　　　449. L. ZULEMA, Sikkim, Bhotan, Assam.

　　　　　　　b[3]. No ferruginous submarginal line on forewing.

　　　　　　　　450. L. DUDU, Sikkim, Assam, Sylhet.

　　　　b[1]. With the white discal band more or less macular, oblique from the costa to the third median nervule.

　　　　　　451. L. TRIVENA, Simla, Kulu, Chumba, Murree, Pangi, Kashmir, Astor, Gilgit, Turkestan.

b. Lower disco-cellular nervule of forewing convex, joining the median nervure far beyond
the point where the second median nervule is given off.

　　a¹. Upperside bright ferruginous, usually with a white spot at the extremity of the
　　　cell of the forewing.

　　　　451. L. (*Moduza*) PROCRIS, India, Andamans, Malay Peninsula and Archi-
　　　　　pelago.

　　b.¹ Upperside dark rufous-brown; with no white spot in the cell of the forewing.

　　　　453. L. (*Moduza*) CALIDOSA, Ceylon.

The first species, *L. austenia*, was originally described as a *Lebadea*, but in the shape of
the cell of the forewing and the position of the præcostal nervure of the hindwing, also in the
outline of the forewing, it corresponds with *Limenitis*, thus lacking all the distinctive features of
Lebadea; it differs from all species of *Limenitis* known to me by the outline of the hindwing, which
is angled at the extremity of the third median nervule, giving it a quadrate appearance,
by the position of the lower disco-cellular nervule in the hindwing, and by the curious
black saggitate markings defined with white on the forewing; these characters are however
not sufficient to establish it as the type of a new genus, and failing that its proper place is
in *Limenitis*.

445. **Limenitis austenia**, Moore.

Lebadea austenia, Moore, Proc. Zool. Soc. Lond., 1872, p. 560, pl. xxxii.fig. 1.

HABITAT : Khasia Hills, Cachar.

EXPANSE : 3·0 to 3·6 inches.

DESCRIPTION : "MALE. UPPERSIDE, *both wings* dark chocolate-brown, with purple
reflections, crossed by a pale lunular band, extending from the costa of the forewing beyond the
cell to hindwing above the anal angle ; exterior to this is a transverse series of pale-bordered
dark brown lunules, those on the forewing being most prominent and zigzag from the costa,
where they are white-bordered, and thence decreasing on to the hindwing ; space outside
these to exterior margin pale brown with a dark brown submarginal and marginal line ; cell
of forewing crossed by six, and that of hindwing by four, black streaks ; *cilia* white [black at
the ends of the veins]. UNDERSIDE greyish brown, whitish grey at base, marked as above,
but having the outer band with all the lunules white-bordered, except the two lower ones
on both wings, which are nearly black. *Palpi, legs* and *body* beneath greyish white."
(*Moore*, l. c.) The FEMALE does not differ in markings from the male, but is rather larger,
and the wings a little broader.

The Indian Museum, Calcutta, possesses a pair of this species taken by Colonel Godwin-
Austen at Sarathu in the Khasi Hills, and another pair taken by Mr. Wood-Mason on
Namotha, Cachar, in September.

The next two species, though differing widely in outline and markings, differ from all the
remaining species in having the cell of the hindwing closed ; the lower disco-cellular nervule
is atrophied and extremely slender, but it can be traced in both species ; they both moreover
have the pale discal band of the upperside in the male tinted throughout not pure white, it
being brown in *L. danava* and pale green in *L. daraxa* ; in *L. danava* the sexes differ, the
band being pure white in the female ; of *L. daraxa* the female is unknown.

446. **Limenitis danava**, Moore.

L. danava, Moore, Horsfield and Moore, Cat. Lep. Mus. E. I. C., vol. i, p. 180, pl. viii, fig. 2, *male,
female* (1857).

HABITAT : Himalayas, Assam.

EXPANSE : 3·0 to 3·5 inches.

DESCRIPTION : "MALE. UPPERSIDE, dark olive-brown from base to disc of forewing, and
from base to one-third of hindwing, the rest being pale olive-brown ; a transverse dark band
crossing the disc of forewing and middle of hindwing ; a dark submarginal wavy line and
two indistinct inner wavy lines crossing both wings ; some indistinct markings within the

discoidal cell with paler centres, and a small green patch at anal angle. UNDERSIDE of a golden-glossed obscure ashy-brown ochreous colour. *Forewing* with markings at the base ; a transverse row of lunulated marks, and an indistinct submarginal row of very small spots, purple-ashy ; also a whitish patch at the apex, and a narrow yellowish line across the disc. *Hindwing* with broad inner and submarginal band purple-ashy ; the latter with small whitish spots along its middle ; two marks within and one above the discoidal cell whitish. FEMALE. UPPERSIDE with portions at the base, as in male, dark brownish-green ; the middle of both wings white, with broad greenish-brown band crossing the disc ; exterior margins broadly paler greenish-brown, with green patch at the anal angle ; markings at base of wings pale. UNDERSIDE pale greenish-yellow, with greenish-golden gloss ; bands and markings as in upperside, but less distinct and whitish." (*Moore*, l. c.)

L. danava differs conspicuously from other species of the genus in the female being very differently coloured and marked from the male. It has a wide range in the Himalayas, occurring from Masuri to Sibsagar in Upper Assam. It differs from all the following species in having two pale discal bands instead of one only, and by having these bands brown throughout in the male ; in the female they are white. Its outline is similar to that of *L. dudu ;* the forewing is more emarginate, and the anal angle is more distinctly produced, giving a slight resemblance in these two species to some of the *Euthalias*, but the inner angle of the forewing does not project beyond the apex of the hindwing.

447. Limenitis daraxa, Doubleday, Hewitson.

L. daraxa, Doubleday, Hewitson, Gen. Diurn. Lep., vol. ii, p. 276, n. 11, pl. xxxiv, fig. 4 (1850).

HABITAT : Kumaon, Sikkim, Bhutan, Sylhet, Cachar, Assam, Naga Hills, Upper Tenasserim.

EXPANSE : 2·25 to 2·85 inches.

DESCRIPTION : MALE. UPPERSIDE, *both wings* black, powdered with obscure ochreous at the base, a brown line near the margin, within which is a series of pale brown spots, each bearing a black spot in the centre, an obscure brown line just beyond the green discal band. *Forewing* with two black lines across the middle of the cell, with a figure of 8 in the interspace below, the disco-cellulars defined with a band of the ochreous powdering ; a discal band of eight pale green spots placed between the nervules, the upper one minute and linear, the next larger and oval, the two following about double the size and kidney-shaped, the next one at the base of the upper median interspace rounded, the three lower ones quadrate, divided only by the nervules. *Hindwing* with some obscure black markings at the base, the discal pale green band in continuation of that on the forewing, continuous, of nearly equal width throughout, but ending in a point at the submedian nervure, divided by the veins ; a rounded deep ferruginous patch at the anal angle. UNDERSIDE with the pale discal band as on upperside but almost white, the ochreous and brown markings of the upperside replaced by violet much brightest on the margin, the ground-colour pale ferruginous, the violet patches on the border each bearing a deep black spot as on the upperside, and inwardly bordered with deep ferruginous lunules, sometimes with an additional whitish spot within the band near apex of forewing. I have not seen a female of this species.

L. daraxa is not a rare species and has a wide range. Mr. Atkinson records it from the Himalayas of the North-Western Provinces, and it appears to occur at a suitable elevation all along the hills as far east as Sibsagar in Upper Assam and the Naga Hills, and Captain C. T. Bingham took it in April in the Upper Thoungyeen forests in Upper Tenasserim.

In all the remaining species of this genus the sexes are alike and the discal band is pure white throughout, except in *L. zayla*, in which it is yellow on the forewing. In all the discoidal cell of the hindwing is open. The first three species have the wings more elongated, and the pale discal band straighter than in typical *Limenitis* ; the outer margin of the forewing is also more emarginate, least so in *L. zayla*, most in *L. dudu*.

448. **Limenitis zayla,** Doubleday, Hewitson.

L. zayla, Doubleday, Hewitson, Gen. Diurn. Lep., vol. ii, p. 276, n. 12, pl. xxxv, fig. 4 (1850).

HABITAT : Sikkim, Assam, Sylhet.

EXPANSE : 3˙5 to 3˙8 inches.

DESCRIPTION : MALE. UPPERSIDE, *both wings* blackish, powdered with ochreous at the base. *Forewing* with a zigzag black line at the base of the cell and in the interspace below, two fine black lines across the middle of the cell and a figure of 8 below both enclosing a ferruginous space, a fine black line beyond, the disco-cellulars enclosed by two black lines surrounding an ochreous space ; a broad discal ochreous band, its inner edge somewhat uneven but sharply defined, its outer edge lanulated and somewhat diffused, the lower portion of this band inwardly white ; three subcostal ochreous elongated streaks in continuation of the band ; the ground-colour beyond brown, gradually deepening into black ; a submarginal series of deep ferruginous lunules, their points joined to a ferruginous outer line ; the margin marked with a black, then a pale, then another black line. *Hindwing* with some obscure black markings at the base ; a broad discal white band attenuating to a point at the submedian nervure where it ends ; a pale band beyond, then a broad black band outwardly bearing a series of prominent deep ferruginous lunules ; beyond which there is a pale band, then a black line, then a very fine pale line, and lastly the margin is black. UNDERSIDE much paler, glossy greenish at the base of the *hindwing*, marked much as above but all the bands more obscure and blurred. *Cilia* alternately black and white throughout. *Sexes* alike.

This is probably the most beautiful species of the genus, it occurs somewhat plentifully on Birch Hill, Darjiling.

449. **Limenitis zulema,** Doubleday, Hewitson.

L. zulema, Doubleday, Hewitson. Gen. Diurn. Lep., vol. ii, p. 276, n. 9, pl. xxxiv, fig. 1 (1850).

HABITAT : Sikkim, Bhutan, Assam.

EXPANSE : 2˙7 to 3˙3 inches.

DESCRIPTION : MALE. UPPERSIDE, *both wings* rich deep brown, crossed by a broad discal white band, divided by the nervules, the upper portion slightly recurved in the forewing, and macular, very straight and even in the hindwing, terminating on the submedian nervure, followed by a pale brown lunulated band, then a series of somewhat quadrate blackish spots placed between the nervules, then a deep ferruginous band, then another series of blackish spots but more elongated, the outer margin pale brown divided by two straight blackish lines. *Forewing* with the base ochreous, a black line in the cell with an annular spot below it, two black lines joined above and below and enclosing a deeper ferruginous space than the ground-colour across the middle of the cell, with a figure of 8 in the interspace below, the disco-cellulars placed on a deep ferruginous band margined with black on both sides. Two subapical small white spots. *Hindwing* with some obscure black markings at the base of the wing and in the cell. UNDERSIDE much paler, the ground-colour being greenish-white, the markings much as above, but more prominent. *Cilia* alternately black and white throughout. I have not seen a female, it will probably be found not to differ from the male in markings.

L. zulema is a rare species which is occasionally received from Sikkim. Mr. A. V. Knyvett has obtained it near Buxa in Bhutan, and there is a single specimen from Cherrapunji in Assam, in the Indian Museum, Calcutta. In general appearance it is very similar to *L. calidasa*, but the neuration is very different.

450. **Limenitis dudu,** Westwood. (PLATE XXIV, FIG. 112 ♂).

L. dudu, Westwood, Gen. Diurn. Lep., vol. ii, p. 276, n. 13, *note* (1850).

HABITAT : Sikkim, Sylhet, Shillong.

EXPANSE : 2˙8 to 3˙6 inches.

DESCRIPTION : " UPPERSIDE fuscous, with a straight rather narrow oblique submedian band across *both wings* white, a little irregular towards the costa of the forewing, with two narrow spots obscurely rufous margined with black towards the base of the *forewing*. *Hindwing* with a broad series of lunules beyond the band and a subapical streak black, with the anal angle acute golden, spotted with black. UNDERSIDE pearly, the band and basal spots as on upperside, but the apical ones obliterated, the anal angle broadly rufescent." (*Westwood*, l.c.)

MALE: UPPERSIDE, *both wings* with the basal half blackish, powdered with obscure ochreous at the extreme base. A broad black band divided from the discal white band by a band of the paler ground-colour, attenuated and macular anteriorly in the forewing, enclosing a series of deep red lunules (which are most prominent at the anal angle) in the hindwing; a submarginal and marginal black line, the former bordered with deep red on both sides at the anal angle of the hindwing. *Forewing* with a small round black spot at the base of the cell, with a similar one in the interspace below; two parallel black lines across the middle of the cell, and a figure of 8 in the interspace below, both enclosing a deep red space; beyond them the ochreous powdered basal area terminates in two sharply defined bands; a wedge-shaped deep red band enclosing the disco-cellulars; a discal white band from the subcostal nervure to the inner margin, the portion above the third median nervule (up to which point the band gradually decreases in width) composed of three spots crossed by the nervules, and separated by a streak of the ground-colour; an oblique series of three white linear spots extending from the lower discoidal interspace (where the spot almost touches the discal band) to the subcostal interspace near the apex; above the upper of these three spots there is an obscure short deep red streak. *Hindwing* with the white discal band of the forewing continued evenly across the wing from the costal margin to the submedian nervure. UNDERSIDE pearly, the apex of the forewing decreasingly to the third median nervule ochreous. *Forewing* with a band across the middle of the cell, a somewhat rounded spot in the interspace below it, and another band enclosing the disco-cellulars composed of an outer fine black line, then a fine line of the ground-colour, the middle ferruginous, as is also the basal half of the costal area; the discal white band as above, but inwardly sharply defined by a dark line, outwardly by a rather broader ferruginous line, beyond which are a double series of obscure lunules and a submarginal line. *Hindwing* with an oval spot across the middle of the cell, another in the interspace above, and a third below the upper disco-cellular, all composed of a very fine outer black line enclosing a pure white area; the discal white band as above, sharply defined on both sides, inwardly by a fine, outwardly by a broader ferruginous line, the latter widening out into a diffused patch at the anal angle; a double series of dark lunules and a submarginal fine line. The FEMALE differs from the male only in the wings being broader, as is also the discal white band, the ground-colour somewhat paler.

L. dudu is a rare species; Major Marshall possesses a specimen taken at Shillong in May.

The figure is taken from a male Sikkim specimen in the Indian Museum, Calcutta, and shows both sides.

The next species, which is the typical Indian species of the genus and most nearly resembles the European *L. sibylla*, has the hindwing shorter and much more evenly rounded than in the other Indian species; it is extremely variable, and the local races have been described under four distinct names, each race being typically very distinct, but numerous intermediate forms connect each local race with the next, and I have found it impossible to draw a line of separation anywhere. The species as a whole is confined to the Western Himalayas and the mountain ranges to the north and west as far as Turkestan. The extreme southern form is typical *L. trivena*, with the white discal band very broad, nearly one-third the breadth of the wing, and with a single row of diffused small whitish spots on the outer border; northwards, as the elevation increases, the white band gradually narrows, till in the forests near the snow line typical *L. ligyes* is found, with the discal band less than one-third the width of that of *L. trivena* and distinctly macular throughout, the black veins separating the spots being also distinctly bordered throughout with black. Further north where the vegetation is sparse the white band remains narrow, but the white border spots are replaced by much larger yellow spots, and an inner series of equally large yellow spots is developed, separated from the outer series by the series of black lunules, and the ground-colour is paler throughout. This is the form that has been named by Mr. Moore *L. hydaspes*. Further north still the form which occurs in Turkestan, and has been named *L. lepechini* by Herr Erschoff, closely resembles *L. hydaspes*, but judging from the figure differs in the disappearance of the black lunules from the space between the two series of yellow spots.

451. **Limenitis trivena,** Moore. (PLATE XXIV, FIG. 113 ♂).

L. trivena, Moore, Ent. Month. Mag., vol. i, p. 133, *note* (Nov., 1864); *L. ligyes*, Hewitson, Trans. Ent. Soc. Lond., third series, vol. ii, p. 246, n. 3, pl. xv, figs. 3, 4, *female* (Dec., 1864) ; id., Lang, Ent. Month. Mag., vol. v, p. 35 (1868) ; *L. hydaspes*, Moore, Proc. Zool. Soc. Lond., 1874, p. 270, n 40, pl. xliii, fig. 2 ; *L. lepechini*, Erschoff, Lep. Turk., p. 14, n. 41, pl. i, fig. 10, *male* (1874) ; id., Hedemann, Hor. Soc. Ent. Ross., vol. xvi, p. 263 (err. 247), *note* (1881).

HABITAT : Western Himalayas, Kashmir, Turkestan.

EXPANSE : 2·25 to 3·10 inches.

DESCRIPTION : "MALE. UPPERSIDE brown, with a broad interrupted white band extending across the disc of *both wings*, beyond which is a marginal series of pale ochrey-red lunules, bordered on each side with black. In the *forewing* are a few small white spots at the apex, before the band, and within the discoidal cell is a transverse white streak, on each side of which is a narrow, pale ochrey-red, black bordered streak, the basal one shewing itself below the cell. UNDERSIDE ochrey-yellow, with the broad band, discoidal and apical spots white. *Cilia* white, at the points black. *Antennæ* at the apex ochrey-red. FEMALE. Darker, fuliginous, tinged with green at the base of the wings, the broad transverse band and spots creamy white, the marginal series of lunules also whitish." (*Moore*, l. c.)

" I have seen but three individuals of this species, all in the Himalaya, 7,000 to 8,000 feet elevation, in forests of oak *(Quercus incana* and *semi-carpifolia)*. Has a quick flight, sometimes slower, floating in and out of the sunlight." (*Note by Colonel Lang).*

As this form was first described it may be considered to be the typical one. It occurs in the outer ranges of the Himalayas and furthest to the south. I took a single female on the top of Jakko, Simla, and there are numerous specimens of both sexes also from Simla in Colonel Lang's collection ; Major Marshall has observed it on the wing in the spring on the road down to Sipi from Mashobra, near Simla ; I found it common at Kujiah near Dalhousie in June, in Chumba and at Mogul Maidan, Kashmir, in the same month ; it occurs also in Murree, and Mr. A. Graham Young has obtained numerous examples in Kulu in May and June. In Colonel Lang's collection are two specimens from Lower Kunawar exactly inter-mediate between typical *L. trivena* and the form or variety described as *L. ligyes*. Some undoubted examples of *L. trivena* have a double series of ochreous spots on the margin on the upperside of both wings, placed one at the apex the other at the base of a series of black conical spots between the nervules, showing in this respect an approach to *L. ligyes*, though the white discal band is twice as broad as in typical specimens of that species. Other examples of *L. trivena* lack the inner series of ochreous spots, and in others again the outer series is white, and the inner also absent. The markings of the underside vary considerably, but the extent and colouration of those on the upperside are the most important.

Var. *ligyes*. " FEMALE. UPPERSIDE dark brown. *Both wings* crossed by a nearly medial band of white spots, followed between it and the outer margin by two bands of lunular black spots. *Forewing* with a black band, a rufous spot and a white band within the cell, and a rufous band at the end of the cell ; three white spots near the apex. *Hindwing* with rufous spots between the two submarginal bands of black spots UNDERSIDE ochreous-yellow. *Forewing* with the basal half rufous, the medial band as above, the lower spots bordered with black ; a lunular white spot below the cell. *Hindwing* (the medial band excepted) immaculate." (*Hewitson*, l. c.) The MALE does not differ from the female except that the outer margin of the forewing is slightly emarginate below the apex, and both wings are rather narrower.

21

This form, or more correctly local race of *L. trivna*, was described ambiguously as from "North India." It is not found in the outer ranges of the Himalayas, occurring always in the middle or inner ranges further north. Colonel Lang took numerous specimens in Upper Kunawar (Pangi, June), I obtained a single male at Mogul Maidan, Kashmir, in June, and Mrs. R. Bazett took numerous specimens at Gulmurg, 9,400 feet in July. The size of the spots in the discal band in these specimens agrees with the figure of *L. ligyes*, but the rufous spots are very feebly developed. I also obtained three males in June at Gagangair, Kashmir, and Major Marshall possesses three males from Baba Marishi, 8,400 feet, also in Kashmir, and one from Pangi, all taken in June. They differ from typical *L. ligyes* in having the discal spots as small as in the next form, *L. hydaspes* ; the development of the rufous spots is inconstant, some of these specimens being quite typical *L. ligyes* in this respect, but in none of them are they as fully developed as in *L. hydaspes* or *L. lepchini*. Lastly Major Marshall possesses quite typical specimens of *L. ligyes* taken at Kutabal, 8,200, and Bayadmalla, 6,500 feet, both in Kashmir, and one from Pangi, all these specimens taken in June. Colonel Lang writes of it : "This species is represented by only one much mutilated specimen in Dr. Jerdon's series [from Kashmir], which resembles the dark 'Kunawar' rather than the light 'Simla' variety ; but it differs from all that I have yet seen, in having an exterior transverse series, nearly obsolete in the forewing, but very distinct in the hindwing, of ochreous-red spots, one being placed at the apex of each of the black borders of the submarginal lunules. The underside is also suffused with ochreous-red. This species is subject to a considerable amount of gradual variation. At the commencement of its range near Simla, all the individuals accord well with the description of *L. trivna*, Moore, having *broad* white fasciæ occupying nearly one-third of the wing ; while at the extreme northern limit of the range, Tibetwards (as also apparently to the west in Cashmere), the fascia is narrow and only macular, and the insects have a dark sombre look. The food-plant of the larvæ is *Lonicera tatarica*, which has a wide range in the N.-W. Himalaya."

The figure of this form (erroneously named *L. hydaspes* on the plate) from a male Pangi specimen in Major Marshall's collection shows both sides.

Var. *hydaspes*. "MALE and FEMALE. UPPERSIDE dark rufous brown ; *both wings* with a transverse discal series of small oval white spots, and two submarginal rows of prominent dentate ochrey-red spots, which are parallelly joined together by an intermediate row of dentate black spots, the outer row being also bordered by a black lunule ; a narrow black and a white streak within, and an ochrey-red streak closing the cell ; two ochrey-white spots before the apex. UNDERSIDE bright ochrey-yellow, the discal maculated band and streak in cell, as above, black-bordered ; middle of the wings, outside the discal band, and a marginal series of lunules ochrey-red ; two black lunules near posterior angle of forewing."

"*Note.* *L. ligyes*, Hewitson, may be distinguished from this species in being of a dark or somewhat greenish-brown colour, the discal maculated band being formed of larger spots, the submarginal series of black dentate spots being bordered outwardly by a whitish (sometimes slightly fulvous white) dentate spot, and outer or marginal hardly apparent blackish lunules ; the underside is paler, and has more black diffused along the borders of the discal bands."

"*L. trivna*, Moore, may also be known by its much paler brown colour, and the very broad discal transverse band, which occupies nearly one-third of the wing, the underside being also of a very pale yellow. *L. ligyes* is apparently confined to the Kumaon [? Kunawar] district, and *L. trivna* to the Simla district of the N.-W. Himalaya." (*Moore*, l. c.)

This form or local race is described as being "common about Kashmir," probably on the authority of the late Captain R. B. Reed who obtained the type specimens. In Major Marshall's collection is a single female taken in Astor, Northern Kashmir in September, and I possess two examples taken by Colonel Lockhart's Mission, one probably near Gilgit, the other in the Astor Valley which are the only typical specimens I have seen. They differ from the figure of *L. ligyes* in having the discal band composed of smaller white spots, and the outer border of both wings bearing two prominent series of ferruginous spots, the inner series becoming white at the apex of the forewing. Several of the specimens mentioned under the previous form approach very closely to this one, notably one from Pangi, which has been here figured as *L. hydaspes*, but the ferruginous spots are not quite so large.

Var. *lepechini*. "MALE. Upperside fuscous, a macular white fascia beyond the middle, two series of fulvous spots before the outer margin. UNDERSIDE greenish-yellow, median fascia white." (*Erschoff*, l. c.)

This form or local race was described from near Maracanda, in Turkestan, and was taken in June. It is very close to our Astor and Gilgit specimens of *L. hydaspes*, but differs in the spots of the discal band being as large as in typical *L. ligyes*. The outer border of both wings on the underside is rich ochreous marked only with a diffused darker band in the middle, more prominent in the forewing. On the upperside also the black spots between the two ferruginous marginal series of spots are not shown in the figure.

The two following species have been generically separated by Mr. Moore (Lep. Cey., vol. i, p. 47) under the name *Moduza*. They differ chiefly from typical species of *Limenitis* in the shape and position of the lower disco-cellular nervule of the forewing. The description is appended.*

452. **Limenitis procris**, Cramer.

Papilio procris, Cramer, Pap. Ex., vol. ii, pl. cvi, figs. E, F (1777); *Nymphalis procris*, Godart, Enc. Méth., vol. ix, p. 404, n. 178 (1819); *Diadis procris*, Horsfield, Cat. Lep. E. I. C., pl. viii, figs. 4, *larva*; 4*a*, *pupa*; 4*b-b*, *structure of imago* (1829); *Limenitis procris*, Horsfield and Moore, Cat. Lep. Mus. E. I. C., vol. i, p. 179, n. 362, pl. v, figs. 12, *larva*; 12*a*, *pupa* (1857); id., Distant, Rhop. Malay., p. 148, n. 1, pl. xvii, fig. 1, *male* (1883); *L. amarta*, Moore, Proc. Zool. Soc. Lond., 1877, p. 585.

HABITAT : India, Burma, Malay Peninsula, Andamans, Sumatra, Banca, Java, Borneo.

EXPANSE : 2·3 to 3·2 inches.

DESCRIPTION ; "MALE and FEMALE. UPPERSIDE bright ferruginous. *Forewing* with the cell crossed by three black lines, and with the same number between the first median nervule and the submedian nervure ; beyond the cell the whole disc of the wing is triangularly blackish, containing an oblique series of five white spots, situated one at end of the cell, three separated by the median nervules, the fifth and smallest on the inner margin ; four or five subapical white spots, of which two linear and smallest are subcostal, two, largest, separated by upper discoidal nervule, and one very small beneath the lower discoidal nervule ; a broad submarginal waved black fascia and two narrower marginal fasciæ of the same colour, which sometimes become fused. *Hindwing* with the cell crossed by two pairs of blackish lines and with a few small black markings above the cell ; a broad medial oblique white macular fascia continuous to the medial spots of the forewing, terminating at the submedian nervure, its inner margin somewhat regular and narrowly bordered with black, its outer margin scalloped and broadly margined with black ; this is followed by a series of blackish spots placed between the nervules and marginal and submarginal fasciæ, much as on the forewing, but the inner one terminating at the anal angle in two small spots. UNDERSIDE with the white markings as above. *Forewing* with the basal area before the white spots (which are margined with black), very pale olivaceous ; the third and fourth lines in the cell including a bright reddish spot, and the same beneath the cell ; the

---

* Genus MODUZA, Moore. " FOREWING, triangular ; *costa* arched, *apex* produced, *exterior margin* oblique, scalloped, convex anteriorly. *Costal nervure* extending two-thirds of wing ; *first subcostal nervule* emitted at nearly one-half before end of the cell, *second* at equal distance between it and end of the cell, *third* at a little more than one-third from the cell, *fourth* and *fifth* at three-fourths beyond ; *upper* [*middle*] *disco-cellular* curved very obliquely outwards and bent near subcostal, *lower* very slender and slightly convex, the *radials* [discoidal nervules] from angle and end of upper disco-cellular ; *discoidal cell* long ; *middle median nervule* emitted at some distance before end of the cell and opposite to its upper end, *lower median* at more than half distance before lower end ; *submedian nervure* straight. HINDWING, broad, *anterior margin* short, *exterior margin* deeply scalloped, convex ; *costal nervure* extending to apex, with a lengthened outward-curved basal spur, its base being opposite to the subcostal ; *first subcostal nervule* at half length before end of the cell ; *radial* at equal distance from the subcostal ; *discoidal cell* open ; *lower median* nervule emitted from opposite base of radial, *second* and *third median* nervules at some distance beyond ; *submedian* and *internal nervures* slightly curved. *Body*, stout, short ; *palpi*, porrect, second joint long, projecting half its length in front of head, third joint very short and pointed, very slightly pilose beneath at upper end ; *legs*, slender ; *antennæ*, with a lengthened slender club. Type, *M. procris*." (Moore, l. c.) In these species the general colouration most nearly resembles that of *L. zulema* ; but the outer edge of the discal band on the hindwing is irregularly scalloped as in typical *L. trivena*. Both the Indian species are tropical or subtropical forms.

black discal area above reddish beneath, the three lower subapical white spots being situated in long and somewhat linear black spots ; submarginal black fascia very much broken and sub-obsolete ; marginal fasciæ as above ; marginal area pale violaceous. *Hindwing* with the whole basal area to just beyond the white fascia, very pale olivaceous ; marginal and submarginal fasciæ as on the forewing, but the last more obsolete and only denoted by a series of spots. *Body* and *legs* more or less concolourous with the wings." (*Distant*, l.c.)

The larva (as figured by Horsfield) is a very extraordinary creature, brown, cylindrical, the head much larger than the following segments and surrounded with numerous pointed tubercles, the three following segments furnished with a pair each of long spined club-shaped tubercles, increasing in length to the third segment, the following segments with similar but shorter tubercles. PUPA rich brown with two foliaceous processes at the head, the wing-cases dilated at the sides, the thorax humped, the dorsal surface of the abdominal segments furnished with irregular projections. In Java Dr. Horsfield records the larva as feeding "on a species of *Nauclea*, bearing the native name of *Kleppu*." In Calcutta I have bred it on *Anthocephalus Cadamba*.

L. procris occurs plentifully in India in the region of heavy rainfall. I have specimens from Sikkim, Assam, Sylhet, Cachar, Burma, Calcutta, Orissa, and throughout South India.

Mr. Moore has described a slight variety of *L. procris* from the South Andaman Isles under the name of *L. anarta*. It is somewhat variable, the white spot in the discoidal cell of the forewing being sometimes entirely absent, in others (and there is every intermediate variety) it is as large as many specimens from continental India. The other distinguishing characters given by Mr. Moore even if they were constant, which they do not appear to be from the specimens before me, are hardly sufficient to warrant the erection of *L. anarta* into a separate species.

Var. *anarta*, Moore. HABITAT : South Andamans. EXPANSE : ♂, 2·5 to 2·7 ; ♀, 3·1 to 3·2 inches. DESCRIPTION : "MALE. Darker than the Indian form of *L. procris*. Differs in the narrower white maculated band on *both wings*, smaller subapical costal spots, and much smaller spot at end of the cell. The outer black markings are also broader ; the marginal black dentate lunules are confluent and similar to those in *L. calidosa*." (*Moore*, l. c.) The late Mr. de Roepstorff has sent many specimens of this form from the South Andamans, the female sex being the one most frequently caught.

453. **Limenitis calidosa,** Moore.

L. calidosa, Moore, Ann. and Mag. of Nat. Hist., third series, vol. i, p. 48, n. 2 (1858) ; *L. calidasa*, Butler, l. c., vol. xvii, p. 285 (1866) ; *Moduza calidasa*, Moore, Lep. Cey., vol. i, p. 48, pl. xxv, figs. 1, *imago* ; 1a, *larva* and *pupa* (1881).

HABITAT : Ceylon.

EXPANSE : ♂, 2·50 to 2·75 ; ♀, 2·9 inches.

DESCRIPTION : "MALE and FEMALE. UPPERSIDE dark rufous-brown, basal area suffused with olive-brown. *Forewing* with a discal transverse series of bluish-white irregular-shaped spots, which continue in a band across the *hindwing* ; *both wings* with basal black streaks, and two submarginal series of black lunules interspaced with dull red ; marginal black lunular lines bordered with pale brown. UNDERSIDE, basal area bluish-grey, outer area pale greyish-purple ; discal nacular band as above ; submarginal spots, apical inter-spaces, and basal streaks, prominently black and red bordered ; marginal lines distinct."

"LARVA pale greenish-yellow or reddish, head spined, the segments armed with short spiny tubercles, and a longer dorsal divergent pair on third and fourth segments. Feeds on *Cinchona, Mussænda, &c.* PUPA reddish-purple-brown, wing cases dilated ; head bifid, twisted and bent outwards at the tips." (*Moore*, l. c. in Lep. Cey.)

L. calidosa appears to occur throughout Ceylon and at all seasons. It is quite distinct from the continental Indian form *L. procris*, the ground-colour of the upperside blackish, with hardly any ferruginous markings, and the white spot at the end of the cell of the forewing so prominent usually in *L. procris* in so far as I know always wanting in *L. calidosa*.

Genus 75.—ATHYMA, Westwood. (PLATE XX).

Athyma, Westwood, Gen. Diurn. Lep., vol. ii, p. 272 (1850); id., Moore, Proc. Zool. Soc. Lond., 1858, p. 11, *Monograph*; id., Felder, Neues Lepid., p. 31, n. 75 (1861); id., Distant, Rhop. Malay., p. 156 (1883).

"BODY, robust ; *wings*, large and strong, generally with transverse white marks on a black ground. HEAD, moderate, with a few long hairs in front ; *eyes*, rather prominent, generally naked, but finely hirsute in some species ; *antennæ* not more than half the length of the forewing, straight ; terminated by a long and gradually formed slender club, slightly obliquely truncate at the tip, and with a fine keel-like line down the underside ; *palpi*, rather slender, obliquely directed upwards, but not reaching above the middle of the eyes ; the tips horizontally porrected and slightly incurved, clothed with closely adpressed scaly hairs, with longer hairs at the base beneath, and towards the extremity of the second joint on the upper side ; the terminal joint very short and obtuse. THORAX, robust ; collar often variously coloured ; dorsum often marked with white spots ; metathorax large, deeply grooved down the middle, finely hairy. ABDOMEN, moderately robust, often party-coloured, especially at the base. FOREWING, large, subtriangular ; *costal margin* rounded ; *apex* rounded ; *outer margin* three-fifths of the length of the costa, slightly convex, straight, or but very slightly concave, and slightly scalloped ; *inner* margin nearly straight, three-fourths of the length of the costa. *Costal nervure* strong, reaching to the middle of the costa ; *subcostal* nervure with its first branch arising at about one-fourth of the length of the wing, followed immediately by the second branch ; third branch arising at about two-thirds of the length of the wing, and extending to the apex ; fourth branch arising at about five-sixths of the length of the wing, extending below the apex ; the terminal portion of the vein rather deflexed. *Upper disco-cellular nervule* almost obliterated, arising from the subcostal nervure at one-third of the length of the wing ; *middle* disco-cellular very short, curved, forming the base of the lower discoidal nervule ; *lower* disco-cellular obsolete in the typical species, the *discoidal cell* being open. In others it is, however, distinct, although very slender, arising from the extremity of the middle disco-cellular, which is in such species curved obliquely towards the base of the wing, and joining the median nervure close to the origin of the third branch. HINDWING, subtriangular ; *costal margin* rather rounded ; *outer* margin rounded, and more strongly scalloped. *Præcostal nervure* strongly curved outwards ; *costal* nervure arched, and extending to the outer angle ; *subcostal* nervure branching very near to its base, and also emitting the upper disco-cellular nervule very near to the base of its branch. *Upper disco-cellular nervule* forming the base of the discoidal nervule ; *lower* disco-cellular obsolete. FORELEGS, of the *male* small, pectoral, finely hairy ; *tibia* not so long as the femur ; *tarsus* rather more than two-thirds of the length of the tibia ; when denuded it is cylindrical, simple, exarticulate, and destitute of claws or spines, as is also the tip of the tibia. Of the *female* rather longer and thicker, scaly ; *tarsus* with well developed joints ; the first being half the length of the tarsus, without spines at the tip beneath ; second, third, and fourth joints with strong short spines on the underside. MIDDLE and HINDLEGS, moderately long ; *tibia* spined beneath, tibial spurs strong ; *tarsi* more thickly spined beneath, the spines arranged in rows."

"LARVA [*A. perius*], long, cylindrical, with setose warts at the sides ; head spinose ; each of the second and third segments with two long, erect, sharp, setose spines ; remaining joints with similar spines, but those of the fourth, sixth, eighth, and tenth joints are shorter than the intermediate ones. PUPA suspended by the tail ; head furcate ; body with a conical protuberance on the dorsal portion of the thorax, and another at the base of the abdomen." (*Westwood*, l. c.)

Athyma is a genus of considerable extent, about forty species being known. It is confined to Asia, occurring almost throughout the outer Himalayas, and eastern and peninsular India (but not in Ceylon), Burma, the Andaman Isles, the Malay peninsula and islands, with several species in China. Many of the species have a superficial likeness to species of the genus *Neptis*, being black with white bands and spots, but the neuration is very different. In several species the females are very differently coloured and marked to the males, but in all cases the style of marking and colouration is similar to that of *Neptis*. Both sexes of *Apatura chevana*, and the female of *Athyma selenophora*, appear to mimic *Athyma opalina*, in which species the sexes are alike. All the species known to me in nature are strong on the wing, but frequently settle, often on the ground with wide-spread open wings, or on leaves of trees and bushes. They are forest-loving insects, occurring only where there is a rich vegetation.

The genus comprises two groups, in one of which the cell of the forewing is open, in the other it is closed; in the first group the sexes are similarly marked in all the species, and all are black with the white bands and spots arranged as in *Neptis*; in the second group the aberrant species occur in which, while the females retain the "*Neptis*" markings, the males diverge in having the bands margined partially with blue, and in some cases the discoidal and submarginal bands obscure, the discal band alone being white and prominent.

Key to the Indian species of Athyma.

First Group.

A. Forewing with discoidal cell open. Sexes alike. Ground-colour black with white markings.
  a. Streak in cell of forewing divided into three portions, a spot beyond.
  　　　454. A. FERIUS, India, Malayana, China.
B. Streak in cell of forewing undivided.
  a¹. A spot in continuation of streak in cell.
    a². White spots forming submarginal band of hindwing on upperside with black centres.
    　　　455. A. ASURA, N.-W. Himalayas, Cachar, Khasi Hills, Upper Assam.
    b². White spots forming submarginal band of hindwing on upperside without black centres.
      a³. Submarginal series of white spots on underside of forewing with black centres.
      　　　456. A. IDITA, Mergui, Malay Peninsula, Java, Borneo.
      b³. Submarginal series of white spots on underside of forewing with no black centres.
      　　　457. A. KANWA, Naga Hills, Borneo.
  b¹. No white spot in continuation of streak in cell.
    a². Underside ferruginous, no dark patches between white bands and spots.
    　　　458. A. JINA, Sikkim.
    b². Underside ochraceous-brown, with dark patches between bands and spots.
    　　　459. A. PRAVARA, Cachar, Assam, Malayana.

454. **Athyma perius**, Linnæus.　(PLATE XX, FIG. 89 ♀; also VOL. I, PLATE II, LARVA AND PUPA).

Papilio perius, Linnæus, Syst. Nat., ed. x, p. 471, n. 79 (1758); idem, id , Syst. Nat., ed. xii, vol. i, pt. 2, p. 766, n. 116 (1767); *Athyma perius*, Aurivillius, Kongl. sv. vet. akad. Handl., vol. xix, pp. 68, 69 (1882); id., Distant, Rhop. Malay., p. 157, n. 1 (woodcut of larva), pl. xvi, fig. 2, *male* (1883); *Papilio plorius*, Linnæus, Mus. Ulr., p. 261, n. 80 (1764); *Papilio leucothoë*, Linnæus, Syst. Nat., ed. x, p. 478, n. 122 (1758); id., Clerck, Icones Ins., vol. iii (inedited), pl. v, fig. 4 (1764); *Acca leucothoë*, Hübner, Verz. bek. Schmett., p. 44, n. 397 (1816); *Nymphalis leucothoë*, Godart, Enc. Méth., vol. ix, p. 430, n. 256 (1823); *Limenitis leucothoë*, Westwood, Donovan's Ins. China, ed ii, p. 65, pl. xxxv, fig. 3 (1842); *Athyma leucothoë*, Horsfield and Moore, Cat. Lep. Mus. E.I.C., vol. 1, p. 170, n. 340, pl. v, fig. 11, *larva*; 11a, *pupa* (1857); *Papilio hylas*, Linnæus, Syst. Nat., ed. x, p. 486, n. 173, *female* (1758); *Papilio crosine*, Cramer, Pap. Ex., vol. iii, pl. cciii, figs. E, F (1779); id , Herbst, Pap., pl. ccxl, figs. 5, 6 (1798); *Najas crosine*, Hübner, Samml., Ex. Schmett., vol. i, pl. lxiii (1806-16); *Papilio leucothea*, Fabricius, Spec. Ins., vol. ii, p. 96, n. 421 (1781); *Papilio polyxena*, Donovan, Ins. China, pl. xxxvii, fig. 4 (1799).

HABITAT : India, Malay Peninsula, Siam, Java, Formosa, China.

EXPANSE : 2·15 to 2·90 inches.

DESCRIPTION : "MALE and FEMALE. UPPERSIDE dark fuscous, with the following lemon-white [almost pure white] spots and markings :—*forewing* with a basal streak and two spots in cell; a subtriangular spot at end of cell; two elongated subapical spots divided by the upper discoidal nervule, beneath which are an oblong discal series of five spots directed inwardly, the upper two smallest, and the fifth linear on inner margin; a submarginal series of six very small spots, the third, fourth and fifth contiguous to the upper three discal spots. *Hindwing* with a wide transverse macular fascia near base, and an outer discal series of six small spots, inwardly margined with dark fuscous spots, placed between the nervules. *Both wings* with a waved pale linear submarginal fascia, and the *cilia* alternately white. UNDERSIDE dark warm ochraceous ; pale spots as above, but whiter and more or less margined with black. *Forewing* with four black spots beneath first median nervule, *viz.*, two beneath cell (the basal very small), the largest before the fourth discal spot, and the last following this spot. *Hindwing* with the apex of præcostal nervure black and situated in a basal transverse whitish fascia ; medial fascia as above, but more or less margined on each side with black, the outer discal spots above fused into a macular fascia beneath, and containing a series of small black spots placed between the nervules (two between the first median nervule and submedian nervure) ; *both wings* with a narrow pale waved submarginal violaceous fascia, outwardly margined with black ; *cilia* as above. *Body* above dark fuscous, the *eyes* castaneous ; *thorax* with some discal linear grey markings and two posterior oblique spots of the same colour ; *abdomen* annulated with greyish. *Body* beneath and *legs* greyish, the under surfaces of the tarsi castaneous." (*Distant*, l. c.)

LARVA cylindrical, of equal thickness throughout its length, head larger than the following segment, black, thickly covered with obtuse castaneous spines, body pale green, beneath and legs castaneous, armed with a subdorsal series of long, and a spiracular series of shorter spined castaneous tubercles, one in each series on each segment, those on the fourth, sixth, eighth, tenth and thirteenth segments in the subdorsal series shorter than the others, spiracles black. PUPA brown, richly gilt, head ending in two points, thorax foliaceous. In Java Dr. Horsfield records the larva as feeding " on a species of *Phyllanthus.*"

A. perius is one of the commonest as well as the most widely distributed species of the genus. It occurs throughout the outer ranges of the Himalayas and in Eastern, South-Western and Southern India to Travancore—but not in Ceylon—throughout Burma, the Malay peninsula, Siam, in Java, Formosa and China. It is very constant in its markings, though Mr. Moore remarks that "specimens from Java are smaller than those from India, and have the medial band broader and the portions closer together." It may be distinguished from all other Indian species, except *A. asura* and *A. sulpitia*, by the white submarginal band on the underside of the hindwing enclosing a series of round black spots. In *A. asura* these spots are in the middle of the band and appear on both upper and undersides ; in *A. sulpitia* these spots are nearer the inner edge of the band and are followed by another row on the ochreous ground-colour within ; in *A. perius* these spots are also near the inner edge of the band, but there is no second row within and no group of black spots near the base, and the ground-colour is very uniform bright ochreous.

The figure shows both sides of a female specimen from Masuri in the Indian Museum, Calcutta. The larva and pupa are figured on Plate II of Vol. I under the synonymic name of this species, *Athyma leucothöe*, by which it was till lately universally known.

Athyma larymna, Doubleday, Hewitson, occurs in Perak and Malacca. It is a very handsome and large species, probably the largest in the genus. Mr. Westwood probably incorrectly recorded it from Northern India. His figure differs from a Perak specimen in the Indian Museum, Calcutta, by the white markings on the upperside being somewhat larger, especially the discal band on both wings. The description is appended.* It closely resembles *A. opalina* in the markings of both upper and underside, but it is much larger, the cell of the forewing is open, and the discoidal nervule of the hindwing is much less curved at the base.

---

* *Athyma larymna*. *Limenitis larymna*, Doubleday and Hewitson, Gen. Diurn. Lep., vol. ii, pl. xxxv, fig. 1 (1850) ; *Athyma larymna*, Westwood, id., p. 274, n. 7 (1850) ; id., Horsfield and Moore, Cat. Lep. Mus. E.I.C., vol. i, p. 172, n. 352 (1857) ; *Athyma larymna.* var., *male*, Distant, Rhop. Malay., p. 150, n. 2, pl. xvi, fig. 1, *male* (1883) ; Northern India? Perak, Malacca, Java, Borneo. EXPANSE : 3¼ to 3½ inches. DESCRIPTION : "MALE and FEMALE. UPPERSIDE dark fuscous, with the following dark cream-coloured markings :—*Forewing* with a [narrow] basal streak followed by two spots in cell, and a large subtriangular spot at end of cell ; two large subapical spots divided by the upper discoidal nervule, and preceded by a small subcostal linear spot ; a large discal spot between the second and first median nervules, and two contiguous spots about middle of inner margin, which are divided by the submedian nervure ; two submarginal series of small spots, the inner one waved and commencing near costa, the outer one commencing beneath the lower subcostal nervule, but fading into pale fuscous beneath the third median nervule. *Cilia* alternately greyish from beneath apex. *Hindwing* with a transverse macular fascia before middle, a transverse series of subconical spots placed between the nervules, gradually enlarging towards abdominal margin, and situated on the outer portion of disc, and a pale fuscous submarginal line. UNDERSIDE brownish ochraceous, the pale markings more or less clouded. *Forewing* with the cellular spots fused into a single fascia, convex, but deeply notched above ; the spot at end of cell elongated, and preceded by an upper subquadrate spot ; discal spots as above, the two series of submarginal spots as above, but of the inner series the two apical spots fuscous,

455. **Athyma asura**, Moore.

A. asura, Moore, Horsfield and Moore, Cat. Lep. Mus. E. I. C., vol. i, p. 171, n. 350, pl. va, fig. 1 (1857); id., Moore, Proc. Zool. Soc. Lond., 1858, p. 17, n. 18.

HABITAT : Western Himalayas, Assam, Cachar, Khasi Hills.

EXPANSE : 2·9 to 3·1 inches.

DESCRIPTION : "UPPERSIDE, smoky-brown, markings creamy-white. *Forewing* with a narrow discoidal streak, which is terminated at a short distance by an angular mark ; a band of spots curving outwards from anterior to middle of posterior margin, the first spot commencing as a very narrow line, second and third long and oval, fourth the smallest, fifth somewhat larger and rounded, sixth larger still and oval, seventh the largest, square, indented at the sides, eighth narrow and on posterior margin ; a submarginal row of well-defined lunular marks, terminated on the apex of the wing by an inner row of three small spots. *Hindwing* with a broad inner band; also a less broad band from abdominal to anterior angle, this being intersected by the nervules, and having a single black spot in the middle between each nervule ; a marginal pale brown line in *both wings* ; a narrow bluish-white collar and band across the base of the abdomen. UNDERSIDE bright ferruginous ; markings as above, but the *forewing* has the submarginal row of marks broad, and having a black spot in the middle of each ; also a marginal row of small spots ; some black lines bordering the discoidal marks ; also a small black circle near base of wing, and a patch of black on posterior margin near the angle. *Hindwing* with the inner, and spotted outer band the same as above ; a bluish-green curved line across the base of wing, and a marginal row of lunular spots ; *body* and upper part of abdominal margin bluish-green. *Sexes* alike. This species may be distinguished from all others by the outer band on the hindwing having a central spot between each vein." (*Moore*, l. c. in Cat. Lep. Mus. E. I. C.)

A. asura is a somewhat rare species. Mr. A. Graham Young has taken it in Kulu, I found it sparingly in a wooded stream below Kotgarh in the autumn, Colonel Lang has taken it in Masuri in June and August, Mr. Wood-Mason took it in Cachar during the summer ; it occurs also at Sibsagar in Upper Assam (*S. E. Peal*), and on the Khasi Hills. The female differs from the male in having the white bands and spots, especially the submarginal band on the upperside of the hindwing, of greater extent. It is a very distinct species, being the only one in which the submarginal white band on the *upperside* of the hindwing bears a series of round black spots placed one on the middle of each interspace.

456. **Athyma idita**, Moore.

A. idita, Moore, Proc. Zool. Soc. Lond., 1858, p. 16, n. 16, pl. li, fig. 3, *male* (1858); id., Distant, Rhop. Malay., p. 160, n. 3, pl. xvi, fig. 9, *male* ; 10, *female* (1883).

HABITAT : Mergui Archipelago, Province Wellesley, Malacca, Java ?, Borneo.

EXPANSE : ♂, 2·3 to 2·5; ♀, 2·8 inches.

DESCRIPTION : "MALE. UPPERSIDE blackish-brown ; markings bluish-white. *Forewing* with the discoidal streak in two portions, the first narrow, the second somewhat round ; from subcostal nervure curving to middle of posterior margin a series of seven spots, the upper two oval, rather long, the third the smallest, fourth larger, the third and fourth widely separated from second and fifth, fifth largest, nearly round, outwardly oblique, sixth and seventh irregularly shaped ; a submarginal row of narrow indistinct marks, that at the posterior angle being largest. *Hindwing* with inner band, and narrow row of six rather square spots curving upwards and outwards from near abdominal angle, the last spot near anterior angle

surrounded by greyish, and the outer series obsolete till beneath the lower discoidal nervule, but then regular and distinctly greyish—this wing is also ornamented with a number of dark fuscous streaks and spots. *Hindwing* marked as above, but with an additional transverse basal fascia, curved and attenuated towards costal margin, the medial fascia deflexed and continued on inner side of submedian nervure, the pale fuscous submarginal fascia above whitish beneath, and the *cilia* somewhat broadly alternately greyish. *Body* above dark fuscous ; *thorax* with an anterior cream-coloured fascia, and *abdomen* with two fasciæ of the same colour, one basal and broad, the second subapical and narrow." (*Distant*, l.c.) The band across the anterior portion of the thorax in a Perak specimen is beautiful iridescent greenish-bluish, and the band across the abdomen and the abdominal fold of the hindwing are also tinted with this colour but more faintly.

centred with a dark brown dot. Front of thorax beautifully variegated with ferruginous, green, brown and blue ; base of abdomen with broad bluish-white band. UNDERSIDE very deep ferruginous. *Forewing* having the discoidal streak with black transverse margins and an ill-defined third portion : curved row of spots as above ; a submarginal row of large white, black-centred spots ; a submarginal and marginal line of white marks ; some dusky patches along posterior margin ; the large portion of the discoidal streak and submarginal row of spots with purple reflections. *Hindwing* with curved streak near the base, inner band, outer row of recurved spots, submarginal line of lunular marks, and marginal row of spots, white ; abdominal margin greyish." (*Moore*, l. c.) "FEMALE. Larger than the male, and with the pale spots and fasciæ larger." (*Distant*, l.c.)

Dr. Anderson obtained two males of *A. idita* in the Mergui Archipelago in the cold weather, and Mr. Distant states that there are "in the British Museum some specimens labelled 'India.'" This too is a very distinct species, being the only one in which the submarginal white macular band on the underside of the *forewing* bears a series of black spots ; the submarginal band of the hindwing is unspotted white.

457. **Athyma kanwa,** Moore.

A. kanwa, Moore, Proc. Zool. Soc. Lond., 1858, p.17, n. 17, pl. li, fig. 2.

HABITAT : Naga Hills ; Borneo (*Moore*).

EXPANSE : 2·25 to 2·50 (*Moore*) ; 2·1 inches, Naga Hill specimen.

DESCRIPTION : "FEMALE. UPPERSIDE brown-black. *Forewing* with discoidal streak in two portions, the first long, slightly clavate, the second large and triangular ; two [three?] small oval oblique spots near the apex, the two outer the smallest ; a round spot in middle of the disc, and a spot and a dot on middle of posterior margin ; an ill-defined submarginal row of narrow marks, white. *Hindwing* with inner and outer narrow band, white, divided by the nervules ; also an indistinct pale brown submarginal line. UNDERSIDE paler, with darker patches between the veins ; markings as above. *Body* with two transverse bluish-white bands." (*Moore*, l. c.) The MALE does not differ in markings from the female.

There is a single specimen of this species from the Naga Hills in the Indian Museum, Calcutta. It has three subapical spots on the forewing, as also has Moore's figure. It is a very small species ; and differs from all the black and white species except *A. asura* and *A. sulpitia* in having the discoidal streak undivided and followed by an elongate triangular spot beyond ; and from these two it differs by none of the white bands bearing black spots. The markings are similar to those of *A. zeroca*, female, but in the latter the bands are all suffused with brown, and it is a larger insect.

The next two species have the discoidal streak entire, with no detached white spot in prolongation of it.

458. **Athyma jina,** Moore.

A. jina, Moore, Horsfield and Moore, Cat. Lep. Mus. E. I. C., vol. i, p. 172, n. 353, pl. va, fig. 3 (1857); id., Moore, Proc. Zool. Soc. Lond., 1858, p 18, n. 21.

HABITAT : Sikkim.

EXPANSE : 2·4 to 3·2 inches.

DESCRIPTION : "MALE. UPPERSIDE smoky-brown ; markings creamy-white. *Forewing* with the discoidal streak entire, long, broad, and thickening to the extremity ; a series of seven spots from subcostal vein curving outwards to middle of posterior margin, the first being small, second larger, broader, third narrow, fourth small, fifth larger, oval, sixth the largest, somewhat square and indented at the sides, seventh narrow, elongated, triangular ; a submarginal row of rather indistinct spots, those on the apex broadest. *Hindwing* with inner band somewhat narrow ; outer band composed of broad lunulated spots ; band across base of abdomen whitish. UNDERSIDE brilliant ferruginous, posterior margin of forewing blackish ; markings the same as above, but the *forewing* with an additional spot to the curved row

22

on costal margin ; extreme posterior margin blackish, bounded inwardly by a submarginal row of white lines. *Hindwing* with the inner band extending across abdominal margin ; space *between* base of wing and costal vein white ; extreme exterior margin blackish, bounded inwardly by a marginal row of narrow lunular marks. *Body* white." (*Moore*, l. c. in Cat. Lep. Mus. E. I. C.)

This very distinct species seems to be confined to Sikkim, and is rare. The FEMALE does not differ from the male. It may be distinguished from *A. pravara*, which also has the discoidal streak entire, with no detached spot in prolongation, by the underside being bright ferruginous almost uniform, and the white bands broad ; in *A. pravara* the underside is brown, and bears numerous dark brown patches on the interspaces.

459. **Athyma pravara**, Moore.

A. pravara, Moore, Horsfield and Moore, Cat. Lep. Mus. E. I. C., vol. i, p. 173, n. 354, pl. va, fig. 4 (1857); Id., Moore, Proc. Zool. Soc. Lond., 1858, p. 19, n. 22 ; id., Distant, Rhop. Malay., p. 160, n. 4, pl. xvi, fig. 11, *female* (1883).

HABITAT : Assam, Naga Hills, Cachar, Penang, Malacca, Singapore, Sumatra, Banca, Java, Borneo.

EXPANSE : 1·90 to 2·45 inches.

DESCRIPTION : "UPPERSIDE smoky-brown ; markings creamy-white. *Forewing* with an *entire* club-shaped [discoidal] streak ; a transverse row of spots curving outwards from costal nervure towards the apex to middle of posterior margin ; the first and second spots being rather large and square, the third much smaller, the fourth a mere dot, the fifth the largest and oval, the sixth large and indented at the sides, the last narrow ; a row of submarginal linear-shaped spots, more or less distinct. *Hindwing* with a broad inner band, and a narrow band of spots curving outwardly from anal angle to anterior angle ; a submarginal line and abdominal margin light brown. *Body* with a narrow bluish-white band across the thorax, and another across the base of the abdomen. UNDERSIDE paler brown, with markings as above, but with dark brown patches between the markings. *Body* and abdominal margin greyish. *Sexes* alike." (*Moore*, l. c. in Cat. Lep. Mus. E. I. C.)

This pretty and very distinct species has never before been recorded from India. It appears to be not uncommon towards our north-eastern frontier. The Indian specimens differ only from Mr. Moore's figure of the Malayan form in having the discal white band rather narrower.

Key to the Indian species of Athyma.

Second Group.

B. Forewing with discoidal cell closed.

 a. Ground-colour black with white markings, with no blue or orange tinting on upperside. Sexes alike.

  a¹. Cell of forewing on underside containing several large white spots occupying its whole width.

   a². Submarginal band on upperside of both wings narrow, sullied with brown.

    460. A. MAHESA, Sikkim, Bhutan, Assam, South India.

   b². Submarginal band on upperside of both wings broader, faintly sullied with brown or pure white.

    461. A. RANGA, Sikkim, Dafla Hills, South India.

  b¹. Cell of forewing on underside containing a longitudinal streak much narrower than the cell.

   a². Underside tinted with violet about outer margins ; discal band on underside of hindwing broad, narrowest at middle ; no black spots along inner edge of marginal band.

    462. A. OPALINA, Himalayas.

   b². Underside with no violet suffusion ; discal band on underside of hindwing narrowest at each end ; a row of black spots along inner edge of submarginal band.

    a³. Discoidal streak long, twice divided.

     463. A. KRESNA, Mergui, Malay Peninsula, Sumatra, Borneo.

b^3. Discoidal streak very short, with a large spot beyond in the cell.
464. A. ABRASA, Mergui, Malacca, Java.
c^3. Underside with no violet suffusion ; two rows of black spots along inner edge of submarginal band ; five or six small black spots at base of hindwing.
465. A. SULPITIA, Western Himalayas, China.
466 A. SANKARA, Masuri.
b. Ground colour black, male with the discal band on upperside margined with pale blue.
   a^1. Male with the submarginal band brown throughout, narrow ; the discal band broad, even, white, well-separated from the white subapical spots.
      a^2. Male with the discal band ending at third median nervule of forewing, no orange markings on upperside. Female black with white markings as in the previous group. *
         a^3. Male with the discoidal streak obsolete on upperside ; twice interrupted on underside in both sexes.
467. A. SELENOPHORA, Himalayas, Assam, Upper Burma, South India.
         b^3. Male with the discoidal streak brown on upperside ; undivided on underside in both sexes.
468. A. ZEROCA, Sikkim, Bhutan, Assam, Upper Burma.
      b^2. Male with the discal band ending at second median nervule of forewing ; the discoidal streak and a subapical spot orange, the streak undivided in both sexes. Female black with orange markings.*
469. A. CAMA, Kumaon, Nepal, Sikkim, Assam, Upper Burma.
   b^1. Male with the submarginal band orange throughout. Female black with orange markings.
      a^2. Male with bands on upperside broad.
470. A. INARA, Northern India.
      b^2. Male with bands on upperside narrower.
471. A. INARINA, Sikkim, Assam, Orissa, South India.
   c^1. Male with the submarginal band orange at apex of forewing, the remainder and on hindwing white. Female black with orange markings.
472. A. ASITA, North India (?), Upper Tenasserim.
473. A. SUBRATA, India (?), Mergui, Malacca, Sumatra, Borneo.
   d^1. Male unknown. Female black with white bands partially suffused with orange.
474. A. RUFULA, South Andamans.
   e^1. Male with the submarginal band white throughout, the discoidal streak typically obsolete, when present short, with no spot beyond the cell on upperside. Sexes alike.
475. A. AMHARA, Upper Tenasserim, Malay Peninsula, Borneo.

The next two species are of a different aspect from the rest of the group, the white bands are more distinctly macular, most of the veins dividing the bands being margined with blackish, the cell of the forewing also lacks the usual discoidal streak which is found in all the other species, the cell in these two being occupied by large white patches, most prominent on the underside, which are separated by irregular dark bands crossing the cell transversely. They are found in the hilly regions of North Eastern India, and again in the Western Ghâts of South India.

460. Athyma mahesa, Moore.

A. *mahesa*, Moore, Horsfield and Moore, Cat. Lep. Mus E. I. C, vol. i., p. 176, n. 360, pl. vii, fig. 7 (1857) ; id., Moore, Proc. Zool. Soc. Lond., 1858, p. 15, n. 14 ; id., Butler, Ann. and Mag. of Nat. Hist., fifth series, vol. xvi, p. 304, n. 36 (1885).

HABITAT : Sikkim, Bhutan, Assam, South India.

EXPANSE : 2·6 to 3·1 inches.

DESCRIPTION : " UPPERSIDE smoky-black. *Forewing* with a green gloss in some lights ; three oblique white ovate spots from subcostal nervure, one-third from the apex ; two white spots in the middle of the wing, the upper one very small, and two white spots on middle of posterior margin, the upper oval, the lower narrow ; two indistinct white spots in discoidal cell, and some indistinct greenish spots at the base of the wing ; a marginal

---

* For the points of distinction between the white banded females of this group and the white banded species of the preceding groups, and also for the points of distinction between the various orange banded females. see detailed remarks on the species.

and submarginal row of light brown spots. *Hindwing* with an inner white band, divided by the veins, and an outer or submarginal row of indistinct brownish-white conic-shaped spots ; also a very indistinct marginal row of small light brown spots. *Body* brown, abdomen with two rows of white spots. UNDERSIDE paler, tinged with ferruginous about the disc ; markings the same, but all very distinct, and more or less white ; the spots within discoidal cell and base of *forewing* divided by black marks ; base of costal margin yellowish-white. *Hindwing* with space between præcostal and costal nervures yellowish-white ; a curved oval black mark, whitish within, between the costal nervure and inner band ; a row of black patches between inner and outer band. *Body*, and broadly on abdominal margin, yellowish-grey. *Athyma mahesa* may be known from *A. ranga* by its larger size and much narrower band." (*Moore*, l. c. in Cat. Lep. Mus. E. I. C.) The FEMALE only differs from the male in the ground-colour of the upperside being decidedly paler, and all the white markings larger an1 more distinct.

    A. mahesa is a common species in Sikkim at low elevations, and occurs eastwards as far as Sibsagar in Upper Assam, and again in South India ; Mr. W. F. Hampson has taken it at Ootacamund and Capt. Macpherson in North Canara. Mr. Butler (l. c.) records "One somewhat melanized male specimen, evidently belonging to this species" from near Assam.

461. Athyma ranga, Moore.

A. ranga, Moore, Horsfield and Moore, Cat. Lep. Mus. E. I. C., vol. i, p. 175, n. 359, pl. va, fig. 6 (1857) ; id., Moore, Proc. Zool. Soc. Lond., 1858, p. 15, n. 13.

HABITAT : Sikkim (*Moore*), Dafla Hills, Western Ghâts.

EXPANSE : 2·2 to 3·0 inches.

DESCRIPTION : "UPPERSIDE smoky-black. *Forewing* with a curved interrupted white band from anterior margin, one-third from the apex, to middle of posterior margin, being composed of eight spots, the first on anterior margin very narrow, second, third and fourth elongate-conical, the fourth being the shortest, fifth triangular and broadly divided from the fourth, sixth broad, largest, and nearly square, seventh narrower and broadly divided from the sixth, eighth long and narrow ; a marginal and submarginal row of rather indistinct whitish spots ; base of wing covered with indistinct white spots. *Hindwing* with broad inner band, intersected by the veins ; and outer or submarginal row of broad conic-shaped indistinct white spots ; a marginal row of very indistinct spots ; also indistinct spots at the base of wing ; abdominal margin whitish. *Body* dark brown, abdomen with two rows of small white spots. UNDERSIDE with the markings the same and very distinct. *Body* and abdominal margin greenish white. *Sexes* alike." (*Moore*, l. c. in Cat. Lep. Mus. E. I. C.)

    This supposed distinct species appears to be an occasional aberration, or still more probably, seasonal form only, of *A. mahesa*, with all the white markings (which are somewhat inconstant in the latter species) very strongly developed. There is a single specimen in the Indian Museum, Calcutta, from the Dafla Hills, and several in my own collection from Sikkim, which appear to grade into *A. mahesa*. Specimens recently received from North Canara have the white markings still larger and purer white than in those from North-eastern India. All the specimens of *A. ranga* of which the date of capture is known have been taken in the winter months, November, December and March, and it is not unlikely that it may turn out to be only the winter or dry season form of *A. mahesa*.

    The next four species, all of which have the discoidal cell of the forewing closed, shew a curious parallelism with the species of the first group in which the cell of the forewing is open. *A. opalina* has the underside very similar to that of *A. larymna*, both having the violet tinting on the outer border of the underside, and the markings, though not identical, are similar in character. *A. kresna* has the underside almost identical with that of *A. pravara* except that the discoidal streak is interrupted, while in *A. pravara* it is entire. *A. abiasa* is somewhat similar also to *A. pravara*, but the markings in the discoidal cell differ even more widely. *A. sulpitia* somewhat resembles *A. perius* on the underside in general characters, but the black dots are more numerous, and the discoidal streak on the forewing is very different in character.

462. **Athyma opalina,** Kollar.

Limenitis opalina, Kollar, Hugel's Kaschmir, vol. iv, pt. 2, p. 427, n. 7 (1848) ; *Athyma opalina*, Horsfield and Moore, Cat. Lép. Mus. E.I.C., vol. i, p. 171, n. 351, pl. va, fig. 2 (1857) ; id., Moore, Proc. Zool. Soc. Lond., 1858, p. 11, n. 2.

HABITAT : Himalayas.

EXPANSE : 2·25 to 2·90 inches.

DESCRIPTION : MALE. UPPERSIDE black with creamy-white markings. *Forewing* with a narrow streak and two spots at its outer end in the cell, a lengthened triangular spot beyond, an oblique subapical series of three spots, (sometimes with one or two very fine streaks below the costa above the upper spot), the upper one oval, the middle one linear and about twice as large, the lower one smallest ; a discal series of four spots from the third median nervule to the inner margin, the two upper ones rounded and well separated, the two lower somewhat quadrate and separated by the submedian nervure only. Two submarginal waved pale lines, the inner one more distinct, especially towards the apex and inner angle. *Hindwing* with a straight discal band from the costal to the submedian nervure divided only by the veins, a submarginal series of lunules placed between the nervules from the first subcostal nervule to the submedian nervure. A pale brown straight fine marginal line. UNDERSIDE, *forewing* ferruginous, the area below the cell marked with black patches between the veins, white markings much as above, the submarginal lines more distinct, a patch of violaceous powdering about the middle of the outer margin. *Hindwing* also ferruginous, outwardly more or less with violaceous powdering. A curved white streak from the base above the costal nervure, the discal band as above but widening out below the costal nervure, the submarginal series of lunules larger, the marginal line broader and violaceous, abdominal area pale greenish. *Cilia* alternately black and white. *Body* black above, with an iridescent bluish-white band at the base of the abdomen, below white. FEMALE differs from the male in the ground-colour on both sides being much paler, and all the white markings considerably larger.

A. opalina is a very common species in the Western Himalayas at about 6,000 feet elevation, becoming rarer towards the east ; in Sikkim and Bhutan it is decidedly rare. Specimens from the latter localities are larger and darker, with the white markings narrower than examples from the North-West, and the violaceous powdering more restricted.

463. **Athyma kresna,** Moore.

A. kresna, Moore, Proc. Zool. Soc. Lond., 1858, p. 12, n. 6, pl. l, fig. 4, *male* (1858) ; id., Distant, Rhop. Malay., p. 161, n. 6, pl. xvi, fig. 3, *male* (1883).

HABITAT : Mergui Archipelago, Province Wellesley, Malacca, Sumatra, Borneo.

EXPANSE : ♂, 2·0 to 2·4 ; ♀, 2·5 inches.

DESCRIPTION : "MALE. UPPERSIDE blackish-brown. *Forewing* with discoidal streak in three portions, the third portion largest and triangular ; an oblique transverse row of three spots near the apex ; a large spot in middle of disc, and two smaller spots on middle of posterior margin, bluish-white ; a submarginal row of small ill-defined whitish spots. *Hindwing* with inner band and narrower outer row of spots, bluish-white ; a narrow marginal line to *both wings*, light brown. UNDERSIDE brown, with markings as above, but all less defined, except the marginal line, which is whitish. *Body* with collar and band across abdomen white. Allied to *A. larymna*, Doubleday, but distinguished by its smaller size and white markings, the discoidal streak in that species being in *four* portions." (*Moore*, l. c.) In Mr. Distant's figure the discoidal streak is in four portions.

"The FEMALE of this species is apparently a difficult insect to find, as all the specimens which I collected in Province Wellesley, as those which I have since received from the Peninsula, have been of the male sex. Both sexes, collected by Mr. Pryer in North Borneo, are now in my collection, and the female differs in no essential respect from the male." (*Distant*, l. c.)

Mr. W. F. Kirby in his Synonymic Catalogue of Diurnal Lepidoptera, Supplement, p. 743, gives *A. kresna*, Moore, as a synonym of *A. jadera*, D'Orbigny,* but the figure does not at all agree with specimens of *A. kresna*; it appears to be much nearer to *A. asita*, and probably the latter name should make way for the *A. jadera* of D'Orbigny. Of this group *A. neftc*, Cramer, from Java may be considered the parent species, *A. nivifera*, from the Malay Peninsula, is hardly separable, both with all the markings on the upperside of the male white; *A. asita* (typical) and *A. jadera* have the submarginal band of the forewing orange anteriorly; while *A. inara* and *A. inarina* have it orange throughout.

Dr. Anderson obtained two males of *A. kresna* in the Mergui Archipelago in the cold weather. Mr. Moore's original figure of this species shows the bands of the upperside of much too deep a shade of bluish: the forewing in his figure is more elongated than in the Mergui specimens.

464. **Athyma abiasa**, Moore.

A. abiasa, Moore, Proc. Zool. Soc. Lond., 1858, p. 16, n. 15, pl. l, fig. 7, *male*; *A. elerica*, Butler, Trans. Linn. Soc. Lond., Zoology, second series, vol. i, p. 540, n. 7, pl. lxix, fig. 5, *female* (1877); *A. abiasa*, var. *elerica*, Distant, Rhop. Malay., p. 161, n. 5, pl. xvi, fig. 8, *female* (1883).

HABITAT : Mergui Archipelago, Malacca, Java.

EXPANSE : ♂, 2·0 ; ♀, 2·3 to 2·6 inches.

DESCRIPTION : "MALE. UPPERSIDE black; markings bluish-white. *Forewing* with an indistinct narrow streak from base, and a large spot near extremity of the discoidal cell; an indistinct narrow transverse disco-cellular line; three spots obliquely from subcostal nervure one-third from the apex, the third spot being minute; two spots in middle of the disc, the upper one small, the lower very large, also a large spot on middle of posterior margin [divided by the submedian nervure]; and a submarginal row of very small whitish spots. *Hindwing* with rather broad inner band, and outer row of recurved small triangular spots; an indistinct brown marginal line. A band of white across base of abdomen. UNDERSIDE dusky-brown, marked as above, with the marginal lines plainer." (*Moore*, l. c.)

Dr. Anderson obtained a single female specimen of this species in the Mergui Archipelago during the cold weather. It does not differ in any important particular from the description and figure of the Javan type, except perhaps that all the markings are rather more prominent. Mr. Distant considers *A. elerica*, Butler, described (inadvertently as a male, but actually a female) from Malacca as a variety only of *A. abiasa*. The original description is appended.†

465. **Athyma sulpitia**, Cramer.

Papilio sulpitia, Cramer, Lep. Ex., vol. iii, pl. ccxiv, figs. E, F (1779); id., Herbst, Pap., pl. cexl, figs. 3. 4 (1798) ; *Nymphalis strophia*, Godart, Enc. Méth., vol. ix, p. 431, n. 257 (1823) ; *Limenitis strophia*, Kollar in Hügel's Kaschmir, vol. iv, pl. 2, p. 429, n. 6 (1844).

HABITAT : Masuri (*Kollar*), China.

EXPANSE : ♂, 2·85 ;? ♀, (Cramer's figure) 3·20 inches.

DESCRIPTION : MALE. UPPERSIDE black, markings white. *Forewing* with a streak in the cell divided towards its end; three short streaks beyond the end of the cell divided by the discoidal nervules; a discal series of eight spots, the five upper ones small and round, the sixth much larger and cordiform, the seventh larger still, outwardly indented in the

---

* *Limenitis jadera*, D'Orbigny (Boisduval, MS.), Dict. d'Hist. Nat., Zoologie, Atlas ii, Lep., pl. iv, fig. 3 (1849).

† *Athyma elerica*, Butler, Trans. Linn. Soc. Lond., Zoology, second series, vol i, p. 540, n. 7, pl. lxix, fig. 5, *female* (1877). HABITAT : Malacca. EXPANSE : 2·6 inches. DESCRIPTION : FEMALE. "Nearly allied to *A. abiasa*, but larger, the spots of the *forewing* more oblique and larger, the subbasal transverse white band of the *hindwing* narrower ; the discal series of spots much larger, more inarched above anal angle, forming a waved band, divided by the nervures ; a well-marked greenish-grey submarginal streak. UNDERSIDE much paler, with the differences of the upperside ; submarginal series of lunate replaced by the submarginal streak, which is rosy greynish (not greenish, as above)." (*Butler*, l. c.) Mr. Butler's figure of *A. elerica* differs from the Mergui example in being larger, the forewing more elongated and the apex more acute, the discal white band on the hindwing a little broader.

middle, the eighth small and linear ; a submarginal series of four lunular spots from the anal angle. *Hindwing* with a discal macular band divided by the veins from the submedian nervure to the middle of the costa ; a submarginal series of somewhat quadrate decreasing spots from the submedian to the costal nervure. UNDERSIDE ochreous. *Forewing* with the middle of the disc to the inner margin blackish, markings much as above, but with some diffused black spots on the outer margin ; a marginal series of white lunules in addition to the submarginal series of the upperside. *Hindwing* with the markings of the upperside, but in addition, there is a series of white lunules on the margin, the inner edge of the submarginal white band bears a series of round black spots, with another series of more diffused dusky brown spots beyond, the base with a diffused white band bearing two small black spots in the cell, and four similar ones above it ; the precostal nervure defined with black. *Cilia* white, black at the end of the nervules. *Body* black above, whitish below.

The above description is made from a specimen without locality in the Indian Museum, Calcutta. Cramer appears to have figured a female, which differs only from the male in being larger, the forewing broader, with the outer margin evenly convex (in the male it is emarginate), all the markings more prominent, and with an additional series of rounded decreasing black spots on the upperside of the hindwing within the submarginal white band, which are hardly traceable in the worn male before me.

Kollar states that Carl Freiherr von Hügel brought this species from Masuri ; there is, however, as far as I am aware, no other record of its occurrence out of China.

466. **Athyma sankara,** Kollar.

Limenitis sankara, Kollar in Hügel's Kaschmir, vol. iv, pt. ii, p 428, n. 3 (1848); *Athyma sankara,* Westwood, Gen. Diurn. Lep., vol. ii, p. 274. n. 6 (1850).

HABITAT : Masuri.

EXPANSE : 2·7 inches.

DESCRIPTION : " Wings on the UPPERSIDE diluted black. UNDERSIDE clouded with fuscous and brown ; with three white bands, the middle one wider, common to *both wings,* the portion on the *forewing* being macular. "

"Larger than *Limenitis* [= *Neptis*] *aceris,* the wings more elongated, on the outer margin un-
dulatingly dentated, upperside dark fawn-colour, with three white bands, the first of which, as in *L.* [= *N.*] *aceris,* arrow-shaped, extending from the base to beyond the middle of the forewing, and only once interrupted ; the second, which extends across both wings, consists in the forewing of eight spots, its medial portion which extends crosswise towards the base of the hindwing being unbroken ; finally the third runs in a slight curve through the middle of the latter. On the underside, besides the three bands just mentioned, is a white curved line extending along the outer margin of both wings, and from the base of the hindwing on either side run two less distinct, short, white bands : the remainder of the wing is clouded with brown of various shades."

"Thorax and abdomen above black, very dark green and metallic ; underside covered with hairs and of a bluish-white colour. Antennæ above black, on underside brown."

"We possess but a single specimen of this splendid species, which Freiherr v. Hugel has lately brought from the Himalayas." (*Kollar,* l. c.)

This species has never been identified since it was described. It most nearly corres-
ponds with the female of *A. selenophora,* of which Kollar described the male from the same locality, but it differs from *A. selenophora* female, so far as the description above goes, in two prominent features : in *A. selenophora* female the discoidal streak of the forewing is more than once interrupted, and the submarginal band as well as the discal one is common to both wings.

The remainder of the species of this group all show a certain amount of blue tinting on the white bands of the upperside of the male, and the discal band is partially and narrowly but distinctly margined with pale blue ; with one single exception (*A. amhara*) the sexes in the Indian species, so far as they are known, are widely differentiated. The greater number of them are subtropical, commonest in the north-east, and found but rarely in Southern India.

In the first three species the males are characterised by having the discoidal streak and submarginal band on the upperside with no trace of white ; the discal band is white, broad and regular, but with the exception of a few white spots beyond the discal band near apex of forewing they present no other white markings whatever ; in the first two species the females are black with all the bands whitish as in the preceding group ; in the third species the female has all the bands orange as in the following group.

467. Athyma selenophora, Kollar.

Limenitis selenophora, Kollar, Hügel's Kaschmir, vol. iv, pt. ii, p. 426, pl. vii, figs 1, 2, *male* (1848) ; *Athyma selenophora*, Horsfield and Moore, Cat. Lep. Mus. E. I. C., vol. i, p. 175, n. 358 (1857) ; id., Moore, Proc. Zool. Soc. Lond., 1858, p. 14, n. 12 ; *A. bahula*, idem, id., p. 12, n. 3, pl. I, fig. 2, *female*.

HABITAT : Sikkim, Assam, Munipur, Cachar, Sylhet, Upper Burma, South India.

EXPANSE : ♂, 2·5 to 3·0 ; ♀, 2·85 to 3·30 inches.

DESCRIPTION : MALE. UPPERSIDE black. *Forewing* with just the slightest trace of the discoidal streak in the cell, an oblique subapical series of three white spots divided by the discoidal nervules ; a somewhat broad discal band composed of four white spots margined with pale blue from the third median nervule to the middle of the inner margin, a submarginal and marginal pale brown macular narrow bands. *Hindwing* with a white discal band in continuation of that on the forewing, also margined with pale blue, from the costal to the submedian nervule, a submarginal pale brown macular band and a marginal similar narrower line. UNDERSIDE, *both wings* with the base more or less greenish pale violet, beyond pale brown marked with darker brown patches between the nervules. *Forewing* with the whitish discoidal streak divided into three portions by two dark lines crossing the cell near its middle, the disco-cellulars inwardly defined by another dark line, with a whitish spot beyond the end of the cell ; the subapical spots and discal band much as above, the former with some fine white streaks in continuation on the costa, a submarginal whitish macular band and some whitish linear marks on the margin below the second discoidal nervule ; two prominent black spots placed one above the other near the base of the submedian interspace. *Hindwing* with a white band between the præcostal and costal nervures, a pair of brown lines in the cell, with another pair in continuation in the costal interspace, the broad discal band as above, followed by a series of diffused rich brown spots, then a submarginal macular whitish band, then a rich brown band, and lastly a whitish marginal line, the margin itself rich ferruginous. *Cilia* alternately black and white. *Antennæ* black, the club ochreous.

"The male may be distinguished from *A. cama* on the upperside by having the oblique subapical spots narrow, and the band on the forewing being composed of *four* spots ; in the underside being of a darker ferruginous colour, and the streak along discoidal cell being divided into four portions, and in having darker black blotches ; also in having on the hindwing four short black lines disposed between the inner band and discoidal nervule." (*Horsfield* and *Moore*, l. c.) FEMALE (separately described under the name of *A. bahula*). "Allied to *A. opalina*, and like that species it has on the *forewing* the discoidal streak divided into four portions, but in *A. bahula* it is narrow, and the terminal portion much elongated, whereas in *A. opalina* this portion is short ; *A. bahula* has also a distinct submarginal row of linear spots ; the bands are also narrower throughout. On the UNDERSIDE *A. bahula* differs in the *forewing* in having the portions of the discoidal streak divided by a blackish line, and a distinct marginal and submarginal row of spots ; the space between the markings blackish. On the *hindwing* between the curved præcostal streak and inner band are some short blackish lines. In *A. opalina*, on the inner band from the middle of its lower margin, there is a descending greyish portion to abdominal margin, whereas in *A. bahula* this is wanting ; space between the two bands with blackish patches ; a distinct marginal row of linear spots." (*Moore*, l. c.)

The female of *A. selenophora* has the discoidal streak twice interrupted in the cell besides the interruption at the end of the cell, in this respect resembling *A. perius*, *A. larymna*, *A. opalina*, and *A. kresna*, in all the remaining black and white species the discoidal streak is entire or only once divided. From *A. perius* and *A. larymna* it may be distinguished by the discoidal cell of the forewing being closed, further from *A. perius* it differs in wanting the conspicuous series of black spots on the white submarginal band on the underside of the hindwing, and from *A. larymna* by the absence of the violet suffusions on the border of the underside. The points of distinction between it and *A. opalina* have been noted above. From *A. kresna* it may be distinguished by the spot beyond the cell in continuation of the discoidal streak being placed on and divided by the lower discoidal nervule, in *A. kresna* this spot is in the interspace below, bounded by the third median nervule and undivided. The markings of the underside closely resemble those of the male, the basal markings being identical on both wings, but the series of diffused dark spots between the discal and submarginal bands are much less prominent and more diffused.

A. selenophora has a very wide range, Kollar described it from Masuri ; it is common in Sikkim and eastwards to Upper Assam, and specimens were obtained by the Yunan Expedition. Mr. Rhodes-Morgan has also taken both sexes in the Wynaad.

468. **Athyma zeroca,** Moore.

A. zeroca, Moore, Proc. Zool. Soc. Lond., 1872, p. 564 ; id., de Nicéville, Journ. A. S. B., vol. lii, pt. 2, p. 94 (1883).

HABITAT : Kumaon, Sikkim, Bhutan, Assam, Munipur, Khasi Hills, Upper Burma.

EXPANSE : ♂, 2·0 to 2·8 ; ♀, 2·85 inches.

DESCRIPTION : "MALE. UPPERSIDE velvety blackish-brown ; a broad median bluish-white band crossing from middle of forewing to abdominal fold of hindwing. *Forewing* with two, and in some specimens three, subapical oblique white spots ; *both wings* with a pale brown-bordered blackish marginal line. UNDERSIDE brownish ferruginous ; bluish-white median band and subapical spots as above. *Forewing* with a straight bluish-white discoidal streak, contiguous dentate spot, and marginal lunular lines ; a blackish spot near base of hind margin. *Hindwing* with a subbasal bluish-white streak, a submarginal and a paler marginal line ; abdominal margin bluish-grey ; between the median band on *both wings* and submarginal line is a blackish maculated fascia. Allied to *A. selenophora.*" (*Moore*, l. c.) "FEMALE. Differs from female *A. selenophora* in having all the white bands and spots on the UPPERSIDE sordid instead of pure white ; the *forewing* has the apex more rounded, the streak in the cell of the UNDERSIDE undivided, markings very much as in the male." (*de Nicéville*, l.c.)

The underside of the female is very similar to that of the male, but in both this species and *A. selenophora* the bands in the female are narrower, wider apart, less upright and more distinctly macular. *A. zeroca* female may be distinguished from the black and white species in which the discoidal streak in the cell is uninterrupted by the following characters :—From *A. asura* by the absence of the series of black spots on the white submarginal band ; from *A. kanwa* by the prolongation of the discoidal streak being along the lower discoidal nervule and well-separated from the third median, in *A. kanwa* it fills the whole base of the interspace and continues along the third median nervule ; from *A. jaina* and *A. pravara* by having a streak beyond the discoidal streak in prolongation, in *A. jaina* and in *A. pravara* there is none ; these four moreover have the cell of the forewing open, while in *A. zeroca* it is closed ; from *A. abiasa* it is distinguished by the uniform width of the discoidal streak and spot in continuation, in *A. abiasa* the streak is very short and narrow, and the large and round spot beyond is within the cell not beyond it ; from *A. sulpitia* it differs in wanting the black spots of the underside, and from all these it differs in having all the white bands of the upperside more or less suffused with brown.

Males of *A. zeroca* are not uncommon at low elevations in Sikkim, but the female (as also that sex of *A. selenophora*) is much less often met with. Females of both these species are wonderful mimics (?) of *A. opalina*, which belongs to the first section of the genus, and may possess some protective qualities not possessed by species of the second section. *A. zeroca* occurs eastwards in the Assam Valley as far as Sibsagar, and was obtained by the Yunan Expedition.

A. urvasi, Felder, described from Malacca, is a remarkable species ; colouration black and white, the latter predominating. The description is appended.* It is probably an extraordinary aberration or " sport" of some species unknown.

469. **Athyma cama**, Moore.

A. cama, Moore, Horsfield and Moore, Cat. Lep. Mus. E. I. C., vol. i, p. 174, n. 357, pl. va, fig. 5, *male* and *female* (1857) ; id., Moore, Proc. Zool. Soc. Lond., 1858, p. 14, n. 11.

HABITAT : Kumaon, Nepal, Sikkim, Assam, Upper Burma.

EXPANSE : ♂, 2·3 to 3·0 ; ♀, 3·0 to 3·4 inches.

DESCRIPTION : "MALE. UPPERSIDE velvety-black. *Forewing* with brown marginal and submarginal lines ; discoidal streak indistinct ferruginous, and dusted over with black ; near the apex a ferruginous spot ; two [sometimes three] oblique spots from subcostal nervure on one-third of the wing from the apex, and a band of three spots from middle of wing to posterior margin, joining a band across *hindwing*, white, bordered with blue ; on the hindwing also a marginal and submarginal brown line. *Body* black, with a broad white band across base of abdomen. UNDERSIDE pale ferruginous ; markings purplish-white ; the curved band as above. *Forewing* with a long broad irregular discoidal streak, submarginal and indistinct marginal lines ; a black patch near the base of wing and posterior angle. *Hindwing* with a curved line near the base of wing, and a rather broad outer band ; a marginal row of marks ; some patches of brown between outer and inner bands. *Body* and abdominal margin broadly grey. FEMALE. UPPERSIDE black ; markings ferruginous. *Forewing* with a long discoidal streak ; an oblique band from anterior to near middle of exterior margin, and nearly joining a band running to middle of posterior margin ; a marginal and submarginal brown line, the latter ferruginous anteriorly and posteriorly. *Hindwing* with a broad inner and narrower outer band ; also a marginal brown line. *Body* black, with a *white* band across base of abdomen, and bounded below with ferruginous ; also a pale white collar. UNDERSIDE ferruginous ; markings as in male, but pinky-white, except marginal and submarginal lines, which are purplish-white. The male of *Athyma cama* may at once be known from that sex of *A. selenophora* in having on the upperside a ferruginous spot close to the apex, and the band on the forewing being composed of *three* spots." (*Moore*, l. c.)

The female of *A. cama* differs from all the orange-banded females of the following species by having the discoidal streak entire and uninterrupted to some distance beyond the cell, its upper edge is irregular but not distinctly dentated, the bands of the underside are white and are all tinted more or less with violet, and the outer edge of the discal band is straight (in the following species it is crenate), the general style of markings of the underside closely resemble those of the male.

A. cama is a common species occurring from Kumaon to Upper Assam. Specimens were also obtained in Upper Burma by the Yunan Expedition.

In the next group the males have the discoidal streak (when present), and also the submarginal band of both wings either white or orange, not brown. The females of all are black with orange markings, except of *A. amhara*, in which the female is marked and coloured as the male.

The females of all the remaining species but the last are very closely allied, and in all those of which I have sufficient specimens to decide the point considerable variation is exhibited ;

---

* *Athyma urvasi*, Felder, Wien. Ent. Monatsch., vol. iv, p. 400, n. 12 (1860) ; idem, id., Reise Novara, Lep., vol. iii, p. 429, n. 683, pl. lvi, fig. 4 (1866) ; id., Distant, Rhop. Malay., p. 164, n. 10, pl. xvi fig. 12 (1882). HABITAT : Malacca Interior. EXPANSE : 2·1 inches. DESCRIPTION : " MALE, upperside black, underside brown, both sides with a white submarginal macular band on *both wings. Forewing* with a white clavate cellular streak coalescing with a broad white discal sinuate band, *hindwing* with a basal band, white. A very distinct species unlike all its allies." (*Felder*, l. c. in Wien. Ent. Monatsch.)

"This beautiful species constitutes a peculiar group, characterised by the shorter palpi, by having the lower discoidal nervule of the forewing distinctly bent downwards before the middle, and also by the slighter curvature of the median nervure of the forewing." (*Felder*, l. c. in Reise Novara.)

they all have the discoidal streak twice or thrice indented on its upper edge, and more or less distinctly interrupted with brown or yellow lines ; the bands of the underside have their edges less distinct, and more or less, sometimes completely, suffused with yellow ; where the yellow suffusion of the bands is complete the interruption of the discoidal streak is most obscure, sometimes barely traceable on the upperside.

470. **Athyma inara,** Doubleday, Hewitson.

Limenitis inara, Doubleday, Hewitson, Gen. Diurn. Lep., vol. ii, pl. xxxiv, fig. 3 (1850) ; *Athyma inara,* Westwood, id., p. 274, n. 12.

HABITAT : Northern India *(Westwood).*

EXPANSE : 2·5 inches.

DESCRIPTION : UPPERSIDE black. *Forewing* with a narrow white discoidal streak tinged with orange, with two white spots beyond, three conjoined subapical white spots, an oblique very wide discal white band, a submarginal irregular orange band, a marginal fine pale line. *Hindwing* with a broad subbasal white band, and a nearly equally broad submarginal orange band, a submarginal suffused pale fascia. *Body* with a pale band at the base of the abdomen.

The above description is taken from the figure in the "Genera of Diurnal Lepidoptera." It differs from all the specimens I have seen of the next species in having both the white and orange bands very much wider. The exact locality of the type specimen is unknown to me ; in the Genera "Northern India" alone is given.

471. **Athyma inarina,** Butler.

A. inarina, Butler, Ann. and Mag. of Nat. Hist., fifth series, vol. xii, p. 304, n. 37 (1883) ; *A. inara,* Moore (*nec* Doubleday, Hewitson), Proc. Zool. Soc. Lond., 1858, pl. l, fig. 6.

HABITAT : Sikkim, Assam, Cachar, Sylhet, Orissa, South India.

EXPANSE : ♂, 2·4 to 2·7 ; ♀, 2·8 to 3·2 inches.

DESCRIPTION : MALE. UPPERSIDE, *both wings* black, the white discal markings margined with pale iridescent blue. *Forewing* with a narrow obscure whitish orange-tinged streak in the cell (obsolete in a Wynaad specimen), a prominent round white spot at its end, with a whitish often obscure spot beyond it (entirely absent in a Wynaad specimen). Three increasing subapical oblique white spots, divided only by the nervules, sometimes with a very fine white line above ; a discal white band composed of four conjoined spots, the upper one very small, the second oval and largest, the third indented at the sides, the fourth linear. A submarginal irregular orange band, widest at the apex, more or less whitish towards the inner angle, followed by a pale marginal line. In the Wynaad example the anterior portion only is orange, below the upper discoidal nervule it is pale brown. *Hindwing* with a discal white band from the costal to the submedian nervure, narrow above the first subcostal nervule (which is pure white for a greater portion of its length). A submarginal series of orange lunules decreasing to the costal nervure, very narrow in the Wynaad specimen, with a terminal whitish spot below the submedian nervure. An even narrow pale marginal line. UNDERSIDE, *forewing* ferruginous, the white markings much as above, the discal ones inwardly marked with blackish streaks between the veins, a prominent rounded black spot below the base of the first median nervule, two subapical ones divided by the upper discoidal nervule, one in the middle of the second median interspace and two others conjoined in the submedian interspace. A submarginal and marginal irregular macular violaceous band from the lower discoidal nervule to the inner angle. *Hindwing* ferruginous, with a basal curved whitish streak above the costal nervure, a discal white band, beyond which are a series of round black spots between the nervules, the submarginal lunules as above but whitish, except the two upper ones, which are inwardly broadly ferruginous ; a marginal pale violaceous line ; abdominal area greenish-white. *Cilia* black, with small white points in the middle of the interspaces. *Body* black above, with an iridescent bluish-white band at the base of the abdomen and across the thorax, below white. In a Wynaad specimen on the underside the ground-colour is bright ochreous rather than ferruginous, and the black markings throughout are less distinct. FEMALE. UPPERSIDE, *both wings* black with orange markings. *Forewing* with a lengthened thrice-indented discoidal streak, a broad subapical oblique band, with three spots beyond it divided by the nervules, a broad discal band from the middle of the second median interspace to the inner margin, with a spot above its upper outer end, and a streak from the first median nervule to the inner angle; an obscure pale marginal line. *Hindwing* with broad even discal and submarginal bands, a pale marginal narrow band. UNDERSIDE marked much as in the male, but all the markings broader and tinged with pale ferruginous.

Mr. Butler (l. c.) in speaking of this species says : " A comparison of the two figures representing *A. inara* will at once decide their specific distinctness, the commoner species figured by Moore having the orange and white bands considerably narrower than in the typical form represented in the ' Genera of Diurnal Lepidoptera.' " The two figures certainly differ as pointed out, but I am not personally aware of the existence of any specimens corresponding with Hewitson's figure, which is probably exaggerated and erroneous.

This is a very common species, occurring in Sikkim at low elevations and in the Tarai, and eastwards as far as Sibsagar in Upper Assam, but it is rare in South India. There is also a single male from the Wynaad taken by Mr. Rhodes-Morgan in the Indian Museum, Calcutta. Mr. W. C. Taylor has taken it in Orissa.

472. **Athyma asita,** Moore.

A. asita, Moore, Proc. Zool. Soc. Lond., 1858, p. 13, n. 8.

HABITAT : Unknown, probably North India (*Moore*), Upper Tenasserim.

EXPANSE : ♂, 2·25 to 2·50 ; ♀, 2·45 to 2·70 inches.

DESCRIPTION : " MALE. Differs from *A. inara* on the UPPERSIDE of the *forewing* in having the basal portion of the discoidal streak white ; the submarginal row of spots being ferruginous at the apex of the wing only, the rest being white ; and on the *hindwing* in having both bands white. UNDERSIDE with markings coloured as on upperside." (*Moore,* l. c.) FEMALE. UPPERSIDE indistinguishable from that sex of *A. inarina*, the discoidal streak of the *forewing* sometimes completely divided into four portions, the submarginal band of the hindwing variable in width. UNDERSIDE with the bands less tinged with whitish than in *A. inarina*. " Intermediate between *A. nefte* and *A. inara*." (*Moore,* l. c.)

In Major Marshall's collection there are three males and three females of this species all from Upper Tenasserim. The males differ in having in one specimen the submarginal band of the hindwing on the upperside white as described by Moore for typical *A. asita*, in another specimen it is tinged with orange, in the last it is wholly orange as in typical *A. inarina*, but all the specimens differ from that species in having the discoidal streak of the forewing white on the upperside. *A. asita* appears to be an inconstant local race only of *A. inarina*.

Athyma nefte belongs to this group and is closely allied to *A. inara*, but the male has no orange markings on the upperside, all the bands and spots are white. A variety of it has been described by Mr. Butler under the name of *A. nivifera*. The descriptions of it by both Butler and Distant are appended ;* it is recorded, but probably erroneously, from Assam ; it occurs in the Malay Peninsula, but has not as yet been found so far north as Tenasserim.

* *Athyma nefte. Papilio nefte,* Cramer, Pap. Ex . vol. iii, pl. cclvi, figs. E. F. *female* (1779) ; *Athyma nefte,* Moore, Proc. Zool. Soc. Lond., 1858, p. 13, n. 7, pl. l, fig. 5. *male* and *female* ; *A. nivifera,* Butler, Trans. Linn. Soc. Lond., Zoology, second series, vol. 1, p. 540, n. 5, pl. lxix, fig. 4, *male* (1877) ; *A. nefte,* var. *nivifera,* Distant, Rhop. Malay., p. 161, n. 8. pl. xvi, fig. 6, *male* ; *7, female* (1883). HABITAT : Assam ? Province Wellesley, Malacca, Java, Borneo EXPANSE : *male,* 2·15 ; *female,* 2·4 inches. DESCRIPTION : " MALE. UPPERSIDE dark fuscous or blackish. *Forewing* with a basal cellular streak closely followed by a rounded spot, succeeded by a triangular spot at end of cell, all more or less suffused with pale bluish ; three subapical bluish-white spots placed obliquely and divided by the discoidal nervules ; an oblique bluish-white macular discal fascia directed inwardly, commencing immediately beneath the second median nervule and extending to about middle of inner margin ; a few small submarginal pale violaceous spots, and narrow fuscous submarginal and marginal fasciæ. *Cilia* alternately whitish. *Hindwing* colour placed between the nervules, and a very narrow pale fuscous submarginal fascia. *Cilia* as on forewing. UPPERSIDE pale olivaceous-brown ; pale markings as above, but with some additional medial pale marginal markings on *forewing*, and a curved basal fascia to hindwing ; on the latter the pale fuscous submarginal fascia

473. **Athyma subrata,** Moore.

A. subrata, Moore, Proc. Zool. Soc. Lond., 1858, p. 13, n. 10, pl. li, fig. 1, *female* ; id., Distant, Rhop. Malay , p. 161, n. 9, pl. xxi, fig. 4, *female* (1883).

HABITAT : India, Mergui, Malacca, Sumatra, Borneo.

EXPANSE : ♀ , 2·3 to 2·5 inches.

DESCRIPTION : " FEMALE, UPPERSIDE deep brown, with the markings disposed as in the female of *A. nefte* ; but they are all narrower, and instead of being of a deep orange colour, are suffused with very pale brown. The UNDERSIDE is also much darker, being of a light smoky-brown, with all the markings white." (*Moore,* l. c.)

Dr. Anderson obtained three females, which I refer to this species, in the Mergui Archipelago during the cold weather. They differ (as do all the Mergui specimens of the different species of the genus obtained by Dr. Anderson) from Mr. Moore's figure in the apex of the forewing being less produced. The markings are arranged as in *Neptis,* and the species may be known from all the other Indian ones by having them very pale brown suffused with dusky ochreous, in this respect being nearest to the female of *A. zeroca.* The male is unknown.

474. **Athyma rufula,** de N., n. sp.

A. reta, Wood-Mason and de Nicéville (*nec* Moore), Journ. A. S. B, vol. I, pt. ii, p. 247, n. 40 (1881).

HABITAT : Andaman Isles.

EXPANSE : ♀ , 2·8 to 3·1 inches.

DESCRIPTION : " FEMALE. UPPERSIDE, *forewing* with the twice divided cellular mark, the triangular spot beyond this, a subapical largish spot, and a much smaller one just in front of the second median nervule in the discal series, orange, and with the curved series of six discal spots, white, diffusedly bordered, from the costal margin increasingly and afterwards decreasingly to the inner margin, with orange. *Hindwing* with the discal band white, decreasingly from the anterior margin narrowly edged externally with orange, and with the submarginal sinuous band narrower, broken up into lunules, and orange-coloured." (*Wood-Mason* and *de Nicéville,* l. c.)

The male of this species has yet to be discovered ; the female differs from that sex of *A. inarina* in having the discoidal streak in the forewing divided into four distinct portions, and the dividing lines being brown not yellow, and most of the spots and bands of the upperside more or less white. The submarginal band on the upperside of the hindwing is very narrow and macular. On the underside there is a very distinct series of rounded black spots beyond the discal band of the hindwing. The late Mr. de Roepstorff obtained several specimens of this species, all females, in the Andaman Isles.

475. **Athyma amhara,** Druce.

A. amhara, Druce, Proc. Zool. Soc. Lond , 1873, p. 341, n. 6, pl. xxxii, fig. 2 ; id., Butler, Trans. Linn. Soc. Lond., Zoology, second series, vol. i, p. 540, n. 6 (1877) ; *A. amhara,* var., Distant, Rhop. Malay , p. 162, n. 7, pl. xxi, fig. 5, *male* (1883)

HABITAT : Thoungyeen Valley, Upper Tenasserim ; Penang, Province Wellesley, Malacca, Borneo.

EXPANSE : 1·8 to 2·2 *(Distant),* 2·65 inches (*Druce's* figure).

above is subviolaceous beneath, and *both wings* have the dark fuscous markings as in *A. amhara* ; abdominal margin pale greenish. *Body* above concolourous with wings ; thorax with an anterior bluish transverse fascia, and abdomen with a subbasal fascia of the same colour ; body beneath and femora greyish ; tibiæ and tarsi pale fuscous. FEMALE. UPPERSIDE very dark brown, with all the markings larger than in male and orange-yellow in hue ; the subapical spots to *forewing* and the outer discal fascia to *hindwing* being prominently broader. UNDERSIDE as above, but much paler, with the fuscous markings as in male." (*Distant,* l c)

Athyma nivifera, Butler. HABITAT : Assam, Malacca, Borneo. EXPANSE : 2 4 to 2 7 inches. DESCRIPTION : " May be at once distinguished from *A. nefte* of Cramer by the much narrower medial band, which in the male is much more distinctly blue at the edges ; by the longer and narrow trifid subapical band on the male, and the deeper colour of the underside." (*Butler,* l c) Mr. Distant (l. c) states that his experience, however, has not allowed him to consider the characters above given for *A. nivifera* by Mr. Butler "as sufficiently constant to indicate a distinct species or race."

DESCRIPTION: "MALE. UPPERSIDE dark fuscous. *Forewing* with some very obscure and slightly paler markings in cell; an oblique discal bluish-white macular fascia, with the margins pale bluish, commencing immediately beneath apex of cell and between the second and third median nervules, and terminating about middle of inner margin; two subapical whitish spots separated by the upper discoidal nervule, followed beneath the second discoidal nervule by a third and very small spot, and two submarginal series of linear spots placed between the nervules, the inner one more or less whitish, the outer entirely pale fuscous. *Hindwing* with a transverse bluish-white fascia, margined with pale bluish near base; an outer discal series of small linear whitish spots placed between the nervules, and a submarginal, narrow, pale fuscous, and somewhat macular fascia. UNDERSIDE pale olivaceous-brown. *Forewing* with the pale whitish spots as above, but larger, the two submarginal series of linear spots almost totally pale violaceous, and with an irregular cellular streak, a spot at end of cell and one beneath cell between the first median nervule and submedian nervure pale violaceous; three slightly oblique dark castaneous linear spots partly crossing cell, and two rounded contiguous spots of the same colour beneath cell near base; a fuscous spot near cell between second and first median nervules; three longitudinal fuscous streaks divided by the discoidal nervules, followed beneath by a series of linear spots of the same colour placed between the nervules. *Hindwing* with the whitish markings as above, but broader; the submarginal fascia pale violaceous; a basal curved whitish fascia, between which and the medial fascia are some linear dark castaneous markings, and a series of dark castaneous spots placed before the outer discal pale fascia; abdominal margin pale greenish. *Body* both above and beneath more or less concolourous with wings; *femora* greyish white; *tibiæ* and *tarsi* pale fuscous. FEMALE. Similar to the male above. *Forewing* with the subapical spots larger; the cell with the base castaneous, and the discal fasciæ to *both wings* rather broader and almost quite without the bluish margins. UNDERSIDE the colour is reddish-ochraceous, instead of olivaceous-brown, the darker markings castaneous, excepting the fuscous spots near the posterior angle of the *forewing*; pale markings as on underside of male, but the discal fasciæ broad as above."

" As Mr. Butler remarks (l. c.) 'In the examples from Malacca the discoidal white streak of the forewing is reduced to one or two dots, connected by a pale brown streak.' These white spots are altogether absent from the Penang specimen figured, but are present in other Province Wellesley specimens. Bornean typical specimens have a whitish streak and two whitish spots in the cell of the forewing." (*Distant*, l.c.)

I possess two males of *A. amhara* from Penang which differ from *A. nivifera* in the forewing in having the discal macular band placed more upright, and consisting of four instead of three spots, the spot in the submedian interspace is much narrower and its edges even, not constricted in the middle as it is in *A. nivifera*; the discal band of the hindwing on the underside is also more even, narrowed to a point at the submedian nervure, but as broad at the costal nervure as it is in the middle; in *A. nivifera* it is narrow at both ends and does not reach the costal nervure anteriorly; the discoidal streak too in the forewing is more or less obsolete, while in *A. nivifera* it is very broad and prominent. The underside is altogether very similar, but in *A. amhara*, the interruptions of the discoidal streak are marked with brown lines.

Genus 76.—ABROTA, Moore. (PLATE XXIV).

Abrota, Moore, Horsfield and Moore, Cat. Lep. Mus. E. I C., vol. i, p. 176 (1857).

"HEAD, of moderate size, tufted in front. *Eyes*, prominent, naked. *Antennæ*, long, filiform at the base, gradually thickening to a slender cylindric club. *Palpi*, elevated above the level of the eyes, hairy, the hairs at the base, side, and in front, long. *Thorax*, robust, clothed with long hairs. *Abdomen*, of moderate size. FOREWING, elongate-trigonate; *costal margin* boldly curved; *apex* slightly rounded; *outer* margin somewhat straight [usually distinctly curved] in the male, concave in the female, slightly waved, two-thirds the length of the costal margin; *inner* margin slightly concave, rather longer than the outer. *Costal nervure* thick at the base, extending to beyond the middle of the costa; *subcostal* nervure with the first branch arising about one-fourth the length of the wing ; second a little beyond it, and before the extremity of the discoidal cell ; third branch arising at two-thirds the length of the wing, and extending in a slight curve to the tip ; fourth branch straight, arising half-way between it and the apex, which it reaches just below the tip ; the terminal portion of the vein deflexed. *Upper disco-cellular nervule* very short, outwardly oblique, arising at one-third from the base of the wing ; *middle* disco-cellular curved outwards ; *lower* disco-cellular long, curved outwards, and uniting with the third branch of the median nervure at a little distance beyond its origin, closing the *discoidal cell* at a little more than one-third the length of the wing. HINDWING, somewhat rounded ; *costal margin* arched at the base, from thence nearly straight to the apex, where it curves slightly downwards ; *exterior* margin rather longer than the costal, rounded and waved. *Præcostal nervure* curved outwards ; *costal* nervure curved, extending to the apex ; *subcostal* nervure branching near its base ; *upper disco-cellular nervule* arising at a short distance from the base of the subcostal branch ; *lower* disco-cellular obsolete, so that the *discoidal cell* is open. FORELEGS, of the *male* slender ; *femur* scaly in front, beneath clothed with fine long silky hairs ; *tibia* as long as the femur, clothed with downy hairs ; *tarsus* two-thirds the length of tibia, conical, covered with uniform hairs. Of the *female* scaly ; *femur* with a few silky hairs beneath ; *tarsus* rather longer than the male, truncated at the tip, where it is finely spined beneath. MIDDLE and HINDLEGS, moderately long, of equal length ; *tibia* shorter than the femur, thickly clothed with short scaly hairs, with two rows of short thick spines ; *femur* thickly scaled ; *tarsus* as long as the tibia, thickly clothed at the sides and beneath with rows of short spines ; *claws* sharp, and much curved." (*Moore*, l. c.)

Abrota is a genus of very small extent, and comprises but two closely-allied if really distinct species, inhabiting a very limited area. The colouration of the males is rich ochreous with black bands, that of the female dark brown with paler ochreous or olive-green bands. In the length of the antennæ, and in habits, such as resting with wide out-spread wings on leaves in dense forest, they closely resemble many species of the genus *Euthalia*. Both species occur in Sikkim from April to July.

Key to the species of Abrota.

A. Male with four distinct well-separated black bands on upperside of hindwing ; female with ochreous bands above.
　　476. A. MIRUS, Sikkim.
B. Male with three black bands on upperside of hindwing, the middle one partially divided by a lunulate ochreous line ; female with olive-green bands above.
　　477. A. JUMNA, Sikkim.

476. **Abrota mirus,** Fabricius. (PLATE XXIV, FIG. 110, ♀ only).

Papilio mirus, Fabricius, Ent. Syst . vol. iii, pt i, p 48, n. 146 (1793) ; *Abrota mirus*, Butler, Cat. Fab. Lep. B. M., p. 61, n. 1 (1869) ; *A. ganga*, Moore, Horsfield and Moore, Cat. Lep. Mus. E. I. C., vol. i, p. 178, n. 361. pl. vie, fig. 1, *male* and *female* (1857) ; *Adolias confinis*, Felder, Wien. Ent. Monatsch, vol. iii, p. 173, n. 7. pl. iv, fig. 3, *female* (1859).

HABITAT : Sikkim.

EXPANSE : ♂, 3·0 to 3·25 ; ♀, 3·6 inches.

DESCRIPTION : " MALE. UPPERSIDE ferruginous. *Forewing* along upper part of discoidal cell, a spot, and disco-cellular mark within it, a broad oblique streak, tapering from middle of costal nervure to middle of lower discoidal nervule, then extending in a zigzag manner to posterior margin near the base, the space between the latter and the median nervure only smeared ; exterior and costal margin, submarginal line, and smeary patches near the apex and lower part of the disc, black. *Hindwing* with marginal, submarginal, third and fourth inner bands, black. *Cilia* with small white spots. UNDERSIDE dull yellow, with duller exterior margins ; a distinct dark narrow streak from near apex of forewing to near abdominal margin [of hindwing] ; two indistinct zigzag lines across the disc, and markings about the base of *both wings* dull ferruginous ; from apex of forewing some white spots.

FEMALE blackish brown. *Forewing* with a streak from the base along the lower part of the discoidal cell to the middle of the wing, with a dentate mark on the disco-cellular nervule; two outwardly oblique spots from near the apex; a broad band from the middle of the disc, inwardly oblique, to posterior margin, and indistinct submarginal series of small spots, pale ferruginous; also two small outwardly oblique white spots at the apex. *Hindwing* with broad inner and narrower outer slightly-curved bands, pale ferruginous. *Cilia* with small white spots. UNDERSIDE pale chocolate-brown, with a patch on the costal margin near the apex, the space about the disc of the forewing and across the middle of the hindwing, yellowish; an ill-defined streak from near the apex of the forewing to the middle of the abdominal margin [of the hindwing]; zig-zag lines across the disc, and patches about the base of both wings, whitish; some spots at the apex of the forewing white." (*Moore*, l. c.)

The male of *A. mirus* (of which I have seen three specimens only in Colonel Lang's collection) is easily distinguished from the only other species of the genus by having the two discal bands on the upperside of the hindwing well-separated, that wing being in fact crossed by four almost equi-distant bands, of which the third from the margin is macular and composed of decreasing rounded spots; in *A. jumna* the wing appears to be crossed by three equi-distant bands only, the middle one being divided by a somewhat lunular line of the ground-colour. The female of *A. mirus* has all the bands on the upperside broad and pale fulvous, the discal band on the upperside of the forewing from the second median nervule to the inner margin being continuous; in the female of *A. jumna* the bands are narrower and olive-green, the discal band on the forewing more macular, its upper portion formed of a well-separated oval spot. Mr. Butler remarks (l. c.) that "the description [by Fabricius] of *A. mirus* is exactly applicable to the female of Mr. Moore's *Abrota ganga*." Dr. Felder also described and figured the female of this species under the name of *A. confosis*.

The figure (of the female only) shows the upperside of a Sikkim example in the Indian Museum, Calcutta.

477. Abrota jumna, Moore. (PLATE XXIV, FIG. 110, ♂ only).

A. jumna, Moore, Proc. Zool. Soc. Lond., 1865. p. 764, *male only*.

HABITAT: Sikkim.

EXPANSE: ♂, 2·9 to 3·2; ♀, 3·5 to 3·9 inches.

DESCRIPTION: "MALE. Similar to *A. ganga* [= *A. mirus*], but differs on the UPPERSIDE in being of a pale yellowish ferruginous, the black markings much less defined, and in having the submarginal and medial lunalated bands of the *hindwing* geminated. On the UNDERSIDE the markings are much less prominent, the geminated sinuous band being apparent as on the upperside." (*Moore*, l. c.) FEMALE. UPPERSIDE blackish. *Forewing* with a streak from the base along lower part of discoidal cell to middle of wing, with a dentate black mark on lower disco-cellular nervule; an oblique, macular, subapical streak, with three small white spots beyond it; a rounded spot in first median interspace, an irregular mark in the interspace below, which is continued widely on inner margin; a submarginal increasing macular band from lower discoidal nervule to inner angle, all suffused olive-green. *Hindwing* with similarly coloured discal and submarginal broad bands. UNDERSIDE marked much as in the male, but the ground-colour is paler, the markings darker and more suffused.

In my opinion (though the matter is still open to doubt) Mr. Moore originally correctly determined the sexes of *A. mirus* when describing that species under the name of *A. ganga*. In describing *A. jumna* he seems to have come to the opposite conclusion (though he does not say so in so many words, nor does he quote his figure of the female *A. ganga* as applying to that sex of his *A. jumna* as he should have done), as he describes the female as follows:—"Differs from that sex of *A. ganga* on the UPPERSIDE in being brown, and in having the markings ferruginous; whereas in *A. ganga* [= *A. mirus*] the upperside is olive-brown, and the markings suffused olive-green."

The male of *A. jumna* is common in Sikkim, the females of both species seem about equally common ; our collections contain ten specimens of that sex of *A. jumna*, and nine of *A. ganga*. The question whether these two species are really distinct or not, also if they are distinct, which are the true opposite sexes of each, must in my opinion remain in doubt till they are bred.

The figure of both species (named *A. mirus* on the plate) shows on the left hand the upperside of a not very typical male Sikkim specimen of *A. jumna* in the Indian Museum, Calcutta. In this example the discal band on the upperside of the hindwing is more widely divided than is usually the case. The right hand half represents the female of *A. mirus*.

Genus 77.—SYMPHÆDRA, Hübner. (PLATE XXI).

Symphædra, Hübner, Verz. bek Schmett., p. 39 (1816) ; id., Westwood, Gen. Diurn. Lep., vol. ii, p. 294 (1850) ; id., Butler, Proc. Zool. Soc. Lond., 1868, p. 612 ; id., Moore, Lep Cey , vol. i, p 34 (1881) ; id , Distant, Rhop. Malay , p. 112 (1883) ; *Adolias (part)*, Moore, Trans. Ent. Soc Lond., new series, vol.v, p. 62 (1857) ; *Adolias*, section 10, Felder, Neues Lep , p. 35 (1861) ; *Lexias*, Boisduval, Voy. Astr., Lep., p. 125 (1832) ; id., Felder, l. c., p. 36, n 83.

"WINGS, short. FOREWING, triangular ; *costa* slightly arched ; *exterior margin* short, slightly scalloped ; *posterior* margin straight ; *first* and *second subcostal nervules* emitted before end of the cell, *third* at one-fifth beyond ; *fourth* and *fifth* at two-thirds beyond ; [*middle*] *disco-cellular* very short, convexly angular ; the *discodal* nervules from the angles ; *discoidal cell* open, short, broad ; *first median nervule* opposite [middle] disco-cellular, the *second* and *third* at some distance beyond ; *submedian nervure* straight. HINDWING, broadly oval ; *exterior margin* very convex, scalloped, *abdominal* margin short ; *neuration* similar to *Euthalia*. BODY, small ; *palpi*, porrect, somewhat pilose ; *legs*, squamose ; *antenna*, of moderate length, stout." (*Moore*, l. c. in Lep. Cey.) The above diagnosis applies to *S. nais*, the only species of the genus which occurs in Ceylon.

"FOREWING, subtriangular ; *costal margin* arched and convex ; *apex* rounded (generally more prominently so in the female) ; *outer margin* slightly waved and slightly concave beneath apex ; *inner* margin nearly straight. *First* and *second subcostal* nervules emitted before the end of the cell, the second longer than the first ; the *third* emitted some distance before the apices of first and second ; the *fourth* and *fifth* bifurcating at about two-thirds beyond end of cell. *Lower disco-cellular* nervule practically obsolete, leaving the *discoidal cell* open, or sometimes slender and faintly visible ; *third median* nervule with the basal portion curved and rounded, and with an apparently common origin with the second at apex of cell [in some species]. HINDWING, ovate ; *costal margin* oblique and slightly convex ; *outer* margin slightly waved and broadly rounded ; *abdominal* margin nearly straight, but becoming obliquely divergent to anal angle. *Neuration* generally as in *Euthalia*. BODY, stout ; *palpi*, porrect and pointed ; *antennæ*, variable in length." (*Distant*, l. c.) This applies to *S. dirtea*, the only species found in the Malay Peninsula.

LARVA (*S. nais*) tapering towards both ends, green, with a dorsal row of rounded spots, the sides furnished with ten laterally-projecting long delicately-branched spines. PUPA broad, the back keeled, head ending in two pointed diverging processes.

Symphædra is very closely allied indeed to the next genus *Euthalia* in all its stages. Mr. Butler, when monographing this group, wrote :—"The structural characters which separate *Symphædra* from *Adolias* [= *Euthalia*] are not very considerable, and from their uncertainty seem almost to indicate a state of transition ; the style of colouration, however, is quite distinct." He excluded *S. nais* and *S. teuta* which have since been placed in the genus *Symphædra*, and included the *ninus* of Felder, which is a *Dichorragia*. About twelve species are known, occurring throughout India except in the North-west, Ceylon, Burma, the Malay Peninsula and islands to New Guinea and Australia. The Indian species form a very heterogeneous group, *S. nais* is brick-red above with black spots and bands in both sexes ; *S. teuta*, *S. teutoides* and *S. recta* are dark brown above with a discal pale green band across both wings, the females being similarly marked but paler, and the bands much whiter ; *S. gupta* is an allied species of which the female only is known, but with the band much reduced on the forewing, entirely absent on the hindwing ; while *S. dirtea* and *S. cyanipardus* are velvety black above, with a broad submarginal purplish-blue band on the upperside of the hindwing in the male ; the females have the upperside regularly covered with rounded spots throughout, and no trace of a purplish band. In *S. nais* the discoidal cell of the forewing is entirely open, in all the rest it is closed ; in the first four species at the bifurcation of the second and third median nervules, in *S. dirtea* and *S. cyanipardus* considerably beyond that point.

Key to the Indian species of Symphædra.

A. Discoidal cell of forewing open. Antennæ a little more than half the length of the forewing. Colouration brick-red above, with black markings.

478. S. NAIS, Eastern, Western and Southern India, Ceylon.

B. Discoidal cell of forewing closed. Antennæ more than two-thirds the length of the forewing. Colouration blackish above.

   a. Upperside with a discal pale green band across both wings.

      a^1. Band on forewing with its inner and outer edges irregular, the upper spot directed somewhat inwards.

479. S. THYELIA, Sylhet, Khasi Hills, Java, Borneo.

480. S. THYELOIDES, South Andamans.

      b^1. Band on forewing with both its edges regular, the upper spot in a straight line with the rest of the band.

481. S. RECTA, Sylhet, Upper Tenasserim.

   b. Upperside, hindwing immaculate, no discal band.

482. S. GUPTA, Upper Tenasserim.

   c. Upperside of hindwing with a broad purplish-blue band in male. Female evenly spotted throughout.

      a^1. Underside of male ferruginous. Female with golden spots on upperside.

483. S. DIRTEA, Bhutan, Assam, Cachar, Upper Tenasserim, Malayana.

      b^1. Underside of male rich indigo-green. Female with bluish-white spots on upperside.

484. S. CYANIPARDUS, Assam, Cachar, Sylhet.

478. Symphædra nais, Forster.

Papilio nais, Forster, Novæ Spec. Ins. Cent., vol. i, p. 73 (1771) ; *Symphædra nais*, Moore, Lep. Cey., vol. i, p. 35 (1881) ; *Papilio thyelia*, Fabricius, Ent. Syst., vol. iii, pt. i, p. 142, n. 437 (1793) ; id., Donovan's Ins. of India, pl. xxxi, fig. 3 (1800) ; *Argynnis thyelia*, Godart, Enc. Méth., vol. ix, p. 257, n. 2 (1819) ; *Symphædra thyelia*, Doubleday, Hewitson, Gen. Diurn. Lep., vol. ii, p. 295, n. i, pl. xlii, fig. 6 (1850) ; id., Forsayeth, Trans. Ent. Soc. Lond., 1884, p. 384, pl. xiv, figs. 3, *larva* ; 3α, *pupa* ; *Symphædra alcandra*, Hübner, Zutrage Ex. Schmett., figs. 1, 2 (1818).

HABITAT : Sikkim, throughout the plains of India except the north-west, Ceylon.

EXPANSE : 2·3 to 2·9 inches.

DESCRIPTION : "MALE and FEMALE. UPPERSIDE fulvous-red. *Forewing* with a broad black disco-cellular spot, a contiguous discal spot, an oblique subapical streak, and a transverse submarginal and marginal narrow lunular band, the two joined by streaks on the veins. *Hindwing* with a large black medial costal spot, a submarginal row of small round spots, and broad marginal band, the black colour slightly ascending the veins. *Cilia* alternated with white. UNDERSIDE brownish-ochreous. *Forewing* with the discal area bright ochreous, two discoidal black ringlet-marks bordered between by white, a black contiguous discal spot, an oblique short subapical white macular band bordered inwardly with dark brown, followed by lower submarginal black lunules. *Hindwing* with transverse medial discal band, which is sometimes broken or consists only of a costal and lower spots [or absent altogether] ; two small discoidal red-centred spots, and a submarginal row of small black spots."

"LARVA dark green, with ten pairs of long green laterally-projecting very delicate branched spines ; a dorsal row of dark blue-bordered red spots. PUPA green, thick, keeled along the back, broadly triangular across the middle, a black-bordered pale band across the triangular back, and some thoracic spots." (*Moore*, l. c.) Dr. Forsayeth describes the larva at Mhow as feeding on the "'Tendu' tree [*Diospyros melanoxylon* ?], a large tree somewhat resembling the ash. General colour a light grass-green ; a row of purple spots along middle of back. Margin of body armed with long, horizontal, fleshy processes, covered with fine green hairs of a non-irritating character. Chrysalis green, angular, with dark and gold spots and lines."

In Major Marshall's collection are two specimens of *S. uais* from Sikkim, a somewhat doubtful locality. It occurs in Oudh, plentifully in the Rajmahal hills, and has been taken at Barrackpore and in Calcutta. It occurs in Orissa and thence throughout the south of the peninsula to Ceylon and up the west coast as far as Bombay, but not apparently in the Punjab. It differs not only conspicuously from the other species of the genus by its quite different colouration, small size and short antennæ, but also has a different distribution ; it apparently thrives best in open and moderately dry country, while the other species of the genus live only in a moist climate and in heavy forest.

A species which apparently belongs to this genus was described by Guérin in Delessert's Voyage dans l'Inde under the name of *Argynuis emalea*. The exact locality from whence the type was obtained is unknown, and so far as I am aware no other specimen has ever been obtained, and nothing further is known about it. The description is appended for reference.*

479. **Symphædra teuta,** Doubleday, Hewitson.

Adolias teuta, Doubleday, Hewitson, Gen. Diurn. Lep., vol. ii, p. 291, n. 5, pl. xliv, fig. 7, *male* (1850). id., Moore, Trans. Ent. Soc. Lond., new series, vol. v, p. 81, n. 42 (1857).

HABITAT : N. India, Assam, Sylhet, Java, Borneo *(Druce)*.

EXPANSE : ♂, 2·75 to 3·25 ; ♀, 3·25 to 4·00 inches.

DESCRIPTION : "MALE. UPPERSIDE, blackish-brown, palest on exterior margins, with a transverse band of pale greenish-yellow spots crossing the middle of *both wings*, the spots being smallest and interrupted on the *forewing*; also a single small spot near the apex, and a minute dot of the same colour within the discoidal cell of the forewing,† a row of indistinct triangular black spots near exterior margins ; and two or three indistinct pale spots from anterior angle of *hindwing*. UNDERSIDE, pale brown, suffused in patches with dusky brown ; band and apical spot as above, pale green ; a [submarginal] row of small black short longitudinal spots from apex of forewing to anal angle [of hindwing] ; a rounded spot and a lunular black mark, centred with crimson, within discoidal cell of *forewing*, and in that of the *hindwing* a small dot and two short black lines ; base of costal margin of both wings tinged with crimson. FEMALE. UPPERSIDE paler, and the row of triangular black spots more distinct ; the marks within the discoidal cell of *forewing* also distinct but black. UNDERSIDE, as in male." (*Moore*, l. c.) The discal series of spots are almost white in the female, the upper ones in the forewing usually larger and lengthened out into streaks, with two additional very fine white streaks on the costa above the uppermost spot of the discal series ; sometimes there are two subapical spots.

* *Symphædra? emalea*, Guérin. *Argynnis emalea*, Guérin, in Delessert's Voy. dans l'Inde, part ii, p. 77 (1843) ; *Symphædra emalea*, Kirby, Syn. Cat., p. 259 (1871) HABITAT : Malay Coast. EXPANSE :) inches. DESCRIPTION : " Wings rather rounded, apex of the forewing subconcave. Above fulvous, the apex of the forewing and tortuous lines and spots on the hindwing, black ; two costal spots, white. UNDERSIDE fulvous-grey, with a pearly gloss, a median common white band, macular, straight externally, toothed internally."

" Nearly allied to *Argynnis thyelia*, Fabricius [= *Symphædra nais*]. UPPERSIDE of a lively reddish [fauve], a little more dull at the base. *Forewing* with the apex [extrémité] black with two undulated [ondées] black bands parallel to the external edge, and less marked [marquées] near the inferior angle, beyond in the middle a toothed and undulated band of black serving to define the more obscure portion of the base ; in the middle of the discoidal cell a small transverse brown band with the middle red ish. *Hindwing,* with three flexuous blackish lines at the external edge, one flexuous line in the middle in continuation of that on the forewing, and between this line and the external ones, a series of six black dots of which the two anterior, and that by the anal angle are a little the larger ; two square [carrée] white marks at the costa [côte], the one at the middle the other near the anterior extremity. UNDERSIDE of a yellowish cindery grey, with violet and pearly reflections ; the nervures reddish ; a macular white band bordered with blackish extends obliquely across the middle, right from the external "côte" to the internal "côte," strongly dented especially on the forewing and "très-élargie" at the "côte" of the forewing ; beyond, on the hindwing, a series of six little black dots corresponding to those on the upperside. The *body* is of a yellowish brown ; the *antennæ* black, with the anterior "côte" reddish." (*Guérin*, l. c.)

† I have not seen a specimen with the discoidal spot mentioned by Mr. Moore.

In the Indian Museum, Calcutta, are numerous specimens of this species from Sylhet ; it has also been recorded* from the " Barak river, on ascent to Manipur from Cachar, December," and from Java and Borneo, the latter, however, may be the *bellata* of Druce.

480. Symphœdra teutiodes, Moore.

S. teutoides, Moore, Proc. Zool. Soc. Lond., 1877, p. 586.

HABITAT : South Andamans.

EXPANSE : ♂, 2·5 to 3·0 ; ♀, 3·25 to 3·60 inches.

DESCRIPTION : " Nearly allied to *S. teuta.* MALE differs in having the maculated band more erect and the lower spots smaller ; the band on the *hindwing* is also straighter, more evenly bordered on the inner edge, and regularly sinuous on its outer edge. FEMALE, on the *forewing* the band is continuous and less broken up into spots ; it is also broader at the costal end ; the band on the *hindwing,* as in the male, is also more evenly edged within and regularly sinuous without. UNDERSIDE, *both sexes* are much paler, are suffused with lilac exteriorly, and have no red in the discoidal marks." (*Moore,* l. c.)

This is a very slightly differentiated local race of *S. teuta,* and hardly worthy of distinct specific rank. In the male the maculated band is not more erect, nor the lower spots invariably smaller, nor are the differences given for the hindwing constant in a long series of specimens. In the female the band certainly is more continuous and broader at its costal end ; the band on the hindwing however is much the same as in *S. teuta.* On the underside some of the differences pointed out by Mr. Moore do exist, but they are all very slight characters indeed on which to base a species, and the discoidal marks are sometimes as prominently red-centred as in *S. teuta. S. teutoides* seems to be a fairly common species in the South Andaman Isles.

481. Symphœdra recta, de N., n. sp.

HABITAT : Sylhet, Upper Tenasserim.

EXPANSE : ♂, 3·0 to 3·3 ; ♀, 3·2 to 3·8 inches.

DESCRIPTION : MALE. UPPERSIDE, both wings black, the outer margins slightly paler. *Forewing* with a perfectly straight, evenly margined, discal pale green band, composed of seven increasing spots, a small whitish spot beyond in the subcostal interspace, a submarginal obscure macular diffused black band. *Hindwing* with a discal pale green macular band, widening from the costa to the first median nervule, ending in a point above the anal angle, its edges even ; a submarginal band composed of quadrate spots as in forewing, with a small crimson spot at the anal angle. UNDERSIDE, *both wings* cinnamon-brown, the discal band as above but defined with black, the submarginal band represented by a large diffused patch towards the anal angle and some linear markings above it in the forewing ; in the hindwing by a linear mark in each interspace. *Forewing* with a crimson spot surrounded with black in the middle of the cell placed against the subcostal nervure, a similar lunular line closing the cell. *Hindwing* with a small black spot in the cell, a double black line on the upper outer end of the cell, a crimson spot at the anal angle. FEMALE. UPPERSIDE, *both wings* with the ground-colour paler than in the male, the discal band broader, paler, almost white, the submarginal black diffused macular band much more prominent than in the male. *Forewing* with two fine streaks on the costal margin in continuation of the discal band, a second white spot beyond above the bifurcation of the fourth and fifth subcostal nervules. *Hindwing* with the crimson spot at the anal angle larger, duplex in one specimen. UNDERSIDE as in the male, with the differences of markings as given for the female.

The straightness and evenness of the discal band of the forewing and the crimson spot at the anal angle of the hindwing will at once distinguish *S. recta* from *S. teuta.* There are two males without locality, and one female from Sylhet in the Indian Museum, Calcutta, and one female taken by Captain C. T. Bingham in March in the Thoungyeen Forests in Upper Tenasserim in Major Marshall's collection.

---

* *Euthalia teuta,* Butler, Ann. and Mag. of Nat. Hist., fifth series, vol. xvi, p. 305, n. 44 (1885).

482. **Symphædra gupta,** de N., n. sp.

HABITAT : Upper Tenasserim.

EXPANSE : ♀, 3·15 inches.

DESCRIPTION : Differs from the same sex of *S. teuta* in its smaller size ; the UPPERSIDE has the ground-colour paler. *Forewing* with the discal macular white band reduced to five decreasing triangular spots, of which the largest is placed beneath the subcostal nervure, the two subapical spots obsolete, and the submarginal diffused black spots very small. *Hindwing* with no trace whatever of the broad white band present in *S. teuta*, the submarginal black dentated band reduced to a fine dentated line with the diffused obsolescent whitish spots above and below it in each interspace. UNDERSIDE, *forewing* with the same differences as above. *Hindwing* with a small white spot on the middle of the costa below the costal nervule, followed by five discal small indistinct blackish spots one in each interspace, with a white linear mark in continuation from the middle of the submedian interspace to the inner margin, and the dentate line of the upperside obsolescent, represented by an obscure diffused dentate mark on the middle of each interspace.

There is a single specimen of this species in Major Marshall's collection taken by Captain C. T. Bingham at Tanaoo Choung, Thoungyeen, in September.

483. **Symphædra dirtea,** Fabricius.

Papilio dirtea, Fabricius, Ent. Syst., vol. iii, pt. i, p. 52, n. 184 (1793) ; *Adolias dirtea,* Gray, Lep. Ins, Nepal, p. 12, pl. 1, figs. 1, *female* ; 2, *male* (1846) ; id., Moore, Trans. Ent. Soc. Lond., new series, vol. v, p 84, n. 48 (1859) ; *Lexias dirtea,* Felder, Wien. Ent. Monatsch., vol, iv, p. 400, n. 25 (1860) ; *Symphædra dirtea,* Butler, Proc. Zool. Soc. Lond., 1868, p. 613, n. 3 ; id., Distant, Rhop. Malay, p. 112, n. 1, pl xii, figs 7, *male* ; 8, *female* (1883) ; *Adolias boisduvalii,* Boisduval, Sp. Gen., vol. i, pl. viii, fig. 2, *male* (1836).

HABITAT : Nepal, Bhutan, Assam, Khasi Hills, Cachar, Upper Burma, Upper Tenasserim, Mergui, Malay Peninsula, Sumatra, Billiton, Banca, Java, Borneo.

EXPANSE : ♂, 3·0 to 3·8 inches ; ♀, 3·3 to 4·7 inches.

DESCRIPTION : " MALE. UPPERSIDE very dark chocolate-brown. *Forewing* with a small whitish subapical spot placed beneath the fourth subcostal nervule [often absent], and a greenish outer marginal fascia, which is almost obsolete at apex and gradually widens to posterior angle [this band is very variable, in some specimens it is obsolete, in others very prominent] ; the inner margin of this fascia is very waved and subdentate. *Hindwing* with a very broad outer bluish marginal fascia, with violaceous reflections, occupying about half of wing [somewhat variable in width, in Indian specimens generally considerably narrower], and containing a submarginal series of blackish spots placed between the nervules and a marginal row of much larger subconical spots of the same colour placed upon and divided by the nervules ; this bluish area is sinuated interiorly, and becomes shaded with greenish and violaceous at and near anal angle ; apical portion of abdominal margin thickly clothed with long pale ochraceous hairs. UNDERSIDE very warm and dark ochraceous. *Forewing* with a small and very pale bluish subapical spot situated beneath the bifurcation of the fourth and fifth subcostal nervules [often with three similar discal spots placed between lower discoidal and third median nervules] ; a cluster of irregular pale spots in cell and a long and irregularly curved one at the termination of the same, which is followed by two very indistinct spots placed one on each side of the upper discoidal nervule ; two pale discal spots on each side of the second median nervule, and one beneath the first median nervule ; inner margin and area of the outer angle broadly suffused with fuscous, the last with two bluish spots placed one on each side of the first median nervule ; above these are a subobsolete and submarginal series of pale spots placed between the nervules. *Hindwing* with two pale spots in cell, a curved discal series of six or seven pale spots placed between the nervules, and a submarginal series of small fuscous spots placed between the nervules, with their surrounding areas somewhat pale. *Body* and *legs* more or less concolourous with wings'; *antennæ* black, their apices warm ochraceous. FEMALE. UPPERSIDE chocolate-brown, with the *cilia* alternately concolourous and pale greyish, and with the following yellowish spots :—*forewing* with three [or four] spots in cell, two at its termination, followed by two placed one on each side of the upper discoidal nervule; an oblique discal series of seven spots placed between the nervules, two beneath cell, situated one on each side of second median nervule, a cluster of five irregular spots near base and between first median nervule and submedian nervure, and an outer submarginal series, placed between the nervules, increasing in size towards outer angle; a small yellowish streak on inner margin near its apex. *Hindwing* with the following yellowish spots :—three beneath costal nervure, three between first and second subcostal nervules, four between lower subcostal and discoidal nervules, three in cell (the first being only a small basal streak), three beyond cell before the third median nervule, two beneath cell placed one on each side of second median nervule, and two on basal half of abdominal margin; and three large spots—denoted by pale bluish margins with anterior and posterior yellowish spots—near anal angle divided by the second and first median nervules. UNDERSIDE, *forewing* greenish ochraceous, darker and somewhat bluish at area of median nervules, marked generally as above, but spots larger and pale bluish grey, those in and at termination of cell fused, and the cluster of spots beneath base of cell obsolete. *Hindwing* pale greenish, the basal half more or less suffused with ochraceous; spots as above, but much paler. *Body* above chocolate-brown, with the following yellowish spots :—six thoracic (two anterior, two central, and two posterior), and four at base of abdomen; a narrow lateral streak on each central side of thorax, and a small spot at extreme base of wings; body beneath and *legs* more or less concolourous with wings."

"In Province Wellesley old fallen fruit was an attraction to this species, and sliced pineapple placed at the proper season in a road where these butterflies frequented was generally sure to be visited by a good supply of both males and females." (*Distant*, l. c.)

This widely distributed species is very common in Upper Assam (*S. E. Peal*), less so to the westward. Captain Bingham has taken both sexes in Upper Tenasserim in the Thoungyeen Valley and Meplay Valley in January, in the Donat range in December, and in the Thoungyeen Forests in March, and Dr. Anderson obtained it in the Mergui Archipelago during the cold weather. In some male specimens on the upperside of the forewing are six ochreous spots in the cell placed in pairs, and a less prominent series placed between the nervules just beyond the cell.

484. Symphædra cyanipardus, Butler. (PLATE XXI, FIG. 96 ♂ ♀).

S. *cyanipardus*, Butler, Proc. Zool. Soc. Lond., 1868, p. 613, n. 4; *Adolias dirtea*, Doubleday, Hewitson, (*nec* Fabricius), Gen. Diurn. Lep., vol. ii, pl. xliv, fig. 1, *female* (1850).

HABITAT : Assam, Khasi Hills, Sylhet, Cachar, Borneo.

EXPANSE : ♂, 4·3 to 4·8; ♀, 5·3 to 5·5 inches.

DESCRIPTION : "MALE. UPPERSIDE, most like *S. dirtea*, larger, but the basal dots of the *forewing* greenish-white not yellow-golden, and the marginal band subobsolete, diffused, with two distinct subapical dots snow-white. *Hindwing* with the violaceous-green band inwardly regularly dentate, the veins not at all tipped with ashy. UNDERSIDE with all the spots most distinctly greenish-white, the ground-colour olivaceous-green not fulvous-ferruginous, the submarginal dots of the *hindwing* obscure scarcely distinguishable." (*Butler*, l. c.) FEMALE. UPPERSIDE with the ground-colour darker than in *S. dirtea*, the markings similar but white, tinged more or less with violet-blue instead of yellowish-golden, the submarginal series of large round black spots on the *hindwing* widely surrounded with bluish towards the anal angle, purplish towards the apex, with an irregular whitish spot given off both above and below from each black spot. UNDERSIDE, similarly marked to *S. dirtea*, the disc and inner margin of the *forewing* much darker.

Mr. Butler (l. c.) describes a local race of this species from Borneo as follows :—" Antennæ in both sexes tipped with fulvous; the female on the upperside a little more greenish."

S. cyanipardus is the largest species of the genus and indeed one of the largest species in the subfamily. Mr. Wood-Mason took it in Cachar during the summer, Mr. S. E. Peal has obtained it at Sibsagar in Upper Assam, Mr. J. L. Sherwill at Jorehât also in Assam, and there are specimens in the Indian Museum, Calcutta, from Sylhet and the Khasi Hills.

The figure shows the uppersides of a male and of a female from the Khasi Hills in the Indian Museum, Calcutta.

Genus 78.—EUTHALIA, Hübner. (Plate XIX).

Euthalia, Hübner, Verz. bek. Schmett., p. 41 (1816); id., Moore, Lep. Cey., vol. i, p. 31 (1881); id., Distant, Rhop. Malay., p. 114 (1883); *Aconthea*, Horsfield, Cat. Lep. E. I. C., pl. viii, fig. 6 (1829); idem, id., Zool. Journ., vol. v, p. 65 (1830); *Adolias*, Boisduval, Sp. Gén., vol. i, pl. iii, fig. 11 (1836); id, Westwood, Gen. Diurn. Lep., vol. ii, p. 289 (1850); id., Moore, Trans. Ent. Soc. Lond., new series, vol. v, p. 62 (1859); id., Felder, Neues Lep., p. 34, n. 82 (1861); id., Snellen van Vollenhoven, Tijd. voor Ent., series i, vol. v, p. 181 (1862); id., Butler, Proc. Zool. Soc. Lond., 1868, p. 599; *Itamus*, Felder, Neues Lep., p. 34 (*Adolias*, section I) 1861; id., Doubleday, Gen. Diurn. Lep., vol. ii, pl. xli, fig. 4 (1848); *Dophla*, Moore, Lep. Cey., vol. i, p. 33 (1881).

" BODY, more or less robust ; antennæ long and straight ; wings large, generally of dull colours, with narrow, irregular, dark marks in the discoidal cell. *Head*, wide, scarcely tufted in front ; *eyes*, large, prominent, naked ; *antennæ*, of very great length, slender, filiform at the base ; beyond the middle very gradually incrassated to a long, cylindrical, abruptly terminated, slightly curved club, having two very slender raised lines on the underside, with an impression between them ; *palpi*, small, very slightly projecting beyond the head, and elevated to the level of the middle of the eyes ; second joint lengthened, and apparently increasing in breadth exteriorly, in consequence of the ridge of hairs on its upperside, beyond the middle ; third joint very minute ; palpi of the males larger than those of the females ; *haustellum*, spiral, of moderate length, robust, compressed towards the extremity, and provided with lateral spreading cilia. *Thorax*, more or less robust, clothed with woolly hairs ; *wings* generally of large size, with moderately strong veins. *Abdomen*, variable in size and thickness, according to that of the thorax. FOREWING, somewhat triangular, with a lengthened, boldly curved *costa* ; *apex* generally but slightly rounded ; *outer margin* variable, but generally a little emarginate in the middle, and scarcely scalloped ; nearly three-fourths of the length of the costal margin ; *inner* margin about as long as the outer one, nearly straight ; *costal nervure* strong, reaching a little beyond the middle of the costa ; *subcostal* nervure with the first and second branches arising before the anterior extremity of the discoidal cell, third branch arising at a little distance beyond, or sometimes close to, the extremity of the discoidal cell, and the fourth branch arising at about four-fifths of the length of the wing ; *upper disco-cellular nervule* extremely minute and almost obsolete, arising from the subcostal nervure at about one-third of the length of the wing ; *middle* disco-cellular short, curved, and directed towards the base of the wing ; *lower* disco-cellular obsolete in the typical species, so that the *discoidal cell* is open ; *median nervure* strong, its third branch moderately curved. HINDWING, rounded, slightly acuminated at the anal angle in the males of some species, slightly scalloped along the *outer margin* ; *costal* margin slightly rounded ; *præcostal nervure* curved outwards ; *subcostal* nervure branching near its base ; *upper disco-cellular nervule* forming the scarcely curved base of the discoidal nervule ; *lower* disco-cellular [usually] wanting, so that the narrow *discoidal cell* is [usually] open. FORELEGS, of the *male* very short and slender ; *femur* clothed beneath with long divergent hairs ; *tibia* nearly as long as the femur, thickly clothed with downy hairs ; *tarsus* consisting of a single elongated attenuated joint, covered with a dense uniform down. Of the *female* scaly, with the first joint of the *tarsi* greatly elongated, the three following short, the last abruptly terminated, with several pairs of spines beneath, indicating the three intermediate joints through the scales of the limb. MIDDLE and HINDLEGS, moderately long, the middle pair in the male with the *femur* nearly one-fourth longer than that of the hindlegs, thickly scaly ; middle *tibia* of the male with a thick coat of very short scaly hairs near the base beneath, and with two rows of short thick spines in all the tibiæ ; *tarsi* considerably shorter than the tibia, rather thickly clothed at the sides and beneath with very short spines ; *claws* rather large and very much curved ; *paronychia* small, bifid."

"LARVA, chilopodomorphous, linear, lengthened, provided on each side with ten long, attenuated, spreading, branchiform appendages of nearly equal length, consisting of a midrib and lateral beards, decreasing in length towards the extremity, and imitating the structure of a very delicate plume, being armed with a terminal spike composed of a dense whorl of short robust spines. Feet short, minute, and entirely concealed by the lateral appendages. PUPA short, angular, attenuated at both ends, with two sides even, and the third or ventral surface gently swelled or rounded ; consisting of unequal pyramidal portions, the abdominal portion being the longest, and provided with two points, whilst the angles are armed with a few short spines, which are more robust at the union of the two pyramids ; the longitudinal and transverse ridges ornamented with a delicate gold streak." (*Westwood*, l. c.)

The genus *Euthalia* is of large extent, about seventy species having been described. It belongs to the Indo-Malayan region, occurring sparingly in the Western Himalayas, but is most fully represented in the Eastern ; in Sikkim they attain their largest size and beauty, and are most numerous both in species and individuals. One or two species occur in all but the very arid tracts of continental India, four in Ceylon, one in the Andaman Isles, and numerous species in Assam, Burma, the Malay Peninsula, and islands as far east as Celebes and the Philippines. It occurs also in China.

There is some variability in structure, *E. evelina* and allies have the discoidal cells of both wings closed. The position of the third subcostal nervule of the forewing is also inconstant, in some species (*E. garuda* and allies) it is given off from the subcostal nervure at one-fourth or less from the origin of the disco-cellular nervules, in others (*E. cocytina* and allied species) it is emitted about midway between end of cell and apex of wing. The outline of the wings shows also great variation, in the male especially. In *E. evelina*, *E. satropaces*, &c., the forewing is distinctly falcate in both sexes, in others the apex is only acuminated, and the outer margin emarginate. In *E. garuda* and its allies the hindwing is sharply acuminate at the anal angle in the male. In *E. lepidea* and its allies, the hindwing is evenly rounded in both sexes. In colouration many species in the males are black on the upperside, with darker bands and irregular linear spots towards the base of the hindwing, and in the cell of the forewing ; the females are paler, and often very diversely coloured ; other males have a broad blue or grey margin to the upperside of the hindwing ; in these the females are in a few instances somewhat similarly marked, in the others they are quite different. Again, there are other species which are alike in both sexes, and have the colouration of the upperside some shade of green, two species with a broad discal pale band across both wings on the upperside, others with the band on the forewing only, and lastly others without any band at all. The larvæ of *Symphædra* and *Euthalia* are similarly formed, and are amongst the most peculiar and interesting in Butterflies. I have often found that of *E. garuda* at rest on the middle of a mangoe leaf, in which position it is very difficult to see, though its form is so remarkable, its body with the pale dorsal line answers to the midrib of the leaf, while the lateral branched spines pass for the other veins of the leaf on which it is resting, forming a remarkable instance of protective colouration, structure and habit combined.

Though the perfect insects differ so widely in outline, and in style of markings as well as in robustness of structure, the genus is separable into two distinct groups ; the first of which has the discoidal cell of the forewing closed by a slender nervule ; the second has the cells of both wings open.

In the first group the sexes, so far as is known, are alike, but the differences between the various species in outline and in style of markings is very considerable ; one, *E. durga*, closely resembles an aberrant *Limenitis* in style of markings, but the strongly arched costa is sufficient to distinguish it, and moreover the white discal band stops short of the first median nervule on the hindwing which in *Limenitis* it never does. In the remaining species the markings are diverse from those of all the allied genera.

Key to the Indian species of Euthalia.

First group.

A. Discoidal cell of both wings closed.
    a. Outer margin of forewing deeply emarginate, apex broadly rounded ; colouration uniform, no sharply-defined pale markings.
        a¹. Upperside brown.
            a². Discoidal spot in forewing marked with crimson.
                485. E. (*Dophla*) DERMA, Sylhet, Assam, Burma, Malayana.
            b². Discoidal spot in forewing unmarked with crimson.
                486. E. (*Dophla*) SOMA, North India, Java.
        b¹. Upperside fuscous, slightly bronze-tinted.
            487. E. (*Dophla*) EVA, North India, Assam, Malay Archipelago.
        c¹. Upperside green.
            488. E. (*Dophla*) EVELINA, South India, Ceylon.
    b. Outer margin of forewing slightly emarginate, apex truncate ; colouration uniform brown, with a discal series of small well-separated pale yellow spots across both wings.
        489. E. (*Dophla*) DUNYA, Lower Tenasserim, Perak, Borneo.
    c. Outer margin of forewing slightly emarginate, apex pointed.
        a¹. Forewing with an oblique prominent macular band on forewing from middle of costa towards anal angle ; no discal band to hindwing.
            a². Macular band pale yellow.
                490. E. PATALA, Himalayas, Chumba to Nepal.
            b². Macular band white or greenish-white.
                a³. With a geminate white spot just beyond middle of submedian interspace on upperside of forewing.
                    a⁴. Spot in first median interspace of forewing four times as long as broad.
                        491. E. IVA, Sikkim.
                    b⁴. Spot in first median interspace of forewing short and conical.
                        492. E. TADDANA, Upper Tenasserim.
                b³. With no geminate white spot in submedian interspace on upperside of forewing.
                  493. E. NARA, Sikkim, N. Khasi Hills.
        b¹. Forewing with no oblique prominent macular band.
            494. E. ANYTE, Sikkim, Nepal.
        c¹. Both wings with a discal macular pale yellow band, directed obliquely from middle of costa towards anal angle in each wing.
            495. E. SAHADEVA, Nepal, Sikkim, Assam.
        d¹. Both wings with a continuous curved pure white discal band from middle of costa of forewing to near first median nervule of hindwing.
            496. E. DURGA, Sikkim, Assam.

The first five species have been generically separated from *Euthalia* by Mr. Moore under the name of *Dophla*,* and have the discoidal cell of both wings closed. They are all large insects, the forewing in several of them deeply emarginate below the apex, giving it a very hooked appearance ; colouration above dark-brown or green, with two black sinuous fine lines across the cell on the upperside of the forewing in the first four species, enclosing anteriorly a crimson spot in three of them. One species (*E. derma*) has been recorded from Masuri, and occurs in Assam, Sylhet and Malayana ; another (*E. evelina*) occurs in South India and Ceylon ; there are two other species described by Felder from North India which appear to be but slight varieties of these two species. Another very distinct species of this group (*E. dunya*) has a series of small but prominent whitish spots across the disc of both wings, and occurs in Lower Tenasserim, Perak and Borneo. In this species the crimson markings are barely traceable.

---

* *Dophla*, Moore, Lep. Cey., vol. i, p. 33 (1881) ; *Adolias*, section v, Felder, Neues Lep., p. 35 (1861). " Forewing, triangular, *costa* much arched, *apex* truncate, *exterior margin* more or less even, angular below the apex, and very concave in the middle, *posterior margin* long, straight ; *first subcostal nervule* emitted at one-third before end of the cell, *second* near its end, *third* at one-fourth beyond and extending to apex, *fourth* and *fifth* at three-fourths beyond ; *upper* (*middle*) *disco-cellular* short, inwardly oblique, waved, *lower disco-cellular* outwardly oblique and slightly concave, *upper discoidal* from close to subcostal, *lower discoidal* from near end of upper (middle) disco-cellular ; *upper median* from end of the cell, *middle* median from imme-diately below its end, *submedian nervure* slightly recurved. HINDWING, bluntly oval, *costa* slightly arched in male, straight in female, *exterior margin* very convex, more or less even ; *discoidal cell* closed by a slender oblique disco-cellular nervule ; other veins as in *Euthalia*. Body robust." (*Moore*, l. c.)

485. **Euthalia derma,** Kollar.

Adolias? derma, Kollar, Hugel's Kaschmir, vol. iv, pt 2, p. 436, n. 2 (1843) ; *Euthalia derma*, Distant, Rhop. Malay., p. 116, n. 1, pl. xix, fig. 4, *male* (1883) ; *Adolias evelina*, race *derma*, Butler, Proc. Zool. Soc. Lond., 1868, p. 600, n. 4.

HABITAT : Masuri (*Kollar*), Assam, Sylhet, Mergui, Malay Peninsula, Java, Borneo, Celebes, Luzon.

EXPANSE : ♂, 3´4 to 3´9 ; ♀, 3´75 to 4´60 inches.

DESCRIPTION : "MALE and FEMALE. UPPERSIDE fuliginous-brown. *Forewing* with the cell crossed by two waved blackish lines in the middle (between which [anteriorly] is a prominent carmine spot), and two lines converging posteriorly at extremity. *Hindwing* with a faint blackish oblique line near the middle, and two prominent black lines at apex of the cell. *Both wings* crossed by a discal curved fuliginous fascia, commencing on the forewing near the end of the cell, where it is broadest, and terminating on the hindwing near middle of abdominal margin, where it is narrowest ; beyond the fascia the colour is slightly paler, the hindwing possessing a somewhat faintly darker and very narrow submarginal fascia. UNDERSIDE pale greenish ; cellular markings of the *forewing* as above, but with the interspaces between the pairs of lines pale brownish ; a subbasal fuscous streak outwardly margined with white, and an irregular spot beneath the cell near the base of the first median nervule ; cellular markings of *hindwing* as above, but with an additional curved black line beyond apex, a similar but shorter mark near and between the bases of the discoidal and lower subcostal nervules ; this is preceded by a rounded spot between the subcostal nervules, and a larger and partly closed one containing a carmine spot between the upper subcostal nervule and the costal nervure ; there is also a small carmine spot in cell ; a darker discal fascia crossing *both wings* as above, a similarly coloured broad submarginal fascia commencing on the forewing at upper discoidal nervule and becoming obsolete on the hindwing at the median nervules, followed by a waved and lunulate fascia broken between the nervules ; the forewing also possesses a broad, darker, oblique, subapical patch, its margins and also the apical margin of the hindwing more or less infuscated." (*Distant*, l.c.)

E. *derma* has a wide range, Kollar described it, probably incorrectly, from Masuri, but it appears to be somewhat common in Sylhet, and occurs through the Malay peninsula to the Philippines. It may at once be known from E. *evelina* by the colouration of the upperside being distinctly brown, while the latter is green.

486. **Euthalia soma,** Felder.

Adolias soma, Felder, Reise Novara, Lep., vol. iii, p. 432, n. 693 (1867) ; id , Butler. Proc. Zool. Soc. Lond., 1868, p. 600, n. 5

HABITAT : North India (*Felder*), Java (*Butler*).

EXPANSE : Not given.

DESCRIPTION : "MALE, UPPERSIDE as in *A.* [= *E.*] *eva*, Felder, but without the bronze tint. *Forewing* with the cellular markings broader, the inner one without the red spot, the diffused fuscous band very obsolete, more excised. *Hindwing* with two cellular marks (the disco-cellular much broader than in *A. eva*), the diffused fuscous discal streak much more dentate than in that species, the submarginal more distinct. UNDERSIDE as in *A. eva*, but much more powdered with bluish-white. *Forewing* with a white diffused but distinct apical spot. *Hindwing* with the basal markings broader than in the species mentioned, the subcostal only including an obliterated red spot and the cellular including a dot of the same colour. The "*orbits*" [? orbits of the eyes, which in E. *derma* and E. *evelina* are red] whitish."

"We received an unique specimen together with the preceding species [*A. eva*] ; the inner and outer margins of the wings are longer and the apex of the forewing much less produced." (*Felder*, l.c.)

"May be only a race of *E. evelina* ; it scarcely differs except in the differently formed discoidal spots without scarlet centres." (*Butler*, l.c.)

The absence of the scarlet markings is a point which should make *E. soma* easily recognized if met with. I have never seen a specimen. *E. annamita*, Moore (Proc. Zool. Soc Lond., 1879, p. 137) from Cochin China belongs to this group.

487. Euthalia eva, Felder.

Adolias eva, Felder, Reise Novara, Lep, vol. iii, p 432, n. 692 [1867].

HABITAT : North India, Assam, Luzon, Java, Borneo, Celebes.

EXPANSE : Not given.

DESCRIPTION : " MALE. UPPERSIDE fuscous, very slightly tinted with bronze, otherwise as in *A.* [= *E.*] *evelina. Forewing* however with the fuscous discal fascia entirely diffused. UNDERSIDE less varied with glaucous [bluish-gray] than in *A. evelina*, with the markings on the border more obsolete. The "orbitæ" red.* FEMALE. Wings paler, *forewing* more produced at apex."

" Up to this it has been confounded in collections with *A. evelina*, Stoll, (*derma*, Kollar), from which it can easily be distinguished by the colouring of the upperside." (*Felder*, l. c.)

I know nothing of this species, but retain it here as distinct on Dr. Felder's authority. Messrs. Butler and Distant both rank it as a synonym of *E. derma*, which is probably correct as Felder appears to have considered *E. evelina* and *E. derma* as one species.

488. Euthalia evelina, Stoll.

Papilio evelina, Stoll, Suppl. Cramer, vol. v, pl xxviii, figs. 2, 2D, *male* (1790) ; *Nymphalis evelina*, Godart, Enc. Méth., vol. ix, p 401, n. 174 (1819) ; *Adolias evelina*, Butler, Proc. Zool. Soc. Lond., 1868, p. 600, n. 4 ; *Dophla evelina*, Moore, Lep. Cey., p. 30, pl. xvii, figs 1, 1a, *male* (1881).

HABITAT : South India, Ceylon.

EXPANSE : 3·0 to 3·5 ; ♀ 4·00 to 4·65 inches.

DESCRIPTION : " MALE and FEMALE. UPPERSIDE, *both wings* aënescent† sap-green, with a transverse discal dusky lunular fascia, and a less distinct marginal fascia. *Forewing* with two discoidal black-lined marks, the upper part of the inner one centred with vermilion. *Hindwing* with one black-lined mark. UNDERSIDE greenish-grey, with dull sap-green transverse discal and a confluent double marginal fascia. *Forewing* with discoidal marks as above, *hindwing* with two discoidal marks, and two rings above them, both of which and the inner discoidal mark are centred with vermilion." (*Moore*, l. c.) The FEMALE differs from the male in being much larger, paler, and with a prominent irrorated whitish discal band, wide on the costa of the foregoing, continued on to the hindwing where it becomes obsolescent near the middle of the wing, its inner margin sharply defined and irregular, its outer margin diffused. In the male there is a trace of the commencement of this band near the costa of both wings ; it is completely absent from both sexes of the preceding species.

In Ceylon *E. evelina* "occurs in the eastern and western provinces in low country forests in June. Flight rapid, along forest-paths, settling on thick parts of trees and sometimes on the ground. Shy" (*Hutchison*). "Rather common in the Kottawa forest, but difficult to capture" (*Wade*). It occurs also at Karwar, Bombay (*J. Davidson*), the Wynaad (*Rhodes-Morgan*), North Canara, January (*Macpherson*), and at Trevandrum.

489. Euthalia dunya, Doubleday, Hewitson.

Adolias dunya, Doubleday, Hewitson, Gen. Diurn Lep., vol. ii, p. 292, n. 6, pl. xliv, fig. 3 (1850); id., Moore, Trans. Ent. Soc. Lond., new series, vol. v, p. 84, n. 47 (1859).

HABITAT : Northern India (*Westwood*), Mergui Archipelago, Perak, Borneo.

EXPANSE : 3·8 to 4·0 inches.

---

* The orbits of the eyes are probably meant
† Bronzy.

DESCRIPTION : " MALE. UPPERSIDE olive-brown, with a row of small yellow spots crossing the middle of *both wings*, each spot being encircled with black ; discoidal marks on *forewing* black, inner mark bounded on each side by a yellow dot ; an indistinct submarginal row of blackish spots. UNDERSIDE pale whitish-green, row of spots indistinct ; discoidal marks and submarginal row of spots blackish." (*Moore*, l. c.)

UPPERSIDE with a small reniform black spot in the middle of the cell touching the subcostal nervure, with two very small yellow marks one on each side, a much larger irregular black mark enclosing the disco-cellulars. Two small subcostal yellow spots ; four small discal ones surrounded with suffused blackish, the one in the second median interspace half the size of the one in the interspace below, two spots in the submedian interspace, the upper one minute. *Hindwing* with an arched discal series of eight yellow spots, the three upper ones conjoined, large and irregularly shaped, the others round and much smaller, the upper one the smallest, all these spots diffusedly surrounded with black.

Dr. Anderson obtained two male specimens of this species in the Mergui Archipelago in the cold weather, and there is one specimen from Perak in the Indian Museum, Calcutta.

The next four species have the outer margin of the forewing nearly straight, very slightly concave ; the apex is neither truncate nor rounded, but bluntly pointed, and the hindwing is broadly rounded. They all have a pale discal macular band on the forewing from the middle of the costa towards the anal angle ; and also some pale spots near the middle of the costa of the hindwing, which distinguish them at a glance from the females of the second group, many of which have the oblique band on the forewing. All the species are large, and have the ground-colour dull green ; the cilia are white between the ends of the nervales.

490. **Euthalia patala**, Kollar.

Adolias patala, Kollar. Hugel's Kaschmir, vol. iv, pt. ii, p. 435, n. 1 (1844) ; *Euthalia patala*, Moore, Proc. Zool. Soc. Lond 1882, p. 239 ; *Adolias doubledayii*, Gray, Lep. Ins. Nepal, p. 13, pl. xiii (1846) ; *Adolias epiona*, Moore, Trans. Ent. Soc. Lond., new series, vol. v, p. 79, n. 37 (1859) ; id., Butler, Proc. Zool. Soc. Lond., 1868, p. 602, n. 16.

HABITAT : Himalayas, from Chumba to Nepal.

EXPANSE : 3˙7 to 4˙5 inches.

DESCRIPTION : " Wings olive-green, with black [marks] in the costal nervure [discoidal cell]. *Forewing* with a spotted white band across the middle, from the middle of the anterior margin towards the posterior angle, and two white spots near the summit [apex]. *Hindwing* with three spots in the middle of the anterior margin. UNDERSIDE like the upper, but of a cinereous colour " (*Gray*, l. c.)

" UPPERSIDE, *both wings* pale olive-green, with two obscure darker narrow lines crossing the disc. *Forewing* with oblique row of yellowish-white spots from middle of costal margin to beyond middle of the wing, opposite posterior angle ; also two smaller spots on costal margin near the apex. *Hindwing* with two [or three] yellowish-white spots on costal margin nearer the angle. Blackish marks at the base of *both wings*. UNDERSIDE pale yellowish-green. *Forewing* with oblique row of spots as above, but less defined, and having two additional very small spots on the lower part of the disc [often absent] ; on the *hindwing* the spots extend by the addition of small ones to the middle of the wing. *Sexes* alike." (*Moore*, l. c. in Trans. Ent. Soc. Lond.)

Colonel Lang writes of this species as follows *:— " Frequents oak-forests at altitudes of 6,000 to 8,000 feet in the Himalaya during the rainy season (July and August). It flies very swiftly over the tops of the trees with a skimming flight like a swallow. Two or three may be seen chasing one another in and out of the shade among the branches of the trees. They pitch abruptly, often with expanded wings, basking in the sun-light, until some passing insect, another *Adolias* or a *Nepta* floating near, tempts the quarrelsome species to dash off, buffet the passer-by, and after a rapid skim. pitch once more, suddenly, near its former

* Ent. Month. Mag., vol. i, p. 121 (1864-65).

resting-place, and bask again. It soon gets battered, and is difficult to capture." Mr. Hocking says* that it "Flies about oaks. June to September." I have taken it commonly in Simla at about 5,000 feet ; it is very partial to over-ripe peaches, plums, &c. Major C. H. T. Marshall has taken it in Chumba ; in Kumaon it is abundant near Naini Tal in the middle of the rains ; and Dr. Scully has sent numerous specimens from Nepal.

491. Euthalia iva, Moore.

Adolias iva, Moore, Horsfield and Moore, Cat. Lep. Mus. E. I. C., vol i, p. 195, n. 395 (1857); idem, id., Trans. Ent. Soc. Lond., new series, vol. v, p. 78, n. 36, pl. viii, fig. 2 (1859)

HABITAT : Sikkim.

EXPANSE : 4 inches *(Moore)* ; 4'4 on plate.

DESCRIPTION : "MALE : UPPERSIDE very dark olive-green. *Forewing* with oblique row of large, long, greenish-white spots from middle of costal margin to near posterior angle, beneath which is a small narrow geminated spot near the middle of the posterior margin ; also two small spots obliquely near the apex, and a small whitish patch at the posterior angle. *Hindwing* with a row of broadly-separated small round greenish-white spots curving from middle of costal margin to middle of the wing ; also black marks within discoidal cell. UNDERSIDE deep greenish-grey, dusky about the anterior half, and blackish along the posterior margin ; markings as above, but the spots on the *hindwing* extending nearly to abdominal margin, Shape of wings as in *Adolias* [= *E. uthalra*] *epiena* [= *E. patala*]. *Adolias iva* may be known from *A. epiena* [= *E. patala*] by its very dark upperside, and by the oblique band being composed of much longer spots, and by its deep greyish-green underside." (*Moore*, l. c. in Cat. Lep. Mus. E. I. C.)

I have never seen this species. In Mr. Moore's figure the three lower spots of the discal series of the forewing are very much elongated and pointed outwardly, and the presence of two small spots just below the middle of the first median nervule, the upper one almost touching it, is an unusual and distinctive feature.

492. Euthalia taooana, Moore.

Adolias taooana, Moore. Proc. Zool. Soc. Lond., 1878, p 831.

HABITAT : Upper Tenasserim, Taoo, 3,000 to 5,000 feet.

EXPANSE : 4 inches.

DESCRIPTION : " Allied to *E. iva. Forewing* with the oblique discal maculated band with shorter lower portions, the penultimate spot quite oval, the last being short and conical ; the two contiguous spots beneath are also smaller, and the two before the apex closer together. *Hindwing*, the three subapical spots are contiguous, the two upper being large, quadrate, and excavated externally." (*Moore*, l. c.)

This species also is unknown to me ; from the description alone it appears to be sufficiently distinct.

493. Euthalia nara, Moore.

Adolias nara, Moore, Trans. Ent. Soc. Lond., new series, vol. v, p. 78, n. 35, pl. viii, fig. 1, *female* (1859).

HABITAT : Sikkim, N. Khasi Hills.

EXPANSE : 3'42 to 4'10 inches.

DESCRIPTION : "FEMALE, UPPERSIDE dark glossy golden olive-green, with blackish marginal and submarginal lines. *Forewing* with oblique transverse row of six white spots, from middle of costal margin to near posterior angle, also two small subapical white spots ; marks within [and below] discoidal cell black. *Hindwing* with two [or three] white spots on costal margin near the angle. UNDERSIDE glossy verdigris-green, apically olive-green. *Forewing* with markings as above, but more defined and whiter ; lower part of disc patched with

---

* Proc. Zool. Soc. Lond., 1882, p. 210.

blue-black. *Hindwing* with transverse row of [five or] six white spots from costal margin to near the posterior angle; indistinct discoidal markings [and a submarginal series of small black spots placed between the nervules]. *Cilia* [alternately] white." (*Moore*, l. c.). The MALE (of which I have seen a single specimen only) differs from the female in the submarginal small black spots on the underside of the hindwing being replaced by a diffused line darker than the ground-colour.

E. nara is decidedly a rare species. It differs from *E. teu* in the shape of the spots in the discal band of the forewing, and in the absence of the two small spots below the first median nervule on the upperside of the forewing, and from *E. patala* in its much deeper tone of colouration, and in having five or six irregular pale bluish-white spots across the disc of the hindwing on the underside.

E. nara is probably the species referred to by Moore in the Proc. Zool. Soc. Lond., 1865, p. 767, under the name of *A. confucius*, Westwood, the letter being a Chinese insect, and is said to be " Closely allied to *A. epiona* [= *E. patala*], but larger; the lower spot on hindwing lunulate and reversely curved."* They are quite distinct species.

The next species, *E. anyte*, differs much in outline from the other species of this group, and closely resembles in this respect, the males of *E. garuda* and its allies, the apex of the forewing and anal angle of hindwing being sharply pointed; the body too is more robust, but the discoidal cell of the forewing is closed; the female is unknown. On the upperside the pale discal band is obsolete, but the pale spots near the costa of the hindwing are almost always prominent.

494. **Euthalia anyto,** Hewitson.

Adolias anyte, Hewitson, Ex. Butt., vol. iii, *Adolias*, pl. ii, fig 5 (1862); id., Butler, Proc. Zool. Soc. Lond., 1868, p. 603, n. 23.

HABITAT : Sikkim, Nepal.

EXPANSE : 2·8 to 3·0 inches.

DESCRIPTION : " MALE. UPPERSIDE, *both wings* green-brown, crossed beyond the middle by two bands of darker brown. *Forewing* with a brown line and a spot of rufous-brown bordered on both sides with black within the cell; a small spot below the last, and a spot just beyond the end of the cell also bordered on both sides with black; the space between the two transverse bands is of a paler tint than the rest of the wing, marked with two indistinct round spots. *Hindwing* with a white [ochreous] spot on the costal margin beyond its middle. UNDERSIDE as above, except that it is much paler; that the *hindwing* has the oblong and transverse black marks near the base common to the species of this group, and that it is crossed in the place of the first transverse band by a band (broken in the middle) of six obscure white spots." (*Hewitson*, l. c.)

This is a rare species, of which I have only seen males : there is one Sikkim specimen in the collection of the Indian Museum, Calcutta, one in Major Marshall's collection, and four from Sikkim and one from Nepal in Colonel Lang's. On the underside it is marked almost exactly as in *E. sahadeva*, except that the discal series of pale spots is narrower on both wings and the white spot near apex of forewing is absent, but the lower half of the disc of the forewing is suffused with black as in *E. sahadeva*, and it lacks the small black linear marks in the middle of the submarginal band of the hindwing present in that species. *E. anyte* is much smaller than *E. sahadeva*, the apex of the forewing more pointed, the outer margin more emarginate, the hindwing much shorter, the anal angle more acute. Mr. Butler says that it " seems to be most nearly allied to *E. garuda*." It is however I think most nearly allied to *E. sahadeva*, differing from that species chiefly in size and shape, and in the absence of the white spots at the apex of the forewing.

In Major Marshall's collection is a single male of this species from Sikkim which differs considerably from the other examples I have seen. The outer margin of the forewing is but very

* Butler, Proc. Zool. Soc. Lond., 1868, p. 603, n. 14.

slightly emarginate, causing the apex to be more acuminate, and on the hindwing there is no trace of the large patch of yellow on the costa which is such a conspicuous feature of *E. anyte* ; the submarginal band is much wider and diffused, especially anteriorly, and placed further from the margin ; it is equally wide on the underside, and the discal series of pale yellow spots on both sides are entirely absent. It is probably only an aberration of *E. anyte* ; at any rate from a single specimen I am disinclined to describe it as a distinct species.

The next species *E. sahadeva* has an oblique pale discal band on the forewing as in *E. patala*, though not so prominent, and also a similar band on the hindwing ; the outline of the wings is as in *E. patala*, but the hindwing is shorter at the costa and more elongated posteriorly.

495. **Euthalia sahadeva,** Moore.

Adolias sahadeva, Moore. Trans. Ent. Soc. Lond., new series, vol. v, p. 80, n. 39, pl. viii, fig. 3, *male* (1859); id., Butler, Proc. Zool. Soc. Lond., 1862, p. 601, n. 11.

HABITAT : Nepal, Sikkim, Assam.

EXPANSE : 3·25 to 3·60 inches.

DESCRIPTION : "MALE. UPPERSIDE olive-green, with darker submarginal band and inner portion of disc. *Forewing* with oblique row of five pale greenish-yellow spots from middle of costal margin ; two small whitish subapical spots ; space between discoidal marks and along outer margin yellowish. *Hindwing* with transverse tapering row of six pale greenish-yellow spots from costal margin to near abdominal angle, bounded below with pale yellow ; two transverse disco-cellular black lines ; abdominal margin greenish-grey. UNDERSIDE greenish-yellow, lighter and darker in portions, marked as above, discoidal markings on both wings, lower part of disc of *forewing* with blackish patches." (*Moore*, l. c.) Mr. Butler (l. c.) says that Mr. Moore has described the female as a male, but his description agrees very well with our male specimens of this species, Mr. Moore informs me also that the type specimen is a male. Mr. Butler redescribes the MALE as follows : " Differs [from *E. sahadeva*, Moore, =female *sahadeva*] altogether in shape : wings smaller, forewing with the apex, hindwing with the anal angle acute, all the bands of the forewing pale concealed with green, of the hindwing most distinct, running together near the costa, but retired on the disc and partly obliterated with black : the marginal spots more obscure." His description agrees fairly well with the *Euthalia anyte* of Hewitson.

I have only seen males of this species ; it is decidedly a rare species, and occurs from Nepal to Shillong. On the forewing there is an oblique discal band of five somewhat obscure yellowish spots, with two smaller spots beyond just below the apex, with an obscure yellowish bar across the cell ; hindwing with a decreasing macular band from the costa to the first median interspace, the lower spots sometimes almost disappeared. Underside marked much as above, but the ground-colour yellowish green. The shape of the hindwing is unusual, being considerably longer than broad, it is longer than broad in some other species, but not nearly to the same extent.

The next and last species of this group is distinguished by having a broad pure white continuous discal band across both wings more or less outwardly margined with blue. In outline it is intermediate between *E. patala* and *E. sahadeva*.

496. **Euthalia durga,** Moore.

Adolias durga, Moore, Horsfield and Moore, Cat. Lep. Mus. E. I. C., vol. i, p. 196, n. 397 (1857); id., Moore, Trans. Ent. Soc. Lond., new series, vol. v, p. 80, n. 41, pl. ix, fig. 2 (1859).

HABITAT : Sikkim, Assam.

EXPANSE : 3·6 to 4·8 inches.

DESCRIPTION : " UPPERSIDE dark olive-green, with a black marginal and submarginal band ; a broad transverse band of irregular-shaped white spots crossing from middle of costal margin of forewing to beyond the middle of the hindwing, near the anal angle, being margined exteriorly with blue from the forewing on its lower half to anal angle [of hindwing] ; the narrow space between marginal and submarginal bands also bluish. Two small rounded white spots near the apex of forewing ; marks within discoidal cells black. UNDERSIDE from inner margin of band to base greenish-grey, from its outer margin to extremity of wing greenish, with band and apical spots as above ; a row of blackish marks from apical spots to posterior angle, which is whitish ; also an indistinct dusky submarginal row on the hindwing, and at the anal angle two patches of black ; marks at the base of wings black. *Cilia* between the indentations on the upper and underside white. *Sexes* alike." (*Moore*, l. c.)

E. *durga* is the largest species of the genus occurring in India and one of the most beautiful. It used to be fairly common in Sikkim, but of late has become much less so. Mr. S. E. Peal has taken it at Sibsagar in Upper Assam.

Key to the Indian species of Euthalia.

Second group.

B.　Discoidal cell of both wings open.

　　a.　Both sexes with a pale yellow well-defined discal band across both wings as in *Limenitis*, its inner edge in the hindwing just beyond the origin of the second median nervule.

　　　　497. E. FRANCIÆ, Nepal, Sikkim, Assam, Sylhet, Upper Burma.

　　b.　Males with no pale discal band, apex of forewing rounded, outer margin of hindwing broadly grey or blue on upperside.

　　　　a¹.　Males with grey or blue marginal band extending on to margin of forewing.

　　　　　　a².　Sexes alike, body slender ; outer margin of forewing emarginate ; apex slightly falcate.

　　　　　　　　a³.　Outer border on upperside whitish-grey.

　　　　　　　　　　498. E. LEPIDEA, Sikkim, Assam, Upper Tenasserim, Orissa, South India.

　　　　　　　　b³.　Outer border on upperside bluish-grey.

　　　　　　　　　　499. E. ANDERSONII, Mergui, Tavoy.

　　　　　　b².　Sexes dissimilar.

　　　　　　　　a³.　Body slender ; forewing highly falcate ; male with grey border broad extending to near apex of forewing ; female with a discal dark brown straight band from apex of forewing to middle of abdominal margin of hindwing, and a discal series of five whitish spots on forewing and an additional one beyond near apex below costal nervure.

　　　　　　　　　　500. E. SATROPACES, Tenasserim.

　　　　　　　　b³.　Body robust ; forewing slightly falcate ; male with blue border narrow, not extending beyond third median nervule of forewing ; female as in E. *entropaces*, but lacking the additional pale spot near apex of forewing.

　　　　　　　　　　501. E. TELCHINIA, Sikkim, Cachar.

　　　　b¹.　Males with blue marginal band not extending on to margin of forewing or to apex of hindwing ; females brown, with two parallel wavy dark discal lines, the space between bearing more or less developed whitish patches near costa of forewing ; body slender.

　　　　　　a².　Male with blue marginal band anteriorly bounded between median nervules by outer black discal band.

　　　　　　　　a³.　Space anteriorly between discal black bands on upperside of forewing in male concolorous with rest of wing ; female with outer margin of forewing slightly emarginate.

　　　　　　　　　　502. E. APPIADES, Sikkim, Bhutan, Cachar, Sylhet, Assam.

　　　　　　　　b³.　Space anteriorly between discal black bands on upperside of forewing brownish-white ; female unknown.

　　　　　　　　　　503. E. BALARAMA, Sikkim, North India.

　　　　　　b².　Male with blue marginal band wider, extending nearly to inner black discal band ; outer black discal band only visible near apex ; female as in E. *appiades*, but discal bands nearer together, inner margin of forewing shorter.

　　　　　　　　　　504. E. XIPHIONES, Upper Tenasserim, Moulmein.

　　c.　Males with apex of forewing acutely angled ; anal angle of hindwing also acute and somewhat produced ; body very robust, sexes dissimilar.

a^1. Male, upperside yellowish olive brown ; underside of hindwing with abdominal margin broadly and about anal angle somewhat green. Female unknown.

505. E. ADIMA, Assam.

b^1. Male, upperside purplish olive-brown, with two parallel discal black lunulated bands and black basal markings on upperside ; underside of hindwing devoid of greenish colour on abdominal margin. Female paler, but marked on upperside as in male.

506. E. JAHNU, Sikkim, Assam, Sylhet, Cachar, Chittagong, Upper Tenasserim.

c^1. Male, upperside black, both wings with broad irrorated discal grey band ; female brown, outer border beyond inner discal band paler ; outer edge of inner discal band marked anteriorly with pale spots on both sides in forewing.

507. E. KESAVA, Sikkim, Bhutan, Assam, Sylhet, Cachar, Burma.
508. E. DISCISFILOTA, Upper Tenasserim.

d^1. Male, upperside dark olive green, with pinky tinge broadly on anterior margin of hindwing, markings above much as in E. garuda and allies, but no small white marks beyond cell of forewing, and the pale discal band much widened at inner margin of forewing ; female with broad discal whitish band on upperside of forewing, bifurcated anteriorly.

509. E. ALPHEDA, ? North India, Java.

e^1. Male, upperside dark brown with a vinaceous tinge, a discal paler broad band bifurcated anteriorly, and marked with white patches within towards the costa ; female paler than male, markings more prominent.

510. E. PARTA, ? India, Borneo.
511. E. SOMADEVA, North India.

f^1. Male, upperside dark bronzy brown ; a series of small white spots beyond cell of forewing on both upper and under sides.

a^2. Female with broad white discal band on both wings, bifurcated anteriorly in forewing.

512. E. ACONTIUS, South Andamans.

b^2. Female with a series of small white spots beyond cell of forewing on both sides.

513. E. GARUDA, India, Ceylon, Malay Peninsula, Java.

c^2. Female with white macular oblique even band across forewing on both sides.

514. E. VASANTA, Ceylon.

g^1. Male with the series of small white spots beyond cell of forewing elongated into narrow white streaks in pairs between the veins.

a^2. Male, upperside, hindwing with broad blue border ; female, hindwing entirely brown, forewing with broad oblique macular white band from middle of costa to first median nervule towards inner angle.

515. E. FRANCIUS, Sikkim, Assam, Naga and Khasi Hills, Sylhet, Cachar.

b^2. Male, upperside, hindwing with no blue border, but with even straight discal brown band from near apex of forewing to middle of abdominal margin on hindwing ; female marked much as in male, but the discal band more curved on hindwing.

516. E. JAMA, Sikkim, Assam, Naga Hills, Cachar, Province Wellesley, Malacca, Banca.

h^1. Male, both wings marked with crimson spots on both sides in addition to the series of small white spots beyond cell ; female also marked with crimson as in male, the discal white spots developed into a broad macular band.

517. E. LUBENTINA, India, Ceylon.

i^1. Male, upperside, both wings profusely irrorated with grey ; female with outer margin of forewing highly emarginate, with a discal series of prominent white spots beyond cell from costa to second median nervule.

518. E. ANOSIA, Sikkim, Assam, Cachar, Chittagong, Mergui, Malay Peninsula.

The second group in which the cell of the forewing is open presents three distinct types. The first section is represented by a single species, which in style of markings corresponds most closely with the last species of the first group, E. durga. It has a broad well-defined pale discal band across both wings, but this band is pale yellow not white, and it extends on the hindwing up to the submedian nervure ; the sexes are alike, and the general aspect is more nearly that of a Limenitis than in any other species of this genus.

26

The second section is distinguished by the shape of the wings in the male, the forewing being more or less falcate, and the hindwing being evenly curved on the outer margin and often somewhat elongate ; the colouration of the males is also peculiar, they have no pale discal markings, the upperside is generally nearly uniform brown or blackish with more or less obsolete dark lines, but the outer margin of the hindwing and sometimes also of the forewing is broadly blue or grey, strongly contrasting with the brown ground-colour. This blue outer border occurs in only one Indian species as yet described, *E. phœmius*, which does not belong to this section, and it may be distinguished not only by its outline, but by the blue patch being bounded outwardly by a pure white streak, and the extreme margin bearing a black line. In this section the body is with one exception (*E. telchinia*) remarkably slender, and the wings are comparatively weak. In this section too the differentiation of the sexes commences, in the first two species the sexes are nearly alike, in the next two the shape and style of markings are the same, but the grey or blue band has disappeared in the female ; the ground-colour is uniform, but the position of the band is marked by a dark transverse band along what would be its inner edge ; in the three remaining species there is no trace even of the outline of the band in the female ; the ground-colour is uniform, but the dark lines follow the same pattern as in the male and are more prominent ; the colouration of the underside also differs conspicuously. In this section again the third subcostal nervule of the forewing arises at a greater distance from the cell than in the third section, but the character is variable, being most pronounced in *E. lepidea*.

The third section is distinguished by the shape of the wings in the male, the forewing having the apex acutely pointed, and the hindwing having the anal angle acutely pointed also and slightly produced ; the body is very robust, and the wings powerful though small ; the antennæ are longer than in the other sections, being often considerably more than half the length of the forewing, and the third subcostal nervule of that wing arises close to the cell. The sexes are differentiated in all the species, the females having larger wings, the forewing with the apex more rounded, and the hindwing broader and more evenly rounded. In many cases the females have prominent white discal bands.

First section. With a well-defined pale yellow discal band across both wings ; sexes alike.

497. **Euthalia franciæ**, Gray.

Adolias franciæ, Gray, Lep. Ins. Nepal, p. 12, pl. xiv (1846); id., Moore, Trans. Ent. Soc. Lond., new series, vol. v, p. 81, n. 13 (1859); *A. franciæ*, Moore, Anderson's Researches, p. 924 (1878) ; *A. sapa*, Felder, Wien. Ent. Monatsch., vol. iii, p. 397, n. 40, pl. ix, fig. 2, *female* (1859).

HABITAT : Nepal, Sikkim, Assam, Sylhet, Upper Burma.

EXPANSE : 2·9 to 4·0 inches.

DESCRIPTION : " Wings olive-green, with a spotted [pale yellow] band across the middle of both wings somewhat in the form of a V, also two white [pale yellow] spots near the apex of the *forewing*, and a series of white [pale yellow] lines along the margin of both wings, and a series of black lines interiorly. UNDERSIDE marked like the upperside, but of a cinereous colour, with a spot of black at the posterior angle of the *forewing*." (*Gray*, l. c.) Sexes alike.

This also is a very beautiful species. It may be known from *E. durga* on the upperside by the ground-colour being a paler green, the discal white (or pale yellow) band much narrower, especially on the forewing, and inwardly deflexed above the third median nervule, this band not defined outwardly with a black line and then a broad blue fascia as in *E. durga* ; a submarginal series of diffused whitish spots. Underside quite different in colour, being of a most beautiful glossy greenish silvery, the discal white band as above but wider on the hindwing, the additional wider portion being pale purplish, a narrow white band across both wings in continuation of the two subapical white spots above, and a wider submarginal band, with a black diffused spot within it at the anal angle of the forewing.

E. francia is not a common species ; it occurs from Nepal to Upper Assam, and was taken by the Yunan Expedition in Upper Burma.

Second section. Forewing more or less falcate. hindwing with outer margin evenly rounded, outer margin broadly blue or grey on upperside ; body slender.

In the next two species the sexes are nearly alike, the forewing is more falcate than in any other species, except *E. satropaces*, and the grey marginal band extends nearer to the apex of the forewing than in any others.

498. **Euthalia lepidea,** Butler. (PLATE XIX, FIG. 78 ♂).

Adolias lepidea, Butler, Ann. and Mag. of Nat. Hist., fourth series, vol. i, p. 71 (1868) : *A. cocytus,* Moore (*nec* Fabricius), Trans. Ent. Soc. Lond., new series, vol. v, p. 76, n 28 (1879) ; id., Pritzwitz, Stettin Ent. Zeit., 1867, p. 272.

HABITAT : Sikkim, Assam, Sylhet, Cachar, Chittagong, Upper Tenasserim, Orissa, South India.

EXPANSE : 2·5 to 3·8 inches.

DESCRIPTION : " UPPERSIDE of the MALE blackish-fuscous, of the FEMALE fuscous ; with the middle disc a little paler, the external margin pale ashy-fuscous ; of the female fuscescent, the discoidal marks black. UNDERSIDE much paler, of the MALE chestnut-fuscous, of the FEMALE ochraceous with the middle disc ochreous ; *hindwing* outwardly whitish ; a submarginal macular streak, another beyond the middle angular lunate ; hindwing ochraceous, the discoidal markings black ; forewing with the outer margin tinged with violet." (*Butler,* l. c.)

" May at once be distinguished by the ashy marginal band widening from apex of the forewing to abdominal margin" [of the hindwing]. (*Moore,* l. c.)

E. lepidea is a very distinct and well-marked species, with the forewing very falcate ; its pale grey margins on the upperside, narrow on the forewing, wide on the hindwing, distinguish it from any other butterfly except *E. satropaces.* It occurs commonly in North-eastern India and Burma, appearing again in Orissa and southwards to Travancore. Mr Butler gives the South Indian form as a variety, but it does not appear to differ from specimens from North-eastern India.

The figure shows both sides of a male specimen from Calicut in the Indian Museum Calcutta.

499. **Euthalia andersonii,** Moore.

E. andersonii, Moore, Journ A. S. B., vol. liii, pt. 2, p. 18 (1884).

HABITAT : Mergui, Tavoy.

EXPANSE : ♂, 2·25 ; ♀, 2·75 inches.

DESCRIPTION : " MALE and FEMALE. UPPERSIDE dark umber-brown, palest in the female ; *both wings* with a marginal bluish-grey band, which extends very narrowly from the apex of the *forewing* and widens across the *hindwing* to broadly above anal angle. Within and beneath the cells the black streaks are most distinct in the female ; across the discal area are two indistinct dusky sinuous fasciæ widening from the costa of the *forewing*, at which end the interspace is slightly paler in the male and distinctly paler in the female. *Cilia* white. UNDERSIDE ochreous-brown in the male and yellowish-ochreous in the female ; the outer borders broadly suffused with purplish lilacine-white ; cell-marks distinct ; across the disc of *both wings* are two dusky lunular fasciæ with pale interspace, most distinct in the female, the fasciæ being disposed across the middle of the disc."

" Nearest allied to *E. cocytus,* Fabricius ; also to *E. lepidea,* Butler, and to *E. macnairii,* Distant." (*Moore,* l. c.) Dr. Anderson took several specimens of both sexes of this species in the Mergui Archipelago during the cold weather. It differs from *E. lepidea* only in having the outer border blue not grey.

The *E. cocytus* of Fabricius belongs to this group, and was described from Siam.   The male has the outer margins of both wings blue on the upperside as in *E. andersonii* ; the female is somewhat similar to that sex of *E. satropaces*, but the apical area of the forewing on the upperside is covered with greenish scales.

Between this species and the next are numerous closely-allied species, six of which, *E. macnairi*, *E. stoliczkana*, *E. maclayi*, *E. cocytina*, *E. puseda* and *E. asoka* have been recorded from the Malay Peninsula.   In all of these the outer border is blue extending on to the forewing in the male, and they exhibit a gradually increasing differentiation of the sexes.   The detailed descriptions are given below. Another species of this group (*E. gopia*) has been described from Assam, but the locality is doubtful ; it is closely allied to *E. cocytina*.   The description of the male is appended, but no description has hitherto been published of the female. I have never seen either sex, and my knowledge of it is confined to the description here republished and the figure which accompanied it, but both sexes are stated to be in the British Museum.

Euthalia macnairi, Distant, Rhop. Malay., p. 123, n. 9, pl. xiv, figs. 6, *male* ; 10, *female* (1883). HABITAT : Province Wellesley.   EXPANSE : *Male*, 2'2 ; *female*, 2'8 inches.   DESCRIPTION : " MALE.   UPPER-SIDE very dark chocolate-brown, the outer margins of *both wings* pale bluish ; on the *forewing* this bluish margin is narrow, commencing a little beneath apical angle, and slightly widening and terminating at posterior angle ; on the *hindwing* it is very broad, especially near the anal angle ; outer margins narrowly black, the *cilia* pearly white ; cell of the *forewing* crossed by four blackish lines, the two innermost nearly straight, the two outer ones prominently bent and sinuated, and a similarly bent black line at end of cell ; the three innermost of these lines are continued beneath the median nervure.   UNDERSIDE pale olivaceous-brown.   *Forewing* with the basal area palest, cellular markings as above, but more distinct, and two discal, narrow, undulating fuscous fasciæ, the inner one waved, the outer entire, but somewhat discontinuous. *Hindwing* with the cell crossed by some indistinct fuscous lines, a similar convex one near its apex, and an elongate ovate spot on each side of the base of the upper subcostal nervule ; two discal and parallel narrow fuscous fasciæ, terminating at about the first median nervule, the inner one broadest, and the outer narrow and somewhat broken.   *Body* and *legs* more or less concolorous with wings.   FEMALE.   Larger and paler in hue than the male ; markings similar, but the *forewing* on the UPPERSIDE exhibiting the discal fasciæ only seen on the underside of the male ; these fasciæ are also slightly broader and the colour between them somewhat paler ; cell of the *hindwing* exhibiting the transverse dark lines as beneath.   UNDERSIDE brighter and warmer in hue than in the other sex ; the markings similar."

" This species and *E. stoliczkana* represent a section of the genus in which the males are strikingly similar to each other and equally dissimilar from the females.   The great interest attaching to the species is that it represents the closest alliance and resemblance between the sexes of this section, the following species showing a gradually increasing tendency to sexually differentiate ; whilst it is to the Indo-Malayan region that this portion of the genus is almost confined." (*Distant*, l. c.)

Euthalia stoliczkana, Distant, Rhop. Malay., p. 124, n. 10, pl. xiv, fig. 11, *female* (1883).   HABITAT : Province Wellesley.   EXPANSE : *Male*, 2'45 ; *female*, 2'80 inches.   DESCRIPTION : " MALE.   Closely resembling the male of *E. macnairi*, but larger, and with the bluish marginal fasciæ on *both wings* on the UPPERSIDE a little broader.   UNDERSIDE with the narrow fuscous outer discal fascia to both wings much more waved and sinuated.   FEMALE.   UPPERSIDE closely resembling the female of *E. macnairi*, but differing on the UPPERSIDE by the absence of the bluish marginal fasciæ, which are only slightly indicated near the posterior angle of the *forewing*, and appear on the *hindwing* as a narrow discal fascia, which becomes obsolete towards the abdominal margin ; on this wing the narrow fuscous discal fasciæ of the forewing are also continued, the innermost distinct, the outer one not distinctly passing the third median nervule.   UNDERSIDE warmer in hue than in *E. macnairi*, and distinctly differentiated from that species by the waved and sinuated outer discal fasciæ to *both wings*." (*Distant*, l.c.)

Euthalia maclayi, Distant, Rhop. Malay., p. 124, n. 11, pl. xiv, fig. 12, *female* (1883).   HABITAT : Province Wellesley.   EXPANSE : *Male*, 2'4 ; *female*, 2'9 inches.   DESCRIPTION : " MALE.   UPPERSIDE almost identical with the male of *E. macnairi*.   UNDERSIDE with the outer discal fascia waved and sinuated as in *E. stoliczkana*, but on the *hindwing* the outer fascia is farther removed from the margin than in that species.   FEMALE. UPPERSIDE closely resembling the female of *E. macnairi*, but the bluish marginal fascia to the *hindwing* inwardly strongly waved and hollowed at the subcostal and discoidal nervules.   UNDERSIDE.   *Both wings* have the outer discal fascia strongly waved and sinuated as in *E. stoliczkana*, but on the *forewing* these fasciæ are wider apart than in that species, and on the *hindwing* the outer fascia is farther removed from the margin."

" *E. macnairi*, *E. stoliczkana*, and *E. maclayi* have so strong a superficial resemblance as to give the impression that they are but varieties of one species, and this was my first conclusion.   The reasons which have impelled me to take the opposite view are that both sexes can be differentiated, and that the forms are not intermediate.   Thus, though *E. maclayi* resembles *E. macnairi* above, it partakes of the character of *E. stoliczkana* beneath, but is yet quite distinctly differentiated from that species by the pattern of those markings. Though I have followed this course I consider the conclusion but tentative.   Some decision must be taken in a work like this, and the proof will ultimately rest with the local breeder of these insects.   In the absence of this information analytic and synthetic empiricism are both to be deplored." (*Distant*, l.c.)

Euthalia cocytina. *Acontheα cocytina*, Horsfield, Zool. Journ., vol. v, p. 67, pl. iv, figs. 3, 3a, *male* (1829); *Adolias cocytina*, Butler, Ann. and Mag. of Nat. Hist., fourth series, vol. i, p. 93, n. 6 (1868) ; *Euthalia cocytina*, Distant, Rhop. Malay., p. 125, n. 12, pl. xviii, fig. 7, *female* (1883) ; *Adolias godartii*, Gray, Lep. Ins. Nepal, p. 14, pl. xii, fig. 2, *male* (1846).   HABITAT : Singapore, Sumatra.   EXPANSE : *Male*, 2'4 ; *female*, 2'8 inches.   DESCRIPTION : " MALE.   UPPERSIDE resembling *E. maclayi*, but the bluish marginal bands wide, as in *E. stoliczkana*.   UNDERSIDE pale but warm ochraceous, the markings generally as in *E. macnairi*, but paler and ochraceous ; the black cellular markings of the *forewing* as in *E. maclayi*.   FEMALE.   UPPERSIDE pale fuliginous-brown, cellular and infra-cellular markings as in *E. maclayi* ; an oblique discal series of six elongate greyish spots, outwardly and obscurely margined with small dark spots placed between the nervules ; of the former the two uppermost, devided by the first discoidal nervule, are largest, and the first is broken at its middle ; the third is smallest, and the sixth, situated beneath the first median nervule, is rather faint and outwardly notched ; a broad pale marginal border, becoming obsolete

at apex and shaded with bluish at posterior angle. *Hindwing* with the apical (outer) half broadly bluish; this area is marked with two series of whitish spots, the first and most distinct at its inner margin, which is preceded by a series of obscure dark spots: the second, which is almost obsolete near its middle; outer margin brownish; the *cilia* of both wings greyish white. UNDERSIDE pale obscure ochraceous. *Forewing* marked as above, the discal series of pale spots large, more continuous, and more obscure and outwardly margined by a narrow waved fuscous fascia. *Hindwing* with the apical (outer) half (which has a narrow transverse dark ochraceous fascia near its anterior margin) somewhat paler. *Body* and *legs* more or less concolourous with the wings."
(*Distant*, l. c.)

Euthalia puseda. Adolias puseda, Moore, Horsfield and Moore, Cat. Lep. Mus. E. I. C., vol. i, p. 191, n. 383 (1857); idem, id., Trans. Ent. Soc. Lond., new series, vol. v, p. 72, n. 18, pl. vi, fig. 5, *female* (1859); id., Felder, Wien. Ent. Monatsch., vol. iv, p. 400, n. 33 (1860); *Euthalia puseda*, Distant, Rhop. Malay., p. 145, n. 13, pl. xviii, fig. 8, *female*; pl. xv, fig. 3, *female variety* (1882); *Adolias monima*, Butler (Fabricius ?), Proc. Zool. Soc. Lond., 1865, p. 608, n. 53, pl. xlv, fig. 4, *male*; idem, id., Cat. Fab. Lep. B. M., p. 89, n. 3 (1869); idem., id., Trans. Linn. Soc. Lond., Zoology, second series, vol. i, p. 539, n. 6 (1877); *Adolias ludekingii*, Butler (nec Vollenhoven), Trans. Linn. Soc. Lond., Zoology, second series, vol. i, p. 539, n. 7 (1877). HABITAT; Perak, Penang, Malacca, Singapore. EXPANSE; *Male*, v1; *female*, 1·5 to 2·9 inches. DESCRIPTION; "MALE. Very closely resembling the corresponding sex of *E. macnairii*, the UPPERSIDE being indistinguishable. UNDERSIDE, *forewing* with a distinct subapical pale fuscous patch, and the two narrow discal fasciæ are placed wider apart, the interior one being almost obsolete and the outer one waved; *both wings* are also somewhat paler in hue. FEMALE. UPPERSIDE pale fuliginous. *Forewing* with the cell crossed by the following dark fuscous lines:—one near base, two near middle with their bases connected, and two at termination, the inner of which is strongly curved and the outer deeply sinuate, both narrowly connected at base; immediately beneath cell are a short line near outer base of first median nervule, a looped line forming an irregular spot at inner base of the same nervule, and a short line near base of the submedian nervure; a submarginal series of large greyish obconical spots separated by the nervules, which occupy about outer half of wing, crossed by a much-waved and dentate narrow brown fascia; the two uppermost of these spots having their centres excavated and suffused with the fuliginous ground-colour, and they are all conically pointed inwardly, except the lowermost, situated above the submedian nervure, which is concavely excavated. *Hindwing* with the outer half (excluding margin) more or less irrorated with pale greyish, its inner margin defined by a narrow waved brown fascia, and crossed by a regularly curved but inwardly dentate narrow brown fascia, the cell crossed by some obscure dark lines. UNDERSIDE pale ochraceous. *Forewing* with the cellular lines as above, the large obconical spots extending to margin and marked as above. *Hindwing* as above, but much paler. *Body* and *legs* more or less concolourous with wings."

"The females are very variable, and I have seen all the intermediate forms between the two specimens figured. The *A.* (= *E.*) *ludekingii*, Vollenhoven (Tijd. Ent., vol. v, p. 189, n. 9, pl. x, fig. 3, *female* (1862) may also be but a variety of this species, but in its typical form, as figured by Vollenhoven, certainly does not appear to be found in the Malay Peninsula."

"Mr. Butler identified the male of this species as the *Papilio monima*, Fabricius, and placed the *P. cocyta*, Fabricius, as a synonym, stating that it is "figured by Jones to his unpublished 'Icones.'" I have not followed him in this course for several reasons:—Firstly, the Fabrician type is not contained in the Banksian collection, and therefore the identification is unreliable; secondly, the index of a number of allied species are so similar that it seems impossible, from the description of Fabricius alone, to decide upon one more than another; and thirdly, as Mr. Moore has figured his species (female specimen) it seems unnecessary to sink the same without more conclusive reason." (*Distant*, l. c.)

Euthalia acola. Adolias acola, Felder, Reise Novara, Lep., vol. iii, p. 433, n. 695, pl. lviii, fig. 1, *female* (1866); id., Butler, Trans. Linn. Soc. Lond., Zoology, second series, vol. i, p. 533, n. 3 (1877); *Euthalia acola*, Distant, Rhop. Malay., p. 147, n. 14, pl. xv, fig. 9, *male*; pl. xiv, fig. 3, *female* (1883). HABITAT; Penang, Province Wellesley, Malacca, Borneo. EXPANSE; *Male*, 2·40; *female*, 2·65 inches. DESCRIPTION; "MALE. UPPERSIDE dark castaneous. Both wings with a bluish outer marginal border, narrowest on the forewing, where it commences a little beneath apex, extending to posterior angle, and very wide on the hindwing, terminating near submedian nervure; this bluish area is more or less suffused with purplish reflections; cell of the *forewing* crossed by four black lines, two medial and two terminal. UNDERSIDE dull and dark ochraceous. *Forewing* with the cellular markings as above, followed by a curved black line connecting the lower discoidal nervule with the base of the second median nervule, and with a very narrow waved dark fuscous discal or submarginal fascia, commencing near lower subcostal nervule, between which and upper discoidal nervule it is strongly angulated; beyond this fascia the colour is violaceous. *Hindwing* with a paler waved submarginal fascia and a very indistinct discal one which is principally visible near the subcostal nervules. *Body* and *legs* more or less concolourous with wings. FEMALE. UPPERSIDE pale brownish. *Forewing* with the cellular markings as in the male; a waved line beyond cell, a small looped line beneath cell at outer base of first median nervule, and a larger one of the same character at inner base of the same nervule, preceded by another small one near base; a discal series of seven pale spots divided by the nervules (the two lower together situated between the first median nervule and submedian nervure), the two upper spots divided by the upper discoidal nervule are largest, and the first is deeply scooped and excavated at its anterior margin; the third is small and subquadrate, the fourth and fifth convex interiorly; beyond these spots the colour is bluish, followed by a waved and narrow brownish fascia outwardly and broadly margined with bluish grey; a marginal fuscous line, and the *cilia* grey. *Hindwing* with a discal curved series of pale spots surrounded by darker brown, placed between the nervules, from which to the outer margin the colour is paler and contains a medial narrow waved dark brownish fascia; a marginal fuscous line, and the *cilia* grey; cell crossed by two pairs of looped lines. UNDERSIDE much paler and ochraceous; markings as above, but the discal series of large spots to the *forewing* much paler, and not outwardly followed by bluish, and the narrow dark fascia placed much closer to them than on upperside. *Body* and *legs* more or less concolourous with wings."

"The female figured somewhat differs from Felder's figure of the same sex by the much less pale colouration of the hindwing between the discal series of spots and the outer margin. Felder, however, refers the species to two localities, viz., "Malacca, interior" and Borneo, but does not specify from which the specimens figured was received. Consequently it is at least possible that the pale form may have been from Borneo, and the species as found in the Malay Peninsula is of a somewhat melanic race." (*Distant*, l. c.)

Euthalia gupia. Adolias gupia, Moore, Trans. Ent. Soc. Lond., new series, vol. v, p. 73, n. 22, pl. v, fig. 4, *male* (1859); id., Butler, Proc. Zool. Soc. Lond., 1867, p. 607, n. 46. HABITAT; Assam and (?) Fiji Islands (Butler). EXPANSE; 3·17 inches. DESCRIPTION; deep pinky brown, with a slight purple shade. *Forewing* with transverse row of whitish irregular spots, each terminating in a point between the veins, the first two long, and ringed with brown across their middle, the rest shorter; basal markings black. *Hindwing* with tapering white band from middle of anterior to middle of abdominal margin, bounded broadly

In all the remaining species the sexes are differentiated. In the first two in which the males have the border grey or blue extending on to the forewing, the female has the ground-colour pale brown throughout, with a straight dark band from the apex of the forewing to the middle of the abdominal margin of the hindwing, and the outer margin of both wings is suffused with the same dark brown colour; they also have a discal series of hyaline spots on the forewing, and the underside is bright ochraceous or orange yellow, dullest at the base, and with no suffusion of bluish gray on the hindwing.

500. Euthalia satropaces, Hewitson.

Adolias satropaces, Hewitson, Ent. Month. Mag., vol. xiii, p. 130 (1876); idem, id., Desc. Lep. Coll. Ath., p. 1, pl. i, figs, 8, *male*; 6, 7, *female* (1879); id., Moore, Proc. Zool. Soc. Lond., 1878, p. 830.

HABITAT : Tenasserim.

EXPANSE : ♂, 2·7 to 2·8; ♀, 3·1 to 3·2 inches.

DESCRIPTION : "MALE. UPPERSIDE, dark brown. *Forewing* projecting at the apex, as in *E. cocytus* [= *E. lepidea*]; marked in the cell by a black line and by two large pale spots border-ed with black, by a spot and two short black lines below these, and by another pale, unde-fined spot nearer the apex; the outer margin, except at the apex, rufous-grey. *Hindwing* with the outer half of the same colour. UNDERSIDE ochreous-yellow. *Forewing* with the spots in the cell and a linear submarginal band of brown. *Hindwing* with some scarcely-seen spots before and after the middle. FEMALE. UPPERSIDE, pale rufous-brown. *Forewing* with the spots in and below the cell as in the male, marked beyond the middle by six transparent spots, fixed in a transverse band, and one near the apex; crossed near the outer margin from the apex by a dark brown band, which is continued to the middle of the inner margin of the *hindwing*: hindwing with two spots in the cell, and a series of submarginal lunular spots of brown. UNDERSIDE as above, except that it is orange-yellow, and that the submarginal band has its origin at a different part of the apex, and is not continued on the hindwing."

"The female of this species very closely resembles *A. aphidas*" [=the female of *E. tel-chinia*]. (*Hewitson*, l. c. in Ent. Month. Mag.)

E. satropaces is also a very distinct species, with a limited geographical range, it having been recorded from Tenasserim only. The type specimens were from Moulmein, Limborg took it in April at Meetan, 3,000 feet, Dr. Anderson obtained three females in the cold weather in the Mergui Archipelago, and Major Marshall has males taken by Captain Bingham in the Thoungyeen Forests in December and in the Donat range in January. In the male the apex of the forewing is more produced, there are two grey patches in the cell and one beyond on the upperside, and the grey marginal band on both wings is broader and darker, than in *E. lepidea*. The female is quite different, and may at once be known from that sex of *E. telchinia* by having an additional transparent white spot beyond the discal series near the apex of the forewing.

501. Euthalia telchinia, Ménétriés.

Adolias telchinia, Ménétriés, Cat. Mus. Pet., Lep., vol. ii, p. 120, n. 1261, pl. ix, fig. 3, *male* (1857); id., Moore, Trans. Ent. Soc. Lond., new series, vol. v, p. 77, n. 31 (1853); id., Butler, Proc. Zool. Soc. Lond., 1868, p. 608, n. 55; *A. aphidas*, Hewitson, Ex. Butt., vol. iii, *Adolias* pl. ii, fig. 8, *female* (1862).

HABITAT : Nepal, Sikkim, Cachar.

EXPANSE : ♂, 2·45 to 3·00; ♀, 3·2 to 3·9 inches.

DESCRIPTION : MALE. UPPERSIDE dark brown. *Forewing* with the costal half of the wing paler, the cell crossed by a fine black line near the base reaching the sub-

---

exteriorly with pale blue, which is centred with a row of whitish spots. UNDERSIDE dull ochreous, with whitish bands and discoidal markings of *forewing only*, as above." (*Moore*, l. c.)

Mr. Butler gives the habitat of this species from both sexes in the British Museum as above, and states that Moore described the "female as male," but when describing the species Mr. Moore speaks of a "female" only. Judging from the outline and style of markings of the figure however it appears to be that of a female, but Mr. Moore informs me that the type specimen is a male, and that the female is somewhat similar to the female of *E. aruna*, Felder, and *E. tociliani*, Butler; that both sexes are in the British Museum, and that he has not seen others.

median nervure, then by a pair of lines which are joined just below the point where the first median nervule is given off, then by another fine line, the space between it and the outer of the pair of lines just described fuscous; a broad fuscous bar beyond the end of the cell. *Hindwing* with some very obscure black basal and cellular lines, the outer margin broadly blue, narrowing towards the apex and continued diffusedly on to the inner angle of the forewing. The margin defined with a very fine black line, the *cilia* pure white. UNDERSIDE much paler brown than above. *Forewing* with a short fine black line near the base of the cell, a pair of lines near the middle, with another pair beyond, the inner one just within the disco-cellular nervules. The disc is crossed by a pair of diffused fuscous lines, the outer one somewhat lunular and evenly curved, the inner one very irregular, inwardly deflexed from the third median nervule to the costa, the space enclosed between it and the outer line somewhat ochreous anteriorly. *Hindwing* with the usual basal and cellular fine black lines, an obscure diffused fuscous discal band and a narrower lunular submarginal line. FEMALE. " UPPERSIDE, *both wings* rufous-brown, crossed by a continuous oblique band of dark brown, commencing at the apex of the forewing and reaching to the middle of the abdominal fold of the hindwing. *Forewing* with a black line, two oblong spots (one within, the other just beyond the cell) and two smaller spots below these ; crossed at the middle by a curved band of five clouded-white spots ; the outer margin dark brown. *Hindwing* with two oblong [dark brown] spots near the base ; crossed beyond the middle by a band of dark brown lunular spots. UNDERSIDE as above, except that it is orange-yellow ; that the band described above as continuous, is much more distinct on the forewing, but scarcely seen on the hindwing ; that the spots near the base of the *forewing* and the band of white spots are all bordered with black ; that there is a sixth white spot below the band of five spots ; that the apex is white ; that the *hindwing* has the usual black spots and lines near the base, but indistinctly marked." (*Hewitson, l. c.*)

The male of this species on the upperside bears a general resemblance to *E. appiades*, but is much darker, and the blue border extends on to the forewing ; on the underside the ground-colour is brown not greenish-ochreous, the two discal bands are continuous, in *E. appiades* they are broken up into round or lunular spots. The female differs from that sex of *E. appiades* on the upperside in having a prominent dark brown band crossing both wings almost in a straight line, and on the underside of the forewing in having six prominent white discal spots. In *E. telchinia* also the body is much more robust than in any other species of this section. *E. telchinia* is a rare species. Mr. Otto Möller has obtained a female in Sikkim in October, Mr. Wood-Mason has taken males on Nemotha in Cachar in September, these are the only exact records of its capture which I possess.

The next three species have in the males the outer margin blue on the upperside of the hindwing only, not extending to the apex or on to the forewing ; the forewing is longer but less emarginate than in *E. lepidea*, and the hindwing is broader. The females are pale brown, with the black lines as in the males but more prominent, and with no trace of blue on the outer margin : they also have whitish patches near the costa of the forewing between the discal lines, sometimes indistinct, sometimes large and prominent. The underside is dusky ochreous with two series of black spots ; in the male the spots of the outer series are circled with blue on the hindwing, and in the female the hindwing is suffused with bluish-grey throughout the inner three-fourths ; deepest along the abdominal margin.

502. **Euthalia appiades,** Ménétriés.

Adolias appiades (*apiades* on plate), Ménétriés, Cat. Mus. Petr., Lep., vol. ii, p. 120, n. 1263, pl. ix, fig. 4, *male* (1857) ; *A. apiades*, Moore, Trans. Ent. Soc. Lond., new series, vol. v, p. 77, n. 32 (1859) ; idem, id., Proc. Zool. Soc. Lond., 1865, p. 766 ; id., Butler, Proc. Zool. Soc. Lond., 1868, p. 609, n. 59 ; *A. sedeva*, Moore, Trans. Ent. Soc. Lond., new series, vol. v, p. 63, n. 10, pl. iv, fig. 3, *female*, var. (1859).

HABITAT : Nepal, Sikkim, Bhutan, Assam, Sylhet, Cachar.

EXPANSE : ♂, 2·50 to 3·25 ; ♀, 3·25 to 3·60 inches.

DESCRIPTION : "MALE. UPPERSIDE dark glossy olive-brown, with two lunulated lines crossing the disc of *both wings*, and markings at base of wings black, the lines obscure at the upper ends on the *forewing* ; a greenish-blue marginal band from anal angle broadly along exterior margin [of *hindwing*]. UNDERSIDE dusky ferruginous, greenish at the apex of forewing, and thickly so on the posterior half of hindwing, and the abdominal margin tinged with yellow ; transverse lines as in upperside, but broader and very black from the anal angle ; also the basal marks. FEMALE.* UPPERSIDE brown. *Forewing* with transverse row of whitish spots, the first two long, each with a point outwards, the rest to the posterior margin very small, along the inner margin of the band only ; the rest of the band being brown, its outer margin defined by a dusky line. *Hindwing* with two transverse zig-zag blackish lines. Discoidal mark blackish. UNDERSIDE. *Forewing* reddish-ochreous, greenish at the base and along outer margin and at the apex ; band as in upper-side, but more defined. *Hindwing* deep glossy greenish-grey, with transverse lines as in upperside, tinged anteriorly within with white. Discoidal marks black." (*Moore*, l. c.) Mr. Butler (l. c.) describes the FEMALE as follows :—"UPPERSIDE yellow-fuscous with the usual basal streaks, two continuous discal fuscous wavy rather diffused lines, both with four whitish dots near the apex of the *forewing*. UNDERSIDE coloured as in *E. jahnu*, but the *forewing* differing altogether in shape."

E. *appiades* is the commonest species of the genus in Sikkim and probably eastwards as far as Upper Assam in suitable localities. The male is at once known by the blue border to the hindwing on the upperside, bounded anteriorly between the third median nervule and discoidal fold by the outer of the two discal zig-zag bands. The two discal bands on the forewing on the upperside at once distinguish it from *E. phemius* and *E. telchinia* ; the underside also is quite different, the discal bands on both wings being broken up into spots, those on the hindwing of the outer band, and towards the anal angle of the inner band, are surrounded with blue. The female is much larger than the male, has no blue border to the hindwing on the upperside, the discal bands on the forewing are more or less marked with white anteriorly ; in specimens from Assam, Sylhet and Cachar this character is very prominent, there being two large oblong white spots filling the interspace between the two bands divided by the upper discoidal nervule. It was this form of the female which was described and figured by Mr. Moore as *E. sedeva*, and which he now maintains as the female of his *E. balarama*.†

503. Euthalia balarama, Moore.

Adolias balarama, Moore, Proc. Zool. Soc. Lond., 1865, p. 766, pl. xli, fig. 3, *male* ; *A. jahnu* (male only), Butler (*nec* Moore), Proc. Zool. Soc. Lond., 1868, p. 609, n. 58.

HABITAT : North India.

EXPANSE : 2·5 inches.

DESCRIPTION : "MALE. UPPERSIDE dark olive-brown. *Forewing* with the basal marks black, two transverse discal suffused black lines, the interspace anteriorly being brownish white. *Hindwing* with the basal marks and two transverse discal sinuous lines black, the space between the outer line of the latter and the exterior margin of the wing slaty blue. UNDERSIDE greenish grey, suffused with yellow. *Forewing* dull chrome-yellow medially ; markings as above, black, the transverse series on the *forewing* formed inwardly by irregular-shaped marks, and outwardly by suffused spots terminating anteriorly with white spots ; those on the *hindwing* by increasing black spots surrounded with slaty blue." (*Moore*, l. c.)

This species differs only from the same sex of *E. appiades* on the upperside in having the space between the discal black bands of the forewing anteriorly brownish white ; on the underside the outer discal macular band of the forewing terminates anteriorly with white spots ; the inner band is formed of almost complete ring-spots as in *E. xiphiones*.

Mr. Butler in his Monograph of the genus states that *E. jahnu* is the female of this species, and gives the habitat of it as follows :—"♀, Darjeeling ; ♂, North India (*Moore*). ♂ ♀,

---

* Described as a distinct species under the name of *Adolias sedeva*
† In Proc. Zool. Soc. Lond., 1865, Mr. Moore correctly gave his *A. sedeva* as a synonym of *A. appiades*.

in British Museum, Sylhet and Darjeeling." The female of *E. balarama*, should it ever be discovered, is almost certain to have the outer discal band on both wings straight ; in *E. jahnu*, which I have no doubt whatever is the female of *E. sananda*, it is highly lunulate. My knowledge of *E. balarama* is confined to what has been published regarding it, but I have a suspicion that it is a "sport" only of *E. appiades*. Mr. Moore believes *E. balarama* to be a good species of which his *E. televa* is the female, but I cannot agree with him. *E. televa* is inseparable from the normal form of *E. appiades*, female, in which the white spots are obsolete.

504. Euthalia xiphiones, Butler.

Adolias xiphiones, Butler, Proc. Zool. Soc. Lond., 1868, p. 609, n. 60, pl. xlv, fig. 6, *male* ; *A. parvata*, Moore, Proc. Zool. Soc. Lond , 1878, p. 831, pl. lii, fig. 3, *female*.

HABITAT : Moulmein, Upper Tenasserim.

EXPANSE : ♂, 2·75 to 2·90 ; ♀, 2·75 to 3·20 inches.

DESCRIPTION : "MALE. Allied to *A.* [= *E.*] *apiades*, smaller. UPPERSIDE more obscure chestnut-fuscous, the discal lines of the *forewing* nearer together. *Hindwing* with the green marginal band much broader. UNDERSIDE, *forewing* yellowish at the base, the dots near the apex whitish. *Hindwing* with the entire ground-colour yellow, the spots of the anal area circled with blue, otherwise as in *E. apiades*. *Body* fuscous above, whitish below. Allied to *E. apiades* and *E. jahnu*, male [Mr. Butler here refers to *E. balarama*], but differing considerably from both." (*Butler*, l. c.) FEMALE. Differs from that sex of *E. appiades* in being smaller, the discal bands nearer together, the space between them on either side of the lower discoidal nervule always more or less whitish (in some examples of *E. appiades* also it is equally white), the outer edge of the inner black discal band also sometimes marked with whitish. UNDERSIDE having much the same differences as above, the discal bands on the *hindwing* somewhat more even.

In Major Marshall's collection are three males of this species taken by Captain C. T. Bingham in the Thoungyeen Forests, Upper Tenasserim, in December. They differ chiefly from *E. appiades* in that the marginal blue band is wider, entirely covering the outer discal black band from the anal angle to the discoidal nervule, and on the underside the inner discal band of the forewing is formed of almost complete ring-spots between the first median and lower discoidal nervules. There are also two females of this species from Mephly, one from Donat taken in January, two from the Upper Thoungyeen Forests taken in April, two from Thoungyeen taken in March, and one from Sekkan, Thoungyeen, taken in February, all captured by Captain C. T. Bingham, in Major Marshall's collection. They show considerable variation in the extent of the white markings between the discal bands of the forewing, and it appears to be a scantily white-marked example that Mr. Moore has described and figured as *E. parvata* as below.* *E. xiphiones* is a smaller species than *E. appiades*, and the male is blacker ; the female differs in the outline of the wings, the forewing having the apex more acute and the inner margin shorter than in *E. appiades*, but the colouration is the same, and the variations in extent of the white patches of the forewing are equally exhibited in both.

E. ramada, from the Malay peninsula, appears to belong to this group ; the male has the margin of the hindwing blue on the upperside, but the discal spots are not ringed with blue on the underside ; the description is appended.† The female is unknown.

E. laverna also from the Malay peninsula appears to be intermediate between this group and the next ; in outline it corresponds with this group, and the markings of the female are

---

* *Adolias parvata*, Moore, Proc. Zool. Soc. Lond., 1878, p. 831, pl. lii, fig. 3, *female*. HABITAT : Upper Tenasserim, Meetan, 3,000 ft (April). EXPANSE : *Female*, ? 75 inches. DESCRIPTION : "FEMALE. Allied to *A.* [= *E.*] *tedeva*, Moore. UPPERSIDE differs on the *forewing*, in the discal band being narrower, the costal portion only partially whitish, and the lower portion without the whitish inner border. UNDERSIDE, with the band on the *forewing* only partially white anteriorly, the lower portion with a slight white lunule to the inner border, and white point with black tip to outer border." (*Moore*, l. c.)

† *Euthalia ramada. Adolias ramada*, Moore, Trans. Ent. Soc. Lond., new series, vol. v, p. 69, n. 12, pl. iv, fig. 5, *male* (1859) ; id , Butler, Proc. Zool. Soc. Lond., 1868, p. 605, n. 37 ; *Euthalia ramada*, Distant, Rhop. Malay., p. 192, n. 8, pl. xiv, fig. 5, *male* (1883). HABITAT : Perak, Malacca. EXPANSE : 1·9 to 2·2 inches. DESCRIPTION : "MALE. UPPERSIDE dark glossy olive-brown, *forewing* with the discoidal marks black, olive-green within ; from posterior margin near angle upwards powdered with green, with a medial zig-zag black line. *Hindwing* with outer margin broadly from abdominal margin to near anterior angle blue, the anterior angle being pale brown,

somewhat similar, but the male has no blue border to the hindwing ; the description* is appended or reference.

Third Section. Males with the body very robust, the antennæ very long, more than half the length of the wing, the wings short, powerful, the apex of forewing acutely pointed, the anal angle of hindwing acutely pointed, and somewhat produced. The third subcostal nervule of the forewing arises nearer to the end of the cell in the typical species of this section than in the preceding.

The first two species have many features which approximate to the preceding section ; the body is only moderately robust, and the outline of the wings is intermediate between the two ; but the males have no blue border on the hindwing on the upperside, and scarcely a trace of blue rings to the marginal spots on the underside. The females so far as known have the underside of the hindwing broadly suffused with pale blue as in the preceding section, but the dark markings are far more prominent, and the outer discal line is highly lunulate and continued distinctly to the abdominal margin of the hindwing.

505. Euthalia adima, Moore.

Adolias adima, Moore, Horsfield and Moore, Cat. Lep. Mus. E. I. C., vol. i, p. 194, n. 392 (1857) ; id., Moore, Trans. Ent. Soc. Lond., new series, vol. v, p. 76, n. 29 (1859) ; *A. sedeva* (*male* only), Butler (*see* Moore), Proc. Zool. Soc. Lond., 1868, p. 609, n. 56.

HABITAT : Assam.

EXPANSE : ♂, 2·5 inches.

DESCRIPTION : "MALE : UPPERSIDE yellowish olive-brown, with two indistinct zig-zag lines crossing the disc of *both wings*, and markings about the base of the wings blackish.

with a submarginal medial zig-zag blackish line along its whole length. UNDERSIDE dusky ochreous, most dusky about the outer margins ; two transverse zigzag lines and discoidal marks blackish." The FEMALE is unknown.

" May be distinguished from the *male* of *A.* (= *E.*) *sedeva* in having the band on the outer margin of hindwing blue, whereas in *A. sedeva* the inner half is pure white." (*Moore*, l. c.)

" The nebulous gloss on the disc of the wings in this species varies from bluish green to violet grey ; its nearest ally is *A.* (= *E.*) *sedeva* [from Java], but the two insects are abundantly distinct." (*Butler*, l. c.)

* *Euthalia laverna*. *Adolias laverna*, Butler (part, —*female* only"), Cist. Ent., vol. i, p. 29 (1870) ; idem, id., Trans. Linn. Soc., Zoology, second series, vol. i, p. 539, n. 4 (1877) ; *Euthalia laverna*, Distant, Rhop. Malay., p. 119, n. 5 pl. xiv, fig. 7, *male*, p. 120, *woodcut of female* (1883). HABITAT : Penang, Malacca. EXPANSE : *Male*, 2·0 ; *female*, 2·4 inches. DESCRIPTION : " MALE. UPPERSIDE fuliginous-brown. *Forewing* with the inner margin and a broad medial transverse fascia, which is outwardly dentate and anteriorly bifurcate from median nervure to near costa, dark brown ; before and a little after the upper portion of this fascia the colour is paler than the remaining outer portion of wing, which contains a submarginal waved and broken black line not reaching posterior angle, where there is a dark brown patch ; there are also two basal black lines. *Hindwing* with the cell crossed by four black lines and a submarginal series of narrow linear black spots placed between the nervules. UNDERSIDE pale greenish, suffused with ochraceous. *Forewing* with the cell crossed by some black lines and a similar waved and broken line near its apex ; two spots beneath cell divided by the first median nervule ; a waved submarginal narrow black fascia starting from a subapical fuscous patch, which contains two whitish spots, and is inwardly margined by the same colour. *Hindwing* paler ; cell crossed by a looped line near its middle and a curved line near its apex—above the last is a short line beneath the base of lower subcostal nervule, a bent line above that nervule, and a looped line beneath the base of costal nervure ; two discal narrow waved ochraceous fasciæ, the outer one more distinct, from which to outer margin the colour is darker. *Body* and *legs* more or less concolourous with wings. FEMALE. UPPERSIDE pale brownish. *Forewing* with the cell crossed by four blackish lines, and with a curved line near apex ; beneath the cell are two spots divided by the first median nervule, the inner one larger ; a transverse series of contiguous, linear, greyish spots only divided by the nervules, their inner apices conical and outwardly margined with a waved and sinuated narrow dark brown fascia ; the two upper spots divided by the upper discoidal nervule are longest, and are preceded by a small whitish subcostal spot, the third spot is shorter than the fourth and fifth, and the lower one beneath the first median nervule is short and notched internally ; all these spots are more or less suffused with pale brownish, and the first, fourth and fifth possess an inner brown looped line. *Hindwing* with two pairs of looped lines crossing cell, the transverse series of large greyish spots as on *forewing*, but not extending to abdominal margin, and with their outer margins defined by a more angulated and inwardly dentate narrow fascia, which is again outwardly margined with greyish, thus dividing the outer dark margin into inwardly angulated spots. UNDERSIDE with the basal halves pale ochraceous ; cell of *forewing* marked as above ; cell of *hindwing* with the looped lines and adjacent markings as in corresponding wing of male ; the transverse series of spots more fused than above, the greyish colour extending to outer margin."

"The female, as Mr. Butler has remarked, bears a striking resemblance to a species of the next genus, *Tanaecia pulasara*, which is also found in this fauna." (*Distant*, l. c.)

* " Some confusion is likely to arise from a consultation of the original description of this species. Mr. Butler (Cist. Ent., vol. i, p. 29, 1870) described a male specimen from Borneo and a female specimen from Penang under the above name, and afterwards figured the first in his ' Lepid. Exot.,' pl. ix, fig. 5. On subsequently receiving both sexes from Malacca, he wrote (Trans. Linn. Soc., Zoology, second series, vol. i, p. 539 (1877), " I find that the male from Borneo figured in my ' Lepidoptera Exotica' is a distinct species," thus electing to make the Penang female the type, of which the only description is—' *Female*. Both wings coloured as in *Tanaecia pulasara*.' " (*Distant*, l. c.)

UNDERSIDE pale ferruginous, palest at the base of *forewing*, with inner row of lunulated marks and outer row of spots crossing the disc of *both wings*, and markings at the base of the wings, black, the spots being deepest from anal angle, where they are margined with bluish-white ; abdominal margin broadly, and about anal angle somewhat green."

"The male of *Adolias* [= *Euthalia*] *adima* may at once be distinguished from *A.* [= *E.*] *apiades* by its plain brown upperside." (*Moore*, l. c. in Cat. Lep. Mus. E. I. C.)

E. adima is unknown to me, but is apparently nearest allied to *E. jahnu*. Mr. Butler (l. c.) places *E. adima* as a synonym of *E. sedeva*, remarking that " *E. sedeva* is not the female of *E. apiades* ; the latter has no large white spots upon the upper surface of the wings." I have above pointed out that the female of *E. apiades* often has large white spots, and I have no doubt that *E. sedeva* is one of the varietal forms of the female of that species. Mr. Moore agrees with me in considering that *E. sedeva* is not the female of *E. adima*. The female of *E. adima* is at present unknown.

506. **Euthalia jahnu**, Moore.

Adolias jahnu, Moore, Horsfield and Moore, Cat. Lep. Mus. E. I. C., vol. i, p. 192, n. 387 (1857); id., Moore, Trans. Ent. Soc. Lond., new series, vol. v, p. 74, pl. vii, fig. 1, *female* (1859); id. (*female only*), Butler, Proc. Zool. Soc. Lond., 1868, p. 609, n. 58; id., Moore, Proc. Zool. Soc. Lond., 1878, p. 832; *Adolias sananda*, Moore, Trans. Ent. Soc. Lond., new series, vol. v, p. 76, n. 30, pl. vii, fig. 3, *male* (1859); id., Butler, Proc. Zool. Soc. Lond , 1868, p. 609, n. 57.

HABITAT : North India, Sikkim, Assam, Sylhet, Chittagong, Upper Tenasserim.

EXPANSE : ♂, 2·4 to 2·8 ; ♀, 3·1 to 3·7 inches.

DESCRIPTION : "MALE [*A. sananda*]. Allied to *A.* [= *E.*] *adima*, but differs in having the UPPERSIDE purplish olive-brown, and the transverse zig-zag lines of *both wings* are wider apart and well defined. The UNDERSIDE differs in having the markings much less defined, and the *hindwing* is devoid of the greenish colour of the abdominal margin, and the spots are without the bluish borders." (*Moore*, l. c. in Trans. Ent. Soc. Lond.) "FEMALE [*A. jahnu*]. UPPERSIDE obscure brown, [very obscurely] glossed with green. *Forewing* falcate, with two indistinct black zig-zag lines across the disc, tinged with white anteriorly ; markings at base of wing large and indistinct. *Hindwing* with two indistinct black zig-zag lines across the disc, also indistinct black basal marks. UNDERSIDE ochreous brown, with transverse zig-zag black lines and basal marks as above ; apex of *forewing* with a white spot and a blackish patch ; exterior margin dusky, basal half of *hindwing*, and along the outer zig-zag line, with a bluish-grey tinge." (*Moore*, l. c. in Cat. Lep. Mus. E. I. C.)

Mr. Butler describes a variety of *E. jahnu* from Sylhet as follows : " MALE. *Hindwing* with about four squamiform blue marginal spots near the anal angle." I have no idea what species he is comparing this variety with, unless it be *E. balarama*, which he erroneously in my opinion identifies as the male of *E. jahnu*. Mr. Moore also agrees with me in referring *E. jahnu* and *E. sananda* to one species.

The male of *E. jahnu* is quite distinct from any Indian species, except *E. adima*, which I have not seen. On the upperside it is of a deep olivous purple, with the usual basal and cellular markings on both wings, and with two common zigzag or lunulated black discal bands. The underside is very similar to that of *E. apiades*, but the outer series of black dots on the hindwing are not surrounded with blue as in that species. The description of the female is rather meagre, so I have re-described it as follows :—UPPERSIDE brown. *Forewing* with a fine black line at the base of the cell continued to the submedian nervure, a pair of lines across the middle of the cell forming a rounded spot, another pair at the end of the cell, the outer one constricted at the lower discoidal nervule, the enclosed space being paler than the ground, a short black line at the base of the first median interspace, a large oval spot in the submedian interspace just within the point where the first median nervule is given off, outwardly constricted on the fold. A discal pair of fuscous bands formed of lunules placed between the nervules, the apex of each lunule directed inwards, the inner band broad, inwardly diffused, starting from the subcostal nervure to the third median nervule and directed obliquely outwards, thence parallel to the outer margin, ending at the submedian nervure; the outer band sharply defined, springing from a black apical oblong patch, and ending on the submedian nervure, the space between the two bands paler, especially anteriorly, than the ground, and bearing a series of sagittate marks between the veins, the upper one in the subcostal interspace alone being prominent, the rest always obscure, sometimes obsolete; the outer margin diffusedly black. *Hindwing* with an oval black-lined spot at the base of the cell, another closing the cell, and with other small black markings around it; the two discal bands as in the forewing. UNDERSIDE, *forewing* ochreous, the basal half of the costa and the base of the wing greyish blue; the markings as above, but the space between the discal bands anteriorly whitish, the outer band often with whitish lunules placed inwardly against it; a whitish diffused spot at the apex. *Hindwing* washed throughout with greyish blue, except the area beyond the inner discal band to the margin from the costa decreasingly towards the anal angle which is ochreous; markings as on upperside, an additional long oval black ring-spot in the subcostal interspace. Mr. Moore's figure of the female shows the apex of the forewing to be more produced than in any specimen I have seen.

E. jahnu does not appear to be a very rare species. I have taken both sexes in Sikkim, in October; it occurs also in Assam, Sylhet, Cachar, Chittagong and Upper Tenasserim, where Limborg obtained it at Hatsiega and Taoo, 3,000—5,000 feet; in Major Marshall's collection also are males taken in March, and in the autumn in the Thoungyeen forests, and females in the Donat range in April, in the Thoungyeen forests in March and April, and at Meplay in January, all by Captain C. T. Bingham.

The next two species have a broad irrorated greyish discal band across both wings, diffused on a blackish ground in the males, defined with dusky lines on a brown ground in the females; the females are very similar to those of the two preceding species; but on the underside the bluish suffusion of the hindwing is more restricted, being usually confined to the abdominal third of the wing.

507. **Euthalia kesava**, Moore.

Adolias kesava, Moore, Trans. Ent. Soc. Lond., new series, vol. v. p. 67, n. 9, pl. iii. fig. 5, *male* and *female* (1859); id., Butler, Proc. Zool. Soc. Lond., 1868, p. 605, n. 31; id., Moore, Proc. Zool. Soc. Lond., 1865, p. 766.*

HABITAT: Sikkim, Bhutan, Assam, Sylhet, Cachar.

EXPANSE: ♂, 2·45 to 2·70; ♀, 2·8 to 3·4 inches.

DESCRIPTION: " MALE. UPPERSIDE, dark dusky brown, powdered across the disc with green [the powdering would be better described as grey or whitish]. UNDERSIDE yellowish-ochreous, more dusky about the margins, with black discoidal marks; two indistinct transverse blackish lines across the disc; below discoidal cell of *forewing* a small patch of black [a white spot on the inner band in second median interspace]. FEMALE. UPPERSIDE olive-brown. *Forewing* with a transverse row of irregular [white] spots, the first and second long, third shortest, fourth and fifth equal, but not so long as the two first, all indented on their outer margin, with the point inwards. *Hindwing* with two blackish transverse zig-zag lines. Discoidal marks blackish. UNDERSIDE ochreous, dusky about the margins. *Forewing* marked as in upperside, but with some suffused white at the apex, and a small patch of black below the discoidal cell, and another near the posterior angle. *Hindwing* with the transverse zig-zag lines tinged with whitish within; broadly from the base of wing along abdominal margin to anal angle greenish-grey. Discoidal marks black." (*Moore*, l. c.)

E. kesava is a very distinct species, and like *E. anosia* has the upperside powdered with grey, this powdering however being confined in the forewing to a broad discal band, broader on the hindwing, and almost reaching the outer margin towards the anal angle;

---

* Mr. Moore at this date considered that his description and figure of *E. kesava* applied to the "male only," he writes me now, however, that his figures of both sexes of this species "are quite correct." I take this opportunity of thanking him for writing to me very fully on the various disputed points regarding the opposite sexes of many of the species of the genus.

the usual black marks in the cell and below it in both wings. Underside bright ochreous yellow, the outer margins narrowly black, the discoidal marks very clear and sharply defined, two suffused black discal lines, the outer one on the forewing widening out into two spots, the lower the larger, towards the anal angle, the inner with a white spot in the second median interspace semi-hyaline and often visible on the upperside through transparency. The female is very variable in the width of the pale discal band on the forewing, and the extent of the semi-hyaline whitish patches, in some specimens they are hardly visible, in others the entire band as far as the first median nervule consists of elongate whitish patches divided by the veins and crossed by a series of diffused brownish lunules. The form figured and described by Moore occurs in Sylhet and Cachar, and even there the space between the discal bands on the forewing is not usually as white as described ; the Sikkim form, which appears to be fairly constant, is dusky brown on the upperside, with a discal band of grey powdering across both wings, on which is placed a black zig-zag line corresponding to the outer discal band on the underside of the male, the inner discal band of the male below represented in the female by a series of highly irregularly-placed pale spots, which are white and very prominent on the underside, and variable in number.

Mr. Butler adds the following to *E. kesava* :—" Sub-species ♂. Discal area fuscous, with a tendency to purple (not to greenish), with a lunule and spot beyond the termination of the cell of the forewing. ♂, East Indies."

E. kesava is a common species at low elevations in Sikkim throughout the year, and occurs eastwards as far as Upper Assam, also in Sylhet and Cachar.

508. **Euthalia discispilota,** Moore.

Adolias discispilota, Moore, Proc. Zool. Soc. Lond., 1878, p. 831.

HABITAT : Upper Tenasserim, Moolai 3,000 to 6,000 feet.

EXPANSE : 2·2 inches (2·4 on plate).

DESCRIPTION : " Allied to *E. kesava*. FEMALE, smaller in size. UPPERSIDE, with the borders uniformly greyish brown ; the transverse discal band with less sinuous dusky outer border ; the whitish spot between the lower subcostal branches, and the spot between the upper median branches prominent. UNDERSIDE, paler ; markings similar, with less blue along abdominal border." (*Moore,* l. c.)

In Major Marshall's collection are two specimens from Upper Tenasserim, a worn male taken by Captain C. T. Bingham in the Donat range in December, and a female from the Thoungyeen forests in September, which, I think, are referable to this species. The male appears to have the grey-powdered discal bands of the upperside less distinct, more diffused, and of a greenish colour ; the underside is yellowish brown, tinged with greenish basally, the two discal bands broader and more diffused. The female, which measures 2·8 inches in expanse, is not distinguishable in its markings from some examples of that sex of *E. kesava*. As pointed out under *E. kesava*, the female is very variable.

In the next three species the males are almost uniform in the colouration of the upperside, the discal pale band being scarcely paler than the rest of the wing, but distinctly divided at the costa by a diffused darker patch ; the females have a pale discal band on both wings, but much whiter than in the preceding species, and on the forewing distinctly divided at the costa by a dark patch ; the underside in these and in all the following species is brown, not ochreous, as in the preceding species.

All three species are unknown to me, except from descriptions and figures, and it is doubtful whether any of them really occur within Indian limits.

509. **Euthalia alpheda,** Godart.

Nymphalis alpheda, Godart, Enc. Méth., vol. ix, p. 384, n. 106 (1823) ; *Adolias alpheda,* Moore, Trans. Ent. Soc. Lond., new series, vol. v, p. 66, n. 6, pl. iii, fig. 4, *male* and *female* (1872) ; idem, id., Proc. Zool. Soc. Lond., 1865, p. 765, id., Butler, Proc. Zool. Soc. Lond., 1868, p. 601, n. 29.

HABITAT : Bengal (*Godart* and *Moore*) ; North India (*Butler*) ; Sikkim (*Kirby*), Java.

EXPANSE : ♂, 2·7 ; ♀, 3·3 inches.

DESCRIPTION : "May be distinguished by the MALE having the UPPERSIDE dark olive green, with a pinky tinge broadly on anterior margin of *hindwing*, and by the deep greenish grey of the UNDERSIDE, and having a greenish gloss over the anterior half of the wings ; also an indistinct white patch at and near the apex [of the *forewing*]. The FEMALE by the very broad whitish band of the UPPERSIDE of the *forewing*, and by the glaucous white UNDERSIDE, and ochreous marking." (*Moore*, l. c. in Trans. Ent. Soc. Lond.)

E. alpheda has been recorded from India by the various authors given above, but its occurrence within our borders must, I think, be considered doubtful. From Mr. Moore's figure the male appears to be very closely allied to *E. jama*, but lacks the white markings on both sides of the forewing ; the description of *E. jama* given by Mr. Distant would apparently almost apply to this species. The female is very different from that sex of *E. jama*, having a broad white discal band across the forewing enclosing a dark spot in the second median interspace, and bifurcated above the lower discoidal nervule. The discal bands of the hindwing are wider apart, the space between them paler than the ground-colour.

510. **Euthalia parta**, Moore.

Adolias parta, Moore, Horsfield and Moore, Cat. Lep. Mus. E. I. C., vol. i, p. 185, n. 373 (1857) ; id., Moore, Trans. Ent. Soc. Lond., new series, vol. v, p. 63, n. 7, pl. iii, fig. 1, *male and female* (1859) ; id., Butler, Proc. Zool. Soc. Lond., 1868, p. 603, n. 76 ; *Adolias apicalis*, Vollenhoven, Tijd. voor. Ent., vol. v, p. 186, n. 5, pl. x, fig. i, *male* (1862).

HABITAT : India (*Butler*), Borneo.

EXPANSE : ♂, 2·37 to 2·90 ; ♀, 2·90 inches.

DESCRIPTION : "MALE. UPPERSIDE dark brown, with a vinaceous tinge. *Forewing* with a paler transverse band, margined broadly on both sides with black, the anterior portion within, from costal margin on both sides, with a series of small white patches ; marks within discoidal cell black, with dark brown centres. *Hindwing* with an inner blackish band and outer row of small black spots. UNDERSIDE paler, marked as above. FEMALE. UPPERSIDE pale brown. *Forewing* with broad whitish curved transverse band, with patch on costa, and dark margins. *Hindwing* with rather broad inner band, and outer zigzag line, the point between each vein with a minute darker dot ; space between inner band and base tinged with white ; marks at base of wings blackish. UNDERSIDE pale dull ochreous, with paler margins ; markings as above, but very indistinct." (*Moore*, l. c. in Cat. Lep. Mus. E. I. C.)

This species is unknown to me. I include it on Mr. Butler's identification, but its occurrence in India is extremely doubtful. He says of it that "the anal angle of the hindwing varies slightly in different individuals of the male."

511. **Euthalia somadeva**, Felder.

Adolias somadeva, Felder, Reise Novara, Lep., vol. iii, p. 437, n. 691 (1866) ; id., Butler, Proc. Zool. Soc. Lond., 1868, p. 602, n. 78.

HABITAT : North India.

EXPANSE : Not given.

DESCRIPTION : "FEMALE. UPPERSIDE as in *A*, [= *E*.] *aconthea*, but the cellular markings of the *forewing* broader, the fascia altogether opalescent-whitish, inwardly deeply cut into (the segment indeed situated between the lower discoidal and third median nervules inwardly truncate), outwardly much more acutely indented, narrowly and equally defined with fuscous, and moreover with a powdery retired whitish streak, in the middle divided by a shortened irregular submacular fuscous fascia, within this powdered with fuscous. *Hindwing* with the disco-cellular markings much narrower than in *A. aconthea*, the cellular separated into two minute [markings], a whitish fascia inwardly increasingly divided within by another submacular diffuse fuscous [fascia], inwardly about the veins alone and unequally excised, outwardly as in the forewing, but equally defined. UNDERSIDE ochraceous. *Forewing* with the fascia of the upperside, but opaline-whitish, outwardly more narrowly circled with fuscous, an l immediately beyond this cincture another marginal ill-defined fascia opaline-whitish, but more violascent. *Hindwing* with the basal markings almost as in *A. acanthea*, but the subcostal longer, the fascia of the upperside but opaline-whitish, divided by another ochraceous [fascia], the black dots on the folds near to the fuscous cincture scarcely conspicuous, the border immediately beyond this much paler."

"Larger than the Javan *A. acanthea*, Cramer ; the inner margin of both wings longer, the outer margin of the forewing less curved." (*Felder*, l. c.)

This species is quite unknown to me and also to Mr. Moore. The male will probably generally resemble that sex of *A. acanthea*, which is of the same type as the male of *A. acontius* ; the former is however nearly uniform paler brown on the upperside with darker dentate discal bands, the space enclosed between them being scarcely perceptibly paler than the rest of the wing, and the discal series of white spots is obsolete. On the underside the discal dark bands of the forewing are continuous dentate lines, not series of dentate spots ; in Cramer's figure these lines are also continuous on the hindwing, but in a male specimen from Java in the Indian Museum, Calcutta, the inner line is obsolete and the outer is represented by a series of dots placed on the folds.

The remaining species of the genus are typical of the robust-bodied section ; in almost all of them the male has some small white discal spots or streaks beyond the cell of the forewing ; and the female has a more or less prominent oblique white discal band on the forewing. The underside in both sexes is pale brown, and in the females the dark discal bands of the hindwing are more obsolete, and the bluish suffusion when present is on the *outer* margin, except in the first species, *E. acontius*, in which it covers almost the entire wing.

In *E. acontius* the female has in addition to the white oblique discal fascia of the forewing a broad white discal band on both wings, in which the discal fascia of the forewing is merged at its lower end.

512. Euthalia acontius, Hewitson.

Adolias acontius, Hewitson, Ann. and Mag. of Nat. Hist., fourth series, vol. xiv. p. 357 (1874); idem, id., Ex. Butt., vol. v, *Adolias* pl. iv, fig. 11, *female* (1875) ; id., Wood-Mason and de Nicéville, Journ A. S. B., vol. l, pt. ii, p. 247, n. 42 (1881) ; *Tanaecia acontius*, Moore, Proc. Zool. Soc. Lond., 1877, p. 586.

HABITAT : South Andamans.

EXPANSE : ♂, 2·72 to 2·80 ; ♀, 3·1 to 3·4 inches.

DESCRIPTION : "MALE. UPPERSIDE almost black, the ground-colour being very dark brown of a bronzy tint, and the prominent cellular and basal marks, the outer margins, and the common discal and submarginal submacular bands velvety-black, the former of the two last-named bounded externally at its anterior end by a series of four indistinct U-shaped white marks, and the latter provided at its inner and anterior extremity with two small elongated subcostal white spots (the posterior of which is the larger), and, in the hindwing, composed of distinct subelongate spots each with an inconspicuous dash paler than the surrounding ground-colour at either end. The *hindwing* strongly glossed with dark greenish-purple anteriorly. UNDERSIDE much as in *A.* [=*E.*] *garuda*, but *both wings* more strongly glossed with amethyst-purple submarginally, and having their basal half coloured greyish-green and conspicuously marked with black as in the female." (*Wood-Mason* and *de Nicéville*, l. c.)

"FEMALE. UPPERSIDE dark rufous brown. *Forewing* with the usual spots in the cell : crossed from the middle of the costal margin to a little beyond the first median nervule (towards the anal angle) by a band (broader as it proceeds) of seven white spots—the first minute, the last, which is below the median nervure, small : a band of three spots, commencing near the apex, joins the band just described at its fourth spot : crossed towards the outer margin by a series of black pyramidal spots, bordered inwardly (between them and the white band) by lilac ; the last black spot near the anal angle bordered on both sides with lilac. *Hindwing* crossed beyond the middle by a broad lilac band, irrorated with white and bordered outwardly by a series of lunular black spots, which have below them hastate lilac spots. UNDERSIDE lilac-white. *Forewing* with the bands as above, bordered by pale ochreous brown, *Hindwing* with five subbasal spots, bordered with black ; the transverse band indistinct, except near the costal margin, where it has a rufous border on both sides." (*Hewitson*, l. c. in Ann. and Mag. of Nat. Hist.)

E. acontius is a rare species even in the Andaman Isles, to which it seems to be confined. The male is hardly distinguishable on the upperside from *E. teutoides*, but all the markings on the underside are more prominent, and there is a complete inner discal series of bluish-white lunules inwardly edged with dark brown on the forewing, and the wings are glossed with purple. The female is widely different from any species of this group, having a broad white band across the disc of both wings on both upper and under sides.

E. decorata is a somewhat allied species occurring in the Malay peninsula. The description of it is given below. *

In the next species, *E. garuda*, the male is very similar to that of *E. acontius*, but in the female the white discal band 'of the forewing is reduced to a short series of white spots along the inner edge of the pale discal area from the cell to the second median nervule, and the hindwing has no white markings.

513. **Euthalia garuda**, Moore. (VOL. I, PLATE II, LARVA).

Adolias garuda, Moore, Horsfield and Moore, Cat. Lep. Mus. E. I. C., vol. i, p. 186, n. 371, pl. xi, figs. 2, *larva* ; *2a, pupa* (1857) ; idem, id., Trans. Ent. Soc. Lond., new series, vol. v, p. 64, n. 3, pl. iii, fig. 2, *male* and *female* (1859) ; id., Butler, Proc. Zool. Soc. Lond., 1868, p. 603, n. 21 ; *Euthalia garuda*, Moore, Lep. Ceyl., vol. i, p. 32, pl. xvi, figs. 2, *male* ; *2a, female* (1881) ; id., Distant, Rhop. Malay., p. 117, n. 3, pl. xiv, fig. 1, *male* ; *2, female* (1883).

HABITAT : India, Ceylon, Burma, Province Wellesley, Malacca, Java.

EXPANSE : ♂, 2·40 to 2·85 ; ♀, 2·9 to 3·3 inches.

DESCRIPTION : " MALE : UPPERSIDE glossy greenish-brown. *Forewing* with costal margin to its middle, a broad irregular band from thence to posterior margin, black, the latter bordered exteriorly, anteriorly from costal nervure, with five white spots ; two small white spots on costal margin one-fourth from the apex ; exterior margin and submarginal band blackish ; within discoidal cell, first a short line, then two reniform marks, black. *Hindwing* with curved dentate blackish band from middle of anterior margin to near abdominal margin ; a submarginal row of small deep black spots ; exterior margin near anal angle blackish ; within discoidal cell some black markings, and two small black spots without, one above, the other below the cell. UNDERSIDE light chocolate-brown, greyish towards the base. *Forewing* with black marks within discoidal cell as above, and a small black spot below it ; the row of five white spots and the two apical spots as above ; from the latter, across the disc to posterior margin, runs a narrow interrupted black band ; at the apex and along the exterior margin some bluish-grey spots. *Hindwing* with four lines within discoidal cell, a small spot, and two oval marks above, black ; an indistinct band across the disc ; submarginal row of black spots as above ; a patch of bluish-grey at anterior angle. FEMALE pale brown, with a greenish gloss. UPPERSIDE with markings as in male, but less defined ; the row of white spots of the *forewing* are larger, and the submarginal row of black spots on the *hindwing* are also larger than in the male. UNDERSIDE as in that of the male. Wings shaped as in *Adolias* [=*Euthalia*] *acontius*." (*Moore*, l. c. in Cat. Lep. Mus. E, I. C.)

---

* *Euthalia decorata*. *Adolias decoratus*, Butler, Proc. Zool. Soc. Lond., 1868, p. 605, n. 39, pl. xlv, figs. 7, *male* ; 9, *female* ; *Euthalia decorata*, Distant, Rhop. Malay., p. 122, n. 7 (with a woodcut of a *female*), pl. xiv, fig. 9, *male* (1883). HABITAT : Province Wellesley, Singapore. EXPANSE : *Male*, 2·15 to 2·25 ; *female*, 2·90 to 3·00 inches. DESCRIPTION : " MALE. UPPERSIDE fuscous. *Forewing* with the costa greenish, the usual basal markings, an irregular hastate green discal band including fuscous macular lituræ, outwardly defined with whitish and margined with fuscous, beyond with pale scales slightly margined with fuscous. *Hindwing* with a regular fascia near the apex snowy-white outwardly defined with a lunular line, at the apex outwardly bordered by three violet lunules, the anal area squarely bronzy-green. UNDERSIDE, *both wings* yellowish, a common band bronzy-whitish, the apex of the forewing bronzy-green. FEMALE. Wings much larger. UPPERSIDE fuscous, the band much broader whitish, and in the *hindwing* inwardly more irregular. UNDERSIDE with the band as on upperside green, margined with opalescent fuscous ; the basal area yellow, the markings blackish-fuscous ; the outer margin to the band altogether whitish opale-cent. *Body* fuscous above, whitish below "

" Allied to *A. zalia*, Moore, from Java, but very distinct ; the underside of the male much like that of *A. bipunctata*, Vollenhoven, from Borneo." (*Butler*, l. c.)

" The males of this species vary in hue ; specimens from Province Wellesley being paler than the Singapore type as delineated by Mr. Butler ; the greyish fascia to the forewing of the former also appears to be slightly broader than that as portrayed in the latter." (*Distant*, l. c.)

A subspecies occurring both in North and South India has been described by Mr. Butler as follows :—" The wings altogether paler fulvescent, the discal spots often obsolete. The figure of the female given by Mr. Moore is applicable to this form of the species, although the discal spots are here distinct." (*Butler*, l. c.)

" LARVA green, with ten pairs of long laterally-projecting very delicate branched green spines ; a pale dorsal line with blue and white spots, head red spotted. PUPA green, thick, keeled along the back, broadly triangular across the middle ; abdominal end short, tubercular at tip, thoracic end long, ending in two tubercular points ; a band across the triangular back, some thoracic spots, and the tubercular points yellow ; a lateral row of black dots on abdomen." (*Moore*, l. c. in Lep. Cey.) The larva is figured on Plate II of the first volume of this work. It feeds on the mango, " *Trophis aspera* and on a species of *Bryonia*." (*Hardwicke*.)

E. garuda is the commonest and most wide-spread species of the genus occurring in India. It is met with throughout the outer ranges of the Himalayas and in the plains, except in the desert tracts, and occurs in Ceylon, Burma, the Malay Peninsula and Java. The female shows some slight variations, the ground-colour in some specimens is paler than in others, and the discal series of white spots is reduced to three placed above the lower discoidal nervule in some specimens, in others the series consists of seven. I have frequently bred the larva in Calcutta from mango trees ; the butterflies frequent these trees, and usually settle with wings widely spread open, sometimes on the underside of a leaf.

In the next two species the males are widely different ; the male of *E. vasanta* very closely resembles those of *E. acontius* and *E. garuda*, while that of *E. phemius* differs both in the character of the white discal markings of the forewing, which consist of fine straight parallel streaks, and in the hindwing having a wide blue patch on the outer border ; but the females are very similarly marked, they have a prominent oblique white macular band from the middle of the costa of the forewing to the first median nervule close to the outer margin, very similar to the band in many species of *Lethe* ; this band is much wider in *E. phemius* than in *E. vasanta*, but similar in shape and character in both.

514. **Euthalia vasanta**, Moore.

Adolias vasanta, Moore, Trans. Ent. Soc. Lond., new series, vol. v, p. 77, n. 33, pl. vii, fig. 2, *female* (1859) ; id , Butler, Proc. Zool. Soc. Lond., 1868, p. 600, n. 17; *Euthalia vasanta*, Moore, Lep. Cey , vol. i, p. 33, pl. xvii, figs. 2, *male* ; 2a, *female* ; 2b, *larva* and *pupa* (1881).

HABITAT : Ceylon.

EXPANSE : ♂, 2·4 to 2·7 : ♀, 2·9 to 3·3 inches.

DESCRIPTION : "MALE. UPPERSIDE blackish purple-brown. *Forewing* with the discal area transversely glossed with greenish-brown and sinuously bordered with black, discoidal black-lined marks and streaks below the cell. *Hindwing* with anal area greenish glossed, discoidal black-lined marks, a discal curved black sinuous band, and marginal row of small black spots. UNDERSIDE ochreous-grey, brownish externally, markings as above, less distinct. FEMALE. UPPERSIDE olive-brown. *Forewing* with an outwardly oblique discal macular white band ; other markings and UNDERSIDE as in male, but paler."

" LARVA dark green, with ten pairs of long paler green laterally-projecting branched spines ; a whitish dorsal line and a lateral row of yellow dots, the segments crossed by a purple line. Feeds on *Mangifera*. PUPA short, green, keeled along the back, broadly triangular across the middle ; a lateral band, a band across the triangular back, and thoracic black-bordered spots yellow ; a lateral abdominal row of black dots." (*Moore*, l. c. in Lep. Cey.)

E. vasanta is apparently confined to the island of Ceylon, where it is " common at Colombo, about mango and cashew-trees. Flight rapid. Settles on the leaves and on the ground" (*Hutchison*). " Plentiful at Galle and Kandy" (*Wade*). The male is very close indeed to *E. garuda*, but the upperside is of a distinct greenish hue, and the discal and apical white spots of the forewing are always smaller, often obsolescent or absent entirely. The underside is usually paler. The female is conspicuously different from that sex of *E. garuda*, as it has an oblique white macular band crossing the forewing from the middle of the costa to near the margin above the first median nervule.

The males of *E. acontius*, *E. garuda* and *E. vasanta*, which are almost identical on the upperside, with the exception that *E. garuda* is on the whole rather paler than the others, may be separated by the following characters of the underside :—

E. acontius has on the inner edge of the pale discal area a complete series of diffused bluish white lunules, the upper of which bear the pure white spots corresponding with those of the upperside ; these bluish white lunules are moreover inwardly defined with dusky ferruginous.

E. garuda has no trace of the bluish white lunules ; the white spots are much more sharply defined, and consist of a curved series of five kidney-shaped spots on an uniform pale brown ground.

E. vasanta also has no trace of the bluish white lunules ; the white spots are four in number (that below the second median nervule being absent), and are arranged in a straight but oblique series from the costa; the ground is not pure brown throughout, but is suffused with greyish on the basal half.

515. **Euthalia phemius**, Doubleday, Hewitson.

Ilanus phemius, Doubleday, Hewitson, Gen. Diurn. Lep., vol. ii. pl. xli. fig. 4. *male* (1850) ; *Adolias phemius*, Westwood, id., p. 291, n. 13; Id., Moore, Trans. Ent. Soc. Lond., new series, vol. v, p. 65. n. 4. pl. iii, fig. 3. *male* (*nec* female), 1859 ; *A. sancara*, Moore, Horsfield and Moore. Cat. Lep. Mus. E. I. C., vol. i, p. 195, n. 394 (1857) ; id., Moore, Trans. Ent. Soc. Lond., new series, vol. v. p. 78, n. 34, pl. ix, fig. 1, *female* (1859); id., Butler, Proc. Zool. Soc. Lond., 1868, p. 602, n. 18 ; *A. hesperus* (part), idem, id., p. 604, n. 32.

HABITAT : Sikkim, Bhutan, Assam, Sylhet, Cachar, Khasi and Naga Hills, China (*Butler*).

EXPANSE : ♂, 2·5 to 2·9 ; ♀, 3·12 to 3·40 inches.

DESCRIPTION : "MALE. UPPERSIDE dark brown. *Forewing* with indistinct black submarginal band, marks within discoidal cell, and two spots and large patch below the cell ; a series of longitudinal narrow white lines tapering from costal margin near the apex to middle of wing. *Hindwing* with basal two-thirds blackish ; from anal angle curving broadly upwards to above middle of exterior margin light blue-green, the margin being white, and a black line along the extreme exterior margin, which is much dentated. Narrow *cilia* white. UNDERSIDE dark brown, paler at the base. *Forewing* with longitudinal white lines, discoidal marks and black submarginal band as above. *Hindwing* with black discoidal marks, indistinct blackish submarginal band ; the bluish-green and white marginal band narrower, and with a small black spot at anal angle ; extreme margin black, with narrow white *cilia*." (*Moore*, l. c. in Trans. Ent. Soc. Lond.) FEMALE. "UPPERSIDE brown. *Forewing* with an outward oblique white band from middle of costal margin to near posterior margin above the angle ; also two small white spots near the apex ; an indistinct blackish transverse band from near apex of forewing to abdominal margin [of hindwing] ; also an indistinct narrow submarginal blackish band on the *hindwing* ; black marks within the discoidal cell. UNDERSIDE greyish-brown, greyer at the base and along exterior margins ; marked as above." (*Moore*, l. c. in Cat. Lep. Mus. E. I. C.)

Much confusion has arisen regarding this species. The male was first figured and named in the Genera of Diurnal Lepidoptera. In 1859 Mr. Moore, in monography the genus, describes and figures the male correctly,[*] but describes and figures as its female what appears to me to be the female of *E. jama*. He also at the same time describes both sexes and figures one sex only, which sex is not stated, of a new species which he names *A. sancara*, it being really the female of *E. phemius*. I can only conjecture that he must have erroneously

* Mr. Moore writes me on the subject that the male and female of *E. phemius* are correctly figured in his Monograph, and that the type specimens of *E. sancara* are both females, that supposed to be the male he has since discovered to be a female, thus proving my conjecture regarding the supposed opposite sexes of Mr. Moore's species being one sex only to be correct. He goes on to say that the male of *E. sancara* "should be something like that sex of *E. vasanta*." I am sorry we differ so widely regarding the sexes of *E. phemius*, but I feel quite sure that I have correctly identified them.

described as male and female of *A. sancara*, two female specimens. At the end of his monograph he gives the *Papilio hesperus* of Fabricius as an *Adolias*, in which course he is followed by Butler in 1868, who gives *phemius* as a synonym of that species, but in the following year places *hesperus* in the genus *Aterica* as a synonym of *dædalus*, which is an African species.*

E. phemius is somewhat rare in Sikkim, but I have taken both sexes at low elevations in October. To the eastwards it occurs as far as Sibsagar, but seems to be nowhere common.

A species of *Euthalia* has been described under the name of *E. mahadeva*, which apparently is allied to *E. phemius*, but it lacks the fine white discal streaks of the forewing. The locality of the species is unknown ; the description is appended for reference.†

The next species *E. jama* has in both sexes the fine white discal streaks on the forewing which characterise the male only of *E. phemius* ; the female has no other white discal markings besides these. In both sexes the dark band which *outwardly* bounds the pale discal area of the forewing is continuous with the band which *inwardly* defines that area on the hindwing, forming a continuous nearly straight dark band from near the apex of the forewing to the middle of the abdominal margin of the hindwing as in the females of *E. satropaces* and *E. telchinia* ; the underside is very similar to that of *E. garuda* in both sexes.

516. **Euthalia jama,** Felder.

Adolias jama, Felder, Reise Novara, Lep., vol. iii, p. 431, n 690 (1866) ; id., Butler, Proc. Zool. Soc. Lond., 1868. p. 604, n. 20 ; idem, id., Trans. Linn. Soc., Zoology, second series, vol. i, p. 539, n. 3 (1877) ; *Euthalia alphæda,* var. *jaina,* Kirby, Syn. Cat. Diurn. Lep , p. 254 (1871).

HABITAT : N. India, Sikkim, Bhutan, Assam, Naga Hills, Cachar, Malacca interior, Banca.

EXPANSE : ♂, 2·6 to 2·8 ; ♀, 3·1 to 3·6 inches.

DESCRIPTION : "MALE. UPPERSIDE as in *A.* [=*E.*] *alphæda,* but much less bronze tinted. *Forewing* with the fasciæ narrower, near the interior a whitish patch almost as in *A. phemius* of longitudinal spots, strongly divided on the folds, bifurcate towards the costa, more or less squeezed out, with a whitish apical powdery spot. *Hindwing* with the discal fascia broader than in *A. alphæda.* UNDERSIDE as in the species mentioned, but yellowish-brown, much paler at the base, the patch of the *forewing* very distinct. FEMALE. UPPERSIDE darker than in *A. alphæda. Forewing* with the discal fascia narrower, not at all powdered with white, nevertheless having the whitish bifid patch very distinct. *Hindwing* with the discal fascia broader, the drawn back [lunulated] streak more distant from the margin. UNDERSIDE as in the male, but much more brightly coloured."

"A local form of the Javan *A. alphæda,* Godart." (*Felder,* l. c.)

E. jama is a very distinct species, the male resembling *E. garuda* in general appearance, but the upperside has a black discal band crossing both wings almost in a straight line, commencing near the apex of the forewing (against which is placed outwardly a pale diffused patch) continued to the middle of the abdominal fold of the hindwing, widest on the inner margin of the forewing ; with a series of elongated white fine lines placed in pairs between the nervules on the disc, the two lowest in the upper median interspace very short, the next pair longer, the pair above longer still, but the upper one broken near its end, the pair above that in the subcostal interspace entirely and widely divided leaving only two very short lines within and two dots outwardly, the latter with a single dot in the interspace above.

* Cat. Fab. Lep. B. M., p. 91, n. 6.

† *Euthalia mahadeva. Adolias mahadeva,* Moore, Trans. Ent. Soc. Lond., new series, vol. v, p. 68, n. 11, pl. iv, fig. 1, male (1859) ; id , Butler, Proc. Zool. Soc. Lond., 1868, p. 605, n. 36. HABITAT : Unknown. EXPANSE : *Male,* 2·37 inches. DESCRIPTION : " MALE. UPPERSIDE dark dusky brown, smeared with purple on exterior margin of *forewing. Hindwing* with a broad band to exterior margin, whitish anteriorly, bluish posteriorly, with a medial longitudinal row of small dusky spots. UNDERSIDE light brown, exterior margins greyish ; discoidal marks and submarginal row of indistinct spots blackish." (*Moore,* l. c.)

"Seems to come near *E. talis* and *E. ketæra.*" (*Butler,* l. c.)

This is apparently a very distinct species, which in outline and general appearance seems to be nearest to *E. phemius.* From the figure the forewing is pale at the base, there is a large oval pale patch enclosing the disco-cellulars, with a similar patch beyond. The outer margin also pale, broad at the anal angle, narrowing to the apex. Nothing is known of it since the type was described.

These white markings are exactly the same as in the male of *E. phemius*, as mentioned by Felder. The female is paler than the male, the discal band narrower and outwardly curved on both wings, the outer band of the hindwing lunular. The white markings of the forewing as in the male.

E. jama is a rare species. It occurs in Sikkim and Bhutan, Mr. S. E. Peal has sent it from Sibsagar, it occurs in the Naga Hills, Mr. Wood-Mason took it on Nemotha, Cachar, in September, and Felder records it from Malacca interior and Banca.

Mr. Distant (probably following Mr. Butler) has described and figured under the name of *E. jama* a species closely allied to *E. alpheda*, but apparently quite distinct from *A. jama* in both the sexes from the absence of the fine white lines on the upperside of the forewing described above. His description is given below.*

The two remaining species are very distinct both from each other and from all the other Indian species of the genus. *E. lubentina* has in both sexes the wings marked on both sides with beautiful crimson spots ; the female has the white oblique discal band very broad and macular extending into the discoidal cell. *E. anosia* in both sexes has the upperside profusely irrorated with grey, not confined to a discal band as in *E. kesava* and *E. discispilota*, but spread over the greater portion of both wings. In outline too the apex is much more acute than in any other species of this section, and the forewing more emarginate on the outer margin ; in the female the forewing is distinctly falcate, and in both sexes the lower half of the outer margin of the forewing is more convex ; the forewing is longer and the hindwing broader than in the other species of this section.

517. **Euthalia lubentina,** Cramer. (VOL. I, PLATE II, PUPA).

Papilio lubentina. Cramer, Pap. Ex., vol. ii, pl. clv, figs. C, D (1777), *female* ; id., Fabricius, Sp. Ins., vol. ii, p. 91, n. 403 (1781) ; idem, id., Mant. Ins., vol. ii, p. 49, n. 486 (1787) ; idem, id., Ent. Syst., vol. iii, pt. i, p. 121, n. 370 (1793) ; id., Donovan, Ins. China, pl. xxxvi, fig. 3 (1799), *male* ; *Euthalia lubentina*, Hübner, Verz. bek. Schmett., p. 41, n. 358 (1816) ; id., Moore, Lep. Cey., vol. i, p. 31, pl. xvi, figs. 1, *male* ; 1*a*, *female* ; 1*b*, *larva* and *pupa* (1881) ; id., Distant, Rhop. Malay., p. 178, pl. xiv, fig. 4, *male* (1883) ; *Nymphalis lubentina*, Godart, Enc. Méth., vol. ix, p. 400, n. 177 (1819) ; *Adolias lubentina*, Horsfield and Moore, Cat. Lep. Mus. E. I. C. vol. i, p. 188, n. 379, pl. xii, figs. 13, *larva* ; 13*a*, *pupa* (1857) ; id., Butler, Cat. Fabr. Lep. B. M., p. 88, n. 1 (1869).

HABITAT : India, Ceylon, (?) Malay Peninsula, China.

EXPANSE : ♂, 2·3 to 3·0 ; ♀, 2·5 to 3·35 inches.

DESCRIPTION : "MALE and FEMALE. UPPERSIDE dark greenish-brown, paler and æinescent externally. *Forewing* with short black transverse discoidal streaks and two dull scarlet interspaces, a black spot below the cell, three white spots beyond the cell, and a

---

* *Euthalia jama*, Distant, Rhop. Malay., p. 119, n. 4, pl. xiv, fig. 8, *male* ; pl. xv, fig. 4, *female* (1883). HABITAT : Province Wellesley, Malacca. EXPANSE : *Male*, 2·7 : *female*, 2·8 inches. DESCRIPTION : "MALE. UPPERSIDE fuliginous-brown. *Forewing* with a black line crossing cell near base and apparently continued between the median and submedian nervures, a dark brown spot crossing middle of cell, the margins of which are black, and which is rounded and closed posteriorly ; a somewhat similar spot at end of cell ; two similarly margined spots obliquely, but not quite, crossing cell of *hindwing* ; a dark brown oblique fascia crossing disc, commencing near termination of cell (where there is an indistinct bronzy area), and terminating on inner margin, about one-third from base ; this is followed by a somewhat narrower oblique fascia crossing *both wings*, commencing near apex of forewing and terminating on hindwing near the abdominal margin at about one-third from anal angle : this fascia is widened at inner margin of forewing. *Hindwing* with a much-waved, narrow, dark submarginal fascia, and outer margins of *both wings* distinctly darker. UNDERSIDE pale greenish ochraceous : cellular markings as above. *Forewing* with a rounded spot beneath, cell on inner side of first median nervule and a smaller dark spot on outer side of that nervule. *Hindwing* with a looped spot beneath and near the base of costal nervure, followed by a smaller rounded spot beneath the first subcostal nervule, and a curved black line beneath the base of second subcostal nervule ; fascia above very indistinctly and narrowly seen beneath. *Body* and *legs* more or less concolorous with wings. FEMALE pale brownish ; cellular markings as in male. *Forewing* with a broad pale fascia, occupying a space equivalent to that between the extreme margins of the two discal pale fasciæ in male—the fascia is pale, obscure, bluish above the second median nervule, and pale brownish beneath that nervule, and its outer margin is brown and prominently waved and angulated ; at costa it possesses an irregular-shaped medial, and a somewhat similar outer subolivaceous spot, the last almost continued to apex above the fourth subcostal nervule. *Hindwing* with fascia as in male, but which are paler and narrower. UNDERSIDE as above but paler ; markings similar, but more indistinct. Hindwing with the outer cellular markings as in male."

"This is but a local race of the Javan *E. alpheda*, Godart, and differs principally in the female sex. Mr. Butler, from an examination of Captain Pinwill's collection, remarked that in Malacca the "species appears to be common," but in Province Wellesley—judging from collections—it appears to be a scarce insect." (*Distant*, l c)

recurved discal series, a submarginal indistinct black lunular fascia. *Hindwing* with costal border purple washed, a black disco-cellular mark, a submarginal row of black-bordered scarlet spots, and a marginal row of black spots, the three apical and anal spots being bordered externally with scarlet. UNDERSIDE, *forewing* greenish purple-brown, suffused with ochreous-brown apically, markings more prominent than above. *Hindwing* ochreous-brown, greenish-brown anally, the scarlet spots very prominent and with scarcely any black border, the costal margin, two discoidal black-bordered spots, and two above them, are also scarlet. FEMALE. UPPERSIDE, *forewing* with a medial transverse outwardly-oblique irregular macular greenish-white band, and three small subapical spots, a dull scarlet discoidal mark. *Hindwing* marked as in male. UNDERSIDE, *forewing* greyish-purple at base, apex ochreous-brown, posterior angle greenish-grey, macular white band and spots as above, two scarlet-streaked black dis-coidal marks and two basal spots. *Hindwing* ochreous-grey, greenish-grey anally, scarlet markings as in male, but less distinct, and the posterior submarginal spots nearly obsolete."

"LARVA green, with ten pairs of long green laterally projecting very delicate branched spines, each pair tipped with crimson ; a large dorsal purple spot centred with white on back of the fourth, sixth, seventh, and ninth to twelfth segments ; head spotted with black. Feeds on *Loranthus*. PUPA short, green, keeled along the back and broadly triangular across the middle ; a pale line along the keel and across the middle, a red lateral line and thoracic spots." (*Moore*, l. c. in Lep. Cey.)

E. lubentina has a very wide range. It occurs at Fyzabad in Oudh, in Calcutta and Sikkim, and eastwards as far as Upper Assam, in Burma, Orissa, Bombay, and thence southwards to Ceylon. It is a very distinct species, the numerous scarlet markings will at once distinguish it from any other species of the genus.

A figure of the pupa under the name of *Adolias lubentina* is given on Plate II of Vol. I of this work.

A species allied to *E. lubentina* has been described from the Malay Peninsula as below.*

* *Euthalia adonia.* Papilio adonia, Cramer, Pap. Ex , vol. iii. pl. cclv, figs C, D, *female* (1779) ; *Euthalia adonia*, Hübner, Verz. bek. Schmett., p. 41, n. 389 (1816) ; *E. adonia*, var., Distant, Rhop. Malay., p. 170, n. 6, pl. xix, figs. 10, *male* ; 11, *female* (1883) ; *Nymphalis adonia*, Godart, Enc. Méth , vol. ix. p. 400, n. 173 (1819) ; *Adolias adonia*, Horsfield and Moore, Cat. Lep. Mus. E. I. C., vol. i. p. 188, n. 378 (1857) ; id., Moore, Trans. Ent. Soc. Lond., new series, vol. v. p. 67, n. 7 (1859) ; *Aceathea lubentina*, Horsfield (*nec* Cramer), Cat. Lep. Mus. E. I. C., pl. v, figs. 5, 5*a*, *male* (1829). HABITAT : Malacca, Java. EXPANSE : *Male*, 2'3 ; *female*, 2'75 inches. DESCRIPTION : "MALE. UPPERSIDE dark olivaceous. *Forewing* with the basal portion of discoidal cell and posterior outer margin greenish ; cell crossed near middle by two black lines, between which the colour is reddish ; these lines are followed by a narrow transverse white fascia, which is outwardly concave, beyond which are two other black lines, with a reddish spot between them ; three white spots beyond cell divided by the nervules, and a waved discal series of five white spots placed between the nervules, the lowest between the third and second median nervules ; these are followed by two larger but obscure spots divided by the first median nervule ; an obscure, broken, fuscous submarginal line. *Hindwing* with the cell crossed by two fuscous lines, and with a broad greenish marginal border : this greenish area contains a medial series of six blackish spots placed between the nervules, with an elongate linear spot at anal angle ; there are also three bright red spots near outer margin at apex and two of the same colour on inner side of the green area, situated one on each side of the lower subcostal oervule,—these are outwardly and inwardly margined with blackish, and are followed by two blackish lines which do not pass first median nervule. UNDERSIDE pale olivaceous-brown. *Forewing* with the cell crossed as above, but with a short basal black line, and the red enclosure brighter and larger, the green shadings on upperside absent. *Hindwing* with costa narrowly red, with the anal margin greenish, and with the two blackish lines crossing cell enclosing two red spots ; at apex of cell and on each side of lower subcostal oervule are two similar black lines enclosing red spots, the first named preceded by a small black spot ; a discal series of four red spots placed between the nervules, the lower one beneath the discoidal nervule ; the submarginal series of black spots as above, but smaller, the upper three with an attached outer red spot, and the linear spot at anal angle broken into two. *Body* and *legs* more or less concolourous with wings. FEMALE larger than male. UPPERSIDE. *Forewing* olivaceous-brown, marked generally as in male, but with all the white spots very much larger, the waved discal series consisting of nine spots, of which the lower five are very large, irregularly rectangular and sinuously following the three placed beyond cell ; a pale and obscure greenish submarginal streak at posterior angle. *Hindwing* olivaceous-brown, with a wide macular, medial white fascia divided by the nervules, outwardly margined with blackish and inwardly margined with the same colour as far as end of cell, which is crossed by two black lines ; outer margin broadly greenish from about discoidal nervule to anal angle ; a submarginal series of seven blackish spots placed between the nervules, the upper three and the seventh attached to an outer red spot. UNDERSIDE as above, but paler in hue. *Forewing* with the cell marked with red as in male, the submarginal fuscous fascia more distinct than above, and with a large white submarginal streak at posterior angle. *Hindwing* as above, but paler, the costal margin narrowly red, cellular black lines enclosing a red spot, a similarly enclosed red spot at end of cell, and the same above and near base of upper subcostal nervule ; submarginal spots smaller, the upper three only attached to outer red spots : abdominal margin pale greenish."

"The male differs from Javan and typical forms of the species by the darker colouration above and the fewer red spots to the hindwing ; the absence of the red spot at anal angle being particularly noticeable ; the colour beneath is also paler, and the red spots to hindwing fewer and paler. The female also differs in several particulars. It is probable that a distinct race of *E. adonia* is found in the Malay Peninsula" (*Distant*, l. c.)

518. Euthalia anosia, Moore.

Adolias anosia, Moore, Horsfield and Moore, Cat. Lep. Mus. E. I. C., vol. i, p. 187, n. 376 (1857); id., Moore, Trans. Ent. Soc. Lond., new series, vol. v, p. 65, n. 5, pl. v, figs. 1, *male* and *female* (1859); *Euthalia anosia*, Distant, Rhop. Malay., p. 117, n. 2, pl. xiv, fig. 5, *female* (1883).

HABITAT : Sikkim, Assam, Cachar, Chittagong, Mergui, Tenasserim, Province Wellesley, Malacca.

EXPANSE : ♂, 2·5 to 3·1 ; ♀, 3·0 to 3·5 inches.

DESCRIPTION : "MALE : UPPERSIDE dark ash-green, with the anterior margin of hindwing broadly pinky-brown. *Forewing* with broad transverse band of ashy-white irrorations ; black markings within discoidal cell, and some below it, bordered with ashy-white irrorations. *Hindwing* with ashy-white irrorations on lower part of the disc, bordering the discoidal marks, and a spot above and below the cell, also bordering a submarginal row of black spots. UNDERSIDE creamy ash-colour, palest on the anterior half, which is covered with rather indistinct darker short transverse striæ ; markings within and about discoidal cell black ; on the *hindwing* an indistinct submarginal row of black spots. FEMALE. UPPERSIDE paler ash-green than the male ; exterior margins brownish ; markings disposed the same. *Forewing* with a curved row of five white spots from middle of costal margin ; the irrorated band paler and more clearly defined ; an indistinct inward oblique row of black spots from near apex to near middle of posterior margin. *Hindwing* with indistinct black curved band from middle of anterior to middle of abdominal margin ; also an indistinct submarginal row of black spots. UNDERSIDE paler than in the male, marked as on upperside, with the curved row of five spots bordered inwardly with dark brown ; the indistinct oblique row of blackish spots from apex only to middle of the disc, the lower part being suffused with dark brown ; exterior margin dark brown. *Hindwing* with indistinct inner band and submarginal row of large dark brown spots. Forewing in both sexes much falcated." (*Moore, l. c. in Cat. Lep. Mus. E. I. C.*)

E. anosia is a very distinct and rare species. The deep emargination of the outer margin of the forewing, the grey irroration of the upperside and the dark striation of the underside, at once distinguish it from every other species of the genus. Mr. F. B. Collins Feilmann has obtained it at low elevations in Sikkim in the spring, Mr. Shirwell took a female in the Jorehát district in June, Mr. Wood-Mason obtained a pair in Cachar, a male at Irangmara in July and a female on Nemotha in September, Mr. S. E. Peal has sent it from Sibsagar, Dr. Anderson took a pair in the Mergui Archipelago in the cold weather, and it has been recorded from Tenasserim and the Malay Peninsula.

Genus 79.—TANAÉCIA, Butler. (PLATE XIX).

Tanaécia, Butler, Proc. Zool. Soc. Lond., 1868, p. 610 (with wood-cut of structure of palpus and hindwing) ; id., Distant, Rhop. Malay., p. 128 (1883).

"*Sexes* nearly alike ; the *palpi* with a slender bristle-like terminal joint, varying somewhat in length in the different species ; the *middle disco-cellular* of *forewing* feebly recurved ; the *first* branch of the *subcostal* nervure in *hindwing* emitted at some distance from the base, the *second* just beyond. Typical species *Tanaécia pulasara.*" (*Butler, l. c.*)

"In general form and neuration this genus resembles *Euthalia*, differing chiefly in the following characters:—the *middle disco-cellular nervule* of the *forewing* is only moderately recurved ; the *first subcostal* of the *hindwing* is emitted at a greater distance from the base of the subcostal nervure than in *Euthalia*, and the *second* subcostal has its origin a little beyond. The *palpi* have a slender bristle-like terminal joint varying in different species." (*Distant, l. c.*) The transformations are unknown.

Neither of the above writers, however, seem to have noticed the remarkable feature of this genus, which distinguishes it from all the other genera in this subfamily except *Prothoë*, and links it to several of the genera of the *Morphinæ*, viz., the anastomosing of the first subcostal nervule of the forewing with the costal nervure at some distance beyond the end of the cell ; the second subcostal nervule also touches the first subcostal below and the third subcostal above before reaching the margin, but does not actually anastomose with either of them. The anastomosing of the first subcostal with the costal occurs in all the species I have seen, but Mr. Distant tells me that it does not do so in *T. orphne*, Butler, which occurs in Borneo.

The cell in both wings is open as in the typical group of *Euthalia*, the body is small and weak, the wings rounded at the apex, giving the insect a weak appearance as in *E. lepida* and allied species. "This genus is much smaller in extent than *Euthalia*, and likewise has a different distribution, for whereas that genus may be said to have its head-quarters in North-Eastern India, *Tanaecia* is almost confined to the Indo-Malayan region, and is apparently absent from Continental India and Ceylon, though found in the Andaman Islands." (*Distant*, l. c.) A single species occurs within our limits, and very much resembles in both sexes the female of *Euthalia acontius*, being dark brown above with the usual Euthaliad basal markings, both wings crossed by a prominent white discal band, the underside washed with pale green almost throughout.

At least seven species occur in the Malay Peninsula, the descriptions of them will be found below.* Some of them are allied in colouration to the blue-banded group of *Euthalias* of which *E. andersonii* is the Indian representative, the others more nearly resemble the females of *E. jahnu*, &c.

519. Tanaecia cibaritis, Hewitson. (PLATE XIX, FIG. 77♂).

Adolias cibaritis, Hewitson, Ann. and Mag. of Nat. Hist., fourth series, vol. xiv. p. 358 (1874); idem, id , Ex. Butt., vol. v, *Adolias* pl. iv, figs. 13, *male*; 12, 15, *female*(1875); *Tanaecia cybaritis*, Kirby, Cat. Diurn. Lep., p. 246 (1877).

HABITAT : Andaman Islands.

EXPANSE : ♂, 2·12 to 3·10 ; ♀, 3·1 to 3·5 inches.

DESCRIPTION : "FEMALE. UPPERSIDE dark rufous brown. *Both wings* with the usual spots in and below the cell : both crossed beyond the middle, from the costal margin of the forewing to the anal angle of the hindwing, by a broad band of white divided by the nervules, sinuated deeply on its inner margin at its fourth spot, bordered outwardly by a series of hastate black spots crowned with lilac. *Forewing* with a small white spot between the band and the apex. UNDERSIDE pale green. *Both wings* with the bands and spots as above, bordered inwardly with black. MALE like the female, except that the white band of the hindwing is narrower, and on the UNDERSIDE bordered on both sides with black spots."

"This is the largest known species of the *T. trigerta* group, to which it belongs." (*Hewitson*, l. c. in Ann. and Mag. of Nat. Hist.) *T. trigerta* occurs in Java.

T. cibaritis is a common species in the South Andaman Isles. Mr. de Roepstorff sent a single specimen from Nankouri in the Nicobars, but its occurrence there is doubtful, probably the specimen was an Andaman one.

The figure shows both sides of a male South Andaman example in the Indian Museum, Calcutta.

---

* *Tanaecia flora*, M. R. Butler, Proc. Zool. Soc. Lond., 1873, p. 235; id., Waterhouse, Aid to the Ident. of Ins., vol. i, pl. xxi (1880); id., Distant, Rhop. Malay., p. 129, n. 1, pl. xviii, fig. 6, *female* (1882). "HABITAT : Province Wellesley. EXPANSE : 2·9 inches. DESCRIPTION : FEMALE. "UPPERSIDE brown, with the usual black markings in cells ; two irregular indistinct transverse discal series of dark brown hastate spots, *Forewing* with two cinereous oval spots between discoidal nervules, just beyond termination of cell ; two similar less distinct spots between the same nervules and just within the outer hastate series ; outer margin pale greenish blue, increasing in width from the apex to the inner angle, and bounded externally by a marginal line of dark brown. Cilia white. *Hindwing* with costal margin broadly pale brown ; external third of wing pale blue tinted with lilacine, becoming whitish at the anal angle ; tridentate internally from discoidal nervule to costa, and gradually widening to inner margin ; six large, but indistinct, flesh-coloured submarginal spots from apex to first median branch ; margin blackish brown. Cilia white. Body above dark brown ; dorsum dark olivaceous ; *palpi* ochreous ; *antennae* black, with minute orange tip. UNDERSIDE brownish ochraceous ; the discal series of spots as above, but lunate ; inner series ill-defined, bounded externally by a series of ovate spots paler than the ground-colour. *Forewing* with black markings in cell ; outer and inner areas clouded with pale lilacine, more prominent at apex and inner angle ; margin brown. Cilia white. *Hindwing* with usual basal markings indistinct ; outer and inner areas pale lilacine ; outer margin indistinctly brown. Cilia white. Body ochraceous white ; tibiae and tarsi of legs ochreous ; *palpi* and cross dirty white ; *antennae* pale brown, club blackish, tip orange."

"This species is especially interesting in its excellent mimicry of the blue-banded male of *Adolias* (= *Euthalia*) *puseda* of Moore, hitherto known to occur commonly in Penang and Singapore." (*M. R. Butler*, l. c.)

"This unique species possesses three distinct and interesting features :—firstly, the palpi have a much shorter slender termination than other species of the genus, thus being somewhat intermediate in that respect between *Euthalia* and *Tanaëcia*, though the position of the first subcostal nervule of the hindwing clearly denotes its relation to the last-named genus ; secondly, it very closely resembles the female of *Euthalia macnairi*, a resemblance which may or may not find its subsequent explanation by the theory of 'mimicry' ; and thirdly, it is a species of extreme rarity." (*Distant*, l. c.) The type specimen is unique, and the male is unknown.

Tanaëcia niceviller, Distant, Ann. and Mag. of Nat. Hist., fifth series, vol. xiv, p. 199 (1884). Habitat : Perak. Expanse : *Male*, 2·9 inches. Description : " Male. Upperside very dark brownish, with a violaceous tinge. *Forewing* with the cell crossed by two basal black lines, continued beneath to the median nervure, two black lines near middle of cell, the innermost of which has a parallel line between the lower median nervule and the submedian nervure, and a single black line at end of cell ; a small bluish spot near apex and a marginal bluish fascia commencing about middle of wing and gradually widening to outer angle, where it possesses two inner lanceolate black spots margined with bluish beneath the lower median nervule, and an inner black streak at inner margin. *Hindwing* with a very broad outer marginal bluish fascia, narrowest at apex of wing, inwardly margined with small blackish spots, and containing a medial series of blackish spots placed between the nervules, which become practically obsolete at the area of the median nervules ; three obscure blackish lines crossing cell, two near middle, and one at apex ; abdominal margin brownish ochraceous. Underside pale brownish ochraceous. *Forewing* with the black linear markings as above, followed by a transverse series of five broad fuscous streaks placed between the nervules, those at end of cell largest ; a pale violaceous marginal fascia with an inner series of lanceolate blackish spots. *Hindwing* with the broader outer bluish fascia as above, but paler and more violaceous, its medial spots smaller, but more continuous and distinct, the three dark lines crossing cell as above, a looped line beneath the costal nervure, and an outer cellular series of three dark spots separated by the lower subcostal and discoidal nervules. Body above and beneath, with *legs*, more or less concolorous with wings."

"This interesting species of *Tanaëcia* belongs to the section of the genus which includes *T. flora*, Butler; and, like it, has the colouration and appearance of an Euthalid above." (*Distant*, l. c.) The type specimen is deposited in the Indian Museum, Calcutta.

Tanaëcia supercilia, Butler, Proc. Zool. Soc. Lond., 1868, p. 610, n. 4, pl. xlv, fig. 7, *male* ; id., Distant, Rhop. Malay., p. 130, n. 2, pl. xv, fig. 8, *male* (1883). Habitat : Penang. Expanse : 2·67 inches. Description : " Male. Closely allied to *T. varuna*, Vollenhoven [from Java]. Upperside coloured as in *T. pelea*, Fabricius [from Java], but with the lunular fascia of the *hindwing* more curved and with basal markings punctiform [dot-shaped], Underside pale fuscous, the intermo-basal area of the *forewing* yellowish, the discal fascia silky-whitish, the spots of the *hindwing* wider black ; otherwise as in *T. varuna*."

"A local representative of *T. varuna*. Lieutenant Roberts has assured me that the nearly allied species of the *Adolias* (= *Euthalia*) group are quite constant to their localities ; otherwise I should have considered this to be a variety of *T. varuna*." (*Butler*, l. c.) Mr. Distant has never seen this species, and the female has still to be discovered. It is entirely without blue markings on the upperside.

Tanaëcia robertsii, Butler, Cist. Ent., vol. i, p. 235 (1874) ; *T. robertsii*, Distant, Rhop. Malay., p. 132 (1883). Habitat : Malacca, Ayerpanas. Expanse : 2·5 inches. Description : " Male. Upperside pale olive-brown ; apical half pearly-white, bounded just beyond end of cell by an irregular blackish undulated line ; a second zigzag line across the middle of disc, interrupted on lower discoidal interspace of the *forewing* ; a series of submarginal hastate black markings ; margin rather broadly pale brown ; ring-like characters at base as usual, blackish. *Body* brown. Underside much paler, the brown area altered to pale ochraceous ; the black lunated lines of disc broken up into spots, the hastate markings only sharply defined at their apices ; basal markings as above, but more sharply defined on the *hindwing*. *Body* pale ochraceous."

"Most nearly allied to *T. supercilia*, Butler, but smaller, with the entire externo-discal area of both wings pearly-whitish, and the hastate submarginal markings distinctly separated from one another as in *T. violaria*." (*Butler*, l. c.) This species also is unknown to Mr. Distant, and the female has yet to be discovered.

Tanaëcia violaria, Butler, Proc. Zool. Soc. Lond., 1868, p. 612, n. 11, pl. xlv, fig. 8, *female* ; id., Distant, Rhop. Malay., p. 130, n. 3, pl. xv, fig. 9, *female* (1883). Habitat : Singapore, Borneo. Expanse : 3·25 inches. Description : " Female. Upperside, both wings fuscous, *Forewing* as in *T. pelea*, Fabricius, but the entire margin fuscous. *Hindwing* with the lunular submarginal fascia increasing at the anal angle, near the apex with snow-white lunules, near the anal angle purple, inwardly defined by fuscous lunules, outwardly with sagittate fuscous spots, terminated on the outside with whitish chiefly near the apex. Underside as in *T. pulasara*, Moore, but the basal area fuscous-yellowish (not ochreous-whitish) and with the arrow marks of the *hindwing* violaceous and longer."

"Allied to *T. vikrama*, Felder [from Sumatra], but very distinct." (*Butler*, l. c.) This species is unknown to Mr. Distant, and the male has yet to be discovered."

Tanaëcia (*Adolias*) *pulasara*, Moore, Horsfield and Moore, Cat. Lep. Mus. E. I. C., vol. i, p. 190, n. 382 (1857) ; idem, id., Trans. Ent. Soc. Lond., new series, vol. v, p. 71, n. 16, pl. vi, fig. 2 (1859) ; *Tanaëcia pulasara*, Butler, Trans. Linn. Soc. Lond., Zoology, second series, vol. i, p. 540, n. 2 (1877) ; id., Distant, Rhop. Malay., p. 130, n. 4, pl. xix, fig. 6, *male* ; pl. xiv, fig. 13, *female* (1883) ; *Tanaëcia varuna*, Butler (nec Vollenhoven), Proc. Zool. Soc. Lond., 1868, p. 611, n. 5, *part*. Habitat : Penang, Perak, Malacca, Singapore. Expanse : 2·7 to 3·1 inches. Description : " Male. Upperside fuliginous-brown, *Forewing* with the cell crossed by four blackish lines, followed by a similar but waved line a little beyond apex ; between the last two lines the colour is somewhat violaceous, the markings beneath cell being much as in *T. violaria* ; a transverse series of six large oblong greyish spots on apical half of wing, placed between the nervules, the upper five of which are margined with fuscous and conically rounded inwardly and acutely excavated outwardly, the third spot being smallest, the sixth situated between the first median nervule and the submedian nervure is doubly angulated outwardly and irregularly truncate inwardly ; these are followed by an elongate spot or streak on inner margin, and are all more or less suffused with brownish and outwardly followed by five small violaceous and inwardly pointed spots, the nervules which separate them are distinctly infuscated to margin. *Hindwing* with the cell crossed by two black lines near base and two near apex, the last being followed by a small black streak on each side of second median nervule ; a transverse series of seven spots on apical half of wing smaller and more regular, but margined and inwardly rounded and outwardly angulated as on forewing,—of these spots the upper three are greyish and outwardly margined with violaceous, the remainder being concolorous with wing ; abdominal margin much paler and somewhat pinky. Underside pale and violaceous. *Forewing* with the basal half ochraceous, with the dark linear markings generally as above, the large transverse spots on apical half as above, but more fused, with the pale colour extending to outer margin. *Hindwing* with the cellular and adjacent markings as above ; a curved black line above and near base of subcostal nervure, and an oblique series of three small black spots separated by the subcostal nervules a little beyond cell ; the transverse spots on upperside only indicated by their black terminal margins, which form two transverse series of spots, between which the colour is tinged with ochraceous. *Body* and *legs* more or less concolorous with wings. Female.

Genus 80.—PYRAMEIS, Hübner. (PLATE XVIII).

Pyrameis, Hübner, Verz. bek. Schmett., p. 33 (1816); id., Doubleday, Gen. Diurn. Lep., vol i, p. 202 (1849); id., Moore, Lep. Cey , p. 49 (1881); id., Felder, Neues Lep , p. 13, n. 21 (1861) ; id., Godman and Salvin, Biol. Cent.-Am , Rhop , p. 217 (1882) ; *Vanessa*, Hübner (*nec* Fabricius), Verz. bek. Schmett., p. 32 (1816) ; *Ammiralis*, Rennie, Consp., p. 10 (1832); *Bassaris*, Hübner, Ex. Schmett., vol. ii (1816-22).

"HEAD, of moderate width, hairy ; *eyes*, nearly round, hairy ; *palpi*, porrect, slightly ascending, convergent, projecting fully half their length beyond the forehead, scaly, slightly hairy in front, more so on the sides and upper surface of the second joint. First joint subcylindric, much curved ; second joint more than three times as long as the first, subcylindric, stouter a little beyond the middle, then narrowed to the apex ; third joint less than half the length of the second, elongate-conic, the apex rather obtuse ; *antennæ*, about three-fourths the length of the body, rather slender, terminating in a short somewhat pyriform club, of which the terminal joints taper to a point. *Thorax*, oval, moderately stout, hairy. *Abdomen*, stout, about half the length of the inner margin of the hindwing. FOREWING, subtriangular ; the *apex* more or less truncate ; the *costal margin* but little curved ; *outer* margin but three-fourths the length of the costal, sinuate, emarginate ; *inner* margin slightly longer than the outer, straight, or slightly emarginate. *Costal nervure* stout, extending to the middle of the costa ; *subcostal* nervure slender, lying close to the costal ; its first and second branches arising near to one another, and but little before the end of the cell, the third arising at about two-thirds of the distance from the base to the apex, terminating at the apex, the *fourth* rather nearer to the origin of the third than to the outer margin ; *upper* and *middle disco-cellular nervules* all but wanting ; *lower* disco-cellular very slender, sometimes nearly atrophied, arising from the second discoidal nervule at a short distance from its origin, nearly straight, directed outwards, anastomosing with the third median nervule at some distance from its origin, at a point where it is slightly angulated. HINDWING, somewhat obovate ; the *inner margin* the longest ; the *costal* and *outer* margins of about equal length, the former rounded, the latter more or less sinuate and subdentate. *Præcostal nervure* simple, or slightly bifid, the outer branch nearly atrophied ; *discoidal nervule* arising from the second subcostal soon after its origin ; *lower disco-cellular* nervule very slender, anastomosing with the median nervure opposite to the origin of its second branch. FORELEGS, of the *male* densely hairy ;

UPPERSIDE generally as in male. UNDERSIDE pale ochraceous. *Forewing* with the greyish spots as above, but clearer, and with the pale colour extending beyond the outer margin. *Hindwing* marked as above, but paler, and with an additional series of three looped dark lines placed near the cell and divided by the subcostal nervules, and three small spots beneath the median nervure, divided by the second and first median nervules."

"*Variety a*" (Distant, Rhop. Malay., p. 131, pl. xviii, fig. 9, *female* (1883); *Adolias inteas*, Vollenhoven, Tijd. Ent., vol. v, p. 194, n. 15, pl. xi, fig. 2, *female* (1862). HABITAT : Malacca, Borneo. EXPANSE : *Female*, 3¼ inches. DESCRIPTION : " FEMALE. UPPERSIDE. Closely allied to the typical form of *T. pulasara*, but differing in having the transverse series of greyish spots on the *forewing* more slender and elongated, the fourth and fifth being much longer than the corresponding spots in Moore's species, the outer dentate margins are also longer and more acute; the transverse spots on *hindwing* are more linear and elongate, particularly the two which are divided by the second median nervule, and their outer dentate margins are also longer and more acute. These characters also apply to the UNDERSIDE."

"This species appears to be almost confined to the Malay Peninsula ; both the typical male and female specimens here figured being from Singapore, whilst the variety (*T. intras*) was collected in Malacca. Of the last Mr. Butler, from a knowledge derived from Vollenhoven's figure alone, remarked, 'this is only the Bornean form of Moore's *pulasara*,' a statement which this Malacean specimen considerably qualifies. Another closely-allied species, or variety, of *T. pulasara* is found in Sumatra, and has been described under the name of *T. tekteawa*, Felder. Females of the typical form of the species are also variable in hue, as in some specimens the transverse series of pale spots on the upperside of the forewing are outwardly margined with small pale violaceous angulated spots, which are absent in the somewhat melanic specimen here figured." (*Distant*, l. c.) There are a pair of this species from Perak in the collection of the Indian Museum, Calcutta, and a male in my own from Penang.

Tanaicia (Adolias) aruna, Felder, Wien. Ent. Monatsch., vol. iv, p. 400, n. 74 (1860) ; *Tanaicia aruna*, Butler, Proc. Zool. Soc. Lond , 1868, p. 611, n. 6 : idem, id., Trans. Linn. Soc. Lond., Zoology, second series, vol. i, p. 510, n. 1 (1877); id., Distant, Rhop. Malay., p. 232, n. 3, pl. xv, fig. 7, *male* (1883); *Adolias pardalis*, Vollenhoven, Tijd. Ent., vol. v, p. 197, n. 17, pl. xi, fig. 5, *male* (1862). HABITAT: Malacca, Java. EXPANSE : 2¼ inches. DESCRIPTION : " MALE. Closely allied to *T. pulasara*, but the transverse series of spots on the UPPERSIDE of *both wings* paler and longer, those of the *forewing* having a medial waved narrow brown fascia, and those on the *hindwing* being also paler and having their outer margins a little nearer to the posterior margin. UNDERSIDE more ochraceous, and with a narrow, distinct, intermediate, dark ochraceous fascia between the dark terminal margins of the transverse spots as seen on the *hindwing*."

"The female has yet to be described, but is probably somewhat similar to the other sex, and not more divergent than are the sexes of the closely-allied species *T. pulasara*" (*Distant*, l. c.)

the *tibia* a little shorter than the femur; the *tarsus* than the tibia; tibia subcylindric, unarmed; tarsus subcylindric, tapering towards the apex, which is obtusely conical. Of the *female* with the femur, tibia, and base of tarsus densely hairy; the proportions of these parts as in the males; *tibia* subcylindric, sparingly spiny within; *tarsus* with the first and second joints spiny below, the latter rather more than one-fifth the length of the former; both armed at the apex, as are the two following joints, with a stout spine on each side, covered by a more or less distinct tuft of hairs at the base of the following joint; third joint little more than half the length of the second, transverse; fourth joint shorter than the third, transverse, obliquely truncate at the apex; fifth joint short, transverse, about equal to the fourth. MIDDLE and HINDLEGS, moderately stout; the *femur* in the former longer than in the latter, equal to the tibia; *tibiæ* with two latero-internal rows of spines, and lateral less regular series; spurs stout, elongate; *tarsi* spiny above, laterally, and, except the fifth joint, below; the spines of the lower surface stout, long, arranged in two nearly regular series; middle tarsi with the first joint about three times the length of the second; the posterior tarsi with the first joint little more than double the length of the second; third joint considerably shorter than the second; the fourth than the third; fifth about equal to the second; claws rather stout, curved, grooved below. *Paronychia* very hairy, bilaciniate; the outer lacinia strap-shaped, as long as the claw; the inner short, subtriangular, or with the inner lacinia rudimentary; the outer elongate, triangular, slender. *Pulvillus* jointed, shorter than the claws, or merely rudimentary."

"LARVA cylindric; all the segments, except the head and prothoracic segment, armed with verticillate* spines. Colouration brown or olive, tending more or less to green, with an interrupted pale longitudinal band on each side. In their habits they are different from *Vanessa*, being always solitary, drawing together the sides of a leaf with silken threads, and thus forming a cylindrical dwelling. PUPA more or less angular and tuberculate; the head rather obtusely bifid. Colouration some shade of brown, grey, or olive, more or less ornamented with golden spots."

"*Pyrameis* differs from *Vanessa* in having the wings less angular; the palpi less hairy, and of somewhat different form; the club of the antennæ rather more pointed; and in other less obvious characters." (*Doubleday*, l. c.) According to Mr. Scudder the name of this genus should fall before *Vanessa*. Except from a profound dislike to upsetting long-established usage, I should have adopted this course, and placed the two species here included in the genus *Pyrameis* in the next genus *Vanessa*, an additional argument in favour of adopting this course being the close agreement in all stages that exists between all the species.

The genus *Pyrameis* is very wide-spread, one species, *P. cardui*, having earned the name of "The Cosmopolitan Butterfly," as it occurs almost throughout the world except in the Arctic regions and in South America. The other Indian species, *P. indica*, occurs in India in the hills wherever they are high enough to produce the nettles on which its larva feeds, in Amurland, China, Teneriffe, Madeira, Spain, and Portugal. Both species have numerous allied forms which replace the typical forms in the countries where the latter do not penetrate, the European "Red Admiral," *P. atalanta*, Linnæus, for instance, replacing *P. indica* in Europe and North America; and other allied species in the Malay Archipelago, Australia, New Zealand, the Sandwich Islands, North and South-Eastern Africa, Madagascar, &c. There are also several allied forms of *P. cardui*, one of them, *P. huntera*, Fabricius, occurring throughout America from Canada to the Argentine Republic; *P. kershawii*, M'Coy, in Australia and again in Costa Rica, and others in South America.

The two species which occur in India are moderate-sized Butterflies, the ground-colour of the upperside of one of them (*P. indica*) black, with a broad irregular oblique scarlet band across the upperside of the forewing, and some whitish spots towards the apex, the outer margin of the hindwing bordered in the middle with scarlet bearing four oblong black spots; the other species (*P. cardui*) has the basal two-thirds of the forewing on the upperside irregularly marked with patches of reddish-ochreous, that colour covering almost the

---

* VERTICILLATE, having parts arranged in a whorl, from *verticillus*, the whirl of a spindle.

whole of the hindwing, but bearing a submarginal series of oval black spots. Both species are usually common where they occur ; they have a bold flight, but frequently settle with outstretched wings, and return again and again to the place from which they may have been driven. The forelegs of the species of this genus as well as of *Vanessa* and *Symbrenthia* are more densely hairy than those of any other subfamily, which feature has earned for them the name of the " Brush-footed Butterflies."

Key to the Indian species of Pyrameis.

A. Upperside, forewing with basal two-thirds, hindwing almost entirely, ochreous-red, marked with irregular black spots and blotches.

520. P. CARDUI, Mundus.

B. Upperside, forewing with broad irregular oblique di-cal scarlet band ; hindwing, outer margin scarlet in the middle.

521. P. INDICA. Hilly portions of India, Ceylon.

520. Pyrameis cardui, Linnæus.

Papilio cardui, Linnæus, Syst. Nat. Ins., ed. x, p. 475, n. 107 (1758) ; idem, id., Faun. Suec., p 276, n. 1054 (1761) ; idem, id., Syst. Nat., ed. xii, vol. i, pt. ii, p. 774, n. 157 (1767) ; id., Esper, Schmett., vol. i, pt. i, pl. x, fig. 3 (1777) ; id., Hübner, Eur. Schmett., vol. i, figs 73, 74 (1793?) ; id., Fabricius, Ent. Syst., vol. iii, pt. i, p. 104, n. 300 (1793) ; *Vanessa cardui*, Hübner, Verz. bek. Schmett., p. 33, n. 271 (1816) ; *Pyrameis cardui*, Horsfield and Moore, Cat. Lep. Mus. E. I. C., vol. i, p. 138, n. 280, pl. v, fig. 3, *larva* ; 30, *pupa* (1857) ; id., Trimen, Rhop. Afr. Aust., p. 119, n. 73 (1862-66) ; id., Butler, Cat. Fab. Lep B M., p. 77, n. 2 (1869) ; id , Moore, Lep. Cey., vol. i, p. 50, pl. xxvii, figs. i, *image* ; 1a, *larva* and *pupa* (1881) ; id., Godman and Salvin, Biol. Cent.-Am., Rhop., p. 217, n. 1 (1882) ; *Papilio carduelis*, Cramer, Pap. Ex., vol. 1, pl. xxvi, figs. E, F (1775) ; " A Cosmopolitan Butterfly," Scudder, Am. Nat. (1876).

HABITAT : Throughout India, Ceylon, the Andamans and Nicobars.

EXPANSE : 2·10 to 2·75 inches.

DESCRIPTION : MALE and FEMALE. " UPPERSIDE, *both wings* ochreous-red. *Forewing* with the basal area ochreous-brown ; an oblique irregular-shaped angular band, the apical area and exterior border black ; before the apex is a short white oblique band and a curved series of four spots ; a pale marginal line ; interspace at end of cell whitish in the female. *Hindwing* with the basal area, a confluent discal fascia, and the costal border ochreous-brown ; a transverse discal row of five black spots, each spot with slightly paler outer ring, a submarginal row of lunular spots, and a marginal row of larger spots." (*Moore*, l. c.) UNDERSIDE, *forewing*, much as above, but the basal area more decidedly red and the apex and outer margin ochreous, some additional black spots in the cell placed just below the subcostal nervure. *Hindwing* ochreous, richly spotted and marbled with deeper shades of ochreous and brown. An oval spot across the middle of the cell, the five round discal spots as above but developed into ocelli, the second and fifth the largest, with blue centres and black outer ring.

" LARVA blackish-brown, with a longitudinal pale interrupted line on each side ; the segments armed with short branched spines. Feeds on *Artemisia*. PUPA tuberculate, head bluntly cleft, pale ochreous or brown, more or less spotted with yellow." (*Moore*, l. c.) Mr. Hocking records (Proc. Zool. Soc. Lond., 1882, p. 240) the larva as feeding on nettle. Mr. Scudder considers this to be a doubtful food-plant. Mr. E. H. Aitken records it as feeding in Bombay " on different species of *Blumea*, all of which are monsoon annuals."

The following account of the transformations of *P. cardui* is taken from a valuable paper by Mr. Samuel Scudder in the "American Naturalist" for July and October, 1876 :—

" The eggs, which are deposited on leaves of plants, vary considerably ; their vertical ribs ranging from fourteen to nineteen, and averaging fifteen and a half to sixteen in number. When about to deposit her eggs, the female alights upon a leaf and moves about with trembling wings, and body generally on a line with the midrib, until it finds a spot to its taste ; the wings, elevated at an angle of about forty degrees with each other, now become quiet, the tip of the abdomen is bent down upon the leaf, and the egg is instantly laid. The same butterfly appears never to lay more than a single egg upon one leaf, although she frequently deposits eggs on different leaves of the same plant, and in one instance laid them on cut leaves lying on the ground."

"The caterpillar feeds principally on plants of the composite order, especially on thistles and occasionally on borages or mallows. It makes its escape from the egg, as usual among lepidopterous larvæ, by biting a slit almost around the crown of the egg, and pushing up this improvised lid; it does not appear to devour the egg-shell, as caterpillars usually do, but, after biting a few little holes partly through the upper surface of the leaf, makes its way to the opposite side and takes up a position, each one apart from its fellow, either between the midrib and curled-up rim if near the tip of the thistle leaf, or next the midrib or a lateral rib, if farther back; here it bites away the silken film and makes a nest, covering itself with a slight open web, into which it weaves the bitten particles of the film. From this retreat it sallies forth to eat irregular patches in the parenchyma, which it often partially covers with an extension of the web."

"Each caterpillar, when it has outgrown this confined abode, builds for itself a separate nest, generally near the summit of a stalk; it spins a thin web on the surface of the leaf, near the edge, if it be a broad-leafed plant, and then draws over a portion of the leaf by means of threads, completing the covering with a silken tent; when half grown it forsakes this and forms a more perfect nest, drawing together leaves, buds, and bitten fragments by the same process, so as to form an oval cavity, about 1·4 inches long vertically, and a little more than half as broad. The narrow, irregular, crisped, and rather distant leaves of the thistle, on which it is most frequently found, cannot, however, be made to cover even a single caterpillar, and the spaces are closed by a thin open web, through which the inmate can readily be seen, but which is sufficiently close to retain all the rejectamenta of the caterpillar. The nest is usually covered, at least in the upper half, with spines of the plant, evidently bitten off for the purpose; there is an opening in the nest, near or at the summit, just large enough to allow the larva to emerge, apparently made by eating away the web. Within this habitation the larva rests with its head downwards, like its congener, *V. atalanta*; but, unlike it, when its earlier stages are passed, it feeds upon the upper surface and parenchyma of the leaf, without touching the under cuticle, and when these are consumed, it crawls out to seek its fortune and weave a more commodious mansion; when, however, it has reached its final stage, it devours the entire leaf."

"When about to undergo its transformation, the caterpillar does not wander far, and frequently remains upon the plant which has nourished it. It weaves a sort of cocoon of no definite shape, but larger than its previous nest, formed of partially dried leaves, connected by open, angular, irregular, silken meshes."

"The butterfly is particularly fond of fields, gardens, highways, open ground, and waste places; it frequently alights on stone walls heated by the sun, and is greatly attracted by flowers, particularly by thistles and other plants on which the caterpillar feeds; here it may readily be taken; not so in other spots, for although very fearless, it is very wary, and its flight is rapid, dashing, and discontinuous; it doubles frequently and abruptly, usually to the right or left, rather than up or down. It loves to return to the spot from which it has been driven, or to the immediate vicinity, often circling about first, as if selecting the best spot."

In India *P. cardui* occurs almost everywhere. In Ceylon Mr. Mackwood states that it is "Found everywhere, but more plentiful in the higher districts." Colonel Swinhoe records it at Karachi as "Plentiful in several months of the year;" in Bombay and the Deccan "Common everywhere from September to December;" he also records it from Quetta and Kandahar. It is decidedly rare in Calcutta; but as far as I am aware it occurs plentifully in every other part of India and in the hills up to a considerable elevation. It has been found in both the Andaman and Nicobar groups of islands, but has not as yet been recorded from the Malay Peninsula.

521. **Pyrameis indica,** Herbst (PLATE XVIII, FIG. 74 ♀).

Papilio atalanta indica, Herbst, Naturs., Schmett., vol. vii, p. 171, n. 64, pl. clxxx, figs. 1, 2 (1794) ; *Pyrameis indica,* Lep. Cey., vol. i, p. 56, pl. xxvii, fig. 2 (1881) ; *P. atalanta,* Cramer (*nec* Linnæus), Pap. Ex., vol. i, pl. lxxxiv, figs. E, F (1775) ; *Hamadryas decora calliroë,* Hübner, Samml. Ex. Schmett. (1805-16); *Pyrameis calliroë,* Hübner, Verz. bek. Schmett., p. 33, n. 272 (1816) ; *P. calliroë,* Horsfield and Moore, Cat. Lep. Mus. E. I. C., p. 138, n. 279 (1857) ; id., Moore, Proc. Zool. Soc. Lond., 1865, p. 761 ; *Vanessa indiana,* Godart, Enc. Méth., vol. ix, p. 320, n. 55 (1819).

EXPANSE : 2·3 to 3·0 inches.

DESCRIPTION : MALE and FEMALE. "UPPERSIDE, *forewing* black, with a broad medial oblique irregular red band, the lower [inner] portion of which is traversed by three irregular-shaped black spots ; basal area and posterior margin golden-brown ; an oblique subapical series of white quadrate spots and an outer series of small dentate spots. *Hindwing* golden-brown, with a marginal red band, [inwardly] bordered by black spots and traversed by a row of black spots and outer lunular line." (*Moore,* l. c. in Lep. Cey.) UNDERSIDE. *forewing* with the costa basally striated with black, two black spots at the base of the cell divided by a white line, a short narrow blue line beyond the end of the cell, the apex ochreous bearing two obscure ocelli divided by the upper discoidal nervule, other markings much as above. *Hindwing* brown, beautifully marked, marbled and irrorated with white, grey, darker brown, black, &c., the veins white on the basal half of the wing. A conspicuous oval white ring-spot in the middle of the cell, with a larger one enclosing a black space beyond, a submarginal series of five cordiform spots, the two divided by the third median nervule with blue centres. the margin marked with a blue irregular line and other grey, black and ochreous ill-defined bands. *Cilia* throughout white, spotted with black at the end of the nervules.

P. indica is a common species wherever its food-plant, the nettle, is found. It occurs commonly in the Himalayas up to considerable elevations. Colonel Swinhoe records it from "Bombay, several examples in 1877, not observed since." In Ceylon it is "rarely seen under 4,000 feet elevation. Settles on pathways or open ground. Very swift of flight. Larva feeds on nettle, *Urtica neilgherriensis*" (*Mackwood*). "Found [in Ceylon] at all times in forest land, Central Provinces, 3,000 to 6,000 feet. Darts about rapidly and settles on the ground. Commonest at the highest elevation" (*Hutchison*). I possess a curious aberration taken in the Dehra Dun in July, 1879, by Colonel Buckley, which almost exactly agrees with a variety of the European *P. atalanta* figured by Herbst.* The European "Red Admiral," *P. atalanta,* differs from *P. indica* in having the red oblique band across the forewing much narrower and very even in width throughout, the basal area darker, merging into uniform black outwardly, the black colour not broken up into spots at the inner edge of the red band as in *P. indica* ; the spots beyond the band larger and pure white.

The figure shows both sides of a female Masuri specimen in the Indian Museum, Calcutta.

Genus 81.—VANESSA, Fabricius. (PLATE XVIII).

Vanessa, Fabricius, Ill. Mag., vol. vi, p. 281, n. 12 (1807) ; id., Latreille, Enc. Méth., vol. ix, p. 10, (1819) ; id., Felder, Neues Lep., p. 12, n. 23 (1861) ; id., Lep. Cey , vol i, p. 48 (1881) ; id., Godman and Salvin, Biol. Cent.-Am., p. 214 (1882) ; *Polygonia, Eugonia,* and *Inachis,* Hübner, Verz. bek. Schmett., pp. 36, 37 (1816) ; *Grapta,* Kirby, Fauna Bor. Amer., vol. iv, p. 292 (1837) ; id., Felder, Neues Lep., p. 12, n. 22 (1861) ; *Grapta* and *Vanessa,* Doubleday, Gen. Diurn. Lep., vol. i, pp. 195, 198 (1848) ; *Comma,* Rennie, Consp., p. 8 (1832) ; *Hamadryas†,* Hübner, Tentamen, p. 1 (1806).

"HEAD, of moderate width, densely clothed with long hairs ; *eyes,* more or less oval, densely hairy ; *palpi,* porrect, ascending, projecting considerably beyond the forehead, scaly and densely hairy all round. First joint scarcely two-fifths the length of the second, sub-cylindric, much curved ; second joint more or less swollen beyond the middle, thence tapering to the apex, which is obliquely truncate ; third joint fully two-fifths the length of the second,

* Pap , pl. clxxx, figs. 5, 6.

† This name was the first applied to species of the genus, and following the law of strict priority, should be used for it.

slender, subcylindric, or nearly acicular, more or less pointed at the apex ; *antennæ*, about three-fourths the length of the body, with two distinct grooves below ; the club rather short, gradually tapering at its origin ; the last joint minute, pointed ; *thorax*, moderately stout, clothed with long hairs ; *abdomen* about two-thirds the length of the inner margin of the hindwing. FOREWING, subtriangular ; the apex truncate ; *costal margin* but little curved, sometimes deeply emarginate at the shoulder ; *outer* margin about three-fourths the length of the costa, sinuate, emarginate ; *inner* margin nearly straight, slightly longer than the outer ; [in the *V. canace* and *Grapta* groups the inner margin is highly sinuous and outwardly excavated] ; *costal nervure* rather stout, extending about to the middle of the costa ; *subcostal* nervure not much slenderer than the costal, and separated from it by a short interval ; its first and second branches thrown off close together, and but little before the end of the cell ; the third arising at about two-thirds of the distance from the base to the apex, and terminating close to the apex, the fourth rather nearer to the origin of the third than to the outer margin ; *upper disco-cellular nervule* very short, all but wanting ; *middle* disco-cellular likewise short ; *lower* disco-cellular atrophied, or nearly so, its position indicated by a faint line, sometimes showing the rudiment of a nervule, which arises from the second discoidal nervule, not far from its origin, and runs obliquely downwards to the third median nervule. HINDWING, somewhat obovate ; *inner margin* longest ; *costal* and *outer* margins about equal, the former more or less rounded, the latter more or less sinuate, dentate, prolonged into a tooth or short tail at the termination of the third median nervule ; *præcostal nervure* simple ; *discoidal nervule* arising from the second subcostal soon after its origin. FORELEGS, of the *male* with the *femur* and *tibia* about equal in length, the latter rather stouter than the former ; *tarsus* of the same length as the tibia, subcylindric, or slightly tapering towards the apex, sometimes with one or two strangulations near the middle. Of the *female* with the *femur* and *tibia* equal in length, the latter unarmed ; *tarsus* about the same length as the tibia, first joint more than three times the length of the second, spiny below, beyond the middle, this and the three following joints armed at the apex with a stout spine on each side, mostly covered by a tuft of hairs at the base of the next joint ; second joint spiny below ; third and fourth about one-third the length of the second ; the latter shorter than the former, very obliquely truncate at the apex ; fifth joint short, transverse, sometimes scarcely visible from below. MIDDLE and HINDLEGS, moderately stout ; *femora* and *tibiæ* about equal, the latter spiny without, and laterally within ; the spurs long, robust ; *tarsi* about as long as the tibiæ, spiny laterally, and, except the fifth joint, below ; the spines of the lower surface arranged in two nearly regular series ; first joint almost four times the length of the second, third and fourth each gradually shorter, fifth longer than the second ; *claws* long, but little curved, grooved below ; *paronychia* with the inner lacinia wanting, or very short, the outer as long as the claw, and slender, but little hairy ; *pulvillus* small, short."

"LARVA cylindric, the head and first thoracic segment unarmed, the rest armed with long spines, set with setæ in whorls. PUPA very angular and tuberculate ; the head deeply bifid, of some shade of brown, sometimes pale green, often bearing brilliant golden spots." (*Doubleday*, l. c., p. 198.)

The genus *Vanessa* is represented by species occurring throughout North America, the whole of Europe, in Asia as far south as the Malay Peninsula, also in North Africa. It does not appear to occur in South America, Central and Southern Africa, the Malay Archipelago, Australia and New Zealand, in other words, in the Southern Hemisphere. Within our limits it occurs in the Himalayas, Maldá, Assam, South India and Ceylon, but it has not been recorded from the Andamans and Nicobars. The species are all very richly coloured, some being blue-black above with a broad blue band, another is rich castaneous with a marginal white or yellow band, others are rich ferruginous marked with black spots and yellow bands and patches, with a submarginal series of blue spots on the hindwing in some species. The colouration of the underside is far less rich than above, being usually black or ochreous, marbled or streaked with dull shades. They are insects of moderate size, have a " rather bold rapid flight, fond of alighting in the sun, and then alternately expanding and closing their wings, producing, by so doing, a faint rustling sound. Most, if not all, of the species hybernate." (*Doubleday*, l. c.)

Key to the Indian species of Vanessa.

A. Upperside blue-black, with a broad blue discal band across both wings.
    a. Blue band on hindwing having its inner edge well removed from apex of cell.
            522. V. CANACE, Himalayas, Malda, Assam, Upper Burma,
                    Malay Peninsula, South India, China, Japan.
    b. Blue band on hindwing having its inner edge touching apex of cell, with a series of blue spots beyond.
            523. V. HARONICA, Ceylon.
B. Upperside rich dark chestnut, with a broad marginal white or yellow band to both wings.
            524. V. ANTIOPA, North and Central America, Europe, North
                    Africa, Central Asia, Sikkim, Japan.
C. Upperside rich fulvous with black and yellow bands and spots.
    a. Costa of forewing evenly arched throughout.
        a^1. Upperside of hindwing with a submarginal series of blue spots.
            a^2. Basal half of hindwing blackish on upperside.
                a^3. Submarginal black blue-centred spots on upperside of hindwing
                    inwardly bordered with a broad dusky band. Of large size,
                    forewing strongly produced or angled at upper discoidal nervule.
                    525. V. CASCHMIRENSIS, Himalayas.
                b^3. Submarginal black blue-centred spots on upperside of hindwing
                    inwardly bordered with a rich fulvous band. Of smaller size, fore-
                    wing less strongly produced or angled at upper discoidal nervule.
                    526. V. RIZANA, Kunawar, Thibet, Kashmir.
                c^3. Submarginal black blue-centred spots on upperside of hindwing
                    inwardly bordered with a rich fulvous band, and then a yellow band.
                    Forewing very slightly produced or angled at upper discoidal
                    nervule.
                    527. V. LADAKENSIS, Himalayas at great elevations.
            b^2. Ground-colour of both wings uniform fulvous throughout on upperside. Of
                larger size.
                528. V. XANTHOMELAS, Eastern Europe, Central Asia,
                    Western Himalayas.
        b^1. Upperside of hindwing with no submarginal series of blue spots.
             529. V. VAU-ALBUM, Eastern Europe, Northern Asia, Kashmir.
    b. Costa of forewing indented at base.
        a^1. Upperside pale fulvous, all the markings small, and with no marginal black band on
          the upperside.
            530. V. (*Grapta*) EGEA, Europe, Central Asia, Quetta.
        b^1. Upperside darker fulvous, often fulvous-red, all the markings larger, a more or less pro-
          minent marginal black band on upperside.
            531. V. (*Grapta*) C-ALBUM, Europe, Central Asia, Himalayas.

522. Vanessa canace, Linnæus.

Papilio canace, Linnæus, Syst. Nat., ed. xii, vol. i, pt. ii, p. 779, n. 173 (1767); id., Johansson, Amœn. Acad., vol. vi, p. 406, n. 68 (1764); *P. charonia,* Drury, Ill. Ex. Ent., vol. i, pl. xv, figs. 1, 2 (1770); id., Cramer, Pap. Ex., vol. i, pl. xlvii, figs A—C (1775); id., Herbst, Pap., pl. clx, figs. 1, 2 (1794); *Vanessa charonia,* Godart, Enc. Méth., vol. ix, p. 308, n. 27 (1819); id. Elwes, Proc. Zool. Soc. Lond., 1881, p. 898; *Papilio kollina,* Meerburgh, Afb. Zeldz. Gew., pl. xlii (1775).

HABITAT : Himalayas, Malda, Assam, Burma, Malay Peninsula, South India, Ammiland, China, Japan.

EXPANSE : 2·5 to 3·2 inches.

DESCRIPTION : MALE. UPPERSIDE, *both wings* deep indigo-blue, crossed by a broad discal paler blue band, which is bifurcated above the third median nervule in the forewing, the outer portion ending in some small whitish spots on the costa, the band gradually increasing in width from the costa to the anal angle, and bearing a series of small black spots between the nervules

---

* The generic name *Grapta* which was established in 1837 should give way to *Polygonia,* the latter having been used for this group of butterflies in 1816. But as *Polygonia* has practically never been adopted, I have in accordance with almost universal use retained the former name here. Messrs Godman and Salvin state that "*Grapta* may be distinguished from *Vanessa* not only by the curvature of the costa and the crenulated margin in both wings, but by the palpi and forelegs being clothed with large densely matted scales." (Biol. Cent.-Am., p. 218).

(sometimes absent) in the hindwing ; two fine marginal blue lines, often more or less obsolete. *Forewing* with the costa more or less striated with bluish. UNDERSIDE most beautifully variegated and striated with black, green, ochreous, pale violet and ferruginous, crossed by a more or less prominent discal dark broad band having its inner edge indistinct, but its outer edge sharply defined with a highly irregular black line. *Forewing* with a small ochreous spot at the outer lower end of the cell touching the median nervure, usually with two ochreous spots near the apex answering to the terminal whitish spots of the discal band above. *Hindwing* with the outer end of the cell usually marked with a prominent ochreous spot, the black spots placed on the blue band above more or less present as obscure ocelli. FEMALE, usually larger than the male, markings similar, but the marginal fine blue lines usually obsolete, the angulations of the outer margins broader and larger.

This very beautiful insect has a swift flight, and in the Simla Hills is often found in the bed of a stream, up and down which it flies within a certain limited distance, often settling on a stone with open wings. It frequents paths in forests, occasionally settling on the ground with open wings ; if disturbed it settles with closed wings on the bark of a tree, where its rich dark colouring completely hides it. It occurs throughout the Himalayas ; Bholáhat, Maldá (*W. H. Irvine*), in Assam, and in Burma having been obtained by the Yunan Expedition. The Indian Museum, Calcutta, has a single female from Perak, and it is found in the hills of South India. It occurs also in China and Japan ; in the latter country occurs also a closely allied species, *V. glauconia*, Motschulsky.

This species has almost universally been known under Drury's name *V. charonia*, but the earlier name of Linnæus must be used, his short description applying very well to this species.

523. Vanessa haronica, Moore.

V. haronica, Moore. Proc. Zool. Soc. Lond., 1879, p. 137 : idem, id., Lep. Cey., vol. i, p. 49, pl. xxv, figs. 2, imago : 2a, larva and pupa (1881).

HABITAT : Ceylon.

EXPANSE : ♂, 2·4 to 2·9 ; ♀, 3·0 to 3·1 inches.

DESCRIPTION : UPPERSIDE. "Differs from the Indian *V. charonia*, Drury [= *V. canace*], in the blue band on the *forewing* being continuous and broader. On the *hindwing* the band crossing the middle, is straight, and has no black spots within it, but has a parallel outer row of small black [blue] spots." (*Moore*, l. c. in Proc. Zool. Soc. Lond.)

"LARVA light red, spotted with black, the segments divided by black and purple lines, armed with eight longitudinal rows of delicate branched spines, anal segment slightly humped. Feeds on *Smilax*. PUPA reddish-brown, abdominal segments tubercular, thorax angular, head produced and bifid." (*Moore*, l. c. in Lep. Cey.)

V. haronica appears to be confined to Ceylon, where it is "found in hilly country from 2,000 to 6,000 feet. Very common on pathways or roads bordered by jungle. Occurs all the year round. Larva feeds on wild yam" (*Mackwood*). "Taken in the Kottawa forest, Galle ; also at Kandy" (*Wade*). In some specimens the blue band on the upperside of the forewing shows traces of bifurcation, the white costal spots being always present ; but the band being broader on the hindwing, placed farther from the margin and not bearing a series of black spots, but with a series of blue spots beyond, will always distinguish it.

524. Vanessa antiopa, Linnæus.

Papilio antiopa, Linnæus, Syst. Nat., ed. x, p. 476, n. 112 (1758) ; idem, id., Faun. Suec., p. 277, n. 1056 (1761) ; idem, id., Syst. Nat., ed. xii, vol. i, pt. 2, p. 776, n. 165 (1767) ; id., Esper, Schmett., vol. i, pt. 1, pl. xii, fig. 2 (1777) ; pl. xxix, fig. 2 (1778) ; id., Hübner, Eur. Schmett., vol. i, figs. 79, 80 (1793 ?) ; var. fig. 931 (1829-1841) ; *Vanessa antiopa*, Godart, Enc. Méth., vol. ix, p. 308, n. 28 (1819) ; id., var., Freyer, Neuere Beitr., vol. ii, pl. cxiv, fig. 1 (1835) ; id., Horsfield and Moore, Cat. Lep. Mus. E. I. C., vol. i, p. 136, n. 272 (1857) ; id., Elwes, Proc. Zool. Soc. Lond., 1881, p. 898 ; *Papilio pompadour*, Pollich, Bemerk. Churpf. Ges. (1779) ; var., *Vanessa hygiaea*, Heydenreich, Verz. Eur. Schmett. (1846) ; var., *V. lintneri*, Fitch, Trans. New York Agric. Soc., 1856, p. 485 ; id., Morris, Syn. Lep. North Amer., vol. i, p. 57, n. 5 (1862).

HABITAT : North and Central America, North Africa, throughout Europe, Central Asia, Amurland, Japan, Eastern Himalayas.

EXPANSE : 2·3 to 3·3 inches.

DESCRIPTION : MALE and FEMALE. UPPERSIDE, *both wings* rich dark chestnut, the outer margin broadly and evenly white or pale straw-coloured, more or less densely striated with black ; along the inner edge of this border is a black band, broader than the pale margin in the hindwing, narrower in the forewing, bearing a series of rich shining blue oval spots between the veins, which become obsolete towards the anal angle of the hindwing. *Forewing* with two short subcostal white or pale straw-coloured bars, the costa striated with the same colour. UNDER-SIDE, *both wings* with the outer border as above but paler and more densely striated, all the rest of the wing black densely striated with deeper black ; sometimes with a more or less prominent ochreous spot at the lower outer end of the cell. *Forewing* with the subcostal bars as above, but less distinct. *Hindwing* with a narrow black irregular discal line.

" LARVA black, with white dots ; from the fifth to the eleventh segments is a row of dorsal light red spots, the spines are black or dark brown. Feeds [in Europe] on *Salix alba*, sometimes on nettle or on birch." (*Lang*, Butt. of Europe, p. 176).

V. antiopa, the "Camberwell Beauty" of English entomologists, has been obtained within our limits by Captain Elwes' and Mr. Otto Möller's native collectors at high elevations in Native Sikkim and across the passes in Chumbi ; it has also been recorded from Bhutan. All the Indian specimens known to me have the pale border on the upperside ochreous not white, this ochreous colour being of a darker shade than in any European specimens I have seen. As will be observed from the localities above, it has an immense range in the Northern Hemisphere.

525. Vanessa caschmironsis, Kollar.

V. caschmirensis, Kollar, Hügel's Kasch., vol. iv, pt. 2, p. 442, n. 1, pl. xi, figs. 3, 4 (1848) ; id., Hors-field and Moore, Cat. Lep. Mus. E. I. C., vol. i, p. 137, n. 276 (1857) ; *V. kaschmirensis*, Moore, Proc. Zool. Soc. Lond., 1882, p. 240 ; id., Doherty, Journ. A. S. B. vol. lv, pt. 2, p. 121, n. 63 (1886) ; *V. kashmeriensis*, Elwes, Proc. Zool. Soc. Lond., 1882, p. 403 ; *V. fixcilla*, Doubleday MS., in Gray's Lep. Ins. Nep., p. 11 (1846).

HABITAT : Throughout the Himalayas at suitable elevations.

EXPANSE : 2·2 to 2·5 inches.

DESCRIPTION : MALE and FEMALE. UPPERSIDE, *both wings* rich chestnut-red, this colour in the hindwing confined to a broad discal band, the base narrowly and inner margin below the first median nervule in the forewing, the base of the hindwing, broadly black, thickly irrorated with ochreous scales, the outer margins black bearing two paler lines, within the latter on the hindwing are a series of prominent deep black lunules with blue centres. *Forewing* with a quadrate black bar across the middle of the cell, then a pale yellow bar, then another much larger black bar, with another narrower pale yellow bar beyond it, beyond which again is a third rather smaller black bar, with a small bluish-white costal spot placed outwardly against it. A round black spot on the disc in the second median interspace, a larger one below it in the next interspace, a still larger but more irregular and diffused spot in the submedian interspace but placed nearer the base of the wing, with a diffused pale yellow patch beyond it. UNDERSIDE, *both wings* brown, thickly striated with black ; a submarginal lunulated black line. *Forewing* with a narrow oval black spot with pale centre at the base of the cell, two fine black zigzag lines enclosing a black space across the middle of the cell, a large black patch at the end of the cell. *Hindwing* with the basal half blackish, this area sharply defined by an irregular deep black fine line, a more or less prominent ochreous spot at the lower end of the cell, and two fine black lines enclosing a blackish space across its middle.

V. caschmirensis is a local race of the European and Japanese "Small Tortoiseshell Butterfly," *V. urticæ*, Linnæus, differing only from that species in the darker and duller tone of colouration and usually larger size. It occurs throughout the outer ranges of the Himalayas at suitable elevations, and specimens were obtained by the Yunan expedition. Captain Elwes (l. c.) writes of it : " Sikkim specimens, as a rule, are darker than those from Kashmir. It occurs at and below Darjiling during winter, and I have taken it on sunny December days at 4,000 feet." In Simla in fine weather it may be seen throughout the year. Mr. Doherty met with it in Kumaon " from the Káli valley (2,500 feet) to the summit of the Lepu Lek, over

18,000 feet, far above the snow line. I also found it abundantly in Nepalese Tibet and in the dry valleys of Hundes (Chinese Tibet). The prehensores as drawn by me are different from those of *V. urticæ* figured by Dr. Buchanan White." The larva like its European congener feeds on the nettle. It is a very common species where it occurs, and is somewhat variable in the tone of colouration, some examples being much darker coloured than others, but it is never as brightly coloured as the European *V. urticæ*.

526. Vanessa rizana, Moore.

V. rizana, Moore, Proc. Zool. Soc. Lond., 1872, p. 559.

HABITAT: Chini (9,000 feet), Middle Kunawar, N.-W. Himalaya.

EXPANSE : 1·87 to 2·20 inches.

DESCRIPTION : "MALE. Differs from *V. cashmirensis* in being a smaller and more compact insect, and having the *forewing* less produced at the apex ; markings and colours disposed as in that species, but more clearly defined and the colours much brighter. *Forewing* with the red colour near the base descending to near the submedian nervure, the posterior black spot being quadrate, well defined, and broadly bordered outwards with clear yellow, this colour also bordering the two upper discal spots ; submarginal black border narrow. *Hindwing* with the black base bordered outwardly by clear yellow ; the submarginal row of dentate blue-centred black lunules being without the broad inner dusky border. UNDERSIDE darker than in *V. cashmirensis* ; markings similar." (*Moore*, l. c.)

The only specimens of this species that I have seen are three in Colonel Lang's collection ; one from Gulmurg taken by Dr. Jerdon,* one from Kunawar, and one from Thibet, 10,000 feet. In all of them the forewing is less angled, the colouration much brighter than in *V. cashmirensis*, (being nearly as bright as in *V. urticæ*), but the chief distinguishing point is that in *V. rizana* the black blue-centred lunules on the margin of the hindwing on the upperside are not broadly inwardly bordered with a dusky band, thus causing the discal fulvous band to be much broader. *V. rizana* appears to be a rare species.

527. Vanessa ladakensis, Moore.

V. ladakensis, Moore, Ann. and Mag. of Nat. Hist., fifth series, vol. i, p. 227 (1878) ; idem, id., Second Yarkand Exp., Lep., p. 2, n. 6, pl. i, fig. 2 (1879) ; id., Elwes, Proc. Zool. Soc. Lond., 1882, p. 403 ; id., Doherty, Journ. A. S. B., vol. lv, pt. 2, p. 122, n. 64 (1885).

HABITAT : Gogra, Changchenmo (15,000 feet), Ladak (October 1873), Karatagh lake, on snow (16,890 feet), Yarkund, October 11th, 1873. Midday temperature 33°. Also in Kumaon and Native Sikkim.

EXPANSE : 1·62 to 2·30 inches.

DESCRIPTION : " Most nearly allied to *V. rizana*, Moore, from Chini. Differing in being (usually) somewhat smaller, less angled below the apex of forewing and at the middle of the hindwing ; the black markings on the UPPERSIDE are much less prominent, the black oblique bands on the forewing merging into the red, and appearing somewhat confluent ; the outer transverse discal yellow band is also broader. Other markings similar. On the UNDERSIDE the interspaces between the markings on the *forewing* are very much paler." (*Moore*, l.c. in Ann. and Mag. of Nat. Hist.)

There is a single male of this species in Colonel Lang's collection from Kunawar, and Captain Elwes' and Mr. Otto Möller's native collectors obtained it at high elevations in Native Sikkim. Mr. Doherty records it from " Near Kálápáni, Nepalese Tibet, 14,000 feet ; another near Hindi, Chinese Tibet, 15,000 feet. The prehensores are quite different from those of *V. kaschmirensis*."

It is distinguished from *V. rizana* by both wings being less angled, and on the upperside there is a pale yellow discal band commencing on the costa of the forewing between the

---

* Probable the specimen referred to by Colonel Lang in Ent. Month. Mag., vol. v, p. 13 (1868) under the name of *V. cashmirensis*.

second and third black quadrate patches and extending across the hindwing beyond the black basal area which inwardly bounds it. Mr. Moore's figure is much too highly coloured, all the markings are duller and less sharply defined. It is a rare species in collections. Captain Elwes writes regarding it in his paper on the Butterflies of Sikkim "About fifteen specimens, mostly worn, of this species, all of which agree in their characters, and can be known at once from the forms of *V. urticæ* by the shape of the forewing, which is rounded at the apex, with hardly a trace of the projecting point below the angle which is conspicuous in *V. urticæ*, *V. kashmeriensis*, and *V. polychloros*. It seems to be an inhabitant of the high cold plateau of Tibet, was first taken at Gogra in Ladak, and has never been sent to England from Sikkim, to my knowledge, before ; so I think we may conclude that it does not occur on this side of the passes."

528. **Vanessa xanthomelas,** Wiener Verzeichniss. (PLATE XVIII, FIG. 73 ♂).

Papilio xanthomelas, Wiener Verzeichniss, p. 176, n. 6 (1776) ; id., Esper, Schmett., vol. i, pt. 2, pl. lxiii, fig. 4 (1780?) ; id., Hübner, Ent. Schmett., vol. i, figs. 85, 86 (1799?) ; id., Ochsenheimer, Schmett. Eur., vol. i, pt. 1, p. 117 (1807). *Vanessa xanthomelas,* Godart, Enc. Méth., vol. ix, p. 820, n. 24 (1823) ; id., Horsfield and Moore, Cat. Lep. Mus. E. I. C., vol. i, p. 137, n. 275 (1857) ; id., Lang, Ent. Month. Mag., vol. v, p. 34 (1868) ; id., Moore, Proc. Zool. Soc. Lond., 1882, p. 240.

HABITAT : Eastern Europe, Central Asia, Western Himalayas.

EXPANSE : 2·0 to 3·0 inches.

DESCRIPTION : MALE and FEMALE. UPPERSIDE, *both wings* rich fulvous, the outer margin broadly black, bearing two indistinct diffused ochreous marginal lines, which are broken by blaish spots at the ends of the nervules. *Forewing* with two black spots in the middle of the cell, often more or less joined, sometimes forming a single quadrate spot, a large quadrate black patch at the end of the cell bounded above by the costa and below by the third median nervule, beyond which is a pale yellow diffused patch on the costa, another black patch beyond decreasing in width from the costa to the lower discoidal nervule ; with a pale yellowish more or less macular streak beyond from the costa to the upper discoidal interspace ; two more or less rounded black spots on the disc, the lower the larger, divided by the second median nervule ; two other larger similar spots in the submedian interspace, the outer one the smaller, less distinct and diffused ; the costa more or less striated with ochreous and black. *Hindwing* with a large somewhat rounded black spot from the middle of the costa to the discoidal nervule, the disco-cellulars defined with two fine black lines, a prominent series of blue lunules on the black margin within the ochreous lines. UNDERSIDE ochreous, densely striated with deep brown and black, the basal half and outer margins of the wings much darker. Both above and below this species is densely hairy, more so than any other Indian species of butterfly known to me.

Dr. Lang* gives Northern India as the only Asiatic habitat of *V. xanthomelas*, but for *V. polychloros* he gives Asia Minor, Armenia, Syria and Siberia. The differences between the two species are very slight. Dr. Lang says that *V. xanthomelas* differs from *V. polychloros* "by the somewhat sharper angular projections of the hind margins, the redder ground-colour of the wings [on the upperside] ; and by the presence of a whitish [in all the Indian specimens of *V. xanthomelas* I have seen, this spot is pale yellow] spot on the apical side of the exterior costal black spot. The blue lunules on the hindwing are rather more definite. The markings of the underside are more defined, and there is on the middle of the hindwing a faint light spot," the latter being also present in *V. polychloros*. There seems to be really no character by which these two species can be satisfactorily separated, but I keep them distinct in accordance with the generally accepted opinions of entomological writers. Dr. Standinger† has also expressed his opinion that they are doubtfully distinct.

In India *V. xanthomelas* is a rare species, and appears to be confined to the Western Himalayas, though it has been recorded in Horsfield and Moore's Catalogue from Darjiling. In Simla and Kulu it appears on the wing in the early summer for a very short period just

---

* Butterflies of Europe, p. 172.

† Hor. Soc. Ent. Ross, vol. xiv, pp. 263, 264 (1878).

after it has emerged from the pupa, it then disappears till the following spring, when the eggs are laid and the early stages of the insect rapidly passed through. Dr. T. C. Jerdon took a single specimen at Gulmurg in Kashmir. I have taken it near Dalhousie. Mr. A. Graham Young has bred it in Kulu on *Pistachia integerrima*, the "larvæ gregarious, under a loose web whilst feeding, when about to change to pupæ they desert the food-plant and disperse amongst low herbage;" Mr. Hocking has reared it on willow. The larva is ferruginous fuscous thickly sprinkled with ochreous; there is a dorsal and two lateral lines devoid of ochreous markings but defined with ochreous on each side, the head is small and black with numerous small black tubercles, the body cylindrical, constricted at each segment, gradually increasing in width to the fourth segment, each segment furnished with six stout black branched spines, of which the upper pair are the largest, the anterior legs black, the posterior ones concolourous with the rest of the body. This description is taken from larvæ preserved by Mr. Hocking.

The figure shows both sides of a male Kulu specimen in the Indian Museum, Calcutta.

529. Vanessa vau-album, Wiener Verzeichniss.

Papilio vau-album, Wiener Verzeichniss, p. 176, n. 7 (1776); *P. v-album*, Fabricius, Mant. Ins., vol. ii, p. 50, n. 489 (1787); id., Hübner, Eur. Schmett., vol. i, figs. 83, 84 (1793?); id., Ochsenheimer, Schmett. Eur., vol. i, pt. 1, p. 112 (1807); *Vanessa v-album*, Godart, Enc. Méth., vol. ix, p. 306, n. 22 (1819); id., Lang, Ent. Month. Mag., vol. v, p. 31 (1868); *Papilio polychloros*, Cramer (*nec* Linnæus), Pap. Ex., vol. iv, pl. cccxxx, figs. C, D (1780); *P. l-album*, Esper, Schmett., vol. i, pt. 2, pl. lxii, figs. 3a, b (1780).

HABITAT: Eastern Europe, Central Russia, Northern Asia, Kashmir.

EXPANSE: 2·0 to 3·2 inches.

DESCRIPTION: MALE and FEMALE. UPPERSIDE, *both wings* deep fulvous. *Forewing* with a black constricted spot across the middle of the cell, a large quadrate spot at its end, reaching from the costa to the third median nervule, with a pale yellow diffused costal patch on each side of it, the apex broadly black bearing a pure white costal spot divided by the fourth and fifth subcostal nervules, a round black spot in the second median interspace, two black spots each in the two following interspaces, the margin broadly black bearing two indistinct ochreous lines, the base and inner margin sprinkled with fuscous scales. *Hindwing* with a large rounded black spot from the middle of the costa to the discoidal nervule, with a white quadrate spot placed outwardly against it, the margin broadly black enclosing a more or less distinct series of rounded spots paler than the ground-colour and two indistinct marginal lines. UNDERSIDE ochreous but very variable, both in the tone of the ground-colour and the extent and disposition of the markings, more or less densely irrorated and striated with various shades of black, brown and white, the basal area darker, sharply outwardly defined with a very irregular black line, the outer margin of the *forewing* between the angulations also darker, and bearing a bluish line; *hindwing* with a small white mark at the end of the cell, often obsolete. It is distinctly transitional to the next group of species.

Dr. Lang (Butt. of Eur., p. 173) describes the larva in Europe as "brownish-red, with a dark dorsal line, and yellowish-white lateral stripes; the spines are yellowish with darker tips. Gregarious on poplar and sallow."

Dr. T. C. Jerdon took this species at Gulmurg, 9,000 feet; it has also been taken at Sona-murg, both in Kashmir, which are the only records of its occurrence in India. It appears to be a rare species. On the upperside it bears a close resemblance to *V. xanthomelas*, especially on the forewing; the hindwing however prominently differs in having a white patch beyond the black patch on the middle of the costa, and in the entire absence of the blue lunules.

The next two species belong to a genus which has been separated from *Vanessa* under the name of *Grapta* by Kirby. Typically the genus differs from *Vanessa* by the costa of the forewing at the base being deeply excavated, the inner margin highly sinuous, and the outer margins more deeply crenulated, but all these characters are variable. In *Grapta egea*, Cramer, they are hardly more prominent than in *Vanessa vau-album*. The palpi and forelegs are less hairy than in *Vanessa*, being clothed with large densely matted scales.

530. Vanessa egea, Cramer.

Papilio egea, Cramer, Pap. Ex., vol. i, pl. lxxviii, figs. C, D (1775) ; *P. l-album*, Hübner, Eur. Schmett., vol. i, figs. 90, 91 (1794 ?) ; *Vanessa l-album*, Godart, Enc. Méth., vol. ix, p. 303, n. 18 (1819) ; *Papilio triangulum*, Fabricius, Ent. Syst., vol. iii, pt. i, p. 125, n. 381 (1793) ; *P. vau-album*, Esper (*vau* Wiener Verzeichniss), Schmett., vol. i, pt. 2, pl. lii, fig. 1 (1780).

HABITAT : Parts of South Europe, the Caspian, Asia Minor, Persia, Turkestan, Kouldja, Quetta.

EXPANSE : 1·75 to 2·4 inches.

DESCRIPTION : FEMALE. UPPERSIDE, *both wings* pale fulvous, the outer margins with two fuscous-ferruginous lines, with a series of indistinct pale yellow lunules within. *Forewing* with two black spots, one above the other in the middle of the cell, a large quadrate spot from the costa to the third median nervule at its end, a round spot in the middle of the submedian interspace, a diffused blackish patch on the costa near the apex, with other indistinct markings of a darker fulvous than the ground-colour on the disc. *Hindwing* with a black spot on the middle of the costa reaching the second subcostal nervule, and another at the end of the cell. UNDERSIDE, *both wings* pale brown, beautifully marbled and streaked with various shades of ochreous, brown and black, a discal irregular pale band. *Hindwing* with a white mark at the end of the cell formed of two straight lines meeting at a very obtuse angle like a broad letter V. The MALE does not differ from the female.

This description is taken from a single female specimen captured at Quetta, 6,500 feet, which is the only occurrence of *V. egea* within Indian limits known to me. It differs from European specimens of the species in the Indian Museum, Calcutta, in lacking the two round black spots on the disc of the forewing on the upperside, divided by the second median nervule, but there are traces of these lost spots, there being spots in their place of a deeper shade of fulvous than the ground-colour. *V. egea* has the inner margin of the forewing almost straight, the costa of the forewing hardly at all excavated at the base, and the outer margin of both wings much less angled than in the following species.

The larva in Europe is described by Dr. Lang (Butt. of Eur., p. 169) as being " blue and spiny, second segment striped transversely with black and yellow. Said to be solitary on *Parietaria officinalis*."

531. Vanessa c-album, Linnæus.

Papilio c-album, Linnæus, Syst. Nat., ed. x, p. 477, n. 115 (1758) ; idem, id., Faun. Suec., p. 279, n. 1059 (1761) ; idem, id., Syst. Nat., ed. xii, vol. i, pt. 2, p. 778, n. 168 (1767) ; id., Esper, Schmett., vol. i, pt. i, pl. xiii, fig. 3 (1777) ; pt. 2, pl. lix, fig. 3 (1780 ?) ; id., Hübner, Eur. Schmett., vol. i, figs. 92, 93 (1794 ?) ; *Vanessa c-album*, Godart, Enc. Méth., vol. ix, p. 309, n. 17 (1819) ; id., Herrich-Schäffer, Schmett. Eur., vol. i, figs. 159, 160 (1844) ; id., Lang, Ent. Mooth. Mag., vol. v, p. 34 (1868) ; id., Elwes, Proc. Zool. Soc. Lond., 1882, p. 403 ; *Papilio g-album*, Fourcroy, Ent. Paris, vol. ii, p. 215 (1785) ; *Vanessa comma-alba*, Miller, Brit. Ent., pl. i, fig. 3 (1821) ; *V. melanostigta*, Stephens, Cat. Brit. Lep., vol. i, p. 11 (1856), var. ; *Papilio c-album*, Hübner, Eur. Schmett., vol. i, figs. 637, 638 (1824), var.; *P. f-album*, Esper, Schmett., vol. i, pt. 2, pl. lxxxvii, fig. 1 (1783), var.; *Grapta agnicula*, Moore, Proc. Zool. Soc. Lond., 1872, p. 559.

HABITAT : Europe, Asia Minor, Persia, Armenia, Himalayas.

EXPANSE : 1·8 to 2·3 inches.

DESCRIPTION : MALE and FEMALE. UPPERSIDE, *both wings* varying in shade from light fulvous to dark fulvous-red, the base irrorated with fuscous, and with a marginal black band, sometimes very broad on the hindwing and enclosing a series of spots of the ground-colour, at others much narrower, with a series of black more or less conjoined spots within, divided from it by a band of the ground-colour, sometimes on the forewing with a series of pale yellow spots placed inwardly against it. *Forewing* with a black bar in the middle of the cell often divided into two well-separated spots one above the other, a black bar at the end of the cell from the costa to the third median nervule, sometimes with a diffused pale yellow costal patch placed outwardly against it, with a wedge-shaped black bar beyond ; with three rounded discal spots and a fourth less distinct diffused spot near the anal angle. *Hindwing* with three discal black spots. UNDERSIDE extremely variable, the ground-colour sometimes ochreous, sometimes umber-brown, sometimes almost black, banded, streaked and striated with various shades of colour. *Hindwing* with a prominent comma-shaped white mark at the end of the cell. Dr. Lang (Butt. of Eur., p. 170) describes the larva in Europe as " greyish-brown, a white dorsal stripe reaching from the 7th to the 13th segment. Head with two horn-like projections. The colour of the head is black, and also that of the second segment, which is covered with minute bristly warts ; the rest of the body is covered with branching spines, brown and white in colour. The spiracles are black, surrounded with white and red-brown."

Colonel Lang writes of it : " This *Grapta*, though apparently common at Gulmurg, Kashmir, occurs but rarely in Kunawar, where, however, I have taken it at several localities far apart, and of diverse altitudes and climates. Thus one very fine fresh specimen was taken on the bleak Hungrung Pass, at about 15,000 feet altitude ; while others were taken 200 miles away on the lower, well-wooded ranges of the Simla district. The species varies considerably in the colouring of the underside." Captain Elwes in his paper on the Butterflies of Sikkim remarks of it : " A single, rather worn specimen was included in the collection, which, until we know more of the Himalayan varieties, I prefer to call *V. c-album*. It is certainly much nearer to Amur specimens of *V. c-album* than to what I have from Mr. Moore as typical *V. agnicula*. I have only seen one specimen from Sikkim before, which differed from this one ; and four others which I possess from various parts of the Himalayas differ from each other as much as a similar number of European specimens from various localities do. Unfortunately, I have but fifty specimens in all of this group—not a tithe of what would be required to illustrate it properly ; but the more I see the more impossible it seems to define them clearly. As far as I can see at present, no one can say to what species a given specimen of any of these forms belongs, unless he was told where it came from ; and if that be so, what more is necessary to prove my theory ?" From the large series of specimens from the Himalayas ranging from Kashmir to Sikkim now before me, I am unable also to find a single constant character by which they can be separated into distinct species or even local races ; they vary in every possible way, in outline, in the extent and distinctness of all the markings, and in the tone of colouration on both upper and undersides. It is very probable some of the variations are due to seasonal dimorphism, the Spring brood being pale, the Autumn brood dark-coloured. Mr. Moore has described one form as a distinct species under the name of *Grapta agnicula*, but the distinctive characters on which it is based appear to me to be quite inconstant. A description of it is given below.*

Vanessa c-album has an enormous range in the Himalayas, from Kashmir to Sikkim at any rate, but appears to be nowhere common. Mr. R. Ellis took it on the Sanch Pass, Chumba, at 13,000 feet, in September, and at Pangi, 9,000 feet, in May, Mr. Doherty met with it in Kumaon, from 8,000 to 15,000 feet elevation, and he remarks that he can separate his own specimens of *G. c-album* and *G. agnicula* by means of slight differences in the prehensores as well as by the shape and colouring. I took it at Chumpur, Kashmir, in June.

Vanessa (*Grapta*) *c-aureum*, Linnæus, has been recorded from Penang.† It occurs in China and Japan, and I know of no other record of its occurrence out of those countries.

Genus 82.—SYMBRENTHIA, Hübner. (PLATE XXIII).

Symbrenthia, Hübner, Verz. bek. Schmett., p. 43 (1816) ; *Laogona*, Boisduval, Sp. Gén., vol. i, pl. x, fig. 3 (1836) ; id., Doubleday, Gen. Diurn. Lep., vol. i, p. 190 (1848).

" HEAD, of moderate width, hairy ; *eyes*, oval, not remarkably prominent, hairy ; *palpi*, ascending, projecting beyond the forehead, clothed with long scales, rather closely appressed, except at the back of the second joint towards the apex, first joint short, subcylindric, curved, two-fifths the length of the second joint, second joint cylindric, scarcely curved, subtruncate

---

* *Grapta agnicula*, Moore, Proc. Zool. Soc. Lond., 1872, p. 559. HABITAT: Katmandu, Nepal ; Goolmurg, North-east of Kashmir. EXPANSE : 2·12 inches. DESCRIPTION : "MALE and FEMALE. UPPERSIDE bright fulvous-red ; *both wings* with prominent black markings disposed as in Kashmir specimens of *G. c-album*, excepting that in the *forewing* the basal spot within the cell is here broken up into two well-separated spots, and the marginal band in the male is nearly obsolete at the apex. FEMALE with a broader marginal blackish-grey band, the band on the *forewing* bordered by an inner row of yellowish spots, and that on the *hindwing* by a medial row of yellow spots. UNDERSIDE very dark greyish-brown, brownest at the base within the irregular medial transverse line, and covered with minute black strigæ ; a transverse discal row of hardly perceptible small black spots with pale borders ; a white comma-like mark on *hindwing*." (*Moore, l. c.*)

† Horsfield and Moore, Cat. Lep. Mus. E. I. C., vol. i, p. 138, n. 273 (1857).

at the apex, third joint elongate, conical, rather shorter than the first joint ; *antennæ*, about three-fourths the length of the body, terminating in a rather short obtuse club. THORAX, oval, stout, hairy. ABDOMEN, about two-thirds the length of the inner margin of the hindwing. FOREWING, nearly triangular, the *apex* very slightly truncate, *costal margin* but little curved, *outer* margin about three-fourths the length of the costal, slightly emarginate, *inner* margin nearly straight, equal to the outer; *costal nervure* rather stout, extending beyond the middle of the wing ; *subcostal nervure* five-branched, its first branch thrown off considerably beyond [before] the middle, its second shortly before the end of the cell, the third at a greater distance from the origin of the second than from that of the fourth, this last nearer to the apex than to the origin of the third ; *upper disco-cellular nervule* very short. *middle* disco-cellular much curved, about half the length of the *lower*, which is nearly straight, and anastamoses with the third median nervule where this last makes a slight angle. HINDWING, angular, the base with a rather prominent shoulder ; *costal margin* curved, *outer* margin curved as far as the third median nervule, then produced into a short tooth, thence sinuate to the anal angle, all the margins of about equal length ; *præcostal nervure* bifid ; *discoidal nervule* separating from the second subcostal close to its origin ; *discoidal cell* open ; *third median nervule* scarcely curved. FORELEGS, of the *male* with the *femur* scaly ; the *tibia*, except at the base, and the *tarsus*, densely clothed with very long hairs, femur longer than the tibia, tibia and tarsus equal in length, the former slenderer at the base than at the apex, the latter cylindric, scarcely curved, rounded at the base and apex. Of the *female* with the femur, tibia, and tarsus scaly, and furnished with long delicate hairs, least numerous on the tarsus, *tibia* much shorter than the femur, equal in length to the tarsus, *tarsus* four-jointed, the first cylindric, spiny below, the spines small, the apex unarmed, second joint about one-fourth the length of the first, armed with a few small spines below, and two stronger ones at the apex, third and fourth joints combined scarcely longer than the second, both armed with two spines at the apex, those of the fourth having a tuft of hair at the base. MIDDLE and HINDLEGS, with the tibiæ and tarsi of equal length, shorter than the femora, which are rather short, *tibia* spiny within except at the base, the spines short, slender, arranged in two nearly regular series, *tarsi* spiny below and at the sides, except the fifth joint, which wants the lateral series of spines ; spines of the lower surface in two somewhat regular series ; first joint longer than the rest combined, second joint less than one-third the length of the first, third joint rather more than half the length of the second, longer than the fourth, fifth joint longer than the second ; *claws* short, curved, grooved below ; *paronychia* bilaciniate, outer lacinia slender, pointed, as long as the claw, inner lacinia shorter, slender, pointed ; *pulvillus* jointed, shorter than the claws." (*Doubleday*, l. c.)

Symbrenthia is a truly Oriental genus, being found only in India and the Malay Archipelago extending into China, being absent however from Ceylon, the Andaman and Nicobar Islands and the Malay peninsula. The species are all of small size, the upperside black with ochreous or fulvous bands arranged as in *Neptis*, the underside is usually paler, and marked with black tesselations with some blue or green conical spots and a marginal line on the hindwing in some species, in others the underside is streaked and lined with ferruginous, with some violet powdering on the hindwing. In all the species the third median nervule of the hindwing is produced into a short tooth or tail. They have a rapid flight, but frequently settle. Mr. Wallace remarks of them that they "are strong and active insects, frequenting sunny places on the skirts of the forests."

Key to the Indian species of Symbrenthia.

A.　Underside profusely marked and spotted with ferruginous, no black tesselations.
　　a.　Upperside, hindwing with discal and submarginal fulvous bands.
　　　a'.　Bands broad, submarginal band on hindwing not dotted with black.
　　　　　532. S. HIPPOCLUS, Himalayas, Assam, Burma, Eastern Ghâts, Java, China.
　　　b'.　Bands narrower, submarginal band on hindwing dotted with black.
　　　　　533. S. KHASIANA, Khasi Hills.

b. Upperside, hindwing with a fulvous spot before the middle, and two spots on the abdominal margin.

534. S. LILÆA, East India.

B. Underside tesselated with black, with a submarginal series of conical blue or green spots.

 a. Underside pale yellow, the apical streak of the forewing and the discoidal and discal bands of both wings of the upperside, white on the underside.

  a¹. The bands and apical streak in the male on the upperside dark fulvous. Male with the apical patch small, not reaching the costa, no spot beyond ; female with the bands uniform paler fulvous.

   535. S. NYPSEUS, Kumaon, Sikkim, Bhutan, Assam, Naga Hills, Cachar.

   536. S. COTANDA, Sikkim.

  b. The bands and apical streak in the male on the upperside pale fulvous. Male with the apical patch large, reaching the costa, with narrow spots beyond ; female marked like the male.

   a². Discoidal streak on the underside narrow, ill-defined, marked with ochreous, lunules green.

    537. S. NIPHANDA, Sikkim.

   b². Discoidal streak on the underside broad, clearly and sharply defined, unmarked with ochreous, lunules cerulean blue.

    538. S. SILANA, Sikkim.

 b. Underside dark yellow throughout.

  a¹. The apical streak in the male small, not reaching the costa, no spot beyond.

   a². Submarginal series of five spots on underside of hindwing with metallic green centres, also similar marginal lunules.

    539. S. ASTMALA, Kashmir, Simla, Masuri, Kumaon.

   b². Metallic green markings on underside of hindwing reduced to a single lunule (the third from the anal angle).

    540. S. BRABIRA, North India.

  b¹. The apical streak in the male large, reaching the costa, lunules blue, a spot beyond.

   541. S. HYSUDRA, Kashmir, Simla, Kulu, Kumaon.

532. **Symbrenthia hippoclus**, Cramer.

Papilio hippoclus, Cramer, Pap. Ex., vol. iii, p. 46, pl. ccxx, figs. C, D, *male* (1779); *Symbrenthia hippoclus*, de Nicéville, Journ. A. S. B., vol. li, pt. 2, p. 57 (1882); id., Doherty, Journ., A. S. B., vol. lv, pt. 2, p. 122, n. 72 (1886); *Vanessa hyppocla*, Godart, Enc. Méth., vol. ix, p. 298, n. 5 (1819); Suppl., p. 818 (1823); *Laogona hyppocla*, Doubleday, Gen. Diurn. Lep., vol. i, p. 191, n. 1 (1848); id., Horsfield and Moore, Cat. Lep. Mus. E. I. C., p. 153, n. 315 (1857); *Hypanartia hippocla*, Hübner, Samml. Ex. Schmett. (1816-1824) ; *Laogona hippocla*, Moore, Proc. Zool. Soc. Lond., 1865, p. 762 ; *Papilio lucina*, Cramer, Pap. Ex., vol. iv., pl. ccxxx, figs. E, F, *female* (1780) ; *Symbrenthia daruka*, Moore, Proc. Zool. Soc. Lond., 1874, p. 570, pl. lxvi, fig. 10.

HABITAT : Himalayas, Assam, Burma, Eastern Ghâts, Java, Amboyna, China (*Cramer* and *Godart*).

EXPANSE : 1·8 to 2·3 inches.

DESCRIPTION : MALE. UPPERSIDE, *both wings* black with pale fulvous markings. *Forewing* with a broad discoidal streak, its upper edge indented before and at the end of the cell, its lower edge irregular, extending beyond and below the cell ; a subapical oblique streak, often divided into two portions, the lower the smaller, sometimes coalescing with the discoidal streak, with a small spot beyond ; a broad oblique discal band from the second median interspace to the inner margin. *Hindwing* with the discal band in continuation of that on the forewing, suddenly widening out at the abdominal fold, a broad patch on the costa between the termination of the discal band and the base of the wing, a submarginal broad band gradually attenuating to the outer angle, a fine marginal more or less interrupted line. UNDERSIDE, *both wings* pale fulvous, marked with dark ferruginous short streaks and spots almost throughout, which assume the form of a somewhat conspicuous discal band, with a small violet spot placed outwardly against it in the second median interspace, and another within it in the submedian interspace of the *forewing*. *Hindwing* more or less irrorated with pale violet on the abdominal margin and towards the anal angle, some bluish metallic submarginal lunules from the discoidal nervule to the anal angle, most distinct in the second median interspace. FEMALE larger, all the markings larger and paler, as is also the ground-colour of the UNDERSIDE, where all the markings are clearer and better defined.

S. hippoclus is the widest spread species of the genus and the most abundant in individuals where met with. It occurs in India throughout the Himalayas and Assam to Upper Tenasserim, and again in the Eastern Ghâts (*Doherty*). It is very variable, a not uncommon form with the fulvous bands on the upperside greatly widened and coalescing throughout, much reducing the black ground-colour thereby, has been described as a separate species as below* under the name of *S. daruka*. This form appears to occur casually wherever *S. hippoclus* is met with, and as it is extremely inconstant, some of my specimens being even more erratically marked than the typical *S. daruka*, I have no hesitation in considering them as all belonging to one variable species.

533. **Symbrenthia khasiana**, Moore.

S. khasiana, Moore, Proc. Zool. Soc. Lond., 1874, p. 564.

HABITAT : Khasi Hills.

EXPANSE : ♂, 1·75 ; ♀, 2·12 inches.

DESCRIPTION : "MALE and FEMALE. Allied to *S. hippoclus*, but differs from N.-W. Himalayan specimens on the UPPERSIDE in having the orange-red bands somewhat narrower, and in the submarginal band on the *hindwing* being dotted with black. On the UNDERSIDE the interlacings and other markings are prominent." (*Moore*, l. c.)

I have never seen a specimen of this species. As stated above *S. hippoclus* is extremely variable in the breadth of the bands on the upperside, the dotting of the submarginal band on the hindwing with black may, however, be sufficient to distinguish *S. khasiana*.

534. **Symbrenthia lilæa**, Hewitson.

Laogona lilæa, Hewitson, Trans. Ent. Soc. Lond., third series, vol. ii, p. 246, n. 4, pl. xv, figs. 5, 6 (1864).

HABITAT : East India.

EXPANSE : 1·8 inches.

DESCRIPTION : "MALE. UPPERSIDE dark brown. *Forewing* with a band from the base to beyond the middle, a minute spot at the apex, two spots below it (one nearly bipartite), a lunular spot (near the end of the first band), and a bifid band between it and the inner margin, all rufous-orange. *Hindwing* with a spot before the middle and two spots on the ventral fold rufous. UNDERSIDE ochreous-yellow, clouded with rufous-brown. *Both wings* crossed beyond the middle by a common rufous band. *Hindwing* crossed near the base by a band of brown ; tinted with lilac from the middle to the anal angle." (*Hewitson*, l. c.)

I have seen no *Symbrenthia* agreeing with the description above or with Hewitson's figure. I feel sure, however, that *S. lilæa* is only a melanoid aberration of *S. hippoclus*, a common form in which the yellow colour prevails being the *S. daruka*, Moore.

All the species that follow are distinguished from the foregoing by having the underside marked with black tesselations.

535. **Symbrenthia hypselis**, Godart.

Vanessa hypselis, Godart, Enc. Méth., vol. ix, Suppl., p. 818 (1823); *Laogona hypselis*, Boisduval, Sp. Gén., vol. i, pl. x, fig. 3 (1836); id., Doubleday, Hewitson, Gen. Diurn. Lep., vol. i, p. 191, n. 2, pl. xxv, fig. 1 (1847).

HABITAT : Eastern Kumaon, Sikkim, Bhutan, Assam, Naga Hills, Cachar, Java (*Godart*).

EXPANSE : 2·0 to 2·3 inches.

DESCRIPTION : MALE. UPPERSIDE, *both wings* black, with dark fulvous markings.

---

* *Symbrenthia daruka*, Moore, Proc. Zool. Soc. Lond., 1874, p. 570, pl. lxvi, fig. 10. HABITAT ; N. India. EXPANSE ; 1·75 inches. DESCRIPTION ; "MALE. Allied to *S. hippoclus* ; differs on the UPPERSIDE in having the orange-red bands very broad, which are irregular marginal and confluent, leaving but little black intervening spaces. On the UNDERSIDE the colour is paler and the interlacings much less prominently defined." (*Moore*, l. c.)

Forewing with a discoidal streak, a short subapical streak divided into two portions by the lower discoidal nervule, sometimes with a third spot placed above it in the next interspace, sometimes with a fourth spot placed outwardly against it in the lower discoidal interspace, the streak however never reaching the costa; a discal oblique band from the middle of the first median interspace to the inner margin, sometimes touching the second median nervule. *Hindwing* with a pale yellow costal streak, a discal band in continuation of that on the forewing, sometimes bounded by the median nervure, in other specimens continued broadly and diffusedly on to the abdominal margin; a broader submarginal band attenuated towards the apex, sometimes with a fine disconnected marginal line. The width and extent of the markings on the upperside are very variable, some Sikkim examples have them fully twice as broad as in others from the same locality. UNDERSIDE, *both wings* very pale yellow, with a marginal and submarginal very fine black line, the black ground-colour above more or less represented by black tessellations; the fulvous bands of the upperside replaced by diffused whitish bands on the underside. *Forewing* with the lower portion of the cell marked with two fulvous marks, some patches of the same colour on the disc below the third median nervule. *Hindwing* with a submarginal series of five more or less heart-shaped or conical black spots profusely powdered with metallic green and surrounded by a fine black line, a lunulated black line on the margin, these lunules from the anal angle to the discoidal nervule broad and also powdered with metallic green, a single similar lunule on the abdominal margin at the termination of the internal nervure. *Thorax* above black thickly clothed with ferruginous scales, *abdomen* ferruginous above streaked with black, *palpi, body* and *legs* beneath pale yellow, the abdomen spotted with black in three rows. FEMALE. UPPERSIDE, *both wings* altogether much paler, all the markings much broader, the subapical band on the *forewing* very large and continued broadly to the costa, a narrow streak beyond. The marginal line on the *hindwing* prominent. UNDERSIDE paler, marked as in the male, but the black tessellations larger and more prominent.

Next to *S. hippoclus* this species occurs most commonly. In India its distribution is much more limited, it is met with only in the hilly portions of the North-East of our Empire, from Eastern Kumaon to Upper Assam and Cachar. Mr. W. Doherty found it abundant in the Kali Valley in Eastern Kumaon at from two to four thousand feet elevation; it occurs in Sikkim at low elevations almost throughout the year, and in Major Marshall's collection are specimens taken by Dr. E. K. Johnson at Shillong in July.

536. **Symbrenthia cotanda,** Moore.

S. cotanda, Moore, Proc. Zool. Soc. Lond., 1874, p. 569, pl. lxvi, fig. 9, male.

HABITAT: Darjiling.

EXPANSE: ♂, 1·87; ♀, 2·00 inches.

DESCRIPTION. "MALE. Allied to *S. hypselis* (figured by Boisduval and Doubleday), but is smaller; bands orange-red, very broad; the band from base of *forewing* with irregular sinuous margins and confluent with cloudy red patches below the cell; narrow marginal line on *hindwing* distinct and extending to near anterior angle. UNDERSIDE white, clouded with dark yellow; tessellations similar; submarginal series of metallic-green conical spots and caudal lunules prominent. FEMALE differs from the male only in having paler bands, and in the oblique subapical spot being irregularly lengthened and extending from the costa to near edge of exterior margin, above which is a small recurved streak." (*Moore, l. c.*)

I possess specimens of *S. hypselis* from Sikkim which approach the figure of *S. cotanda* very closely, but do not quite agree with it. *S. cotanda* has all the markings very broad, but as pointed out in the description of *S. hypselis* this feature is a very variable one. In the broadest-marked male specimens of *S. hypselis* the subapical streak on the forewing is formed of three or four portions; in *S. cotanda* it is formed of two only as in typical *S. hypselis*. This slight character is the only one I can find to separate these two species, and I consider them to be very doubtfully distinct.

537. **Symbrenthia niphanda,** Moore

S. niphanda, Moore, Proc. Zool. Soc. Lond., 1872, p. 559.

HABITAT : Sikkim Himalayas.

EXPANSE : ♂, 1·8 to 2·0 ; ♀, 2·00 to 2·25 inches.

DESCRIPTION : " MALE and FEMALE. UPPERSIDE dark fuliginous brown. *Forewing* with a testaceous [clay-coloured] elongated discoidal streak, an oblique subapical irregular streak (reaching the costa], a small apical lunule, a broad band extending obliquely from near posterior angle to abdominal margin of the *hindwing,* below which band is a submarginal lunular band. UNDERSIDE pale testaceous yellow. *Forewing* tessellated with black along base of costa, at the apex, obliquely from middle of outer margin, and across the base of the *hindwing,* broadly from lower part of abdominal margin, and then decreasing upwards towards the angle, beneath which is a series of broad metallic-green lunules with black double borders ; outside these is a marginal band, the middle portion being metallic-green. The spaces representing the streaks and bands of the upperside are very pale and glossy on the underside." (*Moore,* l. c.)

This very beautiful and distinct species appears to be confined to low elevations in Sikkim, where Mr. Otto Möller has obtained it sparingly. On the upperside it may be at once distinguished from *S. hypselis* by all the markings being pale ochreous-white, the subapical streak of the forewing reaching the costa in both sexes. On the hindwing there is often a fine interrupted submarginal yellow line. On the underside both the white bands and black tessellations are more distinct than in *S. hypselis.* In fine fresh specimens there is a distinct cerulean-blue metallic black-lined spot at the anal angle of the hindwing on the underside, and another similar spot at the termination of the internal nervure, all the other metallic markings being green. The sexes in this species differ but slightly.

538. **Symbrenthia silana,** de N.

S. silana, de Nicéville, Journ. A. S. B., vol. liv, pt. 2, p. 117, pl. ii. fig. 9, *male* (1885).

HABITAT : Sikkim, Bhutan.

EXPANSE : ♂, 2·1 ; ♀, 2·3 inches.

DESCRIPTION : " MALE, UPPERSIDE, *both wings* black. *Forewing* with a very regular streak from the base to beyond the cell extending slightly below the median but not touching the subcostal nervure, a subapical irregular streak not quite reaching the costa or the outer margin, beyond which is a curved narrow lunular line ; a broad band placed obliquely from the second median nervule to the inner margin. *Hindwing* with a broad discal band, a submarginal one less than half the width of the discal band becoming attenuated anteriorly, an obsolete (hardly traceable) very fine marginal line ; all these markings bright ochreous paler in the middle. UNDERSIDE with the markings as above, but glossy opaline white, the black ground-colour replaced by prominent black and yellow tessellations. *Hindwing* with a discal series of five imperfect somewhat cone-shaped spots of moderate size, the three nearest the anal angle centred with brilliant metallic blue ; three lunules of that colour at the anal angle. *Both wings* with the margin black, a submarginal fine line defined with yellow, on both sides. FEMALE larger, the *forewing* broader, the outer margin evenly curved. Markings throughout paler, except the blue ones on the underside of the hindwing, which are larger and more prominent. The subapical streak on the upperside of the forewing touching the costa, and a small narrow spot just within it."

" Near to *S. niphanda,* Moore, which also occurs in Sikkim, but may at once be distinguished from that species by the ochreous bands on the upperside being much wider, and on the underside much paler also. The five cone-shaped imperfect spots are less than half the size of those of *S. niphanda,* and the centres of three of them and the anal lunules are pure cerulean blue instead of green." (*de Nicéville,* l. c.) All the specimens I have seen have been obtained in Sikkim at low elevations by Mr. Otto Möller, except one from Buxa, Bhutan, by the Museum collector, Moti Ram. It is a rare species.

539. **Symbrenthia asthala,** Moore. (PLATE XXIII, FIG. 106 ♂).

S. asthala, Moore, Proc. Zool. Soc. Lond., 1874, p. 269, n. 29, pl. xliii, fig. 9, *male*; id., Doherty, Journ.
A. S. B., vol. lv, pt. 2, p. 122, n. 74 (1886).

HABITAT : Kashmir, Simla, Masuri, North-Western Kumaon.

EXPANSE : 1·75 to 2·00 inches.

DESCRIPTION : "MALE. Differs from *S. hypselis* in being much smaller. On the
UPPERSIDE the bands are of the same orange-red colour, but of a different shape and broader,
the oblique subapical streak of *forewing* being lengthened and extending nearly across the apex.
On the UNDERSIDE the colour is nearly uniform orange-yellow, the tesselations somewhat
different and the submarginal band composed of imperfectly formed conical lunules, partly
dashed with metallic green ; lunules from anal angle to tail similar to those in *S. hypselis.*"
(*Moore,* l. c.) "FEMALE. Differs from the male in the red markings on the UPPERSIDE being
paler, the apical band of *forewing* wider and longer, extending from the extreme costa almost
to the outer margin, approaching the discoidal band, remote from the lower band, having a
deep sinus [indentation] on its lower side and a streak given out upwardly from its outer
end. Lower band broad, its upper part clavate, displaced outwardly above the lower median
nervule ; discoidal band irregular, heavy, its end produced below the middle median nervule.
Lower band of *hindwing* extends only to the second subcostal nervule, with only a trace of a
submarginal line beyond it. UNDERSIDE, nearly uniform orange-tawny, the base of *both wings*
and costa of *forewing* paler ochreous." (*Doherty,* l. c.)

This is a somewhat rare species which I have taken in the bed of the Simla river occasionally. The colour of the bands above is the same as in *S. hypselis,* differing therefore from
S. niphanda and *S. silana* in which they are much paler. The underside also being yellow
throughout will easily distinguish it from all the preceding species. Mr. W. Doherty took
this species in the Pindari Valley in North-Western Kumaon at 7,000 feet.

The figure shows the upper and undersides of a male specimen in the Indian Museum,
Calcutta, from Masuri.

540. **Symbrenthia brabira,** Moore.

S. brabira, Moore, Proc. Zool. Soc. Lond., 1872, p. 558.

HABITAT : N. India.

EXPANSE : 1·75 inches.

DESCRIPTION : "MALE. UPPERSIDE black, with very broad irregular-margined orange-
red bands, disposed as in *S. hypselis.* UNDERSIDE deep yellow. *Forewing* imperfectly
tesselated with black at the base, below and at the apex, and on the middle. *Hindwing*
tesselated at the base and on the abdominal margin ; the submarginal band formed of narrow
lunular lines ; a marginal series of narrow lunules, of which the third from the angle is
metallic green." (*Moore,* l. c.)

I have never seen this species, and the locality given is very vague. It is of course
abundantly distinct from *S. hypselis,* but very close apparently to *S. asthala.* From the description the metallic green markings on the underside of the hindwing appear to be reduced
to a single lunule, which feature, if constant, should be sufficient to distinguish it from
S. asthala.

541. **Symbrenthia hysudra,** Moore.

S. hysudra, Moore, Proc. Zool. Soc. Lond., 1874, p. 268, n. 28, pl. xliii, fig. 8, *male*; id., Doherty, Journ.
A. S. B., vol. lv, pt. 2, p. 123, n. 75 (1886).

HABITAT : Kashmir, Kulu, Simla, North-Western Kumaon.

EXPANSE : 1·87 to 2·30 inches.

DESCRIPTION : "MALE. Differs from *S. hypselis* (figured by Boisduval and Doubleday)
in being smaller, the hindwing more rounded exteriorly and shorter hindwards. On the

UPPERSIDE the bands are of an orange-yellow, much broader and with irregular sinuous margins, the band from the hind margin of *forewing* being joined to the subapical and extending thence inwards to the costa, from which a small streak ascends to near the apex ; on the *hindwing* the submarginal band is narrower, has an even outer edge, and extends to very near the anterior angle ; a narrow marginal line runs from anal to anterior angle. On the UNDERSIDE the tesselations are different, but prominent ; the submarginal band on *hindwing* is formed of short black transverse streaks, the second and third spaces only tinged with metallic greyish blue ; a short black anal spot and two greyish-blue-streaked black-bordered lunules from caudal angle." (*Moore*, l. c.) "The FEMALE is much like the male, but all the red markings are larger and more confluent." (*Doherty*, l. c.)

I have specimens of this species from Simla named by Mr. Moore. It is quite distinct from S. *hypselis*, but it is near to S. *asthala*, differing from that species in the bands of the upperside being much paler in colour and broader, the subapical streak reaching the costa, always coalescing with the discal band in the female, occasionally doing so (according to Mr. Moore) in the male, and with a short streak beyond. In two Simla male specimens taken by me the discal conical spots and submarginal lunules on the underside of the hindwing are very large and centred with cerulean blue, not green ; in two Kulu female specimens they are more or less obsolete. It is a rare species. Mr. W. Doherty met with it in the Pindari Valley in North-Western Kumaon, 5—8,000 feet.

Genus 83.—RHINOPALPA, Felder. (PLATE XXIII).

Rhinopalpa, Felder, Wien. Ent. Monatsch., vol. iv, p. 399 (1860) ; idem. id., Neues Lep., p. 47, n. 100 (1861) ; id., Distant, Rhop. Malay, p. 97 (1883) ; *Enrhinia*, Felder, Reise Novara, Lep., vol. iii, p. 405 (1867).

"Differs from *Precis*, Hubner, Moore, in its longer antennæ and palpi, more robust habit ; in the third subcostal branch of the forewing arising long after the middle of the wing, and the second discoidal nervule of that wing very near to the first, scarcely arched." (*Felder*, l. c. in Wien. Ent. Monatsch.)

FOREWING, triangular ; *costa* very strongly arched, slightly indented near the base ; *apex* truncate ; *outer margin* very deeply emarginate between the upper discoidal and first median nervules, below which it is oblique ; *inner* margin slightly sinuous ; *costal nervure* reaching the middle of the wing ; *subcostal* nervure giving off its first and second branches close together before the end of the cell, third branch emitted nearer to the origin of the fourth than to the apex of the cell, not reaching the apex of the wing, fourth branch reaching the apex ; *upper disco-cellular nervule* short, outwardly oblique ; *middle* disco-cellular practically obsolete, as the *discoidal* nervules spring from the same point, *lower* disco-cellular absent, so that the *discoidal cell* is entirely open ; *third median* nervule gently arched ; *submedian nervure* straight. HINDWING, with the *costal margin* slightly arched, the *outer* margin almost straight to the discoidal nervule which is produced into a blunt tail, afterwards deeply concave to the anal angle, which is produced ; *abdominal* margin deeply excavated below the termination of the internal nervure, and again slightly at the termination of the submedian nervure ; *præcostal nervure* strongly bent outwards ; *costal* nervure strongly arched, *first subcostal nervule* gently arched ; *lower disco-cellular* nervule absent, so that the *discoidal cell* is entirely open ; *third median nervule* almost straight. *Palpi* long, porrect, reaching to the level of the top of the head ; *eyes* not very prominent, naked ; *antennæ* short, less than half the length of the forewing, terminating in a lengthened somewhat large club ; *thorax* stout ; *abdomen* short.

The above description is taken from the typical species, R. *fulva*, Felder, the only other Indian species, which is allied to R. *sabina*, Cramer, presents many points of difference, and has been described as the type of a distinct genus by Mr. Doherty as below under the name of *Yoma*.*

---

* Genus YOMA, Doherty, MS. FOREWING, shaped as in *Rhinopalpa*, with the *costa* similarly indented at the base, the *apex* falcate, but the *outer margin* almost straight below the falcation. *First subcostal nervule* given off one-sixth before the end of the cell, the *second* slightly nearer the end of the cell than to the origin of the first, the third at more than one-third between the end of the cell and the apex of the wing, opposite to the end of the first subcostal, reaching the apex of the wing, the *fourth* and *fifth* midway between the origin of the fourth

These two species agree in having the costa of the forewing slightly excavated near the base, as in some species of *Grapta*, and the apex falcate, the outer margin in *R. fulva* is deeply excavated below the falcation, and produced again at the extremity of the first median nervule, while in *Yoma vasuki* (the Indian species) it is nearly straight; the hindwing in *R. fulva* is tailed at the termination of the discoidal nervule, in *Y. sabina* (described from Amboyna) and *Y. vasuki* the tail is produced at the third median nervule. There are also many differences in venation, in *Rhinopalpa* the discoidal cell of both wings is open, in *Yoma* it is closed, &c. *R. fulva* is rich fulvous on the upperside with a dark brown border on the outer margin, with three or four small round black spots within the dark border on the hindwing, the female paler; *Y. vasuki* is dark brown with a broad discal reddish ochreous band. The genus contains some eight or nine described species, occurring in Assam, Cachar, Arakan, Upper Tenasserim, the Malay Peninsula, Sumatra, Java, Celebes, the Philippines, Amboyna and New Guinea.

Key to the Indian species of Rhinopalpa.

A. Hindwing produced into a tail at the termination of the discoidal nervule.
　　542. R. FULVA, Assam, Cachar, Chittagong, Upper Tenasserim, Malay Peninsula.
B. Hindwing produced into a tail at the termination of the third median nervule.
　　543. R. (*Yoma*) VASUKI, Arakan, British Burma.

542. Rhinopalpa fulva, Felder. (PLATE XXIII, FIG. 102 ♂).

R. fulva, Felder, Wien. Ent. Monatsch., vol. iv, p. 399, n. 21 (1860); id., Butler, Trans. Linn. Soc. Lond., Zoology, second series, vol. i, p. 545, n. 1 (1877); id., Distant, Rhop. Malay., p. 98, n. 1, pl. xii, figs. 1, male; 2, female (1883); *Eurhinia fulva*, Butler, Ann. and Mag. of Nat. Hist., fifth series, vol. xvi, p. 307, n. 54 (1885).

HABITAT : Assam, Cachar, Chittagong, Arakan, Upper Tenasserim, Province Wellesley, Malacca.

EXPANSE : ♂, 2·3 to 3·1 ; ♀, 2·9 to 3·2 inches.

DESCRIPTION : "MALE. UPPERSIDE, deep fulvous, *forewing* with the border, *hindwing* with the external margin black; the latter with four posterior rounded black spots. UNDERSIDE, *both wings* shining brown, with two fuscous basal fasciæ girdled with bluish, near which a pair of undulate bluish strigæ, a third discal and an exterior fascia fuscous. *Forewing* with six ocelli, hindwing with five. Closely allied to *R. polynice*, Cramer." (*Felder*, l.c. in. Wien. Ent. Monatsch.)

"MALE. UPPERSIDE, *forewing* reddish ochraceous, with a broad fuscous outer marginal border, which is inwardly slightly concave. *Cilia* greyish. *Hindwing* reddish ochraceous, with a broad fuscous outer marginal border, narrowing and terminating above discoidal nervule, between which and the anal angle are two submarginal fuscous lines, the outer one broadest, and both preceded by three [or four] round fuscous spots, situated [one in the subcostal interspace] two between the median nervules, and one between the third median and the discoidal nervules—the colour at the area of these spots is distinctly darker ; extreme margin fuscous, with the *cilia* greyish, and a fuscous spot at anal angle posteriorly surrounded with an obovate violaceous margin. UNDERSIDE fuscous, the basal halves darkest, where they are crossed by two irregular almost concolourous fasciæ, denoted by their margins, which are pale bluish and much-waved, sinuated and broken ; about the middle the wings are also crossed by three contiguous, much-waved and sinuated pale bluish lines, the outer one of which is broken and somewhat indistinct—between these lines the colour is paler, and they are outwardly bounded by a waved fuscous line, which in some places becomes confluent

<hr>

and the apex of the wing ; *upper disco-cellular* somewhat long, directed obliquely outwards ; *middle disco-cellular* strongly angled, four times as long as the upper, its upper two-thirds straight, directed inwardly, its lower one-third also straight directed outwardly, *lower disco-cellular* outwardly concave, joining the median nervure just beyond the origin of the second median nervule, half again as long as the middle disco-cellular. HINDWING produced into a short blunt tail at the end of the third median nervule and another at the anal angle, the abdominal margin regularly excavated below the internal nervure, not deeply and sharply and ending in two anal lobes as in *Rhinopalpa* ; the *precostal nervure* slightly bifid, the *discoidal cell* closed by a fine *lower disco-cellular nervule*, somewhat concave, and joining the median nervure some distance before the origin of the second median nervule, the base of the *discoidal nervule* more curved than in *Rhinopalpa*.

Near to *Hypolimnas*, but differs widely in outline and in the shape and position of the disco-cellular nervules of both wings, these latter distinguish it from *Dichorragia*, which in neuration comes nearest to it among Indian butterflies. From *Vanessa* and allied genera it differs in the short broad cell of the forewing, with its deep acute upper angle more remote from the base than its lower one.

with them; these are followed by a broad irregular dark fascia, and a submarginal row of large rounded ocellated spots with blue and black centres and black margins, and situated between the nervules, six on the forewing and five on the hindwing (the lower spot on the forewing is usually bipupillated) ; two fuscous submarginal waved lines, which are preceded near the costal margin of the forewing by an irregularly shaped whitish spot, and the inner one of which is margined on each side with pale bluish ; beyond these the colour is somewhat dull red, and the *cilia* is black, interspersed with greyish ; on anal angle of hindwing, which is reddish, is a looped black spot. *Body* more or less concolourous with wings, *legs* fuscous, and the underside of the *palpi* and *tibiæ* and *tarsi* obscure ochraceous. FEMALE. Larger and much paler in colouration than the male. UPPERSIDE with the black marginal border of the *forewing* broken towards posterior angle, and on the *hindwing* not reaching the outer margin ; the basal third of *both wings* also appears distinctly darker. UNDERSIDE much paler than in the male, being dull reddish ochraceous at base, and then shading into creamy white and pale ochraceous ; the markings are similar to those of the other sex, but of paler and altogether different hue."

" The species is very closely allied to the Javan *R. polynice*, Cramer." (*Distant*, l. c.) In my opinion these two species are very doubtfully distinct, no author has defined the differences between them.

R. fulva has been taken by Mr. Wood-Mason in Cachar from May to August, there are specimens from Cherrapunji and the Naga Hills in the Indian Museum, Calcutta, Mr. J. L. Sherwill took it in the Jorehât district, Assam, in October, Mr. H. M. Parish obtained a female in November in the Chittagong Hill Tracts, and Dr. Anderson in the Mergui archipelago in the cold weather. There is a male taken by Captain C. T. Bingham in the Donat range in Upper Tenasserim in December in Major Marshall's collection, which approaches the typical figure of *R. polynice*, Cramer (pl. cxcv, figs. D, E, *male*, from Sumatra), in having the ground-colour of the upperside much darker than the other specimens I have seen, and the outer black border broad at the apex of the forewing on the upperside, the underside also is much darker. A female, taken by the same gentleman in October also in the Donat range, is also much darker than the Chittagong female mentioned above. *R. fulva* does not appear to be a common species anywhere.

The figure shows the upper and undersides of a male specimen from Cherrapunji in the Indian Museum, Calcutta.

543. Rhinopalpa vasuki, Doherty, MS.

HABITAT : Arakan, Rangoon, Tavoy.

EXPANSE : 3·2 to 3·7 inches.

DESCRIPTION : MALE, UPPERSIDE, *both wings* deep vinous-brown, paler on the outer margins, which bear two somewhat lunulated black lines ; a broad pale reddish-ochreous discal band, its inner edge sharply defined and somewhat irregular, its outer edge blurred and more even, directed somewhat inwardly above the third median nervule of the forewing, becoming gradually narrower towards the anal angle of the hindwing which it does not quite reach. *Forewing* with two whitish spots just beyond the discal band divided by the third median nervule, with two or three subapical ochreous spots, the one in the subcostal interspace always much the largest, a pair of black lines across the middle of the cell, and another pair at its end enclosing the disco-cellulars. *Hindwing* with a very small and obscure black spot on the outer edge of the discal band in the first median interspace outwardly defined with ochreous. UNDERSIDE, *both wings* grey, the basal area darker and sharply defined, the discal band above whitish below, five or six small black dots placed between the veins on a dark band just beyond the pale discal band, the two whitish spots on the upperside of the forewing divided by the third median nervule also white below, not black like all the rest, the marginal lines very obscure. *Forewing* with a prominent quadrate black spot below the submedian nervure at the anal angle. FEMALE exactly like the male, except that the wings are a little broader. *Celia* whitish, tipped with black at the end of the veins.

Differs from *R. sabina*, Cramer (pl. cclxxxix, figs. A, B, *female*; C, D, *male*, from Amboyna and Java) in the male having two whitish spots on the forewing on the upperside and underside divided by the third median nervule (on the underside in *R. sabina* they are black), the discal band less broad, especially on the hindwing, and on the underside all the markings are very obscure. The female differs in having one black spot only on the upperside of the hindwing, in *R. sabina* there are four, on the forewing also in the latter species there is a series of five ochreous lunules within the submarginal black lines, which are not present in *R. vasuki*.

Mr. W. Doherty informs me that "It is found flying rather commonly in the open country at the foot of the Arakan Yoma near Sandoway, Arakan, and has the habits of *Hypolimnas misippus*." In Major Marshall's collection are several specimens obtained from a soldier's box at Rangoon. It occurs also in Tavoy.

Another species, which almost certainly belongs to this genus, but has never been caught as far as I am aware since the type specimen was met with by Delessert, has been described and figured from the Malay Coast. As figured it is very similar to our Chittagong female *R. fulva*, on the upperside the dark apex and outer margin of the forewing, and the submarginal round spots and marginal lines are somewhat more prominent, the underside hardly differs at all. Should it prove synonymic with *R. fulva* (as I believe it to be), the latter name will have to give way to *R. eudoxia*. A translation of the original description is appended.[*]

Genus 94.—CYRESTIS, Boisduval. (Plate XXIII).

Cyrestis, Boisduval, Voy. Astrol., Lep., p. 117 (1832) ; id., Westwood, Gen. Diurn. Lep., vol. ii, p. 260 (1850) ; id., Felder, Neues Lep., p. 24, n. 54 (1861) ; id., Distant, Rhop. Malay., p. 139 (1883) ; *Chersonesia*, idem, id., p. 142 (1883).

"BODY, small, slender ; *wings*, large and delicate. HEAD, small, broader than the neck, but narrower than the middle of the thorax, strongly tufted in front ; *eyes*, very prominent, naked ; *antennæ*, not [sometimes more than] half the length of the forewing, very slender, and terminated by an elongated, very gradually formed, slender club ; *palpi*, long, slender, directed upwards to about two-thirds of the height of the eyes, and porrected to nearly twice the length of the head, somewhat cylindrical, scaly, basal joint clothed beneath with rather short woolly hairs, second joint also similarly clothed on the upperside, the joints not being apparent unless denuded of scales, terminal joint nearly as long as the second, slender, THORAX, squamose, slightly hirsute behind, collar narrow and distinct. ABDOMEN, small and slender, not above one-third of the length of the hindwing. FOREWING, large, subtriangular ; *costa* slightly rounded ; *outer margin* somewhat truncate or slightly rounded, five-sixths of the length of the costa, sinuated along its greater part, *apex* rather acute [sometimes well rounded, sometimes truncate], *anal angle* emarginate and somewhat lobed [sometimes evenly rounded, sometimes acute], *inner margin* not above two-thirds of the length of the costa, rather rounded outwardly towards the base, but emarginate beyond the middle ; *costal nervure* slender, extending to the middle of the costa, *subcostal* nervure rather thicker, its

* *Vanessa eudoxia*, Guérin, Rev. Zool., 1840, p. 44 ; idem, id., in Delessert's Voy dans l'Inde, p. 73, pl xx (1843) ; *Precis eudoxia*, Kirby, Syn. Cat. Diurn. Lep., p. 191, n. 25 (1871) ; *Rhinopalpa? eudoxia*, Distant, Rhop. Malay., p. 99, pl. xvii, fig. 6 (1883). HABITAT : Malay Coast. EXPANSE : 2½ inches. DESCRIPTION ; "*Forewing* subfalcate, *hindwing* outwardly subcaudate. UPPERSIDE, both wings ochraceous, the base fuscous, the apex black. *Hindwing* with two marginal lines and subcostellate dots black. UNDERSIDE, brownish-ochraceous, with dentate striga whitish and fuscous, and ocelli pupilled with blue near the margin."

"This beautiful *Vanessa* perhaps may be placed near the *V. laodora* and *pelarga* of Godart. The *forewing* is of a tawny-yellow ochre colour, highly concave and dentate on the external margin, pale brown at the base, with the apex blackish. The *hindwing* is dentate, with a small tail at the middle of the external margin and a small rounded prolongation at the anal angle. The colour is similar to that of the forewing, with the base equally brown and the apex blackish. It has near the margin two sinuous lines preceded by large black points ringed with a paler colour than the ground, of which the two outermost touch the apical blackish patch, and a small oblique blue streak on the middle of the lobe of the anal angle. The UNDERSIDE is of a yellowish brown ; at the base of the wings, of a paler colour than the middle, deepening in tone towards the margin, with some whitish zigzag lines with violet reflections, and others brown and transverse. The white lines of the middle and those of the external margin are larger and better defined. There is besides on the inner side of the white lines on the border of both wings a line of brown ocelli bordered with black and pupilled with blue, six on the forewing and five on the hindwing. The *cilia* alternately black and white on both sides. *Body* yellowish brown, *antennæ* black." (Guérin, l. c.)

Mr. Distant's figure of this species is a very bad copy of the original, the upperside is made much too dark, and there are a series of broad blue streaks between the veins on both wings, which are entirely absent in the original figure.

first branch arising at the distance of one-third of the length of the wing from its base, second branch arising at a very little distance beyond the first, close to the anterior extremity of the discoidal cell, third branch arising at about two-thirds of the length of the wing, fourth branch arising half way between the base of the third and the tip of the wing, to which it extends, the terminal division of the vein itself being rather deflexed, [sometimes with the second branch arising some distance beyond the end of the cell, the third midway between the origin of the second and the fourth], *upper disco-cellular nervule* very short and longitudinal, forming the base of the upper discoidal nervule, *middle* and *lower* disco-cellulars forming a straight transverse termination to the *discoidal cell*, which forms a triangle occupying about one-third of the length of the wing, the lower disco-cellular being about three times the length of the middle one, very slender, sometimes almost or entirely obsolete, and united with the median nervure exactly at the base of its third branch, which is regularly arched. [In some species the lower disco-cellular is directed obliquely inwards, and meets the median nervure exactly midway between the origin of the first and second median nervules.] HINDWING, somewhat hexagonal, elongated, the *costal margin* nearly straight for more than half its length, when it is emarginate to the outer angle [in some species, in others it is continued straight to the apex], *outer* margin sinuated from the outer angle to the extremity of the third median nervule, where the wing is produced into a short, narrow, curved, and obtuse tail [in some species, in others it is evenly rounded throughout, with no anal lobe] thence to the anal angle the wing appears truncate, the *anal angle* itself being developed into a short, broad, spatulated tail; *præcostal nervure* forming a slender, curved, simple spur, *costal* nervure much curved along its basal portion, then straight to the commencement of the emargination at the outer angle of the wing, *subcostal* nervure branched at about one-fourth of the length of the wing from the base, emitting the *upper disco-cellular nervule* (close to the origin of its branch) which forms the base of the discoidal nervule, *lower* disco-cellular arising at the same distance from the base of the upper disco-cellular as exists between the base of the subcostal nervure and its branch, lower disco-cellular straight, very thin, and united to the median nervure at the base of its third branch. FORELEGS, of the *male* very slender, short, and pectoral; the *femur* as long as the remainder of the limb, curved outwardly about the middle, and clothed beneath with long silky hairs; *tibia* very slender, scaly, clothed within with short hairs, as is also the *tarsus*, which is not above one-fifth of the length of the tibia, very slender, simple, and exarticulate: of the *female* considerably longer than those of the male, slender, and pectoral; *femur* thickly clothed beneath with short silky hairs; *tibia* slender, gradually thickened towards the tip, finely scaly; *tarsus* gradually thickened, short, with several pairs of minute spines near the tip beneath, indicating the very short articulations, the three terminal ones being extremely short, last joint without any claws or their appendages. MIDDLE and HINDLEGS, long and slender, scaly; *tibia* with a few very minute spines, arranged wide apart in two rows, tibial spurs very short; *tarsi* equal in length to the tibiæ, with several rows of minute spines on the under surface, basal joint about half the length of the tarsus, terminal joint furnished with long setæ on its upperside at the tip; *claws* small, much curved; *paronychia* bilaciniated, finely setose, the outer lacinia curved, broader, and obtuse, the inner lacinia small, narrow, slender, and rather pointed. Transformations unknown." (*Westwood*, l. c.)

The structural characters of the genus *Cyrestis* exhibit great variety; like the genera *Hestina*, *Neptis* and *Argynnis* it can be divided into two groups by the position of the second subcostal nervule of the forewing, which in three species which are the smallest in the genus and of a tawny colour, arises long after the end of the cell; in the other group containing the typical species, all of which are larger than those in the first group, though some have the tawny colouration, the second subcostal nervule is emitted before the end of the cell. The former group has been erected into a separate genus by Mr. Distant under the name of *Chersonesia*, his description of it is given below.* The outline of the wings in *Cyrestis*

* Genus CHERSONESIA, Distant, Rhop Malay., p. 142 (1883); Cyrestis, section ii. Felder, Neues Lep., p. 21, n. 51 (1861). "This genus is closely allied to Cyrestis, from which it principally and structurally differs by the neuration of the forewing, of which the first subcostal nervule only is emitted before the termination of the cell, the second being emitted between the apex of cell and base of third subcostal nervule; the other

also exhibits considerable variation ; in *C. periaka* the apex of the forewing is very rounded, and the outer margin is convex ; the hindwing shows just the faintest trace of a tooth at the extremity of the third median nervule, the anal lobe being entirely absent. In *C. rahria* the apex of the forewing is acute, less rounded, and the outer margin is straight, and there are traces of a tail and anal lobe on the hindwing ; in *C. risa* these characters are a little more strongly developed, the outer margin of the forewing is straight, and the apex is sharply angled. In the typical *Cyrestes* the tail and anal lobe are very prominent. In *C. thyodamas* and allies the anal angle of the forewing and the apex of the hindwing are deeply excavated, in *C. risa* the apex of the hindwing only is excised, in the other species the outline of both wings as regards this character is normal. In *C. periander* the apex of the forewing is distinctly truncate. The lower disco-cellular nervule of the forewing also is present in some species and closes the discoidal cell, in others it is absent altogether. It joins the median nervure when present at different points, in *C. risa* exactly midway between the origins of the first and second median nervules, in *C. thyodamas* at the origin of the second and third median nervules. All the species of the genus are very elegant insects, the wings are very large and delicate, and crossed by several black lines forming more or less distinct bands common to both wings and parallel to the body ; the markings throughout are the same in character, the ground-colour being tawny, ochreous, pale buff, greenish or pure white. They are very beautiful insects on the wing, having a floating sailing flight, often settling on the wet sand on the borders of a stream to suck up the moisture with wings very wide outspread and lying flat on the ground, the forewings much advanced in front of the head ; if disturbed they disappear with great rapidity, as they settle suddenly with outspread wings on the *underside* of a leaf, where they are quite invisible from above. They are nearly always found near water, in Simla *C. thyodamas* may often be seen at rest on a bare quartz rock in midstream, its delicately pencilled markings exactly harmonising with the veinings of the stone.

"*Cyrestis* is a genus of not inconsiderable extent, which, although represented in Western Africa and Madagascar, has its head-quarters in the Oriental region. It is found in Continental India, the Andaman and Nicober Isles, Burma, Tenasserim, but not in Ceylon, and in, and from, the Malay Peninsula, throughout the length and breadth of the Malay Archipelago ; it has also recently been received from New Ireland." (*Distant, l. c.*)

Key to the Indian species of Cyrestis.

A. First and second subcostal nervules of forewing emitted before the end of the cell.
  a. Anal angle of forewing and apex of hindwing deeply excavated.
    a^1. Ground-colour white, or yellowish-white or pale buff.
      a^2. Outer margin of forewing narrowly black.
        544. C. THYODAMAS, Himalayas, Assam, Burma, Continental and South India, Andamans.
      b^2. Outer margin and base of costa of forewing broadly black.
        545. C. NIVEA, Upper Tenasserim, Malay Peninsula, Java, Borneo.
    b^1. Ground-colour rich deep fulvous
      546. C. TABULA, Nicobars.
  b. Anal angle of forewing entire, sharply angled, and apex of hindwing evenly rounded, not excavated.
    a^1. Apex of forewing rounded ; of large size, with no prominent outer black border to the wings on the upperside.
      547. C. COCLES, Khasi Hills, Sylhet, Upper Tenasserim, Malay Peninsula, Siam, Orissa, Andamans.
    b^1. Apex of forewing truncate ; of small size, with a prominent outer black border to the wings on the upperside.
      548. C. PERIANDER, Mergui, Tavoy, Java.

---

neural characters are similar to those of *Cyrestis*, [except the point on the median nervure of the forewing at which the lower disco-cellular nervule is joined, which is variable in the different species, but is always *before* the origin of the second median nervule]."

"Two species [a third, *C. periaka*, has since been described] are included in this genus, viz., *C. risa*, Doubleday and Hewitson, a species found in Continental India, and *C. rahria*, Moore, a Javan species, also found in Borneo and in this fauna. Its distribution is probably from Continental India to the confines of the Indo-Malayan region." (*Distant, l. c.*)

B. First subcostal nervule only of forewing emitted before the end of the cell.

    a. Both wings on upperside with eight straight, clearly-marked black lines.

              549. C. (*Chersonesia*) RISA, Kumaon, Sikkim, Assam, Chittagong, Upper Tenasserim, Java.

    b. Both wings on upperside with seven black lines only, the fifth from the base replaced by a diffused blackish fascia, the two lines beyond much curved and uneven.

              550. C. (*Chersonesia*) RAHRIA, Upper Tenasserim, Malayana.

544. Cyrestis thyodamas, Boisduval.

Cyrestis thyodamas, Boisduval, Cuvier's Règne Animal, Insectes vol. ii, pl. cxxxviii, fig. 4 (1835); id., Double-day, Hewitson, Gen. Diurn. Lep., vol. ii, p. 261, n. 4, pl. xxxii, fig. 3 (1850); id., Butler, Ann. and Mag. of Nat. Hist., fifth series, vol. xvi, p. 307, n. 55 (1885); C. thyodamas, var. andamanica, Wood-Mason and de Nicéville, Journ. A. S. B., vol. l, pt. 2, p. 246, n. 31 (1882); Amathusia ganescha, Kollar, Hugel's Kaschmir, vol. iv, pt. 2, p. 430, n. i, pl. vii, figs. 3, 4 (1848); Cyrestis ganescha, Butler, Ann. and Mag. of Nat. Hist., fifth series, vol. xvi, p. 308, n. 56 (1885).

HABITAT : Himalayas, Assam, Khasi Hills, Cachar, Upper Tenasserim, Andaman Isles, Bombay, South India.

EXPANSE : 2·2 to 2·8 inches.

DESCRIPTION : MALE and FEMALE. UPPERSIDE, *both wings* of different shades, varying from pure white to rich ochreous. *Forewing* with the costal area especially basally more or less infuscated, crossed by numerous fine black lines :—first a longitudinal one at the base of the cell, second an oblique one across the cell from the costa to the median nervure, the third crossing the cell obliquely continued to the submedian nervure of the hindwing, the fourth outwardly much arched confined to the cell, the fifth and sixth enclosing the disco-cellulars, the seventh, eight and ninth discal, continued across the hindwing, the eighth with a blackish smudge placed inwardly against it on the costa, and often with a more or less distinct diffused powdery black rounded spot beyond it in the lower discoidal interspace, the ninth the most prominent of all, marked with steel-blue from the second median nervule of the forewing to the anal angle of the hindwing, followed by an irregular series of annular ochreous spots more or less obsolescent in the middle of the wing, most prominent at the inner angle where they are richer coloured ; the margin marked with four more fine black lines, the three outer ones placed upon a more or less decreasing fuscous ground. *Hindwing* with the disco-cellulars marked with a fine black line, the tail black tipped and irrorated with white, the anal lobe and anal angle marbled with numerous irregular ferruginous, steel-blue and white spots, the abdominal margin more or less powdered with black. UNDERSIDE paler, marked much as above, the ferruginous markings at the anal angle and lobe of the *hindwing* more distinct, the latter with a prominent black spot in the middle.

Mr. Butler (l. c.) writing of this species says that it " has long been confounded with the following [C. ganescha], which, if not distinct, must surely, I think, be a seasonal form ; it has probably been assumed (without examination) to be the female of C. thyodamas." He keeps (l. c.) C. ganescha as a distinct species, and adds this note :—" This is a yellow insect, with most of the markings on the wings of a deeper yellow, a few only remaining black ; the apical area is not smoky brownish, as in C. thyodamas. If it be a seasonal form of the preceding [C. thyodamas], one form must have been just disappearing as the other emerged from pupa, for in no other way can one account for both of them having been taken at about the same time." It is not clear on what grounds Mr. Butler says that the typical C. ganescha is a yellow insect ; Kollar in two places describes it as white. The smoky brownish apical area of the forewing is exceedingly variable, and there appears to me to be no grounds whatever for dividing this species into two. The yellow specimens are usually females in the Western Himalayas, but in Sikkim they are quite as often males, this dark colouration may be due to reversion to an ochreous ancestor, and it varies much in intensity in different specimens, every gradation being found between the whitest and the yellowest specimens. This yellow form does not appear to occur in South India. C. thyodamas is usually a common species where met with, but Mr. E. H. Aitken informs me that it is rare at Mahableshwar ; it occurs in the hilly regions of south India as far South as Travancore, but not in Ceylon ; also in Upper Tenasserim, but not in the Malay Peninsula.

Var. *andamanica.* Differs from all continental specimens of *C. thyodamas* " in the blacker apex and outer margin, in the prominent somewhat diffused black spot on the third median nervule between the third and fourth common black strigæ at the point where these bend towards each other in the forewing ; and in having the fulvous marks of the anal half of the abdominal margin, of the anal angle, and of the outer margin as far as the discoidal nervule, of the hindwing, much diffused and darker :—in having, in fact, all the markings and colouring darker and coarser both above and below." (*Wood-Mason* and *de Nicéville*, l. c.) The late Mr. de Roepstorff has sent numerous specimens, including one female, of this local race from the Andamans, which exhibit quite constantly the points of difference given above between it and the continental form.

545. **Cyrestis nivea,** Zinken-Sommer.

Amathusia nivea, Zinken-Sommer, Nova Acta Ac. Nat. Cur., vol. xv, p. 138, pl. xiv, fig. 1, *male* (1831) ; *Cyrestis nivea,* Butler, Trans. Linn. Soc. Zoology, second series, vol. i, p. 545, n. 2 (1877) ; *C. nivalis,* Felder, Reise Novara. Lep., vol. iii, p. 414, n. 634 (1866) ; *C. nivea,* var. *nivalis,* Distant, Rhop. Malay., p. 140, n. i, pl. xii, fig. 3, *male* (1883).

HABITAT : Upper Tenasserim, Penang, Province Wellesley, Perak, Malacca (var. *nivalis*) ; Java, Borneo (*nivea*).

EXPANSE : 1·10 to 2·2 inches.

DESCRIPTION : "MALE. UPPERSIDE, *both wings* pale creamy white, crossed by three obliquely waved fuscous lines commencing about the costa of the forewing, the first near the base, the second a little beyond the cellular apices, both angularly terminating on the abdominal margin, the third crossing the wings at the middle and terminating at the first median nervule of the hindwing. *Forewing* with a broad but irregular fuscous costal margin from the medial fuscous line to base, with an ochraceous basal costal streak ; cell crossed by a fuscous line near base, and with two very slender and waved fuscous lines at about the apex ; a broad apical fuscous patch and a broad outer margin of the same colour, terminating near the first median nervule, the first inwardly containing two waved pale lines with an inner grey spot, and the second possessing three pale submarginal lines ; between second and first median nervules is a submarginal and subovate fuscous spot, with an inner grey spot and inner pale margin, and this spot is connected with the apical patch by a waved fuscous line ; near posterior angle is an ochraceous spot, with a sinuate fuscous inner margin and two small median fuscous spots. *Hindwing* with a submarginal fuscous fascia divided by a medial pale line, followed by a fuscous line which becomes waved beneath the discoidal nervule ; a short straight fuscous fascia from apex to third median nervule, a submarginal fuscous line very broad at area of median nervules, and the margin at apex and also at caudate prolongation fuscous ; basal half of abdominal margin pale fuscous, and apical half of abdominal margin and internal anal-angular area ochraceous, marked with several fuscous spots and pale lines. UNDERSIDE as above, but with the fuscous markings paler, and quite absent from costal margin of forewing and abdominal margin of hindwing. *Head* and *thorax* above fuscous, their lateral margins ochraceous ; the first with the eyes castaneous, and the second with medial pale longitudinal lines ; *abdomen* fuscous, with ochraceous and greyish longitudinal markings ; body beneath and legs more or less concolourous with wings." (*Distant,* l. c.)

Typical *C. nivea* inhabits Java, and Dr. Felder, considering the Malaccan race, to which the above description applies, distinct, described it under the name of *C. nivalis,* as follows :—

"MALE. UPPERSIDE almost as in *C. nivea,* but the *forewing* with the interior discal striga not at all interrupted, arched, the exterior one less arched, submacular, the terminal border narrower, inwardly much less oblique as far as the lower discoidal nervule, almost bent in the shape of an S, the striga emitted from it more bent, with the two glaucescent streaks before the margin more approximating to each other and to the margin, the fulvous anal spot marked externally with another whitish spot on the margin, divided by a small black streak. *Hindwing* with the two discal strigæ closer together, the fuscous fascia bent almost like an S, cut through with a broader glaucous stiga, the apical white patch larger, the whitish streaks before the margin whiter, and the fulvous anal area extending beyond the third median nervule. UNDERSIDE more palely marked. *Hindwing* with the inner whitish streak before the margin hindwardly more dilated."

"A local form of *C. nivea*, Zinken, but with shorter forewing, and the hindwing more deeply cut out at the apex, and longer on the inner margin." (*Felder*, l. c.)

Mr. Distant states that "the variety *nivalis* differs from typical Javan specimens of *C. nivea* in not having a continuous fuscous margin to the forewing, and in the greater amount of ochraceous colouration near the anal angle of the hindwing." (*Distant*, l. c.) I possess no specimens from Java, but a Bornean one in the Indian Museum, Calcutta, is absolutely indistinguishable from Indian specimens, and does not exhibit the differential characters given by either Felder or Distant. The differences between *C. nivea* and *C. nivalis* appear to be so slight even if constant, that I prefer to retain the older name for the Indian representatives of this species. Lieutenant Watson has taken it in Upper Burma in the spring, and Captain Bingham in the Donat range in April and in the Thoungyeen forests in December. There is a single FEMALE from the Meplay Valley in the Indian Museum, Calcutta, which differs in no respect from the male.

546. Cyrestisa tabula, de N.

C. tabula, de Nicéville. Journ. A. S. B., vol. lii, pt. 2, p. 1, pl. 1, fig. 1, *male* [1883] ; id., Doherty, Journ. A. S. B., vol. lv, pt. 2, p. 258, n. 7 (1886).

HABITAT : Great Nicobar.

EXPANSE : 2·2 to 2·5 inches.

DESCRIPTION : "MALE. UPPERSIDE, *both wings* rich deep ochreous or fulvous with black markings ; all the veins more or less defined with black. *Forewing* with a short longitudinal streak at the base of the cell ; immediately beyond this a transverse one reaching from the median nervure to the costa ; then a pair of streaks which are wide apart at the median nervure, but joined at the subcostal nervure ; the disco-cellular nervules defined with a fine black line ; beyond which is a bow-shaped figure composed of two lines joined at their ends, the outer line straight, the inner one curved, with their points resting on the second median nervule and subcostal nervure ; below the cell a pair of streaks reaching the inner margin, the origin of the inner one being where the first median, and the outer one where the second median nervule is given off, the space between them thickly irrorated with black scales, leaving but little of the ochreous ground-colour visible ; two discal lines from the subcostal nervure to the inner margin, the outer one lunulate, the inner one sinuate, the two lines being nearer together at their middle, wider apart at the inner margin, the space between them and within the inner one being irrorated with black scales ; a submarginal series of seven bright ochreous spots, broadly defined inwardly with black, one in each interspace except the two lower, which are smaller and placed between the first median nervule and the submedian nervure ; the outer margin broadly black, bearing two obsolete paler lines. *Hindwing* crossed by four black lines, the space between each pair, and between both pairs being thickly irrorated with black scales, especially at the lower extremity of the outer pair, where the ground-colour is entirely black, at the upper extremity the ground-colour increasingly to the costa is very pale ochreous ; a submarginal line composed of six lunules, each lunule having a bright ochreous spot placed outwardly against it ; the outer margin more broadly black than in the forewing, the black portion ending at the first median nervule, bearing two intensely black lines, the outer one defined on both sides with a pale fine line, the outer of these two pale fine lines becoming almost pure white from the tail to the anal lobe ; which latter, together with a round spot above it, is bright ochreous, defined (especially outwardly) with black. There are also some small white, black, and metallic deep steel-blue markings above the round ochreous spot. The tail black, the extremity white. UNDERSIDE pale ochreous, the outer portion of the forewing, and on either side of the submarginal lunules on the hindwing, somewhat deeper ochreous, becoming ferruginous at the anal angle of the latter. All the markings of the upperside, but narrower and better defined, with no black irrorations, the outer margins (except the extreme margin which is black) concolourous with the rest of the wings ; the veins throughout pale ochreous. *Antennæ* black, the extreme tip ochreous. *Thorax* and *body* rich ochreous above marked with three black lines, beneath pale ochreous." *(de Nicéville,* l. c.) "FEMALE differs from the male in being white below instead of pale orange-ochreous ; above it is only slightly tinged with ferruginous, and is somewhat like *C. thyodamas,* except that the lighter spaces are heavily clouded with grey. When flying it more resembles the white Indian species *C. thyodamas,* for which I at first mistook it." *(Doherty,* l. c.) The outline and markings are very similar to those of *C. thyodamas,* the great difference being in the ground-colour. It is somewhat variable, the type specimen is very much darker than the others subsequently received, in the former alone is the black irroration between the common discal lines of the upperside of both wings present.

"Closely allied to *C. thyonneus,* Cramer (pl. ccxx, figs. E, F) from Amboyna and Bouru in the Malay Archipelago, but differing from the above quoted figure in its much darker colouration throughout on the upperside, more especially on the outer margins ; but on the underside it is much paler." *(de Nicéville,* l. c.)

This beautiful species seems to be confined to the island of Great Nicobar, where the late Mr. de Roepstorff and Mr. E. H. Man have each obtained two male specimens.

547. **Cyrestis cocles,** Fabricius. (PLATE XXIII, FIG. 107 ♂).

Papilio cocles, Fabricius, Mant. Ins., vol. ii, p. 7, n. 53 (1787) ; idem, id., Ent. Syst., vol. iii, pt. i, p. 65, n. 204 (1793) ; id., Donovan, Ins. India, pl. xxiii, fig. 2 (1800) ; *Cyrestis cocles,* Butler, Cat. Fab. Lep. B. M., p. 82, n. 1 (1869) ; id., Moore, Proc. Zool. Soc. Lond., 1878, p. 829 ; *C. cocles,* var. *andamanica,* Wood-Mason and de Nicéville, Journ. A. S. B., vol. l, pt. 2, p. 246, n. 29 (1881) ; *C. formosa,* Felder, Reise Novara, Lep., vol. iii, p. 412, n. 631 (1867) ; id., Wood-Mason and de Nicéville, Journ. A. S. B., vol. l, pt. 2, p. 246, n. 30 (1881) ; *C. horatius,* Wood-Mason and de Nicéville, Proc. A. S. B., 1881, p. 142 ; *C. carli,* Distant, Rhop. Malay, p. 141, n. 2, pl. xiii, fig. 5, *male* (1883).

HABITAT : Khasi Hills, Sylhet, Upper Tenasserim, Malacca, Perak, Siam, Andamans, Orissa.

EXPANSE : 1·9 to 2·8 inches.

DESCRIPTION : MALE and FEMALE. UPPERSIDE, *both wings* with the ground-colour pure white, very pale ochreous just tinted with apple-green at the base, or of a slightly darker shade of ochreous ; the markings also variable in shade and intensity, in some specimens they are hardly traceable, in others of a darker shade of ochreous than the ground, in others again sepia. Both wings crossed at the middle by a band of the ground-colour devoid of markings, outwardly bounded by a straight even narrow band, the inner edge irregular ; the base crossed by numerous broad ochreous or sepia bands more or less defined with fine black lines, the disco-cellular nervules enclosed by fine black lines, the outer portions of the wings crossed by several irregular ochreous or sepia narrow bands, often obsolete at the third median nervule of the forewing, and with a series of rounded and lonulated bluish spots midway between the discal pale band and the margin, a prominent very fine black marginal line. *Hindwing* with the anal lobe and a spot above it at the anal angle irrorated with black scales, and centred with a black spot, often outwardly marked with a rich ochreous patch. UNDERSIDE, *both wings* much paler, many of the markings obliterated, two or three small prominent black spots near the apex of the *forewing,* and a large round one in the first median interspace ; *hindwing* with a large round spot in the subcostal interspace, followed by four fine linear ones between the nervules, the anal lobe with a large round prominent black spot and a small one above at the anal angle, all but the two last mentioned spots answering to the bluish spots on the upperside. *Cilia* pale throughout.

C. cocles appears to usually present three distinct forms wherever it occurs, which, although they differ in the colour of the ground and of the markings, also in the intensity and prominence of the latter, agree in the style and position of the markings and in the shape of the wings ; they also vary much in size. The typical form which has the ground-colour pale ochreous with darker ochreous markings is here figured from a male Sylhet specimen in the Indian Museum, Calcutta, and shows both sides ; exactly similar specimens occur in Orissa, the Andamans and in Perak ; the form which Felder described from the Andamans under the name of *C. formosa** occurs also in Orissa, in Upper Tenasserim and in Perak, it has the markings and ground-colour a little paler than typical *C. cocles*, but the base of both wings is tinted with apple green ; lastly the form described from Malacca by Mr. Distant under the name of *C. earli* † occurs also at Perak, in the Andamans, at Rangoon, in Tavoy, at Shelapunji, Khasi Hills in October, and in Orissa ; the ground-colour is pure white, and all the markings are sepia. Typically each of these forms can be readily distinguished, but they more or less grade into each other, and they do not appear to be due to seasonal variation, but as they occur almost always together, I do not believe them to represent so many distinct and separate species, but one trimorphic one.

548. **Cyrestis periander,** Fabricius.

Papilio periander, Fabricius, Mant. Ins., vol. ii, p. 9, n. 74 (1787); idem, id., Ent. Syst., vol. iii, pt. 1, p. 67, n. 208 (1703); id., Donovan, Ins. Ind., pl. xxxvii, fig. 1 (1800); *Nymphalis periander*, Godart, Enc. Méth., vol. iv, p. 362, n. 42 (1823); *Paphia periander*, Horsfield, Cat. Lep. E. I. C., pl. v, figs. 3, 3a (1829); *Cyrestis periander*, Butler, Cat. Fab. Lep. B. M., p. 82, n. 2 (1869).

HABITAT : Mysore *(Westwood)* ; Assam *(Butler)* ; Mergui Archipelago, Tavoy, Java.

EXPANSE : 1·6 to 1·9 inches.

DESCRIPTION : MALE. UPPERSIDE white. *Forewing* crossed by the following pale ochreous narrow bands :—a short one at the base of the cell, another just beyond reaching the inner margin, a third crossing the cell only, the disco-cellulars marked by a fourth, two others crossing the disc from the costa to the inner margin, the outer one somewhat dilated at the apex. The outer margin broadly blackish, widest anteriorly, bearing a submarginal irregular fine whitish lunular line marked within by some black obscure dots, and an extremely fine marginal black line defined on each side with an equally fine white line. *Hindwing*

* *Cyrestis formosa*, Felder, Reise Novara, Lep., vol. iii, p. 412, n. 631 (1867). HABITAT : Andaman Isles. EXPANSE : Not given. DESCRIPTION : "MALE. UPPERSIDE opalescent-whitish, with the base and the veins towards it slightly tinted with greenish, immediately beyond the middle an ochraceous fuscous striga outwardly waved (especially in the forewing) and joined to a cineraceont fascia opalescent in certain positions, margined with white, broader in the forewing, composed of lunules, decreasing in the hindwing, immediately beyond the fascia another margined with ochraceous-cinereous, broader in the forewing, irregular, submacular, contracted at the third median nervule, bearing six differently formed whitish spots, including an ochraceous pupil powdered with whitish and black (the two lower larger, the lowest bipupilled), in the hindwing decreasing, bearing a decreasing chain of ocellate spots similar to those of the forewing, this outwardly with another narrower whitish fascia, divided in the middle by a cineraceont striga, opalescent in certain positions, in the forewing formed of lunules, in the hindwing nearly entire, and ceasing at the first median nervule, immediately beyond this with the margin as far as the cilia pale ochraceous-yellowish, divided by a very slender black streak bordered with white and outwardly also very narrowly with cinereous, forewing with three fuscous marks below the costa, a violascent-blackish litura and another ochraceous-fulvescent in a pair, a triple ochraceous-fulvescent litura, sullied with black; then an ochraceous-fulvescent litura and another violascent-blackish in a pair cellular, a slender violascent-blackish triple disco-cellular litura bent like an S, the ground between it and the preceding litura irrorated with ochraceous, a diffused ochraceous-fulvous litura and another violaceous-blackish internal below the median nervure, a flexuous broken discal fascia ochraceous-fulvescent, inwardly girdled with whitish and violaceous-blackish, the ground between it and up to the litura irrorated with ochraceous, hindwing with an ochraceous-fulvous striga and another blackish-violascent slender in a pair basal, a triple disco-cellular litura angulated, scarcely beyond the cell a violascent-blackish streak and an ochraceous-fulvous fascia these hindwardly strongly bent, the ground about the disco-cellular litura as far as the above blackish streaks irrorated with ochraceous, an anal whitish spot, slenderly circled with violaceous-blackish, the pupil cinereous, inwardly a blackish lunule bearing a 'freta' and another similar but aborted in the lobe, the little tail whitish."

"This beautiful species is most nearly allied to *C. cassander*, Felder, from the Philippines, but is considerably larger, has distinctly longer and broader wings and the outer border of the forewing between the veins more evenly and deeper undulatingly cut out." *(Felder,* l.c.)

† *Cyrestis earli*, Distant, Ann. and Mag. of Nat. Hist., fifth series, vol. xi, p. 174 (1883); idem. id., Rhop. Malay., p. 141, n. 2, pl. xiii, fig. 5, *male* (1883). HABITAT : Malacca. EXPANSE : 1·7 inches. DESCRIPTION : "MALE. UPPERSIDE, both wings creamy white, with the basal third slightly and palely infuscated and with two narrow oblique brownish fasciæ :—the first commencing on median nervure and at about middle of cell of forewing, and extending to about middle of submedian nervure of hindwing, down which it is continued to near anal angle ; the second commencing on forewing at base of second median nervule, and extending to near apex of first median nervule of hindwing, whence it is strongly sinuated and angulated to submedian nervure. Cell of forewing with four transverse brownish fasciæ, the fourth at end of cell having a medial brownish line ; a similarly formed fascia closing cell of hindwing ; an irregular brownish patch beyond cell of forewing ; at about one-third from apex a narrow brownish fascia crosses both wings. The apex of the forewing is broadly infuscated ; and a submarginal series of obscure spots (absent at middle of forewing) outwardly margined by a narrow brown fascia crosses both wings ; a marginal blackish line ; the extreme margin brownish, with creamy white *cilia* ; an ochraceous patch at anal angle of hindwing, on which are two bluish spots marked with black ; caudate appendages bluish. UNDERSIDE much paler than above ; markings generally similar, but spots darker, with a large black spot at anal angle of hindwing, and the spots divided by the subcostal nervules of hindwing and those between the second and first median nervules of forewing very prominent and black. *Body* and *legs* more or less concolourous with wings."

"*C. earli* holds a somewhat intermediate position between *C. thyonneus*, Butler [from Borneo], and *C. paulinus*, Felder [from the Moluccas]. *(Distant,* l. c. in Rhop. Malay.)

also crossed by several pale ochreous bands in continuation of those on the forewing, *viz.*, a basal one, a subbasal one reaching the submedian nervure, the disco-cellulars defined by a third, another discal reaching the first median nervule, thence to abdominal margin forming a W-shaped figure, a fifth beyond joined to the fourth at the first median nervule. A broad ochreous band from the discoidal nervule to the anal angle, the outer margin marked as in the forewing, but the fine lower black spots placed within the submarginal lunulated white line more distinct. UNDERSIDE marked as above, but all the bands crossing the wings narrower and less distinct, the anal lobe of the *hindwing* marked with a diffused prominent black spot. FEMALE rather larger, the basal portion of both wings has the ground-colour very pale sap green. *C. periander* is the only Indian species with the apex of the forewing truncate.

Dr. Anderson took very numerous specimens of *C. periander* in the Mergui Archipelago in the cold weather, it occurs in Tavoy, Mr. Westwood* records it from Mysore, and it was taken by Dr. Horsfield in Java. Mr. Butler (l. c.) records it from Assam (*Warwick*), but as in the case of all the species given under this reference, the specimens probably came from Burma on the Malay Peninsula.

The remaining species are of very small size, and have the second subcostal nervule of the forewing emitted beyond the apex of the cell.

549. Cyrestis risa, Doubleday, Hewitson.

C. risa, Doubleday, Hewitson, Gen. Diurn. Lep., vol. ii, p. 262, n. 10, pl. xxxi, fig. 4 (1850); id., Moore, Proc. Zool. Soc. Lond., 1878, p. 829; *Chersonesia risa*, Doherty, Journ. A. S. B., vol. lv, pt. 2, p. 122, n. 71 (1886).

HABITAT: Kumaon, Sikkim, Assam, Upper Tenasserim, Java.

EXPANSE: 1·65 to 1·95 inches.

DESCRIPTION: MALE. UPPERSIDE, *both wings* rich ochraceous; crossed by a basal pair of fine black straight lines, the space within irrorated with black scales, another pair beyond, two similar discal lines, the outer one with a series of pale ochreous triangular spots placed inwardly against it, more prominent on the hindwing; followed by a steel-blue line, somewhat macular on the forewing, where it is divided in the middle by a pale ochreous patch and another at the apex, a submarginal fine black line outwardly more or less marked with pale ochreous patches, and a similar marginal line. *Forewing* with a basal line, the disco-cellulars defined on both sides with a fine black line, a single line defining these nervules on the *hindwing*. UNDERSIDE a little paler than above, the spaces between the fine black lines paler and faintly tinged with violet, the markings much as above. FEMALE rather larger, the wings broader, markings similar but paler. Mr. Doherty writes (l. c.) :—" Kumaon specimens are lighter in colour and more delicately marked than Sikkim ones. Three of the bands below are in both sexes beautifully glossed with lilac on the hindwing, and to a less extent on the forewing."

C. risa is a common species in Sikkim at low elevations, and occurs to the eastwards as far as Silsagar in Upper Assam at any rate, and again in Upper Tenasserim, Mr. Moore recording it from "Moulmein to Meetan; Moolai, 3,000—6,000 feet."

550. Cyrestis rahria, Moore.

C. rahria, Moore, Horsfield and Moore, Cat. Mus. E. I. C., vol. i, p. 147, n. 301, pl. iiia, fig. 2, *female* (1857); *Chersonesia rahria*, Distant, Rhop. Malay., p. 147, n. 1, pl. xii, fig. 4, *female* (1883).

HABITAT: Upper Tenasserim, Perak, Penang, Malacca, Nias Island, Java, Borneo.

EXPANSE: 1·3 to 1·7 inches.

DESCRIPTION: " MALE and FEMALE. UPPERSIDE, *both wings* pale ochraceous, crossed by the following fasciæ :—a somewhat curved basal dark ochraceous fascia, margined with fuscous, commencing at about subcostal nervure of forewing and terminating slightly beyond submedian nervure of hindwing; this is followed by a straighter but more irregular fascia of the same colour, which, commencing about costa of forewing, passes the cellular apices of

---

both wings and terminates on hindwing near middle of abdominal margin ; between these
fasciæ on forewing is a short irregular fascia commencing at costa and joining or almost joining
the second fascia near median nervure ; a discal curved fuscous fascia, margined with dark
ochraceous, followed on forewing by a dark ochraceous spot, which precedes a submarginal fascia
bounded by fuscous lines commencing beneath apex, the posterior half of which is dark
ochraceous, and contains two fuscous spots, and the upper portion is preceded by a dark
ochraceous patch also containing a fuscous spot ; an oblique subapical fuscous linear spot and
a fuscous submarginal line. *Hindwing* with a submarginal dark ochraceous fascia, margined
by scalloped fuscous lines and containing a series of fuscous linear spots ; a submarginal
fuscous line preceded by paler and fuscous nebulous shadings. UNDERSIDE paler than
above ; markings similar, but the submarginal fasciæ to *both wings* without the dark outer
margins. *Body* above ochraceous ; *thorax* marked with some longitudinal fuscous lines, and
abdomen with some narrow fuscous annulations. Body beneath and *legs* more or less concolourous with wings." (*Distant*, l. c.) Mr. Distant's figure appears to be that of a female,
the ground-colour of the numerous male specimens in the Indian Museum, Calcutta, is of a
deep reddish-fulvous. *C. rahria* may be at once known from *C. risa* by having the fifth black
line from the base which crosses both wings on the upperside in *C. risa* replaced by a diffused
blackish fascia in *C. rahria*, the two lines which follow in the latter species being very uneven
and curved on the forewing, and nearer the outer margin on both wings. The lower disco-
cellular nervule of the forewing is also much closer to the origin of the second median nervule
in this species than it is in *C. risa*, being in this respect exactly intermediate between the
typical group of *Cyrestis* in which it meets the median nervure at the origin of the second
median nervule, and typical *Chersonesia*, in which it joins the median nervure exactly midway
between the origins of the first and second median nervules.

In Major Marshall's collection is a single male of this species taken in January in the
Donat Range, Upper Tenasserim, by Captain C. T. Bingham, which is the only record I possess
of its occurrence within Indian limits.

Another species of this group (*C. peraka*) occurs in the Malay Peninsula, a description of it
is given below.*

Genus 85.—KALLIMA, Westwood. (PLATE XXIII).

Kallima, Westwood, Gen. Diurn. Lep., vol. ii, p. 324 (1850) ; id., Felder, Neues Lep., p. 14, n. 78 (1861) ;
id., Moore, Lep. Cey., vol. i, p 36 (1881).

" BODY, robust ; *forewing*, large, generally acute at the tip ; *hindwing*, gradually produced into a tail at the anal angle ; *both wings*, traversed across the middle beneath by a
straight dark-coloured line ; *head*, large, densely squamose, with a large rounded tuft of scaly
hairs in front ; *eyes*, large, naked, and prominent ; *antennæ*, scarcely more than two-fifths
of the length of the forewing, nearly straight, terminated by a gradually-formed slender club,
scaly above, finely carinated beneath, rounded off obliquely beneath ; *palpi*, large, porrected
obliquely at least to the level of the top of the eyes, and advanced in front of the face to at least
the length of the head, forming conjointly an elongate conical beak in front, densely scaly
to the tip, the scales concealing the articulations, with a coat of hairs on the back of the
middle joint, applied to the face ; *thorax*, elongate-ovate, very scaly ; *abdomen*, moderately
robust, oval. FOREWING, large, subtriangular ; *costa* very much rounded, slightly emarginate
near the base ; *apex* more or less acute and produced ; *outer margin* five-sixths of the length of
the costa, concave below the apex, but more or less concave [? convex] or subangulated towards
the posterior angle (especially at the extremity of the first median nervule). *Costal nervure*

---

* *Cyrestis (Chersonesia) peraka*, Distant, Ann. and Mag. of Nat. Hist., fifth series, vol. xiv, p. 199
(1884). HABITAT : Perak. EXPANSE : *Male*, 1 1 ; *female*, 1 3 inches. DESCRIPTION : MALE and FEMALE.
"Allied to *C. rahria*, Moore, but smaller, the ground-colour more ochraceous and less rufous ; markings
similar, but with the transverse fasciæ broader, much darker, and placed closer together. The absolute caudate
prolongations in *C. rahria* near the apices of the third and first median nervules are scarcely visible in
C. peraka, and a structural peculiarity exists in the first subcostal nervule of the forewing, which, in this
species, impinges near its base on the costal nervure " (*Distant*, l c.) The FEMALE has the ground-colour
paler than in the male, the wings broader, and the apex of the forewing more rounded. The type specimens are
deposited in the Indian Museum, Calcutta

extends to the middle of the costa ; *subcostal* nervure with two branches arising before the anterior extremity of the discoidal cell, third branch arising beyond the extremity of the discoidal cell, and extending to the tip of the wing, fourth branch arising at about five-sixths of the length of the wing, and extending to the outer margin below the apex ; *upper disco-cellular nervule* very short, almost obsolete, *middle* disco-cellular short, slightly curved and rather oblique, being directed towards the base of the wing, *lower* disco-cellular slender, curved rather obliquely, the curve being towards the base of the wing, and uniting with the median nervure just beyond* the origin of its third branch, which is very much arched ; the anterior extremity of the *discoidal cell* reaches just one-third of the length of the fore-wing, and its posterior extremity is somewhat shorter. HINDWING, elongate, subtriangular ; *costal margin* much arched at the base, *outer* margin rounded, *anal angle* gradually produced into a tail, which is traversed by the submedian nervure. *Precostal nervure* oblique, curved outwardly at the tip, [bifid] ; *costal* nervure extending to the outer angle ; *subcostal* nervure branching nearer the base than the median nervure ; *discoidal cell* closed by a curved lower disco-cellular nervule, rather before the middle of the wing. FORELEGS, of the *male* small, pectoral, moderately hairy, but not forming a dense brush, slender ; *tarsus* about two-thirds of the length of the tibia, simple, exunguiculate ; of the *female* longer than those of the male (especially the tarsus), slender, scaly ; *femur* with a row of short hairs on the inside, set on at right angles ; *tarsus* nearly as long as the tibia, dilated at tip, the inside of which is obliquely rounded off, and armed beneath with four pairs of short spines, indicating the articulations at the extremity, terminal joint very minute and simple. MIDDLE and HINDLEGS, moderately long, not very robust ; *tibiæ* with two rows of very short spines beneath, tibial spurs short ; *tarsi* armed beneath with four rows of small spines ; *claws* slender, very much curved." (*Westwood*, l. c.)

The *Kallimas*, (sometimes spelt *Callima*) or "Oak-leaf" Butterflies as they are called popularly, form a beautiful group. As a general rule, they are some shade of blue on the upperside, the apex of the forewing broadly black, below which is a more or less broad band of fulvous, white, or blue ; in most of the species there are one or more small translucent spots on the forewing. But the underside is the most remarkable feature, the wings are usually closed over the back when in repose, not expanded, and each fore and hindwing together form the exact representation of a leaf, of which the point at the apex of forewing forms the tip, and a long tail at the anal angle of the hindwing represents the stalk ; the latter when the butterfly is in repose frequently rests against the stem on which the butterfly has settled, and produces the impression that the leaf is actually growing out of it : from the tail to the apex a more or less prominent rib-like mark extends, answering to the mid-rib of a leaf, and on either side branching veins extend more or less distinctly marked. A selection of specimens of any one species would show a wonderful series of autumnal tints in these leaf-like representations, and marks are often irregularly scattered here and there over the surface increasing still more the resemblance to a decaying or decayed leaf. The sexes are usually easily discriminated, the apex of the forewing being usually produced into a very much longer process in the female than in the male ; the markings are similar in both sexes in all the Indian species.

They are not as a rule found at any great elevation, and seem confined to the lower valleys in the different mountain and hill ranges ; they frequent rocky nullahs where there is shade, and are strong on the wing and rapid in their movements. When at rest they are extremely difficult to detect owing to the peculiarity noticed above ; and the first indication of their presence is generally the flash of brilliant blue and yellow as they rise with a rapid dart, startled by any movement near their resting place, and exposing the brightly-coloured upper surface of the wings. They do not as a rule fly far, but the rapidity with which they alight again and the concealment with which their colours provide them when settled, render them rather difficult to capture, though few Indian collections are without specimens. In Sikkim they are extremely common butterflies, often settling on the banks of streams to suck up the moisture, also on the trunks of certain trees, which, I presume, furnish them with a juice of which they are fond.

---

* The point of junction of the lower disco-cellular nervule with the median nervure is somewhat variable, in some specimens it is just before, sometimes just after, sometimes at the origin of the second median nervule.

In India they are met with all along the Himalayas, in Assam, Sylhet, Cachar, and Upper Tenasserim ; in Orissa, and the Eastern Ghâts as far south as the Godavery, also in the Western Ghâts, South India, Ceylon, and the Andaman Isles, again in Sumatra and Java, but not in the Nicobars or Malay Peninsula as far as is known.

In a recent monograph of the genus *Kallima* (Trans. Ent. Soc. Lond., 1879, p. 9), Mr. F. Moore has divided the Indo-Malayan species into four groups based on the colour of the oblique transverse band of the forewing, as follows :—

> With oblique band fulvous in male, bluish-white in female.
> With oblique band fulvous in both sexes.
> With oblique band white in both sexes.
> With oblique band blue in both sexes.

The group in which the colour of the band differs in the sexes does not concern us, it contains only two species, *K. paralekta* and *K. hewitsoni*, neither of which are likely to occur in India, the first is a native of Java, and the locality in which the second occurs is unknown ; brief descriptions of them are appended.[*]

The remaining three groups are represented in this country. Of the first of these in which the band is fulvous in both sexes *K. inachis* is the type ; it contains nine species according to Moore, of which all, with the exception of *K. inachis* and *K. huegelii*, are new species described by him either in the paper quoted above or in the Proc. Zool. Soc. Lond. for 1878. He gives the following key for discriminating them :—

A. Forewing produced ; oblique below apex.
    a. Discal spot prominent.   *K. buxtoni*, Sumatra.
                                     K. limborgii, Tenasserim.
    b. Discal spot not prominent.   *K. atkinsoni*, Darjiling.

B. Forewing truncate at apex.
    a. Discal spot prominent.   *K. boisduvali*, Kasowli.
    b. Discal spot not prominent.   *K. huttoni*, Masuri.

C. Forewing acuminate at apex.
    a. Discal spot prominent.   *K. ramsayi*, Nepal.

D. Forewing prolonged at apex
    a. Discal spot prominent.   *K. inachis*, Sikkim.
                                     K. huegelii, Kashmir.
    b. Discal spot not prominent.   *K. buckleyi*, N.-W. Himalayas.

This key I confess I am unable to follow ; all the species, so far as I know, have the forewing "oblique below apex ;" the difference between "forewing produced" and "forewing prolonged at apex" is not very clear ; and the difference between "forewing truncate at apex" in the only sense in which truncation is apparent in this group, and "forewing acuminate at apex" is also not apparent, for the truncation consists of a cutting off of the prolongation, which leaves the apex acuminate ; and the minor divisions rest on a character which, I am convinced, is inconstant in every species.

As will be seen from the remarks I have added to the original descriptions, I have been able to find specimens which more or less agree with the descriptions of all except *K. atkinsoni*. The most important distinction between them appears to be the truncation of the forewing in three of them (*K. boisduvali*, *K. huttoni* and *K. ramsayi*), and the consequent slight prolongation of the apex of that wing. This however seems to be a very inconstant character, some specimens of *K. limborgii* showing it almost as prominently lengthened as

---

[*] *With the band fulvous in male, bluish-white in female.*

Kallima (Paphia) paralekta, Horsfield, Cat. Lep. E. I. C., pl. vi, fig. 4, *male* (1859) ; id., Moore, Trans. Ent. Soc. Lond., 1879, p. 9. HABITAT : Java. EXPANSE : 3·87 inches. DESCRIPTION : " MALE. *Forewing* with an oblique uniformly narrow fulvous band, its inner border terminating at posterior angle ; basal area and *hindwing* deep blue. FEMALE with bluish-purple white band ; basal area and *hindwing* dark rufous-brown ; discal hyaline spot in both sexes small and oval." (*Moore*, l. c.)

Kallima hewitsoni, Moore, Trans. Ent. Soc. Lond., 1879, p. 9 ; *K. paralekta*, Doubleday and Hewitson, Gen. Diurn. Lep., vol. ii, p. 325, n. 3, pl. lii, fig. 3, *female* (1850). HABITAT : Unknown ; (Himalayas ?). EXPANSE : 4·0 inches. DESCRIPTION : " FEMALE. Similar to *K. paralekta*, differing in the shape of the bluish-purple white band and absence of the discal hyaline spot."

"Although the 'Himalaya' is given by Doubleday and Hewitson as the locality of this species, I doubt its correctness. There is no locality label on the type specimen." (*Moore*, l. c.) In this instance the habitat 'Himalaya' has evidently been quoted for this species by those authors because they considered the *paralekta* of the 'Genera' to be identical with *K. horsfieldii*, which was described by Kollar from the Himalayas.

in K. inachis, and there seems to be every gradation to the normal type in which the apex of the forewing is produced and ends in a long process. The next thing appears to be the shade of colour of the ground of the upperside. The eastern forms all seem to have it dark bluish-purple, while typical K. huegelii is much paler. K. buckleyi is probably synonymous with this species, having the upperside uniform greyish-blue. This form is not the only one that occurs in the Western Himalayas, as K. boisduvali and K. huttoni have the ground-colour as dark or nearly so as in the typical eastern forms, and they are both recorded from the Western Himalayas. Mr. Moore seems to consider the size of the discal hyaline spot in the forewing important, in reality it is very variable, even in K. inachis which usually has it the largest, I possess specimens in which it is almost obsolete. Lastly, as regards the colouration, markings, and prominence of the rib-line on the underside. These are all most variable characters, and in my opinion afford no guide whatever to specific determination. To conclude, though typical specimens of all the described species can doubtless be picked out, I am convinced that integrades exist between them all, and that they are all varieties more or less inconstant of a single species which stands as K. inachis. The distribution of the more prominent varieties appears to me to be as follows :—

The typical species, K. inachis, is a very large butterfly with the apex of the forewing considerably produced in both sexes, most of course in the female, and being a resident of the Eastern Himalayas and Assam, the colouring is naturally deep and rich.

In the Western Himalayas it is replaced, as might naturally be expected, by a paler form, K. huegelii, which differs from it in no respect except tone of colouration.

In Burma it is replaced by a rather smaller form, K. limbergii, in which the apex of the forewing is highly produced in the female only. In the male it is usually very slightly or not at all produced ; and as might be expected from the climate, the colouration is deep and rich.

There is still another form found in the Himalayas, in which the apex of the forewing is produced in neither sex ; and wherever it occurs the colouration is dark and rich. It appears as K. boisduvali at Kasowli and Simla, K. huttoni at Masuri, K. ramsayi in Nepal, and K. atkinsoni in Sikkim ; the latter, the Sikkim form, merging into, and being practically inseparable from, K. inachis. It is just possible that this latter form diverging westwards from the head-quarters in a wider and wider degree from the natural variation which takes the form of K. huegelii in the west, may represent a distinct but closely-allied species with its origin in the Western Himalayas, gradually approximating to the larger type, with the apex produced in both sexes, as it extends eastward into the head-quarters of that form. For the present I retain these four forms as distinct for convenience, and the key to the fulvous-banded group of the genus will be as follows :—

Key to the Indian species of Kallima.

First Group.

A. With the oblique band fulvous in both sexes.
    a. Apex of forewing prolonged into a slender point in prolongation of the costa in both sexes.
        a^1. Colouration of base of wings on upperside very dark indigo-purple.
            551. K. INACHIS, Himalayas, Assam, Sylhet, Cachar, Orissa, Eastern Ghâts, Pachmarhi.
        b^1. Colouration of base of wings on upperside much lighter blue.
            552. K. HUEGELII, Western Himalayas.
    b. Apex of forewing typically prolonged in the female only.
        553. K. LIMBORGII, Tenasserim.
    c. Apex of forewing not prolonged in either sex.
        554. K. BOISDUVALI, Himalayas.

As pointed out above the colouration of the underside affords no reliable character as it appears to me, nor do the hyaline spots, both characters being manifestly very variable, and it is impossible to draw the line on these characters between K. buckleyi and K. huegelii. So also with regard to K. boisduvali, K. huttoni, K. ramsayi, and K. atkinsoni, no reliable characters are given on which to separate them, and as all four names bear the same date, I have taken the western form, being the most divergent, as the typical one, which will thus stand as K. boisduvali.

I have at the same time given Mr. Moore's views *in extenso* and all his original descriptions to enable future observers to further investigate the value of them. I have also in the headings to the species given his localities and measurements only.

551. **Kallima inachis,** Boisduval.

Paphia inachus, Boisduval, Crochard's Edit. Cuvier's Règ. Anim., Ins., vol. ii, pl. cxxxix, fig. 3, *female* ; 3*a, front view of head* (1836) ; *Kallima inachis,* Moore, Trans. Ent. Soc. Lond., 1879, p. 11.

HABITAT : Sikkim Himalayas.

EXPANSE : ♂, 3·25 ; ♀, 3·9 inches.

DESCRIPTION : " UPPERSIDE. *Forewing,* with broad fulvous band extending to outer margin, a short apical point in the male and a very prolonged one in the female ; the discal hyaline spot larger than in the other species. *Hindwing* bright violet blue, the outer border paler, and prominently marked with short brown strigæ. UNDERSIDE, ochreous-brown, vinous-tinted, minutely brown-speckled ; rib-line indistinct. A large, dark, bright violet-blue, prominently-marked species." (*Moore,* l.c.)

Mr. Moore remarks that " Dr. Boisduval gives Nepal as the habitat of the species he figures as above. This is doubtless an error." As Sikkim and Nepal are conterminous and have the same climate, it is certain that *K. inachis* occurs in both localities. *K. inachis* is the type of the Indian yellow-banded group of the genus. The original spelling *inachus* should probably be restored, but as it has almost universally been known as *inachis,* I have retained it here. The colouration of the type figure is pale blue like that of the next species.

Typical *K. inachis* has a wide range, extending from Masuri on the west to Upper Assam in the east, I have specimens also from Orissa (*W. C. Taylor*) and Pachmarhi (*J. A. Betham*) which appear to be quite typical. Mr. W. Doherty has taken it on the Eastern Ghâts north of the Godavery.

552. **Kallima huegelii,** Kollar.

Paphia hügelii, Kollar, in Hügel's Kaschmir, vol. iv, pt. 2, p. 442, n. i, pl. ix, *male* and *female* (1848) ; *Kallima hügeli,* Moore, Trans. Ent. Soc. Lond., 1879, p. 12 ; *K. hugeli,* id., Proc. Zool. Soc. Lond., 1882, p. 237 ; *Paphia parakotta,* Westwood in Royle's Himalayan Bot., p. liii, pl. x, figs. 3*a, 3b, male* (1839) ; *Amathusia inachis,* Herrich-Schäffer, Ex. Schmett., p. 77, nos. 7, 8, figs. 7, 8, *female* (1852).

HABITAT : N.-W. Himalayas, Kashmir.

EXPANSE : ♂, 3·4 ; ♀, 3·5 inches.

DESCRIPTION : " May be at once distinguished by the very pale grey-blue colour of the basal area of *both wings.* UNDERSIDE greyish-ochreous, of uniform tint throughout ; frequently black-mottled ; rib-line indistinct. FEMALE, *forewing* with less prolonged apex than in *K. inachis.*" (*Moore,* l. c.)

This is the common form of the genus occurring in the Western Himalayas, and distinguished from the Eastern form (the true *K. inachis*) by its much paler blue colouration on the upperside. The markings of the underside are very variable. Mr. Hocking states that it is " single-brooded in July. Flies about till the cold weather in November, and then hibernates, and comes out again in April. Taken at sugar in April."

Below* is given a description of *K. buckleyi,* which is recorded from the N.-W. Himalayas. As the presence or absence of the hyaline spots on the forewing is very inconstant, and the markings of the underside still more so, I think there is little doubt that *K. buckleyi* is

* *Kallima buckleyi,* Moore, Trans. Ent. Soc. Lond., 1879, p. 11. HABITAT : N.-W. Himalayas. EXPANSE : *Male* and *female,* 4·0 inches. DESCRIPTION : " Allied to *K. inachis,* but larger. UPPERSIDE, outline of wings similar to *K. inachis.* *Forewing,* with a shorter and broader fulvous band than in any of the other species ; the discal spot blind (having no hyaline centre) in the male, and present only as a minute slender one in the female ; basal area uniform greyish-blue. *Hindwing,* uniform greyish-blue. UNDERSIDE, dusky purple-brown in the male, rib-line indistinct ; bright reddish-brown in the female, with greyish-purple sinuous fasciæ." (*Moore,* l. c.)

There is a single male from Simla in the Indian Museum, Calcutta, which agrees with this description, but another Simla specimen which is typical in other respects has a hyaline centre to the discal spot on the forewing. In both these specimens the basal area of both wings on the upperside is darker than in typical *K. huegelii,* but it is lighter than in typical *K. inachis* ; the discal orange band on the upperside of the forewing is wider than in either, and ends at a greater distance from the margin.

synonymous with *K. inachii*. The shape of the discal band on the forewing, and the colour of the base of both wings seem insufficient to specifically separate it from that species.

553. **Kallima limborgii**, Moore.

K. limborgii, Moore, Proc. Zool. Soc. Lond., 1878, p. 828; *K. limborgi*, id., Trans. Ent. Soc. Lond., 1879, p. 10.

HABITAT : Upper Tenasserim, Moolai, 3,000 to 6,000 feet.

EXPANSE : ♂, 3·75 ; ♀, 4·0 inches.

DESCRIPTION : " Allied to *K. inachis* from Sikkim ; but differs in the deeper and more uniform steel-blue colour above in both sexes, the contour of the wings, and the small almost circular discal hyaline spot. *Forewing* less angled on the hindward part of the exterior margin ; the apex more produced in the male, less so in the female, the discal hyaline spot small and almost circular. *Hindwing,* less convex on the exterior margin, and has a much shorter tail. UNDERSIDE luteous-brown, purple-tinted, and rufous-speckled, brightest in female ; rib and basal lines indistinct in male." (*Moore*, l. c, in Trans. Ent. Soc. Lond.)

In Major Marshall's collection are numerous *Kallimas* taken by Captain C. T. Bingham in Upper Tenasserim close to the locality where the type specimens of *K. limborgii* were obtained, and one in Colonel Swinhoe's collection named by Mr. Moore himself. I find that Mr. Moore's description of this species does not hold good as compared with Sikkim specimens of *K. inachis*, the colouration is not deeper or more uniform, the forewing is quite as much angled at the first median nervule, the apex is less (instead of more) produced in both sexes, the discal hyaline spot is very variable in shape, occasionally circular, more usually oval, sometimes linear, and so on. The Tenasserim specimens, however, are uniformly smaller than Sikkim specimens of *K. inachis*, a feature not noticed by Mr. Moore, and as the apex of the forewing is usually not so produced in either sex as in *K. inachis*, *K. limborgii* may perhaps be retained as a distinct species. It would perhaps more rightly rank as a local race.

K. buxtoni from Sumatra appears to be very doubtfully distinct from *K. limborgii ;* the description of it is appended.[*] It is the only species of this group which is not recorded from India.

554. **Kallima boisduvali**, Moore.

K. boisduvali, Moore, Trans. Ent. Soc. Lond., 1879, p. 12 ; *K. huttoni* and *K. ramsayi*, idem, id., p. 12 ; *K. atkinsoni*, idem, id., p. 10.

HABITAT : Kasowli, Masuri, N.-W. Himalayas ; Nepal ; Sikkim.

EXPANSE : 2·9 inches.

DESCRIPTION : Allied to *K. inachis*. "Of smaller size than the other species. *Forewing* truncated and blunt-pointed at apex ; fulvous band narrow, its inner angular border broadly black ; discal hyaline spot small but prominent ; basal area uniformly blue. *Hindwing,* uniformly blue. UNDERSIDE, ochreous-brown, numerously covered with dark brown speckles and strigæ ; rib and basal transverse lines very prominent." (*Moore*, l. c.)

This is the rare dark-coloured *Kallima* which is found occasionally throughout the Himalayas, and which lacks the slender prolongation of the apex of the forewing.

In Major Marshall's collection is a single male *Kallima* from Simla which agrees fairly well with this description in size and outline, but he possesses specimens from Upper Tenasserim (*i. e.* at almost the other extreme of its range) which also have the outer margin of the forewing truncate and the apex blunt-tipped. The Simla specimen has the basal area dark purplish-blue rather than greyish-blue, which latter is the colour usually prevailing in the

---

[*] *Kallima buxtoni*, Moore, Trans. Ent. Soc. Lond., 1879, p. 10. HABITAT : Sumatra. EXPANSE : *Male,* 3·75 ; *female,* 3·0 inches. DESCRIPTION : " Nearly allied to the Javan *K. paralekta*. MALE. Differs in the intensity of the blue of the upperside, broader and more oblique band, the inner border of which terminates at its own width above the posterior angle. FEMALE, paler purple-blue, with broad fulvous band as in male. UNDERSIDE. MALE, dusky greyish-green, vinous-tinted and black-speckled, with broad greyish fascia. FEMALE, pale greenish-ochreous, vinous-tinted ; rib-line only prominent." (*Moore*, l. c.)

Kallimas from the Western Himalayas. The underside does not agree with Mr. Moore's description, but as the colouration and markings are protective and variable, this feature does not seem an important one for specific distinction.

Below will be found descriptions of the three species which I consider to be inseparable from *K. boisduvali.**

The next group contains but a single species which has the band white instead of fulvous ; it is confined to the Andaman Isles.

Second Group.   With oblique band white in both sexes.

555. **Kallima albofasciata,** Moore.

K. albofasciata, Moore, Proc. Zool. Soc. Lond., 1877, p. 584 ; idem, id., Trans. Ent. Soc. Lond., 1879, p. 13.

HABITAT : South Andamans (Port Blair).

EXPANSE : 3·2 to 4·1 inches.

DESCRIPTION : " UPPERSIDE glossy greyish indigo-blue. *Forewing* with a median, oblique, cream-white band with irregular borders ; hind part of wing indigo-blue, tinged with purplish lilac above posterior angle ; apex broadly blue-black, with a small bluish-white subapical spot ; a dark-bordered bluish-white diaphanous spot on middle of the disc ; a submarginal, sinuous, blue-black line. *Hindwing,* indigo-blue, tinged with purplish lilac along upper part of exterior margin ; costa brownish ; a submarginal, sinuous, blue-black line. *Body* greenish. UNDERSIDE, mottled greyish ochreous, black-speckled, varied with confluent brighter fasciæ on outer half, a pale-bordered dusky line from apex to tail ; a subapical and discal spot on *forewing,* and imperfect ocelli on *hindwing.*" (*Moore,* l. c. in Proc. Zool. Soc. Lond.)

The late Mr. de Roepstorff sent numerous specimens of this species to the Indian Museum, Calcutta. As usual no two specimens are similarly marked on the underside, but present every shade of colour and diversity of marking to simulate dead leaves. It is a very distinct species.

Third Group.   With oblique band blue in both sexes.

The third group contains six species according to Mr. Moore, to which a seventh from Bhutan has been added by myself: This group seems to be confined to the true Indian region, the Andaman Isles producing a modified form of it with the band almost white instead of bluish-white as in the continental species. Omitting the two specimens I possess from Bhutan, I have only seventeen specimens in all of this group, not nearly sufficient to enable me to work them out. A female from the Western Ghâts (Khandalla), one from

* *Kallima buttoni,* Moore, Trans. Ent. Soc. Lond., 1879, p. 10. HABITAT : Mazuri, N. W. Himalayas. EXPANSE : *Male* and *female,* 3·75 inches. DESCRIPTION : Allied to *K. inachis.* " Distinguished by the *forewing* being truncated exteriorly and the apex not prolonged. *Forewing,* with the fulvous band narrow and continued to the marginal angle, its upper or apical border less undulated, being nearly even in some specimens ; basal area bright deep dusky vinous blue. Discal hyaline spot minute. *Hindwing* bright deep dusky vinous blue. UNDERSIDE, deep chestnut-brown, with greyish-purple fasciæ ; rib-line prominent " (*Moore,* l. c.).

The Indian Museum, Calcutta, possesses a single female specimen from Mazuri which exactly agrees with the above description, the apex of the forewing being produced but very slightly.

Kallima rumaya, Moore, Trans. Ent. Soc. Lond., 1879, p. 12. HABITAT : Nepal, Khatmandu. EXPANSE : *Male* and *female,* 3·20 inches. DESCRIPTION : Allied to *K. inachis.* " Distinguished by its very dark and prominent markings. *Forewing,* with short sharp-pointed apex ; the upper or apical border of fulvous band very irregular ; the outer marginal parallel sinuous line very prominent ; a single large discal hyaline spot, basal area very dark iron-grey blue. *Hindwing,* very dark iron-grey blue. FEMALE, with the exterior margin of the *forewing* more convex hindward and at posterior angle, and the exterior border of the *hindwing* fulvous-brown. UNDERSIDE, chestnut-brown ; sparsely speckled, and with pale ochreous fasciæ ; rib-line prominent," (*Moore,* l. c.)

There is a single male from Sikkim in Colonel Lang's collection which agrees on the upperside with Mr. Moore's description of this species. The underside is marked quite differently, but this is a matter of no importance in my opinion.

Kallima atkinsoni, Moore, Trans. Ent. Soc. Lond., 1879, p. 10. HABITAT : Darjiling. EXPANSE : *Female,* 3·62 inches. DESCRIPTION : " FEMALE. Outline of wings as in *K. buxtoni.* UPPERSIDE, similar to *K. buxtoni,* but the fulvous band narrower, discal hyaline spot smaller and slender ; blue of base and on the *hindwing* of a purple-violet tint. UNDERSIDE, chestnut-brown, numerously speckled with dark brown ; fasciæ greyish." (*Moore,* l. c.)

As I have never seen the female of either *K. buxtoni* or *K. paralekta,* I am unable to give any indication as to the outline of *K. atkinsoni,* but according to Mr. Moore's key (ante) it is the same as that of *K. hindsrengi.* The description of the markings also is useless unless one has specimens of *K. buxtoni* with which to compare them.

Bassein (Bombay), another from Travancore, and lastly one without locality, agree with Kollar's figure of *K. horsfieldii*, the discal band being broad, no hyaline spot in the Khandalla specimen, and only a minute one in the ones from Travancore, Bassein, and without locality. The main point of distinction, however, between these specimens, and the other females I possess is the great length of the apical process of the forewing, in all the other specimens it is very much shorter, showing a correlation between the species of this group and of the yellow-banded group. A single male of this group from Coonoor, one from Canara, one from Travancore, and two without locality, have the hyaline spots very small, another from the Pulni Hills has no hyaline spots at all. Of the seven other specimens, one without locality, agrees with the Travancore male specimen, except that the discal band is broader, and the discal spots are large. The six remaining specimens consist of a pair from Khandalla, a male from Bassein (Bombay), a female from Coonoor (taken with the Coonoor male mentioned above), and two females from the Wynaad. All these specimens, as stated above, have the apex of the forewing but slightly produced in both sexes and the hyaline spots are very large. The discal band is variable in width, being widest in the Khandalla male, of less width in the Wynaad females, and narrowest in the Khandalla female. All these specimens are probably *K. wardi*. It is however to be noted that Khandalla produces female *Kallimas* with long apical processes and no hyaline spots (*K. horsfieldii*), and others with short apical processes and large hyaline spots (*K. wardi*); also that in the pair from Coonoor the male has very small discal hyaline spots, while the female has these spots large. Arranging them according to localities from which I possess both sexes, I obtain the following contradictory results :—A pair from Coonoor taken *in copulâ* has the discal hyaline spots small in the male large in the female, a Travancore pair have them small in both sexes, a pair from Bassein and another pair from Khandalla have them large in the male and small in the female, but it should be remembered that Khandalla produces two forms of female, one with a long the other with a short process to the apex of the forewing, and I am quite unable to say which female is the correct pair to the male. Mr. Moore in describing *K. wardi* says that it has the discal band "more erect than in any other species." If I have correctly identified my specimens, the band has the same direction as in *K. horsfieldii*. In all the specimens before me the markings on the underside are very variable, Mr. Moore appears to rely somewhat on them to distinguish between his species, but I hardly think that they will prove to be a reliable guide to specific discrimination. I have reproduced Mr. Moore's descriptions of these species without further remark, adding a key to them, derived wholly from his descriptions, except the single character which, as far as I am able to tell, separates *K. knyvettii* from all the rest. *K. wardi* may possibly be distinct, but the five species which precede it will, I think, most probably turn out to be merely varieties of a single species which will stand as *K. horsfieldii*.

Key to the Indian species of Kallima.

Third Group.

A. Outer edge of discal band on upperside of forewing more than half the length of the wing from the base.
    a. With no discal hyaline spots.
        a¹. Base of wings very pale blue.
            556. K. HORSFIELDII,? N.-W. Himalayas, Western Ghâts.
        b¹. Base of wings deep, dusky steel-blue.
            557. K. PHILARCHUS, Ceylon.
    b. With a minute lower discal hyaline spot.
        558. K. ALOMPRA, Burma.
    c. With two discal hyaline spots in male, none in female.
        559. K. DOULEDAYI, Sind.
    d. With two discal hyaline spots in both sexes.
        a¹. Base of wings pale indigo-blue.
            560. K. MACKWOODI, Ceylon.
        b¹. Base of wings greenish.
            561. K. WARDI, South India.
B. Outer edge of discal band on upperside of forewing less than half the length of the wing from the base.
    562. K. KNYVETTII, Buxa, Bhutan.

556. **Kallima horsfieldii,** Kollar.

Paphia horsfieldii, Kollar in Hügel's Kaschmir, vol. iv. pt. ?, p. 434, n. 7, pl. x, *female* (1844); *Kallima horsfieldii,* Moore, Trans. Ent. Soc. Lond., 1879, p 13.

HABITAT :　Himalayas (*Hügel*), Belgaum (*Leith*), Matheran Hill, Bombay (*Newton* and *Smith*).

EXPANSE :　3 5 (*Moore*) ; 4·4 inches (*Kollar's* figure).

DESCRIPTION :　"Oblique band blue in both sexes.　Apex of the forewing prolonged, no discal hyaline spots.　*Forewing,* oblique band broad and bluish-white ; basal portion very pale blue.　*Hindwing* very pale blue, the outer border greenish-ochreous.　UNDERSIDE, ochreous, with greenish-ochreous fasciæ."

"I have not yet seen specimens of this species from the locality given by Hügel, but I possess a specimen of what I doubtfully take to be the same from the collection of the late Dr. Leith, which he stated was captured in Belgaum (2,260 feet, Western Ghâts of South India).　Specimens have also been taken by Mr. Newton and Dr. Smith on the Matheran Hill, near Bombay."　(*Moore*, l. c.)

557. **Kallima philarchus,** Westwood.

Amathusia philarchus, Westwood, Cab. Or. Ent., p. 56, pl. xxvii, fig. 4, *male* (1848) ; id , Moore, Trans. Ent. Soc. Lond., 1879, p. 15 ; idem, id., Lep. Cey., vol. i, p. 32, pl. 11, fig. 1, *male* (1881).

HABITAT : Ceylon.

EXPANSE : 3·75 inches.

DESCRIPTION : Allied to *K. mackwoodi,* "differing in the basal area and hindwing being of a deep, dusky steel-blue colour ; and in the absence of the discal hyaline spots." (*Moore*, l. c. in Trans. Ent. Soc. Lond.)　The FEMALE appears to be unknown.

The original description by Westwood is as follows :—"Wings of a blue-black colour tinged with green, the tip of the *forewing* broadly black, with a white dot near the apex ; beyond the middle is a broad oblique silvery blue fascia, having several dark blue-black obscure short lines near and below the tip of the discoidal cell.　*Hindwing* concolourous, with the anal angle tailed.　UNDERSIDE, obscure greyish-brown, freckled all over with minute brown irrorations ; a slender brown streak extends across both wings (crossing the middle of the hindwing and extending from the apical angle of the forewing to the anal angle of the hindwing, where there is also another short brown parallel streak) ; half way between the middle of the hindwing and the anal angle are two very obscure ocelli surrounded by whitish rings, and there is a very indistinct row of minute whitish dots, running parallel with the apical margin of both wings.　*Body* entirely brown."　(*Westwood,* l. c.)

I have not seen a specimen of this species.　Mr. Moore in redescribing it above says that it has no discal spots on the forewing, but two small ones are shewn in his figure, and in his later description (Lep. Cey.) he states that there are "two minute scarcely discernible hyaline discal spots."　In Ceylon it is "a very rare butterfly.　Taken at Kandy" (*Wade*).

558. **Kallima alompra,** Moore.

K. alompra, Moore, Trans. Ent. Soc. Lond., 1879, p. 14.

HABITAT : Burma.

EXPANSE : 3·0 inches.

DESCRIPTION : "MALE.　Allied to *K. doubledayi* from Sind, but of darker tints.　*Forewing,* basal area of a darker tint than in *K. doubledayi,* the band also of a darker tint, and the male has only a minute hyaline lower discal spot, which is slightly more apparent in the female. *Hindwing,* as in *K. doubledayi,* but of a darker tint.　UNDERSIDE, greenish-brown, tinted with purple ; rib-line prominent, dark brown." (*Moore,* l. c.)

This species is unknown to me, not having specimens of *K. doubledayi,* I cannot identify it.

34

559. **Kallima doubledayi,** Moore.

K. doubledayi, Moore, Trans. Ent. Soc. Lond., 1879, p. 14.

HABITAT : Sind hills, N.-W. India.

EXPANSE : ♂, 3·12 ; ♀, 3·5 inches.

DESCRIPTION : " Smaller than *K. mackwoodi. Forewing,* with the band paler, the basal portion dark dull greenish-grey in the male, and greyish-cyaneous in the female, two hyaline spots in the male, none in the female. *Hindwing,* dark dull greenish-grey in the male, greyish-cyaneous in the female. UNDERSIDE, dull ochreous-brown, markings dark sap-brown." (*Moore,* l. c.)

This species is quite unknown to me.

560. **Kallima mackwoodi,** Moore.

K. mackwoodi, Moore, Trans. Ent. Soc. Lond., 1879, p. 14 ; idem, id., Lep. Cey., vol. i, p. 37, pl. xx, figs. 1, *male* ; 2a, *female* (1881).

HABITAT : Ceylon.

EXPANSE : ♂, 3·12 ; ♀, 3·25 inches.

DESCRIPTION : " UPPERSIDE. *Forewing* with the band very pale in male, almost white in female ; basal portion pale indigo-blue ; both sexes with two prominent discal hyaline spots, the lower spot large. *Hindwing,* pale indigo-blue. UNDERSIDE, greenish-grey in the male, with brown transverse band and outer purplish fasciæ. In the female greenish-ochreous, brown-speckled, with purplish fasciæ, and prominent brown rib-line." (*Moore,* l. c. in Trans. Ent. Soc. Lond.)

" MALE. UPPERSIDE, *both wings* pale indigo-blue. *Forewing* with a broad paler blue oblique transverse discal band, which is outwardly bordered by a black sinuous line and inwardly by interrupted disco-cellular streaks terminating on lower median nervule, apical area blue-black, with a small white spot near the angle, two prominent hyaline discal spots, the lower spot large. *Hindwing* tinged with brown along the anterior and exterior borders, a black lunular submarginal line and indistinct discal spots. UNDERSIDE greenish-ochreous-brown, black-speckled, crossed by three indistinct darker oblique purple fasciæ, with a prominent dark brown narrow transverse band crossing *both wings* from apex to end of the tail. *Forewing* with a series of small black points above the hyaline spots. *Hindwing* with a row of ill-defined and indistinct ocelli on the medial fascia. FEMALE paler above, the oblique band nearly white, with two prominent hyaline discal spots." (*Moore,* l. c. in Lep. Cey.)

I have never seen this species.

561. **Kallima wardi,** Moore. (PLATE XXIII, FIG. 104 ♀).

K. wardi, Moore, Trans. Ent. Soc. Lond., 1879, p. 14.

HABITAT : Calicut ; Malabar Coast ; Conoor.

EXPANSE : 3·12 inches.

DESCRIPTION : Allied to *K. doubledayi.* "Distinguished by having the blue band narrow and crossing the wing more erect than in any other species. *Forewing,* with a narrow blue band, the outer black border extends broadly to the posterior margin, two oval discal hyaline spots ; basal area of a greenish tint. *Hindwing,* of a greenish tint, with the outer border brownish. UNDERSIDE, dark vinous-brown, grey-tinted basally." (*Moore,* l. c.)

The figure shows the upper and undersides of a female specimen from the Wynaad in the Indian Museum, Calcutta. I have thus identified the specimen figured, as it was sent from the district in which *K. wardi* is said to occur, but the discal blue band is not more erect than in the other specimens I possess of this group.

562. **Kallima knyvettii**, de N., n. sp.

HABITAT : Buxa, Bhutan.

EXPANSE : ♂, 4·05 inches.

DESCRIPTION. MALE. Larger than any species of the group to which it belongs known to me, the UPPERSIDE of a darker colour also, being deep indigo-blue glossed with deep obscure green at the base. Forewing with a very broad bluish-white discal band not reaching the outer margin, its inner edge somewhat even, its outer edge irregular, extending broadly on to the costa, its outer edge at the costal end being distinctly less than half the length of the wing from the base, the band has its direction very straight, not curved towards the base of the wing at its costal end as in the other species of this group known to me. The usual opaque white spot at the bifurcation of the fourth and fifth subcostal nervules, a large oval discal hyaline spot in the first median interspace, none in the interspace above ; the disco-cellular nervules defined with a line of the ground-colour, but with no dark linear markings beyond and below it as in all the other species. Hindwing with the usual submarginal irregular line extending on to the forewing as far as the second median nervule. The pale ochreous abdominal margin is thickly clothed with hairs of the same colour, the cell and a broad portion of the wing below it towards the base of the tail is even more densely covered with long hairs, but of a dark brown colour, this setose clothing being very much more dense and conspicuous than in any species of the genus known to me. UNDERSIDE variable.

Described from two male specimens obtained (one with snipe shot) by Mr. A. V. Knyvett in the forest beyond Buxa, Bhutan, in August.

Genus 86.—DOLESCHALLIA, Felder. (PLATE XXIII).

Doleschallia, Felder, Neues Lep., p. 14, n. 24 (1861); id., Moore, Lep. Cey., vol. i, p. 39 (1881); id., Distant, Rhop. Malay., p. 87 (1883); *Kallima* (part), Westwood, Gen. Diurn. Lep., vol. ii. p. 324 (1850).

"FOREWING, subtriangular, *costal margin* arched from base [where it is slightly excavated] and convex, *apex* more or less truncated, *outer margin* sinuated, concave beneath apex, and convex towards posterior angle, *inner margin* more or less concave ; *first* and *second subcostal nervules* emitted somewhat close together near end of cell, *third* emitted beyond cell and extending to apex, *fourth* and *fifth* bifurcating at about one-third from apex ; *upper disco-cellular* nervule short and outwardly angled, [*middle* disco-cellular about three times as long, inwardly oblique], *lower* disco-cellular aborted, leaving the *discoidal cell* widely open ; *median* nervules widely separated, the third prominently rounded at base, *submedian nervure* nearly straight. HINDWING, elongate and subtriangular, the *costal* and *outer margins* convex, *anal angle* produced into a narrow caudate elongation, which is traversed by the submedian nervure, *abdominal margins* convex and contiguous near base, and from thence becoming concavely divergent to anal angle ; *costal nervure* arched and extending to apex, *præcostal* nervure obliquely rounded and curved outwardly towards apex ; *discoidal* [? *subcostal*] nervules well-separated at their origin, *discoidal cell* with the apex quite unclosed, *third median nervule* arched and rounded at a short distance from base. BODY, short, robust ; *palpi* large and porrect, raised above the upper margin of the head, gradually narrowed to an obtuse point at apices, flattened beneath and covered with adpressed hairs, and clothed above (excluding apices) with long semi-erect and well-separated hairs." [*Antennæ* less than half the length of the forewing, with a distinct well-developed club, ending in a short point]. (*Distant*, l. c.)

LARVA long and slender, head rather larger than the following segment, the body gradually increasing in size from the second to about the sixth segment, cylindrical, with dorsal and lateral series of delicately branched spines. PUPA smooth, head ending in two sharp points, thorax humped on the back, constricted beyond.

About fourteen species are included in this genus, but as pointed out by Mr. Distant, two of them inhabiting Western Africa and Madagascar are probably not congeneric, as they have the apex of the forewing acute instead of truncate. The rest occur in North-East India,

Ceylon, the Andaman and Nicobar Isles, Assam, Burma, the Malay Peninsula and Islands and in Australia. The genus is closely allied to *Kallima*, but has the apex of the forewing truncate (in the typical species) instead of acute, and the discoidal cell of both wings open, in *Kallima* they are closed. They are fulvous on the upperside, the apex of the forewing broadly black and including a band and spot of the ground-colour in some species, the underside is of various dark shades of green and brown, with a discal line as in *Kallima*, which simulates the mid-rib of a leaf, to which the whole underside has some resemblance, often with some silvery and brown basal marks, and a discal series of very obscure ocelli.

Much confusion has arisen regarding the specific determination of several species of the genus, which Mr. Distant has lately cleared up.* *D. pratipa* has been erroneously recorded by several writers from Upper Tenasserim and the Andaman Isles, it appears to be confined to the Malay Peninsula and Java ; in the same way *D. bisaltide* has been recorded from India, Ceylon, &c, it appears, according to Mr. Distant, to occur in Java and possibly Sumatra, Cramer giving Surinam as its habitat, a probable clerical error for the latter island. The Indian, Ceylon, Andaman and Nicobar species, which occurs also in Java, Borneo and the Philippines, is *D. polibete*, Cramer.

563. Doleschallia polibete, Cramer. (PLATE XXIII, FIG. 103 ♂).

Papilio polibete, Cramer, Pap. Ex., vol. iii, pl. ccxxxiv, figs. D, E (*nec* pl. ccxxxv, figs. C, D) 1779 ; *Doleschallia polibete*, Distant, Ent. Month. Mag., vol. xxii, p. 41 (1885); *Kallima bisaltide* (*part*), Horsfield and Moore, Cat. Lep. Mus. E. I. C., vol. i, p. 203, n. 477 (1857) ; *Doleschallia bisaltide*, Moore (*nec* Cramer), Proc. Zool. Soc. Lond., 1865, p. 767 ; idem, id., Lep. Cey., vol. i, p. 38, pl. xix, figs. 1, 1a, *imago* ; 1b, *larva and pupa* (1881) ; *Doleschallia pratipa*, Moore (*nec* Felder), Proc. Zool. Soc. Lond., 1877, p. 584 ; idem, id., l. c., 1878, p. 828.

HABITAT : N.-E. India, Upper Tenasserim, Ceylon, Andaman and Nicobar Isles, Java, Borneo, Philippines.

EXPANSE : 2·7 to 3·3 inches.

DESCRIPTION : " MALE. UPPERSIDE deep fulvous. *Forewing* with a very oblique black band from middle of costa joining a marginal band which expands broadly at the apex,† three minute white spots obliquely before the apical angle [often absent]. *Hindwing* dusky fulvous on anterior margin, with a more or less distinct small black upper and lower discal spot and two wavy marginal lines. UNDERSIDE dark fulvous-brown or dark olive-brown, obliquely fasciated with purple. *Forewing* with two more or less prominent black-bordered white discoidal streaks and a lower spot, a red-lined disco-cellular mark, a transverse discal sinuous black line, a submarginal series of white spots, the two lower spots ringed with purple, the upper terminating in a white costal streak, a marginal dark brown lunular line. *Hindwing* with a black-bordered white discoidal spot and another spot above the cell, a transverse discal straight black line, a distinct upper and lower discal ocellus, marginal black line indistinct, and generally terminating in a blue caudal streak, abdominal margin black speckled. FEMALE. UPPERSIDE slightly paler on *forewing*. UNDERSIDE duller fulvous-brown or olive-brown, basal white marks obsolete, other markings as in male, but less distinct."

"LARVA long, somewhat slender, purple-black, with a dorsal and lateral series of short delicate branched blue spines ; a medial lateral row of white spots. Feeds on Acanthads. PUPA slender, head produced into two points, constricted behind the thorax ; pale reddish-purple, numerously dotted with black." (Moore, l. c. in Lep. Cey.)

The markings of the underside are very variable, the forewing in the male has sometimes a prominent silvery quadrate spot in the middle of the cell, an elongated sinuous one at its end, and a third below the base of the first median nervule, in the hindwing there is a large spot at the outer end of the cell, with a small one in its middle, and a large round spot near

---

* Ent. Month. Mag., vol. xxii, p. 41 (1885).

† The markings on this portion of the wing would, perhaps, be best described as the apex broadly black enclosing a broad oblique band of the ground-colour which extends along the costa to the base of the wing, usually with a separate rounded spot beyond the band above the third median nervule, which however sometimes coalesces with the band.

the base of the costal interspace. These silvery spots are sometimes ochreous, often entirely wanting. The colour and marbling of the ground is also exceedingly variable. The female is more uniformly coloured, and the silvery spots are never prominently developed. *D. polibete* is a common species at low elevations in Sikkim, and occurs also in Assam, Cachar, Sylhet, Upper Tenasserim (but not in peninsular India), in Ceylon, and the Andaman and Nicobar Isles.

The figure shows the upper and undersides of a male specimen from the South Andaman Isles in the Indian Museum, Calcutta.

Doleschallia pratipa, Felder, is a closely-allied species, but differs from *D. polibete* in the male in having the fulvous band at the apex of the forewing on the upperside smaller and ending at the lower discoidal nervule, and with no fulvous spot beyond; the female has a broad pale fulvous band outwardly bounded by the black apical border, and with a small black patch at the end of the cell, not joined to the outer black border as in *D. polibete*. It has been recorded from Upper Tenasserim and the Andaman Isles, but is apparently confined to the Malay Peninsula and Java. A description of it is given below.*

Genus 87.—CHARAXES, Ochsenheimer. (PLATE XXII).

Charaxes, Ochsenheimer, Schmett. Eur., vol. iv, p. 18 (1816); id., Felder, Neues Lep., p. 30, n. 92 (1861); id., Butler, Proc. Zool. Soc. Lond., 1865, p. 623, *Monograph*; id., Moore, Lep. Cey., vol. i, p. 28 (1881); id., Distant, Rhop. Malay., p. 101 (1883); *Paphia* (part), Fabricius, Ill. Mag., vol. vi, p. 282, n. 17 (1807); *Eriboea*, Hübner, Verz. bek. Schmett., p. 46 (1816); *Eulepis*, Dalman, in Billberg's Enum. Ins., p. 80 (1820); id., Moore, Lep. Cey., vol. i, p. 29 (1881); *Jasia*, Swainson, Zool. Ill., vol. ii, p. 90 (1832-33); *Nymphalis*, Westwood (*nec* Latreille), Gen. Diurn. Lep., vol. ii, p. 306 (1850); *Haridra*, Moore, Lep. Cey., vol. i, p. 30 (1881).

"BODY, extremely robust; *hindwing* generally with one or two tails [very variable in length]; underside of the wings beautifully ornamented with patches and markings of varied colours. *Female*, scarcely differing in appearance from the male, but larger and sometimes with a paler oblique bar on the forewing. HEAD, moderately large, woolly, not tufted in front; *eyes*, very prominent, naked; *palpi*, large, porrected obliquely; the tip elevated considerably above the level of the top of the eyes, and extending in front of the head nearly as far as its length; rather apart at the base, but approximating at the tip; thickly scaly; the extremity of the second joint above clothed with short erect hairs, resting upon the face in repose; terminal joint somewhat naked, small and conical; inside with the scales more hair-like; *antennæ*, rather short, not half the length of the forewing, strong, straight; terminated by a long, gradually-formed, but not very robust, fusiform club, slightly attenuated at the extreme tip, where it is obliquely

---

* *Doleschallia pratipa*, Felder, Wien. Ent. Monatsch., vol. iv, p. 397, n. 20 (1860); idem, id., Reise Novara, Lep., vol. iii, p. 406, n. 610 (1866); id., Butler, Trans. Linn. Soc. Lond., Zoology, second series, vol. i, p. 537, n. 1 (1877); id., Distant, Rhop. Malay., p. 33, n. 1, pl. xi, fig. 8, *male*; pl. iv, fig. 6, *female* (1883); idem, id., Ent. Month. Mag., vol. xxii, p. 41 (1885). HABITAT: Perak, Province Wellesley, Malacca, Java. EXPANSE: 2 4 to 3 0 inches. DESCRIPTION: "*Male*, UPPERSIDE ferruginous-fulvous. *Forewing* with the discal patch diffused, pale ochraceous-yellow, marked with a blackish-fuscous disco-cellular spot more or less curved, the terminal border immediately beyond it blackish-fuscous, adorned with a whitish subcostal dot and inwardly below the lower discoidal vein an ochraceous spot, subconfluent with the patch. *Hindwing* with the two subapical spots, one hinder punctiform spot, and two streaks before the margin blackish-fuscous, with the anal lobe inwardly irrorated with lilacine-hoary. UNDERSIDE as in *D. bisaltide* but darker, obvaceous-greyish, shining with bronze. *Forewing* with the discal striga more inwardly directed towards the costa. *Hindwing* with the powdery lilascent-hoary streak placed before the hinder margin much broader than in *D. bisaltide* and *D. polibete*."

"In both the specimens which we have before us, the apex of the forewing is less truncate, and the anal process of the hindwing is longer than in *D. bisaltide* or *D. polibete*; Cramer." (Felder, l. c. in Reise Novara). This description is almost undoubtedly that of a female, to which it exactly applies, not of a male as stated by Felder. The differences between both sexes of *D. polibete* and *D. pratipa* are given in my note above.

Mr Distant describes the FEMALE as follows:—"*Forewing* with the apex not prominently falcate; differs from the male by having a large subapical yellowish patch, and by the fuscous oblique fascia being only denoted by an irregular spot at end of cell. *Hindwing* with the marginal fascia only denoted by the marginal borders as in male. UNDERSIDE as in male, but paler, and with the white spots much more obscure."

"This species varies much in the colour of the wings on the underside, and is a very close ally to the Javan species, *D. bisaltide*, Cramer. From this it differs principally in the female sex, which in *D. bisaltide* has the pale subapical patch and also the complete oblique subapical fuscous fascia. *D. pratipa* is clearly a local race of Cramer's species."

"*D. bisaltide* is a somewhat rare species; male and female specimens are contained in the Horsfield collection which agree with Cramer's figure. Several other specimens were confused, however, under the same name, which on examination with Mr. Butler, proved to be both male and female *D. polibete*, Cramer, a species which is quite distinct and not synonymous with *D. bisaltide*, as stated in Mr. Kirby's Catalogue (p. 193). *D. polibete* has both sexes very similar, and not distinct as in *D. bisaltide* and *D. pratipa*; it is also a wide-ranging species, as I possess specimens both from Java and the Andaman Islands. In all these species it appears that the brightest white spots on the underside are developed in the male only." (Distant, l. c. in Rhop. Malay.)

truncate, with a very fine carina [keel] on the undersile, on each side of which is a very slight longitudinal impression. THORAX, very robust, oblong, thickly clothed with wool, especially on the metathorax. ABDOMEN, rather short; nearly ovate in the female. FOREWING, sub-triangular; *costal margin* moderately arched; *apical angle* somewhat acute, but rounded off at its extremity; *outer margin* oblique, slightly emarginate, and almost entire, three-fourths of the length of the costa; *inner margin* straight, about equal in length to the outer margin. *Veins* very strong; *costal nervure* not extending to the middle of the costa; *subcostal* nervure with the first and second branches arising before the anterior extremity of the discoidal cell; third branch arising at a very little distance beyond the cell, [reaching the apex of the wing]; fourth branch arising also at a small distance beyond the third, at rather more than the length of two-fifths of the wing from the base; elbowed downwards towards the tip of the wing; *upper disco-cellular nervule* arising at about the length of one-third of the wing from the base, very short, transverse; as is also the rather longer *middle* disco-cellular; the *lower* disco-cellular still longer, straight, transverse, very slender, and uniting with the third median nervule at some distance from its origin, closing the *discoidal cell* transversely; *third median nervule* gradually arched. HINDWING, large, somewhat ovate, not ocellated beneath; *costal margin* arched; *outer* margin more or less dentate, and tailed; the tails being produced at the extremity of the first and third median nervules. *Præcostal nervure* oblique, the tip rather suddenly bent outwards; *discoidal cell* small and narrow; closed imperfectly by a very fine *disco-cellular nervule*, which unites the discoidal nervure with the median nervure just before its third branch is thrown off. [In some Indian species the lower disco-cellular nervule is absent, leaving the discoidal cell entirely open.] FORELEGS, of the *male* very minute, scaly, and clothed with fine, silky, rather short black hairs above, and white ones below; the *tibia* and *tarsus* being together not, or but little, longer than the femur; the tibia twice the length of the tarsus, which is indistinctly articulated beyond the middle and towards the tip, when denuded of scales. Of the *female* half as long again as those of the male, scaly; the *femur* with a slight row of fine hairs on the inside; *tibia* two-thirds of the length of the femur; *tarsus* about as long as the tibia, compressed, dilated at the tip, which is obliquely rounded off, with several pairs of spines towards the tip on the underside, indicating the articulations; the basal joint being scarcely more than half of the length of the tarsus. MIDDLE and HINDLEGS, rather short, very robust, finely scaly; *tibia* shorter than the femur, flat beneath; intermediate tibia with an oblong patch of delicate plush at the base; each side with a row of fine short spines; tibial spurs short; *tarsi* robust, scaly, with four rows of short spines beneath; *claws* moderate; *paronychia* very small; the inner lobe very short, outer lobe acute, curved."

"LARVA without any spines on the body, which is gradually attenuated behind; terminated by a depressed bicuspidated* tail; the head armed with four obtuse horns. PUPA abbreviated, rounded, subconical, scarcely carinated down the back." (*Westwood*, l. c.)

"The genus *Charaxes*, from its wide distribution, and the beauty of its species, combined with their strength of wing and body, forms one of the most interesting genera of the *Nymphalinæ*. One species is found in Europe, round the shores of the Mediterranean, which has a very close ally in an Abyssinian species. The genus also inhabits Eastern, Western, and the warmer portions of Southern Africa. It is apparently in Western Tropical Africa that *Charaxes* is found in its maximum of size, beauty, and abundance of species. Madagascar possesses some very distinct species, and travelling eastwards the genus has recently been discovered in the Island of Socotra by Professor Balfour. It occurs in Continental India, is found in Ceylon and the Andaman Islands [and Nicobars according to Godart], occurs throughout Burma, Tenasserim, and the Malay Peninsula, Eastern Asia as far north as China, and through the length and breadth of the Malay Archipelago. Its distribution in the Pacific Islands appears at present very limited, but it is found in Australia."

"The smooth spineless larvæ with bifid tails ally *Charaxes* superficially with the *Satyrinæ*." (*Distant*, l. c.)

---

* BICUSPIDATED, two-pointed, from *bi*, two, *cuspis*, a spear point.

All the Indian species of *Charaxes* possess a peculiar character in the neuration of the forewing as pointed out by Professor Westwood, the fourth subcostal nervule arises close to the discoidal cell, being thereby of extraordinary length, and is bent downwards towards the tip of the wing. All the species possess tails on the hindwing placed at the ends of the first and third median nervules, in some species they are both long and narrow, in others the outer tail is shorter and broader, and the inner one obsolete, and there are integrades between these extreme forms. In some species the discoidal cell of the hindwing is closed, in others it is open. Mr. Moore has lately split up the genus into three genera which embrace most, if not all, of the species occurring in India. The larvæ certainly present two types, in the one the sides are marked with oblique stripes, in the other there is a large round spot in the middle of the back, with three smaller ones on the sides; in the European species (*Charaxes jasius*) there are two spots on the middle of the sixth and eighth segments, and none at the sides: the horns on the head are very short in this species. The pupa in the former is much more obtuse anteriorly than in the latter. The genus is very well represented in India, twenty-nine species having been recorded from within our limits, but many of them appear to be varietal forms only. They attain their largest size, and greatest number of species as well as of individuals in the north-east of our empire, but especially in the hot low valleys of Sikkim and Assam.

I have for convenience divided the genus into two groups, the first of which has the discoidal cell of the hindwing open, and embraces the species separated by Mr. Moore under the generic name *Eulepis*.* The second group has the discoidal cell of the hindwing closed, and embraces the typical *Charaxes* and Mr. Moore's genus *Haridra*.

In the first group, both the tails of the hindwing are narrow and elongate. The ground-colour of the upperside is in some of the species very pale straw-coloured, the outer margin more or less broadly marked with black, and in others the ground-colour is deep indigo-blue, with a broad median band white or pale green across both wings, with one or more spots in continuation towards the apex of the forewing. The underside is opalescent whitish with the border as above but much paler, and with other markings differing in the various species.

Key to the Indian species of Charaxes.

First group.

A. Discoidal cell of hindwing open.
  a. Ground-colour of upperside yellowish-white : the apex and outer border of forewing black.
    a¹. Forewing on upperside with one or two spots on the black border near apex, sometimes unmarked.
        564. C. (*Eulepis*) DELPHIS, N.-E. India, Upper Tenasserim, Malayana.
    b¹. Forewing on upperside with a single series of six or seven spots on the black border.
        565. C. (*Eulepis*) DOLON, Kulu, Sikkim.
    c¹. Forewing on upperside with three series of spots on the black border, inner series consisting of two spots only.
        566. C. (*Eulepis*) EUDAMIPPUS, N.-E. India, Upper Tenasserim.
  b. Ground-colour of upperside deep indigo-blue, with a greenish-white or white band across both wings, often very broad.
    a¹. Discal band on upperside white, outwardly and posteriorly broadly margined on both wings with pale blue.
        567. C. (*Eulepis*) SCHREIBERI, Assam, South India, Malayana.
    b¹. Discal band on upperside not margined with pale blue.
      a². Discal band greenish yellow.
        568. C. (*Eulepis*) ATHAMAS, India, Ceylon, Malay Peninsula, Java, China.
      b². Discal band white tinged with very pale greenish.
        569. C. (*Eulepis*) ARJA, N.-E. India, Upper Tenasserim.

---

* Genus EULEPIS, Moore. "Wings similar in form to *Charaxes*; veins of FOREWING also similar; HINDWING with the *second subcostal* and *discoidal nervules* nearer the first subcostal nervule; *discoidal cell* open; *upper* and *middle median nervules* further from lower median nervule; *internal nervure* longer." (*Moore, l. c.*)

564. Charaxes dolphis, Doubleday.

C. *dolphis*, Doubleday, Ann. Soc. Ent. France, second series, vol. i, p. 217, pl. vii (1843); id., Butler, Proc. Zool. Soc. Lond., 1865, p. 635, n. 50; id., Distant, Rhop. Malay., p. 105, n. 3, pl. xv. fig. 1, *male* (1883); C. *concha*, Vollenhoven, Tijd. Ent., vol. iv. p. 162, n. 5, pl. 1, figs. 1, 3 (1861).

HABITAT : Assam, Cachar, Sylhet, Upper Tenasserim, Malacca, Perak, Sumatra, Borneo.

EXPANSE : 3·5 to 4·0 inches.

DESCRIPTION : "MALE and FEMALE. UPPERSIDE, *both wings* pale stramineous. *Forewing* with the costal area slightly infuscated ; a small black streak on upper portion of disco-cellular nervules, and the whole apical third black [something bearing one or two small spots of the ground-colour in the subcostal and upper discoidal interspaces] ; the inner margin of this black area is much waved, and commencing at costa near end of cell really and narrowly terminates at apex of first median nervule, but is apparently continued by two elongated spots, which do not pass the submedian nervure, and do not quite reach the outer margin. *Hindwing* with a submarginal series of greenish lunulate spots placed between the nervules, continued as streaks to the apices of nervules, especially prominent and distinct along the three median nervules. (Some markings of the underside show more or less distinctly near the posterior angle of the forewing, and on the disc of the hindwing.) UNDERSIDE pale silvery white. *Forewing* with the apical third somewhat darker (reflecting the black area of the upperside) ; two small and irregularly-shaped bluish-black spots in cell [these spots in the cell vary in number from two to five] ; a lunulate blue spot with black margins at end of cell, outwardly followed by a contiguous black streak [at base of lower discoidal interspace] ; a narrow black streak above and beneath the upper discoidal nervule ; a rounded blue spot with blackish margins beneath cell and between second and first median nervules, and an outer submarginal series of lunulate bluish markings, outwardly followed by a series of ochraceous spots. *Hindwing* with a blue spot with blackish margins on about middle of costal area [sometimes with a similar spot in the interspace below], three curved blackish lines (diminishing in size) in and near end of cell, a short linear mark of the same colour on each side of the first median nervule, and two similar ones on abdominal margin, about one-third from anal angle ; a discal series of bluish lunulate spots placed between the nervules, closely followed by a series of dark ochraceous spots, and again by a much-waved pale ochraceous fascia ; a submarginal series of bluish elongate and linear spots placed between the nervules, and a marginal corresponding series of rather larger ochraceous spots ; caudate appendages streaked with bluish. *Body* above with the abdomen more or less concolourous with wings, the thorax and head infuscated ; thorax beneath concolourous with wings, the *legs* dull greyish. *Antennæ* fuscous." (*Distant*, l. c.)

This is a rare as well as beautiful species. Mr. Wood-Mason obtained a single male in Cachar in August, Captain C. T. Bingham obtained a male in the Donat range in January and another in the Thoungyeen forests towards the end of the year, and there are specimens in the Indian Museum, Calcutta, from Sylhet, Moulmein and Perak.

565. Charaxes dolon, Westwood. (PLATE XXII, FIG. 100 ♂).

C. *dolon*, Westwood, Cab. Or. Ent., p. 55, pl. xxvii, figs. 2, 3 (1848) ; id., Butler, Proc. Zool. Soc. Lond., 1865, p. 635, n. 49 ; *Haridra dolon*, id., Ann. and Mag. of Nat. Hist., fifth series, vol. xvi, p. 306, n. 52 (1885).

HABITAT : Kulu, Sikkim, near Assam.

EXPANSE : 3·3 to 3·9 inches.

DESCRIPTION : " UPPERSIDE, *both wings* straw-white. *Forewing* having the costa, a con-joined spot at the extremity of the discoidal cell, and a broad apical margin of black, the latter bearing a single row of about eight white spots. *Hindwing* bicaudate, with a subapical [submarginal] narrow fascia of brownish-black, in which are two rows of small whitish lunules ; the tails bluish-grey, the inner one preceded by two blue-white spots. UNDERSIDE, *both wings* pearly-white ; the costa of the forewing (except at the tip) and two narrow fasciæ common to both wings, and more or less edged with black, as well as the apical [outer] margin, dull fulvous ; the *hindwing* with a submarginal row of black dots. *Abdomen* brown."

" This species is closely allied to *C. eudamippus*, Doubleday, but differs in its smaller size, the direction of the dark patch at the apex of the discoidal cell, the single row of white spots in the broad dark apical [outer] margin, the dark costa of the forewing beneath, the single minute black dot in the discoidal cell adjoining the costa, the more regular fascia at the extremity of the discoidal cell, the want of the black oblique line in the anal area of the hindwing, and in the brown abdomen, which is pure white in *C. eudamippus*." (*Westwood*, l. c.)

C. dolon appears to be even rarer than *C. delphis*, as I know of its occurrence only in Kulu (two specimens taken by Mr. A. Graham Young) and in Sikkim. Mr Butler records it from " near Assam."

The figure shows the upper and undersides of a male specimen in the Indian Museum, Calcutta, from Sikkim.

566. **Charaxes eudamippus,** Doubleday.

C. eudamippus, Doubleday. Ann. Soc. Ent. France, second series, vol. i, p. 215, pl. viii (1843) ; id , Butler, Proc. Zool. Soc. Lond., 1865, p. 635, n 47.

HABITAT : Sikkim, Assam, Naga Hills, Sylhet, Upper Tenasserim, Tavoy.

EXPANSE : 3·9 to 4·8 inches.

DESCRIPTION : MALE. UPPERSIDE, *both wings* straw-white. *Forewing* with the costa and upper half of the cell, the apex widely, and the outer margin decreasingly deep indigo-blue almost black ; also a similarly coloured band at the end of the cell enclosing the disco-cellulars, extending on either side of the median nervure almost to the origin of the first median nervule, also along the third median nervule posteriorly for about a third of its length ; with the black apical portion of the wing enclosing a large spot of the ground-colour in the lower discoidal interspace at the end of the cell ; the subcostal and upper discoidal interspaces each bears two rounded spots, the lower discoidal and median interspaces one each, the upper of the three the smallest, in the submedian interspace are a pair of joined lunules, the lower one being tinted with blue ; the margin bears a series of seven or eight smaller spots, one in each interspace, except the submedian which has two ; a blue-tinted spot at the anal angle. *Hindwing* with a submarginal series of somewhat lunular spots of the colour of the ground, surrounded with black and inwardly again with a pale blue band, the margin (except at the anal angle) narrowly black, within which is a broader diffused band of pale blue ; the tails at the ends of the first and third median nervules almost equal in length, narrow, long, and marked like the margin. UNDERSIDE, *both wings* pearly-white, the outer margin with a well-defined dull yellowish-green band ; a similarly-coloured submarginal band, in the forewing commencing on the costa about midway between the apex and the cell, approaching the outer margin at the anal angle, straight, outwardly defined with short black lines between the nervules, which latter become somewhat lunular towards the anal angle ; with two black V-shaped marks in the submedian interspace beyond ; on the hindwing evenly curved and bearing outwardly a series of bluish lunules outwardly defined with black, between which and the outer margin are a series of small round black spots one in each interspace except the submedian which has two ; another similarly-coloured discal band, more or less margined with black on both sides, commencing in the forewing at the subcostal nervure and enclosing the disco-cellulars, hardly extending below the first median nervule, and throwing off a branch along the third median nervule for about one-third of its length, this band on the hindwing commencing on the costa about one-fourth of its length from the base and curving evenly across the wing till it joins the submarginal band in the middle of the submedian interspace. *Forewing* with two prominent round black spots placed obliquely in the cell. *Hindwing* with a short oblique black streak extending from the discal yellow band to the margin near the anal angle. The FEMALE is larger than the male, but does not differ in markings.

C. eudamippus is a common species at low elevations in Sikkim, and extends eastwards as far as Sibsagar in Upper Assam. Captain C. T. Bingham obtained it in March in the Thoungyeen Forests, Upper Tenasserim, it occurs also in Tavoy.

35

C. nepenthes, Smith, from Siam, is very closely allied to *C. eudamippus*. Its description is appended.*

567. Charaxes schreiberi, Godart.

Nymphalis schreiber, Godart, Enc. Méth., vol. ix, Supplement, p. 825 (1823) ; *Paphia schreibera*, Horsfield, Cat. Lep. E. I. C., pl. vi, figs. 3. 3*a*, *female* (1829) ; *Nymphalis schreiberi*, Horsfield and Moore, Cat. Lep. Mus. E. I. C., vol. I, p. 205, n. 418 (1857) ; *Charaxes schreiberi*, Butler, Proc. Zool. Soc. Lond., 1865, p. 633, n. 43 ; id., Distant, Rhop. Malay., p. 104, n. 2, pl. xiii, fig. 2, *male* (1883).

HABITAT : Assam, South India, Malacca, Billiton, Java, Borneo.

EXPANSE : 3 6 to 3 9 inches.

DESCRIPTION : " MALE. UPPERSIDE, *both wings* dark fuscous, the basal third somewhat tinged with bluish, the disc crossed by a medial white fascia, commencing on the forewing immediately beneath the third median nervule and terminating on the hindwing in a subacute point near the third median nervule ; on the forewing this fascia is narrowly margined [inwardly] with pale bluish from beneath the first median nervule, and from the same nervule is outwardly very broadly and somewhat dentately margined with the same colour ; on the hindwing the white fascia terminates in a pale bluish fascia which is inwardly straight and outwardly emarginate, and crosses the wing, terminating very narrowly at the anal angle. *Forewing* with a white spot placed between the discoidal nervules. *Hindwing* with a submarginal series of small whitish spots placed between the nervules, two between the first median nervule and submedian nervure, and a pale bluish narrow submarginal but broken fascia commencing at about discoidal nervule, which becomes ochraceous at anal angle ; abdominal margin pale greyish at base. UNDERSIDE, *both wings* pale silvery white ; crossed by a dull ochraceous fascia margined with blue ; on the forewing this fascia crosses the end of the cell, where it is outwardly bifurcate and terminates, obtusely rounded a little beneath the first median nervule ; on the hindwing the fascia commences at costa and terminates a little beyond the first median nervule. *Forewing* with two dark bluish spots in cell ; an irregularly shaped carmine spot beyond the medial fascia between the lower discoidal and the second median nervule ; a submarginal series of somewhat lunulate spots placed between the nervules, which are obsolete near apex, and suffused with black near outer angle, the lower three being preceded by a lunulate dark line, and the outer margin broadly infuscated. *Hindwing* with a broad submarginal pale fuscous fascia, on the inner margin of which are a series of carmine lunulate spots, the upper three of which have a pale area and are preceded by a continuous bluish line, and the lower and larger three are inwardly margined with white and blue, the one at anal angle being preceded by a transverse dark bluish streak, and a marginal ochraceous fascia, the borders of which are bluish. *Body* more or less concolourous with wings ; posterior and intermediate *femora* much suffused with blackish shadings ; *tibiæ* and *tarsi* ochraceous. FEMALE. Resembling the male, but with the medial white fascia to the wings above only faintly and slightly margined and followed by pale blue, and the marginal fascia to the *hindwing* more ochraceous and continued to apex. On the *forewing* there is an additional small white subapical spot placed above the upper discoidal nervule." (*Distant*, l. c.)

___

* *Charaxes nepenthes*, Smith, Ent. Month. Mag., vol. xx, p. 58 (1884). HABITAT : Siam. EXPANSE : 3 33 inches. DESCRIPTION : " UPPERSIDE straw colour. *Forewing* with the costa and apical portion of the wing as in *C. eudamippus*, Doubleday, dark brown, with a submarginal row of small spots, inside of which is another row of larger spots, and two still larger spots between the subcostal nervules, all straw colour. A quadrangular dark brown spot at the end of the cell, the lower end of the spot, on the outside, extending down the upper and middle disco-cellular nervules. *Hindwing* with a double row of submarginal black spots, the outer row elongate, the inner row hastate, distinct from it, not joined as in *C. eudamippus* and *C. dolon*, two tails bluish-grey, outer margin black. UNDERSIDE silvery-white. *Forewing* with a fulvous band, irregularly marked outside with black, extending from the costa beyond the middle to near the inner angle, beyond which is a row of indistinct dark marks, and a fulvous band on the outer margin ; two black spots within the cell ; two black lines on the upper and middle disco-cellular nervules, the inner one sinuate, under which are two black spots ; near the costa, about halfway between the cell and the first fulvous band, are two more small black spots. *Hindwing* with the double row of submarginal spots as above, the inner row bordered inside with a fulvous band, which, near the anal angle, joins an irregular fulvous band, extending down the wing along the abdominal fold from the costa, near the base, to the anal angle, where it joins a marginal fulvous band bordered with grey. On either side of the band down the wing are several black lines and spots, and two transverse, black, elongate spots on the abdominal fold, a little above the anal angle."

" Near to *C. eudamippus* and *C. dolon*, but quite distinct " (*H. Grose Smith*, l. c.)

In India *C. schreiberi* is a very rare species, the Indian Museum possesses a single male taken in the Wynaad by Mr Rhodes-Morgan, Mr. J. L. Sherwill has sent me another male taken at Jorehât in Assam, and Mr. Harold S. Ferguson has sent a single forewing found on the ground in Travancore. The two former differ from Mr. Distant's description in having the discal white band on the forewing continued up to the lower discoidal nervule, the Wynaad specimen with two quadrate white spots placed above and beyond its upper end—the lower spot four times as large as the upper one—divided by the upper discoidal nervule ; the discal band is also less broad than shown in Mr. Distant's figure ; the Jorehât specimen has the discal band much narrowed anteriorly, with a spot beyond in the upper discoidal interspace. The single wing from Travancore (which is probably that of a female) has the discal band twice as broad as in the Wynaad example, and the two upper spots joined to it and very large. The Jorehât specimen alone has the subapical spot in the forewing between the fourth and fifth subcostal nervules shown in Dr. Horsfield's figure.

568. Charaxes athamas, Drury.

Papilio athamas, Drury, Ill. Ex. Ent , vol. i, p. 5, pl. ii. figs. 4 (1770); id., Cramer, Pap. Ex., vol. i, pl. lxxxiv, figs. C, D (1776); *Nymphalis athamas*, Godart, Enc. Méth., vol. ix, p. 353, n. 11 (1823); id., Horsfield and Moore, Cat. Lep. Mus. E. I. C., vol. i, p. 205, n. 417, pl. vi, figs. 3, larva ; 3a, pupa (1857) ; *Charaxes athamas*, Butler, Proc. Zool. Soc. Lond., 1865, p. 634, n. 45 ; *Jasia achaeus*, Swainson, Zool. Ill. Ins., vol. ii, pl. lxc (1833) ; *Erikta athamis*, Hubner, Verz bek. Schmett., p. 47, n. 430 (1816) ; *Papilio pyrrhus*, Donovan, (*nec* Linnæus), Ins. Ind., pl. xiii, fig. 3 (1800) ; *Charaxes bharata*, Felder, Reise Novara, Lep., vol. iii, n. 438, p. 712 (1867) ; id., Butler, Trans. Ent. Soc. Lond ; 1870, p. 119, n. 3 ; C. *samatha*, Moore, Proc. Zool. Soc. Lond., 1878, p. 851 ; *Eulepis samatha*, id., Lep. Cey., vol. i, p. 79, pl. xiv. figs. 2, *male* ; 2a, *female* ; 2b, *larva*, and *pupa* (1881) ; *Charaxes athamas*, var. *samatha*, Distant, Rhop. Malay , p. 106, n. 4, pl. xiii, fig. 8, *male* (1883) ; *Eulepis houresta*, Moore, Proc. Zool. Soc. Lond., 1882, p. 238 ; *Charaxes agrarius*, Swinhoe, MS.

HABITAT : Throughout the hilly portions of India, Ceylon, Burma, Andaman Isles, Malay Peninsula, Java, China.

EXPANSE : ♂, 2·2 to 3·2 ; ♀, 3·2 to 3·5 inches.

DESCRIPTION : MALE. UPPERSIDE deep indigo-blue. *Forewing* with a small spot in the upper discoidal interspace near the apex, a larger one placed inwardly below it in the next interspace, a broad discal band bounded anteriorly by the third median nervule, not extending into the cell, slightly less than ·3 of an inch* in breadth at the inner margin—all greenish-yellow. *Hindwing* with a similar band from the costa, but rapidly narrowing to a point on the first median nervule above the anal angle, a submarginal series of small whitish spots, two long fine tails at the extremities of the third and first median nervules, a whitish spot on the margin between the inner tail and the anal angle. UNDERSIDE, *both wings* olive brown, with the discal band as above, but paler, its inner margin with a rich chestnut-red band defined on both sides with black in its middle portion, extending as far as the outer edge of the discal band in the forewing. *Forewing* with the lower subapical spot only, two small, black, white-ringed spots placed obliquely above one another in the cell, a series of increasing lunulate spots placed just beyond the discal band, the outer margin broadly darker. *Hindwing* with the outer edge of the discal band prominently defined with a rich chestnut-red line which extends to the abdominal margin above the anal angle, divided by bluish-silvery lunules, the outer margin darker than the rest of the wing, and bearing a submarginal series of diffused whitish spots, with blackish spots placed outwardly against them, then a fulvous marginal line, the tails bluish-silvery.

The above description is taken from the type figure by Drury in which the discal band at the inner margin of the forewing is just under ·3 of an inch in breadth, and there are two apical spots on the forewing. It may be assumed that Drury figured a male specimen. I possess examples agreeing with this form from Sikkim, Sibsagar, Cherrapunji, Sylhet, Cachar, Chittagong, Upper Tenasserim, Orissa, the Wynaad, South Andaman Isles, and Java.

The width of the discal band, the number and the prominence of the subapical spots, and indeed all the markings of the upperside are very variable in this species ; these variations are considered by many authorities to be constant, and no less than four of them have been described as distinct species, as detailed below.

---

* Exactly seven millimetres.

C. bharata. Under this name Dr. Felder has described a form of *C. athamas* as follows :—
" MALE. UPPERSIDE as in *C. athamas*, but the fascia broader, in the hindwing not at all arched outwardly towards the anterior portion. *Forewing* with a much larger spot and another subapical. UNDERSIDE with the fascia of the upperside larger, otherwise as in *C. athamas.*"

" May be distinguished from *C. athamas*, Drury, which we have also received from Upper India, by the forewing which is shorter, much less concave on the outer margin, and but slightly angled, and by the greater length of the inner margin of the hindwing. HABITAT : North India, Darjeeling. EXPANSE : Not given. (*Felder*, Reise Novara, Lep., vol. iii, p. 438, n. 712 (1867).

" This species is perhaps distinct from *C. athamas*; the British Museum has it from Nepal, and white varieties from Northern India ; the typical form is also in the collection of Captain Lang." (*Butler*, Trans. Ent. Soc. Lond., 1870, p. 119. n. 3.) The white varieties above referred to by Mr. Butler I include under *C. arja.*

Under this form I include all the specimens which have the discal band broader than in Drury's figure of *C. athamas*, with those which in the male have three subapical spots. Our collections show that this form occurs in Kunawur, Kulu, Kotgarh, Simla, Mahla, Sikkim, Shillong, Upper Tenasserim, Tavoy, Orissa, Deesa in Rajputana, Matheran near Bombay, the Wynaad, South Andaman Isles, and Java.

C. samatha. Under this name Mr. Moore[*] has described another form of *C. athamas* as follows :—" Smaller than Indian examples of *C. athamas*, the yellow band on both wings one-third less in width, the subapical spot smaller, and the apical [one] either minute or obsolete." HABITAT : Moolai, 3,000 to 6,000 feet, Upper Tenasserim. EXPANSE : 2·37 inches. He redescribes and figures both sexes in his Lep. Cey., the male having a single and the female two subapical spots. Mr. Distant[†] writes as follows regarding it :—" I incline to the opinion that this form should be considered a variety of *C. athamas*. Mr. Moore, in his description of *C. samatha*, describes it as having the 'yellow band on both wings one-third less in width' than in ' Indian examples of *C. athamas*,' and he afterwards figures his species in the ' Lepidoptera of Ceylon.' Now if we compare these figures [figure of the male only] with that of Drury, who originally described and figured *C. athamas*, instead of finding the yellow band of *C. samatha* 'less in width' than in Drury's species, it is, on the contrary, always as broad [in the female it is much broader], and at its apices on both wings *absolutely broader*. There therefore only remains its somewhat smaller size, the frequent absence of the apical spot, and the generally (in the male) smaller size of the subapical spot to differentiate it."

If this form with the band of about the same width at the inner margin of the forewing as in Drury's figure of *C. athamas* is held to have a single subapical spot only in the male (as figured by Mr. Moore), it occurs according to my specimens in Sikkim, the Wynaad, and Ceylon, Mr. Moore records it also from Upper Tenasserim, and Mr. Distant from Province Wellesley.

C. hamasta. Under this name Mr. Moore has described still another form of *C. athamas* as follows :—" Smaller than *C. athamas*. *Forewing* differs in the medial band being broader in the MALE, the subapical spot also broader and more regularly quadrate, its upper angle being nearer the apical spot, of which latter there are two in the FEMALE, one above the other. *Hindwing* with a more prominent submarginal series of white spots, the three lower spots being conspicuously larger and lunular in shape, with contiguous greyish outer lunules." HABITAT : Dharmsala in the Western Himalayas, 6,200 feet, March and June. EXPANSE : 2·5 to 2·75 inches. (*Moore*, Proc. Zool. Soc. Lond., 1882, p. 238.)

" The wildest butterfly that I know. Takes very long flights at a time and returns to the same point. Very shy" (*Hocking*).

Regarding the width of the discal band the matter is a little doubtful, as Mr. Moore (in describing *C. samatha*) does not seem to have consulted Drury's original figure of *C. athamas*. There remains only the size and shape of the subapical spots on the forewing and the submarginal spots on the hindwing in the male, these characters being extremely variable.

C. agrarius. Lastly, Colonel C. Swinhoe has sent me the following description of a form which he names *C. agrarius* :—" Allied to *C. athamas*, Drury, and *C. hamasta*, Moore. Smaller than either, nearest to the latter, but differs [from *C. hamasta*] in having the discal

---
[*] Proc. Zool. Soc., Lond., 1878, p. 691.   [†] Rhop. Malay , p. 196.

band on *both wings* one-fourth narrower in width [it is slightly wider than in Drury's figure of *C. athamas*], the subapical spot on the forewing is smaller [it is larger than in *C. athamas*], whereas in *C. hamasta* this spot is a lengthened square, and in the MALE there are two smaller apical spots. On the *hindwing* the submarginal white spots are prominent, but there is no outer marginal row of ochreous lunules. HABITAT: Mhow and Asirghur in October." EXPANSE: 2·3 to 2·6 inches. (*Swinhoe*, MS.)

The two small subapical spots one above the other in addition to the larger one placed nearer the discal band in the forewing of the male may be considered to be the distinguishing character of this form, the other characters given being variable. I have specimens of it from Simla (taken in the spring) and Bangalore.

It will be seen from an investigation of the localities given above for the different forms of *C. athamas* that have been described, how extremely erratic is the distribution of each, and the only conclusion that I can come to after a patient examination of all the facts in conjunction with a very large series of specimens from nearly every part of India, is that there is but one species, *C. athamas*, which is variable in all the characters which have been taken by different writers in describing the many species which are said to be allied to, but distinct from, the parent species, and that these variations are not confined to any particular geographical ranges of country, nor are they constant.

"LARVA [var. *samatha*] elongated, thickened in the middle, dark green ; head large, wide, flattened, surmounted by four spinous processes ; last segment with two short naked points ; the segments with an oblique yellowish-white stripe, most prominent on the seventh, ninth, and eleventh segments, beneath these a lateral series of small white spots. Feeds on *Cæsalpinia*. PUPA cylindrical, back and thorax convex, head truncated, pointed in front ; green, streaked with white." (*Moore*, l. c. in Lep. Cey.) Professor Westwood (Gen. Diurn. Lep., vol. ii, p. 308) describes a specimen of the pupa obtained in Java by Dr. Horsfield as follows :—"Short and very much swollen, especially the abdominal portion, and is destitute of any conical protuberances ; the head is very broad, and transversely truncate ; the sides of the body, along the inner margin of the cases of the forewings, are formed into two sharp edges ; the body is terminated by a slender horny appendage, armed at the tip with a great number of minute reflexed hooks, enabling the insect to attach itself to the layer of silken thread it had previously spun on the twig, and at the base of this point are several small rounded tubercles." Mr. E. A. Minchin informs that the larva of *C. athamas* feeds in South India on *Adenanthera pavonica*.

C. hebe, *C. moori* and *C. jalysus* have been described as below* from the Malay Peninsula. They are all allied to *C. athamas*, but appear to be quite distinct, the discal band in all of them being very wide. They all have a single spot only in the apical region of the forewing.

---

* *Charaxes hebe*, Butler, Proc. Zool. Soc. Lond., 1865, p. 634, n. 46, pl. xxxvii, fig. 3 ; id., Distant, Rhop. Malay., p. 107, n. 5, pl. xv, fig. 2, *male* (1883). HABITAT : Province Wellesley, Malacca, Sumatra, Borneo. EXPANSE : 3·4 to 3·5 inches. DESCRIPTION : "UPPERSIDE, *forewing* with the basal half, except the cell, pale greenish ; base and inner margin ochreous ; cell grey, brownish in front ; apical half dark brown, with a green oval spot half way between the end of the cell and the apex. *Hindwing* pale greenish, base grey ; inner margin brownish ochreous ; outer margin grey, with brown marginal edge and two submarginal rows of black spots with white spots between them ; a narrow blue line down each of the tails. *Body* fuscous ; thorax grey ; head spotted with ochreous ; antennæ brown, tipped with red. UNDERSIDE pale reddish brown ; outer margin deeper-coloured ; a broad medial greenish silky patch, rounded in front, widest at the inner margin of the forewing, in the hindwing angulated at the median nervure and abruptly tapering to a point at the third median nervule, margined with rich brown, and outwardly by a row of reddish spots extending from near the apex of the fore to the anal angle of the hindwing, lunulate from the middle of the fore to the anal angle of the hindwing, the lunule at the angle of the medial patch margined inwardly with white and outwardly with blue, those below it margined with blue inwardly ; a greenish oval spot on the forewing as above ; a black line near the base, crossing the cells obliquely ; two black lunules on the lower part of the abdominal fold ; a submarginal row of small black spots and a blue and yellow line along the outer margin of the *hindwing*. Tails brown. *Body* brownish ochreous."

"This insect is closely allied to *C. athamas*, but is much more robust ; the forewing is much more rounded and longer, the sinuation of the outer margin is not so deep ; and the wing is more obliquely slanted towards at the anal angle ; the apex is very much rounded ; the hindwing is longer, and the outer tail half as long again as the inner one ; underneath, the medial band is very much further from the outer margin, only extending to the end of the cell." (*Butler*, l. c.)

The specimen from Malacca Mr. Distant has figured † is interesting as showing the varietal character of the colour of the marginal spots to the hindwing. In a Province Wellesley specimen these spots are as pale as in the Sumatran type figured by Mr. Butler." (*Distant*, l. c.)

Charaxes moori, Distant, Rhop. Malay., p. 108, n. 6, pl. xiii, fig. 3, *male* (1883). HABITAT : Province Wellesley. EXPANSE : *Male*, 2·7 inches. DESCRIPTION : "MALE. UPPERSIDE as in *C. hebe*, but the *forewing* with the apex narrower and less produced, the outer black marking narrower, not extending so far inwardly on

569. Charaxes arja, Felder.

C. arja, Felder, Reise Novara, Lep., vol. iii, p. 438, n. 713 (1867); id., Butler, Trans. Ent. Soc. Lond., 1870, p. 119, n. 4.

HABITAT : North-East India, Assam, Upper Tenasserim.

EXPANSE : ♂, 2·3 to 3·2 ; ♀, 3·0 to 3·4 inches.

DESCRIPTION : " MALE. UPPERSIDE as in *C. athamas*, but the fascia a little broader, white, and less well-defined inwardly on the *hindwing*. *Forewing* with a single spot but larger than in *C. athamas*. UNDERSIDE as in *C. athamas*, but the fascia broader."

" The forewing is blunter at the apex than in *C. athamas*, Drury. We possess three males in which the above character separating them from *C. athamas* is very constant." (*Felder*, l. c.)

" I think that there can be little doubt of this being a variety of *C. bharata* ; Captain Lang has several specimens agreeing pretty closely with Dr. Felder's description, but specimens in the British Museum from Sylhet differ in having a second subapical spot in the forewing." (*Butler*, l. c.)

Dr. Felder in describing *C. bharata* says nothing about the discal band being of a different colour to *C. athamas*, in describing *C. arja*, however, he says it is white. I do not therefore agree with Mr. Butler in considering *C. arja* a variety of *C. bharata* ; in my opinion the latter is a variety of *C. athamas*. As identified by me *C. arja* has the discal band white, just tinted with palest green, it is very variable in width as in *C. athamas*, in one extreme it is double the width of the other extreme, and that in the male sex only. The apical spots in the forewing are also variable, there being one, two and occasionally three. The female has the discal band much broader than in the male. I possess this species from Sikkim (where it is less common than *C. athamas*), Sylhet, Jorehât, Sibsagar, Chittagong, and Upper Tenasserim. From these localities it will be seen that it is confined to the north-eastern portion of India and Burma.

An apparently distinct form of this species occurs in Cachar (four males taken by Mr. Wood-Mason), Shillong (two males taken by Dr. Johnson), Jorehât (one male taken by Mr. J. L. Sherwill) and Sibsagar (one male taken by Mr. S. E. Peal). It differs from the common form of *C. arja* in always having a single small subapical spot only in the forewing, the discal band narrow (·25 of an inch in width at the inner margin of the forewing), the ground-colour very deep indigo-blue on the upperside, and all the markings richer and darker on the underside.

C. durnfordi from the Malay Peninsula is not allied to any Indian species. Its description is appended.*

disc and at area of median nervules, and not prominently narrowing at posterior angle : its inner margin much waved. *Hindwing* with the dark submarginal spots with white centres as in the *variety* of *C. hebe* here figured, but prominently widened into a large blackish patch near apex. UNDERSIDE as in *C. hebe*, but with the medial pale fascia to both wings much broader, thus approaching the outer margins much more closely than in Butler's species ; the ground-colour is also considerably tinged with steely blue."

" I have seen none but male specimens of this species. Its natural position is intermediate between *C. hebe*, Butler, and *C. jalysus*, Felder." (*Distant*, l. c.)

Charaxes jalysus, Felder, Reise Novara, Lep., vol. iii, p. 438, n. 714, pl. lix, fig. 5 (1866) ; id., Butler, Trans. Ent. Soc. Lond., 1870, p. 120, n. 5 ; id., Distant, Rhop. Malay., p. 108, n. 7, pl. xiii, fig. 4, *male* (1883). HABITAT : Perak, Province Wellesley, Malacca, Borneo. EXPANSE : 2·7 to 3·3 inches. DESCRIPTION : " MALE. UPPERSIDE with the greenish-white area greatest. *Forewing* with a rather large spot of this colour, otherwise as in *C. athamas*. UNDERSIDE with the area of the upperside but more restricted, somewhat silvery, otherwise as in *C. athamas*, but the lunules outwardly defining the fascia smaller, almost equal. *Forewing* with the ferruginous cincture of the fascia extending to the upper discoidal nervule *Hindwing* with the black submarginal spots much smaller. FEMALE. Wings more dentisulate, the area also broader."

" In the form of the wings nearest to *C. bharata*, Felder, but differing from all hitherto known allies of *C. athamas*, Drury, by the larger and narrower discoidal cell of the forewing. We received the species together with a form of that common Javan species which is figured by Swainson as *Jasia athama*." (*Felder*, l. c.)

" MALE. UPPERSIDE as in *C. moori*, but paler. *Forewing* with the black apical area considerably smaller, its inner margin nearly straight. *Hindwing* with the submarginal border of spots more continuous and amalgamated, but not dilated into a distinct patch at apex. UNDERSIDE paler, and with the pale medial fascia very broad and occupying the whole disc of *both wings* ; on the *hindwing* this fascia is almost straight outwardly, and not concave from costa to third median nervule as in *C. hebe* and *C. moori*." (*Distant*, l. c.) There is a single male specimen of this species from Perak in the Indian Museum, Calcutta.

* *Charaxes durnfordi*, Distant, Entomologist, vol. xvii, p. 101 (1884). HABITAT : Sungei Ujong, Malay Peninsula. EXPANSE : *Male*, 3·7 inches. DESCRIPTION : " MALE. UPPERSIDE dark brownish-ochraceous,

The second group in which the discoidal cell of the hindwing is closed has been divided into two genera by Mr. Moore, the first of these is represented in India by a single species, *C. fabius*, which he retains as typical *Charaxes*, the remainder, which comprise all the fulvous species, he has placed under the genus *Haridra*.

Key to the Indian species of Charaxes.

Second group.

B. Discoidal cell of hindwing closed.

    a. Hindwing with a narrow elongated tail at extremity of first and third median nervules. Both wings black, with a macular discal band of yellow spots.

        570. C. FABIUS, India, Burma, Ceylon, Nicobars.

    b. Hindwing with a short tail (somewhat long in the female) at extremity of third median nervule, and a shorter one at extremity of first median nervule. Both wings fulvous, with margin marked with black on upperside.

        a¹. Both sexes with ground-colour uniform fulvous Upperside, forewing with black border narrow, followed by a distinct black lunular submarginal line.

            a². Lunular fulvous band between black submarginal line and black border extending above fifth subcostal nervule.

                a³. Underside with ground-colour paler fulvous throughout than on upperside, markings indistinct.

                    571. C. *(Haridra)* MARMAX, N.-E. India, Upper Tenasserim.

                b³. Underside with ground-colour buff, all the markings much darker and more prominent.

                    572. C. *(Haridra)* LUNAWARA, Kumaon, Sikkim, Cachar.

            b². Lunular fulvous band ending below fifth subcostal nervule. Underside purplish ferruginous.

                a³. With no fine black lunular lines on disc of both wings ; lunular fulvous band on forewing broad.

                    573. C. *(Haridra)* ARISTOGITON, Sikkim, Sylhet, Upper Tenasserim.

                    574. C. *(Haridra)* DESA, Upper Tenasserim.

                b³. With fine black lunular lines on disc of both wings ; lunular fulvous band on forewing narrow.

                    575. C. *(Haridra)* HEMANA, Nepal, Kumaon.

        b¹. Males with ground-colour uniform fulvous, no pale discal band. Upperside, forewing with black border broader, and no distinct submarginal black line. Females, as far as known, with a broad white discal band.

            a². Black border broad at inner margin of forewing, its inner edge upright.

                a³. Black border of male on hindwing very broad at costa, continuous.

                    576. C. *(Haridra)* PSAPHON, Ceylon.

                b³. Black border of male on hindwing less broad, decreasing to distinct spots towards anal angle.

                    577. C. *(Haridra)* IMNA, Orissa, South India.

            b². Black border narrow at inner margin of forewing, broad on costa.

                578. C. *(Haridra)* BAYA, ? North India, Java, Borneo.

                579. C. *(Haridra)* WATTI, Upper Assam.

                580. C. *(Haridra)* CORAX, North India, Sylhet.

                581. C. *(Haridra)* HARPAX, Upper Tenasserim, Malay Peninsula, Borneo.

                582. C. *(Haridra)* AGNA, Assam, Upper Tenasserim.

        c¹. Both sexes with a pale discal band.

            a². Basal area of both wings on upperside pure fulvous.

                583. C. *(Haridra)* HIERAX, Assam, Cachar, Chittagong.

                584. C. *(Haridra)* HIPPONAX, North-East India.

                585. C. *(Haridra)* JALINDER, North-East India.

                586. C. *(Haridra)* HINDIA, North-East India ? Calcutta, ? Nagpur.

            b². Basal area of both wings on upperside powdered with fuscous.

                587. C. *(Haridra)* PLEISTOANAX, North-East India.

                588. C. *(Haridra)* KHIMALARA, Himalayas, Assam.

                589. C. *(Haridra)* KHASIANUS, N.-E. Bengal, Khasi Hills.

Forewing with the apical half blackish, containing two transverse series of greyish-white angulated spots placed between the nervules, and with a somewhat obscure series of small greyish-white marginal spots, those at the outer angle largest and most distinct ; two small obscure greyish-white spots at end of cell, separated by the upper discoidal nervule. *Hindwing* with a very broad marginal greyish-white fascia, inwardly lunulated

The first species has the tails of the hindwing as long as those in the preceding group, the wings are black and bear across the disc a narrow band of spots, these spots are yellow and distinctly separated on the forewing ; in all the foregoing species the band is continuous, all the spots coalescing. Mr. Moore's diagnosis of the genus *Charaxes* as restricted by him is appended for reference.[*]

570. **Charaxes fabius,** Fabricius.

Papilio fabius, Fabricius, Sp. Ins., vol. ii, p. 12, n 47 (1781) ; idem, id., Mant. Ins., vol. ii, p. 7, n. 52 (1787); idem, id , Ent. Syst., vol. iii, pt. i, p. 62, n. 201 (1793) ; *Nymphalis fabius,* Godart, Enc. Méth., vol. ix, p. 353, n. 8 (1823) ; *Charaxes fabius,* Butler, Cat. Fab. Lep B. M., p 52, n 10 (1869) ; id , Moore, Lep. Cey., vol. i, p. 29, pl. xv, fig. 1 (1881) ; *Paphia fabia,* Gray, Lep Ins. Nepal, pl xi, fig. 3, *larva* (1846) ; *Papilio solon,* Fabricius, Ent. Syst., vol. iii, pt. 1, p. 69, n 216 (1793) ; *P. euphranor,* Esper, Ausl. Schmett., pl. lix, fig. 1 (1785-90).

HABITAT : Himalayas, Oudh, Eastern and Southern India, Ceylon, Burma, Nicobar Isles (*Godart*).

EXPANSE : 2.7 to 3.8 inches.

DESCRIPTION : " MALE and FEMALE. UPPERSIDE, *both wings* blackish olive-brown. *Forewing* with two subbasal small yellow spots [placed one above (touching) the third median nervule a little beyond the end of the cell, the other towards the middle of the subcostal interspace], and a transverse discal recurved series of seven or eight spots, the three lowest widest, a marginal row of minute spots. *Hindwing* with a transverse medial irregular yellow band, a submarginal row of small lunules, and a marginal row of small geminate spots, those at anal angle greenish. UNDERSIDE, *both wings* lilac-grey, dullest at base and purple-tinted externally ; with white discal markings as on upperside, bordered with a black inner line, and basal irregular black streaks. *Forewing* with a submarginal row of black-bordered ochreous-yellow spots, and a marginal row of indistinct purple-white spaces. *Hindwing* with a discal irregular row of black-bordered yellow lunules, each surmounted by an inner purple-white and a black lunule ; a marginal row of ochreous-yellow lunules, each surmounted by an indented black line bordered above and beneath with purple-white." (*Moore*, l. c.)

C. fabius has a wide range, it occurs at Fyzabad and Lucknow in Oudh, Lieutenant-Colonel C. H. T. Marshall has taken it at Chumba in March, Mr. A. Graham Young in Mandi in July and September, it occurs in Sikkim and eastwards through Assam and Cachar, and has been taken again in the Lower Thoungyeen forests in May, and the Meplay valley, Upper Tenasserim, in October ; it is common in Calcutta, and I have frequently taken it drinking the juice of the date palms when cut for the extraction of toddy. Mr. W. C. Taylor

and margined with blackish, containing a medial series of blackish spots with whitish centres, placed between the nervules—that at anal angle duplex—and with a narrow submargin:l blackish line. UNDERSIDE brownish-grey *Forewing* with the cell containing a small black basal spot, and mediality crossed by a darker spot marginal with blackish, an irregular darker fascia margined with blackish crossing wing at end of cell, where it is widest ; beyond the fascia the ground-colour is paler. the whitish spots above are more or less distinctly visible beneath, a waved dark line separating the two discal series. *Hindwing* with two irregular darker fasciæ margined with blackish, one at base, the other crossing disc and terminating on abdominal margin ; the outer white fascia and spots above faintly visible beneath, its margin denoted by two waved or lunulated lines, the innermost bluish, the outer fuscous with the intervening ground-colour ochraceous. *Body* above and beneath and *legs* more or less concolourous with wings."

[*] " This beautiful and exceedingly distinct species seems to find its nearest ally in the Amboinese *C euryalus,* Cramer, and belongs to that division of the genus in which the caudate prolongation to the hindwing, at the apex of the first median nervule, is obsolete, whilst that at the apex of the third median nervule is short but distinct." (*Distant,* l c.)

[*]Genus CHARAXES (restricted). " FOREWING, triangular ; *costa* arched ; *apex* narrow; *outer margin* oblique, uneven, concave in the middle ; *inner* margin straight ; *first* and *second* subcostal *nervules* emitted before end of the cell, *third* immediately beyond the end and extending to the apex, *fourth* and *fifth* at one-third beyond ; *middle disco-cellular* nervule short, angled; *lower* disco-cellular slender and curved ; *discoidal* nervules from angles of the middle disco-cellular ; *median* nervules wide apart, *upper* median nervule curved ; *submedian nervure* curved at the base. HINDWING, triangular ; *costa* very convex at the base ; *outer margin* nearly straight, sinuous ; with a slender tail at end of upper and lower median nervules ; *abdominal* margin long ; *costal nervure* much curved, extending to the apex, with a short bent basal spur [præcostal nervure] ; *subcostals* and *discoidal* equidistant from costal nervure ; *discoidal* cell closed by a slender disco-cellular nervule [which joins the median nervure at the point where the second median nervule is given off]; two *upper median nervules* from end of the cell, *submedian* and *internal nervures* wide apart, the latter short. BODY short, *thorax* robust, *palpi* porrect, pointed at apex, flat beneath, squamose, *legs* squamose, *antennæ* short." (*Moore,* l. c.)

has sent it from Orissa, Colonel Swinhoe records it from "Poona, February, April and November ; Belgaum ; Bombay, November ;" it occurs throughout South India to Travancore. and Captain Wade captured it in Ceylon " at Dambool and Kandy. Not very common." Mr. E. A. Minchin informs me that the larva feeds on the Tamarind tree.

C. echo is a closely-allied species which has been recorded from Singapore and Borneo. It differs chiefly from *C. fabius* in having the discal pale yellow band of the hindwing on the upperside very narrow and its edges very straight and even, the discal series of spots on the forewing consisting of seven instead of eight spots, the upper one being wanting, and only three marginal dots on the forewing at the anal angle.   A description of it is appended. *

The remaining species belong to the genus *Haridra*,† Moore ; in all of them the ground-colour is bright fulvous, and the outer margin of the forewing more or less broadly black, the tails of the hindwing are very slightly developed in the males, more highly developed and more or less spatulate in the females. Many of the species have a broad pale discal band within the black border, sometimes pale yellow, but generally more or less completely suffused with white.

The first five species of this group are easily distinguished by the ground-colour in both sexes being pale fulvous throughout, the marginal black band is narrow as compared with all the other species, and within it is a submarginal narrow black line, sometimes widening out and coalescing with the marginal band towards the costa.

571. **Charaxes marmax,** Westwood.

C. marmax, Westwood, Cab. Or. Ent , p. 43, pl. xvi, *male* and *female* (1848); id., Butler, Proc. Zool. Soc. Lond., 1865, p. 636, n. 57 ; id., Moore, id , 1878, p. 831.

HABITAT : Sikkim, Assam, Sylhet, Upper Tenasserim (Moolai, 3,000 to 6,000 feet).

EXPANSE : ♂, 3·0 to 3·8 ; ♀, 4·30 to 4·75 inches.

DESCRIPTION : "UPPERSIDE, *both wings* of a rich orange colour, the middle portion in the female being [slightly] paler than the rest of the wing, with some small black spots forming two patches near the costa in the middle of the *forewing* (connected in the female with a row of dusky lunules); beyond the middle of the forewing is a row of dusky lunules followed by a marginal series of large black confluent spots ; the *hindwing* is marked beyond the middle with an irregular row of black spots, mostly wedge-shaped, each bearing in the female [sometimes also in the male] a small white spot. UNDERSIDE, *both wings* of a fulvous or yellow buff colour, varied towards the base with darker irregular fasciæ edged by thin black lines which are also margined with greyish white. The *hindwing* has a dark grey transverse

* *Charaxes echo*, Butler, Ann. and Mag. of Nat. Hist., third series, vol. xii. p. 400. pl. viii. figs. 5, 6 (1873); id., Druce, Proc. Zool. Soc. Lond., 1873, p. 345, n. 3 ; id., Distant, Rhop. Malay., p. 193, n. 1 (with a woodcut); 1882; *Nymphalis fabius*, var. ?, Kirby, Cat. Diurn. Lep., p. 269 (1871). HABITAT : Singapore, Borneo. EXPANSE: 2½ inches. DESCRIPTION. "UPPERSIDE blackish-fascious, slightly greenish at the base. *Forewing* with a discal series of seven decreasing fulvous spots ; two spots beyond the cell placed obliquely and three angular anal dots fulvous. *Hindwing* with a slender median fascia, seven oval submarginal dots, and eleven angular marginal dots fulvous ; the inner margin greyish fuscous. *Body* with the thorax blackish-fuscous, the abdomen fuscous. *Antennae* black. UNDERSIDE rosy-ochish, outwardly slightly fuscescent. *Forewing* with three discoidal lines and two below the cell black ; the discal spots as on upperside, inwardly defined with black ; the spot of the upperside beyond the cell enlarged forming a fascicle ; a series of submarginal spots (distinct only near the anal angle) all yellow ; two or three spots joined with these subanal ones, oval, black, the anal one geminate. *Hindwing* with a basal areole and a median fascia which defined with black, this also inwardly margined with silver; seven lunulate ferruginous spots, three lower larger, more rufescent, all inwardly banded with bluish-white and defined with black ; a black subanal line ; seven marginal spots blue, lined with black, and defined outwardly with yellow, inwardly with white. *Body*, ochraceous, the thorax in the middle and the *palpi*, whitish. *Antennae* black."
"Allied to *C. lampedo*, Hübner (Sannd. Ex. Schmett , vol. ii, pl. iii, figs 3, 4), but smaller, the forewing more angular, the hindwing with short obliquely-placed tails, the bands narrower and differently placed." *(Butler, l. c.)*
"This is a so-called "variety," or more correctly designated a "local race" of *C. fabius*, Fabricius, of which several other closely-allied forms or " local races " have been described " *(Distant, l. c.)*
† Genus HARIDRA, Moore. "Similar in form and venation to *Charaxes* ; HINDWING more convex externally, *costal margin* shorter, *costal nervure* more curved ; a short tail only from end of the upper median nervule." *(Moore, l. c.)* The *discoidal cell* is closed by a fine *lower disco-cellular nervule* which reaches the median nervure at the point where the second median nervule is given off. The hindwing has a distinct tooth or short tail at the termination of the lower median nervule.

fascia beyond the middle, succeeded by a pearly space on which are white transverse spots followed by minute black dots; the pearly spots appear of a triangular form on the *forewing* towards the outer margin, between which and the middle of the wing is a dark fulvous row of thin lunular streaks."

"*C. marmax* is very closely allied to *C. bernardus*,[*] Fabricius, but in both sexes of the latter the middle of the wings bears a large, very pale, buff or white patch (which indeed, somewhat reappears in the female of *C. marmax*); the extremity of the forewing in *C. bernardus*, is, however, much darker than in this species. *C. bernardus* appears to be intermediate between this species and *C. psaphon*; the markings of the underside of the wings in all three species is very similar, although the colouring differs. The difference in the length of the tails of the hindwing in the opposite sexes of this species occurs also in *C. bernardus*, whilst the tail at the anal angle of this wing is almost obliterated." (*Westwood*, l. c.)

When the above note was written these three were the only Indian species of yellow *Charaxes* known; they now form the typical species of three groups with numerous intermediate and allied forms. *C. marmax* has the black border of the forewing narrower than in any other species, except *C. lunawara*, and from *C. lunawara* it may be distinguished by its very yellow underside, and all the markings being far less prominent. It is a very distinct and easily recognised species, and in Sikkim at any rate is the commonest species of the *Haridra* group of the genus.

572. **Charaxes lunawara**, Butler.

C. lunawara, Butler, Lep. Ex., p. 99, n. 6, pl. xxxvii. fig. 2, *male* and *female* (1872).

HABITAT : Kumaon, Sikkim, N.-E. Bengal, Cachar.

EXPANSE : ♂, 3·5 to 4·0 ; ♀, 3·6 to 4·7 inches.

DESCRIPTION : "MALE. Allied to *C. marmax*, smaller. *Forewing* with the subapical fasciole broader, confluent with the marginal area, the discal lunules more obscure ; the margin black (not at all blackish-fuscous). *Hindwing* with the virgulæ more slender in the male, none in the female ; the black spots of the external fascia larger, distinctly pupilled with whitish. UNDERSIDE with all the characters better defined ; in the male the external area narrower ; the median fascia of the hindwing twice as wide at the inner margin ; in the female the external area broader, the median fascia of the hindwing comparatively broader at the inner margin ; the discal area much more silky, the subanal tail twice as long."

"Nearly allied to *C. marmax*, *aristogiton*, &c., but perfectly distinct." (*Butler*, l. c.)

C. lunawara is very similar indeed to *C. marmax* on the upperside, all the characters noted above being variable, but the underside is very different, the ground-colour is a pale buff instead of bright fulvous, the markings are much darker and more prominent not only in comparison, but actually, and the inner edge of the irregular dark discal band on the hindwing terminates on the internal nervure much nearer to the base. The characters of the underside appear to be constant and there is no difficulty in recognising this species. It is rarer than *C. marmax*, and all the specimens in the Indian Museum, Calcutta, are either from Sikkim or Cachar. Mr. Doherty found it rare in Kumaon on the Lower Kali.

573. **Charaxes aristogiton**, Felder.

C. aristogiton, Felder, Reise Novara, Lep., vol iii, p. 445, n 727 (1867) ; id., Butler, Trans. Ent. Soc. Lond., 1870, p 121, n. 18 (err. 88).

HABITAT : Sikkim, Sylhet, Upper Tenasserim.

EXPANSE : ♂, 3·6 to 3·8 inches.

DESCRIPTION : "MALE. UPPERSIDE deeper coloured than in *C. harmodius*, [Felder,

---

[*] Figured by Donovan in his Insects of China, pl. xxxiv, which "is a good copy of Jones' drawing, from which Fabricius described the species." (*Westwood*, l. c.)

from Java]. *Forewing* with the subcostal spots placed as in that species, but very distinct ; the external border broader, inwardly well-defined as far as the internal fold, inwardly divided by a bent streak of six increasing spots of the ground-colour (the three lower lunulate). *Hindwing* as in *C. marmax*, sometimes the spots blind, sometimes the apical patch extending as far as the margin. UNDERSIDE almost as in *C. marmax*, [Westwood], but not at all varied with ochraceous, rufescent. *Hindwing* with the fascia ferruginous as in *C. harmodius*, but inwardly more or less ochraceous-brown."

"Shape of the wings as in *C. marmax*, Westwood, the hindwing as shallowly toothed as in *C. harmodius*, Felder, the external tooth of tail however very short." (*Felder*, l. c.)

"I think that this may be distinct from *C. marmax* ; the latter, however, appears to be a variable species, and is represented by two very different-looking forms in Sylhet. *C. aristogiton* is in the collection of Captain Lang, who also has both forms of *C. marmax*, all from Sikkim." (*Butler*, l. c.)

C. aristogiton has the black border broader, especially at the apex, and the series of fulvous spots which it bears always terminates below the fifth subcostal nervule, often below the upper discoidal nervule. The underside too is very distinct from that of both the foregoing species being ferruginous not fulvous or buff, glossed with pale shining purple throughout, except on the ferruginous band and extreme outer margin. All the specimens in the Indian Museum, Calcutta, are from Sikkim. The female is unknown. Captain C. T. Bingham has sent two males of this species from Upper Tenasserim, one taken in the Donat range in January, the other in the Lower Thoungyeen forests in May. These specimens differ from Sikkim examples in having the marginal black spots on the hindwing smaller, very small in one.

574. Charaxes dosa, Moore.

C. *dosa*, Moore, Proc. Zool. Soc. Lond., 1878, p. 832.

HABITAT : Upper Tenasserim, Moolai, 3 000 to 6,000 feet.

EXPANSE : ♂, 3·5 inches.

DESCRIPTION : " Allied to *C. marmax*. MALE differs from *C. marmax* in the following particulars. UPPERSIDE. *Forewing* has the marginal black band broader and extending at the apex further along the costa ; the inner submarginal lunular line is closer to the band. *Hindwing*, the black maculated band is formed of larger angled spots. UNDERSIDE, purplish ochreous. *Hindwing* with a transverse black lunular fascia, which is also further from the outer margin." (*Moore*, l c.)

I have never seen this species ; it is apparently more closely allied to *C. aristogiton* than to *C. marmax*, judging from the colour of the underside, and the characters noted above are precisely those which distinguish *C. aristogiton* from *C. marmax*. The true *C. aristogiton* occurs in the same locality, but Mr. Moore makes no mention of it in describing *C. dosa*, and I cannot discover any character on which they can be separated.

575. Charaxes hemana, Butler.

C. *hemana*, Butler, Trans. Ent. Soc. Lond., 1870, p. 125, pl. iv, fig. 1, *male*; id., Doherty, Journ A. S. B., vol. lv, pt. 2, p. 124, n 97 (1886).

HABITAT : Nepal, Kumaon.

EXPANSE : 3·58 inches.

DESCRIPTION : "MALE. Allied to *C. aristogiton*, Felder. UPPERSIDE, [*both wings*] paler. [*Forewing*] with a duplex litura at the upper angle of the cell and a four-lunate virgula limiting the basal area, the ground beyond it narrowly paler [it is uniformly coloured in the figure], the external border as in *C. harpax*, [Felder], but the margin irrorated with fulvous, and the lunular stria more distinct almost as in *C. aristogiton*. *Hindwing* with a three-lunate virgula limiting the basal area, the area beyond the middle as in *C. bernardus*, [Cramer], paler ; otherwise as in *C. aristogiton*. UNDERSIDE as in *C. eoras*, [Felder]."

"Closely allied to *C. aristogiton*, Felder, but quite distinct." (*Butler*, l. c.)

I have been unable to identify this species. According to the above description it may be distinguished from *C. aristogiton* by the black virgule* on the disc of both wings ; the underside too must be very dark since Felder describes the underside of *C. corax* as much darker than in *C. psaphon*, which is one of the darkest of all. To judge from Mr. Butler's figure of it, this species may also be distinguished by the fulvous line on the border being very narrow and continuous as far as the upper discoidal nervule, and by the black border being considerably broader at the hinder angle and inwardly diffused at its lower half ; the forewing moreover has two small pale spots at the inner edge of the black border separated by the upper discoidal nervule, a feature which is typical of the group of which *C. bernardus* is the type. Mr. Doherty writes of it " my specimens taken in Kumaon in the Gori and Kali valleys, also at Kapkot on the Sarju, perhaps the western limit of the group, seem to correspond well enough with Mr. Butler's figure and description, but the markings are not very constant."

The next two species have the black border of the forewing very broad throughout in the males, its inner edge almost parallel to the outer margin and with no trace of a fulvous line or spots on it, on the hindwing the black band is almost equally broad and uninterrupted in *C. psaphon*, while in *C. imna* the hinder part is typically broken into decreasing well-separated spots towards the anal angle. The females have the black border equally broad, bearing two or three pale fulvous spots on its lower inner edge ; with a broad white discal band, more or less sullied with fulvous towards the inner margin of the forewing, continued diffusedly on to the hindwing as far as the discoidal nervule, where it becomes merged in the ground-colour. The three specimens of the female that I possess I am hardly able to distinguish from the figure of that sex of *C. hindia*, Butler, but they are distinct from all the other species of this group which have the base of the wings on the upperside fulvous in having two or three fulvous spots only on the lower end of the black marginal border of the forewing.

576. **Charaxes psaphon**, Westwood.

C. psaphon, Westwood, Cab. Or. Ent., p. 43, pl. xxi. *male* (1848) ; id., Butler, Proc. Zool. Soc. Lond., 1865, p. 636, n. 52 ; *Haridra psaphon*, Moore, Lep. Cey., vol. 1, p. 30, pl xv, fig. 2, *male* ; *H. screndiba*, id., p. 30, pl. xv, fig. 3, *female* (1881).

HABITAT : Ceylon.

EXPANSE : ♂, 3'37 to 4'0 ; ♀, 3'75 to 4'30 inches.

DESCRIPTION : MALE. " UPPERSIDE, *both wings* of a very rich dark fulvous-red colour, the outer half of the forewing and a very large patch on the hindwing, occupying nearly the outer half, of a black colour. UNDERSIDE, *both wings* varied with glossy brunneous, dull buff and greyish tints, the basal half of the wings varied with irregular slender black lines forming irregular fasciæ, more or less edged with white."

" The outer margin of the forewing scarcely appears to be waved, as in *C. marmax ;* and the transverse vein which closes the discoidal cell [of the forewing] is marked with black. The hindwing has a narrow black lunule preceding the great black patch, which latter is followed by two black spots next the anal angle, which is moreover marked with two small black and white dots. The markings on the underside very nearly resemble those of *C. bernardus*, Fabricius ; but the colours are darker and more varied, with a purplish brown tinge. The hindwing has a submarginal row of black dots preceded by white ones." (*Westwood*, l. c.) I have given below Mr. Moore's more modern description of the male of this species.†

---

* Forming a fine lunular black line.

† " MALE. UPPERSIDE fulvous-red. *Forewing* with the outer half purple-black ; a disco-cellular red-lined black mark, and some indistinct black discoidal streaks. *Hindwing* with a very broad apical submarginal black band attenuated and broken hindwards and ending in two small white-bordered anal spots, a short curved black streak from the costa. UNDERSIDE fulvous-brown, washed with purple-grey, crossed by three basal and two discal zigzag black lines with pale borders. *Forewing* with a submarginal blackish macular fascia. *Hindwing* with a lunular fascia and marginal row of small black-pointed white arch-shaped marks. FEMALE unknown." (*Moore*, l. c.) But in my opinion as pointed out above the insect which Mr. Moore has described as a distinct species under the name of *Haridra screndiba* is merely the female of *C. psaphon*.

Mr. Moore (l. c.) records the male as " taken near Trincomalee in August, fluttering over the ground on the edge of forest jungle " (*Hutchison*).   " Also found at Kandy " (*Wade*).

The FEMALE has been described by Mr. Moore as a distinct species under the name of *H.* [= C.] *tereudibi* as follows :—" UPPERSIDE deep fulvous-red.   *Forewing* with a broad transverse medial discal purple-white band, showing some dusky sinuous streaks of the underside, and bordered inwardly by black streaks, the outer border to external margin being brown-black with a slight fulvous lunular posterior inner streak.   *Hindwing* with a short medial discal purple-white band bordered inwardly by a narrow black streak ; a submarginal black macular band, broad and entire apically, thence attenuated and broken into smaller spots to anal angle and surmounted by a small white medial streak one between each vein.   UNDERSIDE fulvous-brown, darkest basally and externally and washed with purple-grey, the disc transversely fulvous-white, or very pale fulvous, base with transverse irregular zigzag black lines, a short line beyond the cell and a sinuous line across the disc, a submarginal irregular dusky lunular fascia on *forewing*, and *hindwing* with a row of small black-pointed anchor-shaped white marks."

" Taken in the forest at Kottawa, and at Kandy, by Captain Wade."   (*Moore*, l. c.)

C. psaphon is the darkest species of this group known, the upperside of the male having the outer half deep black.   It appears to be confined to the island of Ceylon.

577. Charaxes imna, Butler.

C. imna, Butler, Trans. Ent. Soc. Lond., 1870, p. 122, pl. iv, fig. 2.

HABITAT : India (*Butler*), Orissa, Bombay, South India.

EXPANSE : ♂, 3·75 inches (*Butler*).   ♂, 3·1 to 3·8 ; ♀, 4·7 inches.

DESCRIPTION : " MALE.   Allied to *C. cimon*, [Felder, from Batchian], but the apical area of the *forewing* not at all directed inwardly at the costa and more dentate.   Of the *hindwing* as in *C. corax*, [Felder], the anal half reduced to decreasing spots.   UNDERSIDE almost as in *C. corax*."

" Intermediate in character between *C. cimon* and *C. corax*, the forewing being very similar to that of the former, the hindwing more like that of the latter species." (*Butler*, l. c.) This description is not of much use in the absence of specimens of *C. cimon* and *C. corax*, but from Mr. Butler's figure it is clear that this is the Indian form of *C. psaphon*, which latter typically is confined to Ceylon ; the South Indian specimens approximate very closely to *C. psaphon*, some being barely distinguishable from Ceylon specimens ; further north the divergence increases, and in Orissa, which is the most northerly known locality for this species, typical *C. imna* occurs, with the black spots of the hindwing well-separated and much reduced, but even there specimens are found with the spots coalescing and almost as large as in South Indian specimens.   A female taken with a male by Mr. Rhodes-Morgan in the Wynaad is indistinguishable from that sex of *C. psaphon*.   Two female specimens taken at Calcutta and Nagpur respectively and which I have doubtfully identified as *C. hindia*, as they are nearer to the figure of that species than to the same sex of typical *C. imna*, are not improbably referable to this species.   The character of the markings is the same as in the Wynaad specimen of *C. imna*, but as would be expected from the drier climate of the localities where they were taken, they are much paler throughout.

The Indian Museum, Calcutta, has specimens of *C. imna* from Orissa taken by Mr. W. C. Taylor, and from the Wynaad taken by Mr. Rhodes-Morgan ; Mr. Doherty took it in Travancore and at Beypoor, Mr. G. W. Vidal has sent specimens from Khandalla taken in April; and Mr. E. H. Aitkin from Matheran taken in January.

The next five species may be distinguished from the preceding by the form of the black border to the forewing, it being broad at the costa and very narrow at the anal angle, the inner edge being thus very oblique, sometimes straight, sometimes curved towards the base of the wing at the costa.   The ground-colour is uniform fulvous.   They are all variable, very closely allied, and doubtfully distinct.

The typical species *C. baya* has normally the six black border spots of the hindwing centred with white : we have not a single specimen with this feature fully developed, but it is partially so in all specimens of this group common in North-East India, of which one specimen without locality, now in the Indian Museum, Calcutta, was received from the old East India Museum labelled as *C. baya*. It appears to have the black border of the forewing on the upperside unbroken by spots of the ground-colour towards the anal angle ; the underside is variable, but very similar to that of *C. aristogiton*. It is stated to occur in North-East India, appearing again in Java and Borneo. The type is given as from Java, and I doubt its occurrence in India.

C. watti is recorded from Upper Assam, but I have never seen a specimen. To judge from Mr. Butler's figure of it, it is allied to *C. hierax* both on account of the clay-yellowish ground-colour of the underside, and by the disc of the forewing on the upperside being suffused with paler yellow near the black border. This species also has no spots on the outer black border of the forewing on the upperside, which appears to be exactly as in *C. baya*; the hindwing has a rather small black patch at the apex ending in the middle of the subcostal interspace, then four oval small black spots placed between the veins, and a duplex spot at the anal angle bearing two small white dots.

C. corax is described as having the black border of the forewing divided by three increasing spots of the ground-colour towards the anal angle. It has the spots on the hindwing blind except the anal one as in *C. watti*. Mr. Butler says that these spots are as large as in *C. imna*, but this is not quite correct according to my identification of *C. corax*, nor according to Felder's description, though they are variable in size.

C. harpax is the Malayan form of *C. baya*, and has the underside much paler than in *C. corax*. The outer black border of the forewing in *C. harpax* is said to be as in *C. corax*, but in the apical region more broadly blackish-fuscous. The spots on the hindwing are small, well-separated, and more or less centred with white.

C. agna, which occurs with *C. harpax* in Upper Tenasserim, is more closely allied to *C. baya*, but has the black spots of the hindwing much smaller, more often blind, and the underside more uniform in tone, with the markings less prominent but similarly coloured.

578. **Charaxes baya**, Moore.

Nymphalis baya, Moore, Horsfield and Moore, Cat. Lep. Mus. E. I. C., vol. i, p. 207, n. 424, pl. xii, fig. 14, larva; 14a, pupa (1857); *Charaxes baya*, Butler, Proc. Zool. Soc. Lond., 1865, p. 636, n. 53, pl. xxxvii, fig. 5, male.

HABITAT : ? North India, Java, Borneo.

EXPANSE : ♂, 2·75 inches ; ♀, rather more than three inches.

DESCRIPTION : " MALE. Allied to *N.* [= *C.*] *psaphon*, Westwood, from Ceylon, but differs in having the black exterior border of the *forewing* much narrower, it not extending to the middle of the posterior margin, as in that species, but is confined to the angle. On the *hindwing*, the apical patch is also smaller, and continued in a series of six white-centred spots to anal angle ; a small blackish spot at extremity of the discoidal cell. UNDERSIDE glossy greenish buffy-brown. [Mr. Butler says (Proc. Zool. Soc. Lond., 1865, p. 637) that *C. psaphon* and *C. baya* " exactly agree in the markings of the underside."] FEMALE paler above. *Fore-wing* with a broad medial yellowish band ; a small round yellowish spot near the apex ; a patch of black at extremity of discoidal cell, and narrow zigzag line bordering the black band. *Hind-wing* with the medial upper portion of disc yellowish ; submarginal row of spots clearly defined, and all centred with clear white. UNDERSIDE more variegated than in the male, and much paler. Tails two, short in the male ; *both* long in the female." (*Moore, l. c.*)

LARVA widest in the middle of the body, tapering rapidly towards the anal segment which ends in two short processes or tails, tapering more gradually towards the head. Colouration rich green above, underneath and legs yellow ; a large pink spot on the middle of the back mottled with white, surrounded with a white, then an outer black line ; three similar subdorsal but much smaller spots on each side ; the head encircled by a mottled pink line, with four long pink rugose processes marked with blue at the ends. PUPA pale green, unmarked, head ending in a blunt point.

The only specimens of this species that I have seen are one in Colonel Swinhoe's collection from Borneo, and one without locality in the Indian Museum, Calcutta, which was received under that name from the old East India Company's Museum. I have never seen the female, but it must be quite distinct from any known female of the genus, as the discal band on the upperside is said to be yellowish, in all the others it is white.

579. **Charaxes watti,** Butler.

C. watti, Butler, Proc. Zool. Soc. Lond., 1880, p. 148, n. 6, pl. xv, fig. 2, *male.*

HABITAT : Bishnath, Upper Assam.

EXPANSE : 3·5 inches.

DESCRIPTION : "MALE. Allied to *C. bajes,* Moore, and *C. affinis,* Butler, from Celebes, but differing from the former in the absence of the white pupils in the black submarginal spots on the UPPERSIDE of the *hindwing ;* from the latter in the greater size and more distinctly diamond-like shape of these spots, and the much more regular inner margin of the broad black border of the *forewing ;* and from both in the colouration of the UNDERSIDE, which is dull clay-yellowish washed with shining lilaceous-grey, excepting upon the outer borders and on the lunated discal belt bounding the submarginal ocelloid spots internally ; bands indicated by black lines edged externally with white ; margins and lunated belt dull ferruginous-brownish."

"Only one example was taken in August, 1877, but Dr. Watt says that it is not uncommon" (*Butler,* l. c.) I have never seen this species. From the description it must be very near to *C. bajes,* on the upperside the only distinguishing character I can discover is that *C. bajes* has six white-centred black spots on the upperside of the hindwing, while *C. watti* has the two germinated anal ones only with white centres.

580. **Charaxes corax,** Felder.

C. corax, Felder, Reise Novara, Lep., vol. iii, p. 444, n. 774 (1867) ; id., Butler, Trans. Ent. Soc. Lond., 1870, p. 124, n. 15.

HABITAT : North India *(Felder),* Sylhet *(Butler).*

EXPANSE : Not given.

DESCRIPTION ; "MALE. UPPERSIDE fulvous. *Forewing* with a duplex litura at the upper angle of the cell and the broad external border well-decreasing hindwards, occupying only the internal angle, blackish-fuscous, this [black border] inwardly anteriorly excised, posteriorly most remotely crenate, inwardly posteriorly divided with three increasing elongate spots of the ground-colour (the lowest altogether confluent with the ground). *Hindwing* paler on the anterior border and marked with a black sigmoidal* virgula, the patch occupying the apex† marked with whitish twice and inwardly with an irrorated spot of the ground-colour, the black spots out of this small, the anal one excepted, blind, inwardly truncate and irrorated. UNDERSIDE almost as in *C. psaphon,* Westwood, but much darker [? more obscure), rufescent, more shining, the interior discal streak not at all margined with whitish, in the *forewing* also distant from the cell. *Hindwing* with the deep ferruginous fascia narrower and hindwardly more decreasing than in *C. psaphon,* the submarginal spots better defined, the margin immediately beyond them obscurely rufescent."

"This species belongs to the small group of *C. polyxena,* Cramer, and most resembles *C. marmax,* Westwood, in the form of the forewing, but the apex is less produced, and the hindwing is but shallowly toothed." (*Felder,* l. c.)

---

* Sigmoidal, shaped like a sigma ; that is the Greek letter σ or ς.
† The passage is as follows ; :—" Postica in limbo antico dilutiores virgulaque sigmoidea nigra notatæ plagula apicem occupante albido biss et inus macula atomaria fundi coloris notata." I am unable to translate this accurately, for "albidis" agrees with nothing, but the rendering I have given is the nearest guess I can make to the actual meaning.

"If I have rightly determined this species, it is nearly allied to *C. bays*, though, apparently, quite distinct ; the British Museum has it from Sylhet." (*Butler*, l. c.)

This species appears to chiefly differ from *C. agna* in having the black outer border of the forewing on the upperside marked inwardly towards the inner margin with three elongated spots of the ground-colour. On the hindwing it agrees with *C. watti* in having the black spots on the margin blind, except the geminated anal one. As identified by me, there is one specimen of true *C. corax* from Sylhet and two from Cachar in the Indian Museum, Calcutta. There are, however, numerous other specimens from Cachar taken with the above, and one from Tavoy, which show great variation in the size of the spots and the apical patch on the hindwing, in some examples they are almost as broad as in *C. imna* as pointed out by Mr. Butler. These specimens also show a transition to the next group in having in some of them two small spots of the ground-colour on the upperside of the forewing on the inner edge of the black outer margin divided by the upper discoidal nervule.

581. Charaxes harpax, Felder.

C. *harpax*, Felder, Reise Novara, Lep., vol. iii, p. 444, n. 775 (1867) ; id., Butler, Trans. Ent. Soc. Lond., 1870, p. 121, n. 16 ; id., Moore, Proc. Zool. Soc. Lond., 1878, n. 832 ; id., Distant, Rhop. Malay., p. 19, n. 8, pl. xiii, fig. 1, *male* (1883)

HABITAT : Upper Tenasserim, Province Wellesley, Borneo.

EXPANSE : ♂, 3·2 to 4·0 inches.

DESCRIPTION : "MALE. UPPERSIDE rich fulvous. *Forewing* with a duplex spot at the upper angle of the cell, and the border as in *C. corax*, Felder, but in the apical region more broadly blackish-fuscous. *Hindwing* anteriorly a little paler, the virgula evanescent, the apical patch much smaller than in *C. corax*, and all the spots free, minute, inwardly marked with whitish. UNDERSIDE much paler than in the said species [*C. corax*]. *Hindwing* with a sordid ferruginous-fulvous fascia, decreasing from the second subcostal nervule, very narrowed, the submarginal spots minute, more distant from the margin than in *C. corax* and *C. psaphon*, the marginal region immediately beyond these obscurely ochraceous."

"The specimen we have before us is larger than *C. corax*, Felder, and agrees in the shape of the forewing with *C. marmax*, Westwood, with the exception of the scarcely perceptible toothing of the edge. According to the description *C. baya*, Moore, appears to be a similar species." (*Felder*, l. c.)

Mr. Distant remarks that the specimen of *C. harpax*, Felder, he figures is intermediate between *C. agna*, Moore, and the typical Bornean examples of the former, and that variation must be allowed where no distinct local race has become differentiated.

"There are both sexes of a species allied to *C. corax*, Felder, and agreeing very fairly with Dr Felder's description of *C. harpax*, in the British Museum, from Moulmein : the female of the latter is scarcely distinguishable from *C. bernardus* female, the male is very like *C. baya*." (*Butler*, l. c.)

The characters which distinguish *C. harpax* from *C. baya* have been pointed out above (p. 286). Major Marshall has one specimen of this species, taken by Captain C. T. Bingham, at the Mayla Choung, Upper Tenasserim, in September, and there are three specimens from Perak in the Malay Peninsula in the Indian Museum, Calcutta. Mr. Moore records it from Moulmein to Meetan ; Moolai, 3,000 to 6,000 feet, Upper Tenasserim. I have appended Mr. Distant's very full description of this species.* I have never seen the female.

---

* "MALE. UPPERSIDE reddish ochraceous. *Forewing* with two small contiguous black spots at upper end of cell ; apex and outer margin broadly black ; this black area has its inner margin sinuous and emarginate, it is broadest inwardly and most angulated beyond cell, and commences to diminish in width beneath the lower discoidal nervule, till it narrowly terminates at posterior angle. [At its inner lower end it often bears one, two or three lanular spots of the ground-colour.] *Hindwing* with a submarginal row of black spots placed between the nervules (two at anal angle more or less suffused with grey), and with a black apical patch, [all more or less centred with white]. UNDERSIDE pale castaneous with steely reflections. *Forewing* with the basal half crossed by four waved black lines commencing near the subcostal nervure, the two inner ones crossing cell about middle, and continued on hindwing, terminating near base of internal nervure ; the third commencing a little before, and the fourth some distance beyond end of cell (where there is a terminal black line and a linear ovate black

582. Charaxes agna, Moore.

C. agna, Moore, Proc. Zool. Soc. Lond., 1878, p. 832 ; *Haridra agna*, Butler, Ann. and Mag. of Nat. Hist., fifth series, vol. xvi, p. 306, n. 49 (1885).

HABITAT : Upper Tenasserim, Moolai 3,000 to 6,000 feet ; Tavoy ; near Assam.

EXPANSE : ♂, 3·25 inches.

DESCRIPTION : "Allied to *C. harpax*, Felder [from the same locality], MALE differs in its larger size. *Forewing* has a broader marginal black band. *Hindwing* has a less black apical patch, and the marginal series of spots is also much smaller." (*Moore*, l. c.)

One specimen in the Indian Museum, Calcutta, taken by Dr. Anderson at Mergui in December, one from Tavoy, and two taken by Captain C. T. Bingham in Upper Tenasserim—one in the Donat range in January and the other in the Thoungyeen forests in March—may perhaps belong to this species ; they agree with the description of *C. agna* in the hindwing, but the forewing has the marginal black band less broad instead of being broader, and more upright than in *C. harpax ;* nor are they larger than *C. harpax*. The colouration of the underside of these specimens is lighter than in either *C. baya* or *C. harpax*, but Mr. Moore makes no mention of the underside. Mr. Butler records it from "near Assam." I have never seen the female.

The remaining seven species differ from all the other fulvous *Charaxes* in having the disc within the black border suffused paler, sometimes yellow, more often white, and forming in these latter a distinct broad white discal band. Of these the first four species are all closely allied to *C. bernardus*, Fabricius, from China, which is probably identical with *C. polyxena*. Cramer, from the same locality. They are very closely allied, our collections show numerous gradations between each of the forms, and I have no doubt that they are all varieties of the same species, which should stand as *C. polyxena*, Cramer. Pending further research I republish the descriptions of each, keeping them for the present separate.

Typical specimens of *C. hierax* can easily be distinguished by their having the pale discal band rather narrow and yellow throughout showing no trace of pure white.

Typical specimens of *C. hipponax* on the other hand have the band diffusedly whitish and rather narrow, but numerous intermediate forms occur showing every stage of yellow suffusion from the faintest trace on a limited portion, to complete suffusion of the whole.

C. jalinder and *C. hindia* have the band for a considerable space pure white and broader ; according to the figures of them, *C. jalinder* has on the forewing the six yellow spots on the black border much reduced, the white band terminating abruptly on the submedian nervure, and bearing near its inner edge a black lunular line from the costa to below the first median nervule. *C. hindia* has three lower fulvous spots only on the black border which are large, the white band terminating diffusedly on the submedian interspace, and no trace of the black lunular line on the disc except on the disco-cellular nervules ; but none of these characters hold good as a whole, if one is taken by which to distinguish a species the others fail, and scarcely a specimen can be found with the white band that does not present certain characters of one species in conjunction with other characters of the other, and I cannot even recognise these latter as distinct varieties ; out of our large series not a single specimen corresponds exactly with either figure.

The foregoing remarks apply to the males The females have the wings larger, the tail of the hindwing at the third median nervule longer, and the white discal band considerably broader. I have not many specimens, only twelve in all ; the extent of the black lunular line at inner edge of the discal band of the forewing varies much, and so does the prominence of the white centerings to the submarginal spots of the hindwing ; but the principal variation is in the pale spots on the black border of the forewing ; in one it is immaculate and corresponds in this respect with what Mr. Butler has figured as the female of *C. hindia*,

marginal spot), between which the colour is distinctly darker, and continued and terminating on hindwing at internal nervure (between these on hindwing is a curved terminal line to cell) ; these are followed by a discal and much-waved line of the same colour, followed on hindwing by an oblique bluish-black fascia, which becomes almost fused with the termination of the discal line near anal angle, where there is a large blackish spot. *Forewing* with an apical greyish spot, and an indistinctly dentate submarginal greyish fascia inwardly preceded by a few more or less distinct black spots. *Hindwing* with a submarginal row of bluish spots placed between the nervules and preceded by transverse greyish streaks itwo of these spots at anal angles. *Body* more or less concolourous with wings ; posterior and intermediate *femora* thickly spotted with black." (*Distant*, l. c.)

in others the spots are large and pure white, corresponding so far with his figure of the female of *C. jalinder*. The remainder have the spots of greater or less prominence, and suffused more or less with the fulvous ground-colour.

583. Charaxes hierax, Felder.

C. hierax, Felder, Reise Novara, Lep., vol. iii, p. 412, n. 721, *male* only (1867); id , Butler, Trans. Ent. Soc. Lond., 1870, p. 120, n. 12; *C. bernardus*, Kollar, in Hügel's Kaschmir, vol. iv, pt. 2, p. 434, n. 1, pl. 31, figs. 1, 2, *male* (1848).

HABITAT: Masuri (*Kollar*), North India, Assam.

EXPANSE : Not given.

DESCRIPTION : " MALE. UPPERSIDE paler than in *C. psaphon*, [Westwood]. *Forewing* with a blackish-fuscous discal striga more or less obsolete, the ground-colour immediately beyond it paler, the blackish-fuscous border narrower than in *C. polyxena*, [Cramer], and divided with spots of the ground-colour most often evanescent. *Hindwing* with the patch at the apex broader than in *C. polyxena*, joined with black spots, the uppermost of which often without whitish virgulæ, the margin beyond these narrower than in the species compared [*C. polyxena?*], distinctly no streak before the margin as in *C. polyxena*, but with an antico-discal strigula of blackish-fuscous virgulæ. UNDERSIDE almost as in *C. psaphon*, the two discal streaks in the *hindwing* more distant, and the ferruginous fascia of that wing narrower."

" Nearly related to *C. polyxena*, Cramer, of which we are only acquainted with the figure, larger than *C. psaphon*, Westwood, the apex and inner angle of the forewing of the male more produced, the inner margin of the hindwing shorter, the inner and occasionally the outer tooth of the hindwing very short, not standing out tail-like." (*Felder*, l. c.)

Mr. Butler (l. c.) remarks of *C. hierax* and *C. hipponax* that they "are merely the normal forms of the male *C. bernardus*, from India. Dr. Felder seems to think that the typical form from China may be distinct from the Indian one ; but I find an Indian male agreeing more closely with a Chinese female than do two females from China, or two males from India."

The Indian Museum, Calcutta, has typical male specimens of this form from Sikkim, the Assam Valley, and from Chittagong The specimens from Cachar and Tavoy I have described above as varieties of *C. corax* are almost exactly intermediate between that species and *C. hierax*, but nearer the former, as the discal pale band is hardly visible.

584. Charaxes hipponax, Felder.

C. hipponax, Felder, Reise Novara, Lep., vol. iii, p. 413, n. 722, *male* only (1867) ; id., Butler, Trans. Ent. Soc. Lond , 1870, p 120, n. 13.

HABITAT : North India, Assam.

EXPANSE : Not given.

DESCRIPTION : " MALE. UPPERSIDE richer fulvous than in *C. hierax*, [Felder]. *Forewing* with the blackish-fuscous border broader at the apex, inwardly more oblique than in that species, the space between the discal striga and the border as far as the lowest median fold diffusedly whitish. *Hindwing* with the anterior virgulæ outwardly diffusedly defined with whitish, the margin of the ground-colour beyond the spots broader, otherwise as in *C. hierax*. UNDERSIDE as in that species, but the interior discal streak outwardly defined with ochraceous, of the *forewing* the exterior more receding from it."

" The wings much paler and richer than in *C. hierax*, the two discal streaks more distant, the inner one outwardly more broadly defined with ochraceous-whitish."

"The forewing of the male has the apex less produced than in the male of *C. hierax*. The inner margin of the hindwing in both sexes seems longer than in *C. hierax* and *C. psaphon*. The outer margin of the forewing also in both sexes is longer than in *C. hierax*, the branches of the veins also appear to be longer." (*Felder*, l. c.)

The Indian Museum, Calcutta, has typical specimens of this form from the Assam valley, Cachar, and Sylhet, and also from the Khasi Hills and from Sikkim ; in the latter district it is the prevailing form, while *C. hierax* apparently only occurs rarely there.

585. **Charaxes jalinder**, Butler.

C. jalinder, Butler. Lep. Ex., p. 98, n. 4, pl. xxxvii, fig. 4, *male* and *female* (1872) ; *C. hipponax*, Felder, (*female* only), Reise Novara, Lep., vol. iii, p. 443, n. 722 (1867).

HABITAT : N.-E. Himalayas.

EXPANSE : ♂, 3·6 ; ♀, 4·1 inches.

DESCRIPTION : "MALE and FEMALE. Allied to *C. hipponax*, Felder. UPPERSIDE rich fulvous. *Forewing* with three narrow discoidal nebulæ, a disco-cellular fasciole, four lineoles [little lines] obliquely crossing the middle of the wing, sublunate, and two beyond the cell small, indistinct, black ; a broad fascia outwardly irregularly whitish, extending from the subcostal to the submedian nervure, the external area broadly black, including six spots fulvous in the male, whitish in the female. *Hindwing* almost as in *C. khasianus*, Butler, male. UNDERSIDE, the wings most like those of *C. pleistoanax*, Felder, but more rufescent, the median fascia less whitish, much broader at the costa of the *forewing*."

"This is not a rare species in collections, and, exclusive of other characters, may be picked out at once by the white band of the forewing terminating upon the submedian nervure. Major Roberts took the female of *C. jalinder* at Darjeeling, but I have preferred to figure both sexes from one collection" [that of Mr. Moore] (*Butler*, l. c.)

We have no specimen exactly agreeing with the figure, but specimens closely resembling it are found in all localities where *C. hipponax* is found.

Mr. Butler gives the female of *C. hipponax* as described by Felder as a synonym of his (Butler's) *C. jalinder*. Dr. Felder's description of that sex is given below.*

586. **Charaxes hindia**, Butler.

C. hindia, Butler, Lep. Ex., p. 99, n. 5, pl. xxxvii, fig. 5, *male* and *female* (1872) ; *Haridra hindia*, id., Ann. and Mag. of Nat. Hist., fifth series, vol. xvi, p. 306, n. 50 (1885).

HABITAT : Sikkim ; near Assam.

EXPANSE : ♂, 3·6 ; ♀, 4·2 inches.

DESCRIPTION : "MALE and FEMALE. Allied to *C. jalinder*, Butler. Differs on the UPPERSIDE in having the basal area brighter, the disco-cellular fasciole better defined, the median lituræ obsolete ; no virgula in the fascia ; the whitish fascia broader, tinted with fulvous below the first median branch of the *forewing* ; the external area of the forewing broader, the discal spots larger in the male, but the upper ones obsolete, in the female fulvous, scarcely conspicuous ; the black fascia of the *hindwing* more macular and much narrower. UNDERSIDE much paler ; the median fascia in the *forewing* less oblique, the ochraceous area broader ; the discal area much broader."

"Mr. Moore has two specimens of the female of this species, one of which is scarcely larger than the male. It is a conspicuous form, and may be distinguished without trouble. The female has the external area of the wings much browner than in any other species with which I am acquainted, but this may be partially due to fading." (*Butler*, l. c.)

I have no specimens exactly agreeing with the figure, but there are males closely resembling it from the localities where *C. hipponax* is found. A female most closely resembling the figure was taken by me in Calcutta, the only specimen I have seen from that neighbourhood. Mr. E. A. Minchin took a single female at Nagpur in March. I very doubtfully identify these specimens as *C. hindia*, I think it is very probable they are a dry country form of *C. imna*, being throughout much paler-coloured than the Wynaad female of that species, but not having procured males from the same localities, I cannot be certain about it.

The three remaining species differ from all the foregoing in having the basal area of both wings very dark and powdered with fuscous ; the white discal band is also broader and clearer.

* "FEMALE. UPPERSIDE as in *C. kiesar*, but richer coloured. *Forewing* with the discal strigæ evanescent, a broad diffused whitish fascia extending to the internal nervure, through which the streaks of the underside are seen, the border inwardly divided with six whitish spots. *Hindwing* with an anterior whitish patch extending to the second subcostal branch, and the margin of the ground-colour beyond the spots broader." (*Felder*, l. c.)

C. khimalara and *C. khasianus* are very doubtfully distinct from *C. pleistoanax*, but as Mr. Butler has fully pointed out the distinctions he relies on in separating them, I republish his descriptions to enable others to work out the matter.

C. pleistoanax is found in Sikkim, but not very commonly, and more rarely in Bhutan, and the Assam valley. I have no specimens exactly agreeing with either *C. khimalara* or *C. khasianus*, but the nearest approach to the former which I possess is from Sibsagar, to the latter from Sikkim.

The females like the males differ from the foregoing in having the basal area of both wings powdered with fuscous ; they are larger and the white band is much broader, the spots on the border of the forewing vary, but are usually large and pure white.

587. Charaxes pleistoanax, Felder.

C. pleistoanax, Felder, Reise Novara, Lep., vol. iii, p. 443. n. 723 (1867) ; id., Butler, Trans. Ent. Soc. Lond., 1870, p. 121, n. 14 ; idem, id., Lep. Ex., p. 97, n. i, pl. xxxvii, fig. 3, *male* and *female* (1872).

HABITAT : North India, Assam.

EXPANSE : Not given.

DESCRIPTION : " MALE. UPPERSIDE at the base deer-coloured fuscous, more often indeed altogether deep fulvous. *Forewing* as in *C. hierax*, [Felder], but with the border most often narrower and divided by five spots of the ground-colour or whitish in a bent series before the middle, a discal striga very distinct more or less shortened, within the border a rather broad whitish fascia, most often continued to the inner margin, and inwardly within the striga dissolved in greyish powdering. *Hindwing* with the anterior virgulæ most prominent, outwardly broadly defined with whitish, most often bounded with a rather broad whitish fascia extending to the second median nervule, on this side outwardly most often defined by an obscure ferruginous diffused macular streak, the small apical patch and annexed spots blacker than in *C. hippona x*, Felder, a little more distant from the margin. UNDERSIDE almost as in *C. hierax*, but with the inner discal striga outwardly defined with ochraceous more broadly moreover than in *C. hippona x*. FEMALE. UPPERSIDE as in *C. hipponax*, but at the base more obscurely and sordidly fulvous. *Forewing* with the white discal fascia extending to the inner margin and inwardly best defined beyond the macular streak and there hoary, with the border inwardly divided by seven much larger whitish spots (the uppermost two outside the series, the remainder more or less lunate). *Hindwing* with the anterior virgulæ outwardly defined by a broad white fascia extending beyond the second median nervule, the rhombic spots larger than in *C. hippona x*, a little more receding from the margin. UNDERSIDE with the two discal strigæ more approximated than in *C. hippona x*, much broader and defined with whitish. *Forewing* with the whitish spots of the upperside, but worse defined. *Hindwing* with the ante-marginal zone verging on whitish."

" Confounded, we think, in collections with the Chinese *C. polyxena*, Cramer (*C. bernardus*, Fabricius) of which we are only acquainted with the figure. The forewing of the male has most resemblance to that of *C. hierax*, Felder, but the apex is more produced and the outer margin longer. The female also has the apex of the forewing more produced than in its nearest allies, and the small tail of the hindwing is also longer." (*Felder*, l. c.)

" A white-banded race of *C. bernardus*, Fabricius, the female of which is in most collections : Captain Lang has a series of the males, but only one female." (*Butler* l. c. in Trans. Ent. Soc Lond.) All the latter specimens referred to are from Sikkim, where it is a common species.

588. Charaxes khimalara, Butler.

C. khimalara, Butler, Lep. Ex., p. 97, n. 2, pl. xxxvii, fig. 1, *male* and *female* (1872) ; *Haridra khimalara*, id., Ann. and Mag. of Nat. Hist., fifth series, vol. xvi, p. 306, n. 51 (1885) ; *Charaxes hierax* (*female* only), Felder, Reise Novara, Lep., vol. iii, p. 442, n. 721 (1867).

HABITAT : ? N.-W. Himalayas, Nepal, near Assam.

EXPANSE : ♂, 3·5 ; ♀, 4·0 inches.

DESCRIPTION : " MALE. Allied to *C. pleistoanax*, Felder. Differs on the UPPERSIDE in having the *forewing* more acuminate, much more obscure [darker], the median whitish fascia more slender, inwardly not at all defined with black between the median branches, outwardly very irregular; the discal spots more frequently wanting. *Hindwing* with the black discal fascia almost twice as broad, inwardly more regular, not at all dotted with white Differs on the UNDERSIDE by having the wings more silky; the median fascia more whitish, the virgula of the *forewing* beyond the cell very narrow; the line defining the basal area less irregular; the submarginal ochraceous area broader." (*Butler*, l. c.) "FEMALE. UPPERSIDE as in the male [of *C. hierax*], but the forewing darker at the base, the discal streak much better defined, the space between it and the border beyond the lowest median fold whitish, this [the border] divided with four whitish spots hindwardly and a subapical whitish spot. *Hindwing* with the costal border a little beyond the first subcostal branch between the virgulæ and the patch diffusedly whitish, a diffused ferruginous streak before the margin. UNDERSIDE much more variegated with violascent-ashy, the anterior space between the basal strigæ and the broad cinctures of the discal ochraceous-whitish." (*Felder*, l. c.)

"This species may at once be distinguished from *C. pleistoanax*, Felder, by its darker colouring, narrower white band, the straight inner edge of the broader discal band of the hindwing, and the obsolescent character of all the discal white spots." (*Butler*, l. c. in Lep. Ex.) As figured by Mr. Butler, this species in the male has the broad outer black border of the forewing on the upperside entirely unspotted; in *C. pleistoanax* and *C. khasianus* it bears a curved series of five or six whitish spots. Mr. S. E. Peal has sent male specimens from Sibsagar in Upper Assam agreeing very closely with the figure.

589. **Charaxes khasianus,** Butler.

C. khasianus, Butler, Lep. Ex., p. 98, n. 3, pl. xxxvii, fig. *C*, *male* and *female* (1872).

HABITAT: N.-E. Bengal, Khasi Hills.

EXPANSE: ♂, 3·75; ♀, 4·00 inches.

DESCRIPTION: "MALE and FEMALE. Allied to *C. pleistoanax*, Felder. Differs on the UPPERSIDE in having the basal area paler outwardly, to the least degree bluish; the whitish median fascia broader; the black virgulæ more slender; the virgula of the interno-median interspace of the *forewing* obsolete in the male; the black external area narrower, the discal spots minute, tinted with fulvous in the male; the black fascia of the *hindwing* much broader at the apex; the external area brighter, broader, the tail longer, in the female broader. UNDERSIDE, *both wings* rufescent, the median fascia much narrower, pale ochraceous, not at all whitish; all the black lines very irregular, the curves of the discal line elongated."

"Also allied to *C. pleistoanax*, from which it may be easily separated by the paler basal area of the wings, which exhibits externally a bluish shade peculiar to this species; also by the broader white band, which in the female is carried across the hindwing to the abdominal margin; the slenderness of the transverse black lines and the peculiar reddish tint of the underside." (*Butler*, l. c.) I possess a male from Jorehát, Assam, and two females from Sikkim which agree very well with Mr. Butler's figures and description of this species. The discal white band on the upperside is broader than in any other species, extending on the forewing within the discal fine black lines (virgulæ) towards the base.

Genus 89.—**PROTHOË**, Hübner. (FRONTISPIECE).

Prothoë, Hübner, Samml. Ex. Schmett., vol. ii (1806-16); id., Westwood, Gen. Diurn. Lep., vol. ii, p. 266 (1850); id., Wallace, Trans. Ent. Soc. Lond., 1869, p. 80, *Monograph*; id., Distant, Rhop. Malay., p. 110 (1883).

"BODY, small and rather slender; *wings* large, hindwing slightly tailed; *palpi* applied close to the face. HEAD, as broad as the thorax, clothed with short hairs, and destitute of a frontal tuft; *eyes*, large and naked; *antennæ*, very nearly half the length of the forewing, straight, slender, terminated by a long, very slender, and gradually-formed club, slightly grooved; *palpi*, short, erect, rather compressed, scaly, the inside furnished with short hairs, so that the tips are not applied close together, but are slightly incurved, basal joint not furnished with long hairs, extremity of the second joint hairy on the side applied to the face, terminal joint small and conical. THORAX, small, woolly, tippets very small, metathorax slightly hairy. ABDOMEN, small. FOREWING, large, triangular : *costa*. slightly rounded ; *outer margin* three-fourths of the length of the costa, nearly straight, very slightly scolloped ; *inner margin* the same length as the outer margin, nearly straight ; *costal nervure* strong, extending to half the length of the costa, *discoidal cell* extending to the length of two-fifths of the base of the wing, *subcostal nervure* slender, with its first branch arising at about one-third of the length of the wing, second branch arising a little beyond, and extending to about four-fifths of the length of the costa, beyond this second branch the subcostal nervure is obliquely deflexed for a short distance (to the branching off of the disco-cellular nervule), the third and fourth branches arise almost close together near the middle of the nervure, the third running in a bent manner to the tip of the wing, and the fourth also bent, running into the outer margin ; *upper disco-cellular nervule* very short and oblique, *middle* disco-cellular short and transverse ; *lower* disco-cellular curved in an oblique direction outwards, joined to the *third median nervule* at some little distance beyond its origin, this nervule is but little curved at its base, *submedian nervure* scarcely curved. HINDWING, somewhat oval, the space between the extremities of the second and third median nervules produced into a short, broad, outwardly curved tail ; *costal margin* curved, *outer* margin nearly straight from the outer angle to the tail, from the tail to the anal angle it has two rather deep scallops ; *precostal nervure* reduced to a short, straight, transverse spur arising near the base of the subcostal nervure, and extending to the costal margin, *subcostal* nervure branched at a short distance (not more than one-seventh of an inch) from its base ; *upper disco-cellular nervule* forming the base of the discoidal nervule, and branching from the subcostal nervure at a still shorter distance, *lower* disco-cellular wanting, so that the *discoidal cell*, which is long and narrow, is open ; *median nervure* branched considerably below the branching off of the discoidal nervule, its second and third branches extending to either side of the short tail. FORELEGS, of the *male* very short and pectoral, thickly clothed to the tip with short hairs, the *tibia* shorter than the femur, *tarsus* fully as long as the tibia, cylindrical, simple, exarticulate, and destitute of claws ; of the *female* short, scaly, *tibia* about two-thirds of the length of the femur, *tarsus* as long as the tibia, internally dilated at the extremity, where it is obliquely truncate, with slight indications of the joints. MIDDLE and HINDLEGS, moderately long, and rather thickly clothed with scales, the *tarsus* being nearly as thick as the tibia, *femur* a little curved, thickest at the base, *tibia* as long as the femur, straight, furnished on the underside with two rows of short spines, *tarsus* of the same length as the tibia, rather thickly beset with short spines, especially on the underside, where they form several distinct rows, *claws* small, slender, sickle-shaped, *paronychia* with the outer division as long as the claws, slender, rather pointed and setose, inner division shorter and more obtuse, *pulvillus* small, broadly heart-shaped."

" The beautiful insect [*P. franckii*] upon which this genus is founded is well distinguished, not only by the peculiar character of its colours, but by its short palpi closely applied to the face, the slender club to its antennæ, and the great and nearly equal length of the third and fourth branches of the subcostal nervure of the forewing, which run close together for a considerable distance, and then widen, seeming to take the place of the fourth branch and terminal division of the subcostal nervure, as arranged in *Cyrestis*, &c." (*Westwood*, l. c.) The genus at present contains about nine species, which occur from Assam through Upper Tenasserim and the Malay Peninsula and Islands as far east as New Ireland. The two Indian species are dark indigo-blue or olive-green above, with a broad paler blue band across the forewing on the upperside, which in one species almost reaches the outer margin, and with some white apical spots, the hindwing unmarked, except by two or three white spots at the apex ; underside pale-buff or whitey-brown, marked with numerous fuscous spots and streaks, the outer margin of the hindwing bears a series of very large conical-shaped spots between the veins, of a dark powdery bronzy-green colour. The length of the fourth and fifth subcostal nervules is very unusual, being about equal to half the length of the forewing, and they arise at about the same distance from the origin of the third subcostal nervule as that nervule does from the end of the cell. The neuration of this group differs from that of *P. calcdonia* in the first subcostal nervule of the forewing anastomosing with the costal nervure a little beyond the end of the cell, in *P. caledonia* it is entirely free. In only one other genus of the *Nymphalinæ* (*Tanaccia*) does this anastomosing occur. The direction of the lower disco-cellular nervule of the forewing in *P. caledonia* differs considerably from that of *P. franckii*, being evenly and regularly curved, and closing the discoidal cell much less obliquely.

Key to the Indian species of Prothoe.

A. Upperside, forewing crossed by a broad even straight well-defined blue band, the apical third of the wing black, tail long.

      590. P. ANGELICA, Upper Tenasserim, Malay Peninsula, Sumatra, Borneo.

B. Upperside, forewing crossed by a much broader irregular blue band, almost reaching the outer margin, tail short.

      591. P. REGALIS, Manipur.

590. **Prothoe angelica,** Butler. (FRONTISPIECE, FIG. 120 ♂).

P. angelica, Butler, Ann. and Mag. of Nat. Hist., fifth series, vol. xvi, pp. 53, 54 (1885) ; *P. franckii*, Wallace (*part*), Trans. Ent. Soc. Lond., 1869, p. 80, n. 1 ; id., Moore, Proc. Zool. Soc. Lond., 1878, p. 832.

HABITAT : Upper Tenasserim, Perak, Malacca, Sumatra, Borneo.

EXPANSE : 3·25 inches.

DESCRIPTION : MALE. UPPERSIDE, *both wings* dark indigo-blue, thickly irrorated with lighter blue scales at the base. *Forewing* with a black band at the end of the cell not quite reaching the median nervure, beyond which is a broad discal blue band of equal width throughout, the edges straight and even, occupying nearly the middle third of the costa and extending to the anal angle, and bearing some white indistinct streaks at its upper end and some indistinct white irrorations in the middle, a subapical series of five rounded purplish-white spots, of which the lowest in the lower discoidal interspace and the next but one above it are very small ; the apical area beyond the blue band fuscous. *Hindwing* with two purplish-white elongated spots on the margin divided by the upper subcostal nervule. UNDERSIDE, *both wings* pale buff with fuscous markings. *Forewing* with the inner margin broadly, the middle of the outer margin narrowly, and a wedge-shaped patch from the costa fuscous ; a looped spot at the base of the cell, two annular spots one above the other in the middle, and a W-shaped one near its end continued to the costa, the disco-cellulars enclosed by a double line, some spots outside the cell, on the disc and margin, all fuscous. *Hindwing* with a reniform spot in the middle of the cell, another at its end and continued to the first subcostal nervule, some irregular patches from the costa extending into the disc, and some narrow marks in the median interspaces, and from the median nervure to the abdominal margin, all fuscous ; a submarginal series of large conical-shaped spots placed between the nervules thickly irrorated with dark powdery bronzy-green, the anterior ones inwardly margined with orange, a black lunular spot at the anal angle in the submedian interspace marked inwardly with orange and outwardly with pale blue, a large pale blue quadrate spot on the margin in the first median interspace, beyond which the tail and the margin are decreasingly black, a small black and orange triangular spot on the margin in the internal interspace. This description is taken from a single male from Perak in the Indian Museum, Calcutta, the only specimen of this group I have seen, and from it the figure showing both sides is taken. It is named *P. franckii* on the plate, at the time when the plate was lettered *P. angelica* and two other new and allied species had not been discriminated. I have added in a foot-note* the points of difference between it and the Javan *P. franckii* as given by Mr. Butler. Mr. Moore records it from Meetan, Upper Tenasserim, 3,000 feet, April.

---

  * " *Prothoé angelica*, Butler. " Oblique belt of forewing shining azure or greenish, with a series of irregular white dashes to represent the medial belt ; apical area of hindwing purplish black , prevalent colouring on external area of hindwing below pale green. '

  " *P. angelica* is the brightest of all, the female being slightly less so than the male ; the blue belt is sometimes a little wider than in *P. franckii*, and its outer edge is much less zigzag ; it has white dashes on the belt in both sexes ; the markings below are very similar, but the ground-colour is noticeably different." (*Butler, l. c.*)

"This beautiful insect is not uncommon in Sumatra. It has the habit of settling with closed wings on sticks or the trunks of trees, with which the peculiarly shaded markings of its underside harmonize so as to render it difficult to detect." (*Wallace*, l. c.)

591. **Prothöe regalis**, Butler.

P. regalis, Butler, Ann. and Mag. of Nat. Hist., fifth series, vol. xvi, pp. 53, 54 and 306, n. 53, pl. viii, fig. 1, *male* (1885).

HABITAT : Manipur.

EXPANSE : 3·2 inches.

DESCRIPTION : MALE. "UPPERSIDE, *both wings* with the basal third and *body* olive-green. *Forewing* crossed obliquely from the middle of costa to the third fourth of the inner margin by a broad silvery-blue belt, the external edge of which is irregularly notched and only separated by a blackish submarginal streak from three large spots of the same colour upon the middle of the external border; veins slenderly black, terminating in blackish spots, two of which are placed between the above-mentioned blue spots; two white spots followed by a blackish streak upon the costal part of the blue belt; a large triangular black spot closing the discoidal cell; apical area chocolate-brown; three subapical spots, the upper two large, placed obliquely, bluish, with white centres, the third submarginal, bluish, small. *Hindwing* with the middle of the wing blue-black; apical area and external border chocolate-brown; two linear apical blue dashes and a blue line along the base of the cilia. UNDERSIDE, *forewing* whitey brown, slightly tinted with greenish towards the base and with lilacine along the external border; markings very similar to those of *P. franckii*, but the outline-spots on the discoidal area filled in with dark olivaceous, with no trace of an oblique white band, and with all the internervular submarginal markings cruciform. *Hindwing* with the basal half as in *P. franckii*, excepting that the discoidal spots are filled in with dark olivaceous; external half considerably darker, its inner half greyish olivaceous, enclosing a series of oblong internervular black patches, which are situated in front and bounded by reddish crescentic borders; immediately beyond these reddish crescents is a submarginal series of eight unequal black-edged bronze-green spots, with brighter green borders, these spots are irrorated and more or less suffused with blackish; from apex to second median nervule is a series of gradually increasing marginal black spots, edged externally with pink, the last two crossed by a red stripe; a large bright olive-green semi-circular spot, with black inner border and bluish-white outer border at outer extremity of first median interspace, and a large black spot, crossed by a red A-shaped marking, and bordered along its infero-exterior border with grey, at extremity of interno-median area; a triangular black and red spot at extremity of abdominal fold."

"On the upperside this beautiful species may be at once distinguished from *P. franckii* of Java by the broader, more irregular, and greyer blue belt across the forewing, the absence of a white band on this belt, the blue marginal spots, and the blue or bluish subapical spots; the hindwing also has blue instead of white marginal dashes at apex, and the external border and apical area are chocolate-brown instead of purplish brown." (*Butler*, l. c., p. 306).

I have never seen this species, which appears to be quite distinct. I give below* some further remarks on it by Mr. Butler, which may prove useful.

Prothöe regalis, Butler. "Oblique belt very broad, covering nearly half the wing, three spots of the same colour at middle of external border, only separated from the belt by a blackish submarginal stripe. Hindwing decidedly shorter and less caudate [than in *P. franckii*]; apical markings blue, prevalent colouring on external area greyish olivaceous, black and green."

"*P. regalis* is duller in colouring than *P. angelica*, and corresponds with *P. uniformis* [the habitat of which is unknown], in the absence of white on the blue belt; it, however, differs from *P. franckii*, *P. uniformis* and *P. angelica* in the great width of the blue belt, the blue marginal spots on the forewing, the shorter and less caudate hindwing, the cruciform character of the black submarginal markings on the underside of the forewing, the filled-in discoidal markings on both wings, the inner half of external area of hindwing on the underside being greyish olivaceous crossed by oblong black patches with reddish external borders, the shorter green and black submarginal arched spots, and several other characters. I have seen only one male of this very distinct species." (*Butler*, l. c., pp. 53, 54.)

One of the most beautiful butterflies in the world, *P. caledonia*, occurs in the Malay Peninsula, Borneo and Labuan. A description of it is given below.*

* *Prothoë caledonia*, Hewitson. *Nymphalis calydonia*, Hewitson, Ex. Butt., vol. 2, p. 86, pl. xliii, figs. 3, 4; (1855); *Charaxes calydonia*, Butler, Proc. Zool. Soc. Lond., 1865, p. 638, n. 61; *Prothoë caledonia*, idem, id., 1867, p. 873; idem, id., Distant, Rhop. Malay., p. 110, n. 1, pl. xiii, fig. 9, *male* (1883); *Nymphalis ? caledonia*, Kirby, Syn. Cat. Diurn. Lep., p. 273, n. 58 (1871). HABITAT : Perak, Malacca, Borneo, Labuan. EXPANSE : *Male*, 4 1 to 4 3 ; *female*, 4 3 inches. DESCRIPTION : " MALE. UPPERSIDE *forewing* pale sulphur-yellow, with the base very pale bluish, and with rather more than the apical half dark shining fuscous; the inner margin of this blackish colouration commences narrowly at base of costa, and gradually widening obliquely crosses the cell a little beyond the middle, and crossing the second median nervule near its base extends to near the outer margin between the second and first median nervules, after which it is again directed inwardly and is concavely situated to near apex of inner margin; an oblique subapical series of four sulphureous spots, the first near costa, the second between the fourth and fifth subcostal nervules, the third above and the fourth beneath the upper discoidal nervule; a somewhat obsolete pale apical spot and a very small bright spot on the second median nervule [sometimes absent]. *Hindwing* very pale bluish, with a broad shining fuscous outer margin, which is widest at apex and narrowly terminates at anal angle; two linear pale greyish marginal spots near apex, and apical margin of caudate appendage of the same colour; the costal disc of the wing is somewhat suffused with sulphureous, and the abdominal margin is suffused with very pale brownish. UNDERSIDE, *forewing* dull greyish, beautifully suffused and spotted with bright red, and with the following spots and markings :—four spots on costal area above cell, which contains a basal spot, two placed a little before the middle, followed by an irregular macular fascia, and another and somewhat similar one at apex; immediately beyond cell is a broad curved fascia commencing at costa and terminating at apex of median nervure; a triple series of much broken and irregular fasciæ, the outer margin being also fuscous; beneath the second median nervule the colour is sulphur yellow, becoming paler towards inner margin, with a large irregular fuscous spot near outer angle. *Hindwing* of similar hue and shadings, with the following fuscous spots and markings :—a small rounded spot at base, and another near apex of præcostal nervure; a short broad curved transverse fascia commencing near base and terminating on basal edge of abdominal margin; a linear streak above and near base of costal nervure; a subquadrate spot, followed by a larger and curved spot beneath the costal nervure, three spots in cell, a small rounded one near base, a similar one near origin of first median nervule, and a transverse spot near its termination; a sinuated row of discal spots, consisting of a small one above and a large one beneath the first subcostal nervule, three in oblique series divided by the discoidal and third median nervules; a conical spot between the second and first median nervules, and an obconical one before the submedian nervure, from which to edge of abdominal margin is a broad fascia; the apical area of wings, which is preceded by a transverse pale fascia, is darker and shaded with greenish, and contains some much-waved and somewhat disjointed series of transverse fasciæ; outer margin sulphureous, with its extreme border fuscous, a large fuscous patch on the caudate appendage, and a small red spot near anal angle. *Body* above pale bluish grey; *thorax* beneath more or less concolourous with wings; *legs* brownish, tibiæ and tarsi more or less pale ochraceous; *antennæ* fuscous above, castaneous beneath." (*Distant*, l.c.) The FEMALE differs from the male on the upperside of the forewing in having a small linear white spot on the middle of the costa, the four subapical spots are somewhat larger, and the one at the extreme apex more prominent. All the other markings as in the male.
There are three specimens, two males and a female, of this " glorious butterfly" in the Indian Museum, Calcutta, from Perak. They were captured on bait placed in the forest especially to attract this and other species of butterflies, many of them, including *P. caledonia*, being very foul feeders. It seems to be a little variable, Mr. Butler having recorded the note below* on the subject on procuring a specimen from Malacca, which was also the locality of the type specimen.
* " The specimen from Malacca differs from that figured by Mr. Hewitson in its greater size, and in having the upperside of the hindwing more suffused with greenish; on the underside the markings are slightly different, the basal red bands being broader, the medial band whiter, the discal red band narrower, darker, and rather more irregular, the submarginal green band duller, and the blue lunulate line more irregular and not so deeply margined with black; the large black caudal spot is wanting in Hewitson's figure, which was drawn from an imperfect specimen " (*Butler*, l. c. in Proc. Zool. Soc. Lond., 1867, p. 874).

FAMILY 2.—LEMONIIDÆ.

Lemoniidæ, Kirby, Cat. Diurn. Lep., p. 282 (1871); id., Moore, Lep. Cey., vol. i, p. 67 (1881); *Erycinidæ*, Swainson, Phil. Mag., second series, vol. i, p. 187 (1827); id., Westwood, Gen. Diurn. Lep., vol. ii, p. 415 (1851); id., Bates, Journ. Ent., vol. i, p. 220 (1861); idem, id., l. c., vol. ii, p. 176 (1864); id., Distant, Rhop. Malay., p. 185 (1883); *Erycinina*, Snellin, Lep. v. Midden-Sumatra, p. 20 (1880).

"FORELEGS small, slender, imperfect [in the males], but more developed than in the *Nymphalidæ*; those of the *males* brush-like and clothed with long hairs, the tarsus without claws; of the *females* longer, slender, scaly, tarsus with the joints longer and more distinct than in the *Nymphalidæ*. FOREWING, subcostal nervure generally with only three branches, the disco-cellulars very slender. All of small size." (*Marshall* and *de Nicéville*, Butt. of India, vol. i, p. 18.)

The family *Lemoniidæ* contains four subfamilies, *Libythæinæ*, *Nemeobiinæ*, *Euselasiinæ*, and *Lemoniinæ*; the first embracing but a single genus, the second about fourteen genera, the greater portion of which are American, the two last subfamilies are wholly American. The forelegs in the males are imperfect, the tarsi in the *Libythæinæ* consisting of a single joint ending in a spine, in the *Nemeobiinæ* the forelegs of the males are less hairy, the tarsi consisting of two or three joints. The forelegs of the females are perfect, the tarsi composed of five joints ending in two claws. The forewing in the *Libythæinæ* and in all the Oriental genera of the *Nemeobiinæ* has four branches to the subcostal nervure excluding the terminal portion, in several genera of the new world *Nemeobiinæ* this feature also obtains, but in the majority of them there are three branches only. Throughout the Indian genera of the family the first and second subcostal nervules of the forewing are emitted before the termination of the cell, and the discoidal cells are always closed. All the butterflies appertaining to this family are of small size, though averaging considerably larger than most of the species of the next family *Lycænidæ*. The family occurs throughout both worlds, but is not represented in Australasia.

Subfamily I.—LIBYTHÆINÆ, Bates. (PLATE XXIV).

Libythæinæ, Bates, Journ. Ent., vol. i, p. 220 (1861); idem, id., l. c., vol. ii, p. 176 (1864); id., Moore, Lep. Cey., vol. i, p. 67 (1881); *Libythæidæ*, Westwood, Gen. Diurn. Lep., vol. ii, p. 412 (1851).

"BODY, robust, small; *palpi*, extraordinarily elongated, densely clothed with short hairs, porrected horizontally; *antennæ*, short, gradually incrassated from the base to the tip. FORE-WING, strongly angulated below the apex; *discoidal cell* of both wings closed by a very slender nervule. FORELEGS, short, those of the *male* brush-like, with exarticulate tarsi: of the *female* with ordinary-formed tarsi."

"LARVA cylindrical, not spined, slightly pubescent. PUPA short, not angulated, suspended by the tail." (*Westwood*, l. c.)

This subfamily contains but a single genus, *Libythea*. Mr. Wallace states regarding it that "this small group is of world-wide distribution, and like all such is a frequenter of open grounds, plains, river-banks and sea-shores rather than of the virgin forest. The species are all small, and in the activity of their motions resemble the lesser *Nymphalinæ*." (Trans. Ent. Soc. Lond., 1869, p. 334). In India I have almost exclusively found them near water. Major Marshall informs me that he has more usually seen them in forest glades.

Genus 89.—LIBYTHEA, Fabricius. (PLATE XXIV).

Libythea, Fabricius, Ill. Mag., vol. vi, p. 284, n. 28 (1807); id., Latreille, Enc. Méth., vol. ix, p. 10 (1819); id., Westwood, Gen. Diurn. Lep., vol. ii, p. 412 (1851); id., Moore, Lep. Cey., vol. i, p. 67 (1881); *Lilytheus*, Boitard, Man. Ent., vol. ii, p. 299 (1828); *Hypatus*, Hübner, Catal. Franck., p. 85 (1825); *Hecaërge*, Ochsenheimer, Schneeer. Eur., vol. iv, p. 32 (1816); id., Hübner, Verz. bek. Schmett., p. 100 (1816); *Chilca*, Billberg, Enum. Ins., p. 79 (1820).

"BODY, robust, thickly clothed with soft woolly hairs, rather small in size, and of dark colours; the *wings* with spots of orange, or dirty white, but not ocellated; *head*, small, strongly tufted in front; *eyes*, prominent, naked; *palpi*, extraordinarily elongated, being one third, or even in some species half, the length of the whole body; porrected horizontally, not compressed, thickly clothed with hairs of moderate length, the inner edges uniting together, so as to form conjointly a long conical beak, obtuse at the tip; second joint oval; third joint greatly elongated and slender; *antennæ*, not nearly half the length of the forewing, straight, articulations indistinct, gradually thickening from the base to the tip, which is obtuse; *thorax*, oval, hairy; tippets strongly developed; *abdomen*, small, slender. FOREWING, of moderate size; *costal margin* moderately arched, *apex* acute, *outer margin* strongly angulated below the apex, the lower discoidal nervule extending into the most prominent part of the angle, about five-sixths of the length of the costa, *inner* margin straight, one-fourth longer than the outer margin. None of the veins dilated at the base. *Costal nervure* extending to about half the length of the costa; *subcostal* nervure with the first and second branches free, arising before the anterior extremity of the discoidal cell; third branch arising far beyond the cell, followed at a short distance by the fourth, which extends to the tip of the wing; *upper disco-cellular nervule* minute and sub-oblique, *middle* and *lower* disco-cellulars of nearly equal length, very slender, and uniting into a curve, closing the *discoidal cell* about the middle of the wing, by uniting with the third median nervule at about the same distance from its base as exists between the first and second branches. HINDWING, irregularly and broadly ovate; the *costal margin* produced in the middle into a considerable-sized lobe, *outer* margin strongly scalloped, *abdominal* margin forming only a slight gutter for the reception of the abdomen; *præcostal nervure* short, curved outwards; *costal* nervure extending to the outer edge of the lobe, of which it follows the outline; *subcostal* nervure arising just opposite to the præcostal, branching at a considerable distance from its base; *upper disco-cellular nervule* rather short, almost transverse, arising at a distance from the base of the subcostal branch about equal to the space between the base of the subcostal and its branch; *lower* disco-cellular slender, but distinct, more oblique than the upper disco-cellular, and slightly curved, closing the *discoidal cell* by its union with the third median nervule at a very short distance from its origin; the *third median nervule* considerably curved after its union with the lower disco-cellular nervule. FORELEGS, of the *male* small and brush-like, densely hairy, the *tarsus* rather shorter than the tibia, cylindrical, exarticulate, and destitute of claws. Of the *female* considerably longer than those of the male, but articulated like the middle and hind feet. *Tarsus* armed with short spines beneath. *Claws* curved, dilated at the base, horny, acute at the tips. *Paronychia* slender, membranous, bifid, finely setose; the outer division acute, the inner one shorter and more triangular. *Pulvillus* broadly transverse, the base narrowed. MIDDLE and HINDLEGS, moderately elongated, thickly clothed with scales; *femur* hairy beneath; *tibia* and *tarsus* armed beneath with short spines; *claws* and their appendages formed exactly as in the forelegs of the female."

"LARVA rather slender, subcylindrical, destitute of spines or points. Tail simple. Body finely pubescent, and very delicately shagreened, with pale longitudinal stripes at the sides, very closely resembling those of the *Pierinæ*. PUPA short, suspended by the tail. Thorax-case rather gibbose in the middle of the back. Head-case not produced into a beak."

"The peculiar structure of the forelegs of this genus separates it from all the preceding genera, being imperfect and brush-like in the males, but articulated and furnished with claws and their appendages in the females, exactly as in the tarsi of the hind feet. In other respects, if the gradually clavated straight antennæ and the elongated palpi is excepted, there is no character of importance to remove this genus from the *Nymphalinæ* or *Neurobiinæ*. The structure of the paronychia, and the arrangement of the veins of the wing, offer no distinction; but the larva is entirely like those of the *Pierinæ*, whilst the pupa is simply suspended by the tail. If, therefore, this last-named character is regarded as the primary principle of classification of the Diurnal Lepidoptera, here is a genus which belongs to the great group having the chrysalis suspended. Its larva, however, evidently points out an affinity with the *Pierinæ*; whilst the structure of the feet, and the want of ocellated spots on the wings beneath, seem equally to point to the *Lycænidæ*." (*Westwood*, l. c.)

The genus *Libythea* is in every way peculiar. Mr. Doherty states* that the egg is "ampulliform, shaped like a soda-water bottle, twice as high as wide, forming a short neck or stalk close to the apex, radiate (having ribs diverging from a point at the apex), with strong and anastomosing ribs," in this respect being similar to the *Pierinæ* or "Whites.' The larva and pupa are also strikingly pierid in form, but the latter instead of being girt across the middle as in that subfamily is freely suspended by the tail. In the perfect insect the shape of the palpi and antennæ are entirely peculiar and *sui generis*, the neuration is quite nymphalid, and so is the outline of the forewing with its irregular outer margin, but the forelegs ally this subfamily to the *Lycænidæ*, being imperfect in the male, perfect in the female. As the structure of the forelegs is the primary character on which the classification of butterflies is based in this work, the position of the subfamily will be immediately after the *Nymphalinæ*, to which it is allied by its neuration and its freely suspended pupa, and before the *Lycænidæ*, to which it is also allied by the structure of its forelegs. Taking the egg as the basis of a primary division, Mr. Doherty (l. c., p. 108) places it in one group, the Pieriform, which includes this subfamily and the *Pierinæ*; dividing the butterflies into groups by the legs he places it after the *Lycænidæ* which immediately follow the *Nymphalinæ*, and after the *Neurobiinæ* but before the *Pierinæ*, and states that he has no doubt of the affinity of this remarkable genus with the latter subfamily.

The genus is a small one, and contains about twelve species, of which one inhabits North and one South America, one each in the West Indies and Mauritius, one occurs in the South of Europe and in Asia Minor, one in Africa, four within Indian limits, but no species has been recorded from the Malay Peninsula, the Andamans or the Nicobors, though several occur in the Malay Archipelago.

The different species of *Libythea* are singularly uniform in size and outline as well as in colouration, but the specific distinction in the markings of the upperside are clear and in most cases constant. They all vary from a little under two inches to a little over two inches in expanse; all have the same peculiar outline and strongly falcated forewing. All have the underside clouded and striated with similar protective colouration, varying in tone in each species but uniform in style throughout the genus. In all the upperside is brown, bearing on each wing some tawny or whitish marks, and it is by the variations in these markings that the different species are distinguished.

Key to the Indian species of Libythea.

A. Forewing with streak in cell continued into first median interspace.
   a. Streak in cell of forewing and across disc of hindwing wide, the former extending well below median nervure and base of first median nervule, veins on streak concolourous with it.
     592. L. MYARISTA, Himalayas, Assam, Upper Tenasserim, Java, Borneo.
   b. Streak in cell of forewing and across disc of hindwing narrower, the former not at all or hardly extending below median nervure and base of first median nervule, veins on streak blackish.
     593. L. RAMA, South India, Ceylon.
B. Forewing with streak in cell abruptly widened at its outer extremity, where it nearly fills end of cell, a large rounded spot beyond.
     594. L. LEPITA, Himalayas, Assam.
C. Forewing with streak in cell reduced to a spot at its end, with another well-separated spot beyond, all the markings whitish.
     595. L. ROHINI, Assam.

* Journ. A. S. B., vol. lv, pt. 2, p. 110 (1886).

592. Libythea myrrha, Godart.

L. myrrha, Godart, Enc. Meth., vol. ix, p. 171, n. 4 (1819); id., Boisduval, Sp. Gen., vol. i, pl. x, fig. 8 (1836); id., Gray, Lep. Ins. Nepal, p. 15, pl. xii, fig. 4 (1846); id., Wallace, Trans. Ent. Soc. Lond., 1869, p. 315, n. 1; id., Moore, Proc. Zool. Soc. Lond., 1878, p. 832; id., Swinhoe, Proc. Zool. Soc. Lond., 1885, p. 130, n. 44; *Hecaerge myrrha*, Hübner, Zutrage Ex. Schmett., figs. 789, 790 (1832).

HABITAT: Himalayas, Assam, Upper Tenasserim, Java, Borneo.

EXPANSE: 2'0 to 2'2 inches.

DESCRIPTION: MALE. UPPERSIDE, *both wings* deep vinous-brown, almost black, with tawny markings. *Forewing* with a streak commencing narrowly at the base of the wing, occupying the lower half of the discoidal cell and upper half of the submedian interspace, extending beyond the cell to near the outer margin of the wing and occupying the entire width of the first median interspace and the lower portion of the interspace above; the streak outwardly broadly rounded and widest at the end of the cell: two subapical somewhat whitish spots placed obliquely, sometimes quite separated, sometimes joined into a band, each spot sometimes almost divided into two by the veins, sometimes with a small diffused whitish spot at the extreme apex of the wing. *Hindwing* with a broad discal band wide and diffused at the abdominal margin, elsewhere well defined, and gradually narrowing towards the apex of the wing which it does not quite reach, its apical extremity curved and deflected towards the outer margin. UNDERSIDE, much paler. *Forewing* with the tawny markings as above but paler, the discal streak wider, occupying almost the entire basal area of the cell, the apex irrorated with purplish. *Hindwing* with no tawny discal band, except as far as visible by transparency, irrorated throughout with purplish, which assumes the form of a more or less distinct band across the disc, and another from the middle of the costa to the middle of the cell, the whole wing thickly striated with dark brown. FEMALE, paler throughout, the tawny markings larger. *Cilia* throughout ochreous-brown; *antennæ*, *palpi*, and *body* vinous-brown above, paler below.

Mr. Wallace states (l. c.) that *L. myrrha* "varies much in the width of the bands and the size of the spots; specimens from Ceylon [since described as a distinct species] and South India have these very much reduced and paler, the apical spots being nearly white; specimens from Borneo have the wings somewhat less falcate, and less dentate behind." Some specimens from South India (Ootacamund, Cannanore and the Wynaad) are quite intermediate between this species and typical *L. rama* from Ceylon, other specimens from Ootacamund, the Pulni Hills and Travancore, are typical *L. rama*. In the outer Himalayas *L. myrrha* is rare in the west, but much commoner to the east, generally frequenting streams, and often settling (as does also *L. lepita*) at the end of a dead stick with folded wings, in which position it exactly resembles a dead leaf. It is a common species in Upper Tenasserim, Mr. Moore recording it from "Moulmein to Meetan, Hatsiega." A specimen in my collection from Sumatra hardly differs from typical Indian ones, the markings being ferruginous rather than ochreous only, and a little narrower.

593. Libythea rama, Moore.

L. rama, Moore, Proc. Zool. Soc. Lond., 1872, p. 556; idem, id., Lep. Cey., vol. i, p. 68, pl. xxxiii, figs. 2, 2 a (1881).

HABITAT: South India, Ceylon.

EXPANSE: 1'85 to 2'15 inches.

DESCRIPTION: "Differs from *L. myrrha* in being somewhat smaller, the *forewing* less falcated below the apex, the UPPERSIDE having the discoidal streak and continuous spot very narrow, and the two sets of subapical spots widely separated and ferruginous-white; the streak on the *hindwing* very narrow, short, and placed in the middle of the wing." (*Moore*, l. c. in Proc. Zool. Soc. Lond.)

Typical specimens from Ceylon, Travancore, the Anamalai and Pulni Hills, and some specimens from Ootacamund are quite distinct from *L. myrrha*, but other specimens from Ootacamund, Cannanore and the Wynaad are quite intermediate; *L. rama* appears to be constant in

Ceylon and in the extreme south of the peninsula, but in South India its markings gradually approximate to those of *L. myrrha* as its range extends northwards, till in the Nilgiris typical *L. myrrha* is met with. In Ceylon it is recorded from the "Central Provinces ; hills 4,000 to 6,000 feet, in forest lands during S.-W. Monsoon, May to October. Darts about and settles on the ground. Shy and not very easy to capture" (*Hutchison*). "Plentiful about 3,500 feet and upwards, on the roads and banks of same in vicinity of jungle" (*Mackwood*). "Kandy and Dickoya" (*Wade*).

594. **Libythea lepita,** Moore.

L. lepita, Moore, Horsfield and Moore. Cat. Lep. Mus. E. I. C., vol. i, p. 240, n. 519 (1857) ; id., Swinhoe, Proc. Zool. Soc. Lond., 1885, p. 130, n. 23 ; id., Doherty, Journ. A. S. B., vol. lv, pt. 2, p. 135, n. 196 (1886).

HABITAT : Himalayas, Assam.

EXPANSE : 1·8 to 2·1 inches.

DESCRIPTION : " Differs from *Libythea myrrha* in the ferruginous streak from base of *forewing* being divided into two portions, the first being within the discoidal cell, the second a round terminal spot beyond its extremity." (*Moore*, l. c.) Not infrequently the terminal spot is joined to the discoidal streak, but the upper and lower edges of this combined streak are always highly irregular, the cell portion being shaped just like a tent-peg, while the streak in *L. myrrha* is continuous, with even edges, so there is no difficulty in distinguishing them. Mr. Doherty remarks (l. c.) that "The prehensores [male anal clasping organs] are quite different from those of *L. myrrha*, from which species it seems perfectly distinct."

L. lepita occurs throughout the outer ranges of the Himalayas at moderate elevations, and there is a single specimen from Assam in the collection of the Indian Museum, Calcutta ; Colonel Swinhoe recorded it along with *L. myrrha*, from Bombay;[*] he informs me, however, that this was a mistake. I know of no other locality where it is found within our limits, but it is the nearest ally of the European *L. celtis*, Fuessly, and probably extends through the uplands of Persia and Asia Minor. I have always found it more abundant in individuals than *L. myrrha*.

595. **Libythea rohini,** Marshall. (PLATE XXIV, FIG. 114 ♀).

L. rohini, Marshall, Journ. A. S. B., vol. xlix, pt. 2, p. 248, n. 10 (1880).

HABITAT : Khasi Hills.

EXPANSE : 2·0 inches.

DESCRIPTION : "FEMALE. UPPERSIDE, *both wings* brown with pure white markings. *Forewing* with an oval spot filling the end of the cell, a large quadrate spot on the disc between the first and second median nervules, two spots coalescing one on each side of the lower discoidal nervule, and a spot near the costa divided into three portions by the subcostal nervules. *Hindwing* with a large square spot on the middle of the costa, a straight median band across the wing below the cell not reaching the inner or outer margins, and cut by the discoidal and three median nervules, and a small spot above between the subcostal nervules. All the spots and bands pure white." (*Marshall*, l. c.) UNDERSIDE, *both wings* paler. *Forewing* with the white markings as above, a pale ochreous streak filling the base of the cell, the apex and inner angle whitish, striated with brown. *Hindwing* with the quadrate costal spot and discal band of the upperside but less well-defined, the wing more or less whitish striated with brown. *Cilia* throughout more or less white. The MALE does not differ from the female.

"Taken near Shillong in May by [the late] Mr. J. P. Cock." (*Marshall*, l. c.)

The type specimen is in Major Marshall's collection, other specimens have been obtained in May and October by the late Mr. Cock and by Dr. E. R. Johnson near Shillong. The figure shows both upper and undersides of the female type specimen.

---

* Proc. Zool. Soc. Lond., 1885, p. 130, nos. 43, 44.

Subfamily II.—NEMEOBIINÆ, Bates. (PLATE XXIV).

Nemeobiinæ, Bates, Journ. Linn. Soc., Zoology, vol. ix, pp. 370, 410 (1867, 1868); id., Distant, Rhop. Malay., p. 186 (1883); *Erycinidæ*, Westwood, Gen. Diurn. Lep., vol. ii, p. 415 (1851); *Erycininæ*, Moore, Lep. Cey., vol. i, p. 68 (1881).

"BODY, generally slender. Insects of small size. HEAD, small, not or scarcely tufted in front. *Eyes*, almost always naked. *Antennæ*, generally short and slender, occasionally furnished with short scaly hairs at the ends of the joints. *Palpi*, generally extremely small and slender, scarcely advanced in front of the face as seen from above; the last joint nearly naked. *Wings*, variable in form, colour, and markings, but not [seldom?] ornamented with ocellated spots; generally of large size, in proportion to the size of the body. FOREWING, generally with only three branches to the *subcostal nervure* [always four in the Indian genera excluding the terminal portion]; the first and second arising before the extremity of the discoidal cell, and the third far beyond the cell; the *upper disco-cellular nervule* obliterated; the *upper discoidal* nervule arising at or near the origin of the second subcostal nervule; *discoidal cell* closed by very slender middle and lower disco-cellular nervules, only visible on denuding the wings of its scales. HINDWING, very variable in form; the *discoidal cell* closed by very slender upper and lower disco-cellular nervules; *abdominal margin* forming a slight gutter for the reception of the abdomen. FORELEGS, small and slender; those of the *male* smaller than those of the female, brush-like; the tarsal portion forming an exarticulate mass, destitute of claws at the tip. Of the *female* longer, slender, scaly; *tarsus* articulated, with the joints longer and more distinct than in the *Nymphalinæ* and *Satyrinæ*. HINDLEGS, slender, scaly; spurs short; terminal claws very minute, scarcely exserted."

"LARVA short (but scarcely onisciform*), with tufts of short hairs, or lateral fleshy appendages; the segment behind the head in some species furnished with a pair of erect spines. PUPA short, not angulated, setose, attached by a thread across the body; obtuse at each extremity."

"This is an extensive subfamily of delicately-formed butterflies, chiefly found in Tropical America, although some of the aberrant forms are natives of Africa and Asia, and one even inhabits Europe. They are of small size, and extremely varied in their forms, representatives of many of the remarkable forms of other families occurring amongst the species of the present subfamily. Thus, some of them resemble the tailed species of *Papilioninæ* and *Nymphalinæ*; others the elongated-winged *Heliconiinæ*; others the blue and copper-coloured species of *Lycænidæ*; and some the dusky and spotted *Hesperiidæ*. Structurally, these insects are distinguished from the preceding by the more delicate form of their bodies, the more varied style of their markings, and the short contracted caterpillars and chrysalides, the latter being girt across the body. The forewing appears generally to possess only three branches to the subcostal nervure; the antennæ are very slender, and the palpi very short, although in a few species they are almost as long as in the *Libythæinæ*." (*Westwood*, l. c.)

Mr. Doherty† states that the egg of the subfamily *Nemeobiinæ* is "smooth, prickly or radiate with minute flattened ribs, not so high as wide, opaque, dome-shaped," and that it probably shows an affinity with the *Papilionidæ* and *Hesperiidæ*, and he goes on (p. 110) to define it more particularly as follows:—"Egg not so high as wide, smooth, granulate, prickly or hairy, neither reticulate nor radiate in the few genera examined by me." He places the *Erycinidæ*

---

* ONISCIFORM, shaped like a wood-louse, from *oniscus*, a wood-louse.

† Journ. A. S. B., vol. lv, pt 2, p. 108 (1886).

(= *Nemeobiina*) after the *Lycænidæ* and before the *Libythæinæ*. The larvæ and pupæ as far as known are strikingly like those of the next family *Lycænidæ*, the larva being almost onisciform, and the pupa girt across the middle by a thread as well as attached by the tail. In the perfect insect the palpi are usually exceedingly small, the neuration is very similar to that obtaining in the previous subfamily and in the *Nymphalidæ*; the forelegs however show the affinity of the *Nemeobiinæ* with the *Lycænidæ*, they are brush-like and imperfect in the male, perfect in the female.

Five genera are included within our limits; they present several peculiarities, which are detailed further on, though all the species agree in being small, the largest (*A. fylla*) being under two inches and a half in expanse, most of the remainder being less than two inches. All the Indian genera differ from the family *Nymphalidæ* and the subfamily *Libythæinæ* in the subcostal nervure of the hindwing giving off its branch *after* the end of the cell instead of before its end, except in two species in the genus *Dodona*. This character appears to me to be a very important one, which has not hitherto been noticed or recognized. The costal nervure of that wing is invariably very short also, not extending beyond the middle of the costa, whereas in *Libythea* and all the genera of the *Nymphalinæ* except most species of *Neptis*, it extends to the apex of the wing.

In America most of the species of this subfamily and of the two following (the latter being wholly American) have the habit of resting with wide outspread wings on the underside of leaves, like *Cyrestis*, *Stibochiona*, and many species of *Hesperiidæ*, but some of the American and all the Indian species as far as known to me in the field rest on the upperside of the leaves (over which they frequently walk) with half-expanded wings; and all have an extremely rapid flight, so fast indeed as to be very difficult to follow with the eye, but seldom for more than a few yards, when they settle again. Some species, *Zemeros flegyas* for instance, are enormously abundant in individuals where they occur.

Key to the Indian Genera of NEMEOBIINÆ.

A. Lower disco-cellular nervule of hindwing joined to the median nervure at the point where the second and third median nervules are given off.
XC.—ZEMEROS.

B. Lower disco-cellular nervule of hindwing joined to the median nervure after the point where the second median nervule is given off.

    a. Hindwing lengthened (longer than broad), with an anal lobe and often with a fine tail in addition.
XCI.—DODONA.

    b. Hindwing with anal angle rounded, no anal lobe.

        a¹. Ground-colour of the wings pure white, with a broad outer fuscous border.
XCII.—STIBOGES.

        b¹. Ground-colour of the wings plum-colour or dark brown.

            a². Underside marked with bluish-silvery prominent spots.
XCIII.—TAXILA.

            b². Underside not marked with bluish-silvery spots.
XCIV.—ABISARA.

The first genus of the subfamily, *Zemeros*, is easily distinguished, as the lower disco-cellular nervule of the hindwing joins the median nervure at the point where the second and third median nervules are given off; in the other Indian genera it always meets the median nervure some little distance after the point where the second median nervule is emitted. In colouration the Indian species of *Zemeros* is dark maroon or plum-colour, with numerous whitish spots spread over both surfaces. The next genus, *Dodona*, always possesses an anal lobe to the hindwing, which distinguishes it at once from all the other genera, there is often a fine tail in addition. The colouration is dark brown or fuscous, with numerous spots, often arranged in bands. The genus *Laxita*, which has not as yet been recorded from India, though three species occur in the Malay peninsula, is abundantly distinct, in that the male has the inner margin of the forewing highly convex, covering a glandular patch of differently-formed scales placed on a large shining patch on the upperside of the hindwing below the costa, almost exactly resembling a similar character in the male of *Myrelaus minous*. In both sexes also the disco-cellular nervules of the hindwing are quite differently placed to those in the other Indian genera, being almost at right angles to the subcostal and median nervures. They are also more brilliantly coloured on the upperside than any of the other Indian species of the subfamily. In the other three Indian genera, *Stiboges*, *Taxila*, and *Abisara*, I can find no constant structural feature by which to separate them. *Stiboges* has the lower disco-cellular nervule of the hindwing much longer than the upper, but so also have several species of *Abisara*, but the colouration of the former is very different, the ground-colour being pure semi-transparent white, with a broad outer fuscous border, which extends along the costa of the forewing. *Taxila* can also be easily distinguished by its colouration and markings, the upperside in the male is almost uniformly coloured, being dark plum, blackish or dark purplish-brown, the underside bright reddish-brown, with numerous brilliant bluish-silvery spots inwardly defined with black. The outer margin of the wings of the species of *Taxila* and of *Stiboges* is nearly even and entire, being slightly scalloped, the hindwing in *Taxila* shows a more or less pronounced tendency to a quadrate outline, in *Stiboges* it is regularly convex. The last genus, *Abisara*, has the lower half of the outer margin of the hindwing produced between the third median nervule and the anal angle; it contains two groups, the first group, which may be divided into two subgroups, has the disco-cellular nervules of the hindwing of unequal length, the upper one being much the shorter, the first subgroup (*A. fylla*) has the colouration deep brown, with an oblique pale band across the forewing, the hindwing less produced between the second and third median nervules; the second subgroup (*A. neophron* and allied species) also has the oblique pale band across the forewing, the colouration is brown or black, the produced portion of the hindwing terminating in a long tail between the second and third median nervules; the second group (*A. echerius* and allies) has the disco-cellular nervules of the hindwing of equal length, the colouration is deep plum, with the produced outer margin of the hindwing abruptly terminating in a blunt tooth at the third median nervule.

Genus 90.—ZEMEROS, Boisduval. (PLATE XXIV).

Zemeros, Boisduval, Sp. Gén., vol. i, pl. xxi, fig. 5 (1836) ; id., Westwood, Gen. Diurn. Lep., vol. ii, p. 418 (1851) ; id., Distant, Rhop. Malay., p. 187 (1883) ; *Hamanumida* (part), Hübner, Verz. bek. Schmett., p. 18 (1816).

"BODY, small, slender : *wings*, large, irregular along the [outer] margins ; disc marked with a number of small white dots. *Head*, small, very finely hairy, front with a small truncated tuft ; *eyes*, small, naked ; *palpi*, very minute, almost horizontal, not visible from above, the tip not reaching more than the level of one-fourth of the height of the eyes, rather thickly clothed beneath with hairs, the terminal joint not being visible, except on denuding the palpus ; *antennæ*, short, and very slender, not more than half the length of the forewing, terminated by a short but distinct club, rather slender, obtuse at the tip, annulations very short, and finely ringed with white at the tip. THORAX, rather large, oval ; tippets truncate in front, finely hairy. ABDOMEN, small, slender, scarcely more than half the length of the hindwing. FOREWING, large, broadly triangular ; *costal margin* slightly arched ; *apex* slightly acute in the male, more obtuse in the female ; *outer margin* irregularly scalloped, being more convex in the female than in the male ; *inner margin* not so long as the outer. *Costal nervure* reaching to the middle of the costa ; *subcostal* nervure with four simple free branches, the first and second arising near together, a little before the anterior extremity of the discoidal cell, third and fourth branches arising beyond the cell, at about the same distance apart as occurs between the extremity of the cell and the third branch, the space between the fourth branch and the apex of the wing being still longer ; *upper disco-cellular* nervule obsolete, *middle* and *lower* disco-cellulars of about equal length, slender, forming a transverse arch, the lower united to the third median nervule quite close to [just beyond] its origin ; *upper discoidal* nervule arising simultaneously with the middle disco-cellular a little beyond the middle of the wing, the space between the *first* and *second median* nervules considerably elongated. HINDWING, irregularly oval ; the *outer margin* irregularly scalloped, and somewhat truncate from the anal angle to the extremity of the third median nervule ; *costal nervure* not extending beyond the middle of the costa ; *subcostal* nervure arising near the body, but curved at its base, being deflexed opposite the præcostal nervure, branching at a considerable distance from the base [beyond the end of the cell], the branch extending to the upper end of the first or outer scallop ; *upper disco-cellular nervule* short, arising a little nearer the body than the branch of the subcostal, oblique ; *lower* disco-cellular oblique, slightly longer than the upper, uniting with the median nervure exactly opposite the base of the third branch, which extends to the strongest of the angles formed by the scallops of the margin ; *abdominal margin* of the wing forming a very slight gutter for the reception of the abdomen. FORELEGS, of the *male* very small, and densely clothed with hairs ; *tarsus* simple. Of the *female* more than twice the length of those of the male, slender, but well clothed with scales, so as to conceal the joints of the tarsus, which is about equal in length to the tibia, and is terminated by two small, distinct, very slender claws. MIDDLE and HINDLEGS, slender, and rather short, clothed with fine scales ; *femur* of the middle pair considerably elongated, being as long as the tibia and half the tarsus; *tarsus* of the hind pair rather longer than the tibia ; tibial spurs very slender, short, and acute; *tarsus* armed beneath with very fine, short, acute setæ." (*Westwood*, l. c.)

Zemeros is a genus of but small extent, three species only having been described, and limited distribution. Only one species (*Z. flegyas*) occurs within our limits ; it inhabits the Himalayas, Assam, Tenasserim, Java, and China ; the other two (*Z. albipunctata* and *Z. emesoides*) are found in the Malay Peninsula, Sumatra, and Borneo. *Z. flegyas* and *Z. albipunctata* are rich maroon above with black streaks and white spots placed between the veins. *Z. emesoides* is of somewhat different aspect, the outer margins of the wings are almost entire, the colouration of the upperside is yellow, there are no white spots, but the black streaks are abbreviated and developed into seven even bands across both wings.

596. Zemeros flegyas, Cramer. (PLATE XXIV, FIG. 115 ♂).

Papilio flegyas, Cramer, Pap. Ex., vol. iii, pl. cclxxx, figs. E, F (1780) : *Zemeros flegyas,* Double-day, Hewitson, Gen. Diurn. Lep., vol. ii, p. 410, pl. lxix, fig. 5 (1851) : id., Horsfield and Moore, Cat. Lep. Mus. E. I. C., vol. i, p. 242, n. 520 (1857) ; *Z. phlegyas,* Doherty, Journ. A. S. B., vol. lv, pl. 2, p. 134, n. 194 (1886) : *Papilio allica,* Fabricius, Mant. Ins., vol. ii, p. 52, n. 510 (1787) ; idem, id., Ent. Syst., vol. iii, pt i, p. 244, n. 761 (1793) ; id., Donovan, Ins. India, pl. xxxvii, fig 2 (1800) ; *Hamanumida allica,* Hübner, Verz. bek. Schmett., p. 18, n. 105 (1816) ; *Erycina allica,* Godart, Enc. Méth., vol. ix, p 566, n. 13 (1823) ; *Zemeros allica,* Boisduval, Sp. Gén., vol. i, pl. xxi, fig. 5 (1836).

HABITAT : Himalayas, Assam, Cachar, Sylhet, Burma, Java, China (*Westwood*).

EXPANSE : 1·5 to 1·8 inches.

DESCRIPTION : MALE. UPPERSIDE, *both wings* rich maroon ; each interspace bearing a black streak reaching nearly to the margin, twice interrupted, and each of the sections into which it is divided marked by a white spot at its outer end, those of the inner and outer sections prominent, sharply defined with black, those of the middle section obscure; the submedian interspace bearing two such streaks ; the outer white spots forming a regular submarginal series, the inner spots forming an irregular series on the middle of the wing, of which that on the upper median interspace is out of line, being much nearer the margin. *Forewing* with a small white spot in the middle of the cell, and a longer one below it in the submedian interspace. *Hindwing* with a white streak in the cell, and one or two white spots below it. UNDERSIDE paler, all the markings clearer, the black streaks much reduced, the apices of the marginal series marked with pale ochreous. *Hindwing* with some small basal white spots. *Cilia* throughout black, marked with white on the interspaces. FEMALE paler, all the markings less distinct, the white spots sullied.

Z. *flegyas* is a somewhat variable species even in the same locality, in some Sikkim examples the ground-colour is much duller than in typical specimens, all the markings obscure, on the underside sometimes with three large pale ochreous spots near the apex of the forewing, the middle one the largest, divided by the subcostal nervure and upper discoidal nervule. It is a widely distributed species, occurring in the Himalayas from Masuri eastwards as far as Upper Assam, in Sylhet, Cachar, and Tenasserim, reappearing in Java ; it is also recorded from China. In the Malay Peninsula it is replaced by the closely-allied *Z. albipunctata*, * which occurs also in Sumatra and Borneo.

The figure shows both sides of a male specimen from Sikkim in the Indian Museum, Calcutta.

Z. emesoides occurs also in the Malay Peninsula and Borneo, and differs entirely from *Z. flegyas* and *Z. albipunctata*. The ground-colour is ochraceous, it has no white spots, and the black markings assume the form of even black bands crossing both wings at regular intervals. The description is appended. †

Genus 91.—DODONA, Hewitson. (PLATE XXIV).

Dodona, Hewitson, Ex. Butt., vol. ii, p. 91 (1861).

" Resembles *Nemeobius* and *Melitæa* in colouring, with the hindwing of the male protruded at the anal angle ; the *antennæ distinctly clubbed*." (*Hewitson*, l. c.)

In neuration *Dodona* differs only from *Zemeros* in the lower disco-cellular nervule of the hindwing joining the median nervure some little distance beyond the point where the second median nervule is given off. FOREWING, evenly triangular, the *inner margin* being usually equal in length to the outer, the *costa* very slightly arched, the *outer margin* even, sometimes slightly convex, sometimes almost straight, sometimes slightly concave. HINDWING, with the *outer margin* usually more or less scalloped, sometimes quite even, sometimes angled at the end of the third median nervule, the *anal angle* always produced into a lobe, often with a long fine tail at the end of the submedian nervure. *Palpi*, variable, usually much longer than in *Zemeros ; antennæ*, with a distinct oval club. Sexes generally alike.

Dodona is a small, compact, and well-marked genus, containing at present eight species, all of which are included within our limits ; they occur in the Himalayas, Assam, and Sylhet, with two species from Burma. One species, *D. durga*, is in markings something like the only European species in this subfamily, *Nemeobius lucina*, Linnæus ; all of them have the ground-colour of the upperside dark brown or fuscous, all but three with orange or ochreous spots or bands in both sexes ; in one of these latter the female has a white bar on the forewing only, all the markings of the male being orange, and in the remaining two species with a broad white band across the disc of both wings with white spots beyond. The genus is divisible into two distinct groups, in one of which the anal lobe of the hindwing bears a fine tail outwardly, the other group lacks this feature. The genus is remarkable in having the palpi of very different length, these are very long in *D. durga* and *D. dipæa*, shorter in *D. longicaudata*, shorter still in *D. adonira* and *D. eugenes*, shortest of all in *D. ouida* and *D. egeon*. The genus is still further aberrant in including two species which alone in the subfamily have the subcostal nervure of the hindwing branching *before* the end of the cell. These species are *D. dipæa* and *D. longicaudata*, and not improbably this is the case also in *D. deodata*, which I have not seen. These two species belong to distinct groups, the former having no tail to the hindwing, the latter with a very long one.

---

* *Zemeros albipunctata*, Butler, Cist. Ent., vol. i, p. 156 (1874) ; idem, id., Trans. Linn. Soc., Zoology, second series, vol. i, p. 545, n. 2, pl. lxix, fig. 10, *male* (1877) ; idem, id., Distant, Rhop. Malay., p. 187, n. 1, pl. xviii, fig. 12, *female* (1883) HABITAT : Malay Peninsula, Sumatra. Borneo. EXPANSE : 1'4 to 1'7 inches DESCRIPTION : " Similar in form and colours to *Z. flegyas*, excepting that it is rather darker, and that there are six decreasing well-defined white spots in the *forewing* forming an inner submarginal series, and that none of the black spots on the basal area above or below are white-pupilled " (*Butler*, l. c. in Cist. Ent.)

There is a pair of this species from Perak in the Indian Museum, Calcutta. The female is paler than the male, the forewing more rounded at the apex, as is also the outer margin

† *Zemeros emesoides*, Felder, Wien. Ent. Monatsch., vol. iv, p. 396, n. 10 (1860) ; idem, id., Reise Novara, Lep., vol. ii, p. 289, n. 373, pl. xxxvi, figs. 9—11, *male* and *female* (1865) ; id., Druce, Proc. Zool. Soc. Lond., 1873, p. 347, n. 1 ; id., Distant, Rhop. Malay., p. 188, n. 2, pl. xviii, figs. 3, *male* ; 4, *female* (1883) ; *Z. emesoides*, Kirby, Syn. Cat. Diurn. Lep., p. 285 (1871). HABITAT : Malay Peninsula, Borneo. EXPANSE : 1'1 to 1'7 inches DESCRIPTION : " Wings broad, hindwing somewhat rounded Upperside, both wings in the male ferruginous, in the female dilute fulvous, underside in both sexes paler, both sides with five parallel subdiffuse fuscous bands, and a curved submarginal black streak

" From *Z. flegyas*, Cramer, best distinguished by the shape of the hindwing, in appearance similar to *Emesis* [an American genus of the subfamily *Lemoniinæ*]. (*Felder*, l. c. in Wien Ent Monatsch.)

" MALE. Upperside, *both wings* reddish-ochraceous, and crossed by four broad dark fasciæ, the outer one strongly curved and followed by a submarginal narrow waved fascia of the same colour, the *cilia* also fuscous. *Forewing* with a short basal oblique fascia extending partly through cell. *Hindwing* with a minute and obscure basal fascia. Underside, *both wings* as above, but paler. *Body* and *legs* more or less concolorous with wings. *Antennæ* fuscous, narrowly and obscurely annulated with greyish, but more distinctly so beneath than above, their apices pale ochraceous. FEMALE. Paler in hue than the male, and with the submarginal fascia a little broader." (*Distant*, l. c.)

There is a single of this species from Perak in the Indian Museum, Calcutta.

Key to the species of Dodona.

A. Anal lobe of hindwing not furnished with a tail.
    a Upperside, both wings in both sexes with numerous ochreous or orange spots.
        a¹. Underside with the spots large and pale yellow throughout.
            597. D, DURGA, Western Himalayas.
        b¹. Underside, both wings with many of the spots silvery, spots throughout smaller and less conspicuous.
            598. D, DIPŒA, Himalayas, Upper Burma.
    b Male, upperside, forewing with three orange bands.
        a¹. Underside ferruginous, forewing with some violascent spots at the apex ; hindwing with two discal violascent bands, a costal spot, and two spots at the apex. Female with a single oblique broad white band across the forewing only.
            599. D, OVIDA, Himalayas, Assam.
        b¹. Underside, both wings pale clear yellow without spots, crossed by several straight narrow black lines. Sexes alike.
            600. D, ADONIRA, Sikkim, Bhutan.
    c. Upperside, both wings with the basal half white, crossed near the base by three diffused brown bands.
            601. D, DIPŒATA, Moulmein.
B Anal lobe of hindwing furnished outwardly with a narrow tail.
    a. Upperside, both wings dark brown, with a broad white discal band.
            602. D, LONGICAUDATA, Khasi Hills.
    b. Upperside, forewing with numerous large tawny spots, hindwing almost entirely tawny.
            603. D, EGEON, Nepal, Sikkim, Sylhet.
    c. Upperside, forewing with small ochreous-white spots, hindwing almost entirely dark brown.
            604. D, EUGENES, Himalayas, Assam.

597. Dodona durga, Kollar.

Melitæa durga, Kollar, Hügel's Kashmir, vol. iv, pt. 2, p. 441, n. 1, pl. xiii, figs. 3, 4 (1848) ; *Taxila durga*, Westwood, Gen. Diurn Lep., vol. ii, p. 422, n. 1 (1851) ; *Dodona durga*, Doherty, Journ. A. S. B., vol. lv, pt. 2, p 134, n. 190 (1886).

HABITAT : Outer ranges of the Western Himalayas.

EXPANSE : 1·4 to 1·8 inches.

DESCRIPTION : MALE. UPPERSIDE, *both wings* fuscous, with numerous ochreous spots. *Forewing* with a streak across the cell, continued to the submedian nervure, another at its end, a larger one beyond from the costa to the third median nervule, two spots near the bases of the median interspaces, another in the submedian interspace beyond the lower of these two latter spots, two pairs of spots below the costa divided by the subcostal nervure, a pair of spots placed beneath and between them divided by the lower discoidal nervule, another pair placed outwardly and beneath these latter divided by the second median nervule, another pair at the anal angle divided by the submedian nervure, five linear spots on the margin from the upper discoidal nervule to the submedian nervure. *Hindwing* with the disco-cellulars marked with an ochreous line, an irregular discal series of spots, a submarginal and marginal linear series which coalesce above the anal lobe. UNDERSIDE, *both wings* dark ochreous. *Forewing* with the base and inner margin fuscous, the base of the costa ochreous, also the base of the cell enclosing a black spot, other markings as above, except that the outer spots especially towards the anal angle are of a deep orange. *Hindwing* with all the veins more or less ochreous on the basal half, a short basal ochreous streak from the costa, another subbasal from the costa to the submedian fold, where it meets a fine ochreous line defining the fold, the latter joined at the base to another fine line on the submedian nervure, a short ochreous bar defining the disco-cellular nervules ; a somewhat broad ochreous band from the second median nervure to the submedian nervure above the anal lobe, then recurved and continued up the abdominal margin to the base of the wing, inwardly defined with black, the extreme edge of the abdominal margin ochreous, two short bands on the costa, the inner one defined with black, with another placed beneath and between them from the second subcostal to the second median nervure, the submarginal macular band as above but widened out anteriorly and enclosing two black spots divided by the discoidal nervule, marginal band as above, the anal lobe and a spot beyond black crowned with orange. *Cilia* white, tipped with black at the ends of the veins throughout. FEMALE larger, wings broader, outer margin of forewing more convex, apex less produced, markings similar throughout.

D. durga is a very common species all over the outer ranges of the Western Himalayas as far west as Murree and Kashmir, on the east Mr. Doherty records it as occurring in " Kumaon generally, 2,500 to 8,000 feet."

598. Dodona dipœa, Hewitson. (PLATE XXIV, FIG. 116 ♂).

D. dipœa, Hewitson, Ex. Butt., vol. iii, *Dodona* pl. 1, fig. 3 (1866).

HABITAT : Masuri, Nepal, Sikkim, Upper Burma.

EXPANSE : 1·55 to 1·9 inches.

DESCRIPTION : " MALE. UPPERSIDE, *both wings* dark brown. *Forewing* with macular bands and spots rufous and white. *Hindwing* with a short rufous band near the middle, and two submarginal bands of the same colour. UNDERSIDE, *both wings* rufous-brown. *Forewing* as above. *Hindwing* crossed near the base and inner margin by three bands of paler colour, the third silvery near its base : a silver spot on the middle of the costal margin, a band of pale brown below it which curves upwards towards the inner margin, and bordered inwardly with black : beyond the middle a short band of white also bordered inwardly with black, and below it a band of black which bends upwards to the inner margin when it reaches the anal lobe : two black spots bordered above and below with white, and a submarginal band of brown bordered on each side with white : the lobe black bordered with white." (*Hewitson*, l. c.) FEMALE. Larger than the male, the apex of the forewing less pointed, the outer margin convex instead of straight. UPPERSIDE, *both wings* with the markings rather more prominent. UNDERSIDE marked exactly as in the male.

" I have hesitated before describing this as a species distinct from *D. egeon* ; they are alike on the upperside, but whilst the underside of the hindwing of *D. egeon* is crossed by broad bands of silvery white without any margin, this species has narrow bands of white margined with black." (*Hewitson*, l. c.)

D. dipœa is abundantly distinct from *D. egeon*, not only do the differences Hewitson points out exist, but *D. egeon* has the markings of the upperside tawny, that colour being the predominating one on the hindwing, and it has also a tail in addition to the anal lobe. *D. dipœa* is really more closely allied to *D. eugenes*, but *D. eugenes* has a tail, and the silvery bands of the underside of the hindwing are twice as broad as in *D. dipœa*. The markings of *D. dipœa* are very similar in character to those of *D. durga*, they are all much reduced however, and some altogether wanting. The subcostal nervure of the hindwing branches *before* the end of the cell.

D. dipœa has a limited range as far as is known. It occurs in Masuri, Nepal, and is somewhat common in Sikkim in October and November at about 6,000 feet elevation.

The figure shows both sides of a male Sikkim example in the Indian Museum, Calcutta.

There are two male specimens of a *Dodona* allied to *D. dipœa* in the Indian Museum, Calcutta, obtained by the Yunan Expedition in Upper Burma (probably). They differ on the underside from Sikkim specimens of *D. dipœa* in having the ground-colour clear ochreous instead of dark brown, the markings are similar in character, though smaller throughout, but are pure white instead of ochreous and silvery, and the anal lobe of the hindwing divided into two by a white line through its middle. It may be a local race of *D. dipœa*, or it may be quite a distinct species, but I do not like to name it without knowing its habitat with more certainty.

599. Dodona ouida, Moore.

D. ouida, Moore, Proc. Zool. Soc. Lond., 1865, p. 771 : id., Hewitson, Ex. Butt., vol. iii, *Dodona* pl. 1, figs. 4, 5, *male* ; 6, *female* (1866) ; *Taxila ovato*, Boisduval MS., Horsfield and Moore, Cat. Lep. Mus. E. I. C., vol. 1, p. 243, n. 524 (1857).

HABITAT : Himalayas, Assam.

EXPANSE : 1·7 to 2·1 inches.

DESCRIPTION : " MALE. UPPERSIDE, *both wings* brownish black. *Forewing* with three transverse discal equidistant ferruginous bands, the medial one broadest, the first two oblique ; two white dots at apex. *Hindwing* with transverse discal and two narrow marginal ferruginous bands ; anal lobe with a white bar and border. UNDERSIDE dark ferruginous. *Forewing* with the transverse bands less defined, yellow, terminating on the costal margin in white spots ; two apical white spots. *Hindwing* with bluish basal and purplish medial transverse discal interrupted bands, the latter with an inner border of brown, each having a white spot on the costal margin, that of the latter with a black inner border ; two narrow marginal brown bands, two black purple-bordered dots at anterior angle, and black and white lines bordering the black lobe. FEMALE. UPPERSIDE, *both wings* dull fuliginous-brown, somewhat black apically. *Forewing* with medial broad transverse discal oblique white band, and an outer or submarginal narrow interrupted ferruginous-white line ; two apical dots white. *Hindwing* with two marginal pale brown lines, terminated at the anterior angle with two pale-bordered black spots ; anal lobe black. UNDERSIDE as in male." (*Moore*, l. c.) The outer margin of both wings is entire, not in the least scalloped.

D. ouida is a widely-distributed species, occurring at Masuri, in Sikkim, Bhutan, and eastwards to Upper Assam. The sexes are more strongly differentiated than in any other species of the genus, the male has three ferruginous bands on the forewing, the outer one decidedly macular ; the female has one only, which is white.

600. Dodona adonira, Hewitson.

D. *adonira*, Hewitson, Ex. Butt., vol. iii, *Dodona* pl. i, figs. 1, 2, *male* (1866) ; id., de Nicéville, Journ. A. S. B., vol. lii, pt. 2, p. 95, n. 220 (1883) ; *Taxila fatua*, Boisduval MS., Horsfield and Moore, Cat. Lep. Mus. E. I. C., vol. i, p. 245, n. 523 (1857).

HABITAT : Sikkim, Bhutan.

EXPANSE : 1·5 to 1·8 inches.

DESCRIPTION : " MALE. UPPERSIDE, *both wings* dark brown, paler near the base. *Forewing* crossed transversely by three parallel equidistant rufous bands [the two inner ones broadly united near the inner margin]. *Hindwing* lobed at the anal angle : crossed obliquely by four narrower bands of the same colour [the first, second and fourth long, uniting at the anal lobe, the third short, not extending below the second median nervure] ; the anal lobe marked by two spots of black : rufous above the lobe and spotted with black. UNDERSIDE, *both wings* orange-yellow with the outer margins dark brown ; crossed by five narrow dark brown bands, broken where the wings meet. *Forewing* with a sixth short band beyond the third. *Hindwing* with a sixth and seventh band near the inner margin : orange near the anal lobe and marked with several black spots." (*Hewitson*, l. c.) FEMALE. UPPERSIDE, *forewing* with the rufous bands broader and paler, with a marginal apical series of five small round rufous spots. *Hindwing* with the black spots above the anal lobe in the male, amalgamated with the bands of the ground-colour crossing the wing. UNDERSIDE as in the male.

D. adonira is a very beautiful and distinct species. The upperside is very similar to that of *D. ouida* male, but the underside is pale yellow, crossed by numerous narrow clearly-defined dark brown bands, the hindwing lacking the two round black spots on the outer margin, divided by the discoidal nervule, which occur in all the other species of the genus except *D. longicaudata*. It is a very rare species also with a very limited range, having only been recorded from Sikkim and Bhutan.

601. Dodona deodata, Hewitson.

D. *deodata*, Hewitson, Ent. Month. Mag., vol. xiii, p 151 (1876) ; idem, id., Desc. Lep. coll. Atkinson, p. 3, pl. 1, fig. 1 (1879).

HABITAT : Moulmein.

EXPANSE : 1·7 inches.

DESCRIPTION : "UPPERSIDE, *both wings* white, crossed near the base and parallel to the inner margin [body?] by three bands of brown. *Forewing* with the outer half dark brown, marked by ten white spots; four in a band from the costal margin to the anal angle, and two bands of three spots each near the apex. *Hindwing* with the outer margin broadly brown, traversed by two bands of white spots. UNDERSIDE as above, except that several of the small white spots, near the apex of the *forewing*, meet and form a band; that there are two linear white spots near the anal angle, and a linear band leading to two black spots near the outer margin of the *hindwing*; and that there is a lobe at the anal angle as in the other species, bordered above by orange-yellow, marked by two black spots." (*Hewitson*, l. c. in Ent. Month. Mag.)

This species, except from the descriptions and figure published, is unknown to me, and the exact locality from whence it was obtained seems doubtful, as it is unlikely that a *Dodona* should be found so far south at the sea level. It is apparently nearest allied to *D. longicaudata*, but has much more white on the upperside, and also lacks the tail to the hindwing. The anal lobe as shown in the figure is of very unusual form; it appears to be divided into two short points. Mr. Moore appears to have edited Hewitson's original description when republishing it in the "Descriptions of New Indian Lepidopterous Insects from the collection of the late Mr. W. S. Atkinson," and as this revised description applies better to the figure (apparently a very rough one) of the species, I give it below as a foot note.*

602. **Dodona longicaudata**, de N. (PLATE XXIV, FIG. 117 ♂).

D. longicaudata, de Nicéville, Proc. A. S. B., 1881. p. 121.

HABITAT: Shillong (July and November).

EXPANSE: 1·8 inches.

DESCRIPTION: "MALE. UPPERSIDE, *both wings* deep shining brown. *Forewing* crossed before the middle by a broad white band which does not quite reach the costa, being narrowest at that point and divided by the nervules into two small spots; this band has its inner margin straight, its outer margin evenly convex; a submarginal series of six white spots placed irregularly; an indistinct marginal series of linear spots. *Hindwing* with the white band of the forewing continued in a wedge-shaped figure across the disc of the wing, ending in a point just below the first median nervule; abdominal area paler, with an indistinct white band from the base, and another short transverse one above the anal angle; incomplete submarginal and marginal bands of white linear spots; anal lobe black, encircled with a white line and thickly irrorated with white scales. *Tail* long, black; tip and cilia white. UNDERSIDE, *both wings* rich bright brown, crossed by several silvery-white bands. *Forewing* with narrow basal and subbasal bands, then a broad median band coincident with the band on the upperside, but reaching the costa; then a short narrow costal band beyond; then a very irregular broad band which is broken up into spots on the inner side below its middle; and lastly a marginal series of seven spots, the two upper ones rounded and out of line, the rest increasing, linear; the ground-colour near the outer angle becoming darker and almost forming two dark brown spots. *Hindwing* with the two basal and broad median bands as in the forewing, but all meeting above the anal angle, at which point they are joined by two other white bands traversing the abdominal area; there is also a fourth band from the costa, short, narrow, submarginal, reaching the third median nervule; between which and the broad median band there is another narrow white line not reaching the costa, in continuation of which is an orange fascia terminating on the abdominal margin in a black linear spot, and bearing two black rounded spots at its upper extremity; submarginal and marginal white lines; anal lobe jet-black,

---

* "UPPERSIDE, *both wings* brown, crossed near the middle by a broad common band of white. *Forewing* with the base pale rufous-brown crossed by a band of paler colour; the outer half dark brown marked by ten [eleven in the figure] white spots: four [five] in a band from the costal margin to the anal angle, and two bands of three spots each, near the apex. *Hindwing* with the inner margin broadly rufous-brown, crossed by a band of paler colour, the outer margin dark brown, traversed by two bands of white spots. UNDERSIDE as above, except that several of the small white spots, near the apex of the *forewing*, meet and form a band, that there is a submarginal white line, and two white spots near the anal angle, and a linear band leading to two black spots near the outer margin of the *hindwing*, and that the lobe at the anal angle is bordered above with orange-yellow marked by two black spots."

surmounted by a black white-irrorated space ending in a black spot on the abdominal margin, which space is divided from the lobe by a white line. *Cilia* of the forewing brown, except a small portion near the inner angle, of the hindwing alternately brown and white. *Body* above deep brown, with a somewhat rufous collar ; beneath white, with a black median abdominal line. *Forelegs* pure white, *hindlegs* with tibiæ and tarsi ochraceous. *Antennæ* black, annulated with white."

"This species seems nearest allied to *D. deodata*, from which it may be readily distinguished on the upperside in having only one median white band, being in fact altogether a much darker insect. It is remarkable for the length of its tails which are quite twice as long as those of *D. egeon*, which has them the next longest in the genus." (*de Nicéville*, l. c.) The type specimen is deposited in the Indian Museum, Calcutta, and from it the figure is taken, showing both sides ; there is another male taken in the same locality in Major Marshall's collection, which differs in slight details from the type specimen, but the species is too well-marked to be mistaken. In this species, as in *D. dipæa*, the subcostal nervure of the hindwing bifurcates *before* the end of the cell.

603. Dodona egeon, Doubleday, Hewitson.

Taxila egeon, Doubleday, Hewitson, Gen. Diurn. Lep., vol. ii. p. 422, n. 2, pl. lxix, fig. 2 (1851).

HABITAT : Nepal, Sikkim, Sylhet.

EXPANSE : 1·85 to 2·05 inches.

DESCRIPTION : MALE. UPPERSIDE, *forewing* fuscous, the basal area thickly irrorated with tawny ; markings tawny. A broad band towards the end of the cell extending to the inner margin, then curved outwards and upwards and joining a large quadrate spot in the submedian interspace and another in the interspace above ; a large quadrate spot just beyond the end of the cell ; a smaller one placed outwardly below it in the second median interspace ; an irregular submarginal series of spots, those nearest the costa whitish ; two small white spots at the apex divided by the fifth subcostal nervule. *Hindwing* with the ground-colour tawny, markings black. A discal band from the costa to the submedian nervure above the anal angle ; another shorter one just beyond from the costa to the second median nervule ; the veins tawny, intersecting the black bands ; a submarginal macular band ; the margin black enclosing a fine tawny line ; anal lobe and tail deep black, outwardly margined with white. UNDERSIDE, *both wings* bright ferruginous-brown. *Forewing* with the base of the costa silvery, a broad silvery band towards the base of the cell, other markings as on the upperside but larger and clearer, those on the anterior half of the wing silvery, on the posterior half tinged with ochreous ; four fine linear spots on the margin from the upper discoidal to the first median nervule, also three discal suffused blackish spots within the submarginal series of spots from the third median nervule to the submedian nervure. *Hindwing* with a basal silvery band extending down the submedian nervure to above the anal lobe, then recurved and extending up the abdominal area to the base of the wing ; a broader band beyond from the costa to the middle of the submedian interspace where it ends in a point, broadest in the middle ; a costal spot ; a discal band in continuation enclosing the disco-cellular nervules from the second subcostal nervule to above the anal lobe where it is recurved and extends up the extreme abdominal margin to the base of the wing ; a large wedge-shaped band beyond from the second subcostal to the second median nervule—all silvery ; two round black spots on the margin, broadly surrounded with silvery divided by the discoidal nervule ; some indistinct blackish spots below, beyond which are two indistinct whitish marginal lines ; the anal lobe and tail black, narrowly edged with white, the anal lobe with a broad white line bounding it inwardly, then a zigzag black line extending to the first median nervule, with a short black and white bar above on the abdominal margin, and a large grey space irrorated with white. The FEMALE is apparently unknown.

D. egeon is a rare species. It may be distinguished from all the other species of the genus by the prevailing colour of the hindwing being tawny. Mr. Otto Möller and Major Marshall each possesses a single specimen from Sikkim, and there are two from Nepal and one from Sylhet in the Indian Museum, Calcutta ; these are all the specimens I have seen.

604. **Dodona eugenes**, Bates.

D. eugenes, Bates. Journ. Linn. Soc., Zoology, vol. ix, p. 372 (1867); id., Moore, Proc. Zool. Soc. Lond., 1882, p. 244; id., Swinhoe, Proc. Zool. Soc. Lond., 1885, p. 130, n. 46.

HABITAT : Outer Himalayas from Murree to Bhutan, Assam.

EXPANSE : 1·5 to 1·9 inches.

DESCRIPTION : " MALE. Closely allied to *D. egeon*. Wings of the same shape, and the form of the tail of the hindwing the same. UPPERSIDE dark, blackish brown. *Forewing* with a narrow line across the middle (touching neither the costa nor the hind margin), a curved streak near the hind angle, and about thirteen small spots pretty equally distributed over the apical half of the wing ; all these marks are whitish, except the transverse line and marks near the hind angle, which are slightly tinted with reddish tawny. *Hindwing* with the outer portion traversed by four indistinct brownish tawny lines, converging from the costa towards the anal angle ; at the apex are two black spots edged with light brown. On the broad, square lobe at the anal angle is a quadrate black spot, a slender tail arising from its outer edge. UNDERSIDE, the wings are precisely similar to those of *D. egeon*, being tawny brown, with stripes and spots of white, silky and shining on the hindwing and costa of forewing."

"The species seems to have been confounded hitherto with *D. egeon* ; but the very different colour and small dimensions of the stripes and spots of the upperside well distinguish it." (*Bates*, l. c.)

In *D. eugenes* the outline and markings of the upperside are almost identical with those of *D. dipæa*, the narrow tail beside the lobe being the only distinguishing feature, on the underside although the markings are as stated above precisely similar to those of *D. egeon*, they are narrower and less conspicuous, and the silvery band on the hindwing covering the disco-cellular nervules is continued uninterruptedly to the costa. The markings of the underside of *D. dipæa* are also identical in pattern, but the whitish bars are in *D. dipæa* still more reduced, especially on the hindwing, where they are narrow and inconspicuous. It has a wide range, it has been recorded from Bombay by Colonel Swinhoe, but he informs me that this is probably erroneous. It occurs throughout the outer ranges of the Himalayas from Murree to Bhutan. In Major Marshall's collection is a single male taken at Shillong in July. The FEMALE differs from the male only in being larger, the wings broader, the apex of the forewing more rounded, and the outer margin of that wing convex instead of concave ; all the markings larger and paler. In Simla this species occurs in the summer, the females hybernating and appearing again early the next spring. It is probably the next commonest species to *D. durga*.

Genus 92.—STIBOGES, Butler. (PLATE XXIV).

Stiboges, Butler, Proc. Zool. Soc. Lond., 1876, p. 308; id., Distant, Rhop. Malay., p. 193 (1884).

"Allied to *Abisara*, aspect of *Nymphidium* [a South American genus]. *Wings* with rounded outer margin broad, *costal nervure* of FOREWING terminating abruptly at about the middle of the costa, opposite to the end of the discoidal cell ; *subcostal* nervure with five branches, the last two forking to apex ; *upper radial nervule* emitted from the inferior margin of the subcostal near its origin ;* *lower* radial nearly equally dividing the *disco-cellulars*, which are concave ; *second* and *third median* nervules emitted near together ; *præcostal nervure* of HINDWING short, oblique, directed backwards ; *costal* nervure short, straight, oblique, terminating at basal third of costa ; *subcostal* nervure forking beyond the end of cell, the upper fork running close to the margin from the second third of costa ; *radial nervule* emitted close to the subcostal, reducing the *upper disco-cellular* nervule to a point ; *lower disco-cellular* long, oblique, nearly straight ; *second* and *third median* nervules emitted nearer together than the first and second. BODY, slender : *eyes*, prominent ; *antennæ*, slender, submoniliform† ; *palpi*, very small. Type, *Stiboges nymphidia*." (*Butler*, l. c.)

---

* This is surely a mistake ; the subcostal nervure originates from the base of the wing, the upper radial nervule has a common origin with the middle disco-cellular nervule (the upper disco-cellular is wanting in this genus) from a point on the subcostal nervure beyond the base of the second subcostal nervule.

† MONILIFORM, constricted at the joints so as to resemble a string of beads, from *monile*, a necklace ; SUBMONILIFORM, somewhat constricted, &c.

This diagnosis is evidently drawn up from a female specimen, though the sex is not stated. In the male the inner and outer margins of the forewing are exactly equal in length, the latter is nearly straight, not strongly convex as in the female, and the apex very acute not rounded. It has no secondary sexual characters. The hindwing is much less broad than in the female.

Stiboges is a very remarkable genus, the ground-colour being semi-transparent snow-white, with a broad outer fuscous border spotted with white. It contains but a single species, which occurs in Bhutan, on our North-Eastern frontier, and at Penang.

605. Stiboges nymphidia, Butler. (PLATE XXIV, FIG. 119 ♀).

S. nymphidia, Butler, Proc. Zool. Soc. Lond., 1876, p. 309, n. 1, pl. xxii, fig. 1, *female ;* id., Distant, Rhop. Malay., p. 253, n. 1, pl. xxiv, fig. 11, *female* (1883).

HABITAT : Penang, Naga and Khasi Hills, Bhutan.

EXPANSE : 1·7 to 1·9 inches.

DESCRIPTION : MALE and FEMALE. " *Both wings* semi-transparent, snow-white. *Forewing* with broad costal and external dark brown borders, sinuated internally ; two irregular submarginal series of unequal white spots. *Hindwing* with a broad [dark brown] outer border, undulated internally ; a sinuated disco-submarginal lunulated pale brown line ; a submarginal series of elongated white spots. *Body* dark brown. UNDERSIDE as above. [*Cilia* long, white, very broadly on the forewing, less so on the hindwing, marked with dark brown at the ends of the veins]. *Legs, palpi,* and *venter* white." (*Butler,* l. c.)

The Indian Museum, Calcutta, possesses a worn male specimen from the Khasi Hills, and a female example from the Naga Hills ; from the latter the figure is taken, and shows both sides. Mr. A. V. Knyvett's native collectors obtained a single female example on June 10th beyond Buxa in Bhutan. It was originally described from Penang, and is evidently a very rare species.

Genus 93.—TAXILA, Westwood.

Taxila, Westwood, Gen. Diurn. Lep., vol. ii, p. 421 (1851) ; id., Hewitson, Ex. Butt., vol. ii, p. 91 (1861).

" BODY, robust ; *wings*, large ; *head*, broad, front with a broad transversely truncated tuft, extending over the base of the antennæ ; *eyes*, smooth, naked ; *antennæ*, moderately long and slender, with short joints, the base of each slightly annulated with white, terminated by a long, slender club, ending in a fine point directed outwards ; *palpi*, short, not, or scarcely, visible in front of the face when seen from above, finely scaly, basal joint much curved; finely hairy beneath, terminal joint very small. THORAX, robust, finely hairy at the sides and beneath. ABDOMEN, rather short. FOREWING, subtriangular, or subtriangularly ovate ; *costal margin* slightly convex ; *apex* rounded, or subacute. *Veins* nearly arranged as in *Zemeros ;* the *first* and *second subcostal nervules* arising before the anterior extremity of the discoidal cell, and the *third* and *fourth* at considerable distances beyond it ; *upper disco-cellular* nervule obliterated, *middle* disco-cellular and the *upper disco-cellular* nervules arising together at a little distance beyond the second subcostal nervule ; the *middle* and *lower disco-cellular* nervules forming a nearly continuous curve, the latter uniting with the third median nervule at a very short distance beyond its origin. HINDWING, with the *outer margin* entire, rounded, and very slightly scalloped ; the *costal nervure* scarcely extending beyond the middle of the costal margin ; the *first subcostal nervule* arising considerably beyond the upper disco-cellular nervule ; *lower disco-cellular* nervule uniting with the third median nervule at a short distance from its origin. FORELEGS, of the *male* short, slender, and very densely clothed with soft hairs, forming a thick brush. Of the *female* twice as long, slender, scaly ; *tarsus* well articulated, terminal joint small, oval, armed beneath with a series of very minute spines, and at the tip with two, regularly formed, much curved *claws*, acute at the tip, not above one-fourth of the length of the joint ; *pulvillus* large and leathery. MIDDLE and HINDLEGS, moderately long, slender, and scaly ; *femur* hairy beneath, of the middle pair of legs elongated ; *tibial spurs* very minute, or obsolete ; *claws* small, very strongly curved, broad at the base, with a deep notch at the base of the apical acute portion ; *paronychia* very slender, obliquely truncate, the outer portion of the truncation armed with numerous long setæ; *pulvillus* broad, short, dilated at the extremity." (*Westwood*, l. c.)

Westwood placed several species in the genus *Taxila*, which are now included in the genera *Dodona* and *Abisara*. Mr. Distant in his "Rhopalocera Malayana" places under *Abisara*, the species which I have arranged in this genus, but as they differ in the outline of the wings from typical *Abisara* and also in markings, I have thought it advisable to keep these genera distinct. The species which I have retained in the genus *Taxila* all have the hindwing more evenly rounded, hardly angled, not lobed, or tailed, and the underside is furnished with brilliant bluish-silvery spots. The male of *T. thuisto* and the female of *T. fasciata* have a very "Abisara-like" angle at the termination of the third median nervule, very similar to that in the female of *A. fylla*, but not nearly so prominent as in the *A. neophron* and *A. echerius* groups, but the markings of both upper and underside are sufficient to prevent confusion among the two genera. The males have no secondary sexual characters.

Key to the Indian species of Taxila.

A. A marginal, submarginal and discal series of spots arranged in distinct even bands on the underside of forewing.

606. A. THUISTO, Tenasserim, Tavoy, Malay Peninsula, Sumatra, Borneo.

B. The spots on the underside of forewing placed irregularly, not arranged in distinct bands.

607. A. FASCIATA, Tenasserim, Tavoy.

606. Taxila thuisto, Hewitson.

T. thuisto, Hewitson, Ex. Butt., vol. ii, *Taxila* pl. i, figs. 5, 6, *female* (1861); Id., Druce, Proc. Zool. Soc. Lond., 1873, p. 347, n. 1; *Abisara thuisto*, Distant, Rhop. Malay, p. 191, n. 4, woodcut n 51, *male*, 52, *female* (1883); *A. thuisto*, Butler, Ann. and Mag. of Nat. Hist., fourth series, vol. v, p. 363 (1870).

HABITAT: Mergui, Upper Tenasserim, Tavoy, Sungei Ujong, Singapore, Sumatra, Borneo.

EXPANSE: ♂, 1·4; ♀, 1·7 inches.

DESCRIPTION: "MALE. UPPERSIDE, *both wings* uniform and very dark indigo-blue or black. UNDERSIDE, *both wings* bright reddish-brown. *Forewing* with the apex paler, an oblique bluish fascia crossing cell; a number of irregularly-shaped blue and black discal spots arranged in three series, the outer most distinct, consisting of six spots divided by the nervules, the upper three being very pale, and a submarginal series of linear blue spots margined with black situated between the nervules; the *cilia* black. *Hindwing* with a transverse bluish fascia crossing cell and extending to near costa, and with a number of irregularly-shaped blue and black discal spots as on the forewing, of which the outer are the most prominent, and which are placed between the nervules; submarginal linear spots as on forewing, and the *cilia* black. *Body* above concolourous with wings, beneath somewhat paler; *legs* ochraceous." (*Distant*, l. c.) "FEMALE. UPPERSIDE, *both wings* rufous, clouded at the base, crossed transversely beyond the middle by a band of oblong black spots, each spot marked with dull blue—those near the costal margin of the forewing interrupted by five white spots; a band of lunular black spots near the outer margin, each spot traversed by a line of blue or white. *Forewing* with a transverse band of black spots before the middle. UNDERSIDE does not differ from the male, except that it is lighter." (*Hewitson*, l. c.)

Dr. Anderson obtained several specimens of this species in the Mergui Archipelago during the cold weather; Captain Adamson took a single female in October at Natchoung in Upper Tenasserim which is now in Major Marshall's collection; and there is a single male in the collection of the Indian Museum, Calcutta, from Tavoy, which differs from typical specimens in having the silvery spot on the underside in the subcostal interspace of the forewing showing on the upperside as well.

T. thuisto is a smaller insect than *T. fasciata*, the inner margin of the forewing proportionally longer, giving that wing a squarer appearance; the hindwing too is distinctly quadrate, showing an approach to *Abisara*. The arrangement of the spots in regular bands on the underside will immediately distinguish it from *T. fasciata*.

647. **Taxila fasciata,** Moore.

T. fasciata, Moore, Proc. Zool. Soc. Lond., 1878, p. 832, pl. lii, fig. 1, *male.*

HABITAT : Above Ahsown, Upper Tenasserim ; Mergui, Tavoy.

EXPANSE : ♂, 1·8 to 2·1 ; ♀, 2·0 inches.

DESCRIPTION : " Allied to *T. drupadi,* Horsfield [= *T. haquinus,* Fabricius] from Java. MALE. UPPERSIDE, differs in the apex of the *forewing* being less suffused with red, and having an oblique subapical indistinct whitish fascia. UNDERSIDE similarly marked, with the subapical fascia distinct, well-defined, and pure white." (*Moore,* l. c.) The FEMALE differs from that sex of *T. haquinus* on the UPPERSIDE of *both wings* being duller coloured, the black markings of the underside hardly visible. UNDERSIDE has all the bluish-silvery markings less distinct, their inner black spots obsolete. *Forewing* with the oblique subapical white band more regularly-margined.

T. fasciata is very closely allied to *T. haquinus* which occurs in the Malay Peninsula as well as in Java and Borneo ; the two species will almost certainly hereafter be found to merge into one another.* There is a single male specimen of *T. fasciata* in the Indian Museum, Calcutta, obtained by Dr. Anderson in the Mergui Archipelago in December, and a male and two females from Tavoy ; in Major Marshall's collection are a male taken in the Thoungyeen forests in December, one in the Meplay valley in October, two females in the Thoungyeen forests in February and May respectively, and one in the Donat range in January, all by Captain C. T. Bingham.

In the Malay Peninsula occur three very beautiful species of butterflies, which belong to the genus *Laxita*† of Butler. They differ from all the other species of the subfamily in having on the male a glandular patch of differently-formed scales much as in many species of *Mycalesis* placed on the upperside of the hindwing below the costa, and the inner margin of the forewing strongly convex to cover this patch. The markings of the underside are somewhat similar to those of *Taxila.*

---

* *Taxila haquinus.* Papilio haquinus, Fabricius, Ent. Syst., vol. iii, pt. 1, p. 55, n. 169 (1793) ; *Abisara haquinus,* Butler, Cat. Fab. Lep. B. M., p. 137, n. 2 (1869) ; id., Distant, Rhop. Malay., p. 196, n. 3, pl. xviii, fig. 13, *female* (1883) ; *Taxila haquinus,* Kirby, Cat. Diurn. Lep., p. 286 (1871) ; *Eurygona drupadi,* Horsfield, Cat. Lep. E. I. C., pl. ii, figs. 3 *female* ; 3a, *male* ; 3b–e, *structure of image* (1828) ; id., Boisduval, Sp. Gén., vol. i, pl. vii, fig. 2, *male* (1836). HABITAT : Province Wellesley, Malacca, Singapore, Java, Borneo. EXPANSE : 1·8 to 2·0 inches. DESCRIPTION : " MALE UPPERSIDE, *both wings* dark purplish-brown, apical portion of the nervules paler. *Forewing* with a subapical pale and somewhat ochraceous fascia. UNDERSIDE, *both wings* much paler than above, the discal areas reddish. *Forewing* with a curved pale fascia on upper portion of cell and immediately beneath the subcostal nervure, a subapical pale ochraceous fascia as above, and with the following bluish markings more or less spotted with black, *viz.*, an oblique spot reaching apex of cell, two black spots beyond cell connected by a bluish lunule, above which are some small black spots divided by the subcostal nervules ; these are outwardly followed by a straight series of about four spots (the lower situated above the third median nervule), two on each side of the second median nervule, and one on inner side and at base of first median nervule ; a submarginal series of linear pale continuous lunules becoming obsolete towards apex. *Hindwing* with two short pale oblique fasciæ at base, a discal series of about eleven blue and black markings as on forewing, and a submarginal series of obscure dark conical spots, through which pass two series of pale, transverse, linear spots, the inner series being distinctly linear, &c. *Body* above concolourous with wings, beneath with *legs* greyish brown. FEMALE. UPPERSIDE, *both wings* reddish, the dark spots beneath visible above. *Forewing* with a prominent subapical white fascia. UNDERSIDE generally as in male, excepting the white subapical fascia " (*Distant,* l. c.) In the Indian Museum, Calcutta, are a pair of this species collected by Dr. Horsfield in Java.

† Genus LAXITA, Butler.

Laxita, Butler, Trans. Linn. Soc. Lond., Zoology, second series, vol. i, p. 546 (1877) ; *Abisara* (part), Distant, Rhop. Malay., p. 188 (1883).

" The rounded wings of *Abisara taxita* and the allied species distinguish them from typical *Abisara* ; but I am doubtful of its generic distinction." (*Butler,* l. c.) The characters pointed out on page 306 seem to me to be so well-marked that structurally *Laxita* is the most distinct genus of the subfamily. The genus probably contains several species in addition to the three enumerated below, including *L. orphna,* Boisduval, which has been recorded (*Menetries,* Journ. Linn. Soc. Zoology, vol. viii, p. 149 (1865) from Singapore, but is not mentioned by Mr. Distant in his " Rhopalocera Malayana."

Laxita damajanti, Abisara damajanti, Felder, Wien. Ent. Monatsch., vol. iv, p. 397, n. 13 (1860) ; id., Distant, Rhop. Malay., p. 192, n. 6 (1883) ; *Taxila damajanti,* Kirby, Cat. Diurn. Lep., p. 286, n. 6 (1871). HABITAT : Perak, Malay Peninsula. EXPANSE : 1·7 to 1·8 inches. DESCRIPTION : " MALE. Wings red (ruddy), upperside unmarked, underside with bluish discal spots (each placed on a black spot), hindwing with four submarginal streaks, the first bluish, the second and fourth fuscous, the third whitish."

" An exceedingly beautiful species closely allied to *A. orphna,* Boisduval, but the underside of the forewing ornamented with bluish spots sufficiently distinct." (*Felder,* l. c.)

MALE. UPPERSIDE, *both wings* rich crimson. *Forewing* with the costa and outer margin very narrowly black, the veins defined with black outwardly, and a fine black line on the disco-cellular nervules. *Hindwing* with the costal margin broadly black, with some obscure blackish diffused patches between the veins towards the outer margin. UNDERSIDE, *both wings* rich crimson marked with numerous black and rich shining blue

Genus 94.—ABISARA, Felder. (PLATE XXIV).

Abisara, Felder, Wien. Ent. Monatsch., vol. iv, p. 397 (1860); id., Bates, Journ. Linn. Soc., Zoology, vol. ix, p. 413 (1868); id., Moore, Lep. Cey., vol. i, p. 63 (1881); id. (*part*), Distant, Rhop. Malay., p. 138 (1883); *Sospita*, Hewitson, Ex. Butt., vol. ii, *Sospita* pl. i (1861).

"Genus confounded among English authors with *Taxila*, Doubleday (*T. fylla*, *durga*), to be distinguished by the smaller head, distinct collar, more slender antennæ and shorter palpi." (*Felder*, l. c.)

FOREWING, triangular; *costal margin* gently arched, *outer* margin straight or slightly convex, *inner* margin nearly straight, equal in length to the outer margin, *apex* pointed. *Costal nervure* short, reaching the middle of the wing; *subcostal* nervure giving off its first and second branches close together before the end of the cell, the third nearer to the origin of the fourth than to the end of the cell, the fourth reaching the apex of the wing; *discoidal cell* broad, short, the disco-cellular nervules being emitted at less than half the length of the wing from the base; *upper disco-cellular nervule* wanting, *middle* and *lower* disco-cellulars of equal length, together forming a complete arch, and the lower joining the median nervure after the origin of the second median nervule; *submedian nervure* slightly sinuous. HINDWING, subovate; *costal margin* strongly arched at base, thence nearly straight, *outer* margin evenly rounded and slightly scalloped in the male, slightly angled at the termination of the third median nervule in the female (*A. fylla*), more strongly scalloped and produced into a long tail at termination of third median nervule (*A. neophron* and allies), or, least of all scalloped, but the wing strongly angled at the third median nervule (*A. echerius* and allies). *Præcostal nervure* simple, curved outwardly, *costal* nervure short, reaching the middle of the costa,

spots and streaks. *Forewing* with a submarginal black line becoming macular anteriorly, the inner margin broadly shining fuscous. *Hindwing* with the extreme margin black, then a pink line, then a black line, then an ochreous line, and lastly a black line. FEMALE differs from the male on the UPPERSIDE in being of a paler shade of crimson. *Forewing* with the inner margin straight not lobed, a very indistinct paler fascia towards the apex. *Hindwing* with no glandular patch below the costa, a submarginal even black line replacing the black diffused patches in the male extending on to the forewing as far as the first median nervule, otherwise as in the male.
There are specimens of both sexes of this most lovely insect in the Indian Museum, Calcutta, from Perak.

Laxita tanita. Taxila tanita, Hewitson, Ex. Butt., vol. ii, *Taxila* pl. i, text (1861); id., Druce, Proc. Zool. Soc. Lond., 1873, p. 347, n. 4; id., Kirby, Cat. Diurn. Lep., p. 286, n. 5 (1871); *Abisara tanita*, Distant, Rhop. Malay., p. 192, n. 5, pl. xviii, fig. 14, *female* (1883); *Abisara (Laxita) tanita*, Butler, Trans. Linn. Soc. Lond., Zoology, second series, vol. i, p. 546, n. 4 (1877); *Taxila orphue*, Doubleday, Hewitson (*vere* Bourduval), Gen. Diurn. Lep., vol. ii, p. 422, n. 7 (*part*), pl. lxix, figs. 6, *female*; 7, *male* (1851). HABITAT: Province Wellesley, Malacca, Singapore, Borneo. EXPANSE: 1⅗ inches. DESCRIPTION: MALE. UPPERSIDE, *both wings* pale crimson, the margin narrowly black. *Forewing* with the interspaces streaked with a darker shade, the disco-cellular nervules defined with a black line. *Hindwing* with a discal series of dark red streaks between the veins. Described from Hewitson's figure. "FEMALE. UPPERSIDE, *both wings* bright purplish-red. *Forewing* with the margins, the base, and a broad basal streak between the third median nervule and the submedian nervure pale fuscous. *Hindwing* with the margins (costal and abdominal margins broadly) and some broad streaks situated in the cell and between the nervules pale fuscous. UNDERSIDE, *both wings* bright purplish red. *Forewing* with upper and apical blue streaks in cell, the last margined outwardly with black, and with some blue and black discal spots, of which the largest and most prominent are two beyond the cell, and two divided by the second median nervule; two faint bluish submarginal linear fasciæ which become obsolete at apex, and the costal margin broadly fuscous near base. *Hindwing* with some transverse series of black and blue spots at base, some large elongate black submarginal spots with blue centres between the nervules, and blue and yellow submarginal linear fasciæ, between which the colour is fuscous; posterior margin fuscous. *Body* pale fuscous; *legs* pale obscure ochraceous." (*Distant*, l. c.)
I have not seen this species. Mr. Distant quotes the figure of the female of this species in the "Genera of Diurnal Lepidoptera" as applying to *L. tanita*, but it differs materially from both his figure and description of that sex. He appears to have reversed the sexes, and to have described from the figure the female as a male.

Laxita telesia. Taxila telesia, Hewitson, Ex. Butt., vol. ii, *Taxila* pl. i, figs. 1, 2, *male* (1861); idem, id., Journ. Linn. Soc. Lond., Zoology, vol. viii, p. 149 (1865); id., Kirby, Cat. Diurn. Lep., p. 286, n. 7 (1871). HABITAT: Perak, Sumatra, Borneo. EXPANSE: 1⅘ inches. DESCRIPTION: "MALE. UPPERSIDE, *both wings* dark brown (fuscous). *Forewing* with the apex and outer margin carmine, the inner margin produced, rounded, with near its middle an oval spot of lilac-white. [*Hindwing* with the portion covered by the forewing shining pale ochreous, a large oval glandular patch of closely-packed ochreous scales on either side of the middle of the subcostal nervure, a small patch of carmine on the outer margin about the termination of the discoidal nervule, the black markings of the underside showing through faintly]. UNDERSIDE, *both wings* carmine with bands and spots of blue and black. *Forewing* with the apex rufous (yellow, nearly orange); a longitudinal and a transverse band within the cell blue, a second transverse band also blue, followed by five blue spots, bordered inwardly with black. The inner margin, where the wings touch, light yellow. *Hindwing* with numerous black and blue spots, crossed near the outer margin by a band of light blue and a band of light yellow, each bordered with black, and separated by a band of the same colour." (*Hewitson*, l. c. in Ex. Butt.) FEMALE. UPPERSIDE, *forewing* carmine, the cell, and the interspaces with dull fuscous streaks, an oblique subapical pale ochreous diffused fascia. *Hindwing* almost throughout dull fuscous, the veins slightly margined with carmine. UNDERSIDE, *both wings* marked precisely as in the male.
There are a male and two females of this beautiful species from Perak in the Indian Museum, Calcutta. The female is conspicuously different from the male as it lacks the oval white spot on the upperside of the forewing, the carmine is not confined to the apex and outer margin as in the male, but extends all over the wing, and the inner margin is straight. It also lacks the glandular patch of scales on the upperside of the hindwing.

the *subcostal nervules* bifurcating beyond the end of the cell, *discoidal cell* long and broad, the apex oblique, *disco-cellular nervules* of equal length in *A. echerius* and allies, the upper shorter than the lower in *A. fylla* and *A. neophron* and allies; the lower disco-cellular joining the median nervure after the origin of the second median nervule, almost in the same straight line in *A. fylla* and *A. neophron* and allies, but forming an obtuse angle with the middle one in *A. echerius* and allies. BODY, somewhat small, *head* small, *eyes* hairy, *antennæ* exactly half the length of the forewing, distinctly annulated, with a distinct spatulate club, *palpi* minute.

LARVA [*A. echerius* and allies] oniseiform.* " PUPA recumbent on a leaf or other object, and secured by the tail and a girdle across the middle." (*Moore*, l. c.)

" *Abisara* is distributed over a wide area ; it is found in Tropical Africa and Madagascar, inhabits Continental India, Ceylon, the Andaman and Nicobar Islands, Burma, and the Malay Peninsula, being also represented generally throughout the Malay Archipelago." (*Distant*, l. c.) The type of the genus, *A. echerius*, Stoll, was described from China. In India the genus, as pointed out by Bates, falls into three distinct groups ; the first group which was placed in the genus *Sospita* by Hewitson contains a single species in India, it has an oblique discal band across the forewing, yellow in the male, and white in the female, and the hindwing evenly rounded, not angled (except slightly so in the female) or tailed. The next group, which contains *A. neophron* and *A. chela* in India, and *A. savitri* in the Malay Peninsula, has not, as far as I am aware, been generically separated ; these species also have an oblique discal band across the forewing, but it is white in both sexes, and the hindwing is produced into a long tail at the end of the third median nervule, the base of it wide, extending to the first median nervule ; both these groups are absent from Peninsular India, Ceylon, and the Andamans and Nicobars, but occur throughout the Eastern Himalayas and eastwards to Assam, and thence southwards to the Malay Peninsula. The last group, which contains the typical *Abisaras*, is rich plum colour in the male, and magnificently glossed with purple in certain lights, generally paler in the female with no purple gloss, usually with some pale bands across the forewing, parallel to the outer margin, not obliquely placed, the hindwing bluntly angled, but not tailed at the end of the third median nervule, the outer margin being produced from the tip of the angulation to the anal angle, giving a quadrate appearance. They occur sparingly in the outer Himalayas, Assam, and almost throughout Eastern and Peninsular India, in Ceylon, the Andamans and Nicobars, Burma, the Malay Peninsula, Java and China. The species of this group are all closely allied, many of those which have been described are doubtfully distinct.

Key to the Indian species of Abisara.

A. With a conspicuous pale transverse band placed obliquely on the forewing in both sexes.

    a. Outer margin of hindwing evenly rounded and scalloped, not produced into a tail, and only slightly angulated at the termination of the third median nervule in the female.

        608. A. (*Sospita*) FYLLA, Himalayas, Assam, Sylhet, Upper Tenasserim, Upper Burma.

    b. Outer margin of hindwing produced into a long tail at the termination of the third median nervule.

        a^1. Of large size, the tail long, the submarginal line on the upperside of the forewing not terminating anteriorly in a white spot.

            609. A. NEOPHRON, Sikkim, Assam, Sylhet, Upper Burma.

        b^1. Of smaller size and darker colour, the tail half as long, the submarginal line on the upperside of the forewing terminating anteriorly in a white spot.

            610. A. CHELA, Sikkim, Sylhet.

B. With several obscure pale bands nearly parallel to the outer margin of the forewing, obsolete in the male.

    a. Outer margin of hindwing bluntly and broadly angulated at the termination of the third median nervule.

        611. A. BIFASCIATA, South Andamans.

        612. A. ANGULATA, Upper Tenasserim.

        613. A. ABNORMIS, Upper Tenasserim.

        614. A. SUFFUSA, Sub-Himalayas, Eastern and Peninsular India.

        615. A. FRATERNA, Bombay.

        616. A. PRUNOSA, South India, Ceylon

---

* For explanation of *oniseiform*, see page 305.

608. **Abisara fylla,** Doubleday, Hewitson.

Taxila fylla, Doubleday, Hewitson, Gen. Diurn. Lep., vol. ii, p. 422, n. 8, pl. lxix, fig. 3, *male* (1852).

HABITAT : Himalayas, Assam, Sylhet, Upper Burma, Upper Tenasserim.

EXPANSE : ♂, 1·9 to 2·4 ; ♀, 2·0 to 2·5 inches.

DESCRIPTION : MALE. UPPERSIDE, *both wings* and *cilia* dark brown. *Forewing* with a straight even straw yellow band commencing at the middle of the costa and almost reaching the inner angle, its lower portion narrower and slightly recurved ; a pale brown submarginal line often bearing anteriorly two minute yellow spots divided by the fourth subcostal nervule, often with two additional similar spots near the margin divided by the fifth subcostal nervule, and the cilia beyond white. *Hindwing* with a pale brown curved discal band, a series of six marginal black spots inwardly defined with pale brown, and outwardly bearing a pure white dot, of which the two upper ones divided by the discoidal nervule are always largest, the next two divided by the second median nervule always smallest and often obsolete, the last two at the anal angle placed in the submedian interspace always present. There is sometimes a seventh small spot without a white dot between the subcostal nervules. UNDERSIDE, *both wings* paler throughout, but similarly marked, except that the *hindwing* has a faint subbasal line. FEMALE similarly marked to the male, but much paler, the discal band on the *forewing* very variable in width and pure white or just tinted with palest yellow, and reaching the costa (in the male it does not reach it), wider anteriorly and tapering to a point posteriorly ; the wing broader, apex less produced, outer margin convex. *Body* concolorous with the wings both above and below, the *eyes* with a pure white streak at the sides, the frontal tuft of the *head* also with a pure white streak on both sides, the *palpi* pale brown, the *antennæ* dark brown, annulated with white, the club with a white bar above near its tip.

A. fylla occurs in Masuri and the Dehra Dhun ; Mr. Doherty took it at Askot, the Dhoaj Eastern Kumaon, 4,000 to 7,000 feet ; it is common in Sikkim at low elevations, in Buxa, and in Assam, the Naga Hills, Cherrapunji, and Sylhet ; it was taken by Captain C. T. Bingham in the Upper Thoungyeen forests in Upper Tenasserim in March, and was also brought by the Yunan Expedition. In shape and markings it has no near allies, and might perhaps be advantageously placed in the genus *Sospita* of Hewitson, of which it forms the type.

609. **Abisara neophron,** Hewitson.

Sospita neophron, Hewitson, Ex. Butt., vol. ii, *Sospita* pl. i, fig. 3 (1861) ; *Abisara neophron,* de Nicéville, Journ. A. S. B., vol. lv, pt. 2, p. 253, pl. xi, fig. 8, *male* (1886).

HABITAT : Sikkim, Assam, Sylhet, Upper Burma.

EXPANSE : 1·8 to 2·3 inches.

DESCRIPTION : "MALE. UPPERSIDE, *both wings* rufous-brown. *Forewing* crossed transversely at the middle by a broad band of white, and obliquely beyond the middle by a narrow, obscure, rufous band ; the outer margin pale from the middle to the anal angle, traversed by a dark line. *Hindwing* tailed, crossed beyond the middle and near the outer margin by waved rufous bands, two large black spots at the apex, separated by a line of orange, a submarginal band of white traversed by a black line, the tail white. UNDERSIDE as above." (*Hewitson,* l. c.) FEMALE differs from the male only in being paler throughout, the discal band of the *forewing* usually broader, always reaching the costa (in some male specimens it does not quite touch it), the lower of the two black spots on the upperside of the *hindwing* divided by the discoidal nervule posteriorly defined with an orange line, as indeed it often is in the male, two oval spots on the margin divided by the first median nervule inwardly defined with whitish, outwardly by pure white, with a marginal white line beyond ; *cilia* more or less white.

A. neophron is not uncommon in Sikkim at low elevations ; it occurs also in Assam, Sibsagar, the Naga Hills, and Sylhet, and was brought by the Yunan Expedition.

610.　**Abisara chela**, de N.

A. chela, de Nicéville, Journ. A. S. B., vol. lv, pt. 2, p. 252, p. 4. pl. xx, fig. 7, *male* (1886).

HABITAT : Sikkim, Sylhet.

EXPANSE : ♂, 1·75 to 1·90 ; ♀, 1·90 inches.

DESCRIPTION : "MALE. UPPERSIDE, *both wings* dark fuscous-brown. *Forewing* with an oblique white discal band from the middle of the costa to about the middle of the submedian interspace, variable in width ; a submarginal narrow white line, sometimes distinct throughout its length, at others blurred in the middle, but always ending in a distinct white spot at the costa ; one or two short fine white marginal lines at the anal angle. *Hindwing* with two submarginal rounded black spots divided by the discoidal nervule, the upper one the smaller and outwardly circled with white, the lower one marked anteriorly and posteriorly with white ; the outer portion of the discoidal and third median nervules orange ; three somewhat indistinct black lunular spots on the margin in the median and submedian interspaces, inwardly defined with a pale line, the spots in the submedian interspace geminated ; two fine interrupted white marginal lines ; tail short and marked with white ; an ill-defined discal pale band, inwardly sharply defined, outwardly blurred. UNDERSIDE, *both wings* much paler, all the markings more distinct. *Forewing* with the discal and submarginal bands much broader than above, the latter always well-marked throughout its length. *Hindwing* marked as above, but the space from the discal band to the margin irrorated with white, the outer portion of all the veins orange. FEMALE. UPPERSIDE, *both wings* paler than in the male, tinged throughout with ferruginous, the veins of the *hindwing* more broadly marked with orange. UNDERSIDE with the same differences as above."

"Allied to *A. neophron*, Hewitson, which occurs in the same places with it, and in Sikkim in the same months ; differs from it in its smaller size, usually broader discal band on the forewing, the submarginal line usually more prominent, and always ending anteriorly in a white spot, which is never the case in *A. neophron* ; markedly also in the length of the tail, it being fully twice as long in *A. neophron* as it is in *A. chela*." (*de Nicéville*, l. c.)

Mr. Otto Möller has obtained numerous specimens of this species at low elevations in Sikkim ; there is a single male specimen from Sylhet in the Indian Museum, Calcutta.

An allied species occurs in the Malay Peninsula, which differs chiefly from *A. neophron* and *A. chela* in its paler colouration throughout ; the discal band of the forewing on the upperside is much blurred and very indistinct, as is also the submarginal band, which in *A. savitri* is even broader than the discal band, in the Indian species it is a mere line. A description of it is given below.[*]

The remaining species all belong to the typical group of the genus *Abisara*. The type of the genus and of this group is the *P. echerius* of Stoll (Supplement to Cramer's Pap. Ex.,

---

[*] *Abisara savitri*, Felder, Wien. Ent. Monatsch., vol. iv, p. 397, n. 12 (1860) : id., Butler, Trans. Linn. Soc., Zoology, second series, vol. i, p. 545, n. 1 (1877) ; id., Distant, Rhop. Malay., p. 189, n. 1, pl. xviii, fig. 5, *female* (1883) ; *Sospita suza*, Hewitson, Ex. Butt., vol. ii, *Sospita* pl. i, fig. 2, *male* (1861). HABITAT : India (*Hewitson*), Province Wellesley, Malacca, Ayer Panas, Singapore. EXPANSE : *Male*, 2·1 : *female*, 1·75 to 2·00 inches. DESCRIPTION : "MALE. UPPERSIDE, *both wings* rufous-brown. *Forewing* crossed transversely beyond the middle by two nearly parallel bands of rufous-white, the outer margin from the middle to the anal angle pale, traversed by a dark line. *Hindwing* tailed, crossed by two curved bands, one near the outer margin waved and forming a border to two black spots near the apex, a submarginal band of white traversed by a black line, the tail white. UNDERSIDE as above." (*Hewitson*, l. c.) "FEMALE. UPPERSIDE, *both wings* pale ochreous-brown. *Forewing* with two pale transverse fasciæ crossing the apical half, and with two narrow submarginal pale linear fasciæ, each outwardly bordered with fuscous. *Hindwing* with two broad pale fasciæ continuous to those of the forewing, the first somewhat curved and extending to the abdominal margin, the second situated near the outer margin and containing two large black spots with which surroundings separated by the discoidal nervule, a smaller spot situated between the subcostal nervules, and two small and suboblsolete spots at anal angle ; marginal linear fasciæ as on forewing, the outer margin long and linearly caudate at apex of upper median nervule, this prolongation being white. UNDERSIDE as above. *Body* and *legs* more or less concolorous with wings." (*Distant*, l. c.)

Mr. Hewitson vaguely gives India as the habitat of his *A. suza*. It was described almost simultaneously by Dr. Felder under the name of *A. savitri*, by which name the species should be known. I prefer to unite them under one species as has been done by Messrs. Bates and Kirby, and by Hewitson himself, as I can find no character by which to divide them except the ground-colour which is darker as is usual in Mr. Hewitson's figure of a male than it is in Mr. Distant's figure of a female, the latter author apparently considering them distinct species, as he does not mention *A. suza*. He probably followed Mr. Butler, who remarks that *A. savitri* "is quite distinct from the Indian species, *A. suza* of Hewitson." The male is also unknown to Mr. Distant.

pl. xxxi, figs. 1, 1a, *male*; 1b, *female* (1790), described from China. Stoll's figures are very rough, so I am quite unable to say in what particulars his species differs from Indian ones, and until almost recently his name was used for the Indian species. The style of markings is identical in all the forms described from India, except perhaps *A. bifasciata*, which has the bands on the underside more lunately macular than the rest. If the localities of the specimens are known they can be named. Northern Indian specimens must be *A. suffusa*, because no other forms have been described from there; similarly specimens caught in Tenasserim must be *angulata* (*A. abnormis* is, in my opinion, an easily recognisable occasional variety of this form): specimens from the Andamans must be *A. bifasciata*; if caught in Ceylon they must be *A. prunosa*, but in South India confusion is likely to arise, if caught in the extreme south they will be *A. prunosa*, but further north they may be *A. prunosa*, *A. fraterna*, or *A. suffusa*. *A. prunosa* may typically be recognised by its larger size and intense purple shot in the male. Mr. Moore has pointed out what he considers to be the points of difference between *A. prunosa* and *A. fraterna*, also between the Tenasserim *A. angulata* and *A. suffusa*, but what the differences are between *A. suffusa* and *A. fraterna* I am quite unable to say, unless the inner band on the upperside of the forewing being angulated in *A. suffusa* and rounded in *A. fraterna* should prove sufficient to distinguish them. To sum up the six species described from India. In my opinion *A. bifasciata* might perhaps be kept distinct, though I possess a female specimen from Akyab in British Burma which is almost indistinguishable from it; *A. prunosa* is typically very distinct, and that name might be used for Ceylon and Travancore specimens; but all the rest should, I think, be named *A. echerius* until at any rate the differences, if any, between that species and the Indian ones are pointed out, when the latter might be called *A. kausambi*, which is the oldest of the names applied to the Indo-Malayan forms. In the detailed descriptions below I have given Mr. Moore's localities only for each in the headings.

611. **Abisara bifasciata**, Moore. (PLATE XXIV, FIG. 118 ♂).

A. bifasciata, Moore, Proc. Zool. Soc. Lond., 1877, p. 557, pl. lviii, fig. 1, *female*; id., Wood-Mason and de Nicéville, Journ. A. S. B., vol. l, pt. 2, p. 233, n. 27 (1881).

HABITAT : South Andamans.

EXPANSE : ♂, 1·7 to 2·2 ; ♀, 2·0 to 2·2 inches.

DESCRIPTION : "From the Malayan *A. kausambi*,* Felder, it differs on the UPPERSIDE in the discal transverse bands being sinuous, which are prominent in the FEMALE, and in that sex the two bands on the *forewing* are separated and broadly white anteriorly; the upper and lower spots on the *hindwing* are also larger. UNDERSIDE, the bands are broader and sinuous, and on the *hindwing* there are but two anterior spots instead of three." (*Moore*, l. c.) Regarding this latter point, the two male specimens of *A. kausambi* I possess have three spots on the underside of the hindwing anteriorly, while all the South Andaman male specimens in our collections possess but two; in the females from the Andamans, however, there are always three spots.

There are numerous specimens of this species in the Indian Museum, Calcutta, collected at Port Blair by the late Mr. A. de Roepstorff, and one specimen from Kar Nicobar. As no second specimen has been received from the latter locality, it is probable that the first one was captured in the Andamans.

The figure shows both upper and undersides of a male Andaman example in the Indian Museum, Calcutta.

612. **Abisara angulata**, Moore.

A. angulata, Moore, Proc. Zool. Soc. Lond., 1878, p. 833.

HABITAT : Above Ahsown, Hatsiega, Naththoung to Paboga, Upper Tenasserim.

EXPANSE : 1·92 inches.

DESCRIPTION : " From *A. kausambi*,* Felder, of the Malay Peninsula, this species differs

* *Abisara kausambi*, Felder, Wien. Ent. Monatsch., vol. iv, p. 397, n 11 (1860) ; id., Moore, Proc. Zool. Soc. Lond., 1877, p. 587 ; id., Butler, Trans. Linn. Soc., Zoology, second series, vol. 1, p. 545, n. 2 (1877) ; id.,

in the MALE on the UPPERSIDE being paler plum-colour, the *forewing* showing the transverse discal fascia, and the *hindwing* the apical and anal black spots ; the FEMALE on the UPPERSIDE is also paler purple-brown, the inner discal band is angled at the middle of its inner border on *both wings*, and is only slightly paler at its costal end. On the UNDER-SIDE the discal bands are angled in the middle, the inner band being narrowly bordered with brownish white at its costal end only in the male, its entire length in the female."

"An entirely different insect from the Andaman *A. bifasciata*, Moore." (*Moore*, l. c.)
A. angulata can hardly be said to be "an entirely different insect" from *A. bifasciata* ; in the male of the latter species the pale bands on the upperside of the forewing are slightly more prominent, on the underside also they are more prominent, wider and more lunately macular, the ground-colour is also paler ; in the female the bands on the upperside, especially anteriorly, are more prominent, being wider and paler. All the above-given points of distinction are really very slight, and without knowing the localities from which the specimens come, it would be difficult to distinguish between some specimens of *A. angulata* and *A. bifasciata*.

In Major Marshall's collection is a long series of this species taken by Captain C. T. Bingham in different parts of Upper Tenasserim. The species is very close to, if indeed separable from, *A. suffusa* ; the males are somewhat darker and richer coloured, the discal bands in the female both above and below more distinct. One male from the Donat Range has the inner discal band on the underside of the forewing prominently outwardly defined with white, showing in this respect an approach to *A. abnormis*. The presence or absence of the black spots on the upperside of the hindwing is very inconstant.

613. **Abisara abnormis**, Moore.

A. abnormis, Moore, Proc. Zool. Soc. Lond., 1883, p. 532, pl. xlix, fig. 3, *male*.

HABITAT : Moulmein.

EXPANSE : 1·2 inches.

DESCRIPTION : "MALE. UPPERSIDE, *both wings* dark plum-colour. *Forewing* with a series of distinct whitish spots outwardly bordering the medial dark angular fascia, its lower border pale, and the submarginal fascia also distinctly pale. *Hindwing* less angular on middle of the exterior margin, the apical and anal black spots very indistinct. UNDERSIDE with a very distinct white angular medial fascia crossing *both wings* ; the submarginal line on *forewing* also whitish and slender. *Hindwing* with a continuous marginal row of black conical white-bordered spots." (*Moore*, l. c.)

In Major Marshall's collection is a male specimen of this species from Rangoon, which differs only from Mr. Moore's description in having three anterior and two posterior black spots on the underside of the hindwing, the spots on the median interspaces as usual being of

Distant, Rhop. Malay., p. 180, n. 7, pl. xviii, figs. 10. *male* ; 11, *female* (1883). HABITAT : Zambesi, Nyassa, ? Andaman Isles, Province Wellesley, Sungei Ujong, Malacca, Perak, Singapore, Sumatra, Java, Borneo. EXPANSE : *Male*, 1·7 to 1·8 ; *female*, 1·6 to 1·8 inches. DESCRIPTION : "MALE. UPPERSIDE, *both wings* dark reddish-brown. UNDERSIDE *both wings* somewhat paler, *Forewing* crossed by two pale fasciæ on the apical half and with a submarginal pale linear fascia, outwardly bordered with dark castaneous and becoming obsolete at apex. *Hindwing* with two pale fasciæ as on the forewing, but curved and wider apart, the outer fascia containing three apical black spots surrounded with whitish and separated by the subcostal nervules, and with two smaller spots near anal angle ; a pale and darkly bordered submarginal fascia as on the forewing, but which from apex of upper median nervule (where the outer margin is obtusely angulated) to anal angle is again outwardly bordered with paler colouration. FEMALE. Wings generally much paler in hue than in the male. *Forewing* with a distinct subapical transverse subviolaceous or whitish fascia, and with the submarginal linear fascia distinct as beneath. *Hindwing* with the spots and fasciæ, both above and beneath, as on underside of male ; the subapical pale fascia on the forewing being broader beneath than above."
"The females of this species vary considerably in the size and distinctive character of the pale subapical fascia to the forewing. The most strongly marked or albino specimens in my collection are from Province Wellesley, whilst the most melanic forms I possess are from Malacca and North Borneo. The most interesting fact in connection with the geographical distribution of this species is its presence, unmodified and distinct, in Eastern Africa. The late Mr. Hewitson received it from the Zambesi, and subsequently it reached my hands contained in a small collection made in the neighbourhood of Lake Nyassa." (*Distant*, l. c.)
In my collection is a single male specimen of this species from Malacca which is entirely unmarked on the upperside ; another male however in the Indian Museum, Calcutta, from Perak, has the two discal pale bands of the underside of the forewing showing through, the anterior portion of both of them, but especially the outer, is widened out into a broad diffused fascia above the third median nervule ; and there are two subapical and two subanal black spots on the upperside of the hindwing. These two specimens caught in a limited area are probably as distinct as any two described from India by Mr. Moore.

the colour of the ground defined outwardly with white. I think *A. abnormis* will hereafter be found to be an occasional variety or aberration of *A. angulata*.

614. Abisara suffusa, Moore.

A. suffusa, Moore, Proc. Zool. Soc. Lond., 1882, p. 244; id., Rothney, Ent. Month. Mag., vol. xix, p. 34 (1882); *Sospita echerius*, Moore (*nec* Cramer), Proc. Zool. Soc. Lond., 1865, p. 771.

HABITAT : Chumba, 10,000 feet (*Moore*); Barrackpore (*Rothney*).

EXPANSE : ♂, 1·62 ; ♀, 1·5 inches.

DESCRIPTION : "Allied to *A. angulata*, Moore. Smaller, the MALE being of a deeper tint, with the fasciæ straighter and suffused with grey. FEMALE of a much duller colour and suffused with grey, the medial transverse dark fascia less angular on *both wings*, and the outer fasciæ much less distinct, broader and more suffused." (*Moore*, l. c.)

I possess specimens of this species from the Kangra Valley (*Hocking*), Masuri, Fyzabad, Mahla, Calcutta, Bhutan, Orissa, Karwar and Rutnagherry in Bombay, Ootacamund and Akyab. It is more than probable that a long series of specimens will show that *A. suffusa* merges into *A. fraterna* in Western India, *A. prunosa* in the extreme south of the Peninsula, and into *A. angulata* in Upper Tenasserim and Burma. All these supposed distinct species may be recognizable at their head-quarters, but on the boundary lines separating them it is probable that the distinctive characters of each are lost.

615. Abisara fraterna, Moore.

A. fraterna, Moore, Proc. Zool. Soc. Lond., 1883, p. 532.

HABITAT : Bombay.

EXPANSE : ♂, 1·62 ; ♀, 1·5 inches.

DESCRIPTION : "Nearest to the Ceylonese *A. prunosa*, but smaller. MALE duller-coloured, fasciæ broader. FEMALE of a brighter red colour, the transverse medial dark fascia more decidedly angular in the middle, the two outer fasciæ and the marginal line whitish." (*Moore*, l. c.)

In the Indian Museum, Calcutta, are two female specimens of this species from Karinja, Bombay, which agree with the above description, but others from Bombay in Major Marshall's and my collection agree exactly with Calcutta specimens of *A. suffusa* and some Ceylon ones of *A. prunosa*.

616. Abisara prunosa, Moore.

A. prunosa, Moore, Proc. Zool. Soc. Lond., 1877, p. 137; idem, id., Lep. Cey., vol. i, p. 69, pl. xxxiii, figs. 3, *male*; 3a, *female*; 3b, *larva* and *pupa* (1881).

HABITAT : Ceylon.

EXPANSE : 1·25 to 1·75 inches.

DESCRIPTION. "Differs from the Malacca species, *A. kausambi*,* Felder, in the MALE having more prominent darker bands on the *forewing* and prominent black spots on the *hindwing*. FEMALE differs also in its paler colour, and uniformly pale transverse discal bands without any trace of white at their costal end." (*Moore*, l. c. in Proc. Zool. Soc. Lond.) "MALE, UPPERSIDE, *both wings* deep brownish-purple, with slightly paler transverse discal fasciæ. *Hindwing* with two subapical and two smaller subanal pale-bordered conical black spots margined outwardly by a delicate white line, and two intervening pale conical marks. FEMALE duller coloured, the discal fasciæ and a marginal line paler, and more distinct ; conical spots on the *hindwing* prominent. UNDERSIDE paler, similar in tint and markings to the upperside."

---

* *Vide* footnote on page 313.

" LARVA light green, vermiform, with numerous dorsal and lateral short fine hairs. Feeds on *Ardisia*. PUPA light green, dorsally black spotted, hairy." (*Moore*, l. c. in Lep. Cey.)

In Ceylon *A. prunosa* occurs in the " Western and Central Provinces, in forest land, nearly all the year ; common. Has a rapid darting flight ; settles on the underside of leaves with wings open" (*Hutchison*). " Plentiful amongst the undergrowth of open jungle, or by road-sides. Low country and up to about 4,000 feet" (*Mackwood*). "Galle and Kandy" (*Wade*).

A. prunosa is typically the darkest coloured and in the male most brilliantly purple-shot of this group of the genus, specimens from Travancore being particularly large and dark. Even among Ceylon specimens, however, I find considerable variation ; in some males the inner discal band on the forewing is evenly convex, in others distinctly angled in the middle, and the purple suffusion is also variable ; the size and number of the black spots on both sides of the hindwing is extremely inconstant, in one very abnormal specimen there are two subapical ones only, the anal ones being entirely wanting. From an island one would expect to find some distinguishing characters in a species supposed to be peculiar to it, but I have quite failed to discover any. I can only repeat that in my opinion the name *echerius* should apply to all the species of this group of the genus *Abisara*, except perhaps to the Andaman local race which has been named *bifasciata* ; that as in this case the geographical range of numerous slight local races is not segregated, and each local race must interbreed with the next on the boundary line which is supposed to separate them, it can serve no good scientific purpose to pick out a few apparently different specimens from each local race and to describe them, at the same time ignoring the intergrade specimens which exist.

[Specific names are printed in small type (abiasa); specific synonyms and varieties in italics *(agnicula)*; generic names in small capitals (ABELMOSCHUS); generic synonyms in small capital italics *(ACCA)*; subfamily and family names in large capitals (ACRÆINÆ); and subfamily and family synonyms in large capital italics *(ACRÆIDÆ)*. The number of the page on which a species or variety, genus, subfamily or family is described is printed in italics.]

INDEX.

ERRATA.

Page 19, twenty-one lines from the top, for "*nyctilius*" read "*nyctelius.*"
Page 43, twenty-one lines from the top, for "*clarina*" read "*clarissa.*"
Page 93, six lines from the bottom, for "KALAURA" read "KALLAURA."
Page 143, sixteen lines from the top, omit "*Parnassius davidis,* Oberthür, Etudes d'Ent.t vol. iv, p. 108, n. 17 (1879)." Also eight lines from the bottom, omit para. commencing "I. was these differences" and concluding with "variable species of the genus."
Page 177, eleven and ten lines from the botto n, for "*jaina*" read "*jina.*"
Page 188, five lines from the top, for "**teutoides**" read "**teutoides.**"
Page 197, twenty lines from the top, for "*E. uthalia*" read "*Euthalia.*"
Page 253, eighteen lines from the top, for "**Cyrestisa**" read "**Cyrestis.**"

NOTE.—Volume II, containing the title page, list of illustrations of Vol. II, preface, and pp. 1—332, with Frontispiece to Vol. II and plates XVIII—XXIV, was published October, 1886.

END OF VOL. II.

Printed by the Calcutta Central Press Co., Ld., 5, Council House Street.

Fig 68. DETOTA ISICITESA, BUTLER. ♂

73. VANESSA XANTOMELAS, DEN. VAR. ♂

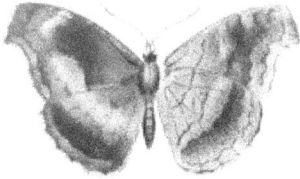

Fig 69. EONTYELA BERNARDIONI, Boldin. ♂

Fig. 74. PYRAMEIS INDICA, HUBN. ♀

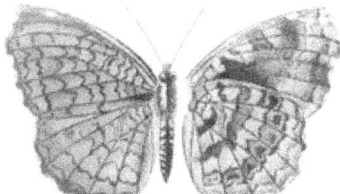

Fig 70. ESGOLIS MERIONE, CRAMER. ♂

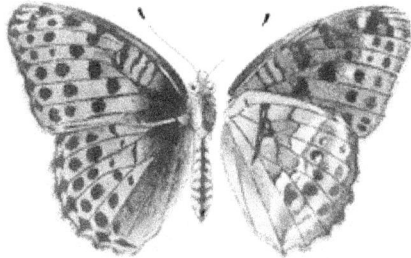

Fig. 75. ARGENNIS NIPHE, LINN. ♂

Fig 71. ACRÆA BALDITA, MOORE. ♀

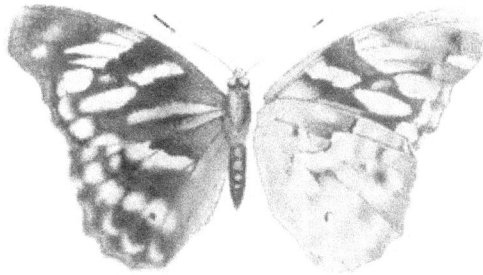

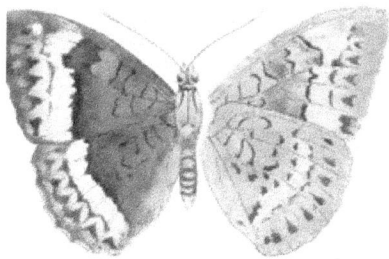

TANCRE... ...

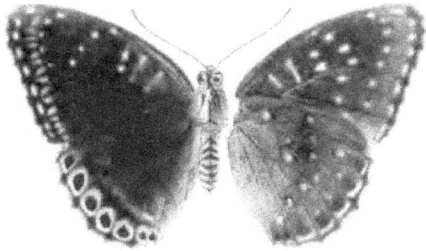

RHIN...

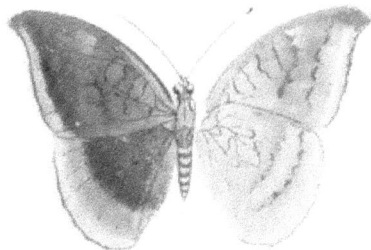

Fig. 7.   EUTHALIA LEPIDEA, Butler.

...

f. 8.   ... ...

HELCYR...

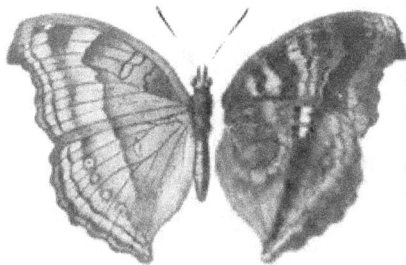

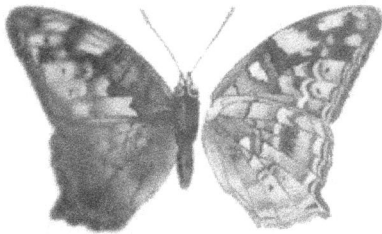

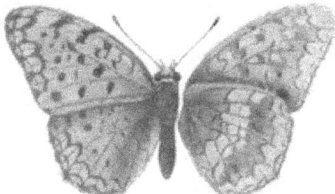

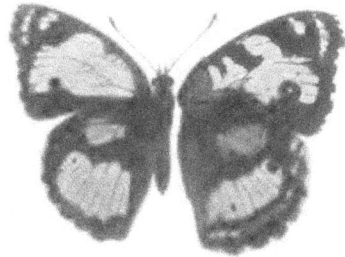

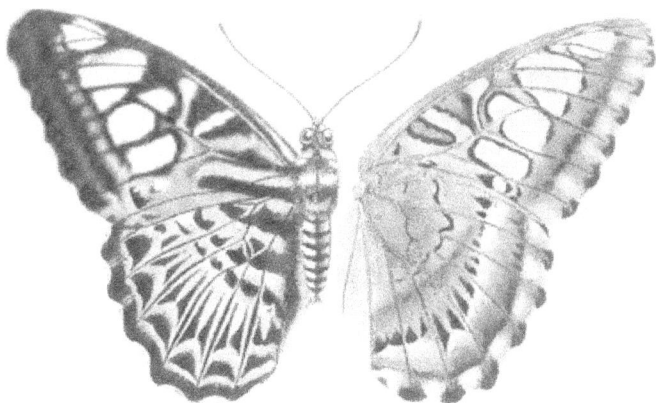

Fig. 95. PARTHENOS CYANEA, Moor.

Fig. 96. SEPHISA CHANDRANA, Butler.

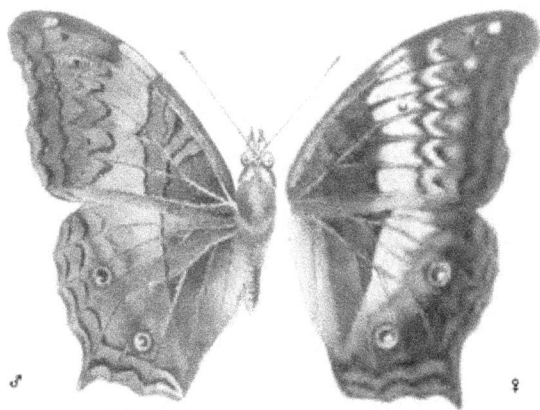

Fig. 97. CYNTHIA ENOTA, Fabricius.

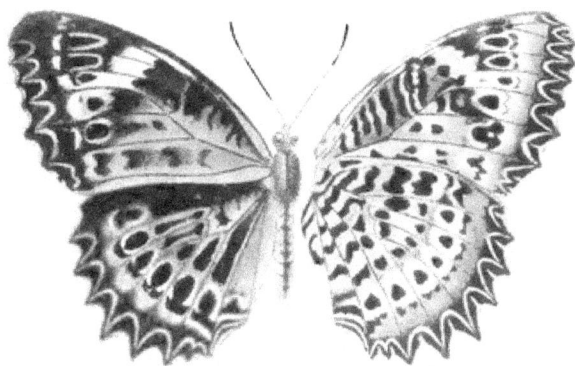

Fig 98.   CETHOSIA MALBATTA, LINEN.   ♀

Fig 99.   HESTINA NAMA, DOUBLEDAY.   ♂

PLATE XIII.

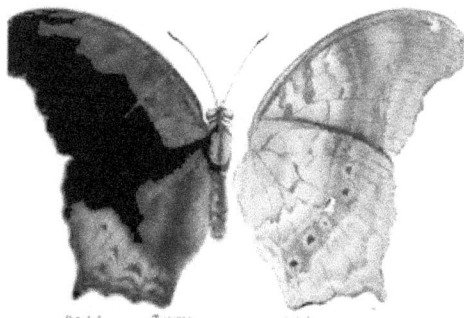

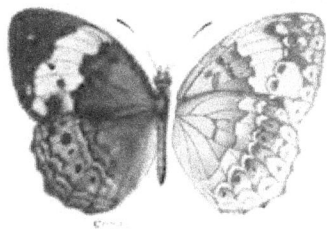

Fig. 11. Tropæa

Cres

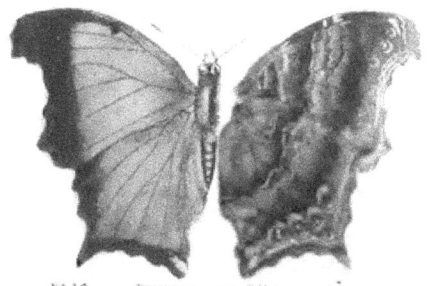

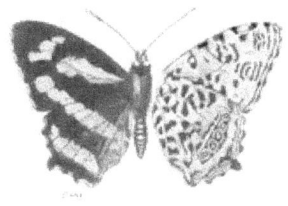

Fig. 12. Kyponeatra

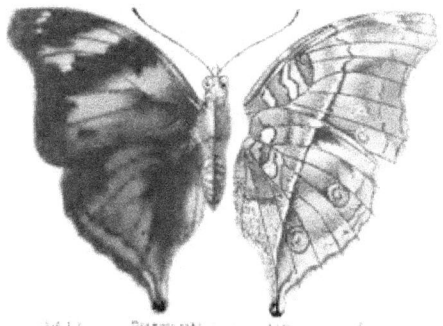

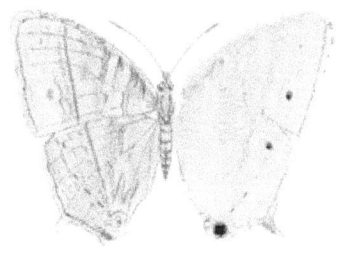

Fig. 13. Diadema

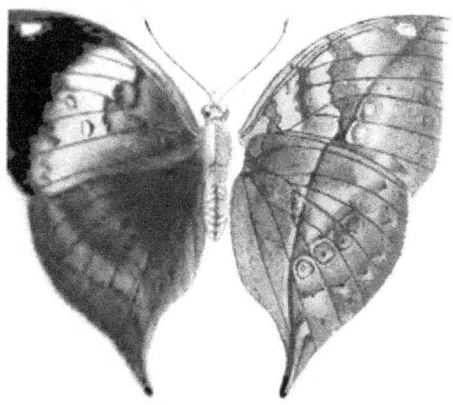

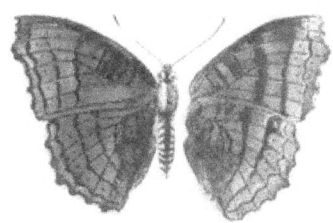

Fig. 14. Kallima inachus

Precis

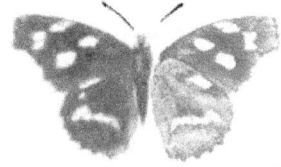

LIBYTHEA BOHEMI, Marshall

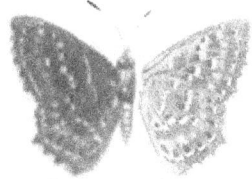

ZEMEROS FLEGYAS, Cramer

Fig. 110. ALCOVA MENZA, Fabricius

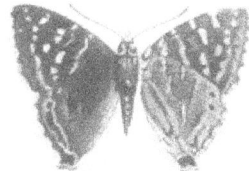

Fig. 116. DODONA DIPŒA, Hewitson.

Fig. 111. CIRROCHROA ... G. & Nicéville

DODONA LONGICAUDATA, de Nicéville

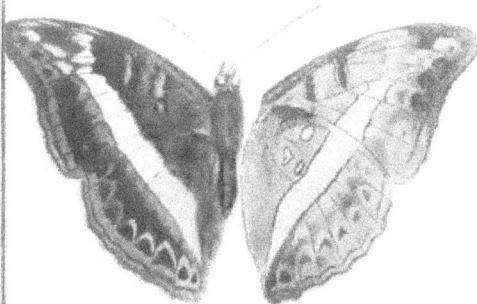

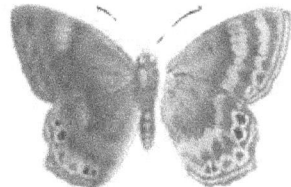

Fig. 11. ABISARA ... ATA, ...

Fig. 112. LIMENITIS DONO, Westwood

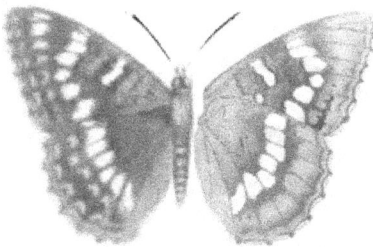

LIMENITIS DUDASI, ... Moor.

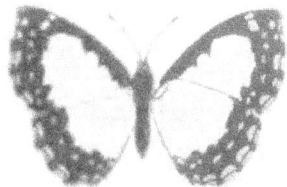

Fig. 119. STIBOGES NYMPHIDIA, Butler.